**AQA A-level**

# Religious Studies

John Frye

**Approval message from AQA**

This textbook has been approved by AQA for use with our qualification. This means that we have checked that it broadly covers the specification and we are satisfied with the overall quality. Full details of our approval process can be found on our website.

We approve textbooks because we know how important it is for teachers and students to have the right resources to support their teaching and learning. However, the publisher is ultimately responsible for the editorial control and quality of this book.

Please note that when teaching the **AQA A-level Religious Studies** course, you must refer to AQA's specification as your definitive source of information. While this book has been written to match the specification, it cannot provide complete coverage of every aspect of the course.

A wide range of other useful resources can be found on the relevant subject pages of our website: www.aqa.org.uk.

**HODDER**
EDUCATION
AN HACHETTE UK COMPANY

## Acknowledgements

The author would like to express his warmest thanks to the following, who have been so kind as to provide comments and advice on various parts of the manuscript:

Revd Patrick Allsop

Revd Tim Fernyhough

Dr Debbie Herring

Mr Chris Hopton

Dr Mel Thompson

Dr Mike Wilkinson

Mrs Sheila Butler

My wife Joy, as an indefatigable proof-reader.

To Dr Debbie Herring I owe a particular vote of thanks for much invaluable help with the Religion elements.

All text and photo credits can be found on page 388.

Orders: please contact Bookpoint Ltd, 130 Park Drive, Milton Park, Abingdon, Oxon OX14 4SE. Telephone: +44 (0)1235 827720. Fax: +44 (0)1235 400454. Email education@bookpoint.co.uk Lines are open from 9 a.m. to 5 p.m., Monday to Saturday, with a 24-hour message answering service. You can also order through our website: www.hoddereducation.co.uk

ISBN: 978 1 4718 7395 9

© John Frye 2017

First published in 2017 by
Hodder Education,
An Hachette UK Company
Carmelite House
50 Victoria Embankment
London EC4Y 0DZ

www.hoddereducation.co.uk

Impression number    10 9 8 7 6 5 4 3

Year        2021  2020  2019  2018  2017

Cover photo © Getty Images/iStockphoto/Thinkstock

Illustrations by Barking Dog Art and Aptara, Inc.

Typeset in India by Aptara, Inc.

Printed and bound by CPI Group (UK) Ltd, Croydon, CR0 4YY

A catalogue record for this title is available from the British Library.

# Contents

# Introduction

When Dorothy uttered these memorable words to Toto, she was not starting out to study a new RS Specification, and Toto might not have been too concerned if she had been. The territory of a new syllabus may not be as uncharted as the lands 'over the rainbow', nevertheless it is new territory, and I hope that at the end of the day you enjoy it. (Note 1)

This AQA Textbook is the first of two volumes published by Hodder. At the time of going to press Volume 1 has been AQA approved and Volume 2 has been selected for the AQA approval process.

Volume 1    AQA Religious Studies AS (7061)

Volume 2    AQA Religious Studies A-level (7062) (publishing August 2017)

Centres will need to be fully aware of the following points:

## A: Government / Ofqual requirements

1  The changes to AS and A-level RS are required by the Government and are specified by the Government department Ofqual (The Office of Qualifications and Examinations Regulation).

2  AQA has interpreted the requirements of Government / Ofqual in the way it feels is most user-friendly and examinable for Centres, at the same time maintaining the maximum continuity with its existing suite of RS papers.

3  For AS students who sit the AQA AS exam after one year of study, after publication of the results, students wishing to improve their grade would need to enter for the following year's exams. The Government no longer allows re-sits within the same academic year.

4  Students doing the full A-level course sit the A-level exam at the end of two years. They do not have to sit the AQA AS exam first.

   However, options at the end of year 1 might include:

   i  Sitting the official AQA AS exam in order to get a diagnostic / prediction of the grade they are likely to get having completed the full A-level.
   ii  Sitting internal end-of-year exams set and marked by their own Centre.

5  For A-level students who take the first of these two options (4(i) above):

   The AS result does not count towards the full A-level result; the full A-level still needs to be sat at the end of the course.

   They do receive an official AS grade.

   The AS grade could be used on a UCAS application.

Having completed the full A-level, students would end up with both an AS and an A-level grade.

# B: The relationship between the Textbooks and the Specification

1 The Textbooks give detailed coverage of the Specification for both AS and A-level.

2 For those intending to end their course of study with AS, it is necessary to study only Volume 1 of the AQA Textbook.

3 For those intending to complete the full A-level, Volume 2 contains all of the material not covered in Volume 1. The natural order of study would therefore be Volume 1 followed by Volume 2, although students / Centres can cover the material for A-level in any order they wish.

4 In terms of the continuity between Volumes 1 and 2:

The content of the AS volume is written at the same standard / level as the A-level volume.

Those who go on to A-level in their second year of study will therefore not need to 'top up' the material covered in the AS Textbook.

5 Differentiation of standard between students who sit only the AS and those who sit the full A-level is achieved naturally by:

The exam paper. The AS exam paper has a different structure that is appropriate to AS.

In particular, the Assessment Objectives for A-level have a higher weighting for AO2. Advanced AO2 skills will develop naturally over the two years of the full A-level.

The 'Dialogue' between Religion & Philosophy and between Religion & Ethics is examined only at A-level. It is not a feature of AS assessment.

# C: General considerations about the Specification and the Textbooks

1 The assessed components are

**Component 1:** Philosophy and Ethics
– Section A: Philosophy of Religion
– Section B: Ethics and Religion
**Component 2:** Study of Religion and Dialogues

'Dialogues' in Component 2 is studied at A-level only, and not AS.

2 Students select one faith option from:

– Buddhism
– Christianity
– Hinduism
– Islam
– Judaism
– Sikhism.

3 AQA (aqa.org.uk/7061 and aqa.org.uk/7062) is committed to supplementing the study of all religions by means of:

- schemes of work
- specimen questions and marked exemplars
- topic guidance
- guidance for assessment
- introduction to resources
- training courses
- subject-expertise courses.

4 Those who have entered students for AQA's Religious Studies exams in the past will note the continuity with much of the bedrock Philosophy and Ethics material from the existing AS and A2 units.

5 The most important message for both AS and A-level is that issues take priority over content. For the new Specification, students are required to focus particularly on the skills of evaluation and critical analysis. You will still need to know enough about the subject content in order to give meaningful analysis and evaluation, but the days of memorising large bodies of material and expecting this alone to generate high grades have now gone, in favour of an emphasis on the skills of understanding, analysis and evaluation.

6 The Textbook content contains the following features:

- an introductory summary of subject content
- key philosophers, theologians and other relevant persons
- extracts from what these various persons actually said
- key vocabulary so you can use the proper technical language of the debate
- activities, discussion points and practice / development tasks
- chapter summaries. You might consider starting each section with the summary in order to get the feel of the subject matter.

7 The Textbook includes a detailed look at exam issues, including:

- the new Assessment Objectives
- the new Levels of Response
- the new structure for exam papers
- Specimen Assessment materials.

8 Finally, it is not unknown for students to describe conversations between modern theologians and people who have been dead for centuries or even millennia. Hence there is an appendix on the time and place of origin of the different philosophers and theologians referred to in the book. You do not get any marks for remembering their dates and personal habits, but such details do flesh out the personalities. It might be of no particular consequence to you that the great Italian Dominican theologian Thomas Aquinas was kidnapped for a year by his own family, but it is the kind of anecdote that might make you appreciate that even the saints were human.

## Please bear in mind that when you sit the AS exam, there are 2 papers

**Paper 1:** Philosophy and ethics

- 2 hours
- 4 questions, each with a 15-mark AO1 and 15-mark AO2

**Paper 2:** Study of religion

- 1 hour
- 2 questions, each with a 15-mark AO1 and 15-mark AO2

The amount of information and explanation in the Textbook is designed to give you a background to the material studied, since any one topic can be studied in different ways. The emphasis should therefore be on quality, and not on quantity, so again: start any section with the summary and go back to it at the end. That is, of course, just a recommendation. The material can be studied in any way that Centres and candidates prefer.

**Final comment:**

The Textbook covers the content of each section in detail. Again, start with the summary in each section, then go back to flesh out the bones.

# Component 1

# Philosophy of religion and ethics

# 1.1

# Arguments for the existence of God

## The Design Argument

This chapter will cover:
- Paley's Analogical Argument
- Criticisms of Design Arguments from David Hume

**You will need to consider seven things for this section**

1 The basis of Paley's Analogical Argument in observation and thought.

2 Paley's Analogical Design Argument.

3 Criticisms of Design Arguments from David Hume.

4 The strengths and weaknesses of Paley's argument.

5 The status of Paley's argument as a 'proof'.

6 The relationship between reason and faith.

7 The value of Paley's argument for religious faith.

### William Paley (1743–1805)

Paley was by all accounts a gifted lecturer, adored by his students. He was also an intellectual powerhouse, having graduated in 1763 as 'Senior Wrangler' from Christ's College, Cambridge, meaning that he was the highest ranking mathematics undergraduate at Cambridge University. He also rose through the ranks of the Anglican Church, becoming Archdeacon of Carlisle in 1782.

This information is useful mainly in order to give you a snapshot of his stature and nature. For everything else about Paley, you should judge him by his writings.

2

# Paley's Analogical Argument: its basis in observation

## Key terms

**a posteriori** Arguments which depend on sense experience: think of 'posterior' – *behind / after* sense experience. For example, that 'oak trees grow from acorns' can only be known by sense experience and not by logic.

**inductive** Arguments which use reasoning in which the premises seek to supply strong evidence for (not absolute proof of) the truth of the conclusion. Inductive arguments are probabilistic. They can be used to argue from what we see in the world back to the supposed cause.

**premise** A proposition that supports, or helps to support, a conclusion.

1 Paley's argument is **a posteriori**, meaning that it is based on sense experience: we observe the world through touch, taste, hearing, smell and sight, and we draw conclusions from what our senses tell us.

2 Further, the argument is **inductive**. Inductive reasoning is where we use **premises** to supply strong evidence for the truth of the conclusion. Inductive arguments are about what is *probably* true, and they give us new knowledge. Since I've owned many cats, here's an example based on my observations about cats:

● All the cats that I have observed have had fur.
● Tomorrow I am going on holiday to Canada.
● The cats I see in Canada will probably have fur.

The third line of the argument gives us knowledge, but it can only be probably true. In fact, until the 1970s, my conclusion would probably have been true for every observation of cats I would ever make, but during the 1970s breeders developed a fur-less cat known as the Canadian Sphynx, and as a matter of fact one turned up two weeks ago in the house next to mine.
Since Paley's argument is *a posteriori* and inductive, his conclusion that the universe was designed is at best probably true, and it might turn out to be false.

3 Paley's argument is based on three particular observations about the world:

● **Its complexity**. Paley goes into great detail concerning his observations about the complexity of the natural world. He looks at the complexity of biological organisms and organs, such as the eye. He also looks at the complexity of the laws of nature by which everything is governed.
● **Its regularity**. Paley observes in particular the regularity of the orbits of comets, moons and planets and the regularity of the seasons of the year.
● **Its purpose**. Paley observes the machines that we make and infers that they are built for a purpose. The complexity and regularity of a watch implies that it has a purpose, even if we do not know what the purpose is. Our observation of the complexity and regularity of the world therefore implies that the world too has a purpose.

4 On the basis of these observations, Paley formulated his inductive Design Argument, which can be summarised as follows:

● Some objects in the world show clear evidence that they were designed because they exhibit complexity and regularity, from which we can infer that they were made for a purpose.
● The universe appears to exhibit complexity and regularity, from which we can infer that it was made for a purpose.
● So it is likely that the universe was designed.

5 In summary, Paley argues inductively from what we can see in the world (the appearance of design) back to the supposed cause (God).

# Paley's Analogical Design Argument

In crossing a heath, suppose I pitched my foot against a *stone*, and were asked how the stone came to be there; I might possibly answer, that, for any thing I knew to the contrary, it had lain there for ever: nor would it perhaps be very easy to show the absurdity of this answer. But suppose I had found a *watch* upon the ground, and it should be inquired how the watch happened to be in that place; I should hardly think of the answer which I had before given, that, for any thing I knew, the watch might have always been there. Yet why should not this answer serve for the watch as well as for the stone; why is it not as admissible in the second case, as in the first? For this reason, and for no other, viz. that, when we come to inspect the watch, we perceive (what we could not discover in the stone) that its several parts are framed and put together for a purpose, *e.g.* that they are so formed and adjusted as to produce motion, and that motion so

regulated as to point out the hour of the day; that, if the different parts had been differently shaped from what they are, of a different size from what they are, or placed after any other manner, or in any other order, than that in which they are placed, either no motion at all would have been carried on in the machine, or none which would have answered the use that is now served by it.

… This mechanism being observed … the inference, we think, is inevitable, that the watch must have had a maker: that there must have existed, at some time, and at some place or other, an artificer or artificers who formed it for the purpose which we find it actually to answer; who comprehended its construction, and designed its use.

▲ Paley: *Natural Theology; or, Evidences of the Existence and Attributes of the Deity collected from the Appearances of Nature,* 1802. Ch.1, 1–3. (Note 1)

### Key term

**natural theology** The view that questions about God's existence, nature and attributes can be answered without referring to scripture or to any other form of special revelation, by using reason, science, history and observation.

Paley's argument here is simple. If, while crossing a heath, I come across two objects, the first a stone and the second a watch, and I ask myself how they came to be there, I would have to give different answers to this question. For the stone, it would not be absurd to suppose it had been there forever; but the watch is quite clearly different, because closer inspection shows that it is a complex artefact.

To put Paley's mention of the watch into context (**Natural Theology** was first published in 1802), remember that watches then were rather different artefacts to the comparatively dainty objects that most of us wear upon our wrists. Paley would be thinking about something like the watch shown here, where unclipping the hinge between the front and the back would reveal a complex arrangement of gears and levers.

▲ Opening a watch reveals a complex arrangement of gears and levers

Looking at these pictures, we could not suppose of Paley's watch what we could suppose of the stone – that it had always been there. For example, the watch would contain brass – a metal that is commonly selected in watch-making because of its elasticity and anti-rusting properties. The front face would be covered with glass, both to protect the hands of the watch and to enable the numbers engraved on the face to be seen. The gears and cogs inside the watch would lead you to suppose that they were responsible for the regularity of the movement; moreover if only one part of the mechanism had been different (such as one cog being too large or too small), then the movement would fail. Eventually you would realise further that the movement had an obvious purpose – to tell the time. From the existence of the watch and its properties we could infer the existence of a watchmaker.

Like a good politician, Paley then anticipated some objections to his argument. For example:

- Some might object that if the watch is broken, or does not work properly, that would weaken his argument. Paley answers that even if that were the case, he would still know that the broken watch was designed.
- The same would be true if he could not work out what all the parts did.
- Some might object to Paley by claiming that there just happens to be a principle of order in material things which had somehow brought the parts of the watch into their present form and situation. Paley sees this as nonsense – watches do not get made by any 'principle of order' other than that found in the mind of a watchmaker.
- Nor would he change his mind if somebody told him he was ignorant of the whole matter – Paley says that he would know enough to understand that the watch was designed.

From here, Paley went on to develop his analogy.

## Paley's analogy

An **inference** is a conclusion reached through evidence and reasoning. An **analogy** is an inference where information or meaning is transferred from one subject to another. Paley is transferring his inference about the organisation and design of watches to the organisation and design of nature.

**Paley's analogy is this:**

1 A watch has complex parts, each with a function, and the parts work together for a specific purpose.

2 So the watch must have been designed by a watchmaker.

3 Similarly the universe has parts that function together for a purpose.

4 So the universe must have been designed by a universe maker.

5 The universe is a far more wonderful design than a watch, so its designer is much greater than any human designer.

6 The universe designer is God.

### Key terms

**analogy** To get to analogy, start with inference. An inference is a conclusion reached through evidence and reasoning. An analogy is an inference where information or meaning is transferred from one subject to another based on similarities / comparison.

**inference** (See analogy)

… Every indication of contrivance, every manifestation of design, which existed in the watch, exists in the works of nature; with the difference, on the side of nature, of being greater and more, and that in a degree which exceeds all computation. I mean that the contrivances of nature surpass the contrivances of art, in the complexity, subtility [subtlety], and curiosity of the mechanism; and still more, if possible, do they go beyond them in number and variety; yet, in a multitude of cases, are not less evidently mechanical, not less evidently contrivances, not less evidently accommodated to their end, or suited to their office, than are the most perfect productions of human ingenuity.

▲ Paley: *Natural Theology* (1802), III, 18.

Paley gives some rather exhaustive examples of what he means, for example:

- The eye in all creatures is superbly adapted for vision. An eye has all the right parts in the right arrangement to achieve its purpose – to enable a person to see – just as a watch has all the right parts in the right arrangement to achieve its purpose – to enable a person to tell the time.
- Fish have fins and gills so that they are perfectly adapted to living in water.
- Equally, birds have feathers, bones and wings that are perfectly adapted to flight.
- Paley considered the grandest of God's works to be the heavenly bodies – the stars, planets and comets – and the awe-inspiring regularity of their orbits.

In summary, Paley's Design Argument is that from the purpose and regularity we observe in nature, we can conclude that these were the intentional design of God. The main argument being from purpose explains why Paley's argument is also called the '**Teleological** Argument', *telos* being the Greek for 'end', or 'purpose'.

We now need to look at Hume's objections to Design Arguments.

> **Key term**
>
> **teleological** *telos* in Greek means 'end' or 'purpose', so 'The Teleological Argument for the existence of God' seeks to show that we can perceive evidence of deliberate design in the natural world.

# Criticisms of Design Arguments from David Hume

> **David Hume (1711–1776)**
>
> Hume was a Scottish philosopher, born in Edinburgh. He was an empiricist, a sceptic and probably an atheist. Hume had a superb intellect and used it to rather devastating effect in his various critiques of religion.

Hume's critique of Design Arguments appears in *Dialogues Concerning Natural Religion* (1779). The text of the *Dialogues* is available online. (Note 2)

In the first place, avoid these three common errors:

1 **Avoid the error of thinking that Hume was commenting on Paley's Design Argument.** Hume died in 1776 and Paley published *Natural Theology* 26 years later, in 1802. Hume showed amazing foresight in so far as many of his comments do apply to Paley's argument.

2 **Avoid the error of assuming that Paley had no knowledge of Hume's critique of Design Arguments.** It is a fact that Paley had read at least some of Hume's *Dialogues*, for the simple reason that he says as much in *Natural Theology*, 1802, XXVI, 512, where he refers to 'Mr. Hume, in his posthumous dialogues ...' It is hard to say whether Paley makes direct replies to Hume. Perhaps Paley decided not to dignify Hume's complaints with an answer.

3 **Do not turn into a parrot.** Students often learn Hume's objections to Design Arguments parrot-fashion, sometimes reducing them to a list of simple phrases or even single words. It is better to engage fully with fewer of Hume's objections than to regurgitate all of them without understanding. Questions on the Design Argument will ask for *explanation* not summary.

## Hume's arguments

The following gives you a selection of some of Hume's main arguments.

1  **Even if we grant that the universe was designed, there is no evidence that this was the God of Christian theism. A lesser being could have designed the universe.**

Hume is using one of his guiding principles here: that **a cause must be proportional to its effect**. Put another way: **a wise man proportions his belief to his evidence**. Imagine yourself hard at work in the classroom, when from the corridor comes the sound of an orchestra playing at full blast. The cause of what you hear might be (a) a full symphony orchestra sitting in the corridor, or (b) someone with a powerful MP3 player. If you apply Hume's principle, you would assume that even though (a) is possible, (b) is all you need to account for what you hear. To apply this to Paley's argument: Paley infers that the designer of the universe is the all-powerful, all-knowing, all-loving God of Christian theism, but although such an inference *might* be true it is nevertheless out of proportion to the evidence. If there *is* a designer, a lesser being could well be responsible.

Hume explores the idea of a limited designer in some detail; also the idea of there being more than one designer:

- Wherever we find intelligent minds, we find them attached to physical bodies, so there is no obvious reason to suppose that the designer of this universe was a metaphysical being. Hume speculated (tongue in cheek) that the designer might have a body, with eyes, ears, nose and mouth. Possibly the designer was mortal and died long ago.
- Design is normally a feature of teamwork, so there is no obvious reason to suppose that the designer of this universe was a single being operating on his own. Think of a set of scales – the kind that used to be used in banks for weighing out gold and silver.

  Imagine that somebody arranges the scales so that one half is hidden by a curtain. On the side that you can see there is a 1 kg weight. Since the scales are balanced, the weight on the hidden side must also be 1 kg, but without observing what is behind the curtain you cannot tell whether the 1 kg weight is balanced by two half-kilograms, or any number of small weights that amount to 1 kg. In the same way, we really have no idea as to how many beings might have designed this world.

For all we know, then, the job of designing this universe could have been carried out by a team of junior gods on a trial and error basis:

▲ Was the universe designed by one being, or many?

> If we survey a ship, what an exalted idea must we form of the ingenuity of the carpenter who framed so complicated, useful, and beautiful a machine? And what surprize must we feel, when we find him a stupid mechanic, who imitated others, and copied an art, which, through a long succession of ages, after multiplied trials, mistakes, corrections, deliberations, and controversies, had been gradually improving? Many worlds might have been botched and bungled, throughout an eternity, ere this system was struck out; much labour lost, many fruitless trials made; and a slow, but continued improvement carried on during infinite ages in the art of world-making …

▲ Hume: *Dialogues Concerning Natural Religion* (FP 1779), 167 [Note 3]

**2  The existence of evil and imperfection in the world does indeed suggest a limited designer.**

Hume noted that Epicurus' questions about the existence of evil are still unanswered.

The inconsistent triad refers to three statements about evil that Epicurus thought were inconsistent with each other, namely:

i   God is **omnipotent** (all powerful)
ii  God is **omnibenevolent** (all loving)
iii Evil exists.

Hume comments:

> Is [God] willing to prevent evil, but not able? then is he impotent.
>
> Is he able, but not willing? then is he malevolent.
>
> Is he both able and willing? whence then is evil?
>
> *Dialogues* (FP 1779), 198

Hume suggests that we only have to think of the long catalogue of ailments that afflict both humans and animals to see this is not what we would expect from a being of infinite power, wisdom and goodness. For all we know, the universe could have been designed by an infant god or a senile god. Instead of confronting such problems, theologians spend much time inventing theodicies to excuse God's behaviour.

**3  Analogies between the way the universe works and the way machines work are unsound.** The world is more like a vast floating vegetable, and the thing about vegetables is that they grow *themselves*, apparently without the need for a designer.

In some parts of Hume's writings he seems to anticipate Darwin's theory of evolution. In the opinion of most evolutionary biologists, evolution is not directed by any external agent such as God. Hume has some powerful support here, then.

**4  To make an analogy between the designers of human machines and the designer of the universe is just anthropomorphism – we are trying to explain the universe in our own image.**

To know that the universe is designed, we would have to have some knowledge of how universes are made, but the fact is that we have no experience at all of universe-making, and therefore we have no idea of what it takes to design one, or what the designer would be like.

Our experience of design is limited to the machines we design ourselves, so in effect we are imagining God to be like a human designer. Again, this is anthropomorphic in the extreme. We cannot assume that we can apply our limited experience of life on this world to the universe as a whole.

**5  The universe could have developed into a comparatively ordered state simply by chance.**

This is Hume's so-called 'Epicurean Hypothesis'. Epicurus (341–270 BCE) taught that the basic constituents of the world were indivisible atoms – an interesting guess in the light of twentieth-century atomic physics. Since the world is nothing more nor less than changing arrangements of

---

**Key terms**

**omnipotent** All-powerful. Omnipotence is an attribute of God.

**omnibenevolent** All-loving. Omnibenevolence is an attribute of God.

**anthropomorphism** The habit of attributing human form or ideas to beings other than humans, particularly to gods and animals. The adjective is 'anthropomorphic'.

its atoms, given infinite time it was inevitable that atoms should arrive at an ordered state. Hume suggested that some such theory accounted for the appearance of design in the world, so it is at least as likely that the world appears in an ordered state purely by chance rearrangement as that it was designed by God.

Twenty-first-century physics offers a refined version of these ideas through multiverse theory, according to which there are vast numbers of universes existing now and perhaps in the past. If some version of multiverse theory turns out to be true, then some universes will be chaotic, some will be semi-ordered, and some will be highly-ordered – all purely by chance. This would not disprove the existence of God, but it would support Hume's argument that we can explain this universe without needing to appeal to God.

# Strengths and weaknesses of Paley's Design Argument

## Weaknesses

The five criticisms we have just looked at from Hume clearly do show some weaknesses in Paley's argument, so the following five points are the same five we have just looked at.

1 **Even if the universe was designed, the all-powerful God of Christian theism is a greater cause than is needed to account for that design.**

   The universe could well have been produced by a team of lesser beings, or even by designers who 'botched and bungled' it.

2 **The existence of evil is a powerful argument against the belief that the designer is all-loving and all-powerful.**

   Evil seems to happen on a cosmic scale. The death of large stars in the universe causes supernova explosions so vast that they would irradiate any nearby civilisation.

   It is difficult to reconcile the sheer amount of evil in this world alone with the existence of a good designer God.

3 **Hume's argument that the universe is more like a vegetable than a machine, and that vegetables do not need designers, is backed up strongly by the theory of evolution.**

   Evolution seems to show that nature designs itself, without the need for God. For example, Richard Dawkins suggested that Paley was 'gloriously wrong' – the heavens are utterly and blindly indifferent to humanity and everything else (*The Blind Watchmaker,* 1986). If there was a 'watchmaker', the watchmaker is evolution, not God, and evolution is as indifferent to our opinions on the subject as the stars themselves. The universe has no purpose, no designer, and no plan.

4 **As Hume says, we have no experience of universe-making, so our ideas about it are anthropomorphic – we lift them from our own limited experience and impose them on the universe.**

   – the design is in our minds, then, and not in the world.

5 **Moreover if nature can design itself, as Hume argues and evolutionary theory supports, Hume is probably right in claiming that the universe designed itself in the first place.**

Multiverse theory suggests one way in which this could be true: there could be so many universes that some will appear designed even though they are not. This could be one such universe.

## Strengths

Commenting first on the five weaknesses identified above:

1 **Paley may be right to argue that the designer is the all-powerful Christian God, because this is the simplest explanation.**

Richard Swinburne claims, against Hume, that the existence of an all-powerful God is a simpler, and therefore better, explanation of the appearance of design in the universe. (Note 4) Swinburne argues that:

' ... simplicity is always evidence for truth'.

You will have to make up your own mind about this.

2 **Paley argued that evil may be unavoidable in order for God to bring about good.** (Note 5)

We can support this in many ways, for example:

- The Free Will Defence: freedom to choose between the highest goods and the highest evils means that there must be such goods and evils in the world.
- Process Theology maintains that God is all-loving but not all-powerful. We study Process Theology in the next section on the problem of evil.
- Perhaps the best theodicy (defence of God against the problem of evil) is that of Irenaeus–Hick. Hick argues that evil is 'soul-making', because without evil we could never learn to love the good. We will study Hick in Chapter 2.

In other words there are any number of possibilities as to why God might allow evil to exist within the design. The important point is not whether one particular explanation is right, but that Paley's argument that 'evil may be unavoidable' may be right.

3 **Evolution does not destroy the Design Argument because (1) evolution does not explain itself, and (2) evolution is compatible with belief in God anyway.**

- Against the likes of Dawkins (*The Blind Watchmaker*), Richard Swinburne maintains that evolution explains *nothing*, since it is regulated entirely by the laws of physics, biology and chemistry, and those laws do *not* explain themselves. We need to ask where the laws of nature come from, and in Swinburne's view, they come from the God who designed them.
- You will have to think carefully about whether or not evolution is compatible with belief in a good designer-God. Humans can treat other humans with indescribable barbarity, and many consider that the lot of animals, particularly in the meat and fur industries and in laboratory testing is foul in the extreme. If such things are 'natural', can we really approve of, or believe in, a God who uses such a process, for whatever purpose?

4 **Paley does draw the conclusion that the designer is metaphysical and transcendent** (above the space–time universe) from evidence that makes the designer seem anthropomorphic. Nevertheless his conclusion that the designer exists beyond the universe seems reasonable, despite the anthropomorphic language he uses to make the point: the designer must be metaphysical, since it would be impossible to design such a system from the inside.

We have neither imagined the laws of nature nor imposed them on the world – science only works because these laws exist. They could only have come from an external source – God.

5 **Paley's argument that 'nature shows intention'** [Note 6] **becomes stronger when supported by the Anthropic Principle**, which is a modern form of the Design Argument. 'Anthropic' means 'relating to humans', so the principle points out that there are 30 or more 'boundary conditions' (such as the 'stickiness' of gravity and the expansion rate of the Big Bang) that have to be 'fine-tuned' for an ordered universe containing intelligent life to develop. The odds against all the boundary conditions being at exactly the right settings are colossal – roughly $10^{180}$ against, so if this is the only universe, then it seems obvious that something must have designed it to bring about intelligent beings such as ourselves.

Be careful here, however, because we have no way of telling how many universes may have existed in the past, or might exist in different space–times alongside our own. The number could easily be far greater than $10^{180}$, in which case this universe would quite possibly *appear* designed but not be. If you are interested in multiverse theory, then there is plenty of material available through internet research. Also, the fact that we result from the way the universe is (and therefore adapted to it) is not evidence that there was a purpose behind it.

6 **One strong point about Paley's argument is its simplicity – it is a simple inductive argument.**

As we have seen, the argument is based on induction – on what we observe – and what we observe does have the appearance of design. Even though Immanuel Kant did not accept the Design Argument as a proof of God's existence, he accepted that it is a powerful argument simply because the order in the heavens he could see above him filled him with awe.

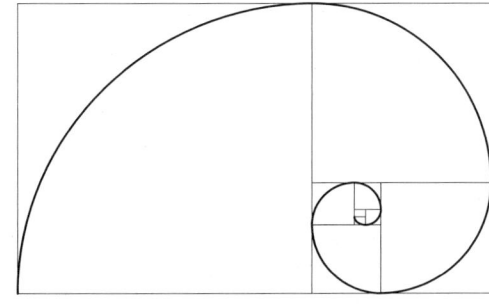
▲ The logarithmic spiral

▲ The Nautilus shell

---

**Key term**

**Anthropic Principle** 'Anthropic' means 'related to humans', so the Anthropic Principle is that there is a direct link between our observation of the universe and the 'boundary conditions' which brought it into existence. In other words, the boundary conditions (also known as 'cosmological constants') had to be 'fine tuned' by God, otherwise intelligent life could never have developed: it is no accident that we are here.

---

**Activity**

There is a view that the strongest indication of design in the universe can be seen in the fact that just about everything has a mathematical description. Research briefly the terms 'logarithmic spiral' and 'Fibonacci numbers', and their appearance in nature. Do these indicate an underlying design principle, and if so, what kind of designer?

# The status of Paley's Design Argument as a 'proof'

Depending on the context, 'proof' can mean different things:

1 **It can mean that there is sufficient evidence for the truth of a proposition** – that the facts of the matter are strong enough to show that something is true. For example, having a receipt is generally taken as 'proof' of purchase. As another example, if by a majority verdict a jury finds you innocent of a crime, this is taken as 'proof' of innocence. In neither case is the proof 100%, because in the first instance you might have found the receipt in somebody's waste-bin, and in the second you might be a guilty party with a convincing lawyer; nevertheless in such cases the evidence can for the most part be taken as *sufficient*.

2 **Proof can be inductive**. If you look back to the start of this section on the Design Argument, we pointed out that Paley's argument is *a posteriori* (based on what we observe) and inductive. Inductive reasoning is where we use reasoning to show the truth of a conclusion. In this case, we argue back from what we observe about order in the universe to the supposed cause – God. Inductive arguments are about what is *probably true*, and they give us new knowledge.

3 **Inductive arguments can amount to 'proofs' when all the evidence points to the truth of the conclusion,** for example that 'Water boils at 100 °C at sea level'. There can be no absolute guarantee that at some stage, somewhere in the world, water will not boil at a different temperature, but for all practical purposes the observations we make about boiling water are taken to be a scientific truth. The test to prove that truth (measuring temperature at sea level) is repeatable and verifiable by anybody who cares to carry it out with reliable equipment. Inductive arguments, therefore, can be very powerful, and in science can have the status of 'proofs'. We use them to uncover scientific laws.

4 **Paley's Design Argument is inductive, but its evidence does not amount to scientific proof,** because we have no clear way of assessing the degree of probability of his argument, because whatever part of Paley's evidence we use, there will always be those who reject it in favour of Hume's view that the universe probably orders itself. Two examples:

● Paley's evidence about the regularity of the orbits of the heavenly bodies is not strong evidence for God, since gravity is what moves the heavenly bodies around the sun, and gravity is just part of the way in which matter behaves.
● Paley's evidence about design in nature is also not very convincing to a scientist, since it is just as likely that some version of multiverse theory is true, so what we see as having been designed might be the product of pure chance.

5 **Nevertheless Paley's inductive argument could well be the best explanation of the order we see in the universe**. In general terms, there are two explanations for the existence of the universe: either it made itself, or something made it. If it made itself, then its apparent orderliness has no explanation beyond itself: there doesn't have to be an explanation. If something made it, then its apparent orderliness shows the maker's design.

Which is the best explanation? The answer can only be one of personal preference. For Hume, the answer could be that there were several designers: so just as ships have many designers for their different parts and functions, there might be many designers of the universe. For those who believe in God, the most obvious solution is a single, all-powerful designer. For many of those who believe in God already, this is an inductive argument that amounts to a *personal* proof. It is also possible that for those who are otherwise undecided about the existence of God, Paley's Design Argument could offer a sufficient level of proof of the existence of God.

6 **For some individuals who believe in God, Paley's Design Argument could not be a proof, because proof could only come through religious experience,** by some kind of psychological certainty that they had experienced God, like some people have in a near-death experience. Nevertheless that kind of 'proof' could never be transferred from one person's brain to another. Not only that, even if everybody *believed* there was a designer God, this would still not *prove* that there is a designer God.

7 **Paley's inductive Design Argument can never have the status of a deductive proof.** The difference between **inductive** and **deductive** arguments will be looked at in the next chapter on the Ontological Argument, which is meant to be a deductive / logical proof of the existence of God. A deductive proof is one in which, if the premises (the propositions on which the argument is based) are true, then the conclusion must logically be true.

No inductive argument can ever be logically true, because inductive arguments are based on observation, and we can never be 100 percent certain that our observations are correct or that they will always remain correct. For example, 'water always boils at 100°C at sea level', is not logically certain, because we can never be sure that at some point in the future water will not boil at a different temperature. To repeat, then: only deductive arguments can be logically certain. Paley's Design Argument is an inductive argument, so it can never be a logically certain proof of the existence of God. At best it is **probably** true.

# The relationship between reason and faith

This discussion is required by the specification. It appears here as a general introduction in connection with arguments for the existence of God. The value of faith for the Design, Ontological and Cosmological Arguments is considered separately for each argument.

1 By reason, we mean the 'rational' part of the human mind: using logic, establishing facts, reaching conclusions, making judgements, supporting our judgements with reasons, and so on. Having faith is having trust, or belief, in something or someone (such as God).

2 **Some argue that belief in God is unreasonable,** because belief in God is about a being who by definition cannot be investigated by science. Those who take this view hold that truth is what we can know through science and our senses, and when people say that they believe in God, they are talking about a being who cannot be known in this way.

We can question this approach. A hypothesis is an explanation of something, made on the basis of limited evidence. There are currently a number of conflicting scientific hypotheses for the origin of the universe, but a complete solution may well remain beyond our grasp. The idea of an intelligent designer is a hypothesis, and the evidence for it is clear: the existence of conscious beings such as ourselves implies that the universe was created by an intelligent Creator. This may or may not turn out to be true, but it is a rational hypothesis. Belief in such a being is neither unscientific nor irrational.

3 **For others, faith is the only thing that gives us certainty**. Such an approach is known as **fideism**, which literally means 'faith-ism'. Fideists hold that in matters to do with religion faith is all-important, and not reason. Faith is about passionate commitment, and people are fully justified in believing something to be true through their own personal experience. People can believe in God with absolute and passionate conviction, and that certainty can never be experienced by using reason.

We can question this approach also. If somebody is absolutely convinced that his faith entitles him to torture others, then fideism might be seen to justify torture on religious grounds, which hardly seems rational. To use another example, well-known in this area of debate, you have probably seen the 'Peanuts' comic strip. One of the characters is Linus, a young boy who believes that every year on Halloween, the Great Pumpkin appears to everyone who sincerely believes in him. Linus, who is a sincere believer, waits every year in his pumpkin patch, but the Great Pumpkin never comes. Although humiliated, Linus never abandons his belief. The cartoon strip does not belittle sincerely held beliefs, but some use 'Great Pumpkin' objections to fideism to argue that it can justify absolutely anything. Should we not expect some rational justification for the beliefs that we hold, however sincerely? (Note 7)

4 **A view which is closer to a middle ground between faith and reason is seen in H.H. Price's distinction between 'belief in' and 'belief that'.** (Note 8) There is an important difference between someone who says 'I believe *that* God exists' and someone who says, 'I believe *in* God'.

> 'Surely belief 'in' is an attitude to a person, whether human or divine, while belief 'that' is just an attitude to a proposition? Could any difference be more obvious than this?' (Note 9)

According to Price, those who have no religious belief tend to trivialise it, but whether they like it or not it is an important phenomenon that they should try to understand by paying attention to the accounts of those who do have it. Belief *in* God is both 'interested' and 'disinterested'. It is *interested* in the sense that the believer can hope for benefits from that belief.

> '… surely it is a good thing for the believer himself (and for all of us) that God is loving, compassionate and merciful, that he answers prayers, that he gives his grace to us, that he is a refuge to us in times of trouble. Nothing could be more advantageous to us than the existence of God, if he is what theists believe him to be … We believe not only that all this is and has been 'a very good thing' for each of us individually and all of us collectively, but also that it will continue to be so.' (Note 10)

Belief in God is *disinterested* in the sense that it is a good thing in its own right that God exists, just as it is a good thing in its own right that friendship exists. It is an intrinsically good thing – good for its own sake – that God exists. In fact it is,

> '... the fundamental 'good thing' without which there would be no others.' (Note 11)

By contrast with this form of belief in God, there are also those who merely **believe that** God exists, and **this is nothing more than the mere acceptance of a proposition**. It is quite possible to believe *that* God exists, in the sense that there 'is a God' (as opposed to there being no God), but such a belief carries with it none of the sense of value that we find with interested and disinterested belief in God.

**We can now see the difference between reasoning about God and having faith in God**. Reason of course has value in the way in which we talk about God, but faith is the vehicle through which we can come to value God as 'the fundamentally good thing'. Faith of this kind, as we just said, '...cannot be reduced to the mere acceptance of an existential proposition.' (Note 12)

5 Nothing in the idea of faith excludes the idea that we can have reasoned evidence for what is believed through faith. Pope John Paul II's Encyclical Letter, *Fides et Ratio* (*Faith and Reason*), argues that truth is known by a combination of both faith and reason, and that the absence of either one diminishes man's ability to know himself, the world and God (see below).

- Using book or internet sources, take notes on how Blaise Pascal (1623-1662) and Søren Kierkegaard (1813-1855) supported fideism. (For example, both are discussed in: https://gotquestions.org/fideism.html)

- Take brief notes on Pope John Paul II's Encyclical Letter, *Fides et Ratio*, on the relationship between faith and reason. The text is available, for example, at: http://w2.vatican.va/content/john-paul-ii/en/encyclicals/documents/hf_jp-ii_enc_14091998_fides-et-ratio.html

## What value does Paley's Design Argument have for religious faith?

1 Perhaps the greatest value of Paley's argument for religious faith is that it supports faith by reasoning.

You will remember that natural theology is the view that the existence of God can be seen in nature through the use of observation and reasoning, without the need for any special revelation from God. Paley's argument supports this view. Again, the argument cannot prove God's existence, but it does demonstrate that theologians and philosophers can use reason and observation to talk rationally and meaningfully about God. This is a clear support for religious faith.

2 Paley's argument can be used as part of the religious defence against atheism.

- Atheists claim that religion is unreasonable because religious faith is nothing more than idle speculation.
- But atheists have no more evidence that God does not exist than theists have for believing that he does, so the atheistic view that religious faith is nothing more than idle speculation is itself nothing more than idle speculation.
- So, if atheists can speculate that 'God does not exist' is reasonable, then it must be reasonable for theists to speculate that God does exist.
- This holds true for Paley's Design Argument: there is nothing obscure or hard to understand about it, so it is a reasonable claim that God exists.
- Some would see it as a reasonable hypothesis because it is a possible interpretation of the evidence. Science and religion can be seen as two different frames of reference looking at the same data.

3 For those who are unsure what to believe, the simplicity of Paley's argument could provide a basis for belief. Moreover belief in God does not depend just on the Design Argument. The Cosmological Argument, for example, is also a powerful argument to support belief in God.

4 Some would argue that Paley's Design Argument has no value for faith, because faith does not depend on any kind of proof or probability: it depends on commitment to God and to a religious way of life.

5 Alternatively, some would use H.H. Price's argument about belief in and belief that. Paley's argument provides evidence for belief *that* God exists but it also comments on the wondrous nature of the design of the universe, suggesting that this supports belief *in* God. .

## What kind of God are we left with?

You will see that criticism of the Design Argument raises some fairly powerful questions about the nature of a designer.

- If we argue that evolution is part of God's design, then some might argue that we are left with a God who does not care about the immense suffering evolution causes. How would Christian belief cope with the idea of a God who is not all-loving?
- Process theologians prefer to accept that God cannot eliminate such suffering because he is not omnipotent. How would Christian belief cope with the idea of a God who is not all-powerful?
- Many deists argue that God designed and created the world and then left it to its own free devices, so what happens in the world is in the hands of the beings that control it, which in our case means ourselves. There are no miracles, and there is no personal revelation through scripture or religious experience. How would Christian belief cope with the idea of a God who is indifferent to humans?

This is not a claim that any of these possibilities is truly the case. It is a suggestion that Christians should think seriously about the nature of God, since traditional answers to that question do not seem to give us consistent answers.

# Technical terms for Paley's Design Argument

**analogy**  To get to analogy, start with inference. An inference is a conclusion reached through evidence and reasoning. An analogy is an inference where information or meaning is transferred from one subject to another. In his Design Argument, Paley is transferring his inference about the organisation and design of watches to the organisation and design of nature. In simple terms his analogical argument is a comparison between two systems.

**Anthropic Principle**  'Anthropic' means 'related to humans', so the Anthropic Principle is that there is a direct link between our observation of the universe and the 'boundary conditions' which brought it into existence. In other words, the boundary conditions (also known as 'cosmological constants') had to be 'fine tuned' by God, otherwise intelligent life could never have developed: it is no accident that we are here.

**anthropomorphism**  The habit of attributing human form or ideas to beings other than humans, particularly to gods and animals. The adjective is 'anthropomorphic'.

**a posteriori**  Arguments which depend on sense experience: think of 'posterior' – behind / after sense experience. For example, that 'oak trees grow from acorns' can only be known by sense experience, and not by logic.

**inductive**  Arguments which use reasoning in which the premises seek to supply strong evidence for (not absolute proof of) the truth of the conclusion. Inductive arguments are probabilistic. They can be used to argue from what we see in the world back to the supposed cause.

**inference**  See analogy

**natural theology**  The view that questions about God's existence, nature and attributes can be answered without referring to scripture or to any other form of special revelation, by using reason, science, history and observation.

**omnibenevolent**  All-loving. Omnibenevolence is an attribute of God.

**omnipotent**  All-powerful. Omnipotence is an attribute of God.

**premise**  A proposition that supports, or helps to support, a conclusion.

**teleological**  telos in Greek means 'end' or 'purpose', so 'The Teleological Argument for the existence of God' seeks to show that we can perceive evidence of deliberate design in the natural world.

# Summary of Paley's Design Argument

1  **Paley's argument is based on his observation of the world, so it is:**

- a posteriori and inductive
- a 'probability' argument and not a proof.

It is based on three main sets of observations:

- The complexity of the biological world (e.g. the eye, and of the laws of nature generally).
- The regularity of the orbits of the heavenly bodies and of the seasons of the year.
- The purpose of a designer (God) seen in this complexity and purpose.

Paley argues inductively from what we can see in the world (the appearance of design) back to the supposed cause (God).

2  **Paley's Design Argument is based on the analogy between the properties of a watch and the properties of the universe**

He begins with the observation of a stone and then a watch. A watch has complex parts put together for a purpose, so it must have been designed by a watchmaker. Similarly the universe has parts that function together for a purpose. So the universe must have been designed by a universe maker. The Design of the universe is far more wonderful than that of a watch, so its designer is far greater than any human: its designer is God. Just as apparent flaws in a watch, and any ignorance we may have about watches, do not destroy the inference to a designer / watchmaker, our lack of knowledge about the universe does not destroy our inference that it was designed. Paley supports his arguments by referring to the perfect design of an eye for vision and to the perfect adaptation of animals such as fish and birds to their environment. Design is also seen in the perfect regularity of orbits of the heavenly bodies.

3  **Hume's critique of Design Arguments**

Avoid three common errors:

- The error of thinking that Hume was commenting specifically on Paley's Design Argument.

17

- The error of assuming that Paley had not read Hume's *Dialogues*.
- The error of giving a 'parrot' recital of Hume's comments.

Hume's critique:

- The cause of design in the universe needs only to be proportional to its effect. Even if we grant that the universe was designed, there is no evidence that this was the God of Christian theism. A lesser being could have designed the universe.
- The existence of evil and imperfection in the world suggests (at best) a limited designer.
- Analogies between the universe and machines are flawed. The world is more like a vegetable, and vegetables design and reproduce themselves.
- Any analogy between the designers of human machines and the designer of the universe is just anthropomorphism.
- The universe could have developed into a comparatively ordered state simply by chance.

### 4 Strengths and weaknesses of Paley's Design Argument

Weaknesses

- Hume seems to be right that the all-powerful God of Christian theism is a greater cause than is needed to account for the appearance of design in the universe.
- There is too much evil in the world to see it as the design of a loving / powerful God.
- Hume's comment that the universe is more like a vegetable than a machine is backed up by Darwin's theory of evolution. Nature appears to design itself without the need for God.
- As Hume says, we have no experience of universe making, so our ideas about it are anthropomorphic and limited.
- Moreover, if nature can design itself, Hume is probably right in claiming that the universe is now in an ordered state purely by chance (his Epicurean Hypothesis).

Strengths

- Paley may be right to argue that the designer is the all-powerful Christian God, and not Hume's lesser gods, because (as Swinburne says) 'God' is probably the simplest explanation of the appearance of design in the universe.
- Paley argued that evil may be unavoidable in order for God to bring about good. Modern

arguments support Paley here, for example, the free will defence; Process Theology; and Hick's Irenaean theodicy.

- Paley is right to see God as the designer of nature: Swinburne argues that evolution simply obeys the laws of science designed by God.
- Paley's language is anthropomorphic, but his conclusion that the designer is metaphysical and transcendent still seems reasonable. Moreover, we know enough about design to show that Paley could be right.
- Paley's argument that nature shows purpose and design is supported by the 'fine-tuning' argument and the anthropic principle, although if it turns out that there is a multiverse, that argument does not work.
- Paley's argument is good because it is based on induction – what we observe; and we *do* observe the appearance of design.

### 5 The status of Paley's argument as a 'proof'

- Proof can mean 'sufficient evidence for a proposition', as in 'proof of guilt'.
- Proof can be inductive, and inductive proof can have scientific status (true in all known circumstances, such as: 'Water boils at 100 °C at sea level'), but Paley's argument amounts, rather, to a reasonable inductive *probability*.
- Paley's argument can be seen as the *best explanation* of the order we see, so is still a powerful argument.
- Some hold that proof can come only through the certainty that people find in faith, for example in religious experience, although this is a proof only to the one who has the experience and the faith.
- Proof can also be deductive, as in Anselm's Ontological Argument. Paley's argument is inductive, so however probable it is, it can never amount to a deductive / logically certain proof.

### 6 The relationship between reason and faith

- Some see faith in God as unreasonable, holding that truth is scientific / empirical. However, the belief that God exists is a *reasonable* hypothesis based on evidence, such as our observation of the universe and its appearance of order and design.
- For others, only faith gives certainty.
- However, fideism itself can be seen as justifying absurd beliefs (such as Linus' belief in the Great Pumpkin).

- H.H. Price distinguishes between *belief that* God exists and *belief in* God. *Belief in* God is evaluative, interested and disinterested, whereas *belief that* God exists is nothing more than the acceptance of an existential proposition ('There is a God').

- Belief *in* God is the most distinctive thing about religion, and is what we mean by **faith**. Belief *that* God exists is reasonable, but reason does not take us as far as faith.

- Pope John Paul II argues that truth can be known only through a combination of faith and reason. Excluding or minimising the importance of either one reduces our ability to understand truth.

7 **The value of Paley's Design Argument for religious faith**

- It *supports* faith by reasoning, which matches Pope John Paul II's argument that faith and reason should be mutually supportive and not exclusive.

- It forms a reasonable defence of religious faith against atheism, which has no more evidence for the non-existence of God than Paley has for God's existence.

- Paley's argument is, in effect, a reasonable scientific hypothesis: a reasonable interpretation of the evidence that we see around us.

- However, some insist that Paley's argument offers no support to faith, since for fideists faith does not depend on reason or proof.

- H.H. Price's distinction between *belief in* and *belief that* can be used to support Paley. Paley's use of natural theology supports *belief that* God designed the universe, and Paley's comments about the wonder of the design promote *belief in* God as the designer.

**At the end of this discussion, we are still left with the issue of what kind of God we are left with.**

Does the nature of evil show that the designer cannot be all-loving? Could Christian belief cope with the view of Process Theology, that God is not all-powerful? Could Christian belief cope with the deistic view that the designer has left us to our own free devices?

## Three suggestions for practice and development

You could use one or more of these three questions / claims as a homework assignment, a class essay, or a focus for practice.

1 'Paley's Design Argument is inductive, so cannot be a proof of God's existence.'

2 How far does the existence of evil defeat Paley's Design Argument?

3 'Evolution supports Paley's Design Argument.'

# Arguments for the existence of God

## The Ontological Argument

This chapter will cover:
- Anselm's *a priori* argument
- Criticisms from Gaunilo and Kant

### You will need to consider six things for this section

1 The basis of Anselm's argument in thought.

2 Anselm's *a priori* Ontological Argument.

3 Criticisms from Gaunilo and Kant.

4 The strengths and weaknesses of Anselm's argument.

5 The status of Anselm's argument as a 'proof'.

6 The value of Anselm's argument for religious faith.

When looking at the Ontological Argument, it is best to start with its technical vocabulary, because the vocabulary defines the argument. Make sure you understand these terms thoroughly before going on to Anselm's Ontological Argument – it will make your studies a lot easier.

## Technical terms for the Ontological Argument

**a priori** and **a posteriori**
These you know from the Design Argument. 'A priori' arguments rely on logical deduction and not on sense experience. An *a priori* argument is prior to / before sense experience. 'A posteriori' arguments depend on sense experience: think of 'posterior' – behind / after sense experience. For example, that 'oak trees grow from acorns' can only be known by sense experience and not by logic.

**inductive** and **deductive**
'Inductive' you already know from the Design Argument. An inductive argument is probabilistic, because the truth of its conclusion cannot be guaranteed by the truth of its premises. In a 'deductive' argument, if the premises are true, then the conclusion must be true. To explain 'deductive', we'll start with 'premise'. A premise is a proposition upon which an argument is based or from which a conclusion is drawn. A deductive argument is one which is intended to guarantee the truth of the conclusion so long as its premises are true. As an example

(in which P1 / P2 stand for Premise 1 / Premise 2 and C stands for Conclusion):

**P1** All horses have manes.

**P2** A Suffolk Punch is a horse.

**C** Therefore Suffolk Punches have manes.

Another example from mathematics:

**P1** If a = b

**P2** and b = c

**C** then a = c.

This kind of reasoning is *a priori*, meaning that it relies on logical deduction and not sense experience. The Ontological Argument is an *a priori* argument which claims to prove that God exists.

### synthetic and analytic
'Synthetic' statements / propositions are those whose truth or falsity are determined by sense experience, for example, 'William has a hairy chest'. 'Analytic' statements / propositions are those that are true by the meaning of the words used, for example, 'A bicycle has two wheels' is analytic because by definition a bicycle is a two-wheeled vehicle. In short, analytic statements are true by definition.

### subject and predicate
Any complete sentence contains a subject and a predicate. The 'subject' refers to who or what the sentence is about and the 'predicate' gives us information about the subject. In the following sentences, the subject is underlined and the predicate is in italics: <u>George</u> *played the piano*. <u>The dog</u> *barked*. <u>The girl</u> *starred in a film*.

### necessary and contingent
We can talk about necessary and contingent 'things' and necessary and contingent 'truths'. A 'necessary truth' is a proposition that could not possibly be false, for example, that 2 + 2 = 4, or 'squares have four sides'. A 'contingent truth' is a proposition that happens to be true but might have been otherwise, for example, 'In the UK police cars use blue flashing lights in an emergency' – it is possible that they could have been red.

A 'necessary thing' is something that could not possibly have failed to exist, for example, some argue that the laws of mathematics exist necessarily. A 'contingent thing' is one which does not exist necessarily and so could have failed to exist. Most things in the universe are said to be contingent, including people – your parents might never have met, for example.

## Activity

Identify which two of the following statements are analytic and explain why.

1. There are mountains on the far side of the Moon.
2. The Sun will rise tomorrow.
3. Frozen water is ice.
4. All bachelors are unhappy.
5. Spinsters are unmarried women.
6. Cows exist.

## Key terms

**subject** Any complete sentence contains a subject and a predicate. The **subject** refers to who or what the sentence is about.

**predicate** Any complete sentence contains a subject and a predicate. The **predicate** gives us information about the subject.

## Activity

Identify the **subject** and **predicate** in the following sentences.

1. Peter Piper picked a peck of pickled peppers.
2. Henry's broken toe will heal itself in about two months.
3. The love of money is the root of all evil.
4. *Tyrannosaurus rex* was one of the largest land predators ever to exist.
5. Happiness is sometimes hard to define.

# The basis of Anselm's argument in thought

1  The term 'ontological' comes from the Greek *ontos*, meaning 'essence', 'existence', 'being'. Anselm's eleventh-century argument was the first of its kind and continues to resurface in different forms. The Ontological Argument is based on the claim that God's existence can be deduced from his definition – that once God is correctly defined, there can be no doubt that he exists.

2  If you look, now, at the technical terms listed above, you will be able to see what it means to say that Anselm's Ontological Argument has its basis in thought.

The Ontological Argument claims that:
- The proposition 'God exists' is *a priori* / **deductive** – it can be known to be true without reference to sense experience, just by thinking about God's nature.
- In the proposition 'God exists', the subject 'God' contains the predicate 'exists', so God must exist.
- God's existence is a **necessary** truth, not a **contingent** one.

Do not worry if this sounds too technical (the Ontological Argument is technical!): these points will become clear as we look at Anselm's argument.

Bear in mind before we start that most of the terminology we have just looked at is not used by Anselm. When he says, for example, that 'God cannot not-exist', we would generally say that God exists 'necessarily', whereas all things exist 'contingently'. The modern wording has been used for clarity, but Anselm's wording can be found in many of the larger commentaries and online. Elsewhere in this book, the various writers have generally been left to speak for themselves.

---

## Key terms

*a priori*  Argument which relies on logical deduction and not on sense experience. An *a priori* argument is prior to / before sense experience.

**deductive**  Argument where if the premises are true, then the conclusion must be true.

**necessary**  A necessary truth is a proposition that could not possibly be false. A necessary thing is something that could not possibly have failed to exist.

**contingent**  A contingent truth is a proposition that happens to be true but might have been otherwise. A contingent thing is one which does not exist necessarily and so could have failed to exist.

---

# Anselm's *a priori* Ontological Argument and criticism from Gaunilo

Gaunilo's criticism of Anselm needs to be considered alongside Anselm's argument, since Anselm's reply to Gaunilo was part of his formulation of the argument. Be aware that we are not dealing with a clear 'dialogue' between Anselm and Gaunilo: rather, their writings make clear the position of each scholar on the Ontological Argument. On that basis we can work out a sequence in what they say.

## Anselm (*c.* 1033–1109)

Anselm is famous (some students might say infamous) for inventing the Ontological Argument. Very much to his credit, Anselm made a meticulous and positive analysis of religious language about 800 years before the logical positivists (of whom you will learn more at A-level) were even thought of. Anselm was many things: a Benedictine monk, Archbishop of Canterbury from 1093 until his death, and of course, eventually, a saint of the Church.

His Ontological Argument appears in *Proslogium* (1077–1078) Chapters 2–4 and also in his *Responsio* to Gaunilo. (Note 1)

Gaunilo was a contemporary of Anselm. He was also a Benedictine monk in the Marmoutier Abbey in France. He wrote *On Behalf of the Fool*, which essentially rejected Anselm's attempt to give an *a priori* proof of the existence of God.

Anselm's Ontological Argument comes in two parts, the whole being couched in a prayerful meditation to God, which we look at later.

## Anselm part 1 The Ontological Argument from *Proslogium* 2

> God is '... a being than which nothing greater can be conceived.' (Note 2)

Here is a summary of Anselm's argument in relatively modern English. The 'fool' in P2 refers to the 'fool' of Psalm 14:1 who says in his heart 'There is no God'.

**P1**  God is a being than which nothing greater can be conceived.

**P2**  This is a definition which even a fool understands in his mind, even though he does not understand it to exist in reality.

**P3**  There is a difference between having an idea in the mind and knowing that this idea exists in reality.

**P4**  For example, a painter has an idea in his mind of what he wants to paint; but when he has painted it, that idea now exists both in his mind and in reality.

**P5**  It is greater to exist both in the mind and in reality than to exist only in the mind.

**P6**  If God existed only in the mind, I could think of something greater, namely a God who existed in reality also.

**C**  Therefore in order to be the greatest conceivable being (**P1**), God must exist both in the mind and in reality.

The two really important claims here are those in **P1** and **P5**.

In **P1**, by describing God as:

> **' ... a being than which nothing greater can be conceived. '**

Anselm means 'greatest' in every possible respect: God is omnipotent and omniscient, and in fact must possess every great-making quality to the highest possible level. Most people who read this think that it is a good 'working definition' of God.

In **P5**, Anselm claims that it is greater to exist both in the mind and reality than to exist only in the mind. This seems like a reasonable claim. You can imagine the necessities of life such as food and water, but to be able to eat and drink in reality is surely a much greater thing than simply thinking about it.

We can therefore reduce Anselm's arguments to two essential premises and a conclusion.

**P1**  God is the greatest conceivable being.

**P2**  It is greater to exist in reality than to exist only in the mind.

**C**  Therefore, as the greatest conceivable being, God must exist in reality.

## Criticism of Anselm by Gaunilo: *On Behalf of the Fool*

Anselm's argument was criticised by a fellow monk, Gaunilo of Marmoutiers. Anselm appears not to have minded the criticism, since it gave him the chance to emphasise a second stage of his argument in his

appear with Gaunilo's criticisms attached. (Note 3)

Gaunilo's attack used a parody of Anselm's argument. He gave an Ontological Argument for the existence of a 'perfect lost island' – an island than which nothing greater can be conceived – in which he used the structure of Anselm's argument.

The following puts Gaunilo's argument in parallel with that of Anselm, using the shorter form above:

**P1**  It is possible to conceive of the most perfect and real lost island.

**P2**  It is greater to exist in reality than to exist only in the mind.

**C**   Therefore the most perfect and real lost island must exist in reality.

Gaunilo clearly believes that the concept of 'the most perfect and real lost island' makes little sense, since we know that such an island cannot exist. Gaunilo is using a method of argument called a *reductio ad absurdum*, which is Latin for 'argument to absurdity'. He is suggesting in effect that Anselm's argument can be used to prove the existence of an endless number of perfect objects – perfect lost cricket bats, perfect oak trees, perfect what you like, and so the real fool would be anybody who argued in this way. We can show that a perfect island does not exist, so Anselm's argument does not work.

## Anselm part 2 Anselm's reply to Gaunilo: The Ontological Argument from *Proslogium* 3 and the *Responsio*

### Activity

In order to get the gist of Anselm's response to Gaunilo, try the following exercise.

Your idea of a perfect island might include some of the following: lots of sunshine, shady palm trees, coconut trees, grape vines, surfing beaches, sun-bathing beaches, swimming beaches, the most magnificent bars, restaurants, hotels and night clubs, swimming pools and an absence of exams.

What is your idea of a perfect island?

Now answer these two questions.

1  Would you ever decide once and for all what your idea of a perfect island would be like, or would your definition change from day to day?

2  If you lived for a million years, would you ever find anybody else with exactly the same definition as yours?

The chances are that you have answered 'No' to both questions in the activity, and therein lies the clue to Anselm's rejection of Gaunilo's argument.

- Anselm's reply is drawn out of his second version of his Ontological Argument in *Proslogium* 3:

> God cannot be conceived not to exist – God is that, than which nothing greater can be conceived – That which can be conceived not to exist is not God. (Note 4)

- This is developed further in the *Responsio*, where Anselm points out the difference between necessary and contingent existence (see the technical terms from earlier).

**First**: as you have probably seen from the Activity, everything that you might want to exist on your 'perfect' island is contingent – it can exist or not exist. What is a beautiful palm tree will one day rot to pieces. A beautiful bar will eventually weather and fall apart or at the very least it will need constant repairs, until eventually it is no longer the same bar.

**Second**: it is impossible to quantify the idea of a perfect island. How many trees must it have to be perfect? If you decided on a number and then changed your mind and added one more, would that number still be perfect? If your perfect drink is a tequila sunrise, but after a few years of drinking you grow to dislike the taste and change to lemonade, what has become of your perfect drink?

We can formulate Anselm's response to Gaunilo in the following way:

**P1**  To be perfect, an island would have to be 'that island than which no greater can be conceived'.

**P2**  An island than which no greater can be conceived would have to exist necessarily, since a contingent island would be less perfect than an island that existed necessarily.

**P3**  But islands are contingent, and so cannot exist necessarily.

**C**  Therefore the logic of the argument related to a perfect island does not apply to God.

Further:

**P1**  God is the greatest conceivable being.

**P2**  The greatest conceivable being cannot be conceived not to exist.

**C1**  Therefore, God, and God alone, possesses necessary existence: God cannot not exist.

In summary, Anselm gives a clear refutation of Gaunilo's 'perfect lost island' argument. He shows that necessary existence is a predicate only of God, and not of things.

Kant's objections to Ontological Arguments are not so easy to dismiss.

# Criticisms from Kant

## Immanuel Kant (1724–1804)

Kant was without doubt one of the most influential of 'modern' philosophers. He lived (and died) in Königsberg, Prussia, which after 1946 became part of Russia. When you refer to him, do resist the urge to reproduce some of the popular stories about him, for example, that he was so regular in his daily walks his neighbours set their clocks by him, or that he never travelled more than 10 miles from home – the second of these is certainly false. Simply, cherish such information to flesh out your picture of Kant's possible character.

Also, do not make the unfortunate mistake of rendering his first name as 'Emmanuelle'. As a matter of fact Kant was christened 'Emanuel' but he later changed it to 'Immanuel', that being a more faithful transliteration of the original Hebrew, which means 'God (is) with us'. (Note 5)

Kant had two major criticisms of the Ontological Argument. These were directed not at Anselm, but at the version of the Ontological Argument written by the French philosopher René Descartes in the mid-seventeenth century, although to some extent they apply also to Anselm's version of the argument. In other words, do not make the mistake of thinking that Kant is offering direct criticism of Anselm's argument.

## Objection 1: Existence is not a predicate

Descartes defined God as 'the supremely perfect being', meaning that God must possess all the perfect predicates such as omnipotence, omniscience, omnibenevolence, and so on. In addition, therefore, God must possess the perfection of existence:

> '... it is quite evident that existence can no more be separated from the essence of God than the fact that its three angles equal two right angles can be separated from the essence of a triangle, or that the idea of a mountain can be separated from the idea of a valley. Hence it is just as much of a contradiction to think of God (that is, a supremely perfect being) lacking existence (that is, lacking a perfection), as it is to think of a mountain without a valley.' (Note 6)

You will see that this is similar to the argument made by Anselm's *Proslogium*, where he states that the greatest conceivable being must possess the perfection / predicate of existence, because it is greater for such a being to exist in reality than to exist only in the mind.

Kant's objection is simple: existence is not a real predicate, because it adds nothing to the concept of a thing. Real predicates give us new knowledge of a subject. If your teacher brings a black cow into the classroom and tells you that it is an Aberdeen Angus, you have gained useful knowledge. If your teacher then tells you that the cow exists, nothing new has been added to the subject. If somebody bursts into a room and shouts out, 'it exists', 'exists' tells you nothing at all about the nature of 'it'.

▲ A Prussian Thaler from the time of Kant

Kant's example was to invite you to imagine 100 Thalers (a coin used in his day).

If you are imagining something like this, you can describe the predicates of Thalers (they are round, metallic, possibly gold, have an image of the king, and so on), and each new predicate adds to our concept of the Thalers. But if you then say, 'Oh, and by the way, the Thalers exist', nothing has been added: there is no difference between our concept of 100 Thalers and our concept of 100 Thalers that exist.

Now apply this to Anselm's concept of God.

Anselm tells us that God is the greatest conceivable being, so we can imagine God with all the predicates that Descartes lists, and each predicate: omnipotence, omniscience, omnibenevolence, and so on, adds to our concept of God. But if I then say, 'Oh, and by the way, God exists', nothing has been added: there is no difference between our concept of God and our concept of a God that exists. Moreover, the only way I can know that Thalers really do exist is to experience them: to touch, smell, see and even taste them, and to hear them if I drop them on the floor. Equally, the only way I can know that God exists is by sense experience. Logic alone gets me nowhere.

## Objection 2: We can accept the proposition that 'existing necessarily' is part of what we mean by 'God', but it does not follow from this that God exists in reality.

We will put this into an understandable sequence. If any of the words confuse you, go back to the definitions of terms at the start of this section.

1 Anselm's Ontological Argument in effect claims that the proposition 'God exists necessarily' is **analytic** – in other words, that it is true by definition.

2 Think, for example, of the statement that 'A bachelor is an unmarried man'. This is obviously analytic – true by definition – because that's how we define a bachelor.

 Think further, for example, of the statement that 'A unicorn is a horse with a horn'. This is also obviously analytic / true by definition, because that's how we define a unicorn.

3 Now take the two following propositions:

- bachelors exist
- unicorns exist.

 How do we know that there are any bachelors? The answer can only be: 'by experiencing them'. If you have an unmarried male in your family of marriageable age, then clearly 'bachelors exist' is true, because you've seen one.

 Now try it with unicorns. How do you know that there really are any unicorns? When did you last see, touch, taste, smell or hear a unicorn? People claim to have seen them, but those claims have never been substantiated. Perhaps at some point in the future somebody will indeed find unicorns; but the obvious point is that this will only happen by sense experience: it can never happen by logic.

4 Now turn your attention to the proposition 'God exists necessarily', which Anselm claims is analytic / true by definition. It follows from 3, above, that I can only know that there is a God by experiencing God

### Key term

**analytic** Statements / propositions that are true by the meaning of the words used. For example, 'A bicycle has two wheels' is analytic because by definition a bicycle is a two-wheeled vehicle. In short, analytic statements are true by definition.

through my senses. Some people do indeed claim to have experienced God, and this may be true or it may be false; but in either case it is a matter of experience and not of logic.

5 To make this as clear as possible:

'A unicorn is a horse with a horn' is logically true because that's how we define a unicorn, but it does not follow that there really are any unicorns.

Equally, 'God exists necessarily' is logically true, because that's how we define God, but it does not follow that there really is a God.

6 Clearer still:

The Ontological Argument fails because it omits one small but powerful word: 'If'.

With unicorns: *If* there are unicorns, then they will be horses with horns.

With God: *If* there is a God, then God will exist necessarily.

# The strengths and weaknesses of Anselm's Ontological Argument

## Strengths

1 It is a deductive argument, so if it succeeds, it is a proof of the existence of God. Put another way, unlike other arguments for God's existence, such as the Design and Cosmological Arguments, it does not depend on anything we observe, and since human observation is not always reliable, that can be seen as a good thing.

In the debate about the Design Argument, for example, it is very difficult to decide whether the appearance of order that we observe in the universe is really the result of design or not. With the Ontological Argument, there is no ambiguity – the argument either succeeds or fails by its logic.

2 The argument can be taken in a different way, namely the interpretation put upon it by Karl Barth, who claimed that Anselm never intended the argument to be a proof of God's existence. Instead, Barth argued that it was the result of a religious experience given to Anselm in which God revealed his nature as:

**' ... that than which nothing greater can be conceived ... '**

In other words, for those with faith, the Ontological Argument is clearly true, because it is an expression of their faith.

We shall assess Barth's argument in the following section on the value of Anselm's argument for religious faith.

3 There is no doubt that the Ontological Argument is a good training ground for learning about the difference between analytic and **synthetic** propositions, necessary and contingent beings, and so on. In other words it is useful in the art of learning how to do philosophy!

**Key term**

**synthetic** Synthetic statements / propositions are those whose truth or falsity are determined by sense experience.

## Weaknesses

1  Although there are several scholars who still defend the Ontological Argument, notably Alvin Plantinga, most scholars reject it, largely on the basis of the two major objections made by Kant, that:

- Existence is not a predicate: to say that something exists, such as, 'Cows exist', tells you nothing about cows that you have not found out from sense experience.
- Even if 'existing necessarily' is part of what we mean by God, it does not follow that God exists in reality. From what we said above about unicorns and God, Kant's objections seem to defeat the Ontological Argument.

You should bear in mind that Kant's objections do not disprove the existence of God: they simply make it extremely unlikely that God's existence can be proved by logic.

2  The starting point of Anselm's argument is that God can be defined as:

' ... that than which nothing greater can be conceived ... '

Some would argue, however, that any attempt to define God would be to limit God. Anything that can be classified and analysed can be understood by humans, and many Christians would argue that this is at best futile and at worst irreligious. Thomas Aquinas, the great Catholic theologian, insisted that we do not know God's definition, so Anselm must be wrong.

You might want to question this, because to say that God is:

' ... that than which nothing greater can be conceived ... '

is really to say that God has no limitation at all, and that this is indeed a concept that we can understand.

# The status of Anselm's argument as a 'proof'

Think back to what we said about the status of the Design Argument as a proof of God's existence: the argument is **inductive**, so cannot be a proof of God, because all inductive arguments are probabilistic. Some people will observe design in the universe; others will not. The former will think that God is the most probable explanation; the latter will not.

Anselm's Ontological Argument, you will now have realised, is a completely different way of arguing.

- It is deductive rather than inductive. In a deductive argument, if the premises are true, then the truth of the conclusion is guaranteed.
- Unlike the Design Argument, it claims to be true without having to use any fallible sense experience, so is *a priori* rather than **a posteriori**.
- Anselm argues that 'God exists necessarily' is analytic – it is true by definition / logically true.
- So, if the premises of Anselm's argument are true, then it is a proof of the existence of God.

---

## Key terms

**inductive** Argument which is probabilistic, because the truth of its conclusion cannot be guaranteed by the truth of its premises.

*a posteriori* Arguments which depend on sense experience: think of 'posterior' – behind / after sense experience. For example, that 'oak trees grow from acorns' can only be known by sense experience and not by logic.

## Is it a proof?

- This is disputed, because various scholars claim that the argument works, including Anselm and Descartes, although most argue that it does not.
- For most scholars, Kant's objections show that the argument is not a proof: it merely shows that 'If' God exists, then he exists necessarily.
- Compare the 'proof' of Anselm's argument with mathematical proof, for example, that 2 + 2 = 4. Nobody doubts that 2 + 2 = 4, but lots of people doubt that Anselm's Ontological Argument is true. If it was really a proof, there would be no doubt.
- Some might argue that it is a proof in Karl Barth's view, as a faith-based acceptance.

# The value of Anselm's argument for religious faith

In *Proslogium* chapter 4, Anselm returns to the idea of the fool of Psalm 14:1, who says in his heart that 'There is no God'. You can read this chapter (it is brief) online at: http://www.sacred-texts.com/chr/ans/ans010.htm

1 Anselm argues that a thing may be conceived in two ways:

   **a** 'when the word signifying it is conceived', and
   **b** 'when the thing itself is understood'.

To explain his meaning, Anselm gives the example of the statement, 'fire is water':

   **a** the **words** in this statement can all be understood without any difficulty
   **b** but someone who **really** understands fire and water cannot understand fire to be water at all.

The same is true (says Anselm), in the fool's statement: 'there is no God':

   **a** the words in this statement can also be understood
   **b** but once you truly understand that God is 'that than which a greater cannot be conceived', according to Anselm you *must* then understand that this being exists.

Anselm in effect is claiming that the God the atheist does not believe in is not the God of Christian faith. **The atheist does not have an *adequate* concept of God**.

Anselm then concludes *Proslogium* 4 with a prayer:

> 'I thank thee, gracious Lord, I thank thee; because what I formerly believed by thy bounty, I now so understand by thine illumination, that if I were unwilling to believe that thou dost exist, I should not be able not to understand this to be true.'

There are some issues here which do not seem to have an obvious answer:

- If, as Anselm claims, the atheist does not have an adequate concept of God, what is to stop the atheist from claiming that Anselm's idea of God is just as inadequate, because he has invented it? Anselm defines God as 'that than which a greater cannot be conceived', but as we said in the objections to the argument, however good that definition is, it still doesn't tell you whether or not such a being exists in reality.
  - Anselm's language can be very difficult to understand, but in the concluding prayer, he seems to be saying that God helped him by making him 'willing to believe', which implies that he was given some kind of religious experience, and that it is this 'illumination' which atheists lack. Perhaps he is saying something similar to H.H. Price (whose views on 'belief in' and 'belief that' we looked at in the section on Paley's Design Argument), that religion is a thing of ultimate value, and so atheists should make every effort to *'believe in'* God. Perhaps the atheist who *'does not believe that'* God exists is just the other side of the coin of someone who just *'believes that'* he does exist. Neither position understands the whole dimension to life that is opened up by *'belief in'* God.

This kind of view is supported by Karl Barth's understanding of Anselm's Ontological Argument as 'Faith Seeking Understanding'.

**2  Karl Barth's view is that Anselm's argument is about faith, not logic.**

In looking at the strengths of Anselm's argument, we did refer to Karl Barth's interpretation of the argument as **a religious experience given by God to Anselm** from which Anselm understood that God exists necessarily.

### Karl Barth (1886–1968)

Barth was a Swiss Protestant theologian. He was emphatically opposed to the liberal Protestantism of his time, primarily since it seemed bent on interpreting the message of Jesus in line with modern culture, whereas Barth insisted that the only allegiance of the Church should be to God (and especially not to the likes of Adolf Hitler).

Barth insisted that God can only be known by revelation, and not by logic, and this led him to have a novel approach to Anselm's Ontological Argument. In 1931, Barth wrote a book on Anselm called, *Faith Seeking Understanding*, in which he claimed that Anselm's argument was never intended to be a logical proof of the existence of God. Rather, and as you can see by the title of his book, Barth saw the Ontological Argument as a way for faith to seek understanding. In other words, according to Barth, Anselm used the Ontological Argument as a way of trying to understand the God he believed in.

Barth's argument in brief:

- At the end of Chapter 1 of the *Proslogium*, Anselm says:

  'I do not seek to understand that I may believe, but I believe in order to understand. For this too I believe: that unless I believe, I shall not understand.' (Note 7)

In other words, for Anselm, belief in God comes before reasoning about God.

- Thus Anselm began with a prayer, praying that God would reveal himself to his understanding.
- Moreover, God revealed a name to Anselm:

  **' ... that than which nothing greater can be conceived.'**

  Anselm's definition of God, according to Barth, was not based on logic – it was given to him by a religious revelation.

- You can see Barth's point if this understanding of Anselm is right: if humans could prove the existence of God purely by logic, then we would not need God's revelation, and God himself could be just another object of human knowledge.

**Against Barth's interpretation:**

- Anselm's *Proslogium* is a prayer directed towards the 'fool' in Psalm 14:4, who says that there is no God. In other words, the prayer is directed at an atheist. If his Ontological Argument is not intended to be a logical proof to convince the atheist, then why does he go to so much trouble to demonstrate the truth of the argument?
- In the preface to the *Proslogium*, Anselm mentions that he is looking for a proof; not that he is merely reinforcing some kind of religious revelation.
- Perhaps the most convincing argument against Barth is that Gaunilo bothers to respond to it. To make that clear: if Anselm was just telling people about his faith in God, why would Gaunilo object to that? Gaunilo objects to Anselm's argument precisely because he thinks it *is* a logical 'proof' that fails, so Gaunilo is telling him why he fails. Moreover, Anselm then responds by telling Gaunilo that only God has necessary existence. In other words, they are having an argument about logic, and not a discussion about faith.

3 **To some extent Anselm's Ontological Argument has value for those who believe in God already,** since perhaps they are more likely to accept it as a logical proof.

4 **Bear in mind, however, that many fideist Christians disagree with this last point.**

  Fideism is the view that faith does not depend on reason, so if faith points one way and reason points another, then fideists are justified in following what they believe. Fideists might therefore reject any attempt to 'contain' God within a system of logic. They would argue that if we could prove God's existence by logic, then faith would lose all of its value: we would not need faith in God if we could show logically that God must exist.

5 To give Anselm the last word, although Anselm is seeking for a logical proof of God's existence, this is not an attempt to replace faith with logic, despite Barth's claims. Faith for Anselm is a volitional state (an act of the will) motivated by love of God:

  **' ... and a drive to act as God wills ... '**

  So 'faith seeking understanding', which is Anselm's 'motto' in the *Proslogium*, means something like:

  **' ... an active love of God seeking a deeper knowledge of God.'** [Note 8]

---

**Discussion point**

Look at the text of Anselm's *Proslogium*, for example, http://www.fordham.edu/halsall/basis/anselm-proslogium.asp#CHAPTER1, and form your own judgement. Do you think that Anselm is talking mainly about logic or faith?

---

**Discussion point**

To what extent do you think that Anselm's Ontological Argument includes both faith and reason equally?

# Summary of Anselm's Ontological Argument

For a start, remember the technical terms and how they define the argument:

● *a priori* and *a posteriori*
● inductive and deductive
● synthetic and analytic
● subject and predicate
● necessary and contingent.

## 1 The basis of the argument in thought

The Ontological Argument is based on the claim that God's existence can be deduced from his definition: once God is correctly defined, there can be no doubt that he exists. Using the list of technical terms above:

● The Ontological Argument claims that the proposition, 'God exists' is *a priori* / deductive – you do not need sense experience to know that it is true: you know it is true just by thinking about it.
● In the proposition, 'God exists', the subject 'God' contains the predicate 'exists', so God must exist. It's as clear as knowing that 'bicycles' (subject) 'have two wheels' (predicate).
● God's existence is a necessary truth, not a contingent one.

## 2 Anselm's *a priori* Ontological Argument and criticism from Gaunilo

### Anselm's Ontological Argument from *Proslogium* 2:

*Use the shortened form of the argument as a basis for remembering the whole:*

**P1** God is the greatest conceivable being.

**P2** It is greater to exist in reality than to exist only in the mind.

**C** Therefore, as the greatest conceivable being, God must exist in reality.

*Now add the bits about fools and painters and you've got it!*

### Criticism by Gaunilo: *On Behalf of the Fool*:

*This uses a parody of Anselm's argument to show that it is absurd:*

**P1** It is possible to conceive of the most perfect and real lost island.

**P2** It is greater to exist in reality than to exist only in the mind.

**C** Therefore the most perfect and real lost island must exist in reality.

*So Gaunilo is saying that the real fool would be anybody who argued in this way (e.g. Anselm!)*

### Anselm's reply to Gaunilo from *Proslogium* 3 and the *Responsio*:

**P1** To be perfect, an island would have to be 'that island than which no greater can be conceived'.

**P2** An island than which no greater can be conceived would have to exist necessarily, since a contingent island would be less perfect than an island that existed necessarily.

**P3** But islands are contingent so cannot exist necessarily.

**C** Therefore the logic of the argument related to the perfect island does not apply to God.

### Further:

**P1** God is the greatest conceivable being.

**P2** The greatest conceivable being cannot be conceived not to exist.

**C1** Therefore, God, and God alone, possesses necessary existence: God cannot not exist.

In summary, Anselm gives a clear refutation of Gaunilo's 'perfect lost island' argument. He shows that **necessary existence is a predicate only of God**, and **not of things**.

*Anselm's response to Gaunilo seems very powerful, but it is hard to see how Anselm would have replied to Kant's objections, given here, which most scholars think defeat Anselm's argument.*

## 3 Criticism from Kant

### Objection 1: Existence is not a predicate

● Kant attacks Descartes' Ontological Argument, that as the supremely perfect being, God must possess all the perfect predicates, such as omnipotence and omniscience and perfect (i.e. necessary) existence.
● But existence is not a real predicate (think 'Thalers' and think 'it exists'), so if we list all of God's predicates (omnipotence, omniscience, and so on) and then add 'existence', we add nothing to the concept of God. The only way I can know that Thalers exist is to experience them; so the only way I can know that God exists is by sense experience, not logic.

**Objection 2: We can accept that 'necessary existence' is part of what we mean by 'God', but it does not follow from this that God exists in reality**

● Think 'unicorn'. 'A unicorn is a horse with a horn' is logically true, because that's how we define a unicorn, but it does not follow from this that there really are any unicorns.
● Equally, 'God exists necessarily' is logically true, because that's how we define God, but it does not follow that there really is a God.
● Think 'if'. If there are unicorns, then they will be horses with horns. If there is a God, then God will exist necessarily.

**4  Strengths and weaknesses of Anselm's Ontological Argument**

**Strengths**

● The argument is deductive, so if it works, it is a proof.
● Not only that, according to Karl Barth and others, the argument succeeds precisely because it is not meant to be a logical proof: it's a confession of faith. For those with faith, the Ontological Argument is clear to their faith.
● The Ontological Argument is a good training ground in learning how to do philosophy!

**Weaknesses**

● Most agree that Kant's two objections defeat all Ontological Arguments. They do not disprove the existence of God, but they do show that God's existence cannot be shown by logic.
● Some reject Anselm's definition of God as 'the greatest conceivable being', but Christians such as Aquinas would reject any attempt to define God, because if we were able to define God that would limit him. Against that, some would say that Anselm's definition is a good place to start and we know what it means.

**5  The status of Anselm's argument as a 'proof'**

● Here you should contrast the deductive / a priori Ontological Argument with inductive / a posteriori arguments (like the Design Argument).
● Inductive arguments can only be probability arguments, but the deductive Ontological Argument is a proof if we agree that the argument works.
● The Ontological Argument does not seem to work, since most agree that Kant's objections defeat it; moreover it does not have the status of

a mathematical proof, where the truth of $2 + 2 = 4$ is obvious to everyone. If the Ontological Argument was really a proof, there would be no argument about the Ontological Argument either.
● You might want to argue that it is a 'proof' in Barth's sense – that it is obvious to faith.

**6  The value of Anselm's argument for religious faith**

**a** ● In *Proslogium* 4, Anselm argues that the fool (the atheist) does not have an adequate concept of God. Someone who truly understands the definition of God as 'that than which a greater cannot be conceived' *must* then understand that this being exists.
● Anselm appears to say that he was helped to this understanding by a religious experience.
● Karl Barth develops a similar view.

**b** This is primarily about Barth's interpretation of Anselm's argument, that:
● It is cast in the form of a prayer rather than a logical proof.
● It is based on a religious experience in which God revealed a name to Anselm:

' ... that than which nothing greater can be conceived.'

● If we could prove God's existence by logic, there would be no need for faith or for trust in God.
Nevertheless:
● Anselm's prayer is directed towards the atheist 'fool' in Psalm 14:4. If the argument is not intended to give an atheist a logical proof of God's existence, why does Anselm go to so much trouble to show that his argument is right?
● In the preface to the *Proslogium*, Anselm says that he is looking for a proof.
● Why else would he bother to respond to Gaunilo? Gaunilo constructs a reply to Anselm's logic and Anselm replies in kind: they are arguing about logic, not about faith.
● For Anselm, 'faith seeking understanding' means:

' ... an active love of God seeking a deeper knowledge of God.'

**c** The argument has value for those who believe in God already, since they are more likely to accept it as a logical proof.
**d** But many Christians disagree about the last point: fideists would argue that if we could prove God's existence by logic, faith would lose all of its value.

## Three suggestions for practice and development

You could use one or more of these three questions / claims as a homework assignment, a class essay, or as a focus for practice.

1 Explain why Christians have differing attitudes towards Anselm's Ontological Argument.

2 Explain what it means to say:

   a that the Ontological Argument is *a priori* / deductive
   b that in the proposition: 'God exists', the subject 'God' contains the predicate 'exists'
   c that God's existence is a necessary truth.

3 'Anselm's Ontological Argument proves nothing.' How far do you agree?

# Arguments for the existence of God

## The Cosmological Argument

This chapter will cover:
- Aquinas' Way 3: The argument from contingency and necessity
- Criticisms from Hume and Russell

Stephen Hawking's *A Brief History of Time* starts with the following anecdote:

A well-known scientist (some say it was Bertrand Russell) once gave a public lecture on astronomy. He described how the earth orbits around the sun and how the sun, in turn, orbits around the center of a vast collection of stars called our galaxy. At the end of the lecture, a little old lady at the back of the room got up and said: 'What you have told us is rubbish. The world is really a flat plate supported on the back of a giant tortoise.' The scientist gave a superior smile before replying, 'What is the tortoise standing on?' 'You're very clever, young man, very clever', said the old lady. 'But it's turtles all the way down!' (Note 1)

**You will need to consider six things for this section**

1 The basis of Aquinas' argument in observation.

2 Aquinas' Way 3: The argument from contingency and necessity.

3 Criticisms from Hume and Russell.

4 The strengths and weaknesses of Aquinas' argument.

5 The status of Aquinas' argument as a 'proof'.

6 The value of Aquinas' argument for religious faith.

Aquinas' Cosmological Argument appears in the first three of his five 'Ways' for proving the existence of God, in his *Summa Theologica*, which is available online, for example, at: http://www.newadvent.org/summa/

Way 1 is his argument from motion and change, and Way 2 is his argument from causation. You need to study only Way 3, the argument from contingency and necessity. The three arguments are interrelated, but Way 3 will give you a good understanding of the trend of Aquinas' argument.

# The basis of Aquinas' argument in observation

▲ The Andromeda Galaxy

Part of our undoubted fascination with the Andromeda Galaxy lies in the fact that it is the nearest major galaxy to the Milky Way (about 2.5 million light years away). It is the largest in the local group of galaxies, and contains over 1 trillion stars. Moreover Andromeda is on a collision course with the Milky Way, at an approach speed of around 68 miles per second, so the two galaxies are expected to collide in about 4 billion years. The result is likely to be a giant elliptical galaxy. Whether or not the Earth could survive such an event is unknown, but at least we have plenty of time to think about it.

It is useful to bear in mind here that when we observe the Andromeda Galaxy, what we observe is 2.5 million years in the past, since the photon stream reaching our eyes takes that long to get here. What we see when we observe the universe, then, is an information stream stemming directly from the Big Bang. This is the way the biophysicist Werner Loewenstein puts it:

> So heaven's vault is crisscrossed with information arrows. The arrows hailing from out there are long – some have been on the fly for nearly 14 billion years. Those are the lines of information issuing from the primordial kernel, the initial state of information in the universe. Eventually that initial state led, in the course of the universe's expansion, to the condensation of matter locally and the formation of galaxies … [and] as those vast structures evolved, more and more structures – stars, planets, moons, etc. – formed inside them.
>
> From our perch in the universe, we ordinarily get to glimpse only segments of the arrows – local arrowlets, we might say. We therefore easily lose sight of the continuity. But as we wing ourselves high enough, we see that those arrowlets get handed down from system to system: from galaxy to stars to planets … to us. (Note 2)

It is this same information stream from the Big Bang that fascinated Aquinas as fascinates us now. Aquinas of course knew nothing of the Big Bang, but his observation of the **cosmos** convinced him that its basic processes did not explain themselves. Galaxies, stars, planets, moons: all things in the universe move and are changed, and those changes are the result of cause and effect.

From here we can make the following points about the basis of Way 3 in observation:

1  As with Paley's Design Argument, Aquinas' third way is *a posteriori* and inductive, so it is based in observation, in Aquinas' case the observation that the universe exists. I am currently looking at a cup of tea currently resting on the table in front of me, and I can touch the mug, taste the tea, see its colour, hear the gurgle of the liquid and smell its aroma; so my senses come together to verify what I observe. The same is true of the universe: sense experience can verify its existence and its properties.

2  Way 3 is the observation that all things that we see in the universe are **contingent**: they are moved, changed and caused; they need not exist, but they do. This applies to galaxies, stars, planets, people and trees;

## Key terms

**cosmos** 'The cosmos' usually refers to this space–time universe. The study of the universe is called cosmology.

**contingent** Contingent beings or things are dependent for their existence on other beings or things. In the Cosmological Argument, contingency implies the existence of something necessary – God.

37

in fact – to everything. Even galaxies can collide, with immeasurable further consequences and changes. Stars can explode and create new stars from their debris. All the heavy elements come from such explosions, including those which make up your body. Metal rots, even stainless steel. All living things die and become compost for new life. Since the first microsecond of the Big Bang, the universe as a whole has been in a relentless process of expansion and change. Nothing stays the same – everything is contingent.

3 From this observation – that all things are contingent – Aquinas concluded that something must exist necessarily. If everything we observe is contingent, then the cause of the universe would seem to lie outside it. There seems to be nothing in what we observe that can explain why contingent things exist. The Cosmological Argument therefore deduces from this that this external reason must itself be necessary.

# Aquinas' Way 3: The argument from contingency and necessity

### Thomas Aquinas (1225–1274)
Aquinas was descended from the Italian aristocracy and was a member of a Catholic religious order called the Dominicans. He had an astonishing intellect and is widely considered as the greatest theologian and philosopher in the Catholic tradition. Tradition has it that shortly before his death he had a religious experience, after which he ceased to write, since what he previously regarded as works of learning were nothing but 'straw' by comparison with one such experience. He was made a saint in 1323CE.

## The text of Aquinas' third way

In Aquinas' third way, he uses the word 'being' to mean both 'beings' (as in human beings) and things – in other words, anything that exists. Where he talks about things that 'are possible to be and not to be', he means contingent things.

The third way is taken from possibility and necessity, and runs thus. We find in nature things that are possible to be and not to be, since they are found to be generated, and to corrupt, and consequently, they are possible to be and not to be. But it is impossible for these always to exist, for that which is possible not to be at some time is not. Therefore, if everything is possible not to be, then at one time there could have been nothing in existence. Now if this were true, even now there would be nothing in existence, because that which does not exist only begins to exist by something already existing. Therefore, if at one time nothing was in existence, it would have been impossible for anything to have begun to exist; and thus even now nothing would be in existence—which is absurd. Therefore, not all beings are merely possible, but there must exist something the existence of which is necessary. But every necessary thing either has its necessity caused by another, or not. Now it is impossible to go on to infinity in necessary things which have their necessity caused by another, as has been already proved in regard to efficient causes. Therefore we cannot but postulate the existence of some being having of itself its own necessity, and not receiving it from another, but rather causing in others their necessity. This all men speak of as God.

▲ Aquinas: *Summa Theologica* (1265–1274) [Note 3]

## The argument in the form it is expressed today

**P1** Everything can exist or not-exist: that is, everything in the natural world is contingent.

**P2** If everything is contingent, then at some time there was nothing, because there must have been a time when nothing had begun to exist.

**P3** If there was once nothing, then nothing could have come from nothing.

**C1** Therefore something must exist necessarily, otherwise nothing would now exist, which is obviously false.

**P4** Everything necessary must either be caused or uncaused.

**P5** But the series of necessary beings cannot be infinite, or there would be no explanation of that series.

**C2** Therefore, there must be some uncaused being which exists of its own necessity.

**C3** And by this, we all understand God.

## Explanation of the argument

The argument has two parts:

In **P1–P3**, the core of the argument stems from **P2**, that: 'If everything is contingent, then at some time there was nothing.' Aquinas is claiming that all contingent beings / things have a finite lifespan: there is no contingent being that is everlasting, (Note 4) so there must have been a time when nothing existed. If there was a time when nothing existed, then nothing would now exist, because *ex nihilo nihil fit* – 'out of nothing nothing can come'. That is obviously false, because vast numbers of contingent beings / things now exist.

**C1**: So something must exist necessarily.

In **P4–P5**, Aquinas deals with the possibility that there might be an infinite series of *caused* necessary beings. That would also be absurd, because then there would be no ultimate cause of the series, and so no series at all.

**C2**: So there must be an 'uncaused' necessary being who brings into existence all caused necessary beings and all contingent beings.

**C3**: This is God.

The difference between a caused necessary being and an uncaused necessary being is that a caused necessary being is one that depends on something else to bring it into existence, but once created is everlasting.

An uncaused necessary being contains the reason for its own existence, in that its essence *is* existence so its very nature is to exist – it cannot not-exist.

By 'caused necessary beings', Aquinas is thinking, for example, of angels and of human souls. He would also be prepared to admit that the universe itself is a 'caused' necessary being – that is, at its most basic level matter may exist necessarily.

# Criticisms from Hume and Russell

### F.C. Copleston (1907–1994) and Bertrand Russell (1872–1970)

▲ F.C. Copleston (left) and Bertrand Russell

Bertrand Russell dismissed Aquinas as a man possessing little of the true philosophic spirit, who before he even begins to philosophise already knows the truth, because:

'… it is declared in his catholic faith.' (Note 5)

Russell's best known critique of Aquinas' Cosmological Argument comes in his 1948 radio debate with the Jesuit priest F.C. ('Freddy') Copleston, during which Russell is very cordial towards Copleston, although Russell's conviction that religion is a generally harmful superstition is never far from the surface.

Hume and Russell have very similar criticisms of the Cosmological Argument, which in Russell's case is probably to be expected, since on occasion his ideas depend heavily on Hume.

## Criticism 1: Russell argues that Way 3 commits the fallacy of composition

A **fallacy** is a failure in reasoning which makes an argument invalid. The 'fallacy of composition' is the fallacy of inferring that something is true of the whole from the fact that it is true of part of the whole, or of every part of the whole.

A simple example of the fallacy of composition is:

1   Hydrogen is not wet; oxygen is not wet.

2   Therefore water ($H_2O$) is not wet.

This is clearly a fallacious argument! It assumes that what is true of the parts of water (hydrogen and oxygen) is true of water as a whole.

Russell's best known example of the fallacy of composition comes in his 1948 radio debate referred to above, where he says to Copleston:

**'I can illustrate what seems to me your fallacy. Every man who exists has a mother, and it seems to me your argument is that therefore the human race must have a mother, but obviously the human race hasn't a mother – that's a different logical sphere.'** (Note 6)

Russell is aiming his criticism mainly at Aquinas and aims it particularly against Way 2, the argument from causation, in which Aquinas argues:

from   1 Every single event in the universe has a cause.

to       2 The universe as a whole has a cause.

Copleston claims that Aquinas is right to argue this way, but Russell rejects it completely: there is no reason why we should not argue:

from   1 Every single event in the universe has a cause.

to       2 The universe itself is uncaused.

What Russell says about Aquinas' Way 2 applies also to Way 3.

In Way 3, Aquinas argues:

from   1 Every thing in the universe is contingent.

to        2 The universe as a whole is contingent.

For Russell, this commits the fallacy of composition, because we can claim that:

**1**   Every thing in the universe is contingent.

**2**   But the universe as a whole is necessary.

## So who is right, Aquinas and Copleston, or Russell?

The following argument suggests that Aquinas and Copleston 'could' be right. It is taken from the online resource the *Stanford Encyclopedia of Philosophy*. (Note 7)

- Russell is correct that arguments from the part to the whole can commit the fallacy of composition. For example:
  Argument 1: 'All the bricks in the wall are small, so the wall is small.'
  Argument 1 is clearly fallacious.
- But this does not apply to *all* arguments from the parts to the whole. For example:
  Argument 2: 'The wall is built of bricks, so the wall is brick.'
  Argument 2 is clearly not fallacious, because here the whole (the wall) has the same quality as the parts (the bricks).
- Bruce Reichenbach (Note 8) suggests that Way 3 resembles Argument 2, so is not fallacious. Compare the form of Argument 2 and Way 3.

| Argument 2 | Way 3 |
|---|---|
| ● The wall is built from bricks. | ● The universe is built from contingent things. |
| ● So the wall is brick. | ● So the universe is contingent. |

If you check lines **P1–P3** in Way 3, you'll see the point.
- On this reading, then, Way 3 does not commit the fallacy of composition. If the things that make up the universe can cease to exist, then the universe, which is no more and no less than the sum total of its parts, can also cease to exist. What can cease to exist requires an explanation beyond itself. An uncaused necessary being, beyond the universe, is a good explanation for the existence of the contingent universe.

As in many philosophical arguments, however, either Russell or Aquinas / Copleston could be right. We do not know enough about the universe to decide one way or the other. What *is* true is that it is not necessarily the case that Way 3 commits the fallacy of composition.

## Criticism 2: Hume and Russell both reject the claim that any *being* can be necessary

The following gives Hume's version of the criticism. (Note 9) (For those who want to read it, Russell's version can be read in the radio debate with Copleston.)

- Any being that exists can also not exist.
- There is no contradiction in thinking that any being does not exist.

41

- This is true of God also, because there is no contradiction in saying, 'God does not exist'.
- So when Aquinas' Way 3 requires God to be a necessary being, this is false logic.

To be clear about this, Hume is assuming that where Aquinas in Way 3 argues that God is a necessary being, Aquinas means that God's existence is 'logically' necessary. You will remember that Hume has already rejected that claim in the Ontological Argument, so he thinks that Aquinas is making the same claim in his Cosmological Argument; so Hume now insists again that all statements about existence are 'synthetic' – they are based on sense experience, so they cannot be 'analytic' (they cannot be logically true). Whereas we have to think of 2 + 2 being 4, because that is logically true, the mind never has to suppose that some object has to remain in existence, so the words 'necessary existence' have no meaning. So Hume holds that Way 3 is making the same mistake as the Ontological Argument. (Note 10)

To make Hume's point clear, consider the following statements:

- Unicorns exist
- Peter Pan exists
- Hume exists
- You exist
- God exists

None of these statements can ever be analytic (logically true). I can only know that they are true or false synthetically (by experience), if I happen to meet a unicorn, Peter Pan, Hume, you or God. All of these five statements are true or false depending on experience, including 'God exists'.

### Reply to Hume (and Russell)

Aquinas' third way does not claim that 'God exists' is **logically** necessary – Aquinas in effect claims that God's existence is 'metaphysically' necessary, so Hume's objection fails.

When Aquinas talks about God as a necessary being in the Cosmological Argument, he is not talking about the logical necessity that we have just been looking at in the Ontological Argument. In fact, Aquinas specifically rejects the Ontological Argument as a logical proof of God, so he can hardly be thought to be introducing it (tongue in cheek) through the back door by way of the Cosmological Argument.

To unpack the idea of metaphysical necessity:

- **Metaphysical necessity** is a form of necessity that derives from the nature or *essence* of things.
- So claims about metaphysical necessity are claims about the way things 'really are'. For example, 'Whatever is water is $H_2O$' seems to be a metaphysically necessary proposition, because whenever you find water it will be made up of molecules that each have 1 atom of oxygen and 2 atoms of hydrogen. That is the essence of water. It is what water really is.
- Next, compare these two propositions:
  1 All bachelors are unmarried males.
  2 Whatever is water, is $H_2O$.
    – Since we define as 'bachelor' as an 'unmarried male', then proposition 1 is logically true – it is true by definition.

> **Key term**
>
> **metaphysical necessity** A form of necessity that derives from the nature or essence of things. Aquinas' third way in effect holds that God has metaphysical necessity.

42

– With proposition **2**, however, 'Whatever is water is $H_2O$', is not logically true: rather it is just part of the way things 'really are': it is always $H_2O$. So we can say that 'Water is $H_2O$' has metaphysical necessity.

● So, you should now be able to see that whereas the Ontological Argument is talking about God's logical necessity, Aquinas in the Cosmological Argument is talking about God's metaphysical necessity. Aquinas is claiming that:

1 In our experience, everything is contingent.
2 The existence of contingent things requires the existence of a being whose necessity is from itself and who causes the necessity in others. This is God.

Note: Although this provides a clear answer to Hume, there is no guarantee that Aquinas is right. In particular, his casual claim at the end of Way 3, that the necessary being is God, is far from obvious. If you remember, we said much the same about the 'designer' in the Design Argument.

## Criticism 3: Hume suggests that the universe itself may be a necessarily-existent being

> Why may not the material universe be the necessarily-existent Being ...?
> (Note 11)

This would be an adequate explanation without having to bring God into it. It conforms with the principle of **Occam's Razor**, that it is simpler to 'make do' with one entity (matter) rather than two (mind *and* matter). You can see the force of Hume's argument: if something has to be necessary, why can't that be the matter which makes up the universe? Why does it have to be an unobservable God?

### Reply to Hume

Aquinas had no problem with the idea that matter might exist necessarily (meaning that once created by God it is everlasting), but for Aquinas, matter would be a caused necessary being (check **P4** in Way 3), and would still need God as an uncaused necessary being to cause its existence (line **C2**).

## Criticism 4: Russell suggests that the universe exists as a 'brute fact'

The simplest explanation of why the universe exists / what caused it is that there is *no explanation*: the universe exists as an unexplainable **brute fact**.

### Reply to Russell

Science works on the assumption that there are no brute facts, otherwise science would not work. If things in the universe are not brute facts, then why should the universe as a whole be a brute fact?

### Who is right: Aquinas or Hume?

The Cosmological Argument is inductive, so like all inductive arguments it is based on probability. It depends which you think is the most probable explanation for the universe:

1 A necessarily existent mind.
2 Necessarily existent matter.

---

### Key term

**Occam's Razor** (Attributed to William of Ockham, c.1287–1347) Given in various forms: if there are competing hypotheses, choose the one that makes the fewest assumptions / entities should not be multiplied unnecessarily / if there are two competing theories that make the same predictions, the simpler one is the better.

**brute fact** A brute fact is a fact that has no explanation.

Those who prefer **1** are likely to believe that an all-powerful mind can explain the existence of matter better than matter can explain itself, so they will say that (God's) mind creates matter.

Those who prefer **2** will point out that matter has produced minds such as ours, so matter creates minds.

### In summary

Aquinas and Copleston can defend Way 3 against the attacks from Hume and Russell. We do not know enough about the universe to be sure one way or another.

## The strengths and weaknesses of Aquinas' argument

In the previous section we have been looking at four alleged weaknesses of Aquinas' argument, and we have concluded that Aquinas' argument does not fail because of those objections. For those who accept the counter-arguments, then obviously those counter-arguments show the strengths of Aquinas' third way:

| Suggested weakness | Counter-argument |
|---|---|
| **1** Russell: Way 3 commits the fallacy of composition. | **1** Not all such arguments are fallacious. Aquinas' argument is the 'brick and brick wall' kind that is not fallacious and might be right. |
| **2** Hume and Russell: We cannot show that the existence of any being is logically necessary. | **2** Way 3 is not talking about God's logical necessity: that would be the Ontological Argument. Way 3 is talking about God's metaphysical necessity and that is a powerful argument. |
| **3** Hume: The universe itself may be the necessary being. | **3** The case for necessarily-existing matter is no stronger than the case for a necessarily-existing mind. |
| **4** Russell (in the radio debate): We do not need to talk about a necessary being at all – the universe exists as an unexplainable 'brute fact'. | **4** Science works on the assumption that there are no brute facts, otherwise science itself would not work. If things in the universe are not brute facts, why should the universe as a whole be a brute fact? |

Remember, in this section that you should aim to talk about the strengths and weaknesses of the third way, and not of the complete argument.

Here are four further areas of discussion, using the same format as above.

| Suggested weakness | Counter-argument |
|---|---|
| **5** Why should there be just one necessary being? Why could there not be a group of necessary beings? | **5** Aquinas admits that here could be any number of caused necessary beings, but unless we admit the existence of an uncaused necessary being, there is no explanation for the existence of caused necessary beings. (Bear in mind here that Aquinas is allowing for the possibility that, once created, the universe itself is a caused necessary being, along with angels, and human souls.) All caused necessary beings are given their necessity, so the giver of that necessity must contain the reason for its own existence. In other words, God is his own existence. To try to go back any further than existence itself would be absurd. |

## Key terms

**infinite regress** In the Cosmological Argument, this is an indefinite sequence of causes or beings which does not have a first member of the series.

**Principle of Sufficient Reason** The doctrine that everything must have a reason or cause: every contingent fact about the universe must have an explanation.

| | |
|---|---|
| **6** Why could there not be a group of uncaused necessary beings? | **6** A clear answer to this comes from Occam's Razor: one uncaused necessary being makes the fewest assumptions and does not multiply entities unnecessarily. |
| **7** Why can there not be an **infinite regress** of contingent beings, without any need for a first necessary being? | **7a** This would still not explain why there is something rather than nothing. Where we look for explanations of things in the universe, we generally find them, or expect to find them as science progresses. This implies that the universe does have an explanation for its existence.<br>**b** Moreover, although we can understand the idea of an infinite past sequence in mathematics (e.g. −1,−2,−3,−4, −5, etc. to infinity), we have no evidence that an infinite past sequence can exist in the real world. |
| **8** Following on from 7, some current cosmological theories suggest that the universe may exist eternally and uncaused, without the need for a necessary being.<br>For example, some theories explain the universe in terms of an infinite cycle of expansions and contractions ('Big Bangs' and 'Big Crunches') | **8** Any such argument still leaves unanswered the question of why such a universe bothers to exist at all. We are still brought back to the idea of a necessary being who is the reason why the reality we experience is a reality in the first place. (You might want to look up Leibniz's '**Principle of Sufficient Reason**'.) No scientific cosmological theories can explain why there is something rather than nothing, whereas the idea of God explains exactly that.<br>Further, it is an open question with cyclic theories about the universe as to whether or not there was a first cycle, and some theorists hold that there probably was, and the idea of God is a good explanation for the explanation of a first cycle.<br>In other words, whichever way we look at it, God is a good hypothesis to explain the existence of the universe. |

## The status of Aquinas' argument as a 'proof'

1  The third way is one part of an inductive argument for the existence of God, and as we have seen in connection with the Design Argument, inductive arguments deal in probabilities rather than proofs.

For most philosophers today, proof would need to be *a priori*, like the Ontological Argument, except that in the opinion of most people, the Ontological Argument is a failed proof.

2  However, there are reasons why we should accept a different idea of proof, namely proof based on overwhelming probability.

In an article written in 2005, which focuses largely on the Cosmological Argument, Gerry J. Hughes argues that as well as the proofs we use in logic and maths, for example, we do accept other kinds of proof based on what we can reasonably conclude about the real world.

> Think for instance of proving that sub-atomic particles exist, on the basis of evidence and experiments. The theories in atomic physics might all be wrong, in the sense that there is nothing illogical, nothing contradictory in supposing that there are no such particles. But given the evidence we now have it [is] surely quite unreasonable to believe that they do not exist. (Note 12)

> **Key term**
>
> **quark** An elementary particle assumed to be one of the building blocks of matter.

To put that in slightly different terms, we have no direct observational evidence that **quarks** exist, since no one has seen an isolated quark, yet the indirect evidence for their existence is so overwhelming that it can be considered to be a proof. The 'Standard Model' of particle physics does not make sense without quarks, so they must exist in some manner.

In short, then, we have what amounts to a sufficient proof of the existence of unobservable entities – quarks – that it would be unreasonable to deny. The implications for the Cosmological Argument are obvious: God is an unobservable entity concerning whose existence it would be unreasonable to deny.

Hughes reduces the structure of the Cosmological Argument to four components:

- Nothing happens without some causal explanation.
- A satisfactory explanation cannot appeal to something which 'just happened' and was not caused. For example, a satisfactory explanation cannot appeal to 'brute facts'.
- The existence of the universe requires an explanation outside itself.
- It is reasonable to think of this 'transcendent' explanation as God.

The crucial line here is the second: Hughes asks what would be a 'satisfactory' explanation of the existence of the universe? It is logically possible, of course, that the universe exists as a brute fact, or that is uncaused, but Hughes suggests that this is about as unlikely as the sudden materialisation of pink sheep or tartan elephants. At this point, Hughes invokes Aquinas' third way:

> The chain of explanations will be complete and satisfying only if in the end one reaches something which has not 'just happened', simply come into existence; in short, the chain will end when it reaches something which cannot not exist, that is to say, exists necessarily. In short, the explanation will stop when one gets to a Necessary Being. [Note 13]

What Hughes claims is simply that the argument is a proof as far as he is concerned, because the chain of reasoning for him means that no explanation will satisfy him apart from the existence of a necessary being. He does admit that he could not claim that somebody who disagreed with him was being unreasonable; moreover there would still be a lot of work to do to identify the necessary being with the God of the Jewish, Christian and Muslim tradition.

Hughes' article is short, eminently readable and easily accessible online (http://www.richmond-philosophy.net/rjp/back_issues/rjp9_hughes.pdf). It is recommended that you read it and reach your own conclusions concerning whether or not the third way can amount to a proof in the modified sense in which he uses the term.

3 Whatever conclusions you reaches concerning Hughes' argument, it has to be said that the third way does not convince atheists, so it can hardly be a proof of God's existence that satisfies even the majority.

Perhaps now is the time to talk about R.M. Hare's concept of '*bliks*', [Note 14] which is often brought up to settle some argument or another, although the usual result is to show that the argument cannot be resolved at all. According to Hare, who follows Hume here, a *blik* is a view of the world, and our *blik* governs what is, and what is not, an explanation. Moreover:

> ' ... differences between bliks about the world cannot be settled by observation of what happens in the world'

and:

> ' ... no proof could be given to make us adopt one blik rather than another ...' (Note 15)

*Bliks* can be sane or insane, rational or irrational; and sometimes we have no *blik* at all. An atheistic *blik* about the universe might be said, therefore, to be a rational *blik* that the universe has no external explanation, whereas a religious *blik* will generally include an equally rational belief in the necessary existence of God. As Hume might say, where you go from there is up to you (and your *blik*).

4 For believers today, Aquinas' third way could give the support of reason and philosophy to what they already believe through faith. For someone who is convinced by faith that God exists, the third way supports this by offering a reasoned proof that God must exist as a necessary being.

**Discussion points**

● How might you use Hare's theory of *bliks* in a discussion about whether or not the Design Argument is a proof of God's existence?

● To what extent (if any) might Hare's theory of *bliks* support Karl Barth's view that Anselm's Ontological Argument is more about faith than reason?

## The value of Aquinas' argument for religious faith

1 Some will argue that Aquinas' third way has value for religious faith because, as part of his Cosmological Argument, it shows faith to be reasonable. The Cosmological Argument is a reasonable hypothesis that the universe owes its existence and its nature to the existence of an uncaused necessary being. There are alternative explanations concerning the origin of the universe, but they have no more probability than the Cosmological Argument.

2 Those with religious faith can easily understand the evidence used by the third way, which is based on what we can observe. With the Cosmological Argument in general, we observe that the universe is in a constant state of motion and change and that events have causes. For the third way in particular, everything we see in the universe is contingent. Although Aquinas' arguments contain some difficult language, the concepts themselves, particularly that of God as a necessary being, are simple, and so can be understood by any believer.

3 It is not the case that all those who have faith in God will accept Aquinas' argument. They might consider that the argument is flawed in one or more ways. For example, Kant believed in God (although the nature of that belief evolved considerably as he got older), but you will remember that he rejected the Ontological Argument. He also argued that the idea of God as a necessary being, as in the third way, is dependent on the Ontological Argument, so he argued that if the Ontological Argument fails, then the Cosmological Argument must fail too. Equally, you will remember that Karl Barth rejected any attempts to prove God's existence, since he believed that God can be known only through Jesus Christ, as revealed in scripture.

## Key term

**grace** The Christian doctrine of God's grace is that God shows humanity an undeserved love and mercy. Roughly speaking, grace is what bridges the gap between the moral standards that God requires and what humans can achieve by their own unaided efforts.

4 For Aquinas, faith in God is supported by reason (hence the Five Ways), but he believed that faith does not come from reasoned arguments but through God's **grace** and by accepting the authority of Church doctrines. Aquinas held that knowledge of God comes from natural theology (what we can know by reason and observation) and by revelation (which we receive through scripture). Revelation is necessary, because we could never reason our way to doctrines like the Trinity and the virgin birth of Jesus. God grants people the light of faith to understand these doctrines, whereas natural theology needs only human intelligence.

5 Following on from point 4, one important question to ask is whether the God of Aquinas' third way is the God of religious faith. Aquinas' argument points to a necessarily existent being, but such a being seems to be the God of philosophy rather than the personal and moral God understood by the Christian faith, with whom one can have a relationship. Is Aquinas justified in believing that the two are the same?

## Technical terms for Aquinas' third way

**brute fact** A fact that has no explanation.

**contingent** Contingent beings or things are dependent for their existence on other beings or things. In the Cosmological Argument, contingency implies the existence of something necessary – God.

**cosmos** 'The cosmos' usually refers to this space–time universe. The study of the universe is called cosmology.

**fallacy** A fallacy is a failure in reasoning which makes an argument invalid.

**fallacy of composition** This is the fallacy of inferring that something is true of the whole from the fact that it is true of part of the whole, or of every part of the whole. Russell argues that Aquinas' third way commits the fallacy of composition.

**grace** The Christian doctrine of God's grace is that God shows humanity an undeserved love and mercy. Roughly speaking, grace is what bridges the gap between the moral standards that God requires and what humans can achieve by their own unaided efforts.

**infinite regress** In the Cosmological Argument, this is an indefinite sequence of causes or beings which does not have a first member of the series.

**metaphysical necessity** A form of necessity that derives from the nature or essence of things. Aquinas' third way in effect holds that God has metaphysical necessity.

**Occam's Razor** (Attributed to William of Ockham, c.1287–1347) Given in various forms: if there are competing hypotheses, choose the one that makes the fewest assumptions / entities should not be multiplied unnecessarily / if there are two competing theories that make the same predictions, the simpler one is the better.

**Principle of Sufficient Reason** The doctrine that everything must have a reason or cause: every contingent fact about the universe must have an explanation. Leibniz used the principle in connection with his Cosmological Argument to ask, 'Why is there a universe at all, and why is it the way that it is?', from which he concluded that God must exist as a necessary being.

**quark** An elementary particle assumed to be one of the building blocks of matter.

# Summary of Aquinas' Way 3

### 1 The basis of the argument in observation

As with Paley's Design Argument, Way 3 is *a posteriori* and inductive, so is based on observation. It is based on the particular observation that all things we see in the universe are contingent: they are moved, changed and caused. From the observation of contingency, Aquinas concluded that something must exist necessarily.

### 2 Aquinas' Way 3: The argument from contingency and necessity

The argument has two parts. In the first part, the core of the argument is that if everything is contingent, then at some time there was nothing. No contingent being is everlasting, so there must have been a time when nothing existed. If there was a time when nothing existed, then nothing would exist now, because 'out of nothing, nothing can come', but of course vast numbers of contingent things now exist. In the second part, Aquinas rejects the idea that there might be an infinite series of caused necessary beings. That would also be absurd, because then there would be no ultimate cause of the series. So there must be an 'uncaused' necessary being who sustains all caused necessary beings and all contingent beings. This is God.

## 3 Criticisms from Hume and Russell

### Criticism 1: (Russell) – Way 3 commits the fallacy of composition

This is the fallacy of inferring that something is true of the whole from the fact that it is true of part of the whole, or of every part of the whole. Russell aims this criticism at Way 2, but it also applies to Way 3, which goes from: **1** every thing in the universe is contingent; to **2** the universe as a whole is contingent. This is fallacious because we can claim that: **1** every thing in the universe is contingent; but **2** the universe as a whole is necessary. In defence of Way 3, Bruce Reichenbach rejects this claim on the grounds that Way 3 resembles the form of the argument: 'The wall is built from bricks, so the wall is brick', which is not fallacious. Way 3 says, 'The universe is built from contingent things, so the universe is contingent.' This may be wrong, but the *form* of the argument is not a fallacy.

### Criticism 2: (Hume and Russell) – the words, 'necessary being' are meaningless

(Hume's version) Having already rejected the claim of the Ontological Argument that 'God exists' is logically true, Hume now rejects Aquinas' claim in Way 3 that God is a *necessary* being, because he thinks that this is the same claim. However, this is not a valid criticism of Aquinas. For a start, Aquinas rejects the Ontological Argument, so where he refers in Way 3 to God as a necessary being, he means that God has 'metaphysical' necessity, and not logical necessity. Aquinas means that the existence of contingent things requires the existence of a being (God) whose necessity is from itself, and who causes all contingent beings and all caused necessary beings to exist.

### Criticism 3: (Hume) – the universe itself may exist necessarily

Aquinas accepts this, but argues that the universe could only exist necessarily if it was brought into existence by an 'uncaused' necessary being. Who is right here depends on what you think is the most probable explanation for the universe: a necessarily existent mind, or necessarily existent matter.

**Criticism 4:** (Russell) – the universe exists as an unexplainable brute fact. Against Russell, if the universe is unexplainable, it seems very odd that science works on the opposite principle.

## 4 Strengths and weaknesses of Aquinas' argument

These are fairly evenly balanced. Aside from the three criticisms and responses above:

**Criticism 5:** Some object that there could be a group of necessary beings rather than just one; however Aquinas argues that unless there is one being who contains within itself the reason for its own existence, then the existence of 'anything' is inexplicable.

**Criticism 6:** Some object that there could be a group of uncaused necessary beings, but Occam's Razor can be used to argue that this multiplies entities unnecessarily.

**Criticism 7:** Some object that there could be an infinite regress of contingent beings, with no need for a first necessary being; but **a** this still would not explain why there is something rather than nothing, and **b** although we can have mathematical infinities, we have no evidence that an infinite past sequence can exist in the 'real' world.

**Criticism 8:** Some object that the universe itself may exist eternally and uncaused; but if so, one wonders why. No scientific cosmological theories can explain why there is something rather than nothing, whereas the idea of God explains exactly that. Some might still object that there could be an infinite cycle of expanding and contracting universes, but even here some theories suggest there was a first expansion, so there is room for God in either scenario.

## 5 The status of Aquinas' argument as a 'proof'

**a** It cannot be a proof in the logical sense, because inductive arguments deal in probabilities rather than proofs.

**b** Gerry Hughes suggests that we should redefine 'proof' to include the idea of 'overwhelming probability'. Nobody has observed quarks, for example, yet their existence is overwhelmingly probable. Equally, nobody has observed God, yet a transcendent God is overwhelmingly probable as the cause of the universe (according to Hughes).

**c** However probable it might be, the argument does not convince atheists. As Hare might say, it depends on whether you have a theistic or deistic or atheistic '*blik*' about the universe.

**d** For modern believers, the third way could give the support of reason and philosophy to what they already believe through faith – that God exists as a metaphysically necessary being.

6 **The value of Aquinas' argument for religious faith**

a It does show faith to be reasonable.

b Anybody with faith can understand the evidence used by the third way.

c However, some believers will not accept Aquinas' argument, for example, Kant and Barth.

d For Aquinas, faith in God is supported by reason, but faith does not come *from* reasoned arguments, but through God's grace.

e Is Aquinas justified in assuming that the necessary being of his philosophical argument is the same as the personal and moral God of Christianity, with whom one can have a relationship?

## Three suggestions for practice and development

You could use one or more of these three questions / claims as a homework assignment, a class essay, or as a focus for practice.

1 Explain the part played by the concept of an infinite regress, both in objecting to Aquinas' third way and in supporting it.

2 'The third way commits the fallacy of composition.' How far do you agree?

3 Evaluate the claim that Aquinas' third way proves the existence of God.

# 2

# Evil and suffering

This chapter will cover:

The problem of evil and suffering
- The concepts of natural and moral evil
- The logical and evidential problem of evil

Responses to the problem of evil and suffering
- The Free Will Defence
- Hick's soul-making theodicy
- Process Theodicy as presented by Griffin
- The strengths and weaknesses of each response

▲ Mother Julian of Norwich

Sin must needs be, but all shall be well. All shall be well; and all manner of things shall be well. (Note 1)

Consider this account written by the author:

These words were read to me by an energetic nun who found me, at the age of 6, eating apples from a tree near St Julian's Church in Norwich. Pointing to the purloined fruit, the nun immediately went into theological overdrive about the consequences of Adam and Eve eating the forbidden fruit in the Garden of Eden: a stolen apple was all it took to bring evil into the world. Since I was not to discover the fact for another dozen years or so, I was not able to tell her that she was mistaken in identifying the fruit as an apple, since this was a confusion based on the similarity between the Latin for 'apple' (malum) and for 'evil' (malus); which was probably just as well, since she had a steely glint in her eye. I was given a one hour lecture on the life and times of the anchoress and mystic Mother Julian, given milk and biscuits, and escorted back to where I lived in St Julian's Street, much to the amusement of my father.

To this day, I have no recollection of the face or name of the nun, since my whole attention was focused on her account of the evils suffered by Julian, and not least on the fact that Julian actually asked God to allow her to experience the agonies of a mortal sickness and of death itself, without experiencing real death. Her aim, it appeared, was to come to a deeper love of Christ so that she could begin to understand why an all-knowing God did not prevent sin at the onset. Her wish was granted: she fell mortally ill, and was given the last rites, following which she experienced 16 visions of Jesus and Mary (Note 2). The passage quoted above is from the thirteenth vision, and by it, she received the reassurance that although sin is inevitable, all will in the end be well. The nun read this to me from memory, and her face was transfigured as she said it, so I suppose that the years spent in contemplation of Mother Julian's visions had convinced her too. By the time you get to the end of this section, you might decide that as an answer to the problem of evil, it is as good as any.

The problem of evil is the single greatest challenge to faith in God, because some people's experience of evil is so great that it destroys their belief in God. Christian philosophy has always maintained that God has a sufficient reason for allowing the continued existence of evil, and it is this sufficient reason that is at the centre of what we study in this section. To begin with a few brief definitions:

**Moral evil** refers to acts committed by human beings, such as murder, theft, rape, etc. It can refer also to evil that comes from human inaction, e.g. where someone does not act to help another person who is in danger, trouble, etc.

**Natural evil** is what the world does to us through things such as disease, starvation, storm, flood, earthquake and tsunami. Whereas moral evil is done by other people's intentions, natural evil is generally seen as being produced by the chance operation of the laws of nature: a flood does not 'intend' to drown you, but if you are in the path of flood water, that is a likely consequence.

**Suffering** is the mental or physical pain / hardship / distress brought about by both moral and natural evil. Both moral and natural evil lead to mental suffering, such as misery, heartache, terror, panic and hopelessness.

The point of this section is to consider specifically Christian responses to the problem of evil, that is, assuming that God exists, how do we account for the amount of evil that we see in the world? For a start, there are no solutions that are accepted by all Christians. There are several traditional answers, but although these may make sense, they are just as likely to be wrong as well as right. Until comparatively recently, most stomach ulcers were traditionally thought to be caused by stress and diet, but it now appears that they are more frequently caused by the *Helicobacter pylori* bacterium, and are treatable by cheap antibiotics rather than by expensive and dangerous surgery.

If traditional answers to the problem of evil at some point turn out to be equally misguided, then different answers will need to be considered, even if they are in turn rejected.

In order to cover these topics, you should study what the Bible says about evil (because this underpins much of what Christians say).

## Here is an overview of this section

An overview is needed so that you can see clearly where the discussion is going.

1 Evil comes in two forms: natural and moral. Natural evil is what the world does to us. Moral evil is what we do to each other. Natural and moral evil can combine, e.g. where people build on known fault lines; spreading a virus.

2 The existence of these two forms of evil leaves us with a logical and evidential problem:

   a The logical problem of how / why an all-powerful and all-loving God can allow evil to exist.
   b The evidential problem: it is not just that God allows evil, but the sheer amount of evil that he allows to exist in the world.

3 Christians seek to solve these problems in different ways, for example:

   ● The 'Free Will Defence' argues that moral evil is not God's fault: he merely allows it, because a world containing free moral beings is better than a world without them.
   ● John Hick's solution is eschatological: everybody will reach into God's Kingdom (heaven).
   ● Process Theology argues that the extent of evil in the world shows that God cannot be omnipotent. God can try to persuade us to choose the good, but he cannot compel us.

## The Bible's perspectives on evil

# Some background information on what the Bible says about evil

**This section is NOT examinable**, *but* it will help you to understand the Free Will Defence, together with John Hick's explanation of evil, and what Process Theology has to say about evil. You can use this information in essays / exams where it is relevant.

The first book of the Bible is the Book of Genesis, and it tells the story of how the first human pair created by God (Adam and Eve) brought moral evil into the world by disobeying God. Good background reading here would be Genesis chapters 1–11. The disobedience of Adam and Eve was punished by the Flood, which is a form of natural evil, so these chapters refer to both moral and natural evil. Some Christians take these stories literally, but this is hard to defend, because the main parts of the stories of creation and the Flood were copied from myths written by the Babylonians at least 1,000 years earlier, and probably nobody would take the Babylonian stories literally. The Babylonian flood story is called the Epic of Gilgamesh: it is

fascinating, and you can listen to it online. [Note 3] Bear in mind that a myth is *not* an untrue story: a myth is an *explanation* for what we see in the world. The myths in the Bible are speculation about the great mysteries of life: Where did we come from? Where are we going? What happens when we die? Why is there so much evil in the world?

The biblical authors believed that everything is under God's control, so God must create evil as well as good (Isaiah 45:7), although it remains a mystery as to why evil can strike good people as well as bad (as in the Book of Job). In the New Testament, St Paul argues that evil can be overcome by having faith in Jesus, because by having that faith, God counts them as righteous and members of God's Kingdom (Romans 3:21–31). [Note 4]

To some extent, the Bible explains evil as caused by Satan, so 1 John 5:19 states that:

'We know that we are of God, and the whole world is in the power of the evil one.'

The Book of Revelation identifies Satan as the Serpent in Genesis 3 who tempts Eve to disobey God by eating the forbidden fruit in the Garden of Eden. Revelation 12:7–9 talks of an apocalyptic (ultimate / end-of-time) war in heaven between Michael and his angels and the evil forces of:

'... the great dragon ... that ancient serpent, who is called the Devil and Satan, the deceiver of the whole world ...'

Christian writers have explained that God allows the Devil to be an evil influence in the world because creation has been given free will. Just as humans can cause evil by their own free choices, Satan used his own free will to rebel against God and to corrupt humans. If you read the story in Luke 4:1–13, you will see that the Devil also tries to tempt Jesus to choose evil rather than good. The idea that humans are *free* to choose between good and evil is at the heart of the 'Free Will defence', which we will look at later.

▲ Ary Scheffer's personification of the Devil, in *The Temptation of Christ*, 1854

# The concepts of natural and moral evil

## Natural evil

We have already defined natural evil as that which the world does to us. It includes: accidents such as car and plane crashes, drought, death, disease, earthquake, famine, flood, forest fire, parasites, plague, storm, tsunami and volcano. The complete list would be incalculable, but the point is that quite apart from moral evil, humans are exposed to a vast catalogue of evils brought about by the physical forces of nature. They range in scale from something like skin irritation caused by bed bugs to full-scale disasters that obliterate whole populations.

Earthquakes alone are a common phenomenon that have been responsible for the death of millions of people and animals and for the destruction of habitat. The 2008 Sichuan earthquake killed about 70,000 people and left around 5 million or more homeless. The 1883 eruption of Krakatoa and subsequent earthquake killed around 36,000, some from tsunamis reaching 150 feet or more in height. Around 628BCE, the Thera / Santorini eruption in the Aegean, estimated as having been six times more powerful than Krakatoa, would have sent a huge tsunami towards northern Crete at around 400 miles an hour. The combined effects of the eruption appear to have destroyed Minoan civilisation.

▲ The Santorini caldera today

Natural disasters are often the most difficult form of evil for religious people to accept. Moral evil can always be put down to human free will; but natural evil is not usually blamed on humans, except where a natural disaster is caused or made worse by human activity, as with global warming. The obvious seat of blame is God, because it should be easy for an omnipotent God to control the forces of nature, particularly since most Christians believe that God created the laws of nature in the first place.

For Christians, the issue is especially hard to understand because in the Bible, God himself uses natural evils in order to punish people, for example, the plagues that were intended to persuade the Egyptian Pharaoh to let the Hebrew slaves go free (Exodus 7:8–11:10), and the Flood, which Genesis 6:5–7 says was brought about because He saw that everybody apart from Noah was evil-minded. There is of course debate about how we should understand these 'acts of God'. Some see them as being literally true, whereas others see them as an interpretation of events.

In the New Testament, the situation is somewhat different, in that Jesus performs a number of beneficial miracles over the world of nature: he heals people from diseases such as blindness and leprosy; he miraculously multiplies bread, fish and wine; and he calms the forces of wind and sea on Lake Galilee in order to save his disciples from drowning. Moreover, the great miracle of the New Testament is that of Jesus' resurrection, where God conquers death itself – an event foreshadowed by Jesus' raising of Lazarus after four days in the tomb (John 11). The point is that if God controlled natural evils 2,000 years ago, why does he not control them now? There is the hint of an answer to this question in John 9:1–13, where Jesus' disciples came across a man who had been blind from birth, and they asked Jesus whether he was being punished for his own sins or for those of his parents. Jesus replied,

**'It was not that this man sinned, or his parents, but that the works of God might be made manifest in him.'**

Jesus therefore shifted the question away from the cause of the blind man's suffering to the purpose: it gives an opportunity for God to act, so Jesus heals the man (9:4–12).

## Moral evil

Humans are regarded as 'moral agents'. The word 'agent' in this phrase refers to any being capable of acting in accordance with what is right and wrong. Moral evil refers to any action where the moral agent uses their will to bring about morally bad consequences. It also refers to 'inaction' by the moral agent. For example, letting somebody drown when the agent could have saved them, or not bothering to seek medical help for someone who is clearly in need of it.

Moral evils include: adultery, arson, bullying, cruelty, deceit, discrimination, dishonesty, genocide, greed, lying, murder, rape, ruthless ambition, slavery, terrorism, theft and torture. As with natural evil, the list goes on, and for some it is significant that it can be easier to think of things that are morally evil than of things that are morally good.

On an individual level, there have always been people whose behaviour classifies them as morally evil, and an internet trawl will reveal many. On a collective level, genocide has brought about moral evil in its most extreme forms. In 1994, the Rwandan genocide was an attempt by the Hutu population (85 per cent) to exterminate the Tutsi (14 per cent), and between 500,000 and 1,000,000 Tutsi (and moderate Hutu) were slaughtered. Perhaps the worst aspect of this situation was the evil of inaction, namely the lack of official condemnation and intervention by the United Nations and by the former colonial powers, despite the fact that preparations for the slaughter were known in advance.

In Europe, the main example of the depths of moral evil is defined by the Holocaust / Shoah, the 1941–1945 genocide brought about by Adolf Hitler's Nazi Germany which exterminated 6 million Jews (about a million of whom were children) together with around 3 million other so-called 'undesirables'. The level of depravity shown by the Nazis and their collaborators is described by some as 'demonic', but to some extent that can be seen as an attempt to excuse humanity for the depth of its own evil. Among the most iconic pictures of that evil are those captured by photograph of the entrance to Auschwitz–Birkenau. One in six of the Jews who died in the Holocaust did so at the Auschwitz complex. Jews from the German-occupied territories were loaded onto trains (mainly in cattle trucks) which from 1944 delivered them straight into the camp via the gatehouse building. Eighty per cent of them were murdered within hours. Most of the remaining 20 per cent were worked to death, or died in unimaginable misery.

▲ The gate-house entrance to Auschwitz–Birkenau

One of the few to survive Auschwitz–Birkenau was Jack Adler, whose reaction to what was happening to him and his family was a complete lack of understanding:

> It's very difficult unless you find yourself in someone's shoes … You just have one word to repeat to yourself. 'Why?' My family did not harm anyone. It shows you that those who preach hate plant the seed of evil. [Note 5]

As a warning to the twenty-first century, this could hardly be more appropriate. The question of whether or not the twenty-first century can understand that message to the point of doing something about it is crucial to say the least. Any major future war will probably be nuclear, and might also be chemical and biological, and all of these military options have the

**Discussion point**

You can read more about Irving Greenberg here: http://www.jewishvirtuallibrary.org/jsource/judaica/ejud_0002_0008_0_07841.html

Why would God create a species capable of the depths of depravity shown by the human race?

capacity to exterminate life on Earth. For some, however much we learn to control human moral evil, there can be no adequate answer to Adler's question. One is reminded of Rabbi Irving Greenberg's comment that:

> 'No statement, theological or otherwise, should be made that would not be credible in the presence of burning children.'

Rabbi Greenberg was talking about the Holocaust, where some accounts tell of children being burned alive in the crematoria at Bergen–Belsen concentration camp. He meant that any answer to the problem of why God allows such evils can be credible only if it can be spoken while watching children die in agony in the flames. Jack Adler experienced the horrors of life in Auschwitz–Birkenau, so his question, 'Why?', has the same kind of force.

# The logical and evidential problem of evil

The logical and evidential problems are grouped together because one is an extension of the other. The logical problem of evil relates to God's omnipotence and omnibenevolence. The evidential problem of evil relates to the further issue of God's omniscience: an all-knowing God knows all about suffering. In brief, so that you can see where the logic leads, the logical problem asks why an all-powerful and all-loving God does not control evil. The evidential problem points to the sheer extent of evil in the world, and asks how this can be reconciled with the fact that at the moment of creation, an *all-knowing God* must have known the full extent of future evil. Why, then, did he bother to create the universe?

## The logical problem of evil

The logical problem of evil is expressed simply by putting together three statements:

1 God is omnipotent (all-powerful).

2 God is omnibenevolent (all-loving / all-good).

3 Evil exists.

These three statements together are known as the 'inconsistent triad', that is, three statements that contain an inconsistency: they cannot all be true. The logical inconsistency arises here because an all-powerful God would obviously be able to remove evil, and an all-loving God would presumably wish to remove evil, yet evil exists. The Greek philosopher Epicurus (341–270BCE) seems to have been the first to point out this contradiction:

> 'Is God willing to prevent evil, but not able? Then he is not omnipotent. Is he able, but not willing? Then he is malevolent. Is he both able and willing? Then whence evil?' (Note 6)

## Solutions that deny one of the three statements
### Solution 1: Denying God's omnipotence
If God is not omnipotent, then the solution is simple: He is not able to control evil, and so cannot be blamed for its continued existence. This is in fact the preferred solution of Process Theology, which holds that evil is a process within matter that is beyond God's direct control. There is an

obvious difficulty with this, because for most believers, a God who is not omnipotent would not be worthy of worship. In effect a non-omnipotent God would not be 'God'. We shall assess Process Theology at a later point in this section, but for now, it is worth noting that there are no arguments that prove God to be omnipotent – it is a matter of faith.

### Solution 2: Denying God's omnibenevolence

For most Christians, this solution is unthinkable. The belief that God is both good and loving supports those who experience evil, and is the basis for the future hope of heaven. It is the basis of the final great expression of hope for those who suffer in the Bible, that:

> **'God ... will wipe away every tear from their eyes, and death shall be no more, neither shall there be mourning nor crying nor pain any more, for the former things have passed away.' (Revelation 21:4)**

The hope that God is omnibenevolent does not of course make it true. According to Freud, this would be a simple case of wish-fulfilment: there is no all-loving God, only the desire for one. Freud's argument does not work, because wishing something to be true does not mean that it is not in fact true; nevertheless it is no more possible to show that God is omnibenevolent than to show that He is omnipotent.

### Solution 3: Denying that evil exists

This was the solution proposed by Augustine of Hippo (354–430CE). [Note 7] Augustine argued that evil is *privatio boni* – a privation of good. By this, Augustine meant quite simply that evil does not exist in its own right but is an absence of good, just as darkness is an absence of light and ignorance is an absence of knowledge.

This looks like a good solution. Dark clearly is the absence of light, so perhaps evil is just the absence of good, and if so, there is no logical 'problem' of evil to solve, and no blame can be attached to God for not solving it.

Unfortunately, denying the reality of evil does not seem to be an acceptable solution. Most people have experienced the power of evil to disrupt their lives, and most people see evil as being as real and tangible as good. One doubts that the mothers who went into the gas chambers with their babies in their arms would gain any consolation from being told that evil has no reality.

## Solutions which argue that there is a *sufficient reason* why God allows evil to exist

You are required to know two of these:

### 1 The 'Free Will' Defence

This argues that God has to allow evil in order to preserve free will. The good has to be freely chosen. In order to bring about the best 'goods' in life, such as love and compassion, we have to be 'free' to choose the opposing vices of hatred and heartlessness. If God controlled evil, there would be no freedom. Humans are therefore morally responsible for moral evil and God is not.

### 2 John Hick's eschatological solution

'Eschatology' is the theology of what will happen at the end of the universe – the theology of death, judgement, heaven and hell. According to Hick, God has all the time he wants in which to bring people to freely love the good, so in the end everybody will reach God's Kingdom (heaven). In this case, evil is a necessary part of the process by which we become fit for heaven.

We shall examine both these views shortly, along with Process Theology.

## The evidential problem of evil

The evidential problem of evil can be expressed simply:

---

- There are known facts about evil that are evidence against the existence of God.

  There are mainly two types of evil which supply such evidence:

  **1** Evil that is overwhelming in quantity and quality.
  **2** Evil that is pointless because it serves no useful purpose.

- The evidential problem of evil is made worse by the problem of God's omniscience.

---

### 1 The evidence from evil that is overwhelming in quantity and quality

The evidential problem of evil is based simply on what we observe about evil. This evidence suggests that the amount of evil and suffering in the world counts against God's existence. Here are two examples:

● **Natural evil: The Permian–Triassic extinction**

This was not the event that killed the dinosaurs 66 million years ago, but an even worse mass-extinction 251–252 million years ago, known as 'The Great Dying', when about 90 per cent of marine species and 79 per cent of land species disappeared, probably through a series of different natural disasters, including a massive asteroid strike. It is understandable that when discussing the problem of evil we are primarily concerned with how evil affects ourselves, but during the Permian–Triassic humans did not exist, so the problem of evil is focused here on the millions of other species that simply ceased to exist. The NASA Science website http://science.nasa.gov/science-news/science-at-nasa/2002/28jan_extinction/ describes this as:

'… almost the perfect crime. Some perpetrator – or perpetrators – committed murder on a scale unequaled in the history of the world. They left few clues to their identity, and they buried all the evidence under layers and layers of earth.' [Note 8]

The perpetrator would appear to be God, since as the creator of the universe, God must be responsible for the evolution of life on Earth. We can grant that evolution runs itself, but evolution is a natural process governed by the laws of nature, so why did God not program those laws to be less destructive, or else intervene to stop the extinction? If cruelty to humans is a bad thing, then surely cruelty to other species is a bad thing too?

Most people will know about the massive eruption of Mount Vesuvius in 79BCE, which obliterated the Roman town of Pompeii along with other Roman settlements. You can read an eye-witness account of this by the Roman poet and administrator Pliny the Younger, at: www.eyewitnesstohistory.com/pompeii.htm (see Note 9). Archaeological excavations have uncovered about 1,500 bodies, although the death toll is unknown. In addition to providing a challenge to belief in the goodness of God, these examples of natural evil provide a powerful challenge to the Design Argument for the existence of God that we looked at previously.

● **Moral evil: Dostoyevsky's view in *The Brothers Karamazov***

Dostoyevsky was a nineteenth-century Russian writer, essayist and philosopher. His 1880 novel, *The Brothers Karamazov*, deals with the central themes of the problem of evil.

It is probably true that Dostoyevsky's exposition of the problem of evil in his novel *The Brothers Karamazov* is the biggest single argument to defeat any defence of God's goodness. It is expounded in the cell of a novice monk, Alyosha. He is visited by his brother Ivan, the public prosecutor, and Ivan challenges Alyosha's faith in the goodness of God by telling him heartrending stories of evil. A feeble little horse has foundered under a too heavy a load, so its peasant owner thrashes it mercilessly and savagely over its 'weeping, meek eyes', until maddened by the pain, the horse, trembling all over and gasping for breath strains and moves sideways down the street with an unnatural spasmodic action.

Ivan moves on to torture Alyosha with a string of case histories in his possession concerning unspeakable cruelties to children.

> There was a little girl of five who was hated by her father and mother … This poor child of five was subjected to every possible torture by those cultivated parents. They beat her, thrashed her, kicked her for no reason till her body was one bruise. Then, they went to greater refinements of cruelty—shut her up all night in the cold and frost in a privy, and because she didn't ask to be taken up at night (as though a child of five sleeping its angelic, sound sleep could be trained to wake and ask), they smeared her face and filled her mouth with excrement, and it was her mother, her mother did this. And that mother could sleep, hearing the poor child's groans! Can you understand why a little creature, who can't even understand what's done to her, should beat her little aching heart with her tiny fist in the dark and the cold, and weep her meek unresentful tears to dear, kind God to protect her? Do you understand that, friend and brother, you pious and humble novice? Do you understand why this infamy must be and is permitted? Without it, I am told, man could not have existed on earth, for he could not have known good and evil. Why should he know that diabolical good and evil when it costs so much? Why, the whole world of knowledge is not worth that child's prayer to 'dear, kind God'! (Note 10)

## 2 The evidence from pointless evil

A well-known example of pointless evil is given by the American philosopher William Rowe (1931–2015). Rowe suggests that we suppose that in some distant forest a lightning strike causes a forest fire. A fawn is trapped in the fire, horribly burned, and lies in agony for several days before death finally relieves its suffering. The fawn's agony appears to be

## Discussion point

In the same chapter, called 'Rebellion' (which you can read online at http://www.bibliomania.com/0/0/235/1030/17183/1/frameset.html), Ivan challenges his brother to imagine that he is God, about to create the universe, knowing (because he is omniscient) that in so doing he will have to torture just one being – the little girl who in the account opposite:

' … beat her little aching heart with her tiny fist in the dark and the cold, and wept her meek unresentful tears to dear, kind God … '

And he asks Alyosha if he would build the universe by accepting that just this one instance of horrible evil would occur. Alyosha says he would not.

You should perhaps at this stage put this question to yourself and then assess it in a group discussion.

pointless: it suffers and dies alone, so no human being ever knows about it, and no eventual good comes from it. It neither preserves human free will nor builds human character by developing virtues like sympathy and compassion (Note 11).

You might by this point have seen that there is one issue that links these examples of overwhelming and pointless evil, namely the belief in God's omniscience.

## The evidential problem of evil and God's omniscience

To make this clear, we can go back to the statement of the logical problem of evil:

1 God is omnipotent (all-powerful).

2 God is omnibenevolent (all-loving / all-good).

3 Evil exists.

What the evidential problem of evil does is to require us to insert one more statement between **2** and **3**:

'God is omniscient (all-knowing).'

'Omniscient' here means that all events that will happen are known to God even before he created the universe.

An omniscient being would know, at the point of creating the universe, that both overwhelming and pointless evils would occur. The evils of mass extinctions during Earth's history, and of Auschwitz–Birkenau, and pointless evils of the kind illustrated by Rowe's example of the fawn would all have been obvious to an all-knowing mind. Why, then, did God bother to create the universe? As Ivan's examples of the foul cruelties practised upon innocent children suggest, the price of building a universe is just too great in terms of its potential for overwhelming and pointless suffering.

## Suffering in relation to evil

We might reply that God has a plan by which all suffering will eventually lead to the perfect harmony of life in heaven; but how satisfying is this?

● How many theologians would accept that there is a place in heaven for all animals who suffer? If there is not, what does that say about the injustice and incalculable amount of animal suffering during 3.5 billion years of evolution? **Where is God's love for all of creation?**
● Are we really sure that there is any kind of atonement that could be made for the sufferings of the children revealed by Ivan?
● If given the choice, what parent would buy the future harmony of heaven at the price of letting their children be thrown into fire pits and watching them being burned alive, as happened during the Holocaust?

Hence Ivan concludes that God asks too high a price now for the harmony of heaven in the future. It is beyond our means to pay so much, and that is the essence of Ivan's 'rebellion' against God: he wants no part in the joys of heaven, even if it turns out that he is wrong about evil.

> 'I hasten to give back my entrance ticket, and if I am an honest man I am bound to give it back as soon as possible. And that I am doing. It's not God that I don't accept, Alyosha, only I most respectfully return Him the ticket.'

(*The Brothers Karamazov*, Ch. 35)

You can see here that Ivan's complaint against God does not apply just to the evidential problem of evil: it applies to all types of evil. The sheer amount of suffering caused by both natural and moral evil leads Ivan to protest that from his point of view, whatever end-plan God has in mind, buying an entrance ticket to heaven at such a price just isn't worth it.

### Evil is the direct cause of suffering, whether it is natural or moral

Natural evil causes people to suffer physically from cuts, bruises, burns, scalding, loss of limbs, blindness, exhaustion … the list is endless. With physical suffering comes mental suffering, because such conditions can bring about a sense of loss, misery, anguish and despair. In fact we can see that natural and moral evil can *combine* to cause suffering. Just about all the suffering caused by nature can also be brought about by human agency: weapons can be used to cut, bruise, blind and kill; fire can be used to burn. Moral and natural evils can go hand-in-hand to produce all the kinds of suffering that we now see in the world.

### Nevertheless we can also accept that some suffering is good

For example, most parents will be prepared to allow the pain of an injection to be inflicted on their children because the pain will bring about the good of immunisation from harmful diseases. Many people view a visit to the dentist with dismay, fearing the pain of having a tooth drilled or extracted, yet most people accept the pain because it brings about the good of dental health, and avoids far greater problems in the future. In the same way people accept the pain and discomfort of surgery in order to restore the body to better health. People can learn from their mistakes in just about all areas of life, in business, social life and relationships, for example. As well as causing some people to despair, some can be restored by suffering through uncovering unsuspected reserves of strength.

### The suffering caused by natural and moral evil brings out some of the best feelings in human nature

When somebody is suffering, we can sympathise with them; we can feel compassion and empathy. Think of the reaction of many countries to natural disasters or war elsewhere in the world, where people will freely give their time and money in order to help the victims. Would we want to live in a world where there was no sympathy or compassion?

These are some ideas to think about as we move on to the Free Will Defence, to Hick's theodicy and to Process Theology, in all of which one of the central ideas is that nature must be 'free' to act in accordance with the laws of nature, and that humans must be free to act for good or for evil in the world.

# The Free Will Defence

In order for you to see the flow of the argument, we shall be looking at the following:

- An introduction to the Free Will Defence.
- John Mackie's account of the Free Will Defence.
- Mackie's rejection of the Free Will Defence.
- Alvin Plantinga's defence of the Free Will Defence.
- Some strengths and weaknesses of the Free Will Defence.

## An introduction to the Free Will Defence

The Free Will Defence argues that God has given up control over human actions in order to bring about a greater good. By giving up control of what humans do, God has given them free will, so humans can make their own decisions and are responsible for their own actions. As a result, they can develop qualities that are valuable in themselves.

However, giving free will is not sufficient to bring about this development, as we must also be placed in situations that require us to make decisions and learn about their consequences. That is why the world is as it is. We experience pain, and see people around us experiencing pain, so that we can choose to develop qualities such as compassion and courage, patience and generosity.

Pain is the stimulus for this development, but the possibility of developing positive qualities is matched with the possibility of developing negative ones – for example, we may choose to develop greed, hate, selfishness and pleasure in inflicting pain, instead of courage and generosity. Moral evil is therefore the price of free will, but free will is worth the price because of the positive qualities the individual may choose to develop.

The risk of pain is not something that everyone is averse to. Risk can be exciting, which explains why many people take up risk sports such as boxing, free-fall parachuting and snow-boarding. For centuries, explorers risked starvation, disease, along with death by drowning, by attack from wild animals and by attack from those whose territory they invaded. There are many for whom being able to survive in the most hostile environment provides the greatest thrill, and those for whom the threat of danger is the spice of life.

The problem with all of this is obvious: free will comes at an enormous price, because genuine *free will* necessarily includes the permission to do evil, the ability to do evil and the opportunity to do evil. Take any of these three away and free will in relation to God is only an illusion.

## Those who would defend the Free Will Defence have two things to prove

1 That free will necessarily leads to moral evil – it is not possible to have free will and not to have moral evil in the world.

2 That the results of having free will are worth the price.

One of the best examples of the Free Will Defence is that of the Australian philosopher John Mackie (1917–1981), and the best-known response to Mackie is by the American philosopher Alvin Plantinga (b.1932). [Note 12]

Note: You are not required to know any particular version of the Free Will Defence beyond the general form given above. Nevertheless, it will greatly improve your knowledge and understanding of the argument if you can refer to a specific example.

## John Mackie's account of the Free Will Defence

John Mackie was an atheist, so do not think that he was trying to show that the Free Will Defence is right: quite the opposite! The title of the book in which he puts forward his version of the Free Will Defence is *The Miracle of Theism*, which is Mackie's tongue-in-cheek way of saying that it would be a miracle for sensible people to believe in God, because (he thinks) God does not exist.

One of Mackie's main reasons for thinking that God does not exist is the problem of evil. Mackie produces his own version of the Free Will Defence, with the aim of showing that it does not work. However, Mackie's is one of the clearest versions of the Free Will Defence, and it seems to show the opposite of what he intended, namely that the Free Will Defence might indeed be the right explanation of why God allows evil to exist. See what you think. Mackie explains the Free Will Defence by constructing and then rejecting his own version of it, which is a matrix of first-, second- and third-order goods and evils.

- We can refer to happiness and pleasure as 'first-order goods'. For example, someone who is experiencing the pleasure of reading a good book or of eating a delicious meal is in a state of first-order good.
- Corresponding to first-order goods, unhappiness, pain and misery are 'first-order evils'. For example, someone who is experiencing the pain of toothache or of the breakdown of a relationship is in a state of first-order evil.
- If we come across somebody in a state of first-order evil, two sorts of reaction are open to us: we can reduce their misery by being sympathetic, understanding, kind, compassionate, loving, generous and self-sacrificing; alternatively we can make their misery worse through spite, meanness, envy, jealousy, greed and selfishness.

  In the same way, if we come across somebody in a state of first-order good, by our reactions we can either increase their pleasure and happiness or perhaps remove it altogether.

- Sympathy, understanding, kindness, compassion, love, generosity and self-sacrifice are therefore higher-order goods than the first-order goods of happiness and pleasure. In effect they are second-order goods.

  In the same way, spite, meanness, envy, jealousy, greed and selfishness are second-order evils.

- We might say, therefore, that second-order good exists to maximise first-order good and to minimise first-order evil.

  Equally second-order evil exists to maximise first-order evil and to minimise first-order good.

- We have a free choice, therefore, to maximise or minimise first- and second-order good or evil in the world.
- Moreover, without the evils of pain and suffering, we could never have the even greater joys and benefits of being able to show courage, sympathy, love – all the things that are best in humanity. But the price for this is that many will reject these goods and will become hateful, envious, jealous and malicious towards others.

- So freedom is a third-order good, that is, it is a higher-order good because it allows us to choose between instantiating (putting in place) first- and second-order goods and evils, and eventually it teaches us to love the good.
- God is therefore justified in allowing evil in the universe, because it permits the freedom to choose or reject the good. It **teaches us to be morally responsible**.

You can see Mackie's version of the Free Will Defence in the following diagram.

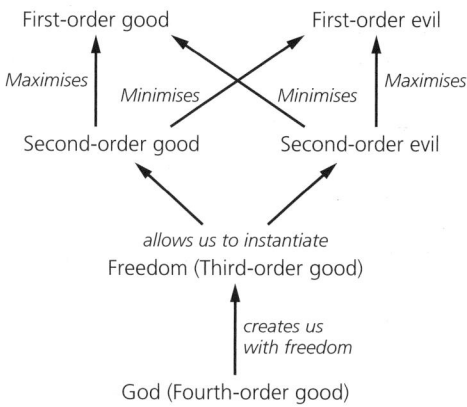

▲ Mackie's account of the Free Will Defence

As clear as this looks, Mackie thinks it is incoherent.

## Mackie's rejection of the Free Will Defence

Here is Mackie's judgement on his version of the Free Will Defence:

> First I should query the assumption that second-order evils are logically necessary accompaniments of freedom. I should ask this: if God has made men such that in their free choices they sometimes prefer what is good and sometimes what is evil, why could he not have made men such that they always freely choose the good? If there is no logical impossibility in a man's freely choosing the good on one, or on several, occasions, there cannot be a logical impossibility in his freely choosing the good on every occasion. God was not, then, faced with a choice between making innocent automata and making beings who, in acting freely, would sometimes go wrong: there was open to him the obviously better possibility of making beings who would act freely but always go right. Clearly, his failure to avail himself of this possibility is inconsistent with his being both omnipotent and wholly good. (Note 13)

### The essence of what Mackie is saying here is this:

1 It is logically possible for a person to make free, good choices, all of the time.

2 God could have created humans so that they would only make free, good choices.

3 God did not do so.

Therefore:

1 Either God lacks the power to do so, or

2 God is not loving enough to do so,

3 Either way, the Free Will Defence fails.

Mackie's obvious conclusion from all of this is simple:

4 God does not exist.

### How strong is Mackie's argument against the Free Will Defence?

Alvin Plantinga has argued that Mackie's Free Will Defence does not work. Mackie claims that God could have created humans so that they always make free, good choices. According to Plantinga, there is no possible world that God could have created in which humans would always make free, good choices. In such a world, even if you wanted to tell a lie you could not, because God would have made that world so that in effect you could not lie. In a world without any kind of evil, you could not even *think* evil thoughts, so clearly you would not be free at all.

To extend this a little, the words 'free to choose' must mean that there is a real choice between real options. Being 'made' in such a way that you can only 'choose' the good is not a free choice – you are doing what God has made you do. The words 'make someone freely choose this' do not describe a possible state of affairs – they are the logical equivalent of a round square, a nonsense. However, the statement 'God cannot do this' does not put a limit on God's power – God can do everything that is logically possible, but it is logically *impossible* to make people so that they always freely choose the good.

It would seem, therefore, that Plantinga is right and Mackie is wrong. This is not to say that the Free Will Defence is the *correct* explanation of why God allows evil, but it does provide a reasonable explanation for evil. Knowing that there is at least one good reason why God allows the existence of evil can be enough to support faith in God.

> What follows here is a more detailed account of Plantinga's defence of the Free Will Defence. It is given here for those who wish to see the flow of Plantinga's argument, but **it is optional reading and not required reading.** Exam questions can refer only to the Free Will Defence, and not to any named version of it.

## Alvin Plantinga's defence of the Free Will Defence

In order to refute (disprove) Mackie, Plantinga has to do two things:

1 He has to show that Mackie's claim that God could have created humans so that they would always, freely choose the good, is logically 'impossible'.

2 He has to provide a logically 'possible' reason why God allows evil. This reason does not have to be the true reason, just one that is logically possible.

Plantinga claims that God allows evil to exist for two 'Morally Sufficient Reasons' (MSR 1 and MSR 2). MSR 1 explains the 'logical' problem of evil. MSR 2 explains *natural* evil. (Note 14)

## MSR 1 and the logical problem of evil

1 Plantinga's MSR 1 is that:

**'God's Creation of persons with morally significant free will is something of tremendous value. God could not eliminate much of the evil and suffering in this world without thereby eliminating the greater good of having created persons with free will with whom he could have relationships and who are able to love one another and do good deeds.'**

As an example of the idea of a greater good, most mothers would allow the small pain (the pain of a needle) to be inflicted on their children because that pain brings about a greater good (immunisation against disease).

2 In MSR 1, Plantinga presupposes the view of free will known as **'libertarianism'**.

Libertarianism is the view that **causal determinism** is false, so that unlike robots / machines, we can make choices that are genuinely free. You can see that this is a necessary (although unprovable) assumption, otherwise a 'free will' defence does not have any foundation.

3 According to Plantinga, libertarian free will is a 'morally significant' kind of free will.

   a This means that people have the chance to put into practice Mackie's second-order goods of sympathy, love, compassion, and so on.
   b This kind of freedom is the most important, because it means that people are morally responsible for their decisions. Moreover they can be praised and rewarded if they do what is right, or blamed and punished if they do wrong.

4 Plantinga's argument aims to show (against Mackie) that there is no logically possible world in which God could have created beings who would always make free, good choices.

Consider these three possible worlds that God could have created (where PW stands for 'possible world'):

### PW1

   a God creates persons with morally significant free will.
   b God does not causally determine people in every situation to choose what is right and avoid what is wrong.
   c There is evil and suffering in PW1.

### PW2

   a God does not create persons with morally significant free will.
   b God causally determines people in every situation to choose what is right and avoid what is wrong.
   c There is no evil or suffering in PW2.

---

**Key terms**

**libertarianism** In the free will debate, this is the view that although some aspects of human existence are determined by physics, biology and chemistry, humans nevertheless have a degree of free will and so can be held morally responsible for their actions.

**causal determinism** The view that every event is determined by antecedent (preceding) events and conditions and by the laws of nature, so humans do not have free will.

**PW3**

    **a** God creates persons with morally significant free will.*

    **b** God causally determines people in every situation to choose what is right and avoid what is wrong.**

    **c** There is no evil or suffering in PW3.***

(If you find this difficult, concentrate on PW1 and PW3.)

If you look carefully at these three possible worlds:

**PW1** is obviously logically possible: people have morally significant free will and make free choices to do good or evil, so there is evil and suffering in PW1. This world describes the real world in which we live.

**PW2** is also obviously logically possible: there is nothing illogical about the idea of God creating people without morally significant free will who are programmed always to make good choices, with the result that there is no evil or suffering in PW2. Its people are moral robots.

**PW3** according to Plantinga would be logically impossible:

- To have morally significant free will (**PW3a** *), people must be able to do morally bad things whenever they want to, but they cannot, because they are causally determined (**PW3b** **).
- So if you wanted to tell a lie, you could not, because causal forces beyond your control, put in place by God (**PW3b**), would not let you; and in the same way, for example, you would be physically incapable of stealing.
- In fact, since **PW3** is a world without evil of any kind (**PW3c** ***), people in **PW3** would not even be able to *think* bad thoughts or desires.

In **PW3**, the three statements **a**, **b** and **c**, are logically incompatible, so **PW3** is logically impossible; therefore God cannot create it.

5 So, Plantinga defeats Mackie's claim that the Free Will Defence is logically inconsistent.

Look back at Mackie's main objection to the Free Will Defence, where he says that God:

> ' ... could have made men such that they always freely choose the good ... '

These words are describing Plantinga's **PW3**, but Plantinga has shown that it was logically impossible for God to make **PW3**:

> 'It would be impossible to causally determine human actions and at the same time allow them to be morally free.'

Again, if you find this difficult, concentrate on **PW3** until you can see why Plantinga has shown that even God could not create such a world.

Then ask yourself: which of **PW1** and **PW2** would you rather live in? The chances are that you do not like **PW2** at all, because you would be a robot; so you would probably choose **PW1**, which describes the world we live in. If **PW3** is impossible, it does not seem so hard, then, to see why God would choose to create **PW1** rather than **PW2**. In any event, Plantinga proves his point: the Christian Free Will Defence is not logically incoherent at all.

## MSR 2 and the problem of natural evil

Plantinga also needs to provide some sort of explanation of natural evil, since natural evil is not caused by human free will. How would it upset your free will, for example, if there were no cancerous diseases, no earthquakes and no tsunamis?

This is where Plantinga introduces his MSR 2 (Morally Significant Reason 2).

1 Plantinga's MSR 2 is that:

  'God allowed natural evil to enter the world as part of Adam and Eve's punishment for their sin in the Garden of Eden.'

2 In the view of nearly all of the philosophers who comment on this, MSR 2 is ludicrous: it is unscientific and relies on the mythological narrative of Adam and Eve.

  But remember that Plantinga does not have to give the true reason or even a convincing reason as to why God allows evil – he merely has to give a logically possible one to refute Mackie.

3 However unlikely, it *is* logically possible that natural evil was created / allowed by God because of human sin in the Garden of Eden.

Therefore Plantinga has successfully refuted Mackie's claim that Free Will Defence is incoherent.

## As a final question: Can the Free Will Defence account for natural evil?

Natural evil is not caused by human free will: it is caused by the forces of nature. We can try to avoid building houses on fault lines in order to avoid death and injury from earthquakes, for example, but most natural evils cannot be avoided. To give just one example, the fourteenth-century outbreak of bubonic plague (the 'Black Death') killed about one-third of the human population of the world, and the vast majority of its victims had little or no chance of avoiding death.

Whereas the Free Will Defence can offer a reasonable explanation for the existence of moral evil, it is often said that God has no excuse for allowing natural evil, because there is no obvious reason why God could not have made the world so that there were no earthquakes, tidal waves, killer storms, asteroid strikes and the like. Was it really necessary for God to create the forces of nature to be so destructive? Moreover, none of these things are under the control of human free will, so in the majority of cases humans cannot be blamed when they happen.

Nevertheless, the Free Will Defence can to some extent account for natural evil:

● Geology shows that the world has evolved from a primitive stage when its surface was so hot that rocks were molten. The cooling of the rocks produced the Earth's crust, and the natural processes of gravity caused the crust to buckle, producing earthquakes and tsunamis that are disastrous for most forms of life. Natural forces such as these seem to be an inevitable part of the way the world works, since everything obeys the laws of nature. The main culprit is gravity, because when a large mass of water gets displaced by an earthquake, for example, the water acts under the influence of gravity to regain its equilibrium, with the kind of results that we saw in the Japanese Tōhoku earthquake and tsunami in 2011.

- Not only does gravity cause large-scale effects like these, it also causes countless accidents in everyday life. If we fall from too great a height, gravity in effect kills us. If cars collide, gravitational forces cause the damage that results, buckling metal and doing worse things to flesh and bone. If God were to intervene to stop all such accidents, picture what would have to happen: the speeding bullet would mysteriously have to stop before it reached its victim; colliding cars would suddenly have to take a different direction; the rock about to fall on your head would be forced to take a curving path to avoid you. In effect it would become impossible to kill or injure another person. The result would be that we would inevitably realise that somebody or something was controlling the world. An entity powerful enough to do this would probably be seen as God, so we would know that God exists. When we look at John Hick's theodicy, one of his main arguments is that if we knew for a fact that God exists, we could never be free, because we would always be conscious of the existence of a superior being, and we would always try to please that being.
- You can see the force of this argument: **nature has to be free to follow the laws by which it works.** Not only that, where we see people suffering as a result of all the accidents and diseases that can happen to us, **this gives us the opportunity to develop Mackie's 'second-order goods' of compassion,** feeling sympathy towards and empathy with their sufferings.

We can therefore make a good case for saying that God has to allow natural evils to exist. Just as we have to be morally free in order to choose between good and evil, the world has to be free to work according to its own rules, without God intervening like an 'almighty magician'.

Bear in mind that we do not have to prove that these are the precise reasons why God allows moral and natural evil. Nevertheless, the Free Will Defence provides a powerful set of reasons why God *might* allow their existence: in the long run, freedom allows us to develop into the kind of beings God wants us to become.

## Some strengths and weaknesses of the Free Will Defence

### Strengths

1 Plantinga's account of the Free Will Defence shows that both his MSR 1 and MSR 2 are logically possible, so Plantinga refutes Mackie.

2 Plantinga is right to insist against Mackie that it would have been logically impossible for God to have created a world (**PW3**) in which people had free will but never made morally bad choices. Even an omnipotent being could not do the logically impossible.

3 It is often argued that the Free Will Defence cannot explain natural evil, since natural evil is not caused by human free will. Nevertheless there is no doubt that natural evils do indeed bring about second-order moral goods such as love, sympathy and compassion, and that such goods are to be valued above simple happiness and pleasure.

4 The Free Will Defence does establish one crucial principle: that a world with free creatures is more valuable than a world without them. Freedom alone is the thing that makes any love or joy or goodness worth having. Without freedom, there is no achievement and no real happiness. It is indeed possible that this is why God allows evil to exist.

5 It is also true, as we suggested previously, that humans value the risk of pain. There are many activities where the risk of injury or even death can increase people's enjoyment. For some, where there is no risk there can be no enjoyment.

## Weaknesses

1 In Plantinga's case, even though his MSR 1 and MSR 2 show that the Free Will Defence is logically coherent, it does not show that it is true. In particular, Plantinga's explanation of natural evil: that it was brought into the world by the free actions of the serpent and Adam and Eve, elevates a mythological story to the status of a philosophical argument, which it is not.

2 The Free Will Defence relies on a libertarian account of free will. Libertarian accounts of free will hold that although humans are to some extent determined by their biology and chemistry, and by the laws of physics, human minds are nevertheless in some way free to make mental decisions and choices, including moral choices. The libertarian account of free will cannot be proved, however: it can only be assumed.

Other philosophers and scientists hold a 'determinist' or **compatibilist** view of free will. A determinist denies it, whereas a compatibilist argues that freedom and determinism are somehow compatible. You do not need to go into the whys and wherefores of these different positions. What is clear is that there is no accepted account of whether or not humans have free will, so of necessity any verdict on the Free Will Defence has to be labelled 'unproved' until we know more about the issue.

3 Perhaps the strongest objection to the Free Will Defence is that it has no convincing response to the evidential problem of evil. Earlier, we pointed out that it is very difficult to reconcile God's omniscience with the sheer extent of evil in the world. The essence of Dostoyevsky's response to this problem was simple: freedom is not worth its price-tag. At the point of creation, God must have known the full extent of human evil, so why did he bother to create such a universe?

We need, then, to find a more likely explanation for why God allows so much evil in the world. This is provided by Hick's 'soul-making' theodicy, to which we now turn.

> Call the world if you Please "The vale of Soul-making". [Note 15]

> **Key term**
>
> **compatibilism** Determinism and free will are compatible where there are no external constraints on a person's actions (such as being tortured), in which case a person is free to act within the constraints of their own motives and desires.

# John Hick's soul-making theodicy

## Hick's theodicy

Hick's task is harder than that of Plantinga, since he attempts to show that there is a plausible explanation for the existence of evil that is probably true. [Note 16]

1 **Hick's starting point is that the traditional Augustinian theodicy is no longer credible.**

The traditional Christian theodicy is that of Augustine (fourth century CE), which is still substantially unchanged within the Catholic Church

▲ John Hick (1922–2012) Hick was an English philosopher of religion, although he spent much of his academic life in America

today. It places the origin of evil and suffering within the mythological story of Adam and Eve and their supposed fall from a state of perfection. This is not to belittle Augustine's theodicy, which was a magnificent achievement for its time. Nevertheless, Hick dismisses it as:

### 'utterly unacceptable' ([Note 17])

In Augustine's account, Satan (in the form of the serpent) used his own angelic freedom to tempt Eve to disobey God, with the result that the creator expelled Adam and Eve from paradise into a new situation of hardship, danger, disease and death, and this situation has been the lot of creation ever since. Then, through the crucifixion and resurrection of Jesus, God made an atonement for human sin and offered free forgiveness for all who commit themselves to Christ as their Saviour. At the Last Judgement, some will enter into eternal life, while others will continue in the 'perpetual living death' of hell. Such ideas, says Hick, are the:

### ' ... product of religious imagination'

In order to pave the way for his own theodicy, Hick begins by pointing out the scientific, moral and logical flaws in Augustine's account. Scientifically, Genesis is a mythological account (based, as we have seen, on the Babylonian Epics of Creation and Flood). Moreover, disease was part of the animal world long before the emergence of humans, as were the natural evils, such as flood and death that were supposedly brought into the world in order to punish Adam and Eve. Morally, punishing the whole succeeding human race for the sins of the first parents is unjust. Logically, Augustine's view that wholly good beings in a wholly good world could become sinful, is incoherent, because if any created being malfunctions from its design, then the only possible reason is that the design was flawed. If Augustine is right, then God is a flawed designer. Augustine's argument is so damaged that any attempts to salvage it stretch credibility beyond breaking point.

2 **For Hick, the earlier (second century CE) ideas of St Irenaeus are a better starting point.**

In the Irenaean tradition, humans did not 'fall' from perfection: rather, they were created as imperfect beings who nevertheless had the capacity to become 'children of God'.

3 **For Hick, just as good parents love their children, humans are made for a love relationship with God.**

Hick describes this by extending the metaphor of humans as 'children of God', pointing out that in Christian thinking, God is consistently described as the Father. No human father can force his children to love him: children learn to love their parents through a free response to their parents' care. Care does not involve treating children like pets whose life is to be made as comfortable as possible, shielding them from all unpleasant things. Having created their children through an act of love, parents then develop their children's character by teaching them how to live responsibly within the world, showing them by example how to respond constructively to the harshness of the physical world and the opportunities these bring for character development.

4 **Hick extends this 'two-step' process of how humans create and develop their children to God's creation and development of the human race.**

- In Genesis 1:26, God decides to create the human race in his own image and likeness.
- Hick calls the image 'Bios', meaning the biological life of human beings. He calls the likeness 'Zoe', by which he means the perfect personal life of humans as seen in Jesus.
- So, just as human parents create their children biologically and then develop their character, God creates the human race through biology and allows it to develop itself until every human being achieves the likeness of Christ.
- So, while now we are capable of a personal relationship with God, eventually humans can become Christ-like. According to Hick, this stage

'... represents the perfecting of man, the fulfilment of God's purpose for humanity, the 'bringing of many sons to glory', the creating of 'children of God' who are 'fellow heirs with Christ' of his glory.' (Note 18)

- This is Hick's way of saying that eventually, just as children can mature and can respond to their parents in freedom and love, the human race will mature, and will respond to its Creator in freedom and love.

5 There is one major difference between how children respond to their parents and how the human race responds to God. The difference is that **whereas some children will never learn to respond to their parents, eventually the human race as a whole will respond freely to God. All will be saved and will enter heaven**. Because God is infinitely persuasive, every individual will be brought into a moral and spiritual relationship with God. This happens at different times for different individuals, and for some, the process may take many lifetimes, in different levels of existence (an interesting thought).

6 **So, whereas in Augustine's theodicy the world is a place of soul-*deciding*, for Hick, the world is a place of soul-*making*.** For Augustine, hell is a reality for those who reject Christ: they will suffer unending torment in hell (Note 19). For Hick, this is an abhorrent doctrine, to say the least, and one that would be unthinkable for a God of love: God's salvation is for all humanity. For Hick, if the doctrine of hell were true, then that would constitute the worst part of the problem of evil, because no loving Father would commit any of his children to hell. Evil can only be overcome if there is some future good that overcomes it.

7 **The accomplishment of this relationship with God can only be achieved through each individual being free to choose between good and evil**, so that eventually individuals freely come to love God and the good. Evil is not simply the absence of good, otherwise there would be nothing to overcome: the denial of evil contradicts the faith of the Bible.

8 **In particular, Hick maintains that humans have to exist at an 'epistemic distance' from God.** An epistemic distance means a 'distance of knowledge'. If humans knew for a fact that God existed, then their

freedom would be lost. Their reason might tell them that there is a God, or it might not, but they cannot *know*, otherwise they would lose their freedom. If they knew absolutely that God existed, they could not be free, because they would do whatever they thought God wanted them to do.

9 **This means that the world has to contain the full range of moral and natural evils**, so that humans can develop the second-order virtues such as courage, sympathy, empathy and compassion. These are qualities by which we become children of God. Hick's theodicy therefore incorporates the Free Will Defence, and is a much wider response to the problem of evil than the Free Will Defence. We need the whole range of first- and second-order evils in order to develop as human beings. Our sufferings make us virtuous.

We made this point as one of the strengths of the Free Will Defence (no.5). It is known technically as the '**counterfactual hypothesis**' – the benefits of this world with all its challenges and hardships are in complete contrast to the experience of living in a world without pain or pleasure, with no incentive in life to do anything. Life as it now is gives us the stimulus for development, but take away the stimulus (the challenges), and the effect is to take away the development.

So, the existence of evil is compatible with the existence of an omnipotent and supremely good God.

10 **Hick, like Plantinga, rejects Mackie's argument that God could have created us so that people always freely choose the good.** God could not have created us with a built-in awareness of the virtues, because the response to God would not then be authentic – it would in effect be compelled. To compel another person to love you would mean that their love was inauthentic, and in the same way, being compelled in any way to love God would be an inauthentic love. Love cannot be forced, otherwise it is worthless.

11 **Hick goes on to deal with three obvious objections to his argument.**

 a **The objection that his theodicy does not justify animal suffering.** Animal pain seems completely unjustified, since they cannot grow spiritually.

 Hick's answer:

 ● Animals have no fear of death or of future evils. Moreover, pain warns animals of danger, so they have to experience pain to exist.
 ● If there were no other animal species alongside humans, we would suspect that our position in the world was privileged. In other words we would no longer be at an epistemic distance from God, because we would be aware of God's existence and our freedom would be compromised. Therefore, other animals have to exist and the whole process of evolution has to exist; and animals have to suffer to a degree that we cannot explain.

 b **The objection that there are pointless evils in the world.**

 Hick's answer:

 ● Such evils (such as William Rowe's example of a fawn dying unseen in agony in a forest fire) must remain a mystery, because if there were no irrational evils in the world, then we would be able to understand and make sense of all forms of evil, and our epistemic freedom would be lost. We would have a very clear piece of evidence for the existence of God.

- Being able to explain all kinds of suffering would leave us without faith or hope, but these are essential to aid our personal development, so some evils have to appear pointless.

c **The objection that his theodicy does not justify the extent of evil in the world. In other words it does not justify the very worst evils.**

Hick's answer:

- All evils are a matter of degree. If we remove evils like the Holocaust, then the next-to-worst evils will seem the very worst.
- The more evil we remove from the world, the less moral freedom and responsibility humans are left with, which defeats the reason for allowing evil to exist in the first place.

## Strengths and weaknesses of Hick's soul-making theodicy

### Strengths

1 The most powerful part of Hick's argument is probably his view that we are created at an epistemic distance from God. Hick can use this to justify any form of evil, including animal suffering and apparently pointless suffering, because his thesis is that the end (heaven for all) justifies the means.

2 Hick's argument that evil is justified because it is necessary for soul-making is also a powerful argument. Individual people, and humanity as a whole, cannot develop without challenge, and suffering develops character. It would be unrealistic to suppose that we can experience great goodness without also being exposed to great evils.

3 Hick argues convincingly that if the doctrine of hell is true, then that alone would constitute the worst part of the problem of evil. If hell exists, then the kind of God who might send you there might be just, but he would hardly be loving. On the 'heaven' side of the equation, it is interesting that Hick believes that we might experience many different levels of existence after this one before reaching heaven. The 'ascent' to heaven is not a kind of frantic scramble to get out of this universe into heaven, but a process of becoming worthy of heaven, whatever heaven turns out to be like. That seems to be a coherent idea, at any rate.

4 Hick's theodicy incorporates evolution as being part of the first stage of human development, so his theodicy fits generally with scientific evidence about the origins of the human race.

### Weaknesses

1 Hick's comments concerning animal pain are strange. He admits that we have no good explanation for the degree of animal suffering, but then suggests that if there were no inexplicable animal suffering then our epistemic distance from God would be breached. That seems to be a very peculiar argument, because he says there is no good explanation for animal pain and then immediately gives one! Moreover, the appeal to the epistemic distance to justify animal suffering fails, since there appears to be no benefit to animals themselves.

Further, the theory of evolution, which Hick accepts, classifies man as an animal, so what is it that separates humans from other animals? In short, the sum total of animal suffering throughout the Earth's history is appalling, and cannot be excused by the kind of comment advanced by Hick, for example, that animals do not know they will die: one wonders whether Hick ever went near a slaughter-house. Following the arrival of humans on the evolutionary scene, the suffering of animals has increased exponentially. If animals are to be excluded from soul-making, then their suffering seems to show that God is callous rather than loving.

2 Closely related to the first suggested weakness is the view that in Hick's theodicy the ends do not justify the means. In other words, the sum total of human and animal pain and suffering is not justified by the promise of heaven. We can make this point in two ways, for example:

● The promise of heaven is not a contract offered to humans for their acceptance or refusal, so is God morally justified in allowing evil without the consent of those on whom it is inflicted?
● We are back to the evidential problem of evil: is the promise of heaven enough to make up for the sheer amount of suffering in the world? You will remember Ivan Karamazov's comment that although he did not reject God, he rejected God's ticket to paradise, because the journey is not worth it.

3 Many Christians reject Hick's theodicy because it does not match up with some Christian teachings. For example:

● If all human beings are saved, what was the point of Jesus' crucifixion? At best, Jesus' life becomes a role model to show Christians how to arrive at God's 'likeness'.
● Hick is a pluralist who sees the world religions as different responses to one Divine Reality. This is not to the taste of those who believe that salvation comes only through Christ.

The fact is, of course, that Hick does not have to give house room for any doctrines he does not accept, Christian or otherwise. It is up to you how you treat such objections.

4 Hick's theodicy argues for universal salvation – everybody will eventually reach God's Kingdom, however long this takes. If that is the case, what is the point of the pilgrimage: if we are all going to get there, what is the point of the journey?

If God wants a Kingdom of spiritually mature people, why not create them as the finished article? Some might answer that it would be necessary to experience the pain of a real journey to the Kingdom to make it worthwhile, but God could have made everybody with a built-in memory of the journey so that they would always believe they had made it.

**Discussion point**

Do you think that this last suggestion is right? Would it have answered God's purposes to create people with a false memory of a journey?

In summary, Hick's theodicy is a reasonably consistent argument, and makes good use of the concept of an epistemic distance between God and humanity. However, Hick incorporates the Free Will Defence within his theodicy, and therefore he has to *assume* that humans have a libertarian kind of freedom to respond to God or not. Moreover, as with the Free Will Defence, the question still remains as to whether or not the whole process is worth the amount of suffering in the world. It is hard to see how anyone can decide on that without experiencing heaven.

We move on now to Process Theology, which is considerably more provocative in its claims than either the Free Will Defence or Hick.

# Process Theology as presented by Griffin

## Griffin's Process Theology

Process thought arose primarily from the work of the English philosopher / mathematician Alfred North Whitehead (1861–1947). Whitehead was fascinated by quantum mechanics, which revealed a world in a constant dynamic of flux and change, and according to Whitehead, God is also growing and changing. This is the background from which Griffin's Process Theology evolved. (Note 20)

▲ David Ray Griffin (b.1939). American theologian / philosopher of religion

### 1 Griffin's rejection of 'creation from nothing'.

The main point from which Griffin starts his theodicy concerns the Christian view of *creatio ex nihilo* – 'creation out of nothing', which most Christians assume is the way that God created the world in Genesis 1:1–3. Griffin insists that this is based on a mistranslation of the text. This is the Revised Standard Version:

> ¹ **In the beginning, God created the heavens and the earth.** ² **The earth was without form and void, and darkness was upon the face of the deep; and the Spirit of God was moving over the face of the waters.**
>
> ³ **And God said, 'Let there be light'; and there was light.**

This translation of the Hebrew shows that God's first creative act is to create the universe ('the heavens and the earth'), and it implies that God called the universe into existence from nothing simply by using words of creative power.

However, a more likely translation of the Hebrew would be:

> ¹ **In the beginning of God's creating the heavens and the earth,** ² **the earth being without form and void, and darkness being upon the face of the deep; and the Spirit of God moving over the face of the waters,** ³ **God said, 'Let there be light'; and there was light.**

If you compare the two translations, you will see that the second gives a completely different sense of the passage, because the phrase, 'the earth *being* without form and void' assumes that the universe already exists. What God is creating, therefore, is not the universe: rather he is creating order out of the 'formless and void' chaos.

According to Griffin, then, the universe is uncreated and eternal, and God is inextricably bound with it. God's creative role was therefore to develop what was already there, by 'persuading' it into a state of greater order and complexity, and the evolution of life on Earth is one aspect of this persuasion.

### 2 Griffin's rejection of God's omnipotence.

The idea of creation out of nothing actually supports the idea that God is omnipotent, because a God who can literally bring the universe into existence from nothing would truly have unlimited power. If the idea of 'creation from chaos' is right, however, then these chaotic materials will probably have had some power of their own by which God's will could be opposed. According to Griffin, they have two types of power: they partially determine themselves, and they can influence each other. On this view, then, God is not omnipotent. We will look at this in more detail below.

3 **Abandoning the key Christian concepts of creation out of nothing and God's omnipotence is a necessary consequence of Griffin's method of doing theology.**

Griffin has a number of ground rules about how to develop (and how not to develop) a theodicy. For example:

● We cannot believe any doctrine just because what the doctrine says is not logically impossible: we need to seek the most probable view of reality that we can find. If you apply this to Plantinga's defence of the Free Will Defence, you should see what Griffin means.
● Any revealed theology must be abandoned if it does not make sense, which is why we should abandon belief in creation from nothing and in God's omnipotence.
● We should accept 'common notions' (commonly accepted ideas) about our existence. For example, most of us have a common notion that we have genuine free will, and that we are therefore responsible for our actions. Most of us also assume that evil is real, so we should also accept that genuinely evil things happen in the world (and we should therefore abandon Augustine's view that evil is just an absence of good).
● Neither the Bible, nor the Church, nor tradition can guarantee the truth of any Christian doctrine.

Using these kinds of rules, Griffin constructs his theodicy, beginning with the view that creation from chaos makes more sense than creation from nothing, and that it is equally sensible to abandon the idea that God is omnipotent.

4 **God and the universe exist necessarily, panentheistically and eternally.**

We do have a common notion, says Griffin, that something probably exists necessarily, because most of us accept that there has to be something necessary to explain why we are here in the first place. Griffin claims that it does not make sense to think of God as being **transcendent** (above, or separate from, the space–time universe); rather, it is sensible to think that both God and the physical universe exist necessarily, and that they exist together in a **panentheistic** relationship, which means that the universe is 'in' God.

What exists necessarily, then, is 'God-and-a-world' (God + the universe). Just as humans have embodied minds, it makes sense to think of God as the soul of the universe. Just as the human body's experiences are integrated by the mind, the experiences of the entire universe are integrated by the mind of God. (Note 21)

The idea that God is eternal whereas matter is not, is false. God + the universe is / are eternal, existing without beginning or end in the panentheistic relationship.

5 **God is therefore not transcendent, and cannot intervene to eliminate evil.**

Griffin first points out what he sees as the disastrous consequence for the problem of evil of the Christian belief in creation from nothing. Following the 'traditional' Christian logic:

a If God creates from nothing, he must exist transcendently: beyond / outside space–time.
b He must also possess the power to intervene to break the laws by which the universe works.

**Key terms**

**transcendent** The idea that God is above and beyond space–time; as opposed to immanent, existing within space–time.

**panentheism** The view that 'all is in God'; in Process Theology, that God is the soul of the universe, so does not transcend the universe.

c  The Bible records many such interventions, including the miracle of Jesus' incarnation, crucifixion and resurrection, by which God redeems humanity from moral evil. Further, Jesus' miracles of healing (for example, raising Lazarus from the dead) and his miracles over the world of nature (such as the Calming of the Storm and the Feeding of the 5,000) show God's power over natural evil.

d  But, if God sometimes intervenes to restrict both moral and natural evil, why does he not intervene to eliminate them completely?

e  This question has been a major headache for Christian theologians, because the answers (according to Process theologians) do not make sense.

f  For example, the Free Will Defence suggests that God permits evil because humans must be free to respond to God. Hick suggests that heaven will justify evil retrospectively (when we get there we will see that it has all been worth it); but the problem with all such answers is that they fail to answer the evidential problem of evil – why did God bother to create such a universe if so much evil would come from it?

6  **Now compare the 'traditional' Christian logic with Griffin's / the Process view:**

a  God 'created' the universe from pre-existing chaotic matter.

b  Both God and chaotic matter exist necessarily and panentheistically: God is the 'soul' of the universe.

c  God cannot control the physical aspect of the universe any more than a human mind can control the internal workings of its body (otherwise nobody would ever feel pain or fall ill). God is therefore powerful but not omnipotent.

d  Over long periods of time, God can persuade chaotic matter into an organised form (such as electrons, atoms and molecules).

e  God's 'creation' therefore amounts to a drive towards increasing complexity in matter, over a period of 13.77 billion years (starting with the Big Bang): first to form stars and galaxies, and then to develop thinking beings such as ourselves through 3.5 billion years of evolution.

f  Nowhere in this process does the idea of a direct / miraculous intervention arise.

g  The evidential problem of evil therefore does not arise, because God cannot 'intervene' to prevent evil. There are no miracles. All there is, is the long process of divine persuasion.

7  **Why did God wish to persuade matter towards complexity?**

- Increasing complexity gives rise to an increased richness of experience, and thereby brings about the possibility of enjoyment. Living cells are probably the lowest level at which enjoyment begins, so it is at this level that we can begin to talk of value.
- From living cells, there is an exponential leap to the animal level, especially animals with a central nervous system: they can experience an increased number of different types of value.

8  **So back to the question: Where did evil come from?**

Janus was the Roman god of beginnings and endings, and is therefore depicted as having two opposing faces, since he looks both to the past and to the future. Evil arose because increased complexity has two faces: on the one hand it brings increased capacity for enjoyment, but on the other it brings increased capacity to suffer. This parallel relationship is probably

▲ The Janus face

metaphysically necessary, built into the nature of things. (Note 22) To get the sense of this, look back at the matrix of first-, second- and third-order goods and evils that we considered with the Free Will Defence, which makes much the same claim. Humans can therefore suffer in ways that other animals cannot.

Moreover, the problem of evil intensifies with the development of complex individuals like ourselves, because the more complex the organism, the more possibility it has to deviate from God's will; and the more power it has to influence others for evil as well as good.

9 **So we are back, yet again, to the evidential problem of evil. Knowing all this, why did God start the process of evolution that led to atrocities such as the Holocaust?** (Note 23)

Griffin admits that the responsibility for this must lie with God, who unilaterally undertook to set chaotic matter on the road to increasing complexity. Griffin maintains, however, that we cannot blame God for this. See whether or not you think Griffin's chain of logic improves on that of the Free Will Defence or Hick:

● God's idea was to produce good, and not to avoid suffering.
● We should be able to understand this: human parents have children despite the suffering this might cause both parent and child. By analogy, God could have avoided bringing forth creatures who could go wrong, but then there would have been no world with any significant value in it.
● For God not to have brought about good would have been evil:

**'I cannot imagine that I would ever conclude that the evils of life have been so great that it would have been better had life never emerged, or that the evils of human life, as horrendous as they have been (and quite possibly the worst is still to come!), are such that it would have been better had human life never been created.'** (Note 24)

● Moreover, God shares all of our suffering. Griffin makes an analogy here to the way 'I' share the pains of my bodily parts: since God / the universe exists panentheistically, God must experience the entirety of pain and suffering in the universe. Griffin here echoes the words of A.N. Whitehead, that God is 'the fellow sufferer who understands'.

10 **Why does God not at least prevent some natural evils?**

Griffin's answer is that the entities that cause natural evils are 'low-grade' entities such as electrons, atoms and molecules and these are very difficult for God to affect, except over long periods of time, so any changes in them are very slow. If your body develops cancerous cells, for example, God cannot lure them into leaving voluntarily; they do not have that much volition – they lack the awareness to respond directly to God.

Also, if we consider 'aggregates', by which Griffin means things like rocks, bodies of water and planets: these have no dominant member. There is no 'lead-molecule' or 'soul' in a puddle of water that God can directly influence in order to change the behaviour of the puddle of water, or a river, or a sea. Therefore, there is no way God can stop a tsunami from drowning you, or the rocks of an earthquake from crushing you, or a speeding car from hitting you.

**Discussion point**

You should now be able to see how radically different Process Theology is. Which do you think offers the most plausible explanation of evil: Process Theology, the Free Will Defence or Hick's theodicy, and why?

## Strengths and weaknesses of Process Theology as presented by Griffin

### Strengths

1 You might have concluded from your discussion that Griffin at least has a sense of realism about what God can and cannot do. His conclusion that God is not omnipotent can be seen as a realistic answer to the problem of evil: God does not have the power to control it.

2 In the same way, the discovery through quantum mechanics that at the sub-atomic scale, reality is a chaotic process of flux and change, gives some support to Griffin's argument that God's creation of the universe was not creation from nothing but instead was the gradual ordering of pre-existing chaotic material.

Whether or not the doctrine of creation from nothing is implied in some biblical texts is a contested point, but Griffin is almost certainly right that the Hebrew of the main creation account in Genesis 1:1–3 is talking about creation from chaotic materials, and this understanding is strongly supported by the fact that the biblical account reflects the Babylonian mythologies of Creation and Flood, where again, 'Creation' means 'putting chaos into order'.

3 The fact that God suffers because He 'contains' the entire sensory experience of the universe, means that believers who suffer know that God understands (although this would be no consolation to animals who would not understand why they suffer).

### Weaknesses

1 God's lack of omnipotence in Process Theology can be seen as a strength in some ways (for example, point **1** above), but a number of commentators consider it to be a major weakness. Thus John Roth comments:

> **'By the implications of Griffin's theory, when Elie Wiesel arrived at Auschwitz, the best that God could possibly do was to permit 10,000 Jews a day to go up in smoke ... A God of such weakness, no matter how much he suffers, is rather pathetic. Good though he may be, Griffin's God is too small.'** (Note 25)

In other words, although the Process God is powerful, for many his lack of omnipotence makes him not worthy of worship.

2 Again, the issue of the evidential problem of evil rears its head. Griffin argues that God cannot be blamed for deciding to bring about this universe from chaotic matter, because having this universe, despite all the evil and suffering in it, is preferable to having no universe at all. You will remember Griffin's comment that even if still greater evils than those we have experienced already are yet to come, he would still judge God to be in the right. How many people believe this?

Moreover, even if the Process God is not omnipotent, at the point when he saw that his persuasion of the universe into greater and greater levels of evolutionary complexity was equally bringing about greater amounts of evil, why then did he not cease in his efforts? Why did God start a process he could not control? Just like Hick, and just like the Free Will Defence, Process Theology does not really answer Ivan Karamazov's complaint that the universe just 'is not worth it'.

3 The suggestion that God cannot control evil is often considered to be the final nail in the coffin of Process Theology, because even though God may do his best, there still can be no guarantee that God will succeed in overcoming evil. Process Theology therefore admits that there is an element of 'risk' in God's strategy, because if advanced entities like humans have sufficient power to reject God's persuasion towards the good, then human existence will probably end in a nuclear, biological and chemical obliteration of all species. As Griffin admits concerning the human race:

> 'In a relatively short time after they learned to write, these individuals could discover that $E = mc^2$; and they can use this knowledge to destroy the world even more quickly.' [Note 26]

If the element of risk is so great, and victory against evil is not guaranteed, then what incentive do we have to join or continue the fight against evil? If victory is not guaranteed, might we not abandon the fight and allow evil to overcome the good?

With Process Theology, analysing it can be difficult, and it is not just a case of detailing the strengths and weaknesses of the theory. For example, for Process theologians, God is 'powerful enough', but that is insufficient for those who are wedded to the notion of God's omnipotence.

It is not unusual for its detractors to describe Process Theology as 'unchristian', but when has there not been a time when one group or another that has professed to follow Christ has *not* been labelled as unchristian?

The simple fact is that we do not know whether or not God is omnipotent, and we do not know whether God created the universe from nothing, from chaotic matter, or in some other way, and no amount of doctrinal table-thumping will decide these issues.

As a final comment, Process Theology is often criticised for having little or no eschatology – no doctrine of what will happen 'at the end of the universe' or when we die. To the extent that this is true, it is simply a reflection of the fact that the metaphysical doctrines of heaven and hell have little interest for Process theologians who believe that reality is contained within this space–time universe. Process theologians therefore tend to believe in 'objective immortality': all individual entities in the universe remain forever in the mind of God, so in that sense they never die. As a matter of fact, however, Griffin argues on the basis of **parapsychology** and near-death experiences that there is a 'strong cumulative case' that the soul could perhaps survive the death of its body and possess subjective immortality. [Note 27] In any event, what is refreshing about Griffin here is that he regards his ideas as probabilities rather than as facts, which might serve as a warning to those who believe they are in possession of religious facts that everybody should bow down to.

## Key term

**parapsychology** The investigation of paranormal and psychic phenomena that lie outside the province of scientific psychology.

# The relationship between philosophy and faith

To conclude, there is clearly no solution to the problem of evil that all Christians accept. The relationship between Christian philosophy and Christian faith is a mixed one.

- In terms of the influence of any particular theodicy, the Catholic Church endorses Augustine's soul-deciding theodicy, as do many Protestant groups for whom the threat of hell is real. Believers will make every effort to live by the moral rules of Christianity in order to avoid hell and have the hope of heaven.

- A practical response to evil is therefore common in Christianity, for example, through prayer and intercession, and by service, for example, contributing to the work of a hospice.

- A common Christian response to evil is to abandon philosophy in preference for faith, following the example of Job in the Old Testament and of Jesus' acceptance of his impending crucifixion and death. Faith does not necessarily mean passive acceptance, as, for example, in the Book of Job, where God commends Job for protesting his innocence to God and demanding an explanation for his treatment.

- Philosophy can cause people to lose their faith. Where the philosophy of religion uses theodicies to defend God against the problem of evil, the conclusions may point away from belief in God, for example, where all theodicies have difficulty in giving a satisfactory explanation for the evidential problem of evil. The death-toll of the Great War of 1914–1918 was around 16 million. Added to the evil of the war, the influenza pandemic of 1918–1920 that followed it infected 500 million and killed up to 40 million, making it one of the deadliest natural disasters in modern history. It contributed significantly to the rise of atheism in the twentieth century, since for many, God was seen to be absent.

- Conversely, the experience of extreme evil and suffering can lead people to ignore rational / philosophical arguments about evil in favour of more radical versions of Christianity, seen, for example, in the emergence of Apocalyptic / **Millenarian** groups. At the end of the 1918–1920 flu pandemic, Millenarian groups developed notably in Nigeria, the Belgian Congo, Southern Rhodesia and South Africa. [Note 28] Such groups can actually be encouraged by increased evil on Earth, which they take as a sign of the impending final battle between good and evil described in the Book of Revelation.

## Key term

**Millenarianism** A belief in a thousand-year reign of Christ on Earth, concluding with a universal resurrection, judgement and the consignment of the just to heaven and the damned to hell.

## Discussion points

1 Do you think that God's omnipotence includes the ability to do the logically impossible? For example, can God make a stone too heavy for Himself to lift? Can He make a square so that it is also circular at the same time? Assuming that omnipotence includes having necessary existence, can a necessary being cause himself to go out of existence? How do you think this issue impacts on the problem of evil?

2 Process theologians argue that God is not omnipotent. Is a non-omnipotent God worth worshipping?

3 Can an omnipotent God do evil? In answer to this question, some would argue that God is by nature all-loving and so his inability to be evil does not stem from his lack of omnipotence, but simply from his nature. Do you think this solves the question?

4 In your view, would a God who is not omnibenevolent be worth worshipping?

5 Are there any good reasons why an omniscient God might consider that it is worthwhile to create a universe containing the kinds of evil that we experience?

6 Which of the following do you think poses the biggest challenge to our ideas about God: problems with God's omnipotence, omnibenevolence or omniscience?

7 Why is the idea of human free will so important in discussions about the problem of evil?

8 'If there is no God, then life is meaningless.' Is this true?

9 'It is meaningless to talk about a God who is beyond space–time.' How far do you agree?

10 'Evil does not exist.' How far do you agree?

## Technical terms for understanding this section on evil and suffering

**causal determinism**   The view that every event is determined by antecedent (preceding) events and conditions and by the laws of nature, so humans do not have free will.

**compatibilism**   Determinism and free will are compatible where there are no external constraints on a person's actions (such as being tortured), in which case a person is free to act within the constraints of their own motives and desires. Consider this: If you are waiting for a train on a crowded platform, and your worst enemy is in front of you, and you wish to push him under the approaching train, then provided: **1** that nobody stops you, and **2** that it is within your nature to be able to commit murder, then you have a real free choice – push, or do not push.

**libertarianism**   In the free will debate, this is the view that although some aspects of human existence are determined by physics, biology and chemistry, humans nevertheless have a degree of free will and so can be held morally responsible for their actions.

**Millenarianism**   A belief in a thousand-year reign of Christ on Earth, concluding with a universal resurrection, judgement and the consignment of the just to heaven and the damned to hell. Millenarian groups arise typically during times of intense evil and suffering.

**panentheism**   The view that 'all is in God'; in Process Theology, that God is the soul of the universe, so does not transcend the universe.

**parapsychology**   The investigation of paranormal and psychic phenomena that lie outside the province of scientific psychology.

**transcendent**   The idea that God is above and beyond space–time; as opposed to immanent, existing within space–time.

# Summary of the problem of evil

1 **The problem of evil is the single greatest challenge to the Christian belief in a loving God.** In the Bible, the origins of evil are generally seen in the story where Adam and Eve disobey God in the Garden of Eden. The cycle of stories concerning Creation and Flood is a re-working of older Babylonian myths. In the New Testament, St Paul argued that the sin of Adam and Eve is made up for by the sacrifice of Jesus on the cross. The Bible does not see evil as something outside God: God creates both good and evil, although in no sense is evil 'in' God. To some

extent, in the New Testament, evil is personified as Satan and Revelation depicts a final war between the forces of God and those of Satan; although Satan is not seen as equal in power to God.

2 **Evil is categorised as natural and moral**, and these give rise to the logical and evidential problems of evil. **The logical problem of evil** is expressed by the inconsistent triad. **The evidential problem of evil** is formed: **1** by the sheer extent of evil in the world, including pointless evils, and **2** by

God's omniscience, because at the point of creation God must have been aware of the full extent of evil.

The problem of the extent of evil is best illustrated by Dostoyevsky's *'The Brothers Karamazov'*, where the public prosecutor, Ivan, alleges that even accepting that God's purposes are good does not excuse the sufferings of innocent children.

3 **Despite the extent of evil in the world we can still accept that some suffering is good**, e.g. the pain of surgery can restore the body to health, and suffering can bring out the best aspects of the human character.

4 **The options**. Aside from denying one of the statements in the logical problem of evil, answers to these problems include the idea that freedom is a higher-order good that is worth the evils it brings and the idea that at some stage it will be shown that the whole process is worth even the worst evils. The first of these ideas is expressed by the Free Will Defence, and the second by Hick's 'vale of soul-making' theodicy.

5 **The Christian Free Will Defence** argues that God is justified in allowing evil to exist in the universe because evil is needed to allow humans to understand and prefer the good. John Mackie describes the Christian Free Will Defence as a matrix of first-, second- and third-order goods and evils, but rejects it on the grounds that it must have been logically possible for God to create the entire human race so that everybody would make free, good choices. Because God has not done so, Mackie concludes that either God is not omnipotent (in which case he is not God), or else he does not exist. In either event, the Free Will Defence is logically incoherent.

In response to Mackie, had God created everybody so that they always made free, good choices, 'good' would be meaningless, because it would have no frame of reference (nothing to identify it by).

Moreover, it would be logically impossible for God to create genuinely free people who would always make good choices, and it is no limitation of God's power to say that he cannot do the logically impossible, because that is not a sensible idea.

Alvin Plantinga rejects Mackie's claim that the Christian Free Will Defence is logically incoherent. Plantinga argues that evil exists because of two 'morally sufficient reasons' (MSR 1 and 2).

**MSR 1 deals with moral evil**, and claims that:

'God's Creation of persons with morally significant free will is something of tremendous value. God could not eliminate much of the evil and suffering in this world without thereby eliminating the greater good of having created persons with free will with whom he could have relationships and who are able to love one another and do good deeds.'

**MSR 2 deals with natural evil**, and says that:

'God allowed natural evil to enter the world as part of Adam and Eve's punishment for their sin in the Garden of Eden.'

However unlikely this is, it is logically possible, so in summary, Plantinga therefore defeats Mackie's claim that the Christian Free Will Defence is logically incoherent.

**Evaluating the Free Will Defence:** the argument is strong because Mackie's claims can be refuted. It would be logically impossible for God to create the kind of world that Mackie thinks God should have created (Plantinga's **PW3**). The Free Will Defence can also explain why natural evils are allowed to happen – they produce second-order goods such as love, sympathy and compassion; so they do bring about a greater good. The Free Will Defence also establishes the crucial principle that a world with free creatures is more valuable than a world without them and this is why God allows evil to exist. It is also true that humans value the risk of pain: where there is no risk there is no achievement.

However, the Free Will Defence has several weaknesses. Plantinga's defence is logically coherent but is not necessarily true. Plantinga's explanation of natural evil is particularly weak; moreover, his defence relies on a libertarian account of free will which cannot be shown to be true. In particular, the Free Will Defence has no convincing response to the evidential problem of evil.

6 **John Hick's 'vale of soul-making' theodicy** has the harder task of trying to give an explanation of evil which is probably true. Hick rejects Augustine's theodicy and argues that humans are made for a love relationship with God. Hick describes this as a two-step process in which humans are created in the *image* of God, and through experiencing hardship and suffering move towards the *likeness* of God, by which he means the perfect personal life of humans as seen in Jesus. The world is not a place of soul-deciding (as in Augustine's account where many go to hell); rather it is a place of soul-making since all will be saved and enter heaven.

Accomplishing this relationship with God can only be achieved by each individual being free to choose between good and evil, and in turn there has to be an epistemic distance between God and humanity: humans cannot be certain that God exists otherwise their freedom would be compromised.

**Evaluating Hick's theodicy:** the epistemic distance is a powerful argument to justify any kind of evil and suffering. His soul-making argument is also powerful: souls cannot be made without challenge and suffering, and great goods cannot be achieved without the experience of great evils. Hick's rejection of the idea of hell also seems coherent, since as he says, hell alone would constitute the worst part of the problem of evil. Hick incorporates evolution into his theodicy as the first stage of human development, which fits well with scientific evidence about human origins.

There are several weaknesses in Hick's theodicy, for example: **1** It does not solve the problem of unfair animal suffering, since their suffering does not benefit the animals. **2** Its ends do not justify the means: humans have never had the opportunity to consent to God's plans. **3** Hick does not solve the evidential problem of evil: is the promise of heaven really enough to make up for the sheer amount of suffering in the world? **4** His theodicy does not match up to some Christian teachings. For example, what was the point of Jesus' crucifixion?

7 **Griffin's Process Theology** rejects the key doctrines of 'creation out of nothing' and of God's omnipotence. The relationship between God and the universe is panentheistic: the universe exists within God and God exists within the universe. Just as humans are embodied minds, God is the soul of the universe, so the mind of God experiences literally everything that happens. God and the universe exist eternally, so God's act of creation was not to create the universe out of nothing but to organise already-existing chaotic matter, and since chaotic matter can resist God's will, God cannot be omnipotent and cannot get rid of evil – evil is not *from* God, but is *within* God. Evil is one aspect of the physical and mental processes of the universe, all of which God experiences.

God's actions are therefore restricted to persuasion, exerted over long periods of time. God persuades chaotic matter (such as electrons, atoms and molecules) into more complex forms, to form stars, galaxies and eventually ourselves. Nowhere in this process does the idea of a direct / miraculous intervention arise. The evidential problem of evil, therefore, does not arise, because God cannot intervene to prevent evil. All there is, is the long process of persuasion.

The problem of evil arises because every increase in the capacity for enjoyment and good is matched by an equal capacity for suffering and evil. Moreover, with beings like ourselves, increased complexity brings about a far greater ability to

oppose God's will and an increased power to influence others towards greater evil also. Why then did God not abandon the drive to complexity? Griffin's answer is that for God not to have brought about the possibility of evil would have been a worse evil than any evil we have so far experienced, so God was right to take the risk. Moreover, the universe is in God, so God shares every instance of pain and suffering in the universe, so he is 'the fellow sufferer who understands'.

**Evaluating Griffin's Process Theology:** it seems more realistic than other theodicies because it abandons the belief in God's omnipotence. The reason we see so much evil is that God cannot control it. On the other hand, Griffin's argument has four major problems. First, is a non-omnipotent God worthy of worship? Second, despite the claim that it would have been evil for God not to have brought about good, would God really be justified in starting a process he could not control? Third, Griffin admits that victory against evil is not guaranteed, so why should we join God in the fight against it? Fourth, most Process theologians believe in 'objective immortality' – people survive only in the sense that they exist forever as part of God's memories. Do you think that is satisfactory?

**Theodicies do influence Christians greatly in the ways in which they lead their lives**. For example, those who follow Augustine's 'soul-making' theodicy make every effort to live by the moral rules of Christianity in order to avoid hell and have the hope of heaven. Protestant groups who live by the rule of scripture will do the same. Many individual Christians follow the example of Job: they abandon philosophy for faith, holding that God must be accounted righteous regardless of what evils happen, although as with Job, protest to God is acceptable: it is right to protest about something you believe to be unjust. Some take a practical approach through prayer and intercession and by service to those who suffer. Some reject all philosophical theodicies and lose their faith, and this was true particularly after the moral evil of the First World War and the natural evil of the influenza pandemic that followed it. Conversely, the experience of intense evil can bring about more radical versions of Christianity, such as Millenarianism. For example, Millenarian groups emerged in Southern Africa and elsewhere after the 1918–1920 influenza pandemic. Millenarianism groups can actually be encouraged by increased evil on Earth because they take it as a sign of the impending final battle between good and evil described in the Book of Revelation.

# Religious experience

This chapter will cover:

**The nature of religious experience:**

- Visions: corporeal, imaginative and intellectual.
- Numinous experiences: Otto; an apprehension of the wholly other.
- Mystical experiences: William James; non-sensuous and non-intellectual union with the divine as presented by Walter Stace.

**Verifying religious experiences:**

- The challenges of verifying religious experiences.
- The challenges to religious experience from science.
- Religious responses to those challenges.
- Richard Swinburne's principles of credulity and testimony.

## The influence of religious experiences and their value for religious faith

There is a tradition about St Thomas Aquinas that the year before he died he had a religious experience so powerful that, by comparison, all his great learning was like 'straw before the wind'. Long after Aquinas' death, the Reverend Alban Butler recorded this tradition:

> During his second ... period in Paris the university was torn by dissensions of different kinds, and in 1272 there was a sort of 'general strike' among the faculties, in the midst of which St Thomas was recalled to Italy and appointed regent of the study-house at Naples. It was to prove the last scene of his labours. On the feast of St Nicholas the following year he was celebrating Mass when he received a revelation which so affected him that he wrote and dictated no more, leaving his great work, the *Summa Theologiae*, unfinished. To Brother Reginald's expostulations he replied, 'The end of my labours is come. All that I have written appears to be as so much straw after the things that had been revealed to me.' [Note 1]

Religious experiences come in a seemingly infinite variety, and there is no doubt, as with that of St Thomas Aquinas, that they can be life-changing. In one sense they are very difficult to write about authoritatively, for the simple reason that those who have had one are in a different ball park to those who have not. Statistics vary, but around 30–40 percent of people will have an experience which they will describe as 'religious', 'mystical', or 'spiritual'.

## Categorising religious experiences

There are many different types of alleged religious experience. The following are some of the more common experiences.

Call experiences (e.g. where someone feels called by God, as with many of the prophets)

Conversion experiences (e.g. conversion to a religion from atheism or from one religion to another)

Crisis apparitions (a form of vision of someone undergoing a crisis, e.g. severe danger or death)

Dream experiences which have a religious message

Hesychasm (a mystical tradition of prayer in the Eastern Orthodox Church)

Meditational experiences

Miraculous healings

Mystical experiences

Near-death experiences

Numinous experiences (experiencing God as the 'wholly other')

Prophetic ecstasy (where prophets prophesy in an altered mental state)

Reincarnational memories

Religious experiences through the power and beauty of nature

Religious vision as discussed further on

Stigmata (marks on the body corresponding to those left on Jesus' body by the Crucifixion)

People inevitably try to put such experiences into neat categories, because categories can be described, tested and labelled. But any one of these experiences can combine with another: for example, visionary and auditory experiences can happen in dreams. Near-death experiences can include a bewildering number of 'nested' experiences, including visions of light, altered states of consciousness, auditory experiences, out-of-body experiences, and a feeling of unity with the universe.

# The nature of religious experience

You have to study three categories from the list above: visions, mystical experiences and **numinous** experiences.

## Visions: corporeal, imaginative and intellectual

The division of visions into these three types comes from St Augustine of Hippo (354–430CE). [Note 2]

### Corporeal visions

Corporeal visions are a form of **empirical** religious experience. Empirical experiences are those which we have through our five senses of touch, taste, hearing, smell and sight. One of the most common forms of religious experience is that of seeing God through nature: for example, through the glory of a beautiful sunset, or the grandeur of mountain scenery. In other words, God is seen through or by means of the object.

---

**Key terms**

**numinous** Relating to the power or presence of a deity.

**empirical** Empirical religious experiences are those which are experienced by the senses of touch, taste, hearing, smell and sight, e.g. a corporeal vision.

A corporeal vision, then, comes through the physical sense of sight. The experiencer sees a supernatural vision of an object that is really present. '**Supernatural**' here means, 'beyond the normal forces of nature'. Light from the object strikes the retina of the eye, and the object is seen in the same way as you would see any normal object, such as a chair or a tree.

A well-known example of a French woman who claimed that she experienced corporeal visions is Joan of Arc (c. 1412–1431). From the age of 12 she experienced visions of angels and saints, accompanied by voices which told her to bring renewal to the French nation. After experiencing these visions she led the French to victory in battle against the English in the Hundred Years War. At her trial (for heresy and for wearing male military clothing), she said that her visions were as real to her as seeing an actual person with her 'bodily eyes'. The visions were often accompanied by heavenly light.

Another equally well-known example from France is the experience of Bernadette Soubirous (1844–1879) at Lourdes.

▲ Bernadette Soubirous

▲ Grotto of Massabielle, Lourdes

Bernadette was the first-born daughter of a miller from Lourdes. While collecting firewood near the Massabielle Grotto with her sister Marie and a friend, she experienced a vision of a 'small young lady' dressed in white with a blue waist-belt. She claimed to have experienced 18 visions in total, in the course of which the lady identified herself as the '**Immaculate Conception**', meaning the Virgin Mary, the mother of Jesus. The visions were accompanied by the appearance of a spring of water, which has since been the source of around 69 documented 'miracles' for which it is claimed there are no scientific explanations.

- The visionary experience was corporeal, since Bernadette saw the physical body of Mary.

- The vision was also private, as her sister and friend claimed to have seen nothing.

- It was also auditory, since during the 16th vision, having asked the lady's name, the answer eventually came in her own dialect of Gascon Occitan: 'I am the Immaculate Conception'.

- The vision had clear religious significance, both in the identity of the person seen, and in the instructions given by the figure to wash in water from the spring and to build a chapel on the site for the faithful to visit in procession. Lourdes is now an international site visited by around 5 million pilgrims each year.

- The similarities with the experiences of Joan of Arc are worth noting, since the visions of both were accompanied by voices and by visions of light.

## Key terms

**imaginative vision** A vision seen in the mind, usually through a dream experience.

**corporeal vision** Relating to a person's body. A corporeal vision is one that comes through the physical sense of sight.

**illumination** To illuminate is to cast light. In religious terms the doctrine of illumination holds (for example) that when the biblical writers wrote their books, the Holy Spirit illuminated their minds with the truth. In intellectual visions, the vision illuminates the soul without any kind of visual image.

## Imaginative visions

While someone who experiences a **corporeal vision** can, to some extent, interact with what is seen and heard (as with Joan of Arc and Bernadette Soubirous), in **imaginative visions** the experiencer has no power to direct the experience, a sign that it comes from God. The vision is given to the experiencer without being perceived by the normal processes of sight.

Imaginative visions often occur most frequently in dreams, where the experience is 'seen' or imagined with the 'eye of the mind', and what is seen is completely beyond the individual's control.

### Example 1 – Pharaoh's dream (Genesis 41)

In this account, the Egyptian Pharaoh (king) receives two powerful dream visions that he cannot interpret. In the first, seven thin cows devour seven fat cows, and in the second, seven withered ears of grain devour seven fat ears. Pharaoh is aware that the dream vision is of crucial importance, but his magicians and wise men are unable to interpret it. Pharaoh's chief butler tells him that they have a young Hebrew in prison who can interpret dreams. This is Joseph, eleventh son of Jacob, sold into slavery by his brothers. Joseph tells Pharaoh that the vision is a warning from God that seven years of plenty will be followed by seven years of famine, so the importance of the vision is that Pharaoh should store surplus grain.

There are several important aspects of this experience:

- The vision was a dream experience, beyond Pharaoh's control, seen with the eye of the mind.

- Pharaoh's account of the dream is vivid, and the effect on him is dramatic: 'Pharaoh saw the things so realistically that when he awoke he first had to adapt himself to reality ...' (Note 3) Being well aware that this is not an ordinary dream, Pharaoh knows that it needs to be interpreted.

- The dream has entered Pharaoh's imagination by God's agency, so Joseph tells him: 'God has revealed to Pharaoh what he is about to do.' (Genesis 41:25) Pharaoh recognises that Joseph is directed by the 'Spirit of God' (41:38), which is the source of Joseph's **illumination** and intellectual power. (Note 4)

- The result of the vision is that by the power of God, Pharaoh stores enough grain to avoid starvation in Egypt. Pharaoh places Joseph in charge of the land of Egypt, and he is eventually reunited with his father Jacob and his brothers.

### Example 2 – Joseph's dream (Matthew 2:13–15)

In this account, an angel appears to Joseph in a dream, and tells him to take Mary and Jesus to Egypt because King Herod is searching for Jesus in order to kill him. Joseph instantly arises and obeys the angel's commands, staying in Egypt till the death of Herod. Matthew adds that the effect of the vision is to fulfil the ancient prophecy of Hosea 11:1: 'Out of Egypt have I called my son.'

Joseph's experience has similar features to the dream of Pharaoh:

- The vision of the angel appears as a dream in Joseph's mind.

- The effect is dramatic – he instantly arises and takes Mary and Jesus to Egypt.

- The vision is from God, by the agency of the angel.

- The result is that Jesus is taken out of harm's way, and prophecy is fulfilled.

## Intellectual visions

While corporeal visions are seen by the eyes, and imaginative visions are seen by the 'eye' of the mind, the **intellectual vision** has *no* image. Nevertheless, those who experience this kind of vision claim to 'see' things as they *really* are. This is a difficult idea to grasp, mainly because intellectual visions are mystical visions, and those who have them claim that they cannot be described using ordinary language.

Some of the most graphic accounts of intellectual visions are those given by the Spanish mystic St Teresa of Ávila (1515–1582).

Sometime before 1567, Teresa wrote an autobiography in which she describes her visions. She recounts an experience of Jesus Christ:

> I was in prayer one day, – it was the feast of the glorious St Peter, – when I saw Christ close by me, or, to speak more correctly, felt Him; for I saw nothing with the eyes of the body, nothing with the eyes of the soul. He seemed to me to be close beside me; and I saw, too, as I believe, that it was He who was speaking to me. As I was utterly ignorant that such a vision was possible, I was extremely afraid at first, and did nothing but weep; however, when He spoke to me but one word to reassure me, I recovered myself, and was, as usual, calm and comforted, without any fear whatever. Jesus Christ seemed to be by my side continually, and, as the vision was not imaginary, I saw no form; but I had a most distinct feeling that He was always on my right hand, a witness of all I did; and never at any time, if I was but slightly recollected, or not too much distracted, could I be ignorant of His near presence. [Note 5]

▲ Teresa of Ávila by François Gérard (1770–1837)

If you look closely at what Teresa says, you can see the difference between corporeal and imaginative visions on the one hand, and intellectual visions on the other:

- 'I saw nothing with the eyes of the body' (the vision was not corporeal).
- 'I saw … nothing with the eyes of the soul … the vision was not imaginary, I saw no form' (the vision was not imaginative).
- 'I had a most distinct feeling … of His near presence' (she saw Jesus Christ as he *really was*: not as an image, but as a 'presence').

Teresa goes on to explain that the 'light' of an intellectual vision is an illumination of the understanding of the soul:

> I went at once to my confessor … in great distress, to tell him of it. He asked in what form I saw our Lord. I told him I saw no form. He then said: 'How did you know that it was Christ?' I replied, that I did not know how I knew it; but I could not help knowing that He was close beside me,–that I saw Him distinctly, and felt His presence … there are no comparisons, in my opinion, by which visions of this kind can be described … He renders Himself present to the soul by a certain knowledge of Himself which is more clear than the sun. I do not mean that we now see either a sun or any brightness, only that there is a light not seen, which illumines the understanding so that the soul may have the fruition of so great a good. [Note 6]

According to Teresa's account of intellectual visions, such visions give spiritual illumination, so they can be about the world of the Holy Spirit, God, the Trinity, and in particular for her, the awareness of the presence of Jesus. To her they represent the highest level of mystical union with God, and reflect the desire to contemplate God as he really is. Similarly, the *Catholic Encyclopaedia* defines mysticism as: '... a religious tendency and desire of the human soul towards an intimate union with the Divinity.' (Note 7)

# Numinous experiences: Otto; an apprehension of the wholly other

Consider this passage from the call of Moses, in Exodus 3:3–6:

> 'And the angel of the LORD appeared to him in a flame of fire out of the midst of a bush; and he looked, and lo, the bush was burning, yet it was not consumed ... God called to him ... 'Moses, Moses!' And he said, 'Here am I.' Then he said, 'Do not come near; put off your shoes from your feet, for the place on which you are standing is holy ground.' ... And Moses hid his face, for he was afraid to look at God.'

## The idea of the Holy

Moses' experience here illustrates one of Otto's central ideas – that religious experiences are encounters with **the Holy** (*Qadosh* or *Sanctus* in Hebrew and Latin respectively), 'holy' being the key-word of all religion. Another word for holy is 'sacred'. The holiness of God is the central feature of another call narrative – that of the prophet Isaiah, who sees a vision of God enthroned in the Jerusalem Temple, surrounded by seraphim who call to one another:

> 'Holy, holy, holy is the LORD of hosts;
>
> the whole earth is full of his glory.' (Isaiah 6:3)

The threefold repetition (known as the *Trisagion*) is the strongest form of emphasis used in Old Testament Hebrew. God's essence is holiness, and in the face of such holiness Isaiah feels impure, until one of the seraphim touches his lips with a burning coal in order to forgive his sins.

Otto does not focus on 'holy' in the moral sense, but in the sense of God being 'transcendent' and 'numinous'. (Note 9)

## The numinous

'Numinous' comes from Latin *numen*, referring to a deity or spirit, so numinous is an adjective meaning 'relating to the power (or presence) of a deity'. According to Otto, the numinous is common to all religious experience, regardless of religion or culture.

One of the best known explanations of the numinous comes from C.S. Lewis (1898–1963). Lewis is famous not least because of his *Chronicles of Narnia*, a seven-book children's series beginning with (in publication order) *The Lion, the Witch and the Wardrobe*. Lewis became an atheist at 15 years old, apparently because he was 'angry with God for not existing'. Some 16 years later, as a result of God's 'compelling embrace'

▲ Rudolf Otto (1869–1937). German Lutheran theologian. His most famous work was *The idea of the Holy*, (Note 8) still regarded as one of the most important works on religious experience

during an ongoing religious experience, he became a theist. Two years after that, influenced by his famous novelist friend, J.R.R. Tolkien, he converted to Christianity, following which he produced a number of books with a Christian basis, including *Mere Christianity, The Screwtape Letters, and The Problem of Pain.*

In *The Problem of Pain* we find the following explanation of the numinous:

> Suppose you were told there was a tiger in the next room: you would know that you were in danger and would probably feel fear. But if you were told 'There is a ghost in the next room', and believed it, you would feel, indeed, what is often called fear, but of a different kind. It would not be based on the knowledge of danger, for no one is primarily afraid of what a ghost may do to him, but of the mere fact that it is a ghost. It is 'uncanny' rather than dangerous, and the special kind of fear it excites may be called Dread. With the Uncanny one has reached the fringes of the Numinous. Now suppose that you were told simply 'There is a mighty spirit in the room', and believed it. Your feelings would then be even less like the mere fear of danger: but the disturbance would be profound. You would feel wonder and a certain shrinking – a sense of inadequacy to cope with such a visitant and of prostration before it – and emotion which might be expressed in Shakespeare's words 'Under it my genius is rebuked'. This feeling may be described as awe, and the object which excites it as the *Numinous.* (Note 10)

Lewis goes on to give a modern example of the numinous from *The Wind in the Willows*, a children's novel by Kenneth Grahame, where Rat and Mole approach the horned god Pan on the island:

> 'Rat,' he found breath to whisper, shaking, 'Are you afraid?'
>
> 'Afraid?' murmured the Rat, his eyes shining with unutterable love. 'Afraid? of Him? O, never, never. And yet – and yet – O Mole, I am afraid.' (Note 11)

### Our feelings about the numinous are *sui generis* ('of their own kind')

Religious experience itself is of God as the wholly other, and God is inherently different from anything and everything else, and is beyond the natural world. The wholly other is beyond apprehension or comprehension – it cannot be grasped or perceived.

Numinous feelings are not just more intense versions of our normal feelings. They are *sui generis*, meaning they are unique or in a class of their own. They are a special faculty in our minds – a faculty that recognises the holy and responds to it.

### Numinous feelings are non-rational

We cannot *reason* our way to understanding numinous feelings, because such feelings are non-rational. They are *beyond* the rational and cannot really be explained. The same is true of all our feelings in general, but numinous feelings are even more beyond rational description. We are left, then, with a '*mysterium tremendum et fascinans*' – a 'tremendous and fascinating mystery'. As John Macquarrie puts it:

**Key terms**

*sui generis* Unique / of its own kind / in a class of its own – applies to numinous feeling.

> ... If the numinous core of religion is inconceivable, how can we talk about or describe it? Otto holds that although it is inconceivable, it is somehow within our grasp. We apprehend it in feeling ... There is on the one side what is called 'creature-feeling' – the feeling of the nothingness of finite being. On the other side is the feeling of the presence of an overwhelming Being – the numinous Being which strikes dumb with amazement. Otto's analysis is summarized in the expression '*mysterium tremendum et fascinans*'. [Note 12]

### The '*mysterium tremendum et fascinans*'

Its tremendous power can chill and numb. It inspires feelings of awe and majesty, alongside dread, fear and terror. Its energy is like the overpowering rush of a tide.

For a more complete list of the feelings Otto is considering see: http://www.bytrentsacred.co.uk/index.php/rudolf-otto/the-idea-of-the-holy-1-summary

It produces feelings of stupor, blank wonder, dumb astonishment, inadequacy, humility and 'creatureliness' in response to that power. When the first disciples encountered Jesus, they perceived this power in Jesus. Peter watched Jesus produce a miraculous catch of fish, and his immediate response was to understand his own inadequacy. Just as Isaiah's response to being called by God gave him a feeling of his sinfulness contrasted with God's holiness, Peter's response to his own call was to fall at Jesus' knees and say, 'Depart from me, for I am a sinful man, O Lord.' (Luke 5:8)

The mystery itself is fascinating – the experiencer is caught up in it. Having recognised that he is a creature confronted by the wholly other, the reaction of Peter is simply to leave everything and follow Jesus. His fishing partners, James and John, are caught up by the same fascination, and do the same thing. (Luke 5:11)

The feeling of fascination is so attractive that it can evoke rapture and love. Again, think of Rat in *The Wind in the Willows*, when he tells Mole that he is afraid, yet at the same time his eyes are 'shining with unutterable love'.

Together, the concept of the numinous as the '*mysterium tremendum et fascinans*' focuses on God as **transcendent:** above and beyond space and time. God is so far removed from humanity that we have no choice but to approach God with numinous awe, dread, fear and terror. The creature is overwhelmed by its own nothingness by comparison with the Holy Spirit.

Notice, then, that God's transcendence is emphasised to the virtual exclusion of the general Christian view that God is also immanent within the universe through Jesus and the Holy Spirit.

**Key terms**

*mysterium tremendum et fascinans* 'A tremendous and fascinating mystery' – part of Otto's description of numinous religious experiences.

**transcendent** The concept that God is above and beyond the space–time universe; for Otto, part of his view that God is 'wholly other'.

## Mystical experiences: William James; non-sensuous and non-intellectual union with the divine as presented by Walter Stace

In Rudolf Otto's approach to mystical experiences, numinous experiences are experiences of a God who is 'wholly other' from humanity. In the approaches of William James and Walter Terrence Stace, however, the object of mystical experiences is union with God.

### William James

**William James (1842–1910)**

American philosopher and psychologist. His well-known work on *The Varieties of Religious Experience* (Note 13) contains his analysis of mystical experiences, and the whole book is an engaging read. You can read the chapter entitled 'Mysticism', which you will find here: https://ebooks.adelaide. edu.au/j/james/william/varieties/chapter11.html

James covers the whole spectrum of human psychology in his investigations, including the clinically insane. In the introduction by Arthur Darby Nock, to the edition of *The Varieties of Religious Experience* referred to above, Nock refers to a comment made by James to some pupils who had visited two mental institutions with him, and had seen a dangerous patient: 'President Eliot might not like to admit that there is no sharp line between himself and the men we have just seen, but it is true.' (Note 14) This is just one of the reasons why Nock concludes that *The Varieties of Religious Experience* is probably 'the only book about the psychology of religion ... which you could conceivably choose to take to a desert island with you.' (Note 15)

It is difficult to do justice to the range of William James's ideas. It is therefore important to consider some of these ideas in a logical order.

1 **Religious experience is primary, and comes from a factually existing God**

Religion, in the sense of organised religion, is secondary. We do not have religious experiences as the result of belonging to any particular religion or Church; rather, organised religion is one response to the religious experiences of our ancestors, so religious experiences are primary and religious dogma and creeds are secondary. Religious experiences are an interaction with God, and they produce positive results, so 'God is real since he produces real effects'. [Note 16]

2 **Although God exists factually, God is not the being described by Judaeo-Christian teaching**

James's views on God are not given as a structured study, but they become apparent by reading his various works on religion. He does not see God as necessarily being omnipotent (all-powerful), so God is likely to be finite rather than infinite. Furthermore God does not have to be a single entity, but could be a collection of god-like selves. [Note 17] God interacts with ourselves in time, so is probably temporal (existing in time), and finite, not knowing the future.

3 **Experience teaches us that the religious life involves the following three beliefs:**

- The most significant thing about the visible world we inhabit is that it draws its chief significance from a more spiritual universe (the realm of God).
- The true end of humanity is union (or harmonious relation) with that higher universe.
- Prayer or inner communion with God is efficacious (it works). Spiritual communion with God through prayer produces real psychological or material effects in this world. [Note 18]

4 **The psychological benefits of this kind of spiritual communion include:**

- an energetic zest for life, from which people can feel a kind of 'lyrical enchantment' or can be inspired to do heroic deeds.
- an assurance of safety, peace, and loving affection.

5 **This kind of personal religious experience has its root and centre in mystical states of consciousness**

There are four criteria by which we judge that someone has had a mystical experience. [Note 19] The first two of these are the most significant in describing such an experience:

a **Ineffability**
This means that the experience cannot be described in words. It has to be directly experienced, and cannot be transferred or imparted to others. An ineffable experience is like a feeling, and no feeling can be understood by somebody who has not experienced it. For example, no one can understand a lover's state of mind unless they too have been in love. Equally, no one can understand a mystical experience unless they too have had one.

**b  Noetic quality**

Although they are similar to states of feeling, mystical experiences also seem to be noetic: they give rise to knowledge, so that those who experience them learn something as a result. They are states of insight in which truths are intuitively realised or felt to be true even though they cannot be described.

For most who experience them, 'they carry with them a curious sense of authority' which affects them thereafter.

Two other qualities are less sharply marked, but are usually found in the mystical experience:

**c  Transiency**

Mystical states cannot be sustained for long. Except in rare cases, the longest they last is half an hour, or at most an hour or two. It is often the case that after a time it becomes difficult to reproduce the experience in memory: although if someone has a further experience they can become conscious of a continuous development in the richness and importance of what is felt.

**d  Passivity**

Once the experience begins, it is beyond the person's control. This is true even when the person concerned has *invited* the experience by going through some of the mental or physical preparations described in manuals of mysticism. The will of the experiencer becomes passive: the mystic does not control the experience – the experience controls the mystic.

**Note:** You will probably have come across a simple device to remember these four criteria: 'PINT', which stands for Passive, Ineffable, Noetic and Transient. But try to remember James's order: INTP, which you can remember by 'PINT IN The Pub'.

6  **There is a wide range of mystical experiences, ranging from those with little religious significance to those in which the religious element is extreme**

For example:

● The strangely moving power of bits of poetry or music. Has your scalp ever tingled when listening to one of these?
● The experience of *déjà vu*, where you are aware that what you are experiencing now you have 'already seen', but you cannot recall when or where, and the feeling takes you beyond normal perception.

Going deeper still into mystical consciousness, James refers to the feelings of the priest and novelist Charles Kingsley:

'When I walk the fields, I am oppressed now and then with an innate feeling that everything I see has meaning, if I could but understand it. And this feeling of being surrounded with truths which I cannot grasp amounts to indescribable awe sometimes …. Have you not felt that your real soul was imperceptible to your mental vision …?' (Note 20)

James moves on to drug-induced states, which he sees as a special state of consciousness. The most common states are those induced by alcohol, anaesthetics, and particularly nitrous oxide gas, by which 'depth beyond depth of truth seems revealed to the inhaler.' (Note 21) James thought that the only time he understood the philosopher Hegel was while under the influence of nitrous oxide. While some would regard drug-induced religious experiences as necessarily false, for James they are clearly not, because they do what all mystical experiences do – they give the experiencer access to different levels of consciousness.

James moves on again to 'mysticism pure and simple ... of sudden realization of the immediate presence of God'. He quotes the following passage:

'I know,' writes Mr Trine, 'an officer on our police force who has told me that many times when off duty, and on his way home in the evening, there comes to him such a vivid and vital realization of his oneness with this Infinite Power, and this Spirit of Infinite Peace so takes hold of and so fills him, that it seems as if his feet could hardly keep to the pavement, so buoyant and so exhilarated does he become by reason of this inflowing tide.' (Note 22)

Among the most powerful mystical experiences are those in which the mystic experiences 'cosmic consciousness', in which '... the universe is not composed of dead matter, but is, on the contrary, a living Presence ...' (Note 23)

James concludes with a survey of those who cultivate mystical consciousness deliberately, for example yoga in India as 'the experimental union of the individual with the divine', where each step in the discipline 'is intended to bring us scientifically to the super-conscious state.' In this state, for the yogi there is no feeling of I, and yet the mind works, desireless, free from restlessness, objectless, bodiless. Then the Truth shines ... and we know ourselves ... for what we truly are, free, immortal, omnipotent, loosed from the finite, and its contrasts of good and evil altogether, and identical with the Atman or Universal Soul.' (Note 24)

When discussing the Christian mystics, James describes Teresa of Ávila as the 'expert of experts' in describing conditions such as union with the divine:

'During the short time the union lasts ... she is utterly dead to the things of the world and lives solely in God ... God establishes himself in the interior of this soul, in such a way, that when she returns to herself, it is wholly impossible for her to doubt that she has been in God, and God in her.' (Note 25)

7  **Finally, the point of mystical experiences is that God meets the individual 'on the basis of his personal concerns'.** (Note 26)

This idea is somewhat alien to science, which deals primarily with analysing and cataloguing the laws by which the universe works. Many scientists tend to view this world and the life forms on it as a 'local accident in an appalling wilderness of worlds where no life can exist' (Note 27), in which religion is just a survival from a more primitive era. 'Not so!' says James. It is on the richer animistic and dramatic aspects of Nature that religion 'delights to dwell':

'It is the terror and beauty of phenomena, the "promise" of the dawn and of the rainbow, the "voice" of the thunder, the "gentleness" of the summer rain, the "sublimity" of the stars, and not the physical laws which these things follow, by which the religious mind still continues to be most impressed; and just as of yore, the devout man tells you that in the solitude of his room or of the fields he still feels the divine presence, that inflowings of help come in reply to his prayers, and that sacrifices to this unseen reality fill him with security and peace.' (Note 28)

According to William James, reality for us is on the level of the personal and private, and not on the level of the cosmic and the general. God is not found in one particular religion or in one set of religious dogmas: each individual *perceives* God, the Absolute or the divine uniquely, and *receives* from God uniquely. Different individuals have different needs: 'sick souls' will require a religion of deliverance, whereas the 'healthy-minded' need no such deliverance. Whatever is wrong with us can be dealt with by connecting with God. For one kind of individual, for example, God will be the God of battles; for another, God will be the God of peace, heaven and home, and God will be whatever it is that 'saves' the individual. Ultimately, 'God's existence is the guarantee of an ideal order that shall be permanently preserved.' (Note 29)

## Discussion points

1 Where James says that mystical experiences are 'ineffable' (indescribable in words) isn't James making a contradiction in terms just by using the word 'ineffable'? Doesn't this describe something?

2 How do we account for the difference between Rudolf Otto's claim, that religious experiences are essentially about something that is 'wholly other' and completely above and beyond humanity, and that of James and Teresa of Ávila, that the ultimate form of religious experience is mystical union with the divine?

Aren't these a complete contradiction, or is this just part of the paradoxical nature of religious experiences that they can involve apparent contradictions?

3 If God is 'wholly other', doesn't this mean that the created world and its beings have no real value?

## Non-sensuous and non-intellectual union with the divine as presented by Walter Stace

### Walter Terrence Stace (1886–1967)

British philosopher well known for his ideas on mysticism. In 1960, Stace published two works on mysticism: *Mysticism and Philosophy*, and *The Teachings of the Mystics*. The latter is a more general summary of his ideas, and is in turn summarised online from the 'textual highlights' found in: http://www.bodysoulandspirit.net/mystical_experiences/learn/experts_define/stace.shtml.
Page references are given in brackets, and are present in the online source.

## Key terms

**non-sensuous** Not involving the physical senses.

**non-intellectual** The 'I' of the rational intellect is replaced by 'pure consciousness'.

**telekinesis** The ability to move objects solely by the power of the mind.

**clairvoyance** The claimed ability to gain information about objects / persons (etc.) by means beyond the normal methods of perception.

**precognition** Foreknowledge of an event through extra-sensory perception.

**extrovertive** In Walter Stace's definition, a kind of 'half–way house' to introvertive religious experience. Unlike the introvertive experience, in the extrovertive type, sense experience is still active although objects are transformed by the 'unity that shines through'.

**introvertive** In Walter Stace's definition, a religious experience in which sense experience is totally suppressed and the conscious 'I' is replaced by pure consciousness / the One / the Void.

**ineffable** For William James – an aspect of mystical religious experiences not describable in words, so cannot be imparted to others.

---

In common with William James, Walter Stace saw little point in trying to prove the existence of God through reason, maintaining that, 'Either God is a mystery or He is nothing at all. To ask for a proof of the existence of God is on a par with asking for a proof of the existence of beauty.' [Note 30] He therefore set himself the task of showing that mysticism makes sense. Interestingly, Stace agrees with James and Teresa of Ávila that the goal of religious experiences is mystical union with God.

Like James, Stace presented a variety of arguments about mysticism. Again, considering these points in a logical sequence can help in understanding his overall argument.

1 Stace defines mysticism as '**non-sensuous** and **non-intellectual**' union with the divine. In its highest form, the senses cease to work, and the rational intellect – the conscious 'I' – ceases to work as well, being replaced by 'pure consciousness'. Stace defines a mystic as someone who has had a mystical experience (and not just someone who talks about mysticism or is sympathetic towards it).

2 Mysticism has nothing to do with 'mystery' or the 'occult', and nothing to do with what are called 'parapsychological phenomena', such as telepathy, **telekinesis**, **clairvoyance** and **precognition**.

3 Visions and voices are not mystical experiences. Mystics are the sort of people who might see visions and hear voices, but according to mystics, a genuine mystical experience is non-sensuous, having no form, shape, colour, smell or sound. A vision, by definition, includes visual experiences including colour and shape, and a voice includes auditory experience. So visions and voices are sensuous experiences.

4 'The most important, the central characteristic in which all fully developed mystical experiences agree, and which in the last analysis is definitive of them and serves to mark them off from other kinds of experiences, is that they involve the apprehension of an ultimate non-sensuous unity in all things, a oneness or a One to which neither the senses nor the reason can penetrate. In other words, it entirely transcends our sensory-intellectual consciousness.'

5 There are two types of mystical experience: extrovertive and introvertive:

- The **extrovertive** mystic still sees the world of normal objects, such as trees and tables, with his physical senses, but these objects are transfigured so that the non-sensuous unity shines through them.
- The **introvertive** mystic, by contrast, achieves the total suppression of sense-experience in which awareness of the world is completely obliterated. 'Ordinary' consciousness is replaced by an entirely new kind of consciousness – mystical consciousness. This kind of experience is non-intellectual in that the normal intellect is not functioning: it is replaced by mystical consciousness in which the 'I' is absent.
- Stace therefore interprets extrovertive mysticism as a kind of 'half-way house' towards the introvertive experience. According to the Hindu Mandukya (Upanishad), the introvertive mystical consciousness is '**ineffable** peace. It is the Supreme Good. It is One without a second. It is the Self'.

6 In *Mysticism and Philosophy,* Stace includes an example of an extrovertive experience had by an American known as 'N.M':

'The room in which I was standing looked out onto the back yards of a … tenement. The buildings were decrepit and ugly, the ground covered with boards, rags, and debris. Suddenly every object in my field of vision took on a curious and intense kind of existence of its own; that is, everything appeared to have an 'inside' – to exist as I existed, having inwardness, a kind of individual life, and every object, seen under this aspect, appeared exceedingly beautiful. There was a cat out there, with its head lifted, effortlessly watching a wasp that moved without moving just above its head. Everything was urgent with life … which was the same in the cat, the wasp, the broken bottles, and merely manifested itself differently in these individuals (which did not therefore cease to be individuals however). All things seemed to glow with a light that came from within them.'

You can see that this fits well with the definition above of an extrovertive experience. Sense experience is still active, but the objects are transfigured so that the non-sensuous unity shines through them. [Note 31]

Another extrovertive experience is that of Meister Eckhart (a 13th to 14th-century German mystic), who could clearly see all objects in the universe as a unity – as one: 'All that a man has here externally in multiplicity is intrinsically One. Here all blades of grass, wood and stone, all things are One.' [Note 32]

7 Compare this with the introvertive experience of Arthur Koestler:

'Then I was floating on my back in a river of peace under bridges of silence. It came from nowhere and flowed nowhere. Then there was no river and no I. The I had ceased to exist. … When I say 'the I had ceased to exist' I refer to a concrete experience. … The I ceases to exist because it has, by a kind of mental osmosis, established communication with, and been dissolved in, the universal pool. It is this process of dissolution and limitless expansion which is sensed as the 'oceanic' feeling, as the draining of all tension, the absolute catharsis, the peace that passeth all understanding.'

You can see that this fits well with the earlier definition of introvertive experience. There is a total suppression of sense experience: the river ceases to exist, and ordinary consciousness ceases to exist. There is no 'I', with the 'I' being replaced by 'the peace that passeth all understanding'. [Note 33]

8 Stace's account of the common characteristics of an introvertive mystical experience:

i    The Unitary Consciousness; the One; the Void; pure consciousness
ii   Nonspatial, nontemporal
iii  Sense of objectivity or reality
iv   Blessedness, peace, etc.
v    Feeling of the holy, sacred, or divine
vi   Paradoxicality (seeming to be self-contradictory)
vii  Alleged by mystics to be ineffable. [Note 34]

Extrovertive mystical experiences differ only in items (i) and (ii), where the extrovertive experience has:

i  The Unifying Vision – all things are One
ii  The more concrete apprehension of the One as an inner subjectivity, or life, in all things. (Note 35)

In the extrovertive experience the mystic still sees with his physical senses the world of normal objects such as trees and tables, but these objects are transfigured so that the non-sensuous unity shines through them.

### Discussion points

1  The distinctive element of Stace's introvertive experience is that ordinary consciousness, or the 'I', ceases to exist. Do you think this is possible, or is it something that the experiencer wants to achieve but cannot?

2  Both James and Stace are examples of scholars who adopt a 'perennialist' approach to religious experiences, meaning that they attempt to identify a 'common core' for religious experiences across all religions, cultures and traditions. James's 'core' has four elements (religious experiences are ineffable, noetic, passive and transient); Stace has seven. Does this difference mean that there is no such common core?

# Moving on to challenges to religious experiences

Within the Christian tradition, we have looked at three broad types of religious experience: visions, numinous experiences and mystical experiences, and some obvious questions come to mind:

- Do they come from an external source? If so, is it reasonable to think that this source is God?
- What part is played by the mind in these experiences? Does the mind act as a receiver, or can we go so far as to say that the mind invents the experience?
- If religious experiences come from God, what is their meaning and purpose?
- If religious experiences are generated by the brain, what is their meaning and purpose?

As you might imagine, religious experiences are often held to be inventions of the brain, or claims made by those who want so much to believe in religious experience that they convince themselves. The table below shows: (i) some reasons why religious experiences are difficult to prove true, and (ii) challenges from science.

| Religious experiences are difficult to prove true because | Religious responses |
|---|---|
| We only have the word of the individual who claims to have had the experience as evidence. | Some religious experiences are group experiences, where the testimony therefore does not rely just on an individual. |
| | Some experiences can be evidenced through their effects, for example where people experience a complete change of lifestyle and a more spiritual outlook on life. |
| | Swinburne's *Principle of Testimony* suggests that we should accept that people's experiences are probably as they report them, unless there are special reasons to think otherwise (see further on). |
| They are subjective / private experiences / feelings, so they are just 'in the mind'. | The fact that they are private does not make them false – reports of dreams and emotional states we have been in cannot be proved true, but we find it reasonable to believe others when they describe how they feel or what they dreamed. |
| They are ineffable – those who experience them cannot describe them, which really means that there is nothing 'real' to describe. | Ineffability is a characteristic of religious experiences and many others. That makes it difficult to compare them with other experiences and difficult to investigate them, but it does not prove them false. |
| | An experience can be considered religious if it conforms to a definition of religious experience. |
| There are natural explanations to account for religious experiences. | We will consider this further on when we look at the challenges from science. |
| There are contradictory religious experiences so they cannot all be true. | How humans understand their experiences is different from what the experiences actually are, and the Ultimate Reality could choose to express it / him / her self in a way suited to the individual. |
| They are so extraordinary and rare as to be unbelievable – because all normal experience counts against them. | There are many reports of religious experience. Statistics vary, but by common report around 30–40 per cent of people have had experiences that range from general spiritual awareness to deep religious insights. |

## The challenges to religious experiences from science and religious responses to these challenges

There are a number of challenges that science can make to religious experiences.

Most of the challenges from science in effect make one major claim about religious experiences, namely that they are a product of the mind, so they are about human psychology and physiology, and not about 'God'. All that is verified when we study people's religious experiences, therefore, is their brain states at any particular moment, and we will not find God when looking at human brain states.

Here are four significant challenges to religious experience:

1 Sigmund Freud (1856–1939) was an Austrian neurologist and physiologist who argued that religion is wish-fulfilment by the unconscious mind. The idea of God helps us to control fear of the unknown and of death, but such fears, according to Freud, are infantile and neurotic. Where people claim to have religious visions and mystical experiences, these are simply hallucinations caused by our need to have some kind of control over our helpless state.

2 People who suffer from temporal lobe epilepsy (TLE) are sometimes prone to have religious visions and mystical experiences. This suggests that religious experiences are nothing more than abnormal states of the brain.

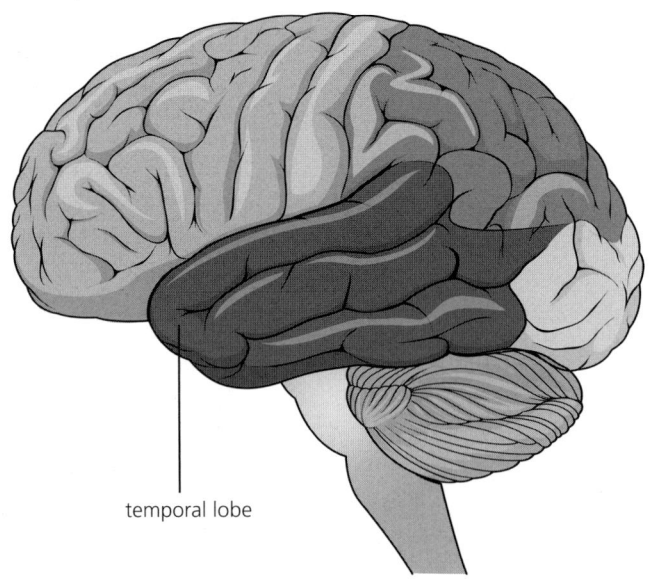

▲ Location of the temporal lobes

Those with TLE can experience strong religious visions, and there have been many suggestions that some of the great religious figures of the past suffered from the condition. For example, in the New Testament, St Paul hints at being afflicted by a condition that he calls a 'thorn in the flesh' (2 Corinthians 12:7). There is no way of knowing the exact nature of his condition, but if you read the accounts of his conversion from Judaism to being a follower of Christ, in Acts 9 and Acts 22, you will see that his conversion was accompanied by seeing light, having visions, hearing voices, suddenly falling to the floor, and temporary blindness, all of which can be associated with TLE. Following this experience, Paul became *the* great Christian missionary, showing intense religious fervour and driving purpose.

Irrespective of whether or not Paul suffered from TLE, there is significant evidence that the condition can result in brain states that produce religious experiences, and this might suggest that such experiences are not from God – they are self-generated.

3  **The research findings on TLE are supported by the science of neurotheology, which suggests that religious experiences are produced by electrical stimulation of the temporal lobes of the brain.**

Neuroscience is the scientific study of the structure and function of the nervous system. Neurotheology attempts to explain religious experience and behaviour in neuroscientific terms. This kind of research was developed in the 1980s, for example by Michael Persinger (b.1945). The results of Persinger's work have been recently confirmed by further studies from Carlos A. Tinoco and João P. L. Ortiz (Note 36).

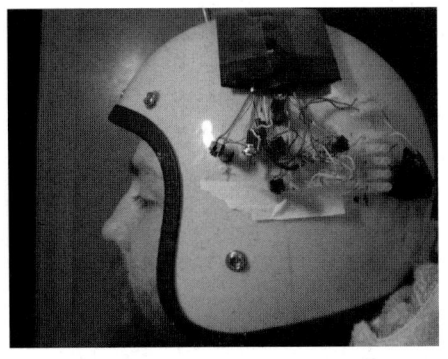

▲ The God Helmet

The God Helmet is an updated version of a device produced by the cognitive **neuroscience** researcher Michael Persinger. It uses magnetic coils placed on either side of the head to stimulate the subject's temporal lobes. The results include (as with Persinger's study) the experience of mystical states, visions of God, and sensing the presence of spiritual beings. The implications are that if neuroscience can duplicate several aspects of religious experiences, then this suggests that religious experiences are specific states of the brain, and are not experiences of God or from God.

**Key terms**

**neurotheology** The attempt to explain religious experience and behaviour in neuroscientific terms.

**neuroscience** The scientific study of the structure and function of the nervous system.

4 **Religious experiences can also be caused by certain types of drugs, which is further evidence that religious experiences are nothing more than the product of brain states.**

The effects of religious experiences are often described in similar terms to the effects of 'hallucinogenic' drugs such as LSD, mescaline and psilocybin. These drugs are called **'entheogens', meaning 'generating / becoming the Divine from within'**, because people who take them can have intense spiritual and religious experiences. Some of the main effects of entheogens are processed by the prefrontal cortex (the grey matter in the frontal lobe of the brain, behind the forehead).

In 1962, Walter Pahnke conducted a scientific study of 20 theology students at Harvard Divinity School, known as the 'Good Friday Experiment'. Ten were given the drug psilocybin while the others were given a placebo. (Note 37) Those who took the drug experienced feelings very similar to those induced by the 'God Helmet', which provides further evidence that religious experience is produced by a particular state of the brain.

From a scientific point of view, then, we might conclude that TLE, neurotheology and the study of **entheogens** show that when certain parts of the brain are stimulated, particularly the temporal and frontal lobes, people access higher levels of consciousness and can have full-blown mystical experiences. They can be convinced that they have experienced God, whereas in reality these experiences have been generated by the brain itself.

## Religious responses

1 **As a response to Freud's view that religion and religious experiences are wish-fulfilment, this is just a hypothesis that cannot be tested, so it remains as a hypothesis. It may of course be true that people wish to have experiences of God, and that these provide comfort, but that does not prove that experiences of God must be false.**

2 **With regard to the challenges that religious experiences are the product of conditions of the brain such as TLE, or that neurotheology shows them to be certain states of the brain or that they are caused by drugs, all three challenges are claiming that religious experiences can be brought about by the individual's own mental state.**

However, the religious believer can make the following reply:

● If God wants to give people religious experiences, these have to be processed by the brain, because the brain is our only way of processing anything.
● So there has to be an area, or several areas of the brain responsible for processing them.
● We know that many such experiences are processed by the temporal lobes and frontal lobes. These are the structures of the brain, therefore, through which God can bring about religious experiences.

3 **The religious believer would have no difficulty in accepting that as well as receiving religious experiences, the mind can generate them and interact with God.**

Most Christians have always held that God is personal – God relates to people in many ways, for example through prayer, through God's incarnation as Jesus (by which God became a person), and through

**Key terms**

**entheogen** 'Generating / becoming the Divine from within' – drugs such as LSD, mescaline and psilocybin that are known to generate religious experiences.

**hallucinogenic** Causing hallucinations, e.g. hallucinogenic drugs.

God's gift to humans of the Holy Spirit as guide and comforter. In the Parable of the Persistent Friend, for example, Jesus makes the point that people should be persistent when they pray to God: 'If you … know how to give good gifts to your children, how much more will the heavenly Father give the Holy Spirit to those who ask him!' (Luke 11:13)

Christians therefore do not have to sit and wait for God to reveal something to them; they can reach out to God. Those who experience God through nature see something of God's power, glory, majesty and love in nature itself. This is one of the main points that William James makes: '… the universe is not composed of dead matter, but is, on the contrary, a living Presence …' (Note 38). Humans can reach out to this Presence.

Equally, William James refers to the great mystics who cultivate mystical consciousness deliberately, for example yoga in India as 'the experimental union of the individual with the divine', where each step in the discipline 'is intended to bring us scientifically to the superconscious state'. (Note 39) Again, the experience begins with those who reach out to God.

You will remember that for William James it makes no difference how the religious experience is arrived at. As far as he is concerned, the mystic can have a religious experience through TLE, through drugs – in fact through any altered state of consciousness, however it is arrived at. Furthermore, the experiencer can take from the experience what he or she needs, because people have widely different needs, and God (or the gods) responds to individuals appropriately. What the experiencer makes of the experience is up to them.

To clarify what we have just said about the two religious responses, we can consider this figure.

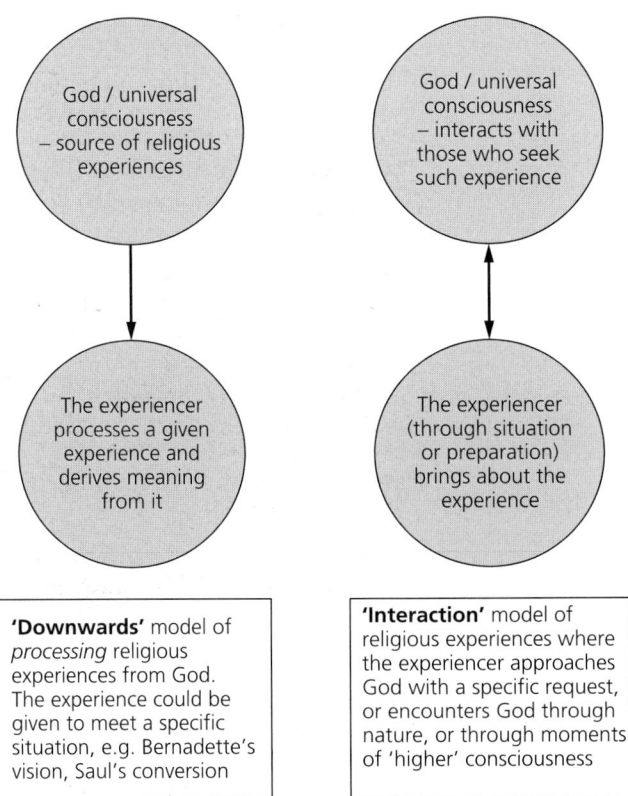

| 'Downwards' model of *processing* religious experiences from God. The experience could be given to meet a specific situation, e.g. Bernadette's vision, Saul's conversion | 'Interaction' model of religious experiences where the experiencer approaches God with a specific request, or encounters God through nature, or through moments of 'higher' consciousness |

▲ The 'downwards' / processing model of religious experience and the 'interaction' model

In conclusion, the religious response to scientific challenges to religious experiences is that it is quite coherent for believers to argue that the mind can both receive experiences from God and initiate the experience by reaching out to God. This still gives us no real basis for deciding which view is correct: the scientific rejection of religious experiences on the grounds that they are simply states of the brain, or the religious counter-argument that religious experiences must be states of the brain, and that they that can be both given by God and asked of God.

## Swinburne's principles of Credulity and Testimony

▲ Richard Swinburne (b.1934): British philosopher, influential in his writings about the existence of God.

Swinburne has a distinctive take on the question of the verification of religious experiences. If you want to read what Swinburne says, look at a copy of his book on *The Existence of God* (Note 40). For Swinburne, though the existence of God cannot be proved by logical arguments (such as the Ontological Argument), nevertheless our experiences of the world suggest that God *probably* exists, and religious experiences are a part of this probability argument.

## The Principle of Credulity

Swinburne begins by talking about our ordinary sense experiences, and then moves from these to religious experiences, which is an interesting leap. Having an experience of seeing a chair or a table, or of listening to a lecture, is good evidence that I do experience seeing the table and the chair and listening to the lecture. From this, Swinburne concludes the following:

> 'I suggest that it is a principle of rationality that (in the absence of special considerations) if it seems ... to a subject that x is present, then probably x is present; what one seems to perceive is probably so.' (Note 41)

Further: 'How things seem to be is good grounds for a belief about how things are.' (Note 42)

Moreover: 'From this it would follow that, in the absence of special considerations, all religious experiences ought to be taken by their subjects as genuine, and hence as substantial grounds for belief in the existence of their apparent object – God, or Mary, or Ultimate Reality ...' (Note 43)

So, Swinburne makes a very simple claim through the Principle of Credulity – the way things seem to be is the way things really are. It is worth noting that he does add a proviso: 'in the absence of special considerations'. He goes on to discuss four of these special considerations, which could perhaps make you think that the way things seem to be might not be the way things really are:

1   The first consideration concerns the **reliability of the claim**. If someone describes to you a religious experience, and it turns out that he has been known to tell lies in the past, then you have good grounds for doubting what he says about his religious experience.

2   The second concerns the **truth of the claim**. For example, if somebody makes unlikely perceptual claims, such as being able to read text of the size you are reading now at a distance of 100 yards, then his claims about a religious experience are not likely to be true.

3   The third is the **difficulty of showing that God was present in the experience**. How can the experiencer do this?

4   The fourth is the possibility that **what is claimed can be accounted for in other ways**. To use an example from what we have said about scientific challenges to religious experiences, someone who claims to have had a religious experience may be suffering from TLE.

Swinburne rejects all four of these special considerations:

1   It cannot be shown that all such claims are unreliable. Just because someone has lied in the past, this does not mean that they are lying now about having a religious experience.

2   It cannot be shown that all such claims are untrue. Again, someone making one claim that is false does not mean that any other particular claim to a religious experience is likely to be untrue.

**3** God is presumably everywhere, so rather than the onus being on the experiencer to show that God was present, the onus is on the doubter to show that he was not.

**4** As the Creator, God underpins all processes, including those that go on in the brain, so if God causes an experience through the temporal lobes, that would be perfectly normal (as William James would argue).

## The Principle of Testimony

The Principle of Testimony is the counterpart to the Principle of Credulity. Swinburne argues that: '... (in the absence of special considerations) the experiences of others are (probably) as they report them'. (Note 44)

In other words, we should believe what people tell us, provided that there are no particular reasons not to. So if someone tells us they have had a religious experience, if they are normally reliable and honest in what they say, we should believe them. Again, it is the sceptic's job to show that religious experiences should be rejected rather than the believer's job to show that they are true.

Swinburne's conclusions:

**1** Someone who has had a religious experience of what seems to be God has, by the Principle of **Credulity**, good reason for believing that there is a God.

**2** The **testimony** of others who report similar experiences supports such a claim.

**3** Without religious experience, the probability of the existence of God is about 50/50. If we add the testimony of religious experience, it becomes greater than 50/50. God probably exists.

## Evaluating Swinburne's claims

There are a number of arguments that can be made against Swinburne's claims:

**1** Swinburne seems to be saying that since normal sense experiences are reliable, religious experiences are reliable evidence for the existence of God. That seems a very dubious claim. Can we really move from being convinced about the reliability of what people claim to touch, taste, hear, smell and see to the reliability of mystical and visionary claims about God?

**2** To explain that further, accounts of ordinary sense experiences are third-person public (meaning that somebody else can confirm your claims as to what you see and hear), whereas accounts of religious experiences are first-person private. How do you get 'inside' someone's head to confirm what they claim to see in a vision?

**3** Even if every single person who has had a religious experience *believed* completely that it was an experience of God, it would not prove that 'God' is the right explanation for such experiences.

You could also argue the following points in favour of Swinburne:

**1** In terms of the Principle of Credulity, Swinburne seems to be on stronger ground where he says that if someone really believes that he has had an experience of God, then this will make measurable differences to his lifestyle (Note 45). His approach to prayer, worship and self-sacrifice might change radically, as might his treatment of others. Since we do often see this change in lifestyle (for example, by those who have had a near-death experience) then this is strong evidence for the reliability of claims about religious experiences.

2 This conclusion is supported by the testimony of others who claim to have had similar experiences of God, and in whom we can see similar changes of lifestyle. (Note 46)

3 Swinburne uses the 'Cumulative Argument'. This suggests that if we consider all of the arguments for the existence of God (such as the Design Argument, the Cosmological Argument and the Ontological Argument), these arguments are stronger when taken together, so the argument that religious experiences show the existence of God strengthens those arguments and is strengthened by them.

## The influence of religious experiences

The influence of religious experiences has been incalculable:

1 **Religious experiences can be foundational**.

By this we mean that religious experiences have been the direct cause of the founding of several religions, so they are the basis for faith and for organised religion.

In Judaism, for example, Genesis 17 records a foundational religious experience given to Abraham in which God makes a covenant (an agreement) with Abraham and his descendants.

In Christianity, Saul the Pharisee has a foundational experience of God while travelling to Damascus to persecute the Christian community there. Saul is portrayed in the Book of Acts as implacably opposed to the Christian sect. He breathes 'murderous threats' against Jesus' disciples (Acts 9:1), and is instrumental in the imprisonment and execution of Christians. Yet Saul receives a foundational religious experience (Acts 9:1-22; also 22:4-16; 26:9-18) which transforms him into the Apostle Paul, who became the real architect of the Christian faith.

Saul did not change his name: 'Saul' is his Hebrew name, but as a Roman citizen he also had a Latin name, 'Paul'. Since he became the apostle to the Gentiles (people who are not Jewish), it was more appropriate to use his Latin name, since most Gentiles would be familiar with that name. In any event, the point is that Saul is portrayed as the very worst kind of material that God could have used for his purposes, yet his religious experience was so powerful that those purposes were still achieved.

2 **Religious experiences are inspirational.**

In particular, the religious experiences of some of the great martyrs and saints of the Church have inspired belief in others. Those who died for the faith convinced others that their faith was worth standing up for. The lives of the saints have inspired people throughout Christian history. Think, for example, of the effects of the visions of Joan of Arc on France during the fifteenth century and ever since.

3 **Religious experiences are at the heart of the experience of pilgrimage.**

To give just one example, think of the experiences of Bernadette Soubirous and the founding of the shrine and pilgrimage centre at

## Activity

Read the accounts of Saul's conversion. Bearing in mind that Saul suffered from a complaint which sounds like TLE, do you think, in Swinburne's terms, that we should accept his testimony as an account of a real experience of God?

Lourdes, where the annual number of pilgrims is around 5 million, many of whom hope for miraculous cures from various diseases and conditions.

4 **Religious experiences are life-changing.**

We have already referred to the effects of religious experiences on individuals. Swinburne, for example, argues that such experiences can be life-changing. The 'fruits' of religious experience include: the development of feelings of sympathy, empathy, hope, courage, endurance, self-esteem and love.

We referred to William James's view that religious experiences bring about psychological benefits such as an energetic zest for life. People can feel a kind of 'lyrical enchantment' or can be inspired to do heroic deeds, as well as an assurance of safety, peace and loving affection.

The fruits of religious experience also include conversion, and you might consider the account of the conversion of C.S. Lewis, for example, in: https://www.ewtn.com/library/SPIRIT/cslewconv.htm

## The value of religious experiences for religious faith

This covers much the same territory that we have just looked at in connection with the influence of religious experiences: they can be foundational, inspirational and life-changing.

Perhaps the most distinctive thing to say here is that **religious experiences confirm faith**. If you read some of the various accounts we have mentioned in this chapter, this element is clear. We referred to Teresa of Ávila's confessor, who asked her how she knew that one particular experience had been of Christ, to which she replied that she did not know how she knew it, but she could not help knowing that Christ was close beside her.

You should now refer back to what we said in the chapters on the arguments for the existence of God about the nature of faith, and the difference between 'belief in' and 'belief that'. For some, the only certainty we can ever have is that which comes from faith, and that certainty is based on a religious experience where God is encountered personally.

This raises one obvious point, that whereas religious experiences will confirm Christianity to the Christian experiencer (or at least to someone who has a Christian cultural background), the same is true for the experiences of those who belong to other religious traditions. This is a problem for those who believe that only their religion holds 'the truth'. For the likes of William James, 'the truth' of religious experiences is much wider than the concerns of any one religion. What you make of this issue is for you to decide.

> **Discussion point**
>
> In what ways does religious experience contribute to the debate about belief 'in' and belief 'that'?
>
> **Action point** When you come to study the section on *Sources of Wisdom and Authority*, in the sections on religion, note that religious experience is: (a) a source of wisdom and authority in religion, and (b) a source of scripture itself. Make a note to explore this link at the point when you arrive at *Sources of Wisdom and Authority*.

## Concluding comments

The simple truth is that religious experiences can bring religious certainty to those who have them, yet 'the truth' is unknowable outside the realms of faith. If that were not the case, then there would be no doubts about what religious experiences are evidence for, whereas of course there are doubts.

You might like to consider the following rationale of religious experiences. Clearly, our experience of the world relies on our own subjective conscious awareness. Although you experience the world through your physical senses, all sense experience is processed and interpreted by your brain, and that is the only way in which any individual can 'see' the world. If you look at the sky and you say that you 'see the Sun', you do not – you experience a photon stream from the Sun, and your visual apparatus converts that stream into images. Light from the Sun takes around 8 minutes and 20 seconds to reach the Earth, so you are seeing the Sun as it was 8 minutes and 20 seconds in the past. With distant galaxies, the light that you see reveals the universe as it was billions of years in the past, and the stars in those galaxies may in the meantime have ceased to shine. Nevertheless, to *your conscious experience*, what you see is 'the truth'.

The point to think about is that consciousness is crucial to the universe, since without it, nothing is experienced. That is why many people see consciousness as the most fundamental thing about existence. In some interpretations of quantum mechanics (the science of the interactions between sub-atomic particles), consciousness conditions the reality that we experience. Whether or not that is true, physical 'reality' seems to have many layers below the everyday objects that we experience in the world. As we go down into the atom, we uncover the world of 'point particles' such as electrons and quarks. We now have a theoretical framework in which the point particles are replaced by one-dimensional vibrating strings, and there is no guarantee that this is the 'bottom' layer. It does not seem unlikely, therefore, that consciousness also operates on different levels. This seems to be a common assumption in mystical religious experiences in all religions, where religious experiences are seen as a means of accessing higher, and more fundamental, levels of consciousness. This idea is at the heart of William James's understanding of religious experiences. If physical reality is layered, then mental reality is layered too.

The best graphical representation of this idea is a 1955 lithograph by the Dutch artist M.C. Escher, entitled *Three Worlds*.

▲ M.C. Escher (1898–1972): *Three Worlds*

As you can see, this lithograph depicts a lake with three perspectives:

● the surface on which the leaves are floating
● the world above the surface, which can be seen by the reflections of trees in the water
● the world below the surface, shown by the fish swimming just below the surface.

The experiences of the fish are confined to its watery environment, although it can gain an impression of the world above that environment when it surfaces to feed on insects. So perhaps our religious experiences are also glimpses of a higher reality. No analogy is perfect, but you can doubtless see several different ways in which this picture can illustrate the idea that religious experiences are altered states of consciousness that are experienced in another dimension.

It is also worth bearing in mind William James's point that religious experiences do not have to be the ultimate mystical or numinous experiences described by Walter Stace and Rudolf Otto. A religious experience can be a simple uplifting of mood, a temporary feeling of elation, or a glimpse of something different. Nor do they need to be confined to the experiences of humans. It is rapidly becoming apparent that consciousness is shared by most if not all living things, so perhaps that consideration should lead us to become far more aware of the fact that human life is not the be-all and end-all of existence, and that human consciousness is not the sole possessor of what we call religious experiences.

## Technical terms for religious experience

**clairvoyance**  The claimed ability to gain information about objects / persons (etc.) by means beyond the normal methods of perception.

**corporeal vision**  Relating to a person's body. A corporeal vision is one that comes through the physical sense of sight.

**empirical**  Empirical religious experiences are those which are experienced by the senses of touch, taste, hearing, smell and sight, e.g. a corporeal vision.

**entheogen**  'Generating the Divine from within' – for example entheogenic drugs such as LSD, mescaline and psilocybin that are known to generate religious experiences.

**extrovertive**  In Walter Stace's definition, a kind of 'half-way house' to introvertive religious experience. Unlike the introvertive experience, in the extrovertive type, sense experience is still active although objects are transformed by the 'unity that shines through'.

**hallucinogenic**  Causing hallucinations, e.g. hallucinogenic drugs.

**illumination**  To illuminate is to cast light. In religious terms the doctrine of illumination holds (for example) that when the biblical writers wrote their books, the Holy Spirit illuminated their minds with the truth. In intellectual visions, the vision illuminates the soul without any kind of visual image.

**imaginative vision**  A vision seen in the mind, usually through a dream experience.

**Immaculate Conception**  The Catholic doctrine of the conception of the Virgin Mary in the womb of her mother (Saint Anne), free from 'original sin' through the merits of her son Jesus Christ. The term is also used as a way of referring to Mary.

**ineffable**  For William James – an aspect of mystical religious experiences not describable in words, so cannot be imparted to others.

**intellectual vision**  A vision without any visual image, where the experience is an 'illumination' of the soul.

**introvertive**  In Walter Stace's definition, a religious experience in which sense experience is totally suppressed and the conscious 'I' is replaced by pure consciousness / the One / the Void.

***mysterium tremendum et fascinans***  'A tremendous and fascinating mystery' – part of Otto's description of numinous religious experiences.

**neuroscience**  The scientific study of the structure and function of the nervous system.

**neurotheology**  The attempt to explain religious experience and behaviour in neuroscientific terms.

**noetic**  For William James – an aspect of mystical religious experience – that such experiences are states of knowledge as well as feelings, but the knowledge is spiritual and non-transferable as well as authoritative.

**non-intellectual**  The 'I' of the rational intellect is replaced by 'pure consciousness'.

**non-sensuous**  Not involving the physical senses.

**numinous**  Relating to the power or presence of a deity.

**original sin**  Refers to the first (original) sin of Adam and Eve in disobeying God in the Garden of Eden. St Augustine taught that original sin is inherited seminally (through sexual intercourse) by all their descendants.

**passivity**  For William James – an aspect of mystical religious experiences, that the experiencer does not control the experience but is controlled by it.

**precognition** Foreknowledge of an event through extra-sensory perception.

*sui generis* Unique / of its own kind / in a class of its own – applies to numinous feeling.

**supernatural** Beyond the normal forces of nature.

**telekinesis** The ability to move objects solely by the power of the mind.

**transcendent** The concept that God is above and beyond the space–time universe; for Otto, part of his view that God is 'wholly other'.

**transiency** For William James – an aspect of mystical religious experiences – that they generally last no more than half an hour, perhaps two hours at the most, although the effects are long-lasting, especially with recurrent experiences.

# Summary of this section on religious experience

## Visions

Visions are usually described using three categories:

- **Corporeal visions** are empirical, involving sense experience, particularly vision and hearing. The eye sees a supernatural vision that is really present, and the experiencer can interact with what is seen and heard, for example the vision of Bernadette Soubirous of the 'Immaculate Conception' at Lourdes, and the visions of Joan of Arc during the Hundred Years War.

- **Imaginative visions** are seen by the eye of the mind rather than by direct sight, usually in dreams, and are beyond the control of the experiencer. Pharaoh's dream in Genesis 41 and the dream of Joseph in Matthew 2 are both cases where the effects of the vision are dramatic.

- **Intellectual visions** have no image, yet what is experienced is 'seen as it really is', for example Teresa of Ávila, who claimed to see Jesus as he really was – not as an image but as a presence. The 'light' of an intellectual vision is through the illumination of the soul.

## Otto and the idea of the Holy

- Religious experiences are encounters with the Holy, as in the call experiences of Moses and Isaiah.

- Encounters with the Holy are numinous, which Otto claims is common to all religious experiences, regardless of religion or culture.

- The numinous is God or the wholly other, and God is inherently different from anything and everything else. God is beyond the natural world, and beyond apprehension or comprehension.

- Numinous feelings are not just more intense versions of our normal feelings. They are *sui generis* – unique or in a class of their own. They are a special faculty in our minds – a faculty that recognises the Holy and responds to it.

- Numinous feelings are non-rational – they are a *mysterium tremendum et fascinans* – a tremendous and fascinating mystery. Before this mystery, we as finite creatures feel our 'nothingness' when faced with the utter transcendence of God.

- The 'tremendous' power can chill and numb. It inspires feelings of awe, majesty and dread, fear and terror, stupor, blank wonder, dumb astonishment, inadequacy, humility and creatureliness. The 'mystery' is 'fascinating', and the experiencer is caught up in it, so that it can evoke rapture and love.

## William James: mystical experiences

For William James, the object of mystical experiences is union with God. Therefore James's account of mystical experiences is radically different from that of Rudolf Otto. For James, religious experiences are primary, and organised religion is secondary. God exists factually, but is probably finite, and may even exist as a collection of god-like selves.

Experience teaches us:

1 that this world draws its chief significance from a more spiritual universe (the realm of God)

2 the true end of humanity is union with that higher realm

3 prayer / spiritual communion with that higher realm has positive effects in this world, such as an energetic zest for life and an assurance of safety, peace and loving affection.

This kind of personal religious experience has its root and centre in mystical states of consciousness. There are four criteria that form a common core to mystical experiences: they are ineffable, noetic, transient and passive. Moreover they range from experiences with little religious significance (such as the effects of music or poetry or the experience of *déjà vu*), to cosmic consciousness and union with the divine. The point of mystical religious experiences is that God / the divine meets each individual on the basis of their personal concerns, be they 'sick souls' or 'healthy-minded'. God's existence is the guarantee that there is an ideal order that will be permanently preserved.

### Walter Stace: non-sensuous and non-intellectual union with the divine

Stace defines mysticism as non-sensuous and non-intellectual union with the divine: non-sensuous because the senses no longer work at this level, and non-intellectual because the normal conscious 'I' of the intellect is replaced by 'pure consciousness'. A mystic is someone who has had a religious experience (as opposed to talking about it or being sympathetic towards it). Mysticism has nothing to do with the occult, and visions and voices are not mystical experiences.

There are two types of mystical experience: extrovertive and introvertive. Extrovertive experiences are a kind of 'half-way house' to introvertive experiences, since in the extrovertive type sense experience is still active and sees the non-sensuous unity that shines through normal objects (all things are one). In the more important introvertive experience, sense experience is totally suppressed, and the conscious 'I' ceases to exist, replaced by Unitary Consciousness / the One / the Void / pure consciousness.

# Challenges to religious experience

Religious experiences are difficult to prove true. For example:

- they are mainly experienced by the unsupported evidence of individuals
- they are subjective and private
- they are ineffable, so *cannot* be understood
- they can be accounted for by natural explanations
- some are contradictory
- all normal experiences count against them

It is not difficult to defend religious beliefs against these challenges.

### The challenges to religious experiences from science

- Freud's argument from wish-fulfilment.

Scientific challenges include the fact that the following conditions or actions can produce religious visions or feelings:

- temporal lobe epilepsy (TLE)
- artificial stimulation of the temporal lobes through the 'God Helmet'
- entheogens (drugs) such as LSD and psilocybin

The scientific conclusion is that religious experiences are generated by the brain, and not by God.

**Religious responses** include:

- religious experiences can *only* be experienced by brain states: how else would God convey them

to the experiencer? The brain of the experiencer simply *processes* what comes from God.

- not only that, there is no reason why the mind should not reach out to God and *generate* religious experiences. According to William James, it makes no difference how religious experiences are generated – experiences of God can come from altered states of consciousness brought about by TLE, by artificial stimulation of the temporal lobes, or by entheogens.

### Swinburne's Principles of Credulity and Testimony

Two principles make part of Swinburne's argument that the existence of God is probable; religious experiences make the existence of God even more probable.

**The Principle of Credulity** is that 'If it seems to a subject that x is present, then (in the absence of special considerations) probably x is present'. How things seem to be is good grounds for a belief about how things are. It cannot be shown that all claims about religious experiences are unreliable, or that they are untrue, or that God was not present, or that religious experiences can more reliably be explained in other ways, so religious experiences are probably true.

**The Principle of Testimony** is that 'In the absence of special considerations, the experiences of others are probably as they report them'. If reliable witnesses report religious experiences, we should therefore believe them. It is the sceptic's job to show that religious experiences are false rather than the believer's job to show that they are true.

**Arguments against Swinburne:**

- It is hard to see how we can go from people's claims about the reliability of their sense experiences to the claim that mystical and visionary religious experiences are also reliable.

- Moreover, unlike sense experiences, religious experiences are first-person private, so we cannot see people's thoughts to confirm them.

- Even if everybody who has had a religious experience believes that they are experiences of God, this would not prove that God really is involved.

**Arguments for Swinburne:**

- Where those who have had religious experiences show a measurable difference in lifestyle, this is good evidence that the underlying experiences are true.

- Moreover, this conclusion is supported by the testimony of others who have had similar experiences and who also make lifestyle changes.

- The cumulative argument supports the argument from religious experience.

**The influence of religious experiences and their value for religious faith**

The influence of religious experiences includes:

- the fact that religious experiences can be foundational, as with St Paul

- they are inspirational, as with Joan of Arc

- they are at the heart of the pilgrimage tradition, as with Bernadette Soubirous

- they are life-changing, as with C.S. Lewis.

These influences obviously have value for religious faith, as most importantly, religious experiences confirm faith. There is good reason to suppose that higher levels of consciousness do exist, and that religious experiences are what we experience when these higher levels are reached, whether we interpret them as God, as Unitary Consciousness, or as Ultimate Reality. Because of this, they can confirm faith of all types.

For some, the only certainty we can ever have comes through faith; through a religious experience in which God is encountered personally.

# Normative ethical theories

## Introduction

This chapter will introduce different approaches to ethical decision-making:

- Deontological
- Teleological
- Character-based

Section B of the specification is concerned in its entirety with three normative ethical theories:

- Natural moral law and the principle of double effect, with reference to Aquinas; proportionalism.
- Situation ethics, with reference to Fletcher.
- Virtue ethics, with reference to Aristotle.

We shall start, therefore, with a brief overview of some of the terminology.

## Normative ethical theories

The word 'normative' is an adjective which comes from the word 'norm', which means a 'standard', or a 'rule', so moral norms are standards or principles with which people are expected to comply.

Obviously, people have different ideas about what these standards are, so the various normative theories of ethics therefore focus on what they claim makes an action a moral action: on what things are good or bad, and what kind of behaviour is right as opposed to wrong.

The three normative theories you are studying therefore illustrate three different sets of ideas about how we should live.

**Deontology**, teleology and character-based ethics are not in themselves ethical theories – they are types of ethical theory.

Natural moral law is seen by most people as one type of deontological theory.

Fletcher's situation ethics is seen as a teleological.

Aristotle's virtue ethics is a type of teleological theory and is also character-based. The different types of ethical theory are not exclusive, however, so we also find teleological ideas in virtue ethics, situation ethics, and natural moral law.

To unpack these words further:

> **Key term**
>
> **deontology** The approach to ethics in which the rightness or wrongness of an act is judged by its conformity to duties, rules and obligations.

## Deontological

The word 'deontological' comes from the Greek *deon*, meaning 'obligation', 'necessity', 'that which is binding'. Generally speaking, those words translate as 'duty', so deontological theories tell you what your moral duties are. As you might guess, once people start telling you what duties you have, those duties form the basis of moral 'rules'. Deontological systems hold that the moral worth of an action lies in your conforming to duties and rules, as opposed to considering the consequences of what you do. Alongside obligations, duties and rules, deontological theories also consider 'rights', because your obligation to follow rules and duties implies that there is an intrinsic (built-in) value of doing so. If you follow the rule, 'Do not murder', then you implicitly have the right not to be murdered.

Deontologists therefore live in a world of moral rules. Apart from, 'Do not murder', some of the obvious ones are:

'Do not steal'

'Do not lie'

'Do not break your promises'

Such rules can also be expressed by using the moral word, 'ought': these actions ought or ought not to be performed.

Since deontologists hold that acts are intrinsically right or wrong (meaning that they are good for their own sake), then their rightness or wrongness is in some sense built into the world and can be discovered by reason, or by studying the world, or (for religious deontology) by knowing the will of God. This intrinsic goodness is why deontologists emphasise the importance of 'motive' and 'intention'.

You can probably see that deontological ethics can lead people to act in ways which bring about bad consequences. For example, if you have a duty not to lie, but following that duty means that somebody dies in consequence, the value of the rule, 'do not lie', can be questioned.

## Teleological

'Teleological' derives from the Greek word *telos*, meaning 'end', 'goal', or 'purpose'. You have already come across this word in connection with the Design Argument for the existence of God, which is also known as the Teleological Argument, because it claims that God's *purposes* are visible in what we can observe about the universe.

In ethics, the *end, goal* or *purpose* which we seek refers to our responsibilities in bringing about specific consequences. For teleological ethical theories, therefore, if you want to find out how you should behave morally, you need to decide what the ultimate goal of ethics is.

Most importantly, teleological ethical theories are *consequentialist*, they look to achieve the best consequence in any particular situation. This will follow the simple reason that to achieve the best consequence in any particular situation will generally contribute to the overall goal.

An example of a teleological ethical theory that you have to study is Fletcher's Situation Ethics. According to Situation Ethics, the purpose of morally good behaviour is to maximise love, so an ethical action is judged by its end result – its consequences.

## Character-based

You will have noticed that deontological and teleological theories are act-centred – we judge that specific acts are good or bad, right or wrong. By contrast, character-based ethics is agent-centred, meaning that goodness is not in the act but *in the person*: we judge whether the agent is by habit and by character a good or virtuous person.

The main example of a character-based theory is Aristotle's Virtue Ethics. Aristotle held that a good person is one who has ideal character-traits. A virtuous person is kind to others, not by obeying rules or by working out the best consequences of an action, but by developing and nurturing kindness over a lifetime.

## Summary of normative ethical theories

Based on what we have said:

- Deontological theories are based on laws / rules; duties / rights. The rules must be obeyed without reference to the consequences, so what is good / right is following moral rules.

- Teleological theories hold that there is a goal or purpose to our moral behaviour: they seek to bring about the best consequences of our actions.

- Character-based ethical theories are based on persons rather than on actions. They emphasise moral character / the virtues rather than rules and duties or the consequences of our actions.

# Normative ethical theories

## Natural moral law

This chapter will cover:
- Natural moral law and the principle of double effect, with reference to Aquinas; proportionalism
- Strengths and weaknesses of natural moral law ethics

## Natural moral law and the principle of double effect with reference to Aquinas; proportionalism

### Two preliminary comments

1 The AQA Specification refers to natural moral law, but many sources will call this theory natural law. The term 'natural moral law' will be used in questions set on this section and throughout the chapter / book.

2 Natural moral law is often described as being deontological, but that would not have been particularly appropriate for Aquinas, since the use of 'deontological' dates from the twentieth century and Aquinas does pay attention to situations. Moreover, natural moral law can operate equally well in a non-religious context, so it is difficult to attach labels to natural moral law in general.

### The origins of natural moral law

The idea of natural moral law does not originate with Christianity. Natural moral law holds that there are **rights** and moral values that can be understood from human nature, and which can be deduced by human reason. Different accounts of this idea appear throughout history. For example:

In the fourth century BCE, Aristotle developed his ethical theory based on **virtue**, which we consider later. Part of that approach also gives a justification for the idea of natural moral law. In brief, Aristotle argued that the distinctive feature of human beings is their ability to reason. Humans can use their reason to discover the end or purpose of human life. Aristotle's approach here is therefore teleological.

121

### Key terms

**rights** Natural moral law is held by many to give all humans certain entitlements (for example, liberty and the pursuit of happiness) which result from their common human nature.

**virtue** A quality / trait / disposition in a person held to be of moral value.

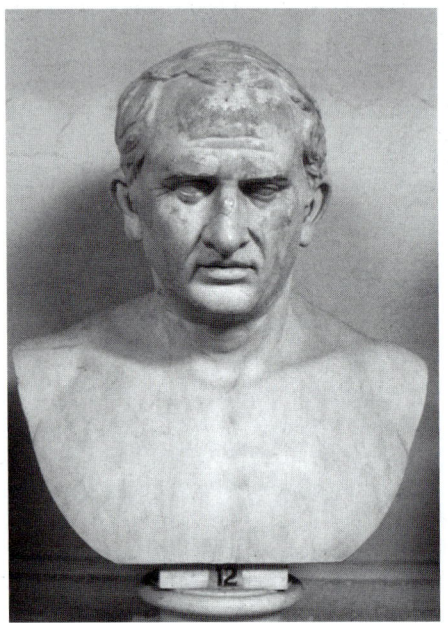

▲ The Roman philosopher and politician Cicero

This is what the Roman philosopher and politician Cicero (106–43BCE) has to say:

> True law is correct reason congruent with nature, spread among all persons, constant, everlasting. It calls to duty by ordering; it deters from mischief by forbidding. Nevertheless it does not order or forbid upright persons in vain, nor does it move the wicked by ordering or forbidding. It is not holy to circumvent this law, nor is it permitted to modify any part of it, nor can it be entirely repealed. In fact we cannot be released from this law by either the senate or the people … There will not be one law at Rome, another at Athens, one now, another later, but one law both everlasting and unchangeable will encompass all nations and for all time. (Note 1)

The most distinctive version of natural moral law is that of Thomas Aquinas. During the thirteenth century CE, Aquinas took up Aristotle's ideas about the end or goal of human life being happiness or complete well-being, and married them to a Christian view of that goal as being union with God in the next life. It is Aquinas' understanding of natural moral law that you need to understand for the AQA Specification.

## Key features of Aquinas' natural moral law

### 1 The four-fold division of law

Aquinas describes law using the following terms:

**Eternal law** This refers to law which comes from God's nature as the Creator. As God is the Creator of everything that is, the universe and nature inevitably reflect the principles of the natural and moral order which existed before creation, as a 'blueprint' in the mind of God.

Humans must, therefore, live a life based on that order, which is objective and absolute and applies to all, because God's blueprint for humans means that we all share a 'common human nature'. What is right for one person must be right for everyone else, with no exceptions.

**Divine law** These principles of natural and moral order are revealed to humans through the divine law, which can be found: **1** in special revelation, for example, the Bible, and **2** through the teachings of the Church.

**Natural moral law** The natural moral order is discovered through human reason and not through revelation. Although the divine law (for example, the Ten Commandments) forbids murder, theft and adultery, that is only by way of a reminder from God, since we can know simply through reason that these things are wrong.

So, Aquinas sees natural moral law as that part of God's eternal law that human beings can discover simply through the application of reason.

**Human law** Through understanding natural moral law, we can then formulate human laws, for example, those which appear in our legal systems. Human law should not contradict natural moral law.

### 2 The main guiding principle is that 'good is to be done and pursued and evil is to be avoided'

> … The first principle of practical reason is one founded on the notion of good, viz. that 'good is that which all things seek after.' Hence this is the first precept of law, that 'good is to be done and pursued, and evil is to be avoided.' All other precepts of the natural moral law are based upon this: so that whatever the practical reason naturally apprehends as man's good (or evil) belongs to the precepts of the natural moral law as something to be done or avoided.
>
> ▲ *Summa Theologica* (1265–1274), I–II, Qu. 94, Art. 2 (Note 2)

All other precepts of natural moral law are based on the guiding principle in this text.

### 3 This main guiding principle brings us to the *primary precepts* (principles)

This key paragraph follows on directly from the one just quoted:

> All those things to which man has a natural inclination, are naturally apprehended by reason as being good, and consequently as objects of pursuit, and their contraries as evil, and objects of avoidance.
>
> Wherefore according to the order of natural inclinations, is the order of the precepts of the natural law. Because in man there is **first of all** an inclination to good in accordance with the nature which he has in common with all substances: inasmuch as every substance seeks the preservation of its own being, according to its nature: and by reason of this inclination, whatever is a means of **preserving human life**, and of warding off its obstacles, belongs to the natural law.
>
> **Secondly**, there is in man an inclination to things that pertain to him more specially, according to that nature which he has in common with other animals: and in virtue of this inclination, those things are said to belong to the natural law, 'which nature has taught to all animals' … , such as **sexual intercourse**, **education of offspring and so forth.**
>
> **Thirdly**, there is in man an inclination to good, according to the nature of his reason, which nature is proper to him: thus man has a natural inclination to **know the truth about God**, and **to live in society**: and in this respect, whatever pertains to this inclination belongs to the natural law; for instance, to shun ignorance, to avoid offending those among whom one has to live, and other such things regarding the above inclination.
>
> ▲ (Note: The emphasis in the text is the author's own, not Aquinas'. Some words have been emboldened in order to make them clear to the eye.)

You can see from this extract from the *Summa Theologica* that Aquinas lists three primary precepts. Numbers 2 and 3 each have two separate ideas.

1 **What human reason has in common with all other substances**:

- the drive to preserve life / the drive to self-preservation.
  All things have a natural desire to carry on existing, including things like trees and rocks.

2 **What humans have in common with other animals:**

- the desire to reproduce / have children
- the drive to educate and care for their offspring / children.

3 **What humans have uniquely as rational beings**:

- to know the truth about God (so to know and worship God)
- to live in society (one that is ordered).

Listing these as five primary precepts was the work of later commentators on natural moral law (known as 'manualists') from the period when natural moral law was adopted in the Roman Catholic Church.

## Discussion point

- Spend 5–10 minutes considering how each of the five primary precepts contributes in various ways to human flourishing.

## Extension activity

- Are there any precepts that you would wish to add? You could compare your ideas here with those of Robert Finnis, a modern natural moral law philosopher, mentioned in point 6 of the strengths of natural moral law (page 137).

## Key term

**beatific vision** The ultimate, direct, self-communication of God to humanity.

## Key term

**teleological** In ethics, refers to views of ethics where the emphasis is on the goal or purpose that an ethical approach is intended to achieve. In natural moral law, the primary precepts are teleological, their aim being to being about complete well-being in this life and union with God in the next. In virtue theory, the goal is the development of character through habitual virtues.

They are often listed in abbreviated form, for example: preserve (innocent) life; reproduction; educate children; worship God; and ordered society. But it is better to remember them in the way Aquinas wrote them.

It seems clear that Aquinas himself was not giving a definitive list of primary precepts. You can see this in his wording, where he uses the phrase 'and so forth'. This is an important point, because it shows that Aquinas' understanding of natural moral law was not as definitive or set in stone as it is often made out to be. (Note 3) His understanding of natural moral law leaves some room for manoeuvre.

## 4 The primary precepts are not deontological rules about specific actions: they are **teleological** – concerned with our final end, which has three points of focus

a **Our *telos* (goal / purpose / end) on Earth is happiness: what Aquinas calls 'human flourishing'.**

The primary precepts are self-evident (obvious) principles understood by reason as being necessary for achieving happiness. It is self-evident, for example, that living in an ordered society provides a stable basis for the education of children, for preserving life, for developing relationships and for the procreation of children.

b **The *telos* of humanity as a whole also has an ultimate focus. Complete happiness cannot be found in something created, but only in the 'beatific vision' of God that is promised in the next life.**

This is how Aquinas puts it in *Summa Theologica* I–II, Qu. 2, Art. 8:

> It is impossible for any created good to constitute man's happiness. For happiness is the perfect good, which lulls the appetite altogether; else it would not be the last end, if something yet remained to be desired. Now the object of the will … is the universal good … Hence it is evident that naught can lull man's will, save the universal good. This is to be found, not in any creature, but in God alone; because every creature has goodness by participation. Wherefore God alone can satisfy the will of man, according to the words of Ps. 102:5: 'Who satisfieth thy desire with good things.' Therefore God alone constitutes man's happiness.

Father Servais Pinckaers summarises this nicely:

> Full happiness does not reside in wealth or glory or honors, or in knowledge of virtue, or in any created reality, but in the loving vision of God. (Note 4)

c **The *telos* for humans after death has an individual as well as a collective focus.**

The *telos* for humanity as a whole is the vision of God – union with God; but Aquinas also thought that each person has an individual *telos* based on their natural abilities (or lack of them).

## 5 From the primary precepts we derive secondary precepts

Secondary precepts are rules that derive from the primary precepts and govern how we should act in specific situations.

To understand them, remember the **teleological** focus of Aquinas' primary precepts that we have just been looking at, which Aquinas copied from Aristotle's doctrine of the Four Causes. This doctrine is Aristotle's explanation of why anything bothers to *do* anything and why things are as they are. Two of these four causes are especially important here, namely the efficient cause and the final cause. The efficient cause is what gets things done and the final cause is the goal or purpose towards which the thing is directed. Here are some examples:

 The efficient cause of a plant is the seed from which it came.

Its final cause, for which it was designed, is to become a mature plant which contains the ability to reproduce itself and repeat the cycle.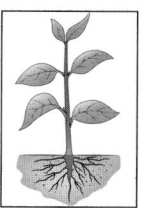

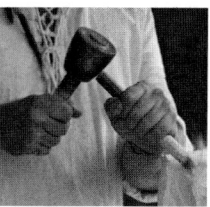 The efficient cause of a sculpture is the sculptor and his tools.

Its final cause is the reason why the sculptor designed it, which is the product, the finished sculpture, which becomes an object of aesthetic appreciation.

- Where Aristotle / Aquinas talk about the final 'cause', bear in mind that we would use the word 'end', 'purpose' or 'goal' rather than 'cause'.
- Whereas efficient causes tell us about facts / descriptions, final causes are about intentions, for example, God intended the 'facts' of sexuality (such as biology, chemistry and psychology) to bring about reproduction.
- It follows from this that whatever promotes the final cause is right and whatever goes against it is wrong. Therefore, if the final cause of sex is reproduction, any act of sex that does not lead directly to the possibility of procreation is wrong: any such act violates the nature and purpose of sexual intercourse. We can see this in the following illustration:

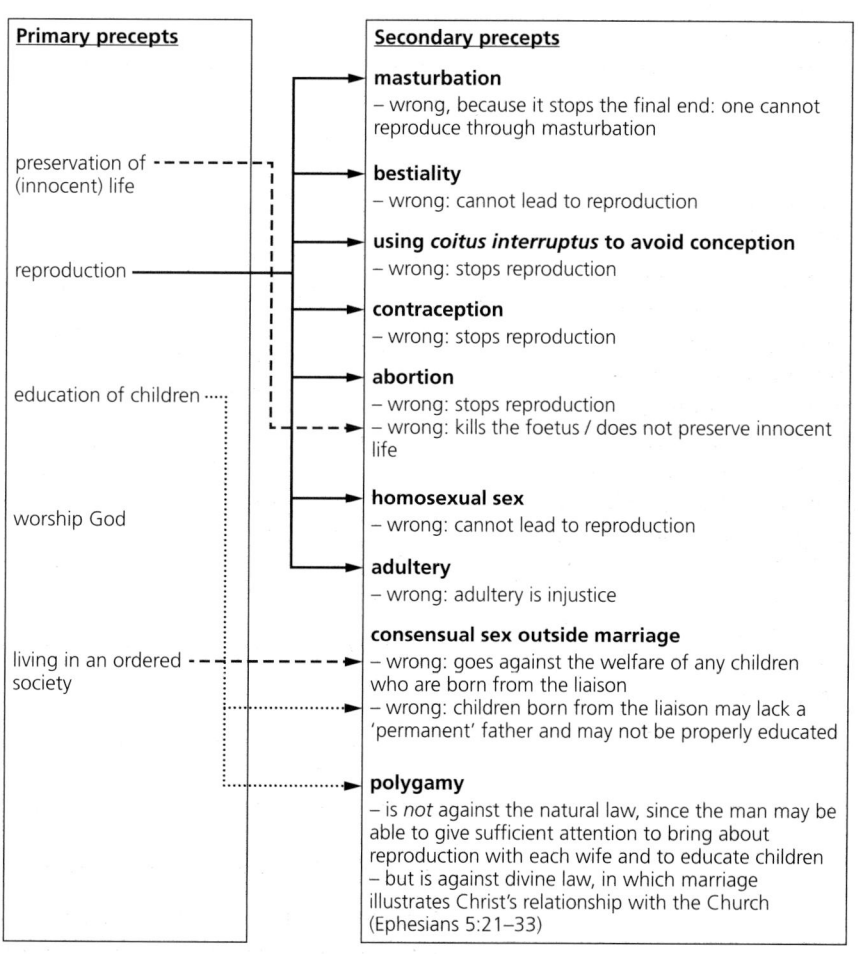

▲ Illustration of secondary precepts concerning sexual behaviour

125

- Note that the secondary precepts shown here are not all based on the primary precept of reproduction. Abortion is ruled out in addition because it does not preserve innocent life and consensual sex is ruled out because it can lead to children not being educated; moreover an ordered society would not benefit from the general lack of welfare given to children born through consensual sex between people who are not married to each other.

## Activity

Aquinas goes into some detail concerning the morality of sex and reproduction, and if you think about it, this emphasis is justified from the number of sexual crimes / offences committed in the UK and worldwide. If you add some of the issues not shown in the table, such as prostitution (including child prostitution), pornography, rape, incest, sex-trafficking and the relation between sexual crimes and hard drugs, the abuse of sexuality remains an enormous moral problem.

Given that, do you think that the list of sexual acts prohibited by Aquinas' secondary precepts are all addressing important sexual issues?

## Activity

Draw a table on your computer or by hand. Put the primary precepts of: 'preservation of life', 'living in an ordered society', 'worshipping God', and 'education' on the left, and make a list of secondary precepts that can be derived from each one.

Do not forget that some of these can overlap. For example, 'Do not murder' as a secondary precept can be included under preserving life and living in an ordered society. **Tip**: do not write 'Do not murder' as 'Do not kill'. The Hebrew *lo tirṣaḥ* refers primarily to murder and most Christians (including Aquinas) accept, for example, killing in a Just War.

### Key term

**cultural relativism** The view that a person's moral beliefs should be judged in the context of their own culture.

- **The secondary precepts are sometimes seen as culturally relative (relative to their own culture).**

  For example, it is often claimed that natural moral law accepts polygamy because polygamy is natural in some countries. That is not the case, and it is certainly not the case with Aquinas, who simply states that on two counts polygamy is not against natural moral law because: **1** it permits the final end of reproduction, and that which permits the final end is good; and **2** it also allows for the educating of children. But on a third count, Aquinas says that polygamy is indeed 'against the law of nature' because it fails to reflect the monogamous nature of the marriage relationship between Christ and the Church.

- **Aquinas does allow some flexibility in the secondary precepts.**

  The 'law' in natural moral law for the Catholic Church has meant 'law' / 'rule', where for Aquinas it meant 'justice' / 'principle', and justice / principle are more flexible than law. For Aquinas, the closer we get to the actual circumstances of a situation, the more variation there will be in what is judged to be morally right in that situation. This is a characteristic which Aquinas adopts from Aristotle's virtue ethics. This is what Aquinas says:

> ... The natural law is altogether unchangeable in its first principles: but in its secondary principles, which, as we have said, are certain detailed proximate conclusions drawn from the first principles, the natural law is not changed ... But it may be changed in some particular cases of rare occurrence, through some special causes hindering the observance of such precepts ...
>
> ▲ *Summa Theologica*, I–II, Qu. 94, Art. 5

Aquinas reaches this conclusion by using the example that sometimes it may not be appropriate to repay a debt:

> Thus it is right and true for all to act according to reason: and from this principle it follows ... that goods entrusted to another should be restored to their owner. Now this is true for the majority of cases: but it may happen in a particular case that it would be injurious, and therefore unreasonable, to restore goods held in trust; for instance, if they are claimed for the purpose of fighting against one's country. And this principle will be found to fail the more, according as we descend further into detail, e.g. if one were to say that goods held in trust should be restored with such and such a guarantee, or in such and such a way; because the greater the number of conditions added, the greater the number of ways in which the principle may fail, so that it be not right to restore or not to restore.
>
> ▲ *Summa Theologica*, I–II, Qu. 94, Art. 4

Aquinas believed that the primary principles of natural moral law are absolute, but as we descend into the detail, the more variation there will be in determining what the moral law requires us to do.

### 6 Given this complexity and detail, how do we avoid making mistakes?

● **For a start, we should avoid becoming confused about the difference between real and apparent goods.**

Aquinas thinks that sin can arise in various parts of our make-up. For example, we can sin by taking delight in thinking about fornication (sexual sins again), and through wrong reason. Reason can be used in different ways. For example, in planning a burglary – but that is not the right use of reason. According to Aquinas, all humans will the good (i.e. they actively desire to bring about good in the world), but we can become confused about the difference between real and apparent goods. For example, adultery can feel like a real good because of its short-term pleasures, but when we consider what adultery involves – betrayal, injustice, lies, putting children at risk – it is clearly not good at all.

● **We should also be aware of the difference between interior and exterior acts.**

For example, the act of giving money to charity is a good exterior act, but can be properly good only if it is accompanied by the right (interior) intention. Someone who gives money to charity in order to be admired by others gets no further than performing a good exterior act, and that is not true morality.

However:

● **The process of following the real good can be aided by following the virtues.**

Following the real good preserves and improves the self and brings us closer to the ideal human nature that exists in the mind of God. In this,

Aquinas argues that it is morally essential for us to cultivate the virtues, and here again he follows Aristotle. For Aristotle, to be a good person is to have a good character, and this is achieved by habit – by practising the virtues as a way of life.

From the virtues listed by Aristotle, Aquinas selected four as the 'cardinal' virtues (from Latin *cardo*, 'hinge'), which he accepted as the foundation of natural morality: **prudence, justice, fortitude (courage)** and **temperance (self-control)**, and these allow the self to fulfil its purpose. Chief among these virtues is prudence, which is practical wisdom – the ability to understand a situation and to use practical reason to work out what to do. Practical wisdom comes only through experience, so the virtuous life can be learned by observing people who habitually practise the virtues, because they will have practical wisdom.

Aquinas also lists three Christian theological virtues: **faith, hope** and **love**, and these derive from St Paul in the New Testament (1 Corinthians 13:13). Together, the Catechism of the Catholic Church lists the cardinal and theological virtues as the 'seven virtues':

> The theological virtues are the foundation of Christian moral activity; they animate it and give it its special character. They inform and give life to all the moral virtues. They are infused by God into the souls of the faithful to make them capable of acting as his children and of meriting eternal life. They are the pledge of the presence and action of the Holy Spirit in the faculties of the human being.
>
> ▲ *Catechism of the Catholic Church* (1992), III.I. Ch.1, Art. 7, 1 [Note 5]

Whereas the cardinal virtues are those that can be achieved by human ability, the theological virtues are given to humans through God's grace:

**Faith** refers to belief in God and belief in what is revealed through scripture and the Church.

**Hope** is the hope of heaven and the beatific vision.

**Love** is sometimes translated as 'charity', but the New Testament Greek is *agape*, which means 'Jesus' other-person-regarding love' (which is the basis of Fletcher's situation ethics, which we study later). It basically means love of God above all things, and love of one's neighbour (everybody) through love of God. Paul's letter to the Colossians (Colossians 3:14) gives a list of virtues, and then states that love:

> ' ... binds everything together in perfect harmony ... '

### 7 We can also avoid making mistakes in difficult moral situations by using the 'principle of double effect'

Double effect is a principle which helps to avoid mistakes in moral reasoning in difficult cases. Aquinas never calls the principle 'double effect', but we get a clear description of the doctrine in his *Summa Theologica*, II–II, Qu. 64, Art. 7, on:

> 'Whether it is lawful to kill a man in self-defense?'

This is what Aquinas says:

> **I answer that**, Nothing hinders one act from having two effects, only one of which is intended, while the other is beside the intention. Now moral acts take their species according to what is intended, and not according to what is beside the intention, since this is accidental ... Accordingly the act of self-defense may have two effects, one is the saving of one's life, the other is the slaying of the aggressor. Therefore this act, since one's intention is to save one's own life, is not unlawful, seeing that it is natural to everything to keep itself in 'being', as far as possible. And yet, though proceeding from a good intention, an act may be rendered unlawful, if it be out of proportion to the end. Wherefore if a man, in self-defense, uses more than necessary violence, it will be unlawful: whereas if he repel force with moderation his defense will be lawful, because according to the jurists ... ' it is lawful to repel force by force, provided one does not exceed the limits of a blameless defense'. [Note 6]

Aquinas argues that killing in self-defence is justified so long as the killing was not intended, but was the unavoidable result of the amount of force necessary to save your own life. Killing your assailant has two effects here: the good one of saving your own life; the bad one of killing your assailant. Moreover, your defence must be proportional – if you use unnecessary violence, it will not be proportional, so will be unlawful. Everybody will have seen a film, or else will have read a passage in a book, in which a murderous assailant is repelled by a violent push, after which the assailant falls on a sharp object or a stone floor and is killed. In such a case, where the intention of the push would be to ward off attack, then the killing of the assailant is lawful.

One of the clearest descriptions of the developed principle of double effect is given by Louis Pojman. [Note 7] Pojman suggests that Aquinas' position and the natural moral law tradition in general are absolutist:

> **'Humanity has an essentially rational nature, and reason can discover the right action in every situation by following an appropriate exceptionless principle.'** [Note 8]

Sometimes, however, we encounter moral dilemmas in which it is not possible to do good without also bringing about evil consequences. The doctrine of double effect was devised as 'a neat algorithm' for solving moral disputes in which an act literally has a 'double effect' – one good and the other bad.

> The doctrine says, roughly, that it is always wrong to do a bad act intentionally in order to bring about good consequences, but that it is sometimes permissible to do a good act despite knowing that it will bring about bad consequences. [Note 9]

In detail: with double effect, there are four conditions that must be satisfied before an act is morally permissible.

1 The **nature of the act** condition:

   The action must either be morally good or indifferent / neutral. Acts such as lying or intentionally killing an innocent person are never morally permissible.

2 The **means–end** condition:

The bad effect must not be the means by which the good effect is achieved.

3 The **right-intention** condition:

The intention must only be to achieve the good effect. The bad effect must be only an unintended side-effect. If the bad effect is a means of bringing about the good effect, then the act is immoral.
The bad effect may be foreseen, but it must not be intended.

4 The **proportionality** condition:

The good effect must at least be equivalent in importance to the bad effect.

You can see that in this doctrine, great emphasis is laid on the person's intentions. Here is an illustration from medical ethics:

---

**Situation 1:** The case of a terminally-ill patient whose death is brought about sooner through doctors administering increasing doses of morphine to control his pain.

There are certain diseases / conditions (some types of leukaemia, for example), in which it is necessary for doctors to use high doses of morphine in order to relieve pain. This will usually happen in the terminal stages of the disease. Morphine is used because of its effectiveness in pain relief by comparison with other treatments, but morphine can act as a respiratory depressant – it makes breathing more difficult. In response to such breathing difficulty, it usually becomes necessary to increase the dosage of morphine, and the doctors who prescribe the drug will be aware that however careful they are in controlling the dose, eventually the morphine can cause breathing failure. In short, the doctor will know that giving doses of morphine sufficient to control the pain can cause the patient to die sooner. (Note 10)

Is this action morally permissible under the doctrine of double effect? Check the answer against the four conditions:

1 The **nature of the act** condition. The act of administering morphine relieves pain, so is a good act which passes condition 1.

2 The **means–end** condition. The bad effect (the earlier death of the patient) is not the means by which the good effect (the relief of the patient's pain) is achieved, so condition 2 is also met. To get the force of this, compare it with a case in which the doctors administered a dose of morphine that they knew would kill the patient immediately.

3 The **right-intention** condition. The doctors' intention is only to relieve the sufferer's pain. The fact that the sufferer dies sooner is an unintended side-effect. Moreover, the bad effect is foreseen (the doctors know that the patient will probably die sooner) but not intended. The act therefore passes condition 3.

4 The **proportionality** condition is also passed, because the good effect – the relief of pain over a period of time – is at least equivalent in importance to the bad effect that the patient dies sooner.

**Conclusion:** The doctrine of double effect allows the actions of the doctor to be judged right in this situation, because the intention is to relieve pain and the hastening of death is considered an unintended but proportional consequence.

---

**Situation 2:** Terror Bombing and Tactical Bombing.

'The terror bomber aims to bring about civilian deaths in order to weaken the resolve of the enemy: when his bombs kill civilians this is a consequence that he intends. The tactical bomber aims at military targets while foreseeing that bombing such targets will cause civilian deaths. When his bombs kill civilians this is a foreseen but unintended consequence of his actions. Even if it is equally certain that the two bombers will cause the same number of civilian deaths, terror bombing is impermissible while tactical bombing is permissible.' (Note 11)

**Activity**

**Situation 3**: Torturing Sally in order to save one million people.

This example is taken from Pojman. (Note 12)

Sally's father has planted a nuclear bomb that will detonate in half an hour. Sally knows the location of the bomb, but has promised her father that she will not reveal the secret; but if the bomb is not found, its detonation will kill 1 million people. Is it permissible under double effect to torture just one person, Sally, in order to save 1 million people?

Work out the answer using the four conditions.

### How should we evaluate the doctrine of double effect?

The logic of double effect can become very convoluted. Here are four comments to think about:

1 Suicide is forbidden in natural moral law. Aquinas forbids it for a number of reasons, for example, that it goes against the inclination of living things to keep themselves in existence. Take the case, then, of a soldier who throws himself on a grenade and thus saves his comrades from harm. Double effect would require him not to intend to sacrifice his own life to save the lives of his comrades, because by intending his own death he is performing a bad act to bring about a good consequence (see condition 3). Instead he has merely to 'foresee' that his act will bring about his own death as an unintended consequence of his action (condition 3). Is this really how the soldier would think? It is more likely that he would consider his act a deliberate act of self-sacrifice for the comrades he loves, and most people would consider his act as heroic and loving, so there is something wrong with the logic of double effect.

2 Many would maintain that it does not matter what your intentions are, because a good act is one that has good consequences, whatever your intention, and a bad act is one that has bad consequences, whatever your intention.

3 In **Situation 3** – torturing Sally to discover the whereabouts of a nuclear bomb – the reasoning seems false. You will have seen that condition 2 is violated: torturing Sally would be using a bad act to bring about a good effect. However, any ruler who permitted the deaths of 1 million people by a refusal to torture Sally would probably be accused of culpable homicide on a grand scale. Consequentialist ethics would generally claim that any act should be judged by its results, so however horrible it would be to torture somebody, failure to do so would amount to the deliberate execution of 1 million people. The inaction would be massively disproportionate.

Some would counter-argue here and ask, 'At what point does torture become permissible? To save 1,000,000? 100? 10?' If no sensible answer can be given then torture should never be permissible.

4 Double effect seems sometimes to be counter-intuitive. For example, Aquinas held that it is not lawful to tell a lie in order to save someone from any danger whatever, but this goes against most people's intuition that in order to save someone from danger or death it is imperative to lie. Who in their right mind would let children be butchered to death if by telling a lie the butchery could be avoided? Aquinas did suggest that it

would be prudent sometimes to hold back the truth, but that looks rather like an admission that there is something wrong with the argument that one should never tell a lie.

What is your view of these claims?

## 8 Catholic natural moral law today in relation to Aquinas

Natural moral law today is still essentially **Thomist** (Aquinas' first name is Thomas, so 'Thomist' means 'coming from Aquinas'). However, whereas for Aquinas the virtues were at least as important as obligations and rules, the Catholic Church gives greater importance to moral rules.

Aquinas accepted that humans have moral obligations to obey rules, but to him such obligations were less important than the virtues that we have just been discussing. When natural moral law was adopted into the Catholic Church during the sixteenth century, however, the reverse happened: obligation and rules were given priority and:

'... invaded the entire domain of moral life ... ' [Note 13]

**Natural moral law became deontological through 'Manualism'**

In the seventeenth century, the preference for a morality of obligation and rules led scholars in the Catholic Church (especially the **Jesuits**) to write manuals of moral theology. These were designed for use in Catholic seminaries, to train the clergy in the application of moral law to specific cases. The manualists gave examples of specific cases which the clergy could refer to in order to decide what to do in similar situations. If you compare this with what judges do today, the manuals were books of case law, so another word for what the manualists were doing is '**casuistry**' (from Latin *casus*, 'case'). You can see, then, that the manualists were producing moral rule-books, so Catholic natural moral law became deontological.

As a matter of fact, the term 'casuistry' today can be used as a criticism of those who are too much concerned with rules and not enough with justice. This captures a key criticism of Catholic natural moral law today, that it is so concerned with rules that it forgets principles and virtues. When the manualists did their work, for example, one of the things they omitted from Aquinas' version of natural moral law was his account of the virtues. For those who write manuals, virtues are far harder to quantify than rules. In other words, Manualism amounted to a considerable narrowing of the scope of Aquinas' natural moral law:

'The moral theology of the manuals lost sight of essential questions: the treatise on happiness and the destiny of the human person ... Obedience to law encroached upon charity and the virtues; the theme of friendship was lost.' [Note 14]

## 9 Nevertheless, there are indications within the Catholic Church of a shift towards a more flexible interpretation of natural moral law

In recent decades there has been a renewal of interest in Aristotle's virtue ethics and this has reminded Catholicism of its roots in virtue theory. The Catechism of the Catholic Church, put forward in 1992 by Pope John Paul

### Key term

**Thomist** Refers to the first name of Thomas Aquinas, so a Thomist position is one that would have been proposed / held by Aquinas, for example, Thomist natural moral law or Thomist Cosmological Arguments.

### Key terms

**Manualism** In the Catholic Church, the tradition of producing manuals for use in Catholic seminaries, to train clergy in applying natural moral law to difficult cases.

**Jesuit** A member of the Society of Jesus: a Catholic priestly order founded by St Ignatius Loyola and others in 1534.

**casuistry** From Latin *casus*, 'case', so case law. The Catholic manuals are compilations of casuistry.

II as a summary of beliefs for the Catholic faithful, includes reference to the cardinal and theological virtues.

Another sign of a more flexible approach to natural moral law is the number of Catholic theologians who accept some form of proportionalism.

# Proportionalism

Proportionalism originated among Catholic scholars in Europe and America. In America, Richard A. McCormick is credited with reshaping Catholic moral thinking.

4.1 Normative ethical theories: Natural moral law

### Richard A. McCormick (1922–2000)

Jesuit priest and moral theologian; expert on Catholic medical ethics. Suggested that Catholic moral theology:

'... was all too often one-sidedly confession-oriented, **magisterium**-dominated, **canon law**-centred, and **seminary**-controlled.'

In 1965, he wrote that:

'... theologians have, without disowning casuistry, disowned an excessively casuistic approach to the moral life.' (Note 15)

The debate about proportionalism among scholars is complex, to say the least. For those who want to trace that debate, the proportionalist movement in relation to natural moral law began with a German scholar, Peter Knauer, whose work was reviewed by McCormick. Bernard Hoose provides a detailed survey in: *Proportionalism: The American Debate and its European Roots.* (Note 16) Amongst many who claim to be proportionalists (or at least they feel attracted to it), the following definition by Vardy and Grosch seems to encapsulate what they are saying:

> Proportionalism holds that there are certain moral rules and that it can never be right to go against these rules unless there is a proportionate reason which would justify it. The proportionate reason is based on the context or situation but this situation must be sufficiently unusual and of sufficient magnitude to provide a reason which would overturn what would otherwise be a firm rule. On this basis, moral laws derived from natural law or similar approaches can provide firm moral guidelines which should never be ignored unless it is absolutely clear that, in the particular situation, this is justified by a proportionate reason. (Note 17)

In other words, where proportionate reasons exist, it would be right to ignore the rule in that situation. This kind of approach is to some extent visible in Aquinas' writings. For example, Aquinas considered the question of whether it would be permissible for a starving man to steal in order to save his life, and considers that this would be lawful:

> If the need be so manifest and urgent, that it is evident that the present need must be remedied by whatever means be at hand (for instance, when a person is in some imminent danger, and there is no other possible remedy), then it is lawful for a man to succor his own need by means of another's property, by taking it either openly or secretly: nor is this properly speaking theft or robbery.
>
> ▲ *Summa Theologica*, II–II, Qu. 66, Art.7

Where a man is starving to death, then, it would be lawful to steal from another – presumably from someone who has more than enough.

However, when it comes to the issue of telling a lie to save someone from death, Aquinas argues that this is not lawful:

> A lie is sinful not only because it injures one's neighbor, but also on account of its inordinateness, as stated above in this Article. Now it is not allowed to make use of anything inordinate in order to ward off injury or defects from another … Therefore it is not lawful to tell a lie in order to deliver another from any danger whatever. Nevertheless it is lawful to hide the truth prudently, by keeping it back …
>
> ▲ *Summa Theologica*, II–II, Qu. 110, Art. 3

Against Aquinas, modern proportionalists would generally argue that if it is acceptable to steal in order to save yourself from starvation, then it makes little sense to prohibit lying in order to save someone's life. Commenting on this, Hoose suggests that:

**'What the proportionalists have done is point out the inconsistency and invalidity of such thinking.'** [Note 18]

Bearing in mind, then, that there are different shades of proportionalist thinking, the modern proportionalist account of natural moral law goes something like this:

1 In order to decide whether an act is moral or immoral, the intention of the moral **agent** has to be considered.

2 If you ignore the intention of the moral agent, then you can only determine what is called the '*ontic*', or 'pre-moral', or 'physical' goodness or badness of the act, and not its morality. Think of the distinction Aquinas makes between exterior and interior acts: only the good interior act is really good.

3 So acts become morally good or bad only when you consider both the proportion of value to disvalue in the act and the intention of the agent. If a surgeon cuts human flesh, for example, you do not immediately say, 'That cut is good', or 'That cut is bad'. It depends on the surgeon's intention in doing it, and the value – or disvalue – that the patient gets out of it.

4 So, there cannot be any acts that are intrinsically evil. The physical act of abortion, for example, is not intrinsically evil. We can only find out whether abortion is morally right or wrong by looking at the value / disvalue of the abortion and at the agent's intention in wanting to bring about an abortion in that situation.

> **Key term**
>
> **agent** The moral agent – the person involved in making an ethical decision.

134

**Example 1:** A woman has become pregnant within marriage. She wishes to terminate the pregnancy because she believes that having a child will interrupt her career pattern.

The **intention** of the agent (the mother; also the father if he agrees with her intention) would be the destruction of an innocent foetus, which goes against the principle of the **sanctity of life**.

The **value** of the abortion would be the uninterrupted progress of her career.

The **disvalue** would include acting against two of the primary precepts: the protection and preservation of life, and reproduction. It would also include acting in a way that could influence other parents in the same situation to make the same decision.

**Conclusion:** the disvalue of the abortion exceeds its value, and the intention of the agent is non-moral. To have an uninterrupted career pattern by means of an abortion is therefore not justifiable in proportionalist thinking.

**Example 2:** A woman has a pregnancy that endangers her life. She wishes to terminate the pregnancy because otherwise, two people will die – herself and the foetus.

The **intention** of the agent is to preserve her life.

The **value** of the abortion would be the preservation of her life. It would also include her continued existence to support the rest of her family. It is possible she might be able to conceive in the future without danger of death.

The **disvalue** would be the destruction of an innocent foetus.

**Conclusion:** the value of the abortion clearly exceeds its disvalue, and the agent's intention includes the moral one of self-preservation. To preserve her life by aborting the foetus is therefore justifiable.

## Activity

Notice that in **Example 2**, the principle of double effect would not permit an abortion.

Using the four conditions of double effect referred to in the section on double effect, explain why not.

Notice that in both examples, the physical act of abortion is 'pre-moral'. What makes abortion a moral or an immoral act in each case is the calculation of value against disvalue and the intention of the agent.

In addition to abortion, proportionalist theologians debate subjects such as contraception and masturbation. The value of using contraceptive devices in sub-Saharan Africa, where the HIV / AIDS epidemic has infected millions, can be held to outweigh the disvalue of going against the Church's teaching on the final end of reproduction, and the intention is to save lives. Similarly, the value of masturbation in a medical procedure such as IVF can be justified because in the case of IVF the intention behind masturbation is to lead to the final end of procreation / reproduction.

## Evaluating proportionalism

### Strengths

1 As a principle, proportionalism has been around for a long time, so is fairly robust. For example, it is a well-known part of 'Just War' theory, which was proposed by Augustine and developed further by Aquinas. The proportionality clause is that the violence used must be proportional to the casualties suffered. To drop a nuclear warhead on a village, for example, would be disproportionate.

2 The proportionalist approach seems to be based on common sense. For example, it seems to be common sense to lie in order to save a life and to steal to avoid dying of hunger.

3 The proportionalist principle is a wide one, and it is used outside natural moral law. As with Just War theory, allowing a proportional response to a threat is built into European Law.

## Key term

**Sanctity of Life Principle** Based on Genesis 1:26–27, that humans were created in the image of God / the gods, from which Christian theologians deduced that (human) life is sacred (dedicated to God). This principle is often used to argue that acts such as abortion and euthanasia are always morally wrong.

## Weaknesses

1 Proportionalism has been condemned by the Catholic Church. For example, by Pope John Paul II's encyclical, *Veritatis Splendor* (*The Splendour of Truth*), on the grounds that it denies that any action can in and of itself be intrinsically evil. Is the Pope right? Many people have the feeling that some acts are indeed intrinsically evil, such as the rape and torture of a child, and if they are right, then the possibility of **intrinsic good** and evil have to be taken seriously.

2 Where proportionalists calculate the proportion of value and disvalue in an act, this looks very much like a consequentialist way of deciding on moral issues. One of the biggest problems with **consequentialism** is that of how we can make accurate predictions about value and disvalue. This is the problem that utilitarians face when they try to calculate how much happiness or pleasure an act will bring. To do that, utilitarians have to be able to predict the future, so some guesswork is involved.

If proportionalism descends to moral guesswork: to a calculation of goods and evils, then the authority of natural moral law is lost. Catholics might just as well become religious utilitarians.

# Strengths and weaknesses of natural moral law ethics

## Strengths

1 In his series *Socratic Ideas*, John Waters puts forward a powerful argument in favour of natural moral law: that it offers a foundational, universal and absolute approach to ethics. (Note 19) Such an approach is for many people very important in the twenty-first-century 'post-modern' world which tends to reject all traditional institutions and authority. Natural moral law provides an objective foundation for ethics during an era where the individual is left to drown in a sea of limitless choice. It is no good telling people that they are morally free when so many people do not know what to do with that freedom. Most need the anchor of an unchanging moral code by which they know what they ought to do.

In summary, natural moral law enables people to establish common rules by which people can live in an ordered society. Natural moral law sets firm boundaries for moral behaviour.

2 Many people think that morality is not just a matter of people's preferences, or of the different customs practised by different societies at different times. Rather, morality is about what is intrinsically good or bad. It is true that different cultures can have different moral ideas: for example, slavery was commonly practised by the European empires and America, but the fact that slavery has been abolished by nearly all cultures shows that human morality has evolved towards a common understanding that there is something intrinsically wrong with slavery.

3 Aquinas' system is realistic in that it acknowledges that people can make mistakes, for example, by being confused about the difference between real and apparent goods.

4 Natural moral law has been a basis for developing our ideas about natural rights, not least in the American Declaration of Independence from Britain. (Note 20)

5 Aquinas' natural moral law is in line with Aristotelian virtue ethics, in that it focuses on the development of good moral character through practising the cardinal virtues of justice, prudence, temperance (self-control) and fortitude, along with the theological virtues of faith, hope and love.

6 Natural moral law is very adaptable. For example, in 1980, the Australian legal scholar and philosopher John Finnis published *Natural Law and Natural Rights*, a version of natural moral law that does not presuppose God's existence. Finnis proposed a list of seven primary / basic goods:

   i life (which includes goods such as health and procreation)
   ii knowledge
   iii play (done for pure enjoyment)
   iv aesthetic experience
   v sociability, including friendship
   vi practical reasonableness, which is the ability to reason correctly for yourself about how you should best act in a situation, both for your own benefit and that of others
   vii spirituality: acknowledging that one is part of a natural ordered system which is the object of our 'ultimate concern'.

This is a theory of both ethics and law, since these goods are all fundamental (like Aquinas' primary precepts), so Finnis argues that the function of the legal system should be to promote these goods for all citizens.

You are not required to know Finnis' natural moral law system. It is mentioned to show the adaptability of natural moral law, which is not so set in stone as is so often presupposed. Aquinas' concept of natural moral law is perhaps the most distinctive of all its adaptations, combining Christian ideas with those of Aristotle.

## Weaknesses

1 One of the greatest weaknesses of natural moral law is its teleological view that we all share a common human nature designed by God. This leads in particular to some very questionable claims about human sexual nature, particularly that God's plan requires human sexuality to be geared specifically to procreation. The list of secondary precepts which derive from this approach includes the condemnation of masturbation, same-sex relationships and artificial contraception. The prohibition of artificial means of contraception alone has arguably led to untold misery for millions. It has also led to the persecution of homosexuals and to the repression of natural sexual instincts.

Pojman comments that:

**'We may have many purposes, and our moral domain may include a certain relativity. For example, heterosexuality may serve one social purpose whereas homosexuality serves another, and both may be fulfilling for different types of individuals. Reason's task may not be to discover an essence of humanity or unchangeable laws, but, rather, simply to help us survive and fulfill [sic] our desires.'** (Note 21)

2 Although some forms of natural moral law can be atheistic, that of Aquinas cannot. Aquinas assumed that it was natural for all humans to worship God, but that is not a natural assumption for an atheist.

3 Even if there is a God, it is not obvious that natural moral law is the best way of looking at morality and the world. Fletcher's situation ethics makes that point very clearly, as you will see when we come to it. For Fletcher, moral systems such as natural moral law amount to legalistic nonsense and should be replaced by an ethic of Christian love.

4 It seems clear that natural moral law can lead to immoral outcomes. For example, despite the fact that the Catholic Church is easily the largest provider of care for HIV / AIDS patients, its prohibition of artificial methods of contraception has contributed to the spread of AIDS.

5 The fact that some Catholics in Europe and America are following a proportionalist approach to natural moral law shows that even some Catholics are dissatisfied with applying exceptionless, absolute rules to moral life. Double effect seems to throw out the 'baby' of common sense with the 'bathwater' of the rule, particularly with the way it approaches the problem of abortion.

## Technical terms for natural moral law

**agent**   The moral agent – the person involved in making an ethical decision.

**beatific vision**   The ultimate, direct, self-communication of God to humanity.

**canon law**   Ecclesiastical (Church) law. In the Catholic tradition, especially that given by the Pope.

**casuistry**   From Latin *casus*, 'case', so case law. The Catholic manuals are compilations of casuistry.

**consequentialism**   The approach to ethics in which the rightness or wrongness of an act is judged by its consequences.

**cultural relativism**   The view that a person's moral beliefs should be judged in the context of their own culture.

**deontology**   The approach to ethics in which the rightness or wrongness of an act is judged by its conformity to duties, rules and obligations.

**intrinsic good**   Something that is (ethically) good in and of itself.

**Jesuit**   A member of the Society of Jesus: a Catholic priestly order founded by St Ignatius Loyola and others in 1534. Regarded by many as the right wing of the Catholic Church. Has produced a disproportionately large number of top physicists.

**Magisterium**   The teaching office of the Catholic Church, composed of the Pope and bishops, having the authority to lay down what is the authentic teaching of the Church.

**Manualism**   In the Catholic Church, the tradition of producing manuals for use in Catholic seminaries, to train clergy in applying natural moral law to difficult cases.

**rights**   Natural moral law is held by many to give all humans certain entitlements (for example, liberty and the pursuit of happiness) which result from their common human nature.

**seminary**   In Catholicism, a school for training clergy.

**Sanctity of Life Principle**   Based on Genesis 1:26–27, that humans were created in the image of God / the gods, from which Christian theologians deduced that (human) life is sacred (dedicated to God). This principle is often used to argue that acts such as abortion and euthanasia are always morally wrong.

**teleological**   In ethics, refers to views of ethics where the emphasis is on the goal or purpose that an ethical approach is intended to achieve. In natural moral law, the primary precepts are teleological, their aim being to being about complete well-being in this life and union with God in the next. In virtue theory, the goal is the development of character through habitual virtues.

**Thomist**   Refers to the first name of Thomas Aquinas, so a Thomist position is one that would have been proposed / held by Aquinas, for example, Thomist natural moral law or Thomist Cosmological Arguments.

**virtue**   A quality / trait / disposition in a person held to be of moral value.

# Summary of natural moral law

Natural moral law [NML] is pre-Christian, its roots being found, for example, in the writings of Aristotle and Cicero. Its most distinctive version is that of Aquinas, which marries Aristotelian virtue ethics with Christian theology.

Aquinas assumes that reality is governed by the eternal law, where the natural and moral order exist as 'blueprints' in the mind of God. These principles of eternal law are revealed to humans through scripture and the teachings of the Church, but the detail of natural moral law is worked out independently of scripture, through human reason, by which we then formulate human laws such as those in our legal systems.

Aquinas' guiding principle of NML is that 'good is to be done and pursued and evil is to be avoided'. Reason leads us to the primary precepts (principles) to which we have a natural inclination. These include: the preservation of life / preservation of the self; reproduction; the education of children; worship of God and living in an ordered society. The primary precepts are teleological: their purpose on Earth is to lead to human happiness / human flourishing / complete well-being. They also have an ultimate focus, both for humanity as a whole in the beatific vision of God (union with God in the afterlife), and for individuals in particular to fulfil their individual *telos*, based on their natural abilities.

From the primary precepts we derive secondary precepts, which are rules that govern how we should act in specific situations. In explaining these, Aquinas follows Aristotle's distinction between efficient and final causes. For example, the efficient cause of sex is pleasure, whereas its final end is procreation, and any act which does not lead directly to the possibility of procreation violates the nature and purpose of sexual intercourse. The secondary precepts are exceptionless in most cases, are the same for everybody and so are not relative to the culture in which you live. However, Aquinas does allow some flexibility in the secondary precepts, because his interpretation of 'law' in NML is 'justice' or 'principle' as opposed to 'rule' or 'law'. He argues that although the primary principles are absolute, in rare cases the secondary principles can vary in relation to particular situations, for example: sometimes it may not be right to repay a debt where that would lead to injury to oneself or one's country.

Nevertheless, there are ways in which we can avoid making mistakes. For example, we can avoid becoming confused about the difference between real and apparent goods. We can also be careful about the difference between interior and exterior acts: someone who gives money to charity in order to be admired by others only performs a good exterior act and not a morally good act. In particular, the process of following the real good can be aided by following the virtues: particularly the cardinal virtues of prudence, justice, fortitude (courage) and temperance (self-control), combined with the theological virtues of faith, hope and love.

We can also avoid making mistakes in difficult moral situations by using the principle of double effect. For example, on the question of whether it is lawful to kill a man in self-defence, Aquinas answers that if killing the aggressor is the unintended second effect of saving one's own life, then this is lawful. However, the amount of force needed to save one's own life must be proportional – it is never legitimate to use more force than is necessary. The developed doctrine of double effect, as described by Pojman, gives four conditions that must be satisfied before an act is morally permissible: **1** the act must be morally good, or at least neutral (so acts such as lying, or intentionally killing an innocent person are never permissible); **2** the bad effect must not be the means by which the good effect is achieved; **3** the intention must only be to achieve the good effect, so the bad effect must only be an unintended side-effect. If the bad effect is the means of bringing about the good effect, then the act is immoral. The bad effect may be foreseen, but it must not be intended; **4** the good effect must at least be equivalent in importance to the bad effect.

Examples of double effect include: the use of morphine to control pain for terminally ill patients; the difference between terror bombing and tactical bombing; and torturing one person to save 1 million people. The method of double effect can be challenged in each of these cases. In addition, for example, Aquinas forbids suicide, but in the case of a soldier who sacrifices his life to save his comrades, double effect would require him not to intend to sacrifice his life, whereas most people would consider an intentional self-sacrifice to be heroic and loving. Aquinas also held that it is not lawful to tell a lie in order to save someone from any danger whatever, but this goes against most people's intuition.

Catholic NML today is still essentially Thomist, although the Catholic Church puts more importance than Aquinas on obligations and rules. Historically, this was the result of Manualism – rulebooks of casuistry designed to train Catholic clergy in the application of moral law to specific cases. The manuals left out Aquinas' treatise on happiness and on the destiny of the human person, for example, together with his emphasis on the virtues.

Nevertheless, there are indications within the Catholic Church of a shift towards a more flexible interpretation of NML. In recent decades there has been a renewal of interest in Aristotle's virtue ethics, and this has reminded Catholicism of its roots in virtue theory. The Catechism of the Catholic Church, put forward in 1992 by Pope John Paul II as a summary of beliefs for the Catholic faithful, includes reference to the cardinal and theological virtues.

Within Europe and America, Catholic theologians such as Peter Knauer and Richard McCormick have introduced proportionalism as a method of rejecting too much casuistry in favour of a more situational approach. Proportionalism is rooted in the work of Aquinas, that where a proportionate reason exists it would be right to ignore a rule in that situation. For example, Aquinas held that it would be lawful for a starving man to save his life by stealing the property of others. Current debate among Catholics produces disagreement on issues such as contraception and masturbation. For masturbation, for example, some hold that it is forbidden in all circumstances because it ignores the final end of procreation; others argue that its use in IVF is a valid exception, because IVF promotes the final end of procreation.

Proportionalism distinguishes between the *ontic*, or 'pre-moral' or 'physical' goodness or badness of an act and its morality. Acts become morally good or bad only where the agent: **1** compares the value and disvalue of an act (such as abortion or contraception or masturbation); and **2** considers his intention in carrying out that act. As a principle, proportionalism seems strong, for example, where it is used in Just War theory; although proportionalism was rejected by Pope John Paul II's encyclical, *Veritatis Splendor*, on the grounds that it denies that any action can be intrinsically evil. Many Catholics argue that proportionalism becomes consequentialism, which reduces morality to guesswork – to a calculation of goods and evils – and that once the authority of NML is lost, Catholics might just as well become religious utilitarians.

## The strengths of NML include:

1  In a time of moral uncertainty, it establishes rules by which people can live in an ordered society;

2  It encourages people to think of some acts (such as slavery) as being *intrinsically* wrong;

3  It is realistic in that it admits that people can make mistakes;

4  It has underpinned our thinking on natural rights & responsibilities;

5  It emphasises virtues;

6  It can be adapted to form a non-theistic system (e.g. Finnis).

## The weaknesses of NML include:

1  Its view that we all share a single, common human nature is arguably false;

2  Aquinas' system does not help atheists who reject his assumptions about God (although Finnis addresses this issue);

3  Many Christians reject its legalistic approach, for example some prefer to follow the approach of Situation Ethics;

4  It can lead to immoral outcomes, as with its approach to contraception and to homosexuality;

5  Some Catholics (e.g. Proportionalists) feel it should be amended.

# 4.2

# Normative ethical theories

## Situation ethics

This chapter will cover:
- Situation ethics, with reference to Fletcher
- Strengths and weaknesses of Fletcher's situation ethics

Fletcher rejected **legalism**, which is the view that it is always right to obey the moral law. For example, he completely rejects the view expressed by legalists such as the German philosopher Kant, that if a mad axe-murderer who is searching for his next victim demands that you tell him the truth about where that person is you must tell him the truth. As far as Fletcher is concerned, anybody who thinks that there is some built-in necessity to tell the truth to homicidal maniacs needs to get a grasp on sanity.

Fletcher also rejects **antinomianism**, which is the view that the laws put in place by societies should be rejected. Fletcher argued that morality should be based on Christian love, which he saw as a mid-point between legalism and antinomianism.

### Key term

**antinomianism** ('Against law') The belief that there should be no laws or principles governing human behaviour.

### John A.T. Robinson (1919–1983)

Robinson became bishop of Woolwich in 1959 and wrote *Honest to God*, in which he suggested that God is not 'out there', but is the 'Ground of Being'. He also followed the Bible's belief that God 'is love' (1 John 4:8).

It is fair to say that Fletcher's book: *Situation Ethics. The New Morality* (Note 1), tends to polarise opinion. John A.T. Robinson, who had already written the well known (and equally controversial) *Honest to God* (1963) referred to Fletcher's approach as the only ethic for 'man come of age', a phrase used by Fletcher in an early article on the subject. Conversely, in 1952 Pope Pius XII had already condemned situationism as an approach to morality, with a warning that such an ethic could be used to justify birth control; this advice being followed in 1956 by the banishment of *The new morality* from all academies and seminaries. (Note 2) The book largely speaks for itself, so by the time you get to the end of the survey given below, you could well find yourself within the ranks of the perplexed as to whether you like it or loathe it.

One question that is worth bearing in mind as you read this concerns the following: Fletcher insists that we cannot 'do' ethics without the real possibility of making mistakes, but he also insists that unless we make our own decisions about what is right or wrong to do in the situation we find ourselves in, we are not being moral at all. To hide behind obedience to moral rules is ethical cowardice and it stops any kind of moral development that might enrich our lives. The question now follows, and it is one that you should ask yourself at different stages of your reading:

*Is the weight of responsibility that Fletcher gives to every individual one that they can realistically bear?*

# Situation ethics, with reference to Fletcher

> ### Joseph Fletcher (1905–1991)
> American professor and notable contributor in the field of bio-ethics. Fletcher advocated the potential value and rightness of abortion, infanticide, euthanasia, eugenics and cloning. He argued that having no life at all is better than some of the forms in which 'life' is led. In 1967, Fletcher abandoned Christianity and became a **humanist**.

> **Key term**
>
> **humanism** A system of thought in which reliance is placed on human intelligence and will, rather than on supernatural guidance.

## A reassessment of Christian morality

**Why did Fletcher believe that a reassessment of Christian morality was necessary?**

Church membership was declining, largely as a result of changing social conditions, for example:

- The insecurity arising from a perceived absence of God during the horrors of two World Wars.
- The rise of science and its apparent displacement of God. For example, Big Bang theory and evolution made it clear that Genesis is not likely to be a factual account.

- The weakening of family and religious bonds through widely available contraception and media impact, particularly TV and permissive periodicals.
- The apparent failure of traditional deontological systems such as natural moral law to provide realistic answers to an increasing number of new ethical problems, especially those arising out of developments in medicine, biology, genetics and neuroscience. Simply following God's commands is not good enough, because in the Bible there are no direct commands concerning IVF, cloning, **cryogenics** and a host of other emerging technologies.

Fletcher's perception was that 'traditional' Christian ethics needed to be given a new focus. Christian ethics is a synthesis of the ethics of ancient Israel (the Law of Moses, centred on the Ten Commandments) with the New Testament ethics of Jesus (as seen, for example, in the Sermon on the Mount in Matthew 5–7) and the ethics of St Paul. Christian ethics has been given different expressions at different times, for example: Catholic natural moral law and Protestant **Divine Command Theory**. Fletcher embraced neither. He was an active Christian in the Episcopal Church, more because of its social ideals rather than because of its doctrines, so *Situation Ethics* was written in a Christian context, but has no Christian presuppositions other than Jesus' ethic of *agape* (Christian love). Fletcher's approach to ethics is teleological / situationist: morality is not about rules (the exception being the rule of love).

Fletcher's Foreword to *Situation Ethics* includes this well-known anecdote:

> A friend of mine arrived in St. Louis just as a presidential campaign was ending, and the cab driver, not being above the battle, volunteered his testimony. 'I and my father and grandfather before me, and their fathers, have always been straight-ticket Republicans.' 'Ah,' said my friend, who is himself a Republican, 'I take it that means you will vote for Senator So-and-So.' 'No,' said the driver, 'there are times when a man has to push his principles aside and do the right thing.' That St. Louis cabbie is this book's hero.

By this anecdote, Fletcher wants to 'set the tone' of what he has to say, which is primarily that he has an ethical 'method' but no ethical 'system'; moreover, there can never be a system of Christian ethics, because Christian living as exemplified by Jesus of Nazareth is not a system at all. It is not particularly Catholic or Protestant or Orthodox or humanist – it is personalistic and contextual, and these are the two main features of Christian situationism: Christian action should be tailored to fit the situation.

The method is focused on Christian love. 'Love' is what Fletcher describes as a 'swampy' word, meaning that it is used in many different senses. Compare his statements from a couple of pages later in *Situation Ethics*:

1  'See it now! Uncensored! Love in the raw!'

2  'I just love that hat. Isn't it absolutely divine?'

3  'Do you promise to love, honor, and obey?'

4  'Aw, come on – just this once – prove your love.'

5  'I love strawberries, but they give me a rash.'

6  'So faith, hope, love abide, these three; but the greatest of these is love.'

7  'And Jonathan loved David.' (Note 3)

Fletcher is concerned with statement **6**, *agapeic* love (we will unpack this concept shortly).

## Key terms

**pragmatism** In Fletcher's system, pragmatism is the presupposition that we should do what is pragmatic, that is, what works in the situation.

**relativism** In Fletcher's system, the idea that morality is relative to the situation, so we should avoid words like: 'always', 'never', 'perfect'. Jesus' *agapeic* love 'relativizes the absolute, it does not absolutize the relative!'

**positivism** In Fletcher's system, the presupposition that ethical norms (for example, those underpinning his situation ethics) are held by faith: that is, that *agape* is the only intrinsically good thing.

**personalism** In Fletcher's system, a presupposition that morality is about persons, not rules.

**intrinsic good** Something that is (ethically) good in and of itself.

**absolute** In ethics, an ethical principle that cannot be challenged, for example, that 'murder is wrong', which an absolutist would hold to be the case at all times, in all places, among all societies.

**norms** (Ethical) standards of proper / acceptable behaviour, so **normative ethics** = laying down standards of moral behaviour.

**normative ethics** Rules or theory by which we make ethical judgements: laying down rules of acceptable behaviour.

# Summary of Fletcher's situation ethics

The structure of Fletcher's work on situation ethics is straightforward and it will help to have an overview of what he has to say before going into detail.

1  There are three approaches to ethics: 'legalistic', 'antinomian' (having no laws or principles) and 'situational'. Fletcher's approach is situational.

2  Fletcher has four presuppositions, or working principles, in addition to conscience.

  **i  Pragmatism**: morality is about facts and actions / about what maximises love in the situation.

  **ii  Relativism**: morality is relative to the situation, so we should avoid words like: 'always', 'never', 'perfect'. Jesus' *agapeic* love:

'relativizes the absolute, it does not absolutize the relative!' (Note 4)

'love relativizes the absolute'

means that there are no absolute rules: rules are always to be interpreted in relation to the situation.

'it does not absolutize the relative!'

means that we cannot take on a relative rule like:

'Do what the situation demands'

and turn it into an absolute rule. Love is the *only* absolute.

  **iii  Positivism**: which is basically affirming the belief in 1 John 4:7–12, that 'we should love one another because love is from God.' (See also 1 John 4:8.)

  **iv  Personalism**: people come before laws. The question to be asked in any situation is, 'Who is to be helped?'

To these presuppositions Fletcher adds conscience, and claims that conscience is a verb, not a noun: it is not a thing. Fletcher sees conscience as a word that can be used for our attempts to make decisions constructively, based on both situations and moral values.

3 There are six fundamental principles of situation ethics proposed by Fletcher:

 i Only one thing is **intrinsically good**: love. Love replaces law. Love is *agape* – Jesus' other-person-regarding love: unconditional, universal, **absolute** for all people. *Agape* was used by the early Christians to refer to God's self-sacrificial love.

 ii Love is the only **norm**, so the ruling norm of Christian decision-making is love, and the most important commandment is to love God and one's neighbour.

 iii Love and justice are the same, because justice is love distributed. Justice is love calculating its duties, obligations, opportunities and resources.

 iv Love wills the neighbour's good, whether we like her or not. Love is not an emotion: love is willed.

 v Only the end justifies the means and nothing else. The end is the most loving result, so anything can be done if it brings about the most loving outcome.

 vi Love's decisions are made situationally, not prescriptively.

In the context of the fifth fundamental principle, Fletcher outlines an important part of his methodology – we need to consider four factors when judging a situation:

 i What **end** do we seek?
 ii What **means** do we use to obtain it?
 iii What **motive** is behind our act?
 iv What are the foreseeable **consequences**?

## Fletcher's situation ethics in detail

### 1 Three approaches to ethics

#### 1 Legalism

Legalism is a web woven by all major Western religious traditions. It has rules for everything, and even rules for bending the rules (such as double effect), but:

> ' … any web thus woven sooner or later chokes its weavers.' [Note 5]

With Catholicism, Fletcher describes casuistry (a process of using rules cleverly in difficult moral situations) as ingenious moral theology:

> ' … homage paid by legalism to the love of persons, and to realism about life's relativities.'[Note 6]

Fletcher means that at some point, even those who are completely dedicated to maintaining moral rules realise that rules are lacking in love, and so they use casuistry to inject a little love into the system. Laws can be sadistic, such as the burning at the stake of homosexuals during the Middle Ages, a process that was in effect supported by Old Testament law.

#### 2 Antinomianism

Fletcher is talking here particularly about those who claim to have special knowledge so that they have no need of laws at all. An example of this during the time of St Paul was Gnosticism. The Gnostics claimed to have special knowledge, so they believed that rules were no longer needed – they would just know what is right. Fletcher describes this kind of thinking as intellectually irresponsible – anarchic ('without a rule'). Others today claim some form of moral intuition or built-in conscience: Fletcher refers in particular to Jean-Paul Sartre, a twentieth-century French philosopher whose philosophy of existentialism rejects all claims to ethical norms that are valid for everybody, and Fletcher insists that those who identify his situation ethics with existentialism are mistaken.

### 3 Situationism

Fletcher agrees with natural moral law that reason is the instrument of moral judgement. He rejects any idea that moral laws had been revealed by God, with the exception of the command to love God by loving one's neighbour (Matthew 22:26–40). Rules can be useful guidelines, but they are not unbreakable.

Situational factors are primary. Situation ethics is:

> ' ... empirical, fact-minded, data conscious, inquiring.'

It is anti-moralistic and anti-legalistic. Situation ethics works with two guidelines from St Paul. First (2 Corinthians 3:6):

> ' ... the written code kills, but the Spirit gives life ... '

Second (Galatians 5:14):

> For the whole law is fulfilled in one word, 'You shall love your neighbour as yourself'.

The only rule is *agape* love. All other rules and laws are:

> ' ... only valid *if they happen* to serve love in any situation.' [Note 7]

Fletcher is keen to point out that he is not the only one to think such thoughts. Apart from John Robinson, he refers to other situationists such as Brunner, Barth, Bonhoeffer, Bultmann, Niebuhr, Lehman and others.

Situation ethics is not antinomian. It is a middle way between legalism and antinomianism. Rules should be set aside only when love demands. Decisions should be made by following the guidelines of situation ethics relative to love.

## 2 Fletcher's four presuppositions: pragmatism, relativism, positivism, personalism

### 1 Pragmatism

Something that is pragmatic is something that works, so the good is, quite simply, 'what works' / what maximises love – what has value. If it does not work and has no value, then it has no point.

Fletcher quotes approvingly from William James:

> 'A pragmatist turns his back upon fixed principles, and pretended absolutes. He turns toward concreteness and adequacy, toward facts, toward actions, and toward power.' [Note 8]

### 2 Relativism

> 'The situationist avoids words like 'never' and 'perfect' and 'always' and 'complete' as he avoids the plague ...' [Note 9]

Everything is relative to the situation, although:

> In Christian situationism the ultimate criterion is 'agapeic', or unconditional love. It relativises the absolute, it does not absolutise the relative!
>
> Fletcher goes on to say:
>
> 'We are always ... commanded to act lovingly, but how to do it depends on our own *responsible* estimate of the situation.' [Note 10]

By this, Fletcher means, for example, that so-called absolute commands such as 'Do not commit adultery' or 'Do not lie', become relative to situations. Sometimes it will be right to commit adultery or to lie, if the situation demands it, if it will maximise love, but that does not mean you can always justify adultery or lying. Only love is constant: everything else is a variable. Laws are abstract, whereas situations are concrete: they are the reality.

### 3 Positivism

Ethical norms (expectations about the way we should behave) are not rational: they are held as an act of judgement and of faith. To understand this, think about the kinds of art, music and literature that you enjoy. In effect you choose paintings, art and books that you like simply because you like them, and you do not have to justify your choices, because they cannot be shown to be reasonable or unreasonable by any empirical test. So when we say that 'God is love', this is simply a choice, and it is equally unverifiable by any kind of external test.

Fletcher means, then, that faith has to come first. Think of the discussion of Anselm's Ontological Argument, at the start of which Anselm says, *'credo ut intelligam'* – 'I believe so that I may understand'. On this basis, Fletcher says:

> The Christian does not understand God in terms of love; he understands love in terms of God as seen in Christ. 'We love, because he first loved us.' This obviously is a faith foundation for love. Paul's phrase (Gal. 5:6), 'faith working through love,' is the essence and pith of Christian ethics. (Note 11)

It is of course true that any sincere person can reject these ideas; nevertheless they are the faith commitments which identify the Christian. In other words, Fletcher's situation ethics is a faith commitment to Christian love.

### 4 Personalism

This means simply that situation ethics puts *people* at the centre of concern, and not *things*: it is immoral to love things and not people. Whereas the legalist asks, 'What does the law say?' the situationist asks, 'Who is to be helped?'

People are to be loved, not rules. Real existence lies in personal relationships. In Christian situation ethics, the personal element is emphasised by the belief that God became incarnate as a person: Jesus, and that humans are created *imago Dei* – 'in God's image'.

### Conscience

There are (says Fletcher) four theories about conscience: **1** that it is an innate (built-in) faculty; **2** that it is guidance by the Holy Spirit, or by an angel or by some other entity; **3** that it is the internalised values of society; **4** (Aquinas) that conscience is reason making moral judgements.

According to Fletcher, however, conscience is not like the Roman Catholic confessional: it is not a 'review officer' judging what you have done: it is prospective, not retrospective: it is choosing what love demands in the present situation. It is this calculation which is the conscience in situation ethics, so the conscience is not a noun: it is not something we have; it is a verb – something we *do* when we are deciding and calculating how love is best served in a situation. Fletcher's six propositions now give us his ideas on how to do that.

## 3 Fletcher's six propositions

### 1 Love only is always good

> Only one 'thing' is intrinsically good; namely, love: nothing else at all. (Note 12)

Further:

> In Christian situation ethics nothing is worth anything in and of itself. It gains or acquires its value only because it happens to help persons (thus being good) or to hurt persons (thus being bad). (Note 13)

Good, then, depends on the situation. It is good to lend cash to a father to feed his starving family. It may be wrong to do so if he is a compulsive gambler or an alcoholic.

The only intrinsically good thing is love and nothing else. It is the one and only regulative principle of Christian ethics. Only in God does love have real existence. With humans, love (like value, worth, goodness or badness, right or wrong) is only a **predicate**: it is not objectively real. Love is not something we have, or are: it is something we do. Love is a principle expressing what kinds of real actions Christians are to call good. Love is the only principle that is good and right in every situation. Our task is to act so that more good (loving-kindness) will occur than with any possible alternatives. Love is an attitude, a disposition, a leaning, a preference, a purpose. Whatever is loving is right, even though it can lead situationally to:

> '... complicated, headaching, heartbreaking calculations and gray rather than black or white decisions.' (Note 14)

> The situationist holds that whatever is the most loving thing in the situation is the right and good thing. It is not excusably evil, it is positively good. (Note 15)

For example, for a soldier to commit suicide rather than betray his comrades to the enemy is a positively good act.

### 2 Love is the only norm

> The ruling norm of Christian decision is love: nothing else. (Note 16)

> **Key term**
>
> **predicate** Love is a predicate in Fletcher's system, meaning that it describes action in a situation and is not a thing in itself. Love is not a thing or a property, it is a formal principle expressing what kinds of real actions Christians are to call 'good'.

Love replaces law: love employs law when it seems worthwhile, otherwise love can break any or all of the Commandments (the ones that deal with ethics, for example: prohibiting murder, theft, and false witness. We should:

'... drop the legalist's love of law, and accept only the law of love.'
(Note 17)

## Activity

Here are three situations in which Fletcher sees the action carried out by the person concerned as loving. For each situation:

- Explain whether or not you would have acted in the same way as the person concerned.

- Explain the reasoning by which a situation ethicist would support the person's decision.

- Explain why somebody who takes a legalist approach to religious ethics might have reservations about how each person acted.

▲ Dietrich Bonhoeffer (1906–1945)

**Situation 1**: Dietrich Bonhoeffer was a German Lutheran pastor. Bonhoeffer decided that as a response to the Nazi atrocities against the Jews, comforting the wounded and burying the dead was an inadequate response for a Christian. He therefore became involved in a plot to assassinate Hitler. The plot was discovered, and Bonhoeffer was executed, along with three other members of his family.

**Situation 2**: Fletcher refers to the hypothetical situation of a man caught hopelessly in the wreckage of a burning plane, who begged to be shot. Fletcher refers to this in order to ask the question of whether Bonhoeffer would have shot him, even though he was innocent as opposed to Hitler, who was guilty. In other words, Fletcher is saying that it could still be the most loving thing for Bonhoeffer to shoot an innocent man.

▲ Mother Maria before she was systematically starved at Ravensbrück concentration camp

**Situation 3**: From the possibility of killing a guilty man, to the possibility of killing an innocent one, Fletcher now moves to the possibility of a self-sacrificial death that was in effect suicide. Mother Maria was a Russian nun in Ravensbrück concentration camp, who (according to some accounts) chose to die in a gas chamber in the place of a young ex-Jewish girl Communist. The girl survived the war and became a Christian. Fletcher describes Mother Maria's sacrificial death as being on the model of Christ. The girl concerned knew that she was about to die and was becoming hysterical. Rather than allow the inevitable beating that the girl would have received before being killed, Mother Maria walked into the gas chamber in her place.

You will appreciate Fletcher's strategy here. Although many of those who follow a legalistic form of Christian ethics would argue that one or more of these actions is morally justifiable, it is perhaps likely that this kind of response would be tempered by saying something like, 'Well, doing this was morally wrong, but it was nevertheless the right thing to do'. A situation ethicist would probably conclude in all three cases that the acts of the persons concerned were both morally good and morally right, since in each situation they were motivated by love. As Fletcher goes on to expand what he means by 'love', see whether or not your assessment of his position changes.

Fletcher's dislike of natural moral law intensifies as his argument develops. Love has no equal; it expects nothing in return; it is neighbour-regarding, and everybody (even your enemy: Luke 6:32–35) is your neighbour. This kind of love is not like the love of natural moral law:

> In the name of a 'natural law' of secrecy they have been known to admonish a doctor to withhold from an innocent girl the fact that she is about to marry a syphilitic man. No such cut-and-dried, coldly predetermined (prejudiced) position could or would be taken by a situationist. [Note 18]

At this point, Fletcher anticipates some common objections to situation ethics, for example, that we are not bright enough to use it and that freedom is too hard to live by. Fletcher's response is that we will have to grow up and get used to it: as St Paul says, we are now set free from the Law (Galatians 5:1). Freedom is openness – it is responsibility – it is danger. Law tries to remove these. In England and in the USA, we can just keep out of the way of the car in front whose wheel is wobbling and no law will convict us for avoiding the moral responsibility of taking action to help that person. Law minimises what we have to do, so people hide behind the letter of the law to escape the higher demands of the spirit of the law.

### 3 Love and justice are the same

> Love and justice are the same, for justice is love distributed, nothing else. [Note 19]

Love becomes justice. Love in society has to be calculating, careful, prudent, distributive in caring for all; and that *is* justice. Justice is the 'many-sidedness' of love. Love is not just one-to-one: love is in union-management relations, international affairs, trade treaties, UN policy and the like; so again, we need to talk about love of neighbours, not neighbour. Love and justice need to be reunited, because justice is nothing more than love working out its problems. Justice is simply Christian love 'using its head', calculating its duties and obligations.

At this point, Fletcher comments that situation ethics needs to form a coalition with Utilitarianism, with the utilitarian goal of happiness and pleasure being replaced by *agape*. Also, where Bentham used his pleasure calculus to calculate the amount, duration, intensity, (and so on) of pleasure generated by an action, this should be replaced by an **agapeic calculus** to calculate the amount of love generated by an action. Situation ethics here is seeking the goal of the most love in every possible situation.

### Key term

**agapeic calculus** Fletcher's parallel to Jeremy Bentham's pleasure calculus; just as Bentham believed that happiness / pleasure can be measured by its intensity, duration, likelihood of giving rise to further pleasures, how near or far away the pleasure is in time, and so on, Fletcher proposed that *agapeic* love can be similarly measured.

## Activity

Fletcher gives a number of examples of how an *agapeic* calculus might work, for example:

● The decision of British Intelligence during the Second World War to let a number of female agents return to Germany to certain death, in order to keep secret the fact that they had broken the German code.

▲ The 'mushroom cloud' from the atomic bomb dropped over Hiroshima in August 1945

● President Truman's '*agapeic* calculation' of the effects of dropping an A-bomb on Hiroshima and then on Nagasaki. These killed around 200,000 people. Truman's aim was to end the Second World War as soon as possible, and it was estimated that winning the war by conventional means would cost the lives of up to 2 million US servicemen.

Do some brief online research of Truman's decision. To what extent would you agree that this was an '*agapeic* calculation'?

## 4 Love is not liking

> Love wills the neighbour's good whether we like him or not. [Note 20]

Love is not sentimental: love based on emotions like sympathy and affection amounts to self-love (ask yourself why). Love is **conative** (meaning that it is about the will) – you should will yourself to promote other people's well-being. Willed love can be commanded, whereas emotions cannot; so love is goodwill / benevolence. Love does not seek out the deserving, nor does it make judgements about the people it wants to serve:

> *Agape* goes out to neighbors not for our own sakes nor for theirs, really, but for God's. We can say quite plainly and colloquially that Christian love is the business of loving the unlovable, i.e., the *unlikable*. [Note 21]

That does not mean to say that we have to like everybody – that would be cheap hypocrisy. Virtues like kindness, generosity, patience, concern, righteous indignation (the kind of virtues listed by St Paul, in for example, Galatians 5:22) are all conative – we must will them.

*Agape* can, however, include love of self. Jesus' summary of the Law is to love your neighbour as yourself, so love of self teaches you to do for others those things that you need for yourself. As Kierkegaard puts it:

> **The commandment 'Love thy neighbour as thyself' means 'Thou shalt love thy self in the right way'.** [Note 22]

However, love needs calculation: it is right to deal lovingly with an enemy, but if he hurts too many friends, and only some can be saved in a situation, you would not calculate to save the enemy. If you are asked, 'Which should you save if you can carry only one from a burning building, a baby or da Vinci's *Mona Lisa*?', you take the baby if you are a personalist. If the choice is your father or a medical genius with a cure for a lethal disease, then you carry out the medical genius if you understand *agape*.

Only those who sentimentalise love would look upon such calculation as a betrayal of love. Fletcher gives the clear example from a TV play called *The Bitter Choice*, in which a nurse in a military hospital deliberately chooses to make wounded soldiers detest her, because that is the only way she can find of giving them a good reason to get better, get away from her and the hospital and make a complete recovery. [Note 23] Love can make people angry, and love can be angry if it does the job.

## 5 Love justifies its means

> Only the end justifies the means; nothing else. [Note 24]

Fletcher complains that Christian ethics through the centuries has clung to the absurd doctrine that 'the end does not justify the means', whereas if the end does not justify the means, what does? The answer is – nothing! Unless some action has an end or purpose, any action we take is literally meaningless and random.

Not any old means will do, however. The means has to be selected with the greatest care. For example, in most situations, birth control is better than abortion. We have to remember that:

> '… what is sometimes good may at other times be evil, and what is sometimes wrong may sometimes be right when it serves a good enough end – *depending on the situation*.' [Note 25]

So, 'the end does not justify the means' is obviously false, and the legalists do not have the wit to see it.

> Surgeons have to mutilate bodies to remove cancers, some priests have to give up married love and children for their vocation's sake, nurses lie to schizophrenics to keep them calm for treatment. But in such cases it is *worth* it. [Note 26]

If killing and lying are to be used, however, as in the French Resistance during the Second World War, it must only be under the most urgent purpose of social necessity, and with a profound sense of guilt that no better way can be found. Consider one further example from Fletcher.

### Activity

Fletcher refers to the 'Wilderness Road' in the eighteenth century, westward through Cumberland Gap to Kentucky, where many families and trail parties lost their lives in border and Indian warfare. Compare these two episodes in which pioneers were pursued by 'savages'. [Note 27]

1 A Scottish woman saw that her suckling baby, who was ill and crying, would betray her and her three other children, and the whole company, to the Indians. But she clung to her child, with the result that they were caught and killed.

2 A Negro woman, seeing how her crying baby endangered another trail party, killed it with her own hands, to keep silence and reach the fort.

Which woman made the right decision?

Fletcher is clearly inviting you to suggest that the second woman made the right decision. Being faced with a horrifying choice, her *agapeic* calculation was that strangling her baby was the means to the end of saving everybody else. Whether or not you personally could make such a decision does not affect the fact that this particular woman, in this particular situation, was able to make a genuinely loving choice. If we ask, then, 'Does an evil means always nullify (cancel out) a good end?', Fletcher's answer is an emphatic, 'No!'.

Fletcher now moves on to an important element in his situation ethics.

We need to consider four factors when judging a situation:

i What **end** do we seek?

ii What **means** do we use to obtain it?

iii What **motive** is behind our act?

iv What are the foreseeable **consequences**?

This is Fletcher's illustration:

i  A student wants to buy a new and highly useful thesaurus (a book listing alternative terms for words).

ii  The **means** he uses to obtain it might be stealing or borrowing or buying, and to get money to buy it, he might steal or save or beg or borrow or gamble.

iii What then is his **motive** – is he moved by covetousness or charity or scholarship or ostentation or bibliomania (an obsessive love of books)?

iv  Finally, what are the foreseeable **consequences** of what he does? What are the direct and indirect effects, and the immediate and remote consequences? This last question points out that there are more results entailed than just the end wanted, and these will have to be weighed and weighted. Along with getting the thesaurus, other things might come, such as impoverishment, the increase of a neurosis (bibliomania), professional growth, resentment by a wife or creditor, successful completion of an important thesis.

The moral responsibility of love is therefore no light thing, and love has to weigh relative values. Fletcher at this point refers to those who use 'wedge arguments' against any attempt to weigh relative values. A wedge argument is one which says that if we break an important rule by allowing just one exception, then the rule becomes useless. The exception will drive a wedge between the rule and the need to obey it. The wielder of the wedge argument will say, 'What will happen if we allow everybody to do this?' (for example, if we allow euthanasia in a case where a parent has killed a suffering infant, or where a husband has killed his wife out of mercy, and at her request? We cannot allow this, because if everybody did it would mean chaos and cruelty). Fletcher rejects this as legalistic nonsense which simply takes away our moral responsibility and ignores love. What do you think?

Fletcher's conclusion here is that *we* cannot refuse to do a deed which has a mainly good end just because it entails some evil. He ends this section with another powerful example:

> Several years ago Congress passed a special bill giving citizenship to a Roumanian Jewish doctor, a woman, who had aborted 3,000 Jewish women brought to the concentration camp. If pregnant, they were to be incinerated. Even accepting the view that the embryos were 'human lives' (which many of us do not), by 'killing' three thousand the doctor saved three thousand and prevented the murder of *six thousand!* [Note 28]

Fletcher is referring to Gisella Perl (1907–1988), known as 'The Angel of Auschwitz'. The picture shown is from the cover of her memoirs of the operations she performed in Auschwitz. Apart from her daughter, who she managed to hide during the war, her parents, her husband, her only son and her extended family were murdered in the concentration camps. The 'means' by which she managed to perform the abortions were her bare hands, justified by her ethic of love.

### 6 Love decides there and then

> Love's decisions are made situationally, not prescriptively. [Note 29]

▲ Dr Gisella Perl, 'The Angel of Auschwitz'

People often want the crutch of an ethical system to lean on – they want to cower behind the security of rules; but we have to accept that morality has grey areas that we must wrestle with. The following is one of Fletcher's examples of such 'wrestling':

A few years ago a lady in Arizona learned that she might bear a defective baby because she had taken the drug thalidomide. Thalidomide was used to alleviate the symptoms of morning sickness during pregnancy. As a result, about 10,000 babies were born with an absence or malformation of their limbs. There were many other side-effects of the drug, including blindness, deafness and heart problems. She asked the court to support her doctor and his hospital in terminating the pregnancy, but the law prohibited non-medically indicated abortions, so the judge refused. Her husband took her to Sweden, and she was aborted there. Fletcher argues that this decision was brave, loving and right – and would have been right even if it turned out that the embryo had not been damaged by the drug. As things turned out, the lady was right in her belief that the embryo would be damaged. (Note 30)

Fletcher complains that politicians and others sit behind ideologies to protect themselves, but all that does is to abandon freedom and strangle morality. Jesus did not do this – he was a situationist, and appears, for example, not to have been bedevilled by legalistic sexual morality. For many people, sex is so much a moral problem, largely due to the repressive effects of legalism, that newspaper references to somebody's 'morals' generally means a sex complaint. Look at the following Discussion point and Activity (page 157) which are based on what Fletcher says next.

---

## Sexual ethics

Fletcher makes the following observations about sexual ethics in the New Testament (Note 31):

- The only comments that Jesus makes about sexual ethics are to condemn adultery and divorce.

- He says nothing about whether people should have large or small families, or about birth-control, childlessness, homosexuality, masturbation, abortion, sex play, courtship, sex before marriage, sterilisation and artificial insemination.

Given the silence concerning Jesus' views on these subjects, Fletcher says that love has to decide in the situation: 'there and then'. He makes (or implies) these suggestions:

1 Whether any form of sex is good or evil: heterosexual, homosexual, or autosexual (gratifying oneself sexually), depends only on whether love is fully served. In other words, homosexuality and autosexuality are merely alternative forms of sexual expression, and should not be condemned by the Church or by anybody else. Any type of sexual expression is to be judged purely and simply by its capacity to bring about good or evil in the situation.

2 We can have love without sex and sex without love; moreover baby-making can be (and often ought to be) separated from love-making. Sex is for recreation as well as procreation.

3 If people do not believe that having sex outside marriage is wrong, then it is not, unless they hurt themselves, their partners or others. Fletcher admits that this is a big 'if'.

---

## Discussion point

As a group, or in pairs, discuss Fletcher's claims in points **1** and **2**. Contrast them with the claims of Aquinas' natural moral law concerning:

- non-heterosexual sex, and

- sex and procreation.

Do you prefer the rule-based approach of natural moral law or Fletcher's situational approach, and why?

**Activity**

- As an evaluative exercise, think of one argument to support the claim that Fletcher makes in point **3** (concerning sex outside marriage), and another to oppose it.

## 4 Postscript

Fletcher concludes with a number of warnings, particularly against moralism, which trivialises morality. Moralism makes the moral life a matter of petty disciplines; it condemns things like smoking, Sunday fun, kissing and petting, missing church and having sinful thoughts, but shows little concern for the great issues of love and justice. It is more concerned with the idea that we are 'saved' by being 'good' and by the even more peculiar idea that we can be saved by following such petty, puritanical prohibitions. (Note 32)

**Activity**

Fletcher ends his book with four cases to test the methods of situation ethics.

- Christian cloak and dagger

- Sacrificial adultery

- 'Himself might his quietus make'

- Special bombing mission no. 13

Using his four presuppositions, six fundamental propositions and four situational factors, as summarised on pages 144–145, research these four cases through using the internet or books, and justify your opinion as to whether or not what is done in each case effectively meets the demands of Christian love.

# Strengths and weaknesses of Fletcher's situation ethics

Lists of strengths and weaknesses of situation ethics (wherever you find them) tend to be very long, so some kind of selection process should be employed. The following suggestions are not, therefore, all-inclusive, and if there are other strengths and weaknesses that you would prefer to focus on, then that of course is fine.

## Strengths

1 Basing a Christian ethical approach on the principle of *agape* seems right, since the principle itself is clearly grounded in the life of Jesus. Jesus acted situationally, not legalistically, so Christians should follow Jesus' example. Jesus taught the central message that we should love God and love our neighbour: everything else, including the Law, hangs on this kind of love. One of the clearest examples is the story of the woman taken in the act of adultery (John 8:1–11). The Pharisees would have stoned her in accordance with the Law of Moses, whereas Jesus refused to condemn her, told her to sin no more, and thereby probably effected a major change for the better in her life. Love is motivational.

Balanced against that, Fletcher's choice of *agape* as the central principle of situation ethics seems arbitrary when one considers that most Christians view the Bible as a much wider construct in which we see the working out of experience, law, wisdom, prophecy *and* love. If Fletcher feels that it is legitimate to focus on *agape*, in effect this is a licence for the individual to pick and choose whatever he or she likes, so there can be no real reason, other than personal preference, to focus on *agape*. However, the situationist can reply to this that in the Bible, Jesus gives love priority over everything, saying that the love of God and of one's neighbour are at the heart of Scripture (Matthew 23:36–40).

**Key term**

**autonomy** ('Self law') The principle of self-determination, that people should be able to decide for themselves what is in their best interests.

2  Fletcher's presuppositions seem to be good ones. An ethic that is 'personalist', putting people before rules; 'situational', looking at the situation as it really is; and 'pragmatic', selecting a solution that works, is based on a platform of moral common sense.

3  Situation ethics promotes individual **autonomy** – people are empowered to make their own decisions in the situations that they encounter. Religious legalism can often do the opposite – it requires people to act counter-intuitively, against both reason and emotion, by following rules that may not fit the situation. Moreover, situationists do not discard moral rules, since they can accept that rules are formed from the entire experience of the human race, although laws which do not fit a situation should be ignored in that situation.

4  Whereas legalism can struggle to accommodate new technologies, situation ethics adapts readily to any developments in medical science and to developments in understanding human sexuality. In other words, situation ethics can be flexible about new technologies, whereas legalistic ethics tend to ban some of these technologies merely because they contradict pre-scientific beliefs about the nature of the body.

5  Situation ethics focuses on helping people, whereas legalistic ethics often amounts to worship of laws that have no real moral force. For example, many of the 'crimes' punishable by death in the Old Testament are about sex. The death penalty was decreed for: sex with an animal, incest, adultery, homosexual acts, prostitution by a priest's daughter, false claims about virginity prior to marriage, and sex between a betrothed virgin and a man other than her betrothed. [Note 33] As Fletcher points out, the fact that rules such as these are hardly ever enforced today shows that even legalists have moved away from the letter of the law towards the law of *agape*, which is a recognition that living by outdated rules is pointless.

6  Similarly, situation ethics promotes social justice, because it forces people to analyse situations in terms of the desired end. It motivates people to change things for the better and to get rid of the various types of discrimination that plague society.

## Weaknesses

1  One of the main problems with Fletcher's situation ethics is the amount of responsibility it puts upon the individual. In effect the individual ends up with more moral responsibility and authority than either the Bible or the Church. It is asking a lot of the average individual to put the welfare of their neighbour before that of themselves. Many people have a natural tendency towards selfishness, and whereas this might be held in check by the requirement to follow moral rules, a requirement to act autonomously could easily end up with people serving their own ends.

2  Situation ethics sidelines 2,000 years of Church tradition and authority together with something like 3,000 years of biblical authority. In effect, the accumulated wisdom of the great moral teachers can be thrown away at the whim of the individual. This is one of the reasons why John Robinson eventually rejected situation ethics – it runs too great a risk of

descending into moral chaos. As William Barclay argued, religious law is the distillation of experience that has been found to be beneficial, so to discard moral rules is to discard this experience. There needs to be an institutional authority outside the individual, since:

'... not all men are angels'. [Note 34]

3 There may be no consensus on what the most loving action may be in a specific situation, which would make the decision arbitrary.

4 With regard to Fletcher's case studies, it is commonly objected that they reflect extreme situations rather than 'real life'. If you completed the case study on 'Sacrificial Adultery', where a female prisoner of war decided to commit 'sacrificial' adultery with a guard in order to be sent back to her family: this is hardly a common situation in which to assess adultery. Having said that, one could say that Fletcher chooses extreme examples simply to show that situation ethics can find a possible answer where legalistic ethics would have no option but to leave the prisoner where she was: that is, to leave her in a situation where in all probability the family would never be reunited.

5 Situation ethics puts a lot of emphasis on motivation and appears to argue that doing something with the sincere motive of love justifies what you do, but that is a doubtful assumption to make. Parents who are motivated by love for their children can give them obsessive love that stifles their development. Obsessive love can be possessive, where the human object of what one loves can be treated as a possession. People can love their country to the extent that they are prepared to attack or ridicule other cultures on the grounds that they are less lovable.

6 Obsessive love is not *agape* love, but parents might *think* that it is. A valid ethical theory (it is argued) needs to be consistent, coherent, rational and objective, otherwise it cannot stand the test of time. With Fletcher's method, this appears to be true, since it has not stood the test of time. Many scholars and theologians have turned their backs on it, including John Robinson.

# Summary of situation ethics

To remind you, a summary of situation ethics is at the start of this chapter, on pages 144–145. As a concluding Activity, practise summary skills by summarising the preceding sections on the strengths and weaknesses of Fletcher's situation ethics.

## Technical terms for Fletcher's situation ethics

**absolute**  In ethics, an ethical principle that cannot be challenged, for example, that 'murder is wrong', which an absolutist would hold to be the case at all times, in all places, among all societies. Absolutes can be derived from, for example, nature, human nature and God's commands.

*agapeic* **calculus**  Fletcher's parallel to Jeremy Bentham's pleasure calculus; just as Bentham believed that happiness / pleasure can be measured by its intensity, duration, likelihood of giving rise to further pleasures, how near or far away the pleasure is in time, and so on, Fletcher proposed that *agapeic* love can be similarly measured.

**antinomianism**  ('Against law') The belief that there should be no laws or principles governing human behaviour.

**autonomy** ('Self law') The principle of self-determination, that people should be able to decide for themselves what is in their best interests.

**conative** Brought about by the (human) will.

**cryogenics** The science of freezing bodies shortly before death in the hope that future technology will discover the means to reanimate the body and cure it of whatever was responsible for its death.

**dilemma** A moral dilemma is a situation where two or more courses of action are available, but it is not clear which course of action will be in the best interests of those concerned.

**Divine Command Theory** An ethical theory held by many Protestants, that morality consists in following God's absolute commands, as laid down in Scripture.

**humanism** A system of thought in which reliance is placed on human intelligence and will, rather than on supernatural guidance.

**intrinsic good** Something that is (ethically) good in and of itself.

**norms** (Ethical) standards of proper / acceptable behaviour, so normative ethics = laying down standards of moral behaviour.

**normative ethics** Rules or theory by which we make ethical judgements: laying down rules of acceptable behaviour.

**personalism** In Fletcher's system, a presupposition that morality is about persons, not rules.

**positivism** In Fletcher's system, the presupposition that ethical norms (for example, those underpinning his situation ethics) are held by faith: that is, that *agape* is the only intrinsically good thing.

**predicate** Love is a predicate in Fletcher's system, meaning that it describes action in a situation and is not a thing in itself. Love is not a thing or a property, it is a formal principle expressing what kinds of real actions Christians are to call 'good'.

**pragmatism** In Fletcher's system, pragmatism is the presupposition that we should do what is pragmatic, that is, what works in the situation.

**relativism** In Fletcher's system, the idea that morality is relative to the situation, so we should avoid words like: 'always', 'never', 'perfect'. Jesus' *agapeic* love 'relativizes the absolute, it does not absolutize the relative!'

# Normative ethical theories

## Aristotle's virtue ethics

This chapter will cover:
- **Virtue** ethics, with reference to Aristotle
- Strengths and weaknesses of Aristotle's virtue ethics

For one swallow does not make a spring, nor does one day. And in this way, one day or a short time does not make someone blessed and happy either. (Note 1)

### Key term

**virtue** (*arete*) A disposition – a character trait – which is to be valued, for example, courage, truthfulness, self-control, generosity, friendliness, justice, and so on.

This quotation encapsulates an important point about Aristotle's virtue ethics: virtue is not something we do in one-off situations; it is the goal of life.

In recent years there has been a move away from act-based moral systems such as natural moral law and situational ethics towards virtue ethics. This re-emphasis is generally said to have begun with an essay published in 1958 by the British philosopher Elizabeth Anscombe (1919–2001). (Note 2) In effect, Anscombe recommended a more Aristotelian approach to ethics that pays more attention to the workings of human psychology. As a result, several modern versions of virtue theory have developed, and these have been particularly influential in the field of medical ethics. You are not required to study any of these modern versions, they are mentioned primarily to point out the attraction of Aristotle's theory. For many people, following moral rules and regulations does not work, because the rules often seem unfair, particularly where the rights of rapists, murderers and thieves are often seen to be taken more seriously than those they have raped, murdered and robbed. Perhaps what is needed is a return to the practice of doing ethics by copying the behaviour of those who are held to be virtuous.

# Virtue ethics, with reference to Aristotle

### Aristotle (384–322BCE)

Aristotle was born in Stagira in northern Greece. He joined Plato's Academy at the age of 18 and stayed there until around 347BCE. Aristotle eventually set up his own school called the Lyceum. His writings cover a vast range of subjects, including science, politics and morality. He wrote several books on ethics, including the *Nicomachean Ethics* (often referred to just as his 'Ethics'), dedicated either to his father or to his son, who were both called Nichomachus. The book is probably a compilation of some of Aristotle's lecture notes.

The theme of the book concerns how we should live, so it is a practical work examining the best life for humans. As we have seen, in about the thirteenth century CE, Thomas Aquinas synthesised (merged together) Aristotle's ethics with Christian ethics, and that synthesis is still used today in Roman Catholic ethical teaching and practice.

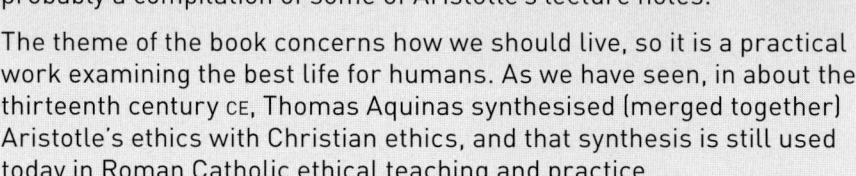

> The problem with people who have no vices is that generally you can be pretty sure they're going to have some pretty annoying virtues.

This comment, apparently from Elizabeth Taylor, tends to sum up a view of virtue which is a far cry from that of Aristotle. We tend to use the word 'virtue' in the sense that we think of 'stodgy Victorian values' (Note 3), (for example, old-fashioned rules about children being seen and not heard; or women supporting their husbands without being granted equal rights in property or work or politics), but this is not the sense in which Aristotle uses it, so do not be dismayed! 'Virtue' translates the Greek term *arete*, which is why virtue ethics is often referred to as 'aretaic' ethics.

To give you a few more pointers about Aristotle's world:

Aristotle's audience is made up of *spoudaioi* (a word that you do not need to remember), meaning 'serious' human beings (Note 4). These were the citizens of the Greek city states: adult males who governed each city. The bulk of the rest of the population was made up of slaves, non-citizen labourers, women and children. In other words, Aristotle is writing for the group of people in whom he observed the virtues that he goes on to write about. Aristotle's ethical ideas are often held to be elitist, therefore, in so far as they were not intended to apply to the whole population; but his ethical theory can be applied to everyone in a modern context. If we grant that virtue can be cultivated by habit and training, then there is no reason why most people could not be virtuous. You can judge that for yourself through Aristotle's account of virtue.

# Outline of Aristotle's theory

## 1 Aristotle begins the *Nicomachean Ethics* with the following claim:

> Every art and every enquiry, and similarly every action as well as choice, is held to aim at some good.
>
> ▲ [1094a 1]

You can see from the start that this is a teleological claim. There is a large variety of ends at which we can aim, because there is a large variety of activities we can take part in. Whatever it is: ship-building, medicine or war; each activity has its end. However, some ends are subordinated to others: for example, those who make horse bridles serve the higher ends of horsemanship; horsemanship in turn serves the ends of military strategy; military strategy leads to victory in war, and so on. This suggests that there is some final end to which all activities are directed.

## 2 Discovering this final end is a process that is likely to be directed by politicians

It is politicians who hold the power, and who therefore decide what sciences ought to exist in city states, what each group of citizens has to learn, and how proficient they must be. [1094a 28–b 2] Remember here that the politicians Aristotle refers to will be from the families of the citizens he is addressing.

## 3 There is disagreement about the final end, but most people agree that this final end is happiness (*eudaimonia*)

Note that there is some disagreement as to precisely what happiness / **eudaimonia** is. [1095a 17–20]

- Some say that happiness is pleasure, but Aristotle rejects that, because even cattle experience pleasure.
- Others say that happiness is receiving political honour, but that is given to us by others, so honour can hardly be the final end; moreover, honour is easily lost!
- Others say that it is wealth, but wealth is just a means to an end, and is also easily lost.

Aristotle now goes on to give his own account of *eudaimonia*, based on his Function Argument.

> **Key term**
>
> **eudaimonia** (For Aristotle) that which is the good for humans, defined (and rejected) variously as: pleasure, honour, happiness, complete well-being; defined finally as the intellectual virtue of *theoria* (scientific) contemplation.

## Activity

Before we look at the Function Argument, try this Activity, to see whether or not your ideas run in the same direction as those of Aristotle.

The following list gives 20 items – goods that some people find desirable because they lead to happiness. The list includes the three that Aristotle has dismissed, since you might disagree with him:

1 pleasure
2 high intelligence
3 wealth
4 power
5 a close family
6 friendship
7 a satisfying career
8 a satisfying sex life
9 a good character
10 environmental good
11 the car of your dreams
12 good for all
13 religious values
14 a long life
15 beauty
16 musical skills
17 other artistic skills
18 scientific skills
19 foreign travel
20 a good memory

**As a class:**

- Discuss these 20 items and select the **three** that by vote or agreement are considered the most important. Feel free to add any goods to the list that you think have been omitted.

- Now reduce the three to just the **one** item that by vote or agreement is the greatest of these goods. Make a note of it for when you reach the end of Aristotle's analysis.

- Aristotle makes the interesting claim that people do many things in the hope of achieving happiness, but that nobody seeks happiness in order to achieve something else. Does this prove that happiness is the final goal?

## Key term

**function** (*ergon*) 'work', or 'accomplishment'. Something is 'good' if it fulfils its function.

## 4  The Function Argument: The human good is a function of the soul in accord with virtue

There is a relation between goodness and **function**. 'Function' in Greek is *ergon*, meaning 'work', or 'accomplishment'. So, for example, a good knife is one that works well and fulfils its purpose: its blade will be sharp, its handle will be engineered for the best grip and it will cut well. You might take some time to consider the *ergon* / function of a good:

- artist
- soldier
- tree
- tiger
- virus.

The function of a good tiger might be to bite and to claw its victims (human or otherwise), because that is what a good tiger does in order to survive. Equally, we need to find the right function for humans, because whatever the human function is, human goodness will be in fulfilling that function.

Virtue in a human is defined by the natural characteristics of the human **soul**. 'Soul' for Aristotle does not refer to a non-physical aspect of humans: instead, the soul is the form or blueprint of the body. Aristotle defines this as a **hierarchy**:

▼ Table of the hierarchy of souls

| Soul | | Characterised by |
|------|------|------------------|
| plants | vegetative | nutrition and growth |
| animals | sensitive | • nutrition and growth<br>• movement<br>• sense perception<br>• (low-level) thought |
| humans | rational | • nutrition and growth<br>• movement<br>• sense perception<br>• reason |

Function, therefore, depends on the nature of the soul, so plants, animals and humans fulfil their function by doing the work / activity that is characteristic of them. So what is especially characteristic of humans?

- It cannot be nutrition and growth, because even plants have these.
- It cannot be sense-perception and movement, because animals have these too.
- So it can only be the exercise of reason / the rational part of the soul, which according to Aristotle is unique to humans.

Aristotle therefore concludes that the *telos* – the end or purpose of human beings – is focused on the rational soul. The good life will be one in which reason is exercised well, so *eudaimonia* is:

> … an activity of the soul in accord with virtue, and if there are several virtues, then in accord with the best and most complete one.
>
> ▲ [1098a 16–18]

> Thus the good life is not the kind in which we eat, reproduce, sense, move, remember or imagine well [plants and animals do that], but that in which we exercise reason well. (Note 5)

## 5 Reasoning well means exercising virtue (exercising moral excellence)

Aristotle now goes into a lengthy exposition of moral virtue. Moral virtue in someone's life is not to be evaluated over a short period, or by seeing how they operate in isolated situations, but is to be assessed over someone's complete life.

Aristotle states that there are two aspects of the human soul: one is the rational part and the other is non-rational. The non-rational soul does not mean irrational – it refers to emotions and appetites, for example, as in the diagram shown here:

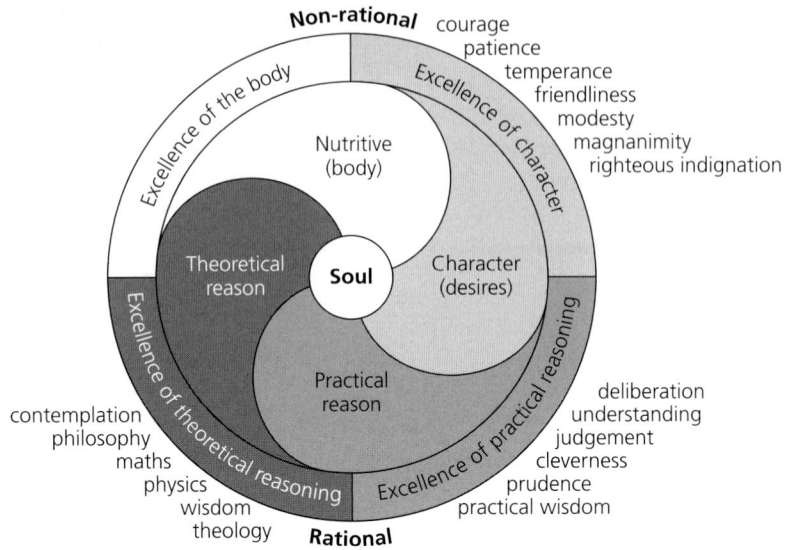

▲ Aristotle's division of the soul

● Some virtues are intellectual; others are moral.

**The non-rational soul has moral virtues** (virtues of character), such as: courage, patience and modesty.

● **The rational soul has intellectual virtues**: theoretical virtues, such as doing maths, physics and philosophy; and practical virtues, such as understanding, judgement and practical wisdom.

● The intellectual virtues are those which contribute most to the good life, because they are under the control of reason.

● **The moral virtues are formed by habit** [1103a 17], but not by blind habit: they are helped by the rational soul and particularly by the virtue of practical wisdom. Just as we become physically strong by nourishment and exercise, we become moderate by abstaining from pleasures and we become courageous by the habit of ignoring frightening things and putting up with them. [1104a 30–1104b 3]

● By nature, we are neither good nor evil; but we have the capacity to become good or evil by training, and training must start as soon as possible, because children acquire good or bad moral habits by following role models, usually their parents. In other words, we do not become just and virtuous by learning rules, but by imitating virtuous people.

● Not only that, a virtuous person must:

 – **know** what he or she is doing in any situation, and not act through ignorance, and
 – must **choose** to act virtuously.

For example, if a man performs a heroic deed, such as rescuing a child from a burning building, he would not be acting virtuously if:

**a** he did not believe or know he was really in danger, and
**b** if he acted in this way only because he wanted to impress his girlfriend.

He is acting virtuously only if:

**a** he *knows* that he runs the risk of injury or death, and
**b** he chooses to save the child because he is convinced that this is how a virtuous person should act.

We cannot read people's minds to know their motives: only the moral agent knows whether he or she is acting virtuously in rescuing the child.

### 6 How do we perform the virtues well? – The doctrine of the mean

Specific virtues lie between two extremes (usually called vices, but they are better called the 'excess' and the 'deficiency').

> Virtue, therefore, is a characteristic marked by choice, residing in the mean relative to us, a characteristic defined by reason and as the prudent person would define it. Virtue is also a mean with respect to two vices, the one vice related to excess, the other to deficiency …
>
> [1106b 36–1107a 3]

There are some crucial key terms here:

- **Choice** means **rational deliberation** about what to do. Choice is rational, and not non-rational: we choose for specific reasons.
- The **mean** is the *median*, which is **relative** to each individual. If you are training to be an athlete or a wrestler, then your trainer will prescribe a diet for you. If 10 pounds is the maximum weight of food you can consume and 2 pounds the minimum, the trainer will *not* prescribe 6 pounds for everyone: how much food you are allowed depends on your body size, your metabolism, your activity levels, your appetite and so on. So the food allocation will vary from individual to individual. [1106a 29–1106b 4] So the mean is what is appropriate / right for each individual.
- The mean is not hit or miss; rather it is as defined by a '**phronimos**' – meaning 'a man of practical wisdom'. A *phronimos* is a good judge of ethical matters. The individual concerned in this situation could be the *phronimos*, or else it could be another person, but the mean will be **rationally** designed by the *phronimos* for each individual and *not* simply laid down as a universal prescription or rule.
- The mean lies between two extremes: the **excess** and the **deficiency**:

> Moral virtue … is concerned with passions [emotions] and actions, and it is in these that excess, deficiency, and the middle term [the mean] reside. For example, it is possible to be afraid, to be confident, to desire, to be angry, to feel pity, and, in general, to feel pleasure and pain to a greater or lesser degree than one ought, and in both cases this is not good. But to feel them when one ought and at the things one ought, in relation to those people whom one ought, for the sake of what and as one ought - all these constitute the middle as well as what is best, which is in fact what belongs to virtue.
>
> [1106b 16–23 The parts in the square brackets are the author's own.]

---

**Key terms**

**mean** The median – specific virtues lie between two extremes – the excess and deficiency. The mean is relative to the **disposition** of each individual.

**dispositions** Character traits. Virtue is a disposition in relation to a mean.

**phronimos** The man of practical wisdom who, in Aristotle's system, is best qualified to define virtuous behaviour in any situation, his practical wisdom having been acquired by constant practice and habit.

In simple terms, Aristotle is saying that your emotions and your actions can be extreme either by being excessive or deficient, or else they can lie in the middle ground between those extremes: for example, you can feel too much anger, not enough or the right amount. Being virtuous is to act and feel in the middle ground when you should, at the things you should, with proper regard to the people you are dealing with.

Note the importance Aristotle gives to emotions ('passions') within the rational character. Our emotional reactions to situations and to people are part of the way in which we assess those situations and people. Martha Nussbaum puts this well:

'Aristotle's norm of a reasonable person is one whose character is infused completely by the correct reasons for action, which have shaped all their motives and attitudes. Because he aims to describe the cultivation of a whole person and way of life, rather than simply to prescribe a list of duties, he has ample scope for discussing emotional self-shaping.' (Note 6)

The emotion of grief, for example, is not morally useless: it shapes our attitudes of compassion, caring and empathy towards others, and so develops virtue. Also, it is important that people should enjoy acting virtuously, because if such behaviour is both enjoyable and rational, it becomes self-reinforcing.

## 7 Aristotle develops the doctrine of the mean with reference to specific moral virtues

**Key term**

temperance The virtue of self-control.

**Activity**

Here is Aristotle's list of virtues, each with its excess and deficiency. In pairs, try to fill in the missing words. Check your answers with the complete list on page 178.

| The moral virtues | | | |
|---|---|---|---|
| **Area** | **Excess** | **Virtue** | **Deficiency** |
| fear and confidence | | courage | |
| pleasure and pain | licentiousness (lack of restraint in moral and sexual behaviour) | **temperance** (self-control) | insensibility |
| getting and spending – small amounts | | generosity | |
| getting and spending – large amounts | | magnificence | parsimony (being very unwilling to spend money or use resources) |
| honour – large honours | small-mindedness | high-mindedness | vanity |
| honour – small honours | | having right ambition | |
| anger | | good temper | |
| truth | | truthfulness | self-deprecation (disparaging or undervaluing oneself) |
| pleasantness | buffoonery (amusing but silly behaviour) | wittiness | boorishness (being crude and insensitive) |
| in daily life | | friendliness | |
| shame | shamelessness | modesty | |
| the fortune of others | envy | just resentment | spite |
| | | justice * | |

(Note 7)

* According to Aristotle, justice has no excess or deficiency. Justice is missing from Aristotle's list, but he discusses it later.

## Discussion of specific virtues

### Courage (Book III, 6–9)

- Courage is an activity in the area of fear and confidence. Its deficiency is cowardice and its excess is foolhardiness.
- The kind of courage that Aristotle is talking about is specifically the threat of death in battle, because war was the normal state of existence in Greece. Those who show fear would be cowardly; so courage means overcoming fear to the extent that you do not show it, and it also means not acting rashly and getting yourself killed, because then you are of little use to anybody in a battle! In the appropriate situation, a courageous person would not fear death in battle for a noble cause.
- The mean of courage does not mean showing *moderate* courage, and equally the mean is not about finding *moderation* in all things. In the face of an enemy charge, being moderate in courage would be useless, because it would end by everybody on your side getting killed. In such a situation, then, courage would need to be extreme, so the mean would need to be appropriate for this situation: **the mean would become the excess.**
- However, courage is not, for example, facing danger for fear of punishment, or for fear of being shamed. Nor is somebody courageous who acts bravely out of ignorance of what might happen to him. Nor is somebody brave who is driven to do dangerous things by violent passions such as anger or lust, because they might encounter a situation in which violent passion will not sustain them.

### Temperance (Book III, 10–12 and Book VII.1–10)

- Temperance is an activity in the field of pleasure and pain. Its deficiency is insensibility and its excess is licentiousness or self-indulgence.
- By temperance, Aristotle means self-control, and he is talking about the pleasures of the body, specifically those of eating, drinking and sex.
- Aristotle comments that if people do go wrong in the area of their natural desires, they do so in only one direction, namely, toward the excess.
- The self-controlled person trains himself to enjoy moderate natural appetites, and is disgusted by the things that licentious people get up to. Reason dictates that people should lead a life of habitual self-control.

### Justice (Book V)

- Some virtues benefit the self, and some can benefit the self and others: for example, a courageous soldier who dies in a battle will thereby benefit those who survive it. Justice considers the good of others as an end in itself, meaning that it is an altruistic virtue.
- Aristotle talks about justice in two senses. In the broad sense, justice is not just legality, but the whole system of law, rule and custom. Justice is a virtue, but one that has no mean – it is a simple extreme. The law / justice unites all the other virtues, because it requires people to be brave, temperate, courageous, and so on, both for themselves and for the good of the community. In justice:

'... every virtue is summed up.' [1129b 29]

- In the narrower sense, justice is concerned with fairness, first in a distributional sense and second in a rectifying sense. In the distributional sense, justice is making sure that all goods in the community should be distributed so that each person receives what is directly proportional to his merit. In the rectifying sense, justice means restoring the distribution of gain and loss between two people, for example, where loss has occurred during trading, or through theft, or through assault (for example, the loss of, or damage to, a limb).
- The moral agent is responsible for acts of injustice which he does voluntarily. He is not responsible for acts of injustice done through ignorance, unless the ignorance is wilful (for example, where somebody turns a blind eye to the possible consequences of what they are doing).

### Friendship (Books VIII and IX)

- Like justice, friendship is an altruistic virtue, because it considers the good of others as an end in itself. Friendship in Greek is *philia*, which is broader in meaning than our word, 'friendship', because it includes everyone dear to the person, including their family.
- Aristotle thinks that friendship is similar in function to justice, but if anything is more important:

> It seems too that friendship holds cities together and that lawgivers are more serious about it than about justice … When people are friends, they have no need of justice, but when they are just, they do need friendship in addition … friendship is not only necessary but also noble, for we praise those who love their friends, and an abundance of friends is held to be a noble thing. Further, people suppose good men and their friends to be one and the same.
>
> [1155a 23–32]

- Aristotle discusses three kinds of friendship, based on usefulness, pleasure and goodness. For usefulness, the affection that people have for each other comes from the good that each receives from the other. When friendship is based on pleasure, the same is true, for example, witty and humorous people give us pleasure. Friendship based on goodness is the perfect type of friendship that exists between good men who are alike in excellence or virtue: they wish each other's good because they are good men. [1156b 7–9). This kind of friendship is longer-lasting, because they love the friend as another version of themselves. Love of self and love of another in this way are fully rational: acting for the good of a friend is a rational extension of acting for the good of yourself, so **altruism** (love of others) and egoism (love of self) rationally coincide.

To look at descriptions of the other virtues, there are many websites that will give you a good summary, for example: http://www.gradesaver.com/aristotles-ethics/study-guide/summary.

### Key terms

**altruism** Love of others, as opposed to egoism (love of self).

**voluntary action** Action brought about by the will.

## 8  Only **voluntary actions** can be virtuous

You will have gathered by now that to be virtuous involves your will: you cannot be virtuous by accident, and we can only be praised or blamed for what we do voluntarily, that is, what we do by choice, because what we do by choice reveals our character.

Consider the following four cases:

i   A sailing ship is boarded by pirates; the sailing master is put in chains, and the cargo is looted.

ii  A sailing ship is caught in a major storm. The captain feels that he has no choice but to throw the cargo overboard if he wants to save the ship and the lives of his crew, even though he knows that the cargo owners will be furious.

iii As case **ii**, with the difference that the sailing master jettisons the cargo out of fear for his own life.

iv  In the Athenian tragedy *Oedipus Rex*, written by Sophocles, Oedipus is told by the Oracle at Delphi that he is destined to kill his father and mate with his mother. Despite desperate attempts to avoid his fate, that is exactly what happens. All three parties remain in ignorance of the truth, but when later it is revealed, his mother hangs herself and Oedipus blinds himself with the pins from her robe.

In case **i**, the master's act is non-voluntary because he does not contribute to the action and cannot be blamed for it. An intention is something that one has the power to do and here the master has no power to do anything.

In case **ii**, the master's act is partially voluntary, because he makes the choice. Yet if he feels pain at having to act as he did, then he should not be blamed for his choice, since feeling this pain shows that his intention was virtuous.

In case **iii**, the master's act is again partially voluntary, since he feels compelled by fear. He will probably feel pain in acting as he did, but this is through self-contempt, and as a sailing master with experience of facing hard weather, he can be blamed for not showing appropriate courage in the circumstances.

In case **iv**, Oedipus' acts are caused by ignorance. The test of true ignorance is that when the agent discovers the truth, it should cause him pain and repentance, even though he was not intentionally doing wrong. If he would have acted differently if he knew all the facts, then his acts are caused by ignorance and he should not be judged by them. When Oedipus learned the facts, his pain and repentance were such that he blinded himself, so he could not be blamed for his actions.

### Conclusion

● A proper intention is necessary in order to carry out a virtuous action.
● A proper intention does not include things like desire, or a wish, or an opinion: a proper intention must involve deliberation and choice made on the basis of reason.
● One can only intend something which one has the power to do.

It follows that whenever we desire to act with courage, temperance, generosity, magnificence, high-mindedness, right ambition, good temper, truthfulness, wittiness, friendliness, modesty, just intention, justice and friendship, we can only do so by having a proper intention. Nobody can be virtuous by accident.

### 9 Aristotle concludes: the good life for humans is *theoria* (contemplation)

At the end of his discussion of the virtues, Aristotle returns to the issue of the good for humans. Having rejected pleasure, honour and wealth, and having lined up the life of flourishing through moral virtue as the major candidate, Aristotle now decides in favour of the intellectual virtue of **theoria** – contemplation.

**Aristotle's argument is as follows:**

- We began with the idea that happiness is an activity which conforms to the highest virtue, which must be the best thing in us.
- The highest thing in us is reason, that is, our intelligence – our intellect. [1177a 20–21]. We use our intelligence to do science, to discover what the world is really like, and there can be no achievement of reason greater than that.
- Since scientific discoveries are the highest objects of knowledge, contemplation of them gives us our greatest happiness, not least because we can contemplate whenever we like.
- And contemplation is done for its own sake, and not for the sake of anything else, so it has intrinsic (built-in) value. [1177a 32–b 1]
- Not only that, contemplation, being pure reasoning, is in effect contemplation of the divine, so theoretical reasoning has to be the greatest thing we can do – practical reason is merely human. [1177b 26–35]

**What are we to make of this?**

- Is it obvious, for example, that intellectual contemplation brings more happiness than practical activity? For Aristotle, it might well do, since he was the world's first real scientist, and wrote many scientific works, but perhaps all he is doing, then, is to support his own preferences rather than those of other people.
- Does contemplation of the divine / the gods make us happy? For some, it clearly does, although for others it seems a bit rarefied.
- By Aristotle's own admission, there are two parts to the intellect, with the corresponding virtues of theoretical and practical wisdom. Why do we have to choose which is 'higher'? Would it not seem a more holistic approach to suggest that both are indispensable and equally important parts of human nature? Are the pleasures of the body really inferior to those of the mind? One might argue that simple physical pleasures are necessary to the wellbeing of even the greatest minds. Equally, Aristotle's preference for the intellectual virtue of contemplation perhaps over-values one aspect of human nature.

Did you include 'studying science' in your selection from the 20 items in the Activity on page 164?

## The strengths and weaknesses of Aristotle's virtue ethics

To get an idea of the strengths and weaknesses of Aristotle's virtue ethics, to some extent the theory has to be translated into a twenty-first-century context. This can be difficult, for the simple reason that the virtues discussed by Aristotle have their immediate context in the

> **Key term**
>
> **theoria** The intellectual virtue of contemplation, which Aristotle finally decides constitutes the good life for humans.

Greece of the fouth century BCE. The virtue of courage for Aristotle was exercised primarily by men in battle, since not only was Greece under constant threat from the Persians, but it was beset by its own internal wars. Aristotle became tutor to Alexander the Great in 343, and Alexander went on to build one of the largest empires of the ancient world. Although empire-building continues unabated in the twenty-first century, the virtue of courage is seen by many people to operate within a much wider sphere, not least in medical ethics.

One of the best examples of the attraction of virtue ethics is Barry Schwartz's, *Our loss of wisdom*, a 21-minute film in which Schwartz begins by referring to Barack Obama's 2009 inaugural presidential address, in which Obama asked for a return to basic virtues such as honesty, truth and justice. In support of this, Schwartz begins with a job description for a hospital janitor. The description contains 15 items, including shampooing carpets, cleaning upholstery, stripping and waxing floors, mopping and cleaning out the toilets. There is nothing on the list that includes involvement with other human beings, so the janitor's job could just as well be done in a mortuary as in a hospital. When psychologists interviewed hospital janitors to get a sense of what the job was like, they encountered a number of people who thought that their job encompassed the primary virtues of kindness, care and empathy towards people in hospital as opposed to slavish obedience to a list of jobs. They encountered moral will and moral skill, and these, says Schwartz, are what Aristotle sees as 'practical wisdom'.

A person with practical wisdom knows:

● when to ignore a rule
● how to improvise
● how to use their moral skills in pursuit of the right aims
● that wisdom is made, not born: wisdom depends on experience.

A person with practical wisdom also knows:

● that failure is OK
● that people need mentoring by wise teachers on how to care
● that people do not need to be brilliant to be wise
● that without wisdom, brilliance will get you into a lot of trouble.

**Discussion point**

Watch this video on YouTube: https://www.youtube.com/watch?v=VYu0kMCxFEE. Take a few notes on the case of *The Father, his son, the Detroit ball game and the 'lemonade'*. Then discuss:

● What does this case teach about rules and incentives?

● What are your general reactions to what Schwartz is saying about morality?

The last part of Schwartz's argument is the call to re-moralise work, which involves celebrating moral exemplars / moral heroes, because 'any moral work depends upon practical wisdom'. Schwartz ends with the example of a drive to get 'inner-city kids' into college, where he says that the single most important thing to learn is character: to have self-respect, to respect one's schoolmates, to respect one's teachers. The primary role of teachers should be to embody virtue.

Finally, practical wisdom enables other virtues, such as kindness, honesty and courage, all of which should be displayed at the right time and in the right way.

In so far as lists can sometimes help you to be virtuous in your manner of learning, we are perhaps now in a position to list some of the virtues of virtue ethics and to ask where the shortcomings of Aristotle's claims about virtue might be found.

## Strengths

1 Virtue ethics is holistic, the whole personality is considered: excellence of character; the development of theoretical reasoning, such as maths, physics and philosophy; and the development of practical skills such as judgement, practical wisdom and deliberation.

2 It is a human-centred ethic. It values strength of moral character above following rules regardless of whether the rules are good, bad or indifferent. Think of the hospital janitor.

3 It allows for moral judgement, so it does not have the problem of deontological ethics where rules conflict. It also avoids trying to guess the future, which is one of the main issues with consequentialist ethics. As a result, you do not have the consequentialist problem of doing bad actions to get good results or the deontological problem of obeying rules even when they cause harm.

4 It does not make the claim that there is a perfect solution for every moral problem, but instead it equips people to deal with those problems.

5 It has a teleological focus of *eudaimonia* – complete well-being, so is good for society.

6 You do not have to be mentally equipped to deal with natural moral law's difficult doctrine of double effect. Instead, you follow the example of virtuous people, and if you make mistakes, so do virtuous people. Virtue is developed over a complete lifetime, so there is always room for development and improvement.

7 The doctrine of the mean, means that virtue ethics is flexible with regard to situations and persons. For example, soldiers in a war zone will need a different degree of courage from that required in combating a disease.

8 It sees human emotions as important.

## Weaknesses

1 Perhaps the greatest weakness of Aristotle's virtue ethics is that although the mean is relative to individuals in a situation, it ignores cultural relativism. Different societies have different virtues, and what is virtuous in one century might be a comparative vice in another. Consider the following examples. Note that none of these is intended to be complete or completely accurate.

| Virtues in different times and places | | | |
|---|---|---|---|
| **Aristotle's Athens** | **Victorian England** | **Secular Europe** | **Modern China** |
| male dominance | modesty | tolerance | propriety |
| courage | patience | individualism | wisdom |
| bravery | courtliness | respect for rights | obedience |
| friendship | obedience | self-expression | modest appearance |
| justice | piety | | diligence in work |
| wisdom | conformity | | |
| | hard work | | |

If different societies have different sets of virtues, whose virtues should be the role model? Aristotle's virtues could be seen as ideal for the life of a fourth-century BCE Athenian nobleman, in a society in which something like 50 per cent of people would be slaves and male domination was accepted. One suspects that they would not do for secular Europe. Where national ideologies conflict, how do we solve the question of which set of virtues is right?

2 Closely related to the first point, Aristotle's argument does seem to be circular: how should we behave? We should act virtuously. What is a virtuous act? An act done by someone who is virtuous. How does someone become virtuous? By acting virtuously. Moreover, as point **1** above suggests, virtues are culturally relative, so all Aristotle is doing is recommending the virtues of his own time and social class.

3 Although virtue ethics has much to recommend it for individual morality, it is less useful in both national and international politics because governments (except where they are run by an individual) cannot make ethical decisions based on individual character. Political morality in the UK tends to run on consequentialist principles, where politicians aim to bring the greatest happiness to the greatest number, so the ethics of virtue might seem less effective in the wider context.

4 How accurate is Aristotle's Function Argument? He claims that since each part of the body has a specific function, a human being as a whole must have a specific function, but is either claim true?

– You will remember that Aquinas adopted Aristotle's Function Argument into natural moral law, for example, in his claim that the function (the 'final end') of human sexuality is reproduction, so anything which stops reproduction, such as abortion and contraception, is immoral. But that seems a weak argument, since human sexuality might have many functions, such as to form loving relationships, to find physical pleasure and to develop empathy.

– For Aristotle to claim that since each part of the body has a specific function therefore the whole human must have a specific function seems to be an example of the fallacy of composition (we looked at this in connection with Aquinas' Cosmological Argument).

– Aristotle's view that humans have a specific function – that they have an end, or goal, or purpose – is teleological. Many scientists today would reject that claim, arguing that evolution is not goal-directed, but works through random mutations. On the other hand, others would claim that evolution does seem to be moving towards increasing complexity in species, so perhaps it is teleological after all.

**Key term**

**anthropocentric** Human-centred: used, for example, as a criticism of Aristotelian virtue ethics – that it applies human values to everything, so animals do not figure as objects of moral concern for Aristotle.

5  It is often claimed that virtue ethics is **anthropocentric**. Aristotle's system is focused on the good for humans. Aristotle's argument that humans are unique in having rationality, whereas the animal soul is restricted to basic knowledge and sense-perception, is clearly wrong, since the least intelligent humans are considerably less intelligent than the most intelligent animals. If the animal kingdom is not included in the system, then the environment as a whole is likely to be ignored. Aquinas' natural moral law was influenced by Aristotle's view here, so Aristotle's system has contributed to over 2,000 years of undervaluing animals.

6  It is difficult to apply virtue ethics to moral dilemmas such as embryo research and cloning. Virtue is practised over a complete lifetime, whereas many moral issues require immediate answers and radically different ways of thinking.

7  Following on from point **6**, people need laws in order to have a clear understanding of what they should and should not do. There are many people who would refuse to act virtuously and who would go on refusing to act virtuously throughout their lives. Such people need the guidelines of moral rules to know that breaking them will bring about harsh consequences for themselves.

8  Virtuous people can be dull, whereas most people admire the kind of character that does not conform to rules or to common ideas about virtue. Think of the kind of TV series or films that you like to watch. These may include shows such as *Breaking Bad* and *Star Wars*. The first of these involves a chemistry teacher who makes millions by making a particularly pure kind of 'crystal meth'. The second features Darth Vader, who embraces the 'dark side', and thereby appears as the most fascinating villain in the series. Think of characters such as Hannibal Lecter in *The Silence of the Lambs*, and Norman Bates in *Psycho*. What does this say about the value of virtue as the basis for an ethical system?

**Activity**

1  In pairs, select (and justify) what you consider to be the four greatest strengths and four greatest weaknesses of Aristotle's Virtue Ethics.

2  Select two each from your list, and think out a counter-argument for each.

# Summary of Aristotle's virtue ethics

Aristotle's virtue ethics takes an agent-centred approach to morality, unlike natural moral law and situation ethics, which are act-centred. This difference of emphasis, and a dissatisfaction with rule-based ethics in particular, has led to a revival of virtue ethics in recent years.

Aristotle's virtue ethics is developed in the *Nicomachean Ethics*. Aristotle begins with the claim that every art and enquiry, and every action as well as choice, is aimed at some good. Most agree that this good is happiness (*eudaimonia*), although there is disagreement as to what *eudaimonia* really means. Aristotle argues that it does not mean pleasure, political honour or wealth. Instead, Aristotle uses his Function Argument to suggest that 'the human good is a function of the soul in accord with virtue'. If we compare the excellence of plant, animal and human souls, we can see that the unique aspect of the human soul is the exercise of reason, so: *eudaimonia* is:

'... an activity of the soul in accord with virtue, and if there are several virtues, then in accord with the best and most complete one.'

Reasoning well means exercising virtue (moral excellence). The soul has both a rational and a non-rational aspect, with corresponding intellectual and moral virtues. Moral virtues are formed by habit, and by imitating virtuous people, and the virtuous person must act through knowledge of a situation (and not out of ignorance) and through choice, since the absence of either means the absence of virtue.

Here Aristotle introduces his doctrine of the mean. In addition to knowledge and choice, specific virtues lie between two extremes (often called vices, but better referred to as the 'excess' and 'deficiency'). The mean is relative to the **disposition** (the natural character) of the individual, and can be chosen by the individual, or by the advice of a *phronimos* – a man of practical wisdom. Within this framework, emotions are important because they do in fact form part of our rational assessment of a situation. It is also important that virtuous behaviour should be enjoyed, since if virtuous behaviour is both enjoyable and rational, it becomes self-reinforcing.

Aristotle exemplifies the virtue, excess and deficiency of: courage, temperance, generosity, magnificence, high-mindedness, right ambition, good temper, truthfulness, wittiness, friendliness, modesty and just resentment; and he later adds justice and friendship as altruistic virtues. Throughout his account, Aristotle argues that only voluntary actions can be virtuous: a proper intention is needed to carry out a virtuous action. This does not include desire, wish or opinion, but must involve deliberation and choice made through reason. Nobody can be virtuous by accident.

Almost as an afterthought, Aristotle decides that the intellectual virtue of *theoria* (contemplation) is more important than moral virtue, because contemplation is the 'highest' aspect of the soul, being based on scientific thinking, which is 'divine', done for its own sake and productive of the greatest happiness. Having spent most of his energy in the 'Ethics' in explaining the moral virtues, this seems a surprising conclusion.

| The moral virtues – complete table | | | |
| --- | --- | --- | --- |
| **Area** | **Excess** | **Virtue** | **Deficiency** |
| fear and confidence | recklessness | courage | cowardice |
| pleasure and pain | licentiousness | temperance (self-control) | insensibility |
| getting and spending – small amounts | extravagance | generosity | stinginess |
| getting and spending – large amounts | vulgarity | magnificence | parsimony |
| honour – large honours | small-mindedness | high-mindedness | vanity |
| honour – small honours | being over-ambitious | having right ambition | being ambitious |
| anger | short temper | good temper | apathy |
| truth and self-expression | boastfulness | truthfulness | self-deprecation |
| pleasantness | buffoonery | wittiness | boorishness |
| social conduct in daily life | flattery | friendliness | surliness |
| shame | shamelessness | modesty | bashfulness |
| the fortune of others | envy | just resentment | spite |
| | | justice ** | |

** According to Aristotle, justice has no excess or deficiency.

## Technical terms for Aristotle's virtue ethics

**altruism**   Love of others, as opposed to egoism (love of self).

**anthropocentric**   Human-centred: used, for example, as a criticism of Aristotelian virtue ethics – that it applies human values to everything, so animals do not figure as objects of moral concern for Aristotle.

**dispositions**   Character traits. Virtue is a disposition in relation to a mean.

*eudaimonia*   (For Aristotle) that which is the good for humans, defined (and rejected) variously as: pleasure, honour, happiness, complete well-being; defined finally as the intellectual virtue of *theoria* (scientific) contemplation.

**function**   (*ergon*) 'work', or 'accomplishment'. Something is 'good' if it fulfils its function.

**hierarchy**   A system in which the parts / members are ranked according to status or authority. Aristotle, refers, for example, to the hierarchy of souls: vegetative, sensitive and rational (plant, animal and human), in which humans rank highest, since they alone possess rationality.

**mean**   The median – specific virtues lie between two extremes – the excess and deficiency. The mean is relative to the disposition of each individual.

*phronimos*   The man of practical wisdom who, in Aristotle's system, is best qualified to define virtuous behaviour in any situation, his practical wisdom having been acquired by constant practice and habit.

**soul**   The form or blueprint of the body; so souls can be attributed to plants, animals and humans. These form a 'nested' hierarchy, in that each level of the hierarchy has all the characteristics of the lower degrees, so humans possess all the functions and capabilities of plants and animals and possess rationality in addition.

**temperance**   The virtue of self-control.

*theoria*   The intellectual virtue of contemplation, which Aristotle finally decides constitutes the good life for humans.

**virtue**   (*arete*) A disposition – a character trait – which is to be valued, for example, courage, truthfulness, self-control, generosity, friendliness, justice, and so on.

**voluntary action**   Action brought about by the will.

# Application of ethical theories

This chapter will cover:

The application of the three normative ethical theories (Aquinas' natural moral law, Fletcher's situation ethics and Aristotle's virtue ethics) to the following ethical issues:

- Theft
- Lying

Application to issues of human life and death:

- Embryo research; cloning; 'designer' babies
- Abortion
- Voluntary euthanasia and assisted suicide
- Capital punishment

Application to issues of non-human life and death:

- Use of animals as food; intensive farming
- Use of animals in scientific procedures; cloning
- Blood sports
- Animals as a source of organs for transplants

## How to use this section

- As a general 'health warning' the application of Aquinas' natural moral law, Fletcher's situation ethics and Aristotle's virtue ethics to these ethical issues does not require you to know large amounts of facts concerning each issue. You should know in outline the appropriate facts, and then consider how the theories deal with them.
- What the three theories say about each issue is not an exact science. Aristotle was born 24 centuries ago, and what he would have thought

about modern medicine, for example, is a matter for conjecture. The society that Aristotle (and Aquinas) lived in was very different from UK society in the twenty-first century. So, always start by asking yourself, 'If that is what they said in the context of their age and society, what might they have said about this moral issue today?'

- Each issue is dealt with across the three theories, so that you can compare them. As you consider each issue, evaluate which aspects are dealt with better (or worse) by one theory rather than another. Also, consider whether each of the theories works as a whole, or whether the flaws in a theory are fatal to its success.
- Note: Where you come across variant spellings in the quotations, such as 'neighbor' rather than 'neighbour', or 'defense' rather than 'defence', that is because the original spelling of the source has been retained, which may have used American English spelling.
- Remind yourself of the methods used by each theory:

**When applying Aquinas' natural moral law to any issue, where relevant you could consider, for example:**

- Which of the primary precepts affect the issue.
- Which secondary precepts have produced a ruling on the issue.
- Whether double effect applies.
- Whether the situation requires an unusual response.
- The view of the Catholic Church.
- Reference to the virtues.
- What a proportionalist response might be, in terms of the value / disvalue of the act and the intention of the moral agent in carrying it out.

Note that this is not a list of things to go through in an exam answer. You should select, for each theory, the issues that are relevant and most appropriate for the question asked.

**When applying situation ethics to any moral issue, you could consider, for example:**

- What will work in the particular situation.
- How love is affirmed by the action taken.
- Whether what you propose to do puts people before laws.
- What end is aimed at: understanding the nature and demands of *agape* love.
- What means we use to obtain that end.
- What motive lies behind our act.
- What the foreseeable consequences are.
- How we then calculate love's demands and act accordingly.

**When applying virtue ethics to any moral issue, you could consider, for example:**

- Which virtues are to be taken account of / developed in the situation – you do not have to deal with Aristotle's entire list: focus on those virtues most appropriate to the situation.
- Which vices are being demonstrated.
- How the possible actions available will encourage good habits / good character, both for individuals, and for society as a whole, and answer 'what would virtuous people do?'.
- What the motives are for the various courses of action that could be taken.
- Whether there are factors in the situation that we cannot account for by using virtue theory.

- With virtue ethics, remember that Aristotle's list of virtues is not meant to be complete or exhaustive. When applying virtue theory to situations, therefore, you should refer to whatever virtues (or vices) that you think are appropriate to that situation.
- Remember also, the mean is not a hard and fast rule that can be applied to all situations – there will always be exceptions, unusual situations and complications, so you will need to develop skills of practical wisdom.

This kind of understanding of the different theories could be useful, but you will not be asked to summarise / parrot these lists. They show the content from which you can select.

# Issue 1: Theft (1) Natural moral law

When applied to the issue of theft, the most relevant primary precept is that of living in an ordered society, since theft generally contributes to disorder. A clear secondary precept can be followed here, namely: 'do not steal', and this is supported by the biblical commandment that prohibits stealing. Moreover, the cardinal virtue of justice would condemn any act of stealing.

However, as we have seen, Aquinas held that where proportionate reasons exist, it would be right to ignore a rule in that situation, and Aquinas considered the question of whether it would be permissible for a starving man to steal in order to save his life, and considers that this would be lawful:

> If the need be so manifest and urgent, that it is evident that the present need must be remedied by whatever means be at hand (for instance when a person is in some imminent danger, and there is no other possible remedy), then it is lawful for a man to succor his own need by means of another's property, by taking it either openly or secretly: nor is this properly speaking theft or robbery.
>
> ▲ *Summa Theologica* (1265–1274), II–II, Qu. 66, Art. 7

Where a man is starving to death, it would be lawful to steal from another, presumably from someone who had enough for themselves. Aquinas also suggests that it would be lawful for a man to take someone else's property in order to help a neighbour in dire need.

It also seems clear that a modern proportionalist view of the situation outlined above by Aquinas could take a similar view. The value of a starving man stealing someone's goods or money in order to save his own life would be that he does preserve his life, which would be in accordance with the primary precept of preserving life; moreover, the fact that he is still alive enables him to help his family if he has one. The disvalue of his act is the injustice to the person from whom he steals, and the possible bad effects on society from those who might copy his act in different and less urgent circumstances, such as mere hunger. On balance, the theft here produces more value than disvalue. Moreover, the man's intention is to save (his own) life and not to steal from somebody merely to increase his own stock of money or goods.

**Discussion points**

● Is Aquinas' example of a man stealing in order to save his life an example of double effect?

● Why would someone need the virtue of prudence (practical wisdom) in discussing cases such as theft?

● How might someone who follows natural moral law react to the suggestion that in a war of self-defence, it is morally right to steal enemy property?

● How might someone who follows natural moral law react to 'socially acceptable' theft such as: 1 asking for payment in cash to avoid paying VAT; 2 making a pirate copy of a DVD that has already sold millions of copies?

● Consider the following case:

You are in the first term of a university degree course. You are told that you must buy a specialist textbook which costs £90. You have spent all your available money on accommodation and other essentials. Two possibilities come to your mind:

1 You could steal a copy of the book from the university library.
2 You might be able to make an illegal download of the book.

You have a major test on the contents of the textbook within two weeks. You choose the first possibility and steal the book with the intention of returning it at the first opportunity. Would you be justified, under natural moral law, in taking the book from the library?

● Under natural moral law, would you be justified in stealing a gun from a mentally disturbed individual who is likely otherwise to use it to harm himself or others?

# Issue 1: Theft (2) Situation ethics

Whereas natural moral law can refer to those primary and secondary precepts that tell us that theft is wrong, together with the biblical commandment that prohibits it, the situation ethicist takes a different approach: the question, 'Is it right to steal?' can only be answered with reference to an actual situation.

You will remember that Fletcher gives this illustration of possible theft:

A student wants to buy a new and highly useful thesaurus (a book listing alternative terms for words). The means he uses to obtain it might be stealing or borrowing or buying, and to get money to buy it, he might steal or save or beg or borrow or gamble.

Fletcher does not reach a conclusion on what the student should do, because the possibilities are endless, but we formulated a similar question in the previous section on natural moral law, concerning whether you would be justified in stealing an expensive textbook from the library, with the intention of returning it. Let us assume here that you are the student, and you do exactly that: you walk into the library with a bag, you take the book off the shelf, and after a time you put it in the bag and walk out with it. At the conclusion of the exam, you return the book by the same method. Is this act justifiable by the reasoning of situation ethics?

Your motive is simply the desire to pass an important test. The means that you use to do so involve theft, since the book belongs to the library and not to you, and you have it in your possession, however temporarily, without the permission of the owner. The foreseeable consequences might involve detection and punishment, but they are more likely to achieve your desired result of passing the test. Your action is therefore pragmatic: it will probably work; it may maximise love, which is the essence of pragmatism for Fletcher, and it addresses your particular situation; moreover, it puts you as a person before the law which says that you shall not steal.

Is the action then justified in situation ethics? Almost certainly not, because it ignores what should be the 'end' of all action, namely love. Fletcher insists that love is justice distributed. Your act cannot be just, because it deprives other students of the possibility of using the book that you have stolen, so they could be in the same situation as you. Love 'wills the neighbour's good', whether we like him or not and whether we know him or not. *Agapeic* love is 'other-person-regarding', and the only love considered in the situation is love of the self. Love of the self is permitted in situation ethics, but only where it leads at the same time to love of one's neighbour.

## Discussion points

- Looking at the situation of the theft of the book, what were your conclusions concerning the same situation that you looked at under natural moral law? Remember that the most important thing in each case is the reasoning by which you reach your decision.

- Using the methods of situation ethics, on what grounds might a situation ethicist justify the act of a starving man who steals from another person in order to stay alive, or of a man who steals in order to save someone else from starving to death?

- How might a situation ethicist react to the suggestion that in a war of self-defence, it is morally right to steal enemy property?

- How might a situation ethicist react to 'socially acceptable' theft such as: 1 asking for payment in cash to avoid paying VAT; 2 making a pirate copy of a DVD that has already sold millions of copies?

- Under situation ethics, would you be justified in stealing a gun from a mentally disturbed individual who is likely otherwise to use it to harm himself or others?

# Issue 1: Theft (3) Virtue ethics

With virtue ethics, the focus is not so much on what to do in particular situations but on the development of a person's character over a lifetime. In Aristotle's view, people do not become morally good by wading their way through moral dilemmas but by learning how to act so that in any situation they encounter they will behave virtuously. As we have seen, this is achieved by habituation: by taking the advice and following the example of a man of practical wisdom – somebody who is acknowledged to have a virtuous character. Virtue theory can be applied to situations, since a virtuous life is made up from the sum total of situations in which people develop a good character.

When we look at Aristotle's view of theft, he is quite explicit:

> … Not every action or every passion admits of the mean, for some have names that are immediately associated with baseness – for example, spitefulness, shamelessness, envy, and, when it comes to actions, adultery, theft, and murder. For all these things, and those like them, are spoken of as being themselves base, rather than just their excesses or deficiencies. It is never possible, then, to be correct as regards them, but one is always in error; and it is not possible to do what concerns such things well or not well – by committing adultery with the woman one ought and when and as one ought. Rather, doing any of these things whatever is simply in error.
>
> ▲ *Nicomachean Ethics:* 1107a 9–18

Theft, then, is always a base action, and just as there is no way one can commit adultery well or not well, or with the woman one ought, there is no way one can steal well or not well, with the victim one ought.

Aristotle appears to be even more hard-line on theft than Aquinas, since Aquinas at least permits a starving man to steal from somebody else in order to save his own life, or else allows a person to steal from somebody in order to feed someone else who is starving to death.

The problem is that we cannot ask Aristotle whether he would forbid stealing in such a context. You may remember that Aristotle talked about the virtue of justice in two senses: first in a broad sense, meaning the whole system of law, rule and custom, and second in a narrower sense, where justice is about fairness, for example, in restoring the distribution of gain and loss between two people where the loss has occurred through theft. It is perhaps this kind of theft which Aristotle is thinking about where he says that theft is always a base action. There is clearly a difference between somebody who steals another person's goods purely for personal profit and Aquinas' example of somebody who steals in order to save the life of a starving man.

Bear in mind also that Aristotle's audience is the adult males who alone governed Greek society, and who were generally of Aristotle's social class. Theft between members of this class would be viewed as base. However, theft for the express purpose of saving a starving man might better be described as distributional justice, not least since: **a** the intention behind the act is not at all one of stealing for personal profit; and **b** the 'redistribution' would be from someone who had more than enough.

## Discussion points

- If in fact Aristotle does see all theft as base, does this in effect mean that he is making an exceptionless rule, 'do not steal'?

- In the case we looked at earlier, where a student steals and returns a library book in order to pass an important test:

  1 What virtues and vices can be identified in the situation?
  2 What course of action might be likely to encourage good habits in the student?

- Leonardo da Vinci's *Mona Lisa*, regarded by some as the world's greatest painting, hung at one time in Napoleon's bedroom. Eventually it ended up in the Louvre museum. Vincenzo Peruggia, a former worker at the Louvre, was passionately convinced that the painting should be restored to Italy. On Sunday 20 August 1911, when the museum was closed, he stole the painting, hid it under his coat and took it to Florence. Two years later he was arrested and the *Mona Lisa* was returned to the Louvre. Peruggia was hailed as an Italian patriot and was given a mere seven months in jail. What criteria would you use to decide whether or not Perrugia's actions were virtuous?

- Under virtue ethics, would you be justified in stealing a gun from a mentally disturbed individual who is likely otherwise to use it to harm himself or others?

- Daniel Cardinal, Gerald Jones and Jeremy Hayward give an interesting case study on theft. (Note 1) In brief, your partner is dying of liver cancer. The drug that he has recently taken has been helpful, but has been withdrawn because the medical authorities are not convinced of its value, and it costs £30,000 a year for each patient. Your partner's condition has as a result deteriorated. You have a friend who works in the hospital's cancer wing. He visits you (to help care for your partner) and leaves his hospital pass and keys on the table, so you have the opportunity to get hold of large amounts of the drug. Do you steal the drug?

  Aristotle's uncompromising approach would clearly rule out the theft; however, modern virtue ethicists might take a different approach, and argue, for example, that in some cases the appropriate thing to do would be to take the 'mean' to the extreme. To remind you about taking the mean to the extreme, see page 169 on courage and justice. With courage, for example, the extreme is 'foolhardiness', and in a desperate situation in war it would be virtuous for your soldiers to be brave to the point of foolhardiness in order to win the battle. Similarly in the case of stealing in order to save a life, the extreme of theft becomes the mean, in which case most people would probably judge that it becomes the right thing to do. Do you think that applies in the case raised by Cardinal, Jones and Hayward? (Note 2) That case raises a range of questions for the virtue ethicist, for example: the dispositions of honesty towards others as opposed to love and compassion for the partner, and the virtues of justice and consideration towards society as a whole. Where might practical wisdom lead you in such a case?

  Which do you think is the most appropriate ethical theory to apply to this case: virtue ethics or situation ethics?

# Issue 2: Lying (1) Natural moral law

As with the issue of theft, lying violates the primary precept of living in an ordered society, since there can hardly be an ordered society where people habitually lie to each other. If people lied in business arrangements, no property would ever be safe. If husbands lied to wives (or vice versa), no marriage would ever be safe. The secondary precept 'do not lie' is generally held to be included in the biblical commandment which forbids people to bear false witness. Bearing false witness is what people sometimes do in court, but the principle is the same: 'tell the truth: do not lie'.

The importance of telling the truth is thoroughly rooted in natural moral law. Someone who says one thing and thinks another in effect lies to himself, and breaks Aquinas' virtues of courage and justice.

> Lying is the most direct offense against the truth. To lie is to speak or act against the truth in order to lead into error someone who has the right to know the truth. By injuring man's relation to truth and to his neighbor, a lie offends against the fundamental relation of man and of his word to the Lord.
>
> ▲ *Catechism of the Catholic Church* (1992) 2483 ([Note 3])

Aquinas picks up specifically on the fact that lying is wrong because it is an unnatural failure to represent what is in one's own mind:

> Now a lie is evil in respect of its genus, since it is an action bearing on undue matter. For as words are naturally signs of intellectual acts, it is unnatural and undue for anyone to signify by words something that is not in his mind. Hence the philosopher says … that 'lying is in itself evil and to be shunned, while truthfulness is good and worthy of praise.' Therefore every lie is a sin …
>
> ▲ *Summa Theologica*, II–II, Qu. 110, Art. 3

Thus for Aquinas, whereas it can be right for a man to save his life by stealing from another person, when it comes to the issue of telling a lie to save someone from death, Aquinas argues that this is not lawful:

> A lie is sinful not only because it injures one's neighbor, but also on account of its inordinateness, as stated above in this article. Now it is not allowed to make use of anything inordinate in order to ward off injury or defects from another … therefore it is not lawful to tell a lie in order to deliver another from any danger whatever. Nevertheless it is lawful to hide the truth prudently, by keeping it back …
>
> ▲ *Summa Theologica*, II–II, Qu. 110, Art. 3

## The issue of the necessary lie

In this last phrase from Aquinas, that it is lawful to hide the truth by keeping it back: this issue has been discussed endlessly by philosophers and theologians, and surfaces most memorably in Immanuel Kant's argument that whatever the disadvantage that may arise for the person concerned, or for anybody else, it is everybody's duty to tell the truth. The most colourful example of this is the scenario where a mad axeman comes to your door and asks the whereabouts of his victim, who is your friend, and who is hiding inside your house. Doing your moral duty, you may not lie, even if it leads to the death of your friend; however it is permitted to tell a 'misleading truth', for example, you could say, 'I saw him at a football match two hours ago'. This might be the kind of answer that Aquinas would give (if he knew what football was), since it states the exact truth without revealing the truth that the homicidal axeman wants to hear.

## Discussion points

- Where Aquinas allows a starving man to steal in order to save his life, yet forbids someone to lie in order to save a life, is the second case really any different from the first?

- Do you think that Aquinas' solution of 'prudently keeping back the truth' is the morally right solution to the problem of telling the truth to the mad axeman? If the axeman is unconvinced, and ends up killing both you and your friend, can we really say that nevertheless, moral good has been upheld? Should we not tell a 'necessary lie'?

- If, instead of considering the mad axeman, we ask: 'Could Christians hiding Jews in Nazi Germany morally lie to those seeking them to destroy them', would a 'prudent holding back of the truth' be morally right?

- What might a proportionalist response be to the issue of the 'necessary lie'? In particular, how might a proportionalist deal with the intention of the moral agent in telling a necessary lie?

- In a world where lying is forbidden, the responsibility moves to the person who asks the question – they have to be certain that they want the truth. In our world the 'white lie' is so generally accepted that when the question 'does my bum look big in this', is asked, the person replying does not actually know if the truth is wanted or not. Perhaps a world in which no-one lied would be simpler.

# Issue 2: Lying (2) Situation ethics

We have referred, in Chapter 4.2 Situation ethics, to a number of situations in which Fletcher suggests that lying would be morally right or else morally wrong, depending on the situation.

> In the name of a 'natural law' of secrecy they have been known to admonish [meaning that he has been sternly instructed] a doctor to withhold from an innocent girl the fact that she is about to marry a syphilitic man. No such cut-and-dried, coldly predetermined (prejudiced) position could or would be taken by a situationist.

In this case, Fletcher is talking about **lying by deliberately withholding information** because of a legal principle. The 'natural law' Fletcher refers to is not the natural moral law of Aquinas, but a legalistic principle in American medical ethics at the time which prohibited the disclosure of a person's medical details to somebody else, even his fiancée. A legalistic principle like this prejudges a situation, and in effect means that the principle must be observed without reference to the likely consequences.

In reality, such a decision could not serve love's ends. The actions of a syphilitic man in marrying an innocent girl without informing her of his condition are unjust, not least because she will probably contract the disease. Moreover, the infection can be spread to any child born from the marriage, through the placenta during pregnancy or through contact with a syphilitic sore during birth. Someone who in effect lies about his condition in order to marry someone is likely to lie about other important issues as well. Such actions show a lack of love for one's neighbour. In the situation, then, the syphilitic man and the doctor, and those who have instructed the doctor, have omitted to tell the truth, and the outcome to the girl is dangerous and unloving. It would hardly be possible to do all this and at some stage not to tell a direct lie: the syphilitic man must at some point have lied to the girl about his general medical condition; the doctor, if he is instructed to deceive the girl at some point must also have lied; and, those who instruct the doctor must be aware that he will have to lie.

> The decision of British intelligence during the Second World War to let a number of female agents return to Germany to certain death, in order to keep secret the fact that they had broken the German code.

In this case, Fletcher is again talking about lying **by withholding information**, but this time **acting out of love for the majority of people** concerned in the situation. The action was pragmatic, because it worked. It addressed the particular situation, considering the likely effects had the Germans become aware that their code had been broken. The means was the lie of not telling the women concerned the truth about the situation although the deceit could hardly have been carried out without telling the woman direct lies. The end was that love was served. Without such action, perhaps thousands would have died and the war might have lasted longer. Note that for Fletcher, the action here is decided by an *agapeic* calculus that considers the amount of risk, the distribution of love in the best interests of the majority and the love brought about in the long term. No guarantee could be given of the success of lying to the female agents: the moral agent or agents concerned had to assume the responsibility for making the decision. Appealing to moral laws in order to decide what to do would for Fletcher have been morally useless. In the situation, then, Fletcher judged that withholding information is morally justifiable.

> Nurses lie to schizophrenics to keep them calm for treatment. But in such cases it is *worth* it.

By this example, Fletcher illustrates a **lie by reassurance**. Schizophrenia has a whole raft of different symptoms. These include delusions, disconnection from emotions, hearing voices and having feelings of acute anxiety. Fletcher clearly suggests that where a nurse lies to schizophrenic patients about their delusions and anxieties, this affirms Christian love.

Notice the simple point that in all of the situations, Fletcher insists there is no intrinsic right or wrong with regard to lying. The rightness or wrongness of such an act is situational and the only absolute in each situation is to affirm Christian love.

## Discussion points

- Here is another of Fletcher's scenarios concerning lying: this time, lying by misrepresentation:

'In a TV play, *The bitter choice*, a nurse in a military hospital deliberately makes wounded soldiers hate her enough to motivate them to get them on their feet again and out of her care on the way to full recovery! Love can simulate, it can calculate. Otherwise, it is like the bride who wanted to ignore all recipes and simply let her love for her husband guide her when baking a cake.'

Aquinas argues that it can be lawful to 'hide the truth prudently, by keeping it back'. Do you think that Fletcher and Aquinas would reach the same conclusion in this situation? Construct such an argument.

● What might natural moral law say about the situation of the syphilitic man marrying an innocent wife? Explain your reasoning.

● Would it be loving to lie to a drunk driver who has caused an accident in which an innocent family has been killed, when the driver, who is about to die, asks a medic if he has killed the people in the other car?

● How might a situation ethicist respond to the mad axe-murderer's request to be told where his victim is?

● In the case of the syphilitic patient who wants to marry an innocent girl, do you think that the patient's doctor has a duty of love to tell the girl about her fiancé's condition or is patient confidentiality something that should never be breached? Explain your reasoning.

# Issue 2: Lying (3) Virtue ethics

With the issue of telling lies, Aristotle's virtue ethics would point to the virtues of honesty and truthfulness, which forbid them. The situation could also require the courage to tell the truth and the justice of admitting a fault. Where the aim would be to have a society in which people habitually tell the truth, lying can more easily become habitual. How often do people lie to get themselves out of trouble? Is there a difference between the murderer who lies in order to avoid imprisonment and someone who accidentally damages your property but does not own up to it? Lying in either case is part of a mental state in which people become accustomed to distorting reality for their own benefit.

One of the most quoted passages in the *Nicomachean Ethics* that concerns lying is given in the context of a longer discussion about 'falsehood relating to speeches and actions' (1127a–b):

> In itself, what is false is based on the blameworthy, whereas what is true is noble and praiseworthy.

At first sight this looks like a blanket condemnation of lying, but this is probably not the case. If you check Aristotle's table of virtues, you will see that lying is discussed under the virtue of 'truthfulness'; and 'boastfulness' is the excess and 'self-deprecation' (making yourself less worthy than you really are) is the deficiency. Moreover truthfulness is put into the area of 'truth and self-expression'. **In other words, lying is an issue which concerns how we interact socially with each other.** For example, false promises are about being unjust rather than about being untruthful. In this approach, truthfulness is about how you present yourself in the context of socialising with others. If you boast about what you do and what you achieve, then you are presenting a false image of yourself; equally if you are self-deprecatory, habitually underselling yourself, then that is just as false. The 'mean' is neither to exaggerate nor to underrate yourself.

Aristotle goes on to suggest that the person who is properly in the 'mean' of truthfulness is:

> … a kind of 'plain dealer', since he is given to truthfulness, both in his life and his speech, acknowledging that the qualities he possesses are his own and neither exaggerating nor diminishing them.

What Aristotle appears to be saying is that truthfulness is not just a matter of telling the truth or telling a lie, it is concerned essentially with your social interaction: the way in which you fit into society. Within a society, once a person acquires a disposition for presenting themselves truthfully, then they are likely to be honest and to tell the truth in all contexts. For example, a truthful person will admit to damaging your property simply because in his social interactions he is a truthful person. If called to the witness stand in court, a truthful person will habitually tell the truth.

What Aristotle is getting at here is that **the virtues together form a synergy**, which means that the individual virtues work together to form something greater than the power of each virtue working on its own. As a rough analogy, think of the individual parts of a car before they are assembled to form the finished product: you can have a good engine, a good transmission system, comfortable seating, excellent steering and so on; but the value of each part becomes fully operational only when they are combined into the complete car. Equally, a life spent practising the individual virtues will produce a virtuous character that is greater than the sum of its parts.

Truthfulness itself is a synergy of different virtues: we need honesty to express the truth; we need courage and temperance to face the truth; we need to be high-minded and friendly in the sense of giving others their due; and we should feel just resentment when others are not given their due. Practical wisdom shows us, therefore, that we cannot isolate honesty from the other virtues: honesty is one aspect of what it means to be virtuous.

Let us apply what Aristotle says to two situations:

**Situation 1:** This is the case we raised earlier, with Fletcher's situation ethics.

> The decision of British Intelligence during the Second World War to let a number of female agents return to Germany to certain death, in order to keep secret the fact that they had broken the German code.

Remember that in this situation the women must inevitably have been lied to in order to make the intentional deceit convincing.

On the one hand, honesty requires that the female agents are told the truth, since for them it is a matter of life or death. On being arrested in Germany, they would feel a just resentment at not having been told the truth. On the other hand, the agents would recognise that their situation is not just about the different societies in which they move, but is really about their place in the 'society' of the world as a whole. Theirs was one of several situations during the Second World War when the war could have been lost. The concentration camps could have finished their work, the Russian campaign could have ended in disaster for the allies. German scientists could have developed and used atomic weapons on allied cities. Perhaps the female agents who did survive the war concluded that British Intelligence was virtuous in lying to them, and perhaps again this is a case where it was the right decision *to make the mean the extreme: the lie became virtuous.* It also requires great courage and temperance to lie with the appearance of conviction. Also it would have required pain and regret on the part of British Intelligence to make their decision, which for Aristotle would show that their intention was virtuous. (See Chapter 5.3 'Only voluntary actions can be virtuous' page 171)

**Situation 2:** This is the case we discussed earlier under natural law.

> A mad axeman comes to your door and asks the whereabouts of his victim, who is your friend, and who is hiding inside your house. Do you lie to him?

If you look back at the discussion of lying, in Aquinas' natural moral law, we concluded that Aquinas in the same situation might have returned an evasive answer, for example: 'I saw him at a football match two hours ago', which would be a truth, but an evasive truth. With Aristotle's virtue ethics, an evasive answer is of course a deception, since you are not telling the mad axeman what he wants to know. Nevertheless, virtue ethics can deal with the situation effectively.

The virtues involved are the friendship, loyalty and honour that you should show to your friend, balanced against the honesty and truthfulness you should show to other people. If your character is truthful and honest, then you will be justified in telling a lie on this occasion because in this situation, as in situation 1, lying / being dishonest becomes the mean. Common sense would tell you that in such a situation, saving your friend's life is the right thing to do. (Note 4) Moreover, telling a lie on this occasion will not lead you to become an untruthful or dishonest character in the future. You make the decision through your own virtuous character as a man of practical wisdom. The same would hold if you lied to save the life of a stranger, in which case you would also practise the virtues of empathy, compassion and understanding.

## Discussion points

- To what extent do you think that the decisions of virtue ethics are common sense?

- Situation: You are a medical doctor and you are a firm believer in Aristotelian virtue ethics. You come across a traffic accident in which you know that one of the people concerned will die. She asks you whether she will be alright. What do you reply?

- Adultery almost always involves lying. Are there any situations in which someone who follows Aristotelian virtue ethics could accept adultery as a virtuous act?

- You are married to a man you think of as the epitome of virtue. You overhear a telephone conversation in which it is clear that your husband has killed somebody. You confront him, and he tells you that this is the case, but he insists that the killing is justified, because the person X he has killed was someone who has used his wealth and power to attack women. One of the women he has attacked and raped is your husband's sister. The police interview you concerning the whereabouts of your husband on the occasion of the death of X. Are you morally justified (in terms of virtue ethics) in giving your husband a false alibi?

# Application to issues of human life and death

You are required to look at four issues:

- embryo research; cloning; 'designer' babies
- abortion
- voluntary euthanasia and assisted suicide
- capital punishment.

# Issue 1: Embryo research; cloning; 'designer' babies

## Embryo research and cloning

### The facts include:

An embryo here refers to the earliest stage of the development of a human up to the beginning of the third month of pregnancy, after which it is called a foetus. Embryo research is where scientists extract 'embryonic stem cells' from human embryos, mainly from those that have been left over from IVF (*in vitro* fertilisation). Embryonic stem cells are those from which all the 200+ kinds of tissue in the human body originate. Human embryo research is undertaken because animal embryos are not sufficiently compatible to be used in research affecting humans.

The aim of embryo testing is to find cures for the diseases that affect humans, such as Alzheimer's and Parkinson's. UK law allows experimentation on human embryos up to the fourteenth day, on the grounds that this is the point in an embryo's development when the individual person starts to develop. This is disputed, since there are many different definitions of when a person becomes a person.

A more reliable method for carrying out this research is to make an 'embryonic clone' of the patient. Cloning is the name given to a process by which scientists make biological duplicates of an organism. The embryonic clone is destroyed in order to harvest its stem cells. This is called 'therapeutic cloning', and since the cells are cloned from the patient, they are less likely to be rejected by the patient's immune system. Therapeutic cloning has the potential to lead to cures for a whole range of diseases and conditions, including diabetes, stroke, arthritis, multiple sclerosis and heart failure.

### The main ethical issues include:

- 'Harvesting' embryonic stem cells destroys the embryo. Is the embryo to be seen as a person? If the embryo is regarded as a person, then it has rights and killing it can be seen as murder.
- Cloning, in particular, is seen by some as 'playing God'.

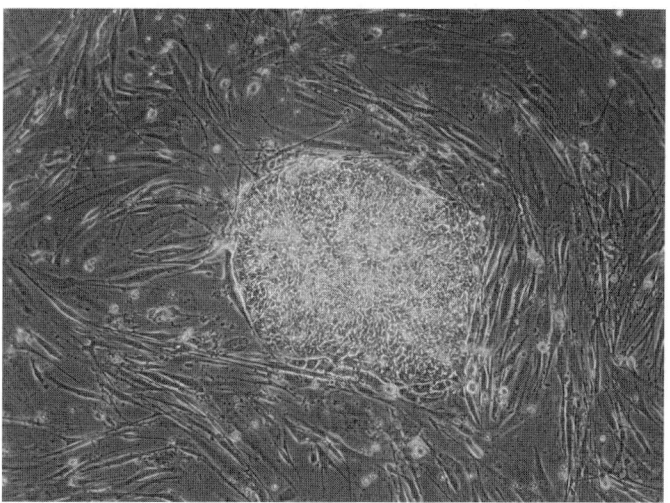

▲ Embryonic stem cells

### 'Designer' babies

**The facts include:**

Designer babies are the result of the editing of DNA cells or embryos. An embryo is first made by IVF. Within five days a single cell is removed from the embryo and genetically tested. If the parents decide to go further, it is implanted in the mother's womb or else it is destroyed. The process of genetic selection of the embryo is called Pre-implantation Genetic Diagnosis (PGD), which means that doctors can check for conditions such as Down's syndrome and cystic fibrosis. This information can be used to select the sex of a child, to treat a sick sibling (a brother or sister) and eventually it will become possible to engineer the intelligence and appearance of children.

**The main ethical issues include:**

- This might contribute to a 'dystopia', meaning one of the worst kinds of societies one can imagine, where parents who can afford it create a kind of super-race, whereas those who cannot are seen as second-class citizens.
- Valuing a child for what you want it to be rather than what it is.
- The likelihood that the human race would become trans-human, where people would choose (and pay) to have all sorts of different body-types and mental abilities, and eventually post-human, where people will no longer be recognisable as humans as we define ourselves today.
- The belief that in doing all this, humans are taking over God's function as the Creator.

## Issue 1: Embryo research, cloning, 'designer' babies (1) Natural moral law

### Embryo research and cloning

- Aquinas' natural moral law would reject both, since they abandon the usual methods of procreation through loving sexual relationships. Aquinas would see them as a failure to worship God, who is the creator of life. They would also violate a third primary precept, namely the requirement to live in an ordered society: 'scientific' reproduction could lead to the breakdown of the marriage relationship. The Catholic Church rejects such procedures for the same kind of reasons.

- Natural moral law can appeal to a number of biblical texts to support its rejection, for example: Job 31:15, which refers to the belief that God fashions each person in the womb, and particularly Jeremiah 1:5, where (during God's call to Jeremiah to be a prophet) God tells Jeremiah:

> **'Before I formed you in the womb I knew you, and before you were born I consecrated you; I appointed you a prophet to the nations.'**

- The genetic blueprint of a human is present at the moment of conception, so biologically, a human becomes an individual person at that point. The rule which allows experimentation on human embryos up to the fourteenth day can therefore be seen as breaking the commandment not to murder. How strong do you think this argument is?
- The argument that stem cell research / therapeutic cloning has the potential to cure all types of human diseases does not pass the law of double effect, since it is not permitted to do a bad act to achieve a good result.

## 'Designer' babies

- Human life is created *imago Dei* – 'in the image of God' (Genesis 1:26–27), so human reproduction is not something to be tampered with. To design babies so that the image of the human race is eventually changed into a trans-human state seems to go against God's intentions: the 'image' of God would no longer be seen in the human form.
- The production of designer babies would violate the primary precept of living in an ordered society, since it would lead to an even greater gap between the rich and the poor. How convincing do you find such arguments? Can you think of a strong argument to justify creating a child through PGD in order to cure a sick sibling?

# Issue 1: Embryo research, cloning, 'designer' babies (2) Situation ethics

- Fletcher's situation ethics is not in principle opposed to any of these procedures. Humans are (in Fletcher's view) makers, selectors and designers, so if adequate controls are in place then there is no reason why humans should not be redesigned to banish disease and to improve the species.

In *Ethical Aspects of Genetic Control* (Note 5), Fletcher says this:

> **'Take cloning of humans, for example ... There might be a need in the social order at large for one or more people specially constituted genetically to survive long periods outside bathyspheres at great marine depths, or outside space capsules at great heights. Control of a child's sex by cloning, to avoid any one of 50 sex-linked genetic diseases, or to meet a family's survival need, might be justifiable.'**

- Fletcher goes on to say that he would favour making and using man-machine hybrids rather than genetically design people for dull, unrewarding or dangerous roles, even though we cannot see clearly what the promises and dangers of such procedures are. Moreover:

> **' ... All this is going to destroy to some extent our traditional grounds for ethical beliefs.'** (Note 6)

- One of the key elements in situation ethics is love for persons. Fletcher is, in effect, directing the love concerned towards the persons who will benefit from embryo research, cloning and designer babies, rather than towards the embryo or the clone. For Fletcher, the good for 'actual persons' is more important than the good for 'potential persons'.

- Given that these procedures will almost certainly happen in the not-too-distant future, do you think that Fletcher is right to base his *agapeic* calculations on their potential good rather than their potential evil?

## Issue 1: Embryo research, cloning, 'designer' babies (3) Virtue ethics

- In modern contexts, the key virtue referred to by virtue ethicists is that of compassion, since compassion operates in a wide range of contexts such as medical ethics and animal ethics, where empathy and understanding for the plight of others are particularly important. As with situation ethics, compassion is likely to focus on people whose well-being is destroyed by disease rather than on a collection of cells in a petri dish.

- Having said that, virtue ethics is not particularly well equipped to handle some of the questions here. How can we tell the character traits and dispositions of designer babies, for example? With trans-humans, individuals might be bred for specific character traits, such as excessive aggression in a soldier. In other words the dispositions required of potential human beings in the future may not match Aristotle's understanding of the mean. A cloned soldier might operate at the extreme of uncontrolled aggression, anger and malice.

- Part of the problem here is that (as Fletcher says above) physical and mental modification of humans is probably inevitable, since what one country does, others will feel compelled to do also. Can there be a recognisable set of virtues that would go across the huge range of human types that might begin to appear by the middle of this century?

- In the short term, virtue ethicists might argue that stem cell research and therapeutic cloning offer the opportunity to increase human well-being and to develop the virtues of courage and vision through the removal of some or all of the diseases that afflict human beings. It would be right to control unnecessary suffering. The failure to use PGD where it could prevent suffering makes parents / medics / society responsible for the suffering that follows.

- It may be true to say that neither Aristotle nor a modern virtue ethicist would be happy with the future developments of embryo research, cloning and designer babies. They will arguably lead to a society in which there are specific sets of virtues for the different types of future humans. The effect of that will be that the teleological aspect of Aristotle's virtue ethics will be lost: there will be no common set of virtues and no set of dispositions or character traits that will produce a person of practical wisdom. What do you feel about the prospect of such a society?

## Issue 2: Abortion

Abortion is the ending of a pregnancy by removing the foetus or embryo before it can survive outside the uterus.

195

**The main ethical issues include:**

- Is an embryo a person and if so does it have a right to life?
- How should the life of the embryo / foetus be valued against the life of the mother?

# Issue 2: Abortion (1) Natural moral law

- Aquinas held that a human person with a rational soul is present at around 60–80 days after conception. In the *Summa Theologica* (II–II, Qu.64, Art.8) he says:

> 'He that strikes a woman with child does something unlawful: wherefore if there results the death either of the woman or of the animated fetus, he will not be excused from homicide, especially seeing that death is the natural result of such a blow.'

By this he means that whoever causes the death of a foetus in which the rational soul is present is guilty of homicide / murder. Some take this to mean that abortion is justified before the rational soul is present, but Aquinas nowhere makes such a claim. (Note 7)

- It is certainly the case that abortion at any stage fails all the tests for Aquinas' natural moral law. It violates the primary principle of defending innocent life (that of the foetus). It also violates the primary precept of worshipping God: God is the creator of human life, so abortion murders that which God creates.
- The Catholic Church reinforces the approach of natural moral law by forbidding abortion at any stage and for any reason except indirectly, through the principle of double effect. For example, if a woman's life is endangered by pregnancy, an abortion is not allowed because it violates the means-end condition: it uses a bad means (killing the foetus) to achieve the good end of saving one's life. However, to take another example from Pojman (Note 8), if the woman's uterus happens to be cancerous, then she may have a hysterectomy in order to save her life, which will result in the death of the foetus. Removing a cancerous uterus is morally good, and the death of the foetus is the unintended side-effect of the hysterectomy. The death of the foetus is not the means of saving the woman's life – the hysterectomy is. Finally, saving the woman's life is at least as good as saving the foetus. If you look back at the four conditions of double effect (Chapter 4.1 pages 129–130), you will see that this satisfies all four conditions of double effect.
- This approach to abortion is supported by the strong Sanctity of Life Principle based on Genesis 1:26–27 – human life is sacred because it is created in God's image.
- Having said that, the Catholic stance is very hard-line, with no exceptions, even pregnancy resulting from rape or incest. Pojman's comment on the above case is that:

> ' ... given the doctrine of double effect, the woman is really lucky to have a cancerous uterus.' (Note 9)

# Issue 2: Abortion (2) Situation ethics

- Fletcher's approach to abortion is entirely situational. You will remember this, and the following scenario from the Chapter 4.2 Situation ethics (see page 55):

'Several years ago congress passed a special bill giving citizenship to a Roumanian Jewish doctor, a woman, who had aborted 3,000 Jewish women brought to the concentration camp. If pregnant, they were to be incinerated. Even accepting the view that the embryos were 'human lives' (which many of us do not), by 'killing' three thousand the doctor saved three thousand and prevented the murder of *six thousand!*

Is Fletcher right in this situation to make abortion a matter of *agapeic* calculation based on the number of lives saved?

● Fletcher also refers to the following case:

A few years ago a lady in Arizona learned that she might bear a defective baby because she had taken the drug thalidomide. Thalidomide was used to alleviate the symptoms of morning sickness during pregnancy. As a result, about 10,000 babies were born with absence or malformation of their limbs. There were many other side-effects of the drug, including blindness, deafness and heart problems. She asked the court to support her doctor and his hospital in terminating the pregnancy, but the law prohibited non-medically indicated abortions, so the judge refused. Her husband took her to Sweden, and she was aborted there. Fletcher argues that this decision was brave, loving and right. As things turned out, the lady was right in her belief that the embryo would be damaged.

Morally, do you think that a diagnosis of possible physical deformity should give the mother the absolute right to abort a child? Do parents / medics / society have a responsibility, through love, to prevent unnecessary suffering?

● In *Situation Ethics*, (Note 10) Fletcher refers to a case in 1962 where an unmarried girl, ill with radical schizophrenic psychosis, was raped by another patient in a state mental hospital. The girl's father demanded an abortion to be performed at once. The hospital authorities refused, on the grounds that the criminal law prohibited all abortion except when the mother's life is at stake. Fletcher asks:

'May we rightly ... terminate this pregnancy, begun in an act of force and violence by a mentally unbalanced rapist upon a frightened, mentally sick girl?'

In terms of Fletcher's principles of pragmatism, relativism, positivism and personalism, do you agree that abortion is the most loving response to this situation?

● In contrast to natural moral law, Fletcher's *agapeic* calculus is always situational, puts people before rules and assesses the foreseeable consequences. Do these factors mean that situation ethics is always in the best position to make judgements about abortion?

## Issue 2: Abortion (3) Virtue ethics

Aristotle says in his *Politics* that if parents have too many children, abortion should be brought about:

' ... before sense and life have begun.'

(*Politics*: 7, xvi)

Abortion here is a matter for the rules of the city state. For Aristotle, then, abortion should take place before there are signs of an individual human being having been established. We know that these signs appear very early, which is why we have the fourteen day rule about experimentation on human embryos, so Aristotle seems to be taking a similar approach to our own – that it is better to abort 'potential' babies rather than 'actual' babies.

Remember that although there is no requirement to go beyond Aristotle's virtue ethics, you are at liberty to do so if you wish. Rosalind Hursthouse is particularly noted for her work on virtue ethics. Writing on virtue theory and abortion, Rosalind Hursthouse (Note 11) suggests that:

- Abortion is a moral issue that has little to do with what the rules about abortion might say, and nothing to do with someone's rights. Acting within your rights does not mean that you are acting virtuously: you might be acting callously or selfishly.
- The morality of abortion also has nothing to do with whether or not the foetus is a person – we do not know enough about the biological facts to be sure of the status of a foetus.
- The act of abortion is not at all like deciding whether or not to have a tooth out: it is a supremely important decision about whether or not to end a life.
- Thus the reason for having an abortion should not be something comparatively trivial, like the woman worrying about how she will look, or deciding that she does not like morning sickness, or does not want to give up her job: the reason has to be something weighty. Cutting short a life is, otherwise, morally evil.

  **'The virtuous woman has such character traits as strength, independence, resoluteness, decisiveness, self-confidence, responsibility, serious mindedness, and self-determination.'** (Note 12)

  These are virtues that count, and depending on the situation, they are what should govern whether or not an abortion takes place.

- Equally, men and boys (no less than women and girls):

  **' ... can, in their actions, manifest self-centredness, callousness and light-mindedness about life and parenthood in relation to abortion. They can be self-centred or courageous about the possibility of disability in their offspring; they need to reflect on their sexual activity ... and take responsibility for their own actions and life in relation to fatherhood.'** (Note 13)

There is no suggestion that Hursthouse is right in everything she says here, but you can see that her approach gives an excellent example of how virtue theory (as opposed, for example, to natural moral law or situation ethics) can approach the issue of abortion. Comparing the three accounts of abortion we have looked at, does one approach feel 'right'? Are there elements of more than one approach that seem 'right'?

# Issue 3: Voluntary euthanasia and assisted suicide

For a start, do not get hung up on the terminology, since some sources use 'voluntary euthanasia' and 'assisted suicide' interchangeably, and there is certainly overlap in meaning. Some include voluntary refusal of food and fluids as voluntary euthanasia, whereas others see this as a form of suicide. Voluntary euthanasia and assisted suicide are illegal in the UK, although from 2002, euthanasia and physician-assisted suicide became legal in Holland.

Note that you do not have to study involuntary or non-voluntary euthanasia: just voluntary euthanasia. Also, bear in mind that these issues need to be discussed from the point of view of natural moral law, situation ethics and virtue ethics, and not simply in general terms.

## Voluntary euthanasia

- 'Euthanasia' comes from two Greek words meaning 'good death'. To euthanise someone therefore means to induce a gentle and easy death in order to end suffering.
- The request comes because the pain is unbearable and the condition causing it is terminal (or at least life-threatening), and the patient refuses to continue with intrusive medical treatment that can be as unbearable as the suffering caused by the condition itself.
- Euthanasia is therefore a deliberate termination/shortening of life, usually by a doctor.
- *Voluntary* euthanasia is where someone who is mentally stable / in their right mind requests his / her own death.
- The person concerned usually is unable to die without help (from a doctor / physician).

### The ethical issues include:

- The claim that persons are autonomous (free to act independently), and so have an autonomous right to death as well as a right to life.
- The effects on human society where the right to death is granted.

### Assisted suicide

- The person concerned is usually given the means / medicine to *kill himself / herself*, and the patient *asks for* the medicine.
- The medicine is usually a lethal drug administered in the form of a drink provided by a doctor, although it can sometimes involve someone such as a close relative.
- Once the medicine is provided, it can be used at a time of the patient's own choosing.
- The patient's condition may be similar to that described for voluntary euthanasia, including mental competency, although in some cases the condition might not be life-threatening.

### The ethical issues include:

- As with voluntary euthanasia, the right to die.
- The question of whether or not those who assist are guilty of murder.

# Issue 3: Voluntary euthanasia and assisted suicide (1) Natural moral law

- Aquinas in effect rejected any form of euthanasia or suicide:

    ' … The passage from this life to another and happier one is subject not to man's free-will but to the power of God. Hence it is not lawful for man to take his own life that he may pass to a happier life, nor that he may escape any unhappiness whatsoever of the present life, because the ultimate and most fearsome evil of this life is death ... Therefore to bring death upon oneself in order to escape the other afflictions of this life, is to adopt a greater evil in order to avoid a lesser.'

(*Summa Theologica*, II–II, Qu.64, Art. 5)

- According to Aquinas, then, the most fearsome evil is not pain or disability but death itself. Suicide (he argues) is contrary to the natural inclination of any life form to stay alive; it injures the community as a whole; and life is God's gift to humans, so is subject to his power. Do you agree with these claims?
- In terms of natural moral law, neither voluntary euthanasia nor assisted suicide can be justified, because they reject the primary precepts of preserving life and worshipping God (since life is God's gift to humans). They also reject the precept of living in an ordered society, and this is a fear shared by many governments today, where the fear is that following the example of the Netherlands and legalising voluntary euthanasia and physician-assisted suicide might eventually open the door to compulsory euthanasia.
- The 1980 *Declaration on Euthanasia* is the Catholic Church's official document about euthanasia and reinforces Aquinas' judgements. Euthanasia and assisted suicide ignore the value of suffering for salvation (as seen in the value of Christ's suffering on the cross).

However, the Catholic Church allows dying to proceed without medical intervention that would become extraordinary or disproportionate. As the nineteenth-century English poet, Arthur Hugh Clough said, in his poem, *The Latest Decalogue*:

'Thou shalt not kill; but needst not strive

Officiously to keep alive ... '

- Most Christians refer to the Sanctity of Life Principle when arguing against voluntary euthanasia or assisted suicide, or refer to the 'dignity of life'. Consider this case:

### The case of Chantal Sébire

Chantal Sébire was refused the right to die by a French court. She suffered from a disfiguring and incurable facial tumour. Shortly after the court's refusal, she was found dead, apparently through her own act.

'[Her] case caught France's attention when the media published heart-breaking before-and-after pictures that made her suffering instantly apparent. The tumour burrowed through her sinuses and nasal cavities, causing her nose to swell to several times its original size, and pushing one of her eye sockets out of her head.' (Note 14)

Try to be objective in answering this question: Where is 'dignity' to be found in this case? In the rejection by the French court as a matter of law? In the rejection of her action through the arguments of natural moral law? In her own actions? Is there a clear answer?

# Issue 3: Voluntary euthanasia and assisted suicide (2) Situation ethics

With cases of physician assisted suicide (PAS), in countries where this is legal, a doctor provides the patient with the means to commit suicide, and the drugs are usually self-administered so that the act is seen to be the patient's own decision.

Take the hypothetical case of Jim, 45, who has a terminal disease. His life expectancy is 8 months, and the condition will deteriorate to the point that he will be in great pain for several months.

How would situation ethics view his case? There are no set rules to be applied – a situation ethicist would probably think that Jim has a right to die as well as a right to life. The case has to be judged on its own merits, for example:

● Is his choice rational, made without family pressure?

● Is he suffering from depression, which might at some point change?

● How correct is the diagnosis likely to be, given that some people can live for years rather than months, for example when a disease goes into remission?

● Has his choice to die been approved by more than one competent medical authority?

In summary, then, situation ethics would try to find a rational, pragmatic and personal decision appropriate to Jim's case.

In your opinion, should someone who follows situation ethics campaign to make PAS legal in the UK?

● In his discussion of euthanasia in *Morals and Medicine* (1954), [Note 15], Fletcher asks what purposes are sufficient to justify the loss of one's life, and suggests that relief from demoralising pain where there is no further possibility of serving others, is sufficient. We should believe in the sacredness of personality, but not in mere existence in terms of the length of time that we live.

'To prolong life uselessly, while the personal qualities of freedom, knowledge, self-possession and control, and responsibility are sacrificed is to attack the moral status of a person.' [Note 16]

● Fletcher always admits that there are risks in the decisions of *agape*. Given that we cannot know where all the risks will lead, do you agree with Fletcher that risk is justified in the name of love?

# Issue 3: Voluntary euthanasia and assisted suicide (3) Virtue ethics

If a person is in a state where he or she is no longer able to achieve *eudaimonia*, then further living would seem to be pointless, in which case Aristotle might accept that voluntary euthanasia or assisted suicide are the courageous option. Alternatively, enduring pain might be equally courageous, depending on one's disposition and occupation.

Cardinal, Jones and Hayward offer a useful discussion of assisted suicide in the context of virtue ethics, (Note 17), citing the case of Michael Haneke's film *Amour* (2012), which is about a married couple, Anne and George, both ex-piano teachers in their 80s, living in a flat in Paris:

> Anne suffers a stroke and undergoes surgery, leaving her paralysed and unable to play the piano. Anne tells George that she doesn't want to go on living. George tries to look after her, but she suffers a second stroke and now has severe dementia and is incapable of speech. Both George, as a carer looking after his dying loved one, and his wife, Anne, are undergoing unbearable suffering. At the end of the film, George tells the non-responsive Anne a story and then kills her by smothering her with a pillow. He then adorns the bed with flowers – his last act of love for her. (Note 18)

Cardinal, Jones and Hayward discuss this as a case of competing virtues: the virtues of charity and love that prompt George to kill his wife, and the virtue of justice, which normally prevents killing. There is no doubt that Aristotle would place justice above charity and love, since he regards murder in the same light as theft and adultery: as actions that can never be justified. In the case of George and Anne, George could have opted to take a stand based on courage and justice by not killing her and by sharing her pain. Nevertheless the competing virtues of charity and love, also mercy and compassion, suggest that George's act is not murder at all, but is the kind of justifiable homicide that happens when people defend themselves from attack and where George is enabling his wife's wish to die. In this case, the attack is from the twin enemies of stroke and dementia, in which case we can perhaps hold that assisted suicide in this case is not murder at all, but justified homicide. You will remember that Aristotle holds that a sense of regret is a strong indication of a virtuous intention, and there is no doubt that George feels intense regret.

Consider the following questions:

● Virtue ethics does not show us how to act in such a situation: the decision depends on practical wisdom. Is this satisfactory in dealing with voluntary euthanasia and assisted suicide?
● In the modern context, which virtues should govern the actions of doctors when confronted with people who ask to be euthanised because of unbearable pain and the imminence of death, for example, in the case of Chantal Sébire referred to above?
● What virtues and dispositions might a virtue ethicist refer to in Fletcher's case of Jim, referred to above?
● 'Rules cannot decide on the rightness or wrongness of voluntary euthanasia and assisted suicide: only virtues can decide.' How far do you agree with this claim?

# Issue 3: Capital punishment

Capital punishment is state-sanctioned killing, either on the basis of retribution or deterrence.

**The ethical issues include:**

● Does capital punishment amount to unjustified killing?
● Is retribution, or deterrence, a sufficient justification for allowing capital punishment?
● Does capital punishment brutalise the society that practises it?

Consider these three issues in relation to the following case; where many people feel that the death penalty should have been given.

> On August 15, 1990, Angel Diaz, age nineteen, was sentenced in the Bronx for the murder of an Israeli immigrant who had employed one of Diaz's friends. After strangling the man with a shoelace and stabbing him, Diaz and four friends donned Halloween masks to rob, beat and gang-rape the man's wife and sixteen-year-old daughter. The women were then sexually tortured while the murdered man's three-year-old daughter watched from her crib.
>
> Angel Diaz already had been convicted of burglary four times before he was sixteen years old. Diaz's lawyer, Paul Auerbach, said that Diaz was an honest boy forced by poverty to do bad things. (Note 19)

- Diaz was sentenced to prison. Do you think this was an appropriate response to his crimes, or should he have received the death penalty?
- What should have been the motive for punishing Diaz: retribution, deterrence or the hope of reformation in prison?
- Do you think that execution of Diaz would have had a brutalising effect on society?

# Issue 3: Capital punishment (1) Natural moral law

In *Summa Theologica*, II–II, Qu.64, Art. 3, Aquinas has this to say:

> Now it is lawful for any private individual to kill a wild beast, especially if it be harmful. Therefore for the same reason, it is lawful for any private individual to kill a man who has sinned.
>
> … It is lawful to kill an evildoer in so far as it is directed to the welfare of the whole community, so that it belongs to him alone who has charge of the community's welfare. Thus it belongs to a physician to cut off a decayed limb, when he has been entrusted with the care of the health of the whole body. Now the care of the common good is entrusted to persons of rank having public authority: wherefore they alone, and not private individuals, can lawfully put evildoers to death.

In other words, Aquinas says that capital punishment is legitimate, but is not the responsibility of individuals, because that becomes mere revenge and can get out of hand; so capital punishment has to be carried out by somebody appointed for the task by the state. This does not mean that the executioner becomes a murderer, because just as God authorised the Israelites to kill their enemies, the state authorises the executioner to kill criminals.

With regard to the case of Angel Diaz, then, Aquinas would probably have argued that just as it is lawful to kill a harmful wild beast, it would be right to execute Diaz because his actions threatened society. Moreover, Aquinas' views suggest that Diaz's guilt would require execution as a just punishment (retribution) to serve as a deterrent to others.

**The Catholic Church gives qualified assent to the principles of Aquinas' natural moral law.**

Article 2267 of the *Catechism of the Catholic Church* states:

Assuming that the guilty party's identity and responsibility have been fully determined, the traditional teaching of the Church does not exclude recourse to the death penalty, if this is the only possible way of effectively defending human lives against the unjust aggressor. If, however, non-lethal means are sufficient to defend and protect people's safety from the aggressor, authority will limit itself to such means, as these are more in keeping with the concrete conditions of the common good and more in conformity to the dignity of the human person. Today, in fact, as a consequence of the possibilities which the state has for effectively preventing crime, by rendering one who has committed an offense incapable of doing harm – without definitely taking away from him the possibility of redeeming himself – the cases in which the execution of the offender is an absolute necessity are very rare, if not practically non-existent.

The Catechism still refers to protection and deterrence as the motive for allowing capital punishment, but places more emphasis on the possibility of reforming the criminal. As Michael Wilcockson points out:

> **'Total exclusion of capital punishment would weaken the Church's view of war and the principle of legitimate killing of the wicked in that context.'** [Note 20]

Some natural moral law theorists support capital punishment by referring to the law of '*talion*', meaning 'retribution'. This law is found, for example, in Genesis 9:6:

> **'Whoever sheds the blood of man, by man shall his blood be shed.'**

# Issue 3: Capital punishment (2) Situation ethics

Situation ethics has no set view on capital punishment. Its response to the crime carried out by Angel Diaz and his friends would, like any other situation involving the possibility of capital punishment, be assessed situationally in terms of how an average individual would interpret the demands of love.

In the case of Angel Diaz, it would be false simply to claim that somebody who follows situation ethics would automatically follow one particular course of action. Some situationists might disagree as to whether or not Jesus was a pacifist, which would then affect their view of the appropriateness of capital punishment. Some might have different ideas about whether or not capital punishment brutalises society. Some might disagree about the aims of punishment, so those who accept the value of retribution and deterrence might demand capital punishment, whereas those who prefer the idea that even murderers like Diaz should have the chance to reform might recommend imprisonment.

Fletcher's point would be that there are no rules which compel you to respond one way or the other, so you have to decide in the light of your own views as to what love demands in the situation. The tools that you use to make your decision are always the same: they are the basic presuppositions and principles of Christian action. Moreover, we are free to decide, and because we cannot escape freedom we cannot avoid decision.

An example of the difficulties of decision-making would be the arguments of situation ethics in favour of capital punishment for a man the state knows to be innocent but executes in order to maintain public order – a typical situation in which the established rules seem to result in an unloving outcome. The decision to execute one man would be unloving towards him, but would be pragmatic in applying love to the majority. Just as the theory of utilitarianism might reach this decision by applying its principle of the 'greatest happiness for the greatest number', situation ethics could use its principle of maximising love: 'the greatest love for the greatest number'.

# Issue 3: Capital punishment (3) Virtue ethics

When it comes to capital punishment, virtue ethics is no more of an exact tool for making decisions about the issue than is situation ethics. This is probably true both for the time of Aristotle and in the modern era.

Capital punishment is not discussed by Aristotle. As a punishment for various crimes, capital punishment was in use in Athenian society, so Aristotle presumably assumed that its use was part and parcel of life in the Greek city states. By the time of Socrates, execution by poison was one way of doing things, since he was sentenced to death by drinking poison hemlock, allegedly for 'impiety' and for corrupting the youth of Athens.

Capital punishment is, of course, about justice, a virtue for which Aristotle says there is no excess and no deficiency. Justice is altruistic – it is about the good of others and is an end in itself. Justice requires people to be brave, considerate, temperate, courageous and magnanimous – in fact, says Aristotle, in justice:

'... every virtue is summed up.'

(*Nicomachean Ethics* 1129b 29)

As we saw in the section on Aristotle's virtue ethics, in one sense justice is about rectifying / balancing / restoring the distribution of gain and loss between two people, for example, where loss has occurred during trading, or through theft, or through loss of, or damage to, an eye or a limb when one person assaults another. In this respect, then, where one person murders another, the balance still has to be rectified, even though the victim is dead, and the only way this can be done is for the state to kill the murderer. Perhaps, then, this is how Aristotle would deal with the issue of capital punishment.

In terms of what Aristotle says about voluntary actions, we are clearly responsible for any actions we intend. If someone murders someone else for vicious reasons, through the vices of spite, malevolence, hatred, envy, jealousy, anger or lust, then this is simply a matter for justice. A person of practical wisdom behaves justly quite simply by obeying the law and by being seen to obey it. For somebody who voluntarily and viciously disobeys the law by murder, then justice really requires restoration in kind, which requires capital punishment. This is not an issue of choosing between retribution and deterrence on the one hand or reformation on the other.

You can, of course, disagree with Aristotle, but you may find that in doing so you adopt another ethical system and reject virtue theory.

# Application to issues of non-human life and death

To remind you, you are required to look at four issues:

- use of animals as food; intensive farming
- use of animals in scientific procedures; cloning
- blood sports
- animals as a source of organs for transplants.

Since each of these issues has as its theme the potential misuse of animals, the ethical issues are very similar for each one, so for each of the three normative ethical theories, we shall discuss all four issues together under the following headings:

1  The moral status of animals

2  The facts about each of the four issues and ethical issues that arise from the facts

3  How natural moral law, situation ethics and virtue ethics address these issues

## 1 The moral status of animals

There is no agreed definition of the moral status of animals. Animals are denied moral status, for example, by those who claim that they have no rationality, that they have no souls, that they have no consciousness or that they cannot speak. They are given moral status by those who claim they have rationality, that they do have souls, that they are conscious and that they can communicate. The utilitarian philosopher, Jeremy Bentham, argued that having moral status comes from the ability to feel pleasure and pain; animals can feel both pleasure and pain, therefore according to Bentham they have moral status.

The facts are relatively simple:

- Animals have consciousness and are sentient (self-aware). To think otherwise is to ignore the facts. (Note 21)
- Animals exhibit complex social and co-operative behavioural patterns, emotional responses and self-directed behaviour. They can grieve and show empathy.
- The most intelligent animals possess long-term memory and can understand simple symbolic language. Chimpanzees can use computer imagery to demonstrate a vocabulary of 1,500 words, and in some short-term numerical memory tests can out-perform humans. (Note 22)

Clearly, other animals are not as intelligent as humans, but intelligence is not the only measure of value, otherwise we would not protect the mentally weaker members of our society. It is difficult to make any judgement about moral awareness in animals beyond what we observe in their patterns of social behaviour, although much the same can be said of a considerable proportion of the human race.

In summary, other animals possess sentience, social organisation and cognitive skills.

## 2 The facts about each of the four issues and the ethical issues that arise from the facts

### 1 Use of animals as food; intensive farming

Note: 'Intensive' farming does not refer just to factory farming of animals. It includes the mechanisation of agriculture to produce the maximum yield of crops, and this is associated with all sorts of environmental issues, particularly deforestation and environmental warming. Since there is no scope to discuss all these issues here, we shall confine ourselves to intensive farming in the sense of the factory farming of animals.

**The facts:** The two parts of this issue amount to the same thing, since the most widespread use of animals for food is found in the context of intensive farming, or 'factory farming'. Intensive farming can include farming animals in tiny crates for their fur, particularly where it is reported that mink and sable farms often skin the animals alive for the benefit of humans who wish to wear fur or fur accessories. In the food industry, most animals live in crowded and filthy conditions, and suffer painful procedures such as branding, de-horning, de-beaking, having their tails cut off and their teeth sawn off, and again it is reported that this is generally without anaesthetic.

**The ethical issues:** These include:

- The moral right of humans to inflict such pain and suffering on other animals who possess sentience, social organisation and cognitive skills.
- The issue of whether animals have a right to life.
- The fact that the meat industry contributes to human starvation, since, for example, cattle consume around fifteen times more grain than they can produce as meat. It might be ethically preferable, therefore, to decrease meat production and increase that of grain and other crops.

▲ Conditions for factory-farmed chickens

### 2 Use of animals in scientific procedures; cloning

**The facts:** 'Scientific procedures' refers, for example, to using animals to develop drugs and medicines to treat human conditions and diseases; using animals as test-subjects for new therapies. Vaccines and drugs to treat

HIV / AIDS came from research on similar viruses in chickens, cats and monkeys. Penicillin was developed through research on mice and other rodents. Animals are widely used in oncology (study of the prevention, diagnosis and treatment of cancer / tumours), for example: for understanding the growth of cancer cells, the role of viruses in causing cancer, the use of hormone treatment to limit tumour growth, and the effects of chemotherapy and radiotherapy.

Cloning refers to the process of producing genetically identical copies of a plant or an animal. The copied individual is the clone. The technology has a number of applications, for example: preserving endangered species; 'improving' animals to make them disease-resistant or to increase the meat or fur yield; therapeutic cloning of cells in order to understand diseases and test medicines; mass-production of animals for scientific research.

**The ethical issues:** These include:

- The moral right of humans to do research without consent on other animals who possess sentience, social organisation and cognitive skills.
- The fact that despite the commitment of many scientists to control animal pain, there are still many scientists who use no anaesthetics at all.
- Duplication of experiments in different countries: there is no co-ordination to lessen the impact on animals.
- For cloning, one of the main concerns is where the technology might lead, for example, with human–animal hybrids.

## 3  Blood sports

**The facts:** 'Blood sports' is a term commonly used to refer to sports that involve animal bloodshed; also to sports that involve the death of the animal. The list is long, and includes, for example: hunting, fishing, hare-coursing, badger-baiting and bull-fighting. Blood sports are for the entertainment of those who participate.

**The ethical issues:** These include:

- The moral right of humans to kill or maim for their own amusement, other animals who possess sentience, social organisation and cognitive skills.
- The negative effect on human psychology, in so far as those who participate can become hardened (or desensitised) to animal suffering and can transfer it to their treatment of humans.

▲ The blood sport of bull-fighting

## 4 Animals as a source of organs for transplants

**The facts:** The technical term for this is 'xenotransplantation', which is the transfer of cells / tissues / organs from one species to another, for example, the transplantation of human tumour cells into mice for research on tumours / cancers. One aim is to use pig hearts that have been genetically engineered (to prevent rejection and blood clotting) in order to give life-saving heart transplants for humans.

**The ethical issues:** These include:

- The moral right of humans to use (and thereby kill) animals who possess sentience, social organisation and cognitive skills as sources of body parts for humans.
- The risks of the various procedures, particularly the transfer of diseases and viruses from animals to humans. For example, human contact with chimpanzee blood possibly transmitted an immune deficiency from chimpanzees to humans, where it mutated into HIV. HIV / AIDS is now a global pandemic.

# 3 How natural moral law, situation ethics and virtue ethics address these issues

## Natural moral law

Aquinas adopted Aristotle's hierarchy of the souls of plants, animals and humans:

Table of the hierarchy of souls

|  | Soul | Characterised by |
|---|---|---|
| plants | vegetative | ● nutrition and growth |
| animals | sensitive | ● nutrition and growth<br>● movement<br>● sense perception and (low-level) thought |
| humans | rational | ● nutrition and growth<br>● movement<br>● sense perception<br>● reason |

In this hierarchy, the ability of animals to have sense perception and to move means that they are able to make use of plants as a food supply for nutrition and growth. Equally, Aquinas follows Aristotle in assuming that humans, at the top of this hierarchy, have the same right in relation to animals. Animals were created, in Aquinas' view, for any use to which humans choose to put them.

Aquinas refers to humans and 'other animals', holding that:

> Although man is of the same 'genus' as other animals, he is of a different 'species.'
>
> ▲ *Summa Theologica*, I, Qu. 75, Art. 3

From this, Aquinas concluded that humans are the only rational beings. Humans alone are capable of determining their actions, so they are the only beings towards which we should extend concern for their own sakes. Animals have instrumental value only, meaning that they exist for the sake of the humans that use them. Only humans are capable of achieving the final end of union with God, so all other beings exist for humans to achieve that end. This includes killing animals if we want to:

> There is no sin in using a thing for the purpose for which it is [made]. ... Wherefore it is not unlawful if man use plants for the good of animals, and animals for the good of man ... Now the most necessary use would seem to consist in the fact that animals use plants, and men use animals, for food, and this cannot be done unless these be deprived of life: wherefore it is lawful both to take life from plants for the use of animals, and from animals for the use of men. In fact this is in keeping with the commandment of God Himself: for it is written: 'Behold I have given you every herb . . . and all trees . . . to be your meat, and to all beasts of the earth': and again: 'Everything that moveth and liveth shall be meat to you' ... Hence, as Augustine says ... 'by a most just ordinance of the Creator, both their life and their death are subject to our use.
>
> ▲ *Summa Theologica*, II–II, Qu. 64, Art. 1

In the same passage, Aquinas goes on to claim that:

> He that kills another's ox, sins, not through killing the ox, but through injuring another man in his property. Wherefore this is not a species of the sin of murder but of the sin of theft or robbery.

In other words, the killing of another person's ox is nothing more than a property-theft so no restitution is or can be done to the animal: only to its owner.

All in all, therefore, you can see why many people today see Aquinas (along with Aristotle) as a source of more than seven centuries of cruelty towards animals. Where animals are in effect held to have instrumental value, as objects for human use, then cruelty may often result.

## 1 Use of animals as food; intensive farming

- If animals are for human use then Aquinas' natural moral law justifies using animals as food, and it justifies intensive farming procedures.
- Given that it is reportedly not uncommon in factory farming for individuals to bludgeon animals to death as a cheaper method of killing them than sending them to a properly regulated abattoir, then as we have seen, on Aquinas' logic this is not a moral issue.
- The issue of whether animals have a right to life is not relevant to Aquinas' system, since any potential rights for animals are subsumed under the rights of humans, which include the right to use animals in any way they wish.
- The whole approach is justified further by Aquinas' appeal to the Bible.

### Is there any substance to Aquinas' view?

Those who support Aquinas see humanity as having greater value than animals, and that animals were created for human use.

However, it is difficult to see a rational justification for Aquinas' view. For a start he relies on Aristotle's account of the hierarchy of souls, according to which *all* souls have a final end, in which case it must be wrong to interfere with that final end. Consider this argument by Judith Barad:

> The tusks of an elephant are for fighting, and this takes precedence over their use as material for chess pieces … The natural end of an animal is to grow to the state of maturity characteristic of its species; if an activity contributes to the efficient functioning of the animal, then its natural end is to make that contribution. **An animal's capacities have value independent of their usefulness to human beings.** [Note 23]
>
> ▲ [The bold emphasis is the author's own.]

## 2 Use of animals in scientific procedures; cloning

● If the status of animals is no greater than being human property, then the use of animals in scientific procedures is not in itself immoral, particularly as experiments may develop cures for a variety of human diseases. If the animal dies as a result of any scientific procedure, that would be acceptable to Aquinas.

● The use of animals in scientific experiments is acceptable to the Catholic Church, which has presumably been influenced by Aquinas:

> '**Medical and scientific experimentation on animals is a morally acceptable practice, if it remains within reasonable limits and contributes to caring for or saving human lives.**'
>
> (*Catechism of the Catholic Church*, 2417)

● The use of scientific procedures to cure terminal diseases in humans would fulfil the primary precept to preserve (human) life.

● The pain inflicted on animals during experiments would be accepted by Aquinas if it was necessary to the experiment. If the pain was not necessary, and was inflicted by human cruelty, Aquinas would have a different view. Aquinas holds that if a person is cruel to an innocent animal, this is morally wrong, not for the sake of the animal, but because the person concerned:

> ' … **might go on to do the same to men.**'
>
> (*Summa Contra Gentiles* (c.1260–1264), III–II, Ch. 112)

In other words, Aquinas would be concerned about the effects of excessive pain on animals only if it meant that the person inflicting pain developed a tendency to do the same to human beings.

● The nature of some of the experiments done on animals would give Aquinas concern, particularly experiments which would change the nature of the animal, for example, experiments to produce beings that are part-animal and part-human, or that mix the genetic structure of different animals. Given the enormous potential of animal cloning to change the very nature of animal species, Aquinas would probably condemn all such procedures, since each species was created by God to fulfil its purpose as that species. Genetic experimentation within species would probably be acceptable, for example, to increase milk yield, animal size and resistance to disease, and the Catholic Church generally takes this approach.

The *Catechism of the Catholic Church* says further:

> Man's dominion over inanimate and other living beings granted by the Creator ... requires a religious respect for the integrity of creation ... Animals are God's creatures. He surrounds them with his providential care. By their mere existence they bless him and give him glory. Thus men owe them kindness. (2415–2416)

It is fair to say that most people accept experimentation on animals in order to provide cures for human diseases, provided that adequate pain-relief is given. Whether the general approach of Aquinas' natural moral law is based on such kindness is for you to decide.

● The Pontifical Academy of the Roman Catholic Church says that:

**'... There is a place for research, including cloning, in the vegetable and animal kingdoms, wherever it answers a need or provides a significant benefit for man or for other living beings, providing that the rules for protecting the animal itself and the obligation to respect the biodiversity of species are observed.'** [Note 24]

● Animal cloning is now available at a cost for cloning pets: for example, the recent survey of a couple whose dog died of cancer – the dog was cloned and the couple now have one puppy. [Note 25] Given that animal welfare bodies such as the RSPCA are critical of dog cloning on the grounds that they cause pain and distress, with high failure and mortality rates, and that cloned animals frequently suffer physical ailments, natural moral law might reject cloning if the process amounts to unjustified abuse:

**'... even when done to ... animals who are without rational souls.'** [Note 26]

## 3 Blood sports

The use of animals in blood sports meets with little or no objection from Aquinas' natural moral law approach:

● Humans can use animals as they see fit, which includes blood sports.
● The pain and suffering inflicted upon animals is acceptable as part of that use.
● If the animal dies as a result of the blood sport, then that too is acceptable, since it is a result of legitimate use.
● Although the general tone of the *Catechism of the Catholic Church* is that of Aquinas, nevertheless it does say the following:

**' ... Men owe [animals] kindness. We should recall the gentleness with which saints like St. Francis of Assisi or St. Philip Neri treated animals.'** (2416).

**'It is contrary to human dignity to cause animals to suffer or die needlessly.'** (2418)

Given that there is nothing 'kind' about blood sports, and that blood sports cause animals to 'suffer and die needlessly', these comments do amount to a more reasonable approach than that of Aquinas. Little of this is translated into action, however, although Catholic groups have called on the Pope to take action over blood sports in line with Church ideas about the human responsibility for the 'stewardship' of creation (Genesis 1:26).

- It is hard to see how an animal that is killed or maimed as the result of human blood sports can have a chance of fulfilling the end for which it was created by God.

## 4 Animals as a source of organs for transplants

As with animal cloning, the use of animals as a source of organs for transplants is not an issue that Aquinas would have thought about, nevertheless his account of natural moral law would on the whole approve of it:

- Humans do have the moral right to use animals in any way they see fit, so with certain safeguards, using animals as a source of organs for transplants would probably be acceptable to Aquinas' natural moral law. The safeguards would include a ban on any attempt to modify the human germline*, which would be a modification of God's blueprint for humans at creation.

This safeguard is reflected in the recommendations of the Catholic Medical Association (UK):

'... We are opposed to any xenotransplantation which might modify the germline*, and particularly to any transplantation of sex organs or gametes**. We are opposed to any use of human tissue for transplantation into animals.' [Note 27]

[*The term 'germline' means inherited material that comes from the eggs or sperm and which is passed on to offspring. **A gamete is the male or female reproductive cell.]

- Whereas the Catholic Medical Association insists that all such procedures be carried out with due concern for animal pain and suffering, no such concern would be required by Aquinas.
- It is hard to see how an animal that is killed as the result of having its organs removed for transplantation into humans can have a chance of fulfilling the end for which it was created by God, unless it is accepted that this end is to serve human beings.

# Situation ethics

With situation ethics, it is sometimes difficult to see where the theory takes us. Perhaps the main issue is that of 'personalism'. By definition, Fletcher's situation ethics is concerned with persons. *Agape* love in the Bible is also primarily concerned with persons. This does not mean that animals are of no concern in situation ethics, but it does mean that human interests will generally be put first.

Many who agree with situation ethics do see animals as being included in God's love. *Agape* love is inclusive rather than exclusive, and there is no intrinsic reason why it should not apply to animals as objects of human care. Having said that, in life or death situations, most situation ethicists would put human life before animal life.

With Fletcher's situation ethics, then, much of what we discuss here will depend on your own interpretation of how *agape* love might be applied to particular situations regarding animals.

# 1 Use of animals as food; intensive farming

Bear in mind that Fletcher urges people to make *agapeic* calculations: we need to ask ourselves:

What end do we seek? What means do we use to obtain them? What motive is behind our act? What are the foreseeable consequences?

The use of animals as food would seem to be a habit as old as humanity itself. Without the existence of animals, it is probable that the human race would have died out, since hunting for food went on for thousands of years before the development of agriculture. The human digestive system is adapted to eating meat, so it would seem 'natural' for humans to use animals as food.

Two main things have affected this point of view:

1 First, the introduction of intensive farming of animals means that 'hunting animals for food' has changed to 'exploiting animals for food', since the methods used in factory farming are almost universally exploitative, cruel and unjust.

2 Further, the mechanisation of agriculture has contributed to a huge population increase globally.

These two factors are mutually reinforcing, since continual population growth fuels the need for intensive farming, so the cruelty to animals increases on a massive scale.

- Current estimates are that about 795 million people are undernourished, having insufficient food to lead an active and healthy life. This is particularly true in less economically developed countries, where around 12.9 per cent of the population is undernourished. (Note 28)
- Some who follow situation ethics would argue that the most loving thing to do in this global situation is to increase intensive animal farming and the mechanisation of agriculture, since this puts persons first. They might argue that the spectacle of starving children is worse than the practice of intensive animal farming.
- Other situation ethicists could argue that this is not loving, because the calculations maximise misery rather than love, and look for short-term rather than long-term solutions to the problem. The fact is that the meat industry contributes to human starvation, since, for example, cattle consume around fifteen times more grain than they can produce as meat and it could be seen as more loving to abandon intensive animal farming for more productive methods. Factory farming of animals should therefore be abandoned in favour of the production of crops. Moreover, new technologies should be developed for growing meat in laboratories, where the meat does not come from any kind of animal. Solutions such as these are pragmatic and treat animals as objects of loving concern.

# 2 Use of animals in scientific procedures; cloning

- Fletcher himself was involved in cloning research and had clear views on bio-ethics. In particular, he advocated the use of animals in scientific procedures as the means to the end of human welfare, and as a pragmatic way of saving human lives by the development of vaccines for the major diseases that cause so much human suffering.

- Various surveys taken in the UK show a fairly steady support (around 80–90 per cent) for the use of animals in scientific experiments for developing cures for major diseases such as diabetes, HIV / AIDS, cancer, coronary artery disease and stroke. Most people at the same time stress the need for adequate control of pain for the animals concerned. Most of those who support situation ethics would probably agree with both these points as the most practical, effective and *agapeic* ways of addressing the general problem of human diseases.
- On this kind of approach, for situation ethics, the *agapeic* end of human welfare is achieved by the means of animal testing. The end justifies the means.
- Some argue, however, that it can never be loving to subject an animal to the kinds of test that experimentation requires. Moreover, although it is claimed that pain controls for animals are extensive, this is often disputed. Here is one of the comments from the PETA(UK) website (People for the Ethical Treatment of Animals), concerning their investigations into the practices of pharmaceutical companies, universities and other institutions:

> For example … mice had tubes inserted into their brains, then were subjected to major organ damage and surgical mutilation, starved and deprived of water for days, and forced to run on treadmills to avoid electric shocks. When no longer needed, animals were killed using disturbing methods such as carbon dioxide poisoning in gas chambers or decapitation of infant rats with scissors. (Note 29)

- When it comes to animal cloning, public opinion is generally not in favour, because of the effects on the animal itself (see previously under natural moral law), and because of uncertainty about where animal cloning (as well as human cloning) will lead. Since situation ethics does not attempt to provide 'right' answers to ethical issues and situations, individuals are required to make up their own minds, and this may (or may not) involve an element of risk, depending on the *agapeic* calculations that people make in different situations.

## 3 Blood sports

- It is likely that most situation ethicists would not put the interests of humans before those of animal species in cases where human pleasures are gained at the expense of animal pain and suffering.
- In particular, the nature of the human pleasure can be said to degrade those who take part in blood sports, for example, because it may damage the character, perhaps leads to other forms of violence, and desensitises people into allowing people to inflict pain for pleasure.
- There is arguably nothing *agapeic* about blood sports. This quotation comes in various forms, but Oscar Wilde described the occupation of the English country gentleman galloping after a fox as, 'the unspeakable in pursuit of the inedible'. Its ban in England, Wales and Scotland would appear to support the view that fox-hunting is unethical. Limitations on blood sports have been enacted in many parts of the world.
- It is probably the case that a situation ethicist could construct a case that fox-hunting is *agapeic*, for example, on the grounds that: foxes reputedly do great damage to stocks of chicken and lamb; hunting is

215

part of the human make-up, and is less unloving than factory farming; and fox-hunting conserves the environment. You should make your own *agapeic* judgement.

## 4 Animals as a source of organs for transplants

The same general considerations that we have referred to in connection with the use of animals in factory farming, for scientific procedures and in blood sports, apply also to their use as a source of organs for transplants.

- Fletcher's situation ethics is directed at persons. For most people, animals do not qualify as persons in the strict sense, although for others they do; so again, answers to questions about the use of animals as a source of organs for transplants will depend on the situation and on what the individual thinks about the status of animals.
- It seems likely that the main question here is, 'Who is to be helped?', and an immediate answer includes 'all those in need of transplants for organs', not least the heart, so transplantation from animals to humans would help persons.
- An *agapeic* calculus here needs to be future-looking, since the technology does not yet exist in usable form. The most likely donors are pigs, since their body organs are similar in size to ours, and pigs are readily available (whereas chimpanzees are an endangered species). The calculus would also have to consider the possibility of transmitting infections from donor to recipient, although Fletcher points out that *agapeic* calculations always carry some risk, otherwise there would be no need for calculation in the first place.
- Some situation ethicists will of course insist that as beings with social and cognitive functions, other animals qualify as persons, so donors should be dead or consenting humans. That does not solve the problem, since there will probably never be sufficient human donor organs available to meet the demand. At the moment, then, humans are the only pragmatic source of donor organs, so the most loving thing might be to pursue other technologies as they are developed.

# Virtue ethics

Aristotle is of course the source of Aquinas' hierarchy of souls in which plants are for animal use and animals are for human use. Cows eat grass and humans eat cows. There were no factory farms in Aristotle's time, and no scientific procedures in the modern sense, although Aristotle did dissect animals as part of his own investigations into animal behaviour.

As we said about Aquinas, this kind of hierarchical approach has dominated European thinking for a long time – in the case of Aristotle for more than 2,300 years. His whole approach to animals is based on his teleological view that all things have a final end – a reason which governs their existence, what they do and what they can achieve.

In terms of the four issues to be discussed, we therefore have to adapt Aristotle's thinking into a modern context.

# 1  Use of animals as food; intensive farming

- Given Aristotle's hierarchy of souls, Aristotle himself would have had no ethical problem with eating meat, since he considered that animals existed for the sake of humans.

- In a modern context, however, it is not clear how Aristotle would have reacted to the methods of intensive animal farming. Let us take just one example: the factory farming of chickens. These unfortunate animals live in crowded and filthy conditions. It is estimated that around 60 per cent of chickens are produced in industrial systems, in some of which they are fed drugs to encourage abnormal growth. They can become so heavy that their legs break, being unable to bear their body weight; they live in their own filth, unable to turn round; the overcrowding makes them aggressive, so many have untreated body-sores. Male chicks cannot produce eggs, so are useless to the egg industry, so a common treatment is that they are thrown into trash bags and left to suffocate, or else they are ground up alive. This is only one small part of the mass of animal suffering caused by intensive farming. The sum total is unimaginably vile. What virtues could Aristotle refer to in support of eating factory-farmed food?

▲ Discarded male chicks

- Here, perhaps the main virtue we need to consider is that of compassion. Compassion cannot be compartmentalised so that we talk about compassion just for humans: you are either a compassionate person or you are not. If you are, then compassion must apply to all animals, human and non-human. Factory-farming of animals is not even remotely compassionate.

- We might reply that the virtues must be directed towards persons, and not towards animals, but again, if Aristotle were to be brought back to life and given a tour of the conditions under which factory-farmed animals live, what could he point to in such conditions that could lead a person to develop a virtuous character?

## 2 Use of animals in scientific procedures; cloning

Given what we have said previously concerning the opinion of most people that animals should be used in scientific procedures, this issue presents somewhat different concerns for a virtue ethicist.

● Aristotle himself used animals in his own scientific researches, so quite clearly he would regard such procedures as compatible with a virtuous character.

● Moreover, you will remember that Aristotle insisted that the highest thing in us is reason, that is, our intelligence – our intellect (*Nicomachean Ethics* 1177a 20–21) – we use our intelligence to do science, to discover what the world is really like, and there can be no achievement of reason greater than that. Using animals in scientific procedures extends our intellect and increases knowledge, and so is virtuous on that level.

● Moreover, the benefits of scientific research include the ability to develop drugs and medicines to control diseases such as HIV / AIDS and cancer. The same is true with animal cloning, which has the potential for controlling specific diseases and conditions in animals, thereby improving animal health. Compassion directed towards humans might therefore suggest that using animals for such research is morally good.

● However, one of the biggest objections to using animals for scientific experiments is that animal pain is not always properly controlled, primarily because some researchers do not care about the suffering of the animals. Some argue that the very fact of using animals in this way can lead researchers to be cruel. At the very least, then, a person of good character would insist upon the control of pain by anaesthetics, since this would be a minimum requirement of the compassion that should be felt for animal suffering as well as for the humans who benefit from the research.

● Other virtue ethicists would object that the use of animals in scientific experiments is not compassionate at all. It is obviously done without the consent of the animals; there is no regulation to avoid experiments being duplicated in different parts of the world; and there are now a number of alternative technologies that are at least as effective as the use of research animals.

● Rosalind Hursthouse argues that experiments on other animals are generally not necessary: the benefits of these experiments are out of proportion to the suffering they cause:

> 'Just as the exercise of virtues such as charity, generosity, justice, and the quasi virtue of friendship, necessarily involve *not* focusing on oneself and one's virtue but on the rights, interests, and good of other human beings, so the exercise of compassion and the avoidance of a number of vices, involves focusing on the good of the other animals as something worth pursuing, preserving, protecting, and so on.' (Note 30)

## 3 Blood sports

● It would be difficult to find convincing arguments against blood sports in Aristotle's writings, since hunting was a common Greek pastime and was a source of food.

● In terms of the modern debate, hunting animals in public will upset and offend some people, as is the case with fox-hunting, where the general disquiet about hunting foxes has led to a ban on the practice in England, Scotland and Wales.

- Some people judge a person by his or her treatment of animals, for example, in terms of the consideration shown to animals that cannot defend themselves. Participation in blood sports suggests to some a lack of consideration for humans as well as for animals.
- Some might appeal to the virtue of temperance, arguing that experiencing pleasure at the expense of other beings is not conducive to developing a good character. In this respect, Rosalind Hursthouse argues that blood sports show the vice of 'callousness' – they are indifferent to the feelings of both the animals concerned and of those who sympathise with the animals. Against that, the philosopher Roger Scruton has delivered several public lectures in which he argues that some blood sports are 'courageous': for example, the matador who faces an enraged bull in the bullring takes his life in his hands.

Who is right? Someone who risks injury or death at the 'hands' of an enraged bull is undoubtedly courageous, but in the context of the bull-ring, Aristotle would probably see this as an inferior form of courage. In the *Nicomachean Ethics*, he says that:

> ' ... It is more courageous to be fearless and calm amid unforeseen dangers than amid those that are clear beforehand ... In the case of foreseen dangers, a person would make his choice on the basis of calculation and reason, whereas in the case of sudden dangers, he would choose in accord with his characteristic.' (1117a 18–22)

The matador facing the bull clearly does show courage, but his courage is based on calculation and reason: since he is skilled in bull-fighting, he will reason that it is unlikely that the bull will kill him. If the matador did assume that the bull would win, the chances are that there would be comparatively few matadors left in the world.

- There are many sports in which a person can demonstrate reasoned courage, for example: heli-skiing, karate, base-jumping, cave diving and mountain climbing, none of which involve being callous to animals. Showing reasoned courage by killing or maiming animals in blood sports would seem to be more callous than courageous.

## 4 Animals as a source of organs for transplants

Most of the arguments concerning the use of animals in scientific experiments apply also to the use of animals as a source of organs for transplants:

- Aristotle's approval of scientific research.
- His emphasis on the development of useful knowledge.
- The compassion shown to humans who might survive through organ transplants.
- The callousness to animals by judging that their lives are expendable.
- The callousness shown towards those in society who are distressed at the prospect of using animals in this way.

219

As a final comment that applies to all the issues discussed here, bear in mind that virtue ethics is not just about which virtues apply to a particular situation. Its main emphasis is on the development of a virtuous character, which brings together all the characteristics of being human. Do you think that virtues are exclusively about how we treat each other or do they apply also to other animal species? If they apply to other animal species, how would a virtuous person act consistently with regard to the issues we have discussed?

## Activity

1 Make your own summary of the responses of Fletcher's situation ethics and Aristotelian virtue ethics to these issues, so that you have a study resource. Use the same approach as shown here for natural moral law.

2 You might want to consider making some general comments about each theory that you could use for evaluating its approach to any ethical issue. For Aquinas' natural moral law, for example:

- Is the theory too rigid for use in modern society?
- Natural moral law is a religious (specifically Christian) ethic. Does it have value for agnostics or atheists?
- Aquinas' natural moral law is based on the views of Aristotle. How relevant to us are moral ideas that were developed over 2,000 years ago?
- The primary precepts of natural moral law include procreation, which has produced a number of secondary precepts that forbid artificial contraception, masturbation, homosexual sex, abortion, IVF, cloning and so on. How useful is this approach to sexual behaviour and to medical research and developments?

# Summary of the application of ethical theories

Below is a summary of the approach of Aquinas' natural moral law to the ethical issues we have looked at.

| Aquinas' natural moral law |
| --- |
| Abbreviations<br>CCC = *Catechism of the Catholic Church*<br>ST = Aquinas' *Summa Theologica*<br>ANML = Aquinas' natural moral law<br>FSE = Fletcher's situation ethics<br>AVE = Aristotle's virtue ethics |

| Issue | Natural moral law response |
| --- | --- |
| Theft | • Violates primary precept of living in an ordered society<br><br>• Secondary precept: 'Do not steal'<br><br>• Aquinas ST: it would be lawful for a man who is starving to death to steal from someone who has more than enough; or for someone to save someone from starvation by stealing on his behalf<br><br>• This would probably be a proportionalist response also<br><br>• The role of double effect in these exceptions<br><br>• Application, for example, to the case of the student who wants to steal (then return) a library book in order to pass an important exam; or stealing a gun from a mentally disturbed individual<br><br>**Evaluation**<br><br>• Is ANML too rigid? Is there such a thing as socially acceptable theft?<br><br>• Which approach to theft is best: ANML, FSE or AVE? Why? |

| | |
|---|---|
| Lying | • Violates primary precept of living in an ordered society<br>• Secondary precept: 'Do not lie'<br>• Links to the biblical commandment not to bear false witness<br>• CCC – lying:<br>' ... offends against the fundamental relation of man and of his word to the Lord ... '<br><br>• Aquinas ST, it is:<br>' ... unnatural ... for anyone to signify by words something that is not in his mind ... '<br><br>• Aquinas ST, therefore:<br>' ... it is not lawful to tell a lie in order to deliver another from any danger whatever ... '<br><br>but it is permissible to:<br>' ... hide the truth prudently, by keeping it back ... '<br><br>• application to the mad axe-murderer<br>**Evaluation**<br>• Is it not common sense to lie to achieve the best outcome?<br>• Are there situations where *not* to lie would be immoral?<br>• Which approach to lying is best: ANML, FSE or AVE? Why?<br>• The white lie |
| Embryo research (ER)<br>Cloning (C)<br>'Designer' babies (DB) | **ER and C**<br>• Harvesting embryonic stem cells seen by the Catholic Church as murder<br>• Therapeutic cloning destroys embryos, so seen as murder<br>• Cloning seen as playing God / usurping God's role as Creator<br>• Such procedures violate the primary precept of procreation (for example, most embryonic stem cells are taken from embryos left over from IVF, which involves masturbation)<br>• Violates primary precept to worship God (the creator of life)<br>• Violates primary precept of living in an ordered society – 'scientific' reproduction could lead to breakdown of the marriage relationship<br>• Biblical statements showing that God fashions and knows each person in the womb (Job 31:15, Jeremiah 1:5)<br>• The genetic blueprint of a human is believed to be present at the moment of conception, so the 14-day rule leads to embryo murder<br>• Stem cell research / therapeutic cloning do not pass the law of double effect – they use a bad act to obtain a good result<br>**DB**<br>• Edits DNA cells or embryos; uses PGD to select embryos / aims at the good of checking for diseases like cystic fibrosis and Down's syndrome / used to select sex of child / treat a sick sibling / other designer features<br>• Uses IVF, so violates primary precept of procreation<br>• Destroys embryos, so seen as murder<br>• Genesis 1:26–27 – *imago Dei* text – designer babies will lead to God's 'image' no longer being seen in human form<br>• Usurps God's role as Creator<br>• Will lead to dystopia, so will violate the primary precept of living in an ordered society |

| | |
|---|---|
| | **Evaluation** |
| | • Do you think that ANML is right to value the potential life of the embryo over the welfare of existing humans? |
| | • In particular, do the potential benefits of ER, C and DB outweigh ANML's concerns about the treatment of embryos? |
| | • Are ANML's views on sex and procreation simply wrong? |
| | • Which approach to ER, C, DB is best: ANML, FSE or AVE? Why? |
| Abortion (A) | • Aquinas ST: a human person with a rational soul is present at around 60–80 days after conception |
| | • Aquinas ST: anyone who causes the death of a foetus with a rational soul is guilty of homicide |
| | • Aquinas does not justify A before the rational soul arrives |
| | • A violates the primary precept to defend innocent life |
| | • The Catholic Church forbids A at any stage for any reason, except indirectly through the principle of double effect, for example, a woman with a cancerous womb may have a hysterectomy to save her life |
| | • This uncompromising approach is supported by the strong Sanctity of Life Principle |
| | • Catholicism allows no exceptions on A, even for pregnancy through rape or incest |
| | **Evaluation** |
| | • The coherence of ANML's stance on A is called into question by its rigidity. In situation ethics, for example, A can be the most loving thing to do in a situation. Rape and incest seem to qualify as appropriate situations |
| | • There is no agreed definition of when a person becomes a person. Does this suggest that until this issue is decided upon, the Catholic Church is right to forbid A? |
| | • Is there any act that is intrinsically evil? If so, is killing the foetus intrinsically evil? |
| | • Would a proportionalist approach to A be preferable to that of ANML? |
| | • Which approach to A is best: ANML, FSE or AVE? Why? |
| Voluntary euthanasia (VE) Assisted suicide (AS) | • Aquinas ST: suicide is contrary to the natural inclination to stay alive; life is God's gift to humans, so is subject to his power |
| | • VE and AS violate the primary precept to preserve life |
| | • They violate the primary precept to maintain an ordered society |
| | • 1980 Catholic Church *Declaration on Euthanasia* – VE and AS ignore the value of suffering for salvation (as seen in the value of Christ's suffering on the cross) |
| | • The Catholic Church does allow dying to proceed without extraordinary or disproportionate medical intervention |
| | • The Sanctity of Life Principle argues against VE and AS |
| | • Case of Chantal Sébire |
| | **Evaluation** |
| | • If humans have a right to life, should they not also have a right to die? |
| | • Aquinas insists that there is a natural inclination to preserve life. Is it not true that at some point there is a natural inclination to die? |
| | • Some suffering can be horrendous, and it is arguably wrong to prevent someone from ending it |
| | • Forbidding VE and AS can be seen as taking away free will |
| | • Which approach to VE and AS is best: ANML, FSE or AVE? Why? |

| Capital punishment (CP) | ● Aquinas ST: it is lawful to kill a wild beast, especially if it is harmful, so it is lawful to kill an evildoer who harms the community |
| --- | --- |
| | ● Aquinas: this must be done by someone appointed by the state, to avoid revenge getting out of hand |
| | ● This does not make the executioner a murderer. Just as God authorised the Israelites to kill their enemies, the state authorises the executioner to kill the state's enemies |
| | ● This allows the use of CP for both retribution and deterrence |
| | ● Case of Angel Diaz |
| | ● CCC gives qualified support. If the criminal will not reform, then CP can be justified to safeguard society |
| | ● Principle of *talion* (retribution) legitimises CP, as in Genesis 9:6: 'Whoever sheds the blood of man, by man shall his blood be shed.' |
| | **Evaluation** |
| | ● ANML in effect argues that retribution and deterrence are more important than reform of the criminal. How far do you agree? |
| | ● Is the principle of *talion* natural justice? |
| | ● If the Bible allows CP, does this mean that ANML must be right in it approach to CP? |
| | ● Which approach to CP is ethically the best: ANML, FSE or AVE? Why? |
| Use of animals as food (F) Intensive farming (IF) | ● Aquinas' approach is governed by Aristotle's hierarchy of souls: animals were created for any human use, including F and IF |
| | ● Aquinas ST: only humans are rational, so animals have instrumental value only, which includes using them for F and IF |
| | ● Aquinas ST: there is no sin in using something for the purpose for which it was intended. Scripture allows us to control and eat animals |
| | ● Aquinas ST: if someone bludgeons another man's ox to death, that is just property theft. Equally, F and IF are just property issues |
| | **Evaluation** |
| | ● 'Aristotle's "hierarchy of souls" is pre-scientific nonsense.' How far do you agree? |
| | ● How useful is Aquinas' view that animals are merely 'property'? |
| | ● Should the Christian virtue of compassion be extended to all animals? |
| | ● The Genesis texts about 'dominion' over animals can also be interpreted to mean that humans should be responsible stewards of other animals. How responsible are F and IF in terms of stewardship? |
| | ● Which approach to F and IF is best: ANML, FSE or AVE? Why? |

| | |
|---|---|
| Use of animals in scientific procedures (SP)<br><br>Cloning (AC) | ● If animals amount to 'property', then SP must be acceptable<br>● CCC: accepts SP if the procedures 'remain within reasonable limits', especially if they lead to saving human lives<br>● Using SP to cure terminal illnesses fulfils the primary precept of preserving (human) life<br>● Aquinas might accept SP even when animals are not given pain relief, since in the ST he says that cruelty to animals is morally wrong only where the person concerned:<br>**'might go on and do the same to men.'**<br><br>● Aquinas might probably condemn AC because it changes the nature of a species, whereas God created each species to fulfil its purpose<br>● The Catholic Church accepts AC to increase milk yield, animal size, resistance to disease, and so on<br>● CCC accepts SP / AC to provide cures for human diseases, provided that adequate pain-relief is given |
| | **Evaluation**<br>● Same as for F / IF, since SP and AC involve much the same considerations<br>● CCC and the Catholic Church make the point that animals must be given pain relief where required, which is an advance on Aquinas<br>● Which approach to SP and AC is best: ANML, FSE or AVE? Why? |
| Blood sports (BS) | ● As for F / IF and SP / AC, 'property' can be used for BS<br>● The pain and suffering inflicted on animals through BS is morally wrong only if it leads humans to be cruel to humans<br>● The death of the animal must be a legitimate use of property<br>● CCC, however, modifies Aquinas' views: Men owe animals kindness, following the example of saints like Francis of Assisi<br>● CCC:<br>**'It is contrary to human dignity to cause animals to suffer or die needlessly.'**<br><br>**Evaluation**<br>● Aquinas' views would allow BS, but the thinking is still outdated: ANML refuses to acknowledge the moral status of other animals<br>● Even on Aquinas' thinking, it is hard to see how animals that are killed or maimed in BS can have a chance of fulfilling the end for which they were created by God, unless we accept that their purpose is for human use<br>● Catholic groups have called on the Pope to take action over BS in line with Church ideas about responsible stewardship<br>● Which approach to BS is best: ANML, FSE or AVE? Why? |

| Animals as a source of organs for transplants (AOT) | ● As with other animal issues, AOT is not an issue that Aquinas would have thought about, but his account of NML would accept it |
|---|---|
| | ● ANM would accept AOT so long as there was no attempt to modify the human germline (that is, to alter God's 'blueprint' for humans) |
| | ● This specific safeguard has been recommended by the CMA – the Catholic Medical Association (UK) |
| | ● The CMA insists that all procedures should minimise animal pain and suffering. |
| | **Evaluation** |
| | ● As with BS, it is hard to see how an animal that is killed as the result of AOT can fulfil the end for which it was created by God |
| | ● It is fair to say that most people accept animal experimentation / AOT where adequate pain relief is given and where animal suffering is minimised. The Catholic Church and the CMA accept this |
| | ● Which approach to AOT is best: ANML, FSE or AVE? Why? |

# Component 2

# Christianity

# 6

# Sources of wisdom and authority

This chapter will cover three sources of wisdom and authority:

● The Bible
● The Church
● The authority of Jesus

A note on Component 2 of the specification: Study of the Christian Religion.

This section of the specification has five parts:

● Sources of wisdom and authority
● God
● Self, death and afterlife
● Good conduct and key moral principles
● Expressions of religious identity.

When studying these parts, it will become apparent that they help you to understand the sections on the Philosophy of religion, and on Ethics and religion. For those who complete the A-Level, the Dialogue section of A-Level looks at the discussion between Christianity and the Philosophy of religion, and between Christianity and Ethics.

In other words, the Specification makes an organic link between its three parts: Christianity, Philosophy of religion and Ethics.

## The Bible

For those whose knowledge of the contents and structure of the Bible is limited, some 'Background information about the Bible' is included later in this book. It is **not** examinable, but think of it (very approximately) in terms of learning a foreign language: you do not need to know the rules of grammar to learn a language, but it does help!

For the Specification, you need to know about:

**The Bible**

● Different Christian beliefs about the nature and authority of the Bible and their impact on its use as a source of beliefs and teachings, including the Bible as inspired by God but written by human beings.

# Introduction

The authority of the Bible is an important issue for Christians. The extent to which the Bible has authority is the extent to which it has the right to demand obedience or belief. Whatever belief particular Christians have about the Bible's authority must take the following into account.

There are many different types of writing in the Bible. Can we assume that they all have the same authority? In the Old Testament (the scriptures of Judaism), for example, there are many apparent contradictions: for example there are two different creation accounts in Genesis 1 and 2. The present versions of the New Testament, dealing with the life of Christ and the teaching of the Early Church, are based on hand-written texts produced long after Jesus' death. These are written in Greek and include variant readings (different readings) in many passages. They are in Greek, but the language of Jesus and his **disciples** is assumed to have been Galilean Aramaic, so these texts are translations, and they include errors of translation.

The texts included in the New Testament were agreed by the Church (the earliest, largely complete, list appears around 170CE), but the Church authorities left out other Gospels circulating at the time – can we really be sure that they made the right decisions concerning what to include and what to exclude?

The teaching recorded in the Bible may depend for its authority on the authority of the main individuals such as Jesus and Paul. Can we really be sure that they had the authority claimed in the texts?

These questions have led to many different views within Christianity including:

- God gave the writers the words to write: the teaching as it came from Jesus was perfect, and the original Gospels were perfect, but what we see today is not a perfect record but one damaged by human interference.
- God inspired the writers to write, but only the Catholic Church can correctly interpret the teaching, because not only is the record of the teaching fallible (includes errors) but the style and intention of the writers are not always clear. For example, the Church alone can identify what is history and what is a teaching story.
- The Bible is a human interpretation of the way God expressed himself through Jesus' life. As the work of human beings it is fallible, but the personal experience of the presence of God, stimulated by reading scripture, makes the Bible authoritative for the believer.

**Consider these six sentences from the Bible:**

> 1 'Like a dog that returns to his vomit is a fool that repeats his folly.' (Proverbs 26:11)
>
> 2 '[Elisha] went ... to Bethel, and while he was going up on the way, some small boys came out of the city and jeered at him, saying, "Go up, you baldhead! Go up, you baldhead!" And he turned around, and when he saw them he cursed them ... And two she-bears came out of the woods and tore forty-two of the boys.' (2 Kings 2:23–24)

**Key term**

**disciples** A disciple is a pupil / student / apprentice of a teacher. Jesus' 12 Apostles would have been disciples of Jesus, but not all disciples were Apostles (see Apostles).

> 3 'My beloved is to me a bag of myrrh that lies between my breasts.
>
> My beloved is to me a cluster of henna blossoms in the vineyards of Engedi.' (Song of Solomon 1:13–14)
>
> 4 'The king of Babylon slew the sons of Zedekiah before his eyes … He put out the eyes of Zedekiah, and bound him in fetters, and the king of Babylon took him to Babylon, and put him in prison till the day of his death.' (Jeremiah 52:10–11)
>
> 5 'You have heard that it was said, "An eye for an eye and a tooth for a tooth." But I say to you, do not resist one who is evil. But if any one strikes you on the right cheek, turn to him the other also …' (Matthew 5:38–39)
>
> 6 'But the angel said to the women, "Do not be afraid; for I know that you seek Jesus who was crucified. He is not here; for he has risen, as he said. Come, see the place where he lay".' (Matthew 28:5–7)

These six sentences are a selection from the many different literary types in the Bible.

Consider the question of the **authority** of these six statements (in reverse order):

- Statement 6, that Christ rose from the dead, is the central doctrine of Christian belief, and is held by most Christians to be literally true and authoritative, because through Christ's death on the cross, humans are given salvation: they are 'saved' from sin.
- 5 is a moral command from Jesus, so most Christians accept its moral authority.
- 4 is a historical statement about the end of the independent kingdom of Judah, and is generally held to have historical authority.
- 3 is part of an erotic poem.
- 2 is a salutary tale warning small boys not to mess with prophets.
- 1 is a somewhat humorous proverb (especially if you know about the habits of dogs).

If you accept 6, then you are convinced about **the authority of the Bible's main claim about the resurrection of Jesus.**

If you accept 5, then you are convinced about **the Bible's Christian moral authority**.

If you accept 4, then you accept that the Bible has **historical authority**.

You might also say that these types of authority are revealed by God. Revelation is God's disclosure of himself to humanity. It refers also to the content of what is disclosed, for example, Scripture / the Bible, and most Christians believe that the human authors of the Bible were inspired to write by God.

What about items 3, 2 and 1? Would you think that these kinds of literature are also inspired and authoritative? In addition to these literary types, the Bible contains (for example) funny stories, riddles, wisdom sayings, myths and legends. Do we need to think of all of these different literary types as inspired by God? Does the truth of a proverb depend on God's authority? Does the story of Elisha's annoyance at being called 'baldy' by small boys appear in the Bible because God inspired it?

You can see the problem: it is one thing to say that the accounts of Jesus' resurrection are given or inspired by God, but it is quite another to say that *everything* in the Bible is inspired by God. Some Christians therefore think that where the Bible deals with matters of belief and morality, it is inspired, whereas proverbs, erotic poems, myths and the like are not; but this still leaves a large body of material where things are not so clear. For example, in 1 Samuel 15:2–3, the prophet Samuel gives Saul (the king) a message from God to destroy the Amalekite tribe, down to the last man, woman and infant – even babies suckling at the breast – not to mention all the animals. Is this command really inspired by God? If you decide that this is too bloodthirsty to come from God, where do you draw the line? What about the account of the world-wide flood (Genesis 6:5–8:22), where God exterminates all human and animal life except for Noah, his family, and the pairs of animals and birds that are taken to re-stock the world after the deluge?

It is questions like these which are assessed when considering the nature and authority of the Bible. As a word of warning, do not get bogged-down in the precise terminology, because different scholars and interpreters use different labels for the different theories of **inspiration** and authority. The ones used here will get the main points across.

## Three different theories about the inspiration and authority of the Bible

### 1 Conservatism

We shall illustrate conservative accounts of the inspiration and authority of the Bible by looking at (1) **evangelical** Protestantism, and (2) Catholicism.

**Evangelical Protestantism**

Evangelical Protestantism is a world-wide movement within Protestantism. Evangelicals hold that Christians are saved by grace (God's free gift), through faith in Jesus' **atonement**. The doctrine of the atonement is part of the theology of St Paul, who held that after the original sin of Adam, God and the world became 'reconciled' by the sacrificial death of Jesus (for example, Romans 5:1–11). Evangelicals are committed to spreading the word about Jesus, and those who are converted have the experience of being saved from sin by receiving salvation by being 'born again'.

Do bear in mind that Evangelical Protestants do not all believe the same things, so the comments here apply to many, but not to all Evangelicals.

- Evangelical views of the inspiration and authority of the Bible are based on a number of texts, in particular 2 Timothy 3 and 2 Peter 1:

> All scripture is inspired by God and profitable for teaching, for reproof, for correction, and for correction in righteousness, that the man of God may be complete, equipped for every good work. (2 Timothy 3:16–17)

The word 'inspired' comes from a Greek word that is often translated as 'God-breathed', in the sense of being 'breathed out' by God: in other words, God wrote Scripture.

**Key term**

**inspiration** In the biblical sense, the doctrine that God in some sense influenced the authors and editors of the Bible, so that what they recorded was 'the word of God'.

**Key terms**

**evangelism** The Greek 'euangelion' means 'good message' / 'good news'. The word 'Gospel' was its Old English equivalent. To evangelise /evangelism is to spread the good news about Jesus the Messiah. The writers of the four Gospels are also known as the Four Evangelists.

**atonement** Part of the theology of St Paul, who held that after the original sin of Adam, God and the world were 'reconciled' by the sacrificial death of Jesus; for example, Romans 5:1–11.

> First of all you must understand this, that no prophecy of scripture is a matter of one's own interpretation, because no prophecy ever came by the impulse of man, but men moved by the Holy Spirit spoke from God.
> (2 Peter 1:20–21)

- Some interpret such texts to mean that God literally dictated the books of the Bible, so that the authors were in that sense 'dictating machines'.
- The text is therefore 'inerrant' – that which comes from God must be without error.
- For many Evangelicals, the text of the Bible is literally true. If the Bible says that God created the world in six days, then it is literally the case that God created the world in six 24-hour periods. If there is any conflict between religion and modern science, then religion is authoritative and dictates what the science really is. Many Evangelical Protestants believe that the story of the creation of the world in Genesis is historically and scientifically accurate in all its details.
- Another common phrase is: 'verbal plenary inspiration'. 'Plenary' means 'full', or 'complete', so it suggests that God inspired all of Scripture, from Genesis to Revelation, including the erotic poetry and Elisha's reaction to those who called him 'baldy'. This does not mean that God approved of Elisha's actions – they are simply recorded as the truth of what happened.

God inspired the authors to produce the precise words he wanted, but at the same time the human authors were allowed to express their own personalities in the writing. For example, we can see that the author of Matthew's **Gospel** was mainly addressing a Jewish audience, whereas Luke wrote to spread the message about Jesus to Gentiles (non-Jews).

Bear in mind that the view of Evangelical Protestants accounts for only one part of Protestant thinking about the inspiration and authority of the Bible. Do not be concerned about this, since it is simply a clear example of one type of Christian belief.

### Catholicism

Catholicism believes that the Bible is inspired by God, but the approach is quite different from that of Evangelical Protestantism.

Catholic teaching on the inspiration and authority of the Bible forms an organic whole. The following account is taken mainly from the Catechism of the Catholic Church (Note 1). Two of the key terms, to begin with, are the Apostolic Tradition and the Apostolic Succession.

**The Apostolic Tradition** is the tradition that stems from Jesus' Apostles. Jesus commanded them to preach the Gospel to all men. This was done orally, from the teachings they had received from Jesus and from the Holy Spirit; also in writing by the Apostles and by others associated with them, again under the inspiration of the Holy Spirit.

The Apostolic Tradition was continued in **the Apostolic Succession**. Jesus' apostles appointed bishops to be their successors, and the bishops were given teaching authority, and this established a continuous line of succession that would last till the end of time.

In Catholicism, it is essential to understand that its Tradition is seen as a **living** tradition. It is called 'Tradition' to distinguish it from Sacred Scripture, with which it is closely connected through the work of the Holy Spirit, and the Holy Spirit is seen as remaining *active within the Church*. To describe the Catholic approach to the Bible as conservative, then, does not at all mean that it is cast in stone, since the tradition is seen as essentially **dynamic**, so that (for example) new truths can be discovered in Scripture. We can illustrate this with an extract from a teaching document of the Bishops' Conferences of England and Wales, and of Scotland: 'The Gift of Scripture', which you can read online at http://www.cw.org.uk/ content/ download/34862/258906/ file/gift-of-scripture-2005. pdf. [Note 2]

> Centuries of reflection and prayer have led Christians to discover new truths and new senses of biblical passages. Catholic teaching has treasured the 'spiritual sense' of Scripture, which has been defined as 'the meaning expressed by the biblical texts when read, under the influence of the Holy Spirit' … the text itself is often richer than the author's intention and contains potentialities which the Holy Spirit actuates in the course of history. Modern insights about the nature of language have explored and clarified the potential of the written word to give rise to new meanings and insights through reading in new contexts and times. [Note 3]

Scripture, then, remains eternally dynamic and alive because Tradition finds new interpretations of Scripture to address modern situations and needs.

To return to the Catechism: Tradition and Scripture spring from the same divine source, **so share the same divine authority**. Scripture is the 'speech of God', put down in writing under 'the breath of the Holy Spirit'. Tradition transmits the *active* word of God given by Jesus and the Holy Spirit to the successors of the **Apostles**. So: the Church does not derive its certainty about revealed truths just from Scripture – both Scripture and Tradition have equal standing and authority, and the authoritative body for interpreting both is the **Magisterium** – the bishops in communion with the Pope, who as the Bishop of Rome is the direct successor of St Peter. The whole body of the Catholic faith is '**inerrant**' (it cannot err / make mistakes) in matters of belief, because there is a *sensus fidei* – an 'instinct of faith' that allows the faithful to recognise authentic Christian doctrine and to reject what is false. [Note 4]

**Article 3 of the Catechism goes on to look at the nature of inspiration in some detail:**

- Sacred Scripture is not a human word: it is the word of God, written under the inspiration of the Holy Spirit:

> For Holy Mother Church … accepts as sacred and **canonical** the books of the Old and the New Testaments, whole and entire, with all their parts, on the grounds that, written under the inspiration of the Holy Spirit, they have God as their author, and have been handed on as such to the Church herself. [Note 5]

> **Key term**
>
> **Apostles** From a Greek word meaning someone who is 'sent out'; applied particularly to Jesus' original 12 Apostles; also to a wider group of Christian figures such as St Paul.

> **Key term**
>
> **canon** A collection of books which a religious group regards as inspired by God, and which therefore forms a body of authoritative scripture, for example, the Christian Canon of the books of the Old and New Testaments.

- In writing the books of the Bible, God chose the human authors and inspired them, but allowed them full use of their own faculties to write what he wanted and no more.
- As the inspired word of God, both the Old Testament and the New Testament are without error, and contain the saving truth.
- Truth comes through **all** the literary forms in the Bible, be they historical, moral or poetic, for example, since the forms together cover the whole range of human thinking and expression.
- Whereas the inspiration of the Holy Spirit meant that the original books of the Bible were without error, over the course of time mistakes may have arisen, for example through imperfect copying; so the Scriptures may need to be interpreted in order to understand their original meaning, and, where appropriate, to apply them to modern issues (such as those arising from science in general and medicine in particular).
- In order to interpret Scripture: (1) Scripture as a whole must be seen as a unity; (2) it must be read within the *living* Tradition of the Church; and (3) the interpreter must be attentive to the 'analogy of faith' (the unchanging faith of the Church, so that no scholar will interpret any passage in such a way that it forgets the unity of Scripture and sets the truth of one passage against the truth of another).

## 2 Neo-orthodoxy

Whereas the Catholic approach can be termed 'orthodox', in that it confirms the creeds of the Early Church established by Jesus, neo-orthodoxy means 'new orthodoxy'. It refers to the work of a number of theologians such as Karl Barth, Reinhold Niebuhr and Paul Tillich, although many of those who are labelled as 'neo-orthodox' reject that label. Broadly speaking, this is their argument:

- They reject the conservative belief in biblical inerrancy, largely because modern forms of studying the Bible suggest that parts of the Bible are not true, because there are many historical and scientific errors, not least in the account of creation in the Book of Genesis, which is a re-write of an older Babylonian myth. Also, the Bible contains apparent contradictions: for example in Mark 10:11 Jesus says that anybody who divorces his wife and marries another commits adultery against her, whereas in Matthew 19:9 Jesus says that anyone who divorces his wife – except for marital unfaithfulness – and marries another woman, commits adultery.
- Karl Barth held that the Bible is not the Word of God; instead it *contains* the Word of God. Barth held that other religions are humanity's attempt to reach God, whereas Christianity is God's attempt to reach humanity. [Note 6]
- So, God does not reveal himself in the words of the Bible; rather, God reveals himself in Jesus, who is the Word who becomes flesh for the salvation of humanity, and who should be worshipped.
- Reading the Bible we become aware that we are sinners in need of forgiveness and we feel the presence of God the forgiver in Jesus.
- For Barth, scripture is a vehicle through which God may be experienced. At the moment that the presence of God is experienced, the text becomes personally meaningful, and the experience is authoritative for the believer.

**Activity**

Read an online version of the *Catechism of the Catholic Church*, for example at: http://www.vatican.va/archive/ENG0015/_INDEX.HTM

Look at Part 1, Chapter 2, on 'God's Revelation ('God comes to meet man').

## 3 Liberalism

'Liberalism' is an umbrella term which is used here to refer to the views of those Christians who reject any idea that the Bible is literally the inspired Word of God. Here are two examples of the Liberal approach:

### 1 The Social Gospel Movement

The Social Gospel Movement was founded by Protestant intellectuals at the end of the nineteenth and beginning of the twentieth centuries, where the idea was to use Christian ethical principles to address social issues ranging from poverty and crime to racism and war. This is not to say that Christians within the Social Gospel Movement had no identifiable doctrinal beliefs; merely that for many, the social action of the movement was more important than worrying about which doctrines are true. In other words, the Bible is authoritative for recommending how we should live.

You can see the point: in the aftermath of two world wars, with political and social unrest on a large scale in many countries, it might seem more important to put the gospel into practice rather than to debate insoluble questions about inspiration and authority.

### 2 Process Theology

Process Theology is a form of Christianity which fully takes on board the discrepancies between some of the claims made in the Bible and what we know to be true from science. As with all forms of Christianity, there is a wide range of Process thought. Here are some of the ideas held by different Process theologians:

- God is not the Creator; 'he' exists panentheistically with the physical universe, meaning that God is 'in' the universe and the universe is 'in' God.
- God is not all-powerful, because he can do no more than to 'persuade' matter into more complex arrangements. God certainly cannot remove the problem of evil.
- God does not intervene in the world – there are no miracles; Jesus is not God incarnate; and God does not answer prayer.
- The Bible is an entirely human document. It is inspired only in the sense that it contains passages that people might find uplifting.

You will come across some of the ideas of Process thought in the three sections on: Self, death and the afterlife; God; and the Problem of evil. In the discussion of evil, Process Theology begins its account of the Bible by rejecting the idea that Genesis / the Bible contains any factual or scientific knowledge of the origins of the universe or of humans. The discussion there will improve your understanding of the different ideas discussed here about the inspiration and authority of the Bible.

# The Bible as inspired by God but written by human beings

This belief can take different forms. For example, we find it in one sense in the Catholic view, and in another in Karl Barth's Neo-orthodox view.

## The Catholic view

In the Catholic view, we have seen that God's Holy Spirit is the main author of Scripture; nevertheless the human authors also used their own faculties and powers: unless that were the case, there would be no point, for example, in the four Gospels being associated with four named human beings – Matthew, Mark, Luke and John. Not only that, each book in the Bible has a characteristic style and language. For example, it is impossible to read the Old Testament Book of Jeremiah without coming 'face to face' with Jeremiah the individual who felt so isolated that he wished he had never been born: 'Woe is me, my mother, that you bore me, a man of strife and contention to the whole land!' (Jeremiah 15:10) Statements such as this are showing the human concerns of the authors.

Near the start of this section, we looked at different types of literature found in the Bible, including the erotic poetry of the Song of Songs and the humour of some of the proverbs. We asked whether or not these types of literature can really be called inspired. From our account of the Catholic view of inspiration, the answer is clearly, 'Yes!', because the humour and the eroticism are again the result of the human authors using their own faculties and powers. Inspiration covers the whole human response to God, since God is the 'author' of humanity.

We quoted earlier from a teaching document of the Bishops' Conferences of England and Wales, and of Scotland: 'The Gift of Scripture', and the same document says this about the human dimensions of Scripture:

> Our God comes willingly to be immersed in our humanity. The Son comes to live human life to the full, and the words of God share fully in the dynamics of human language. It follows that in order to understand the word of God in Scripture we should seek to know the intention of the human author. [Note 7]

In other words, the human contribution to Scripture is important: so much so that it must be studied.

## Karl Barth's Neo-orthodox view

We said above that Barth did not see the words of the Bible as being inspired, nevertheless he believed that Scripture becomes inspired when it provides those who read it with a personal encounter with Jesus.

> For Barth revelation always comes to us in a fallible human vehicle … The Bible is veiled by fallible human words and can only be unveiled by a revelatory act of God. Barth had no time for any doctrine of Scripture which attempted to remove the offence of the humanness of the biblical text by denying or qualifying its human side. Barth proposed that the text is both fully divine and fully human. He insisted that the Bible contained scientific, historical and religious error but … the fallibility of the Bible is essential to its intended theological function, namely, preventing humans from setting it up as a false absolute and leaving revelation under the control of God. (Joshua Hoffman) [Note 8]

By 'fallible', Barth means 'capable of being wrong or mistaken', so he means that God's revelation is hidden behind human language that can be confusing. Nevertheless it is impossible to try to remove that human side to Scripture, because Scripture IS fully human as well as being fully divine. Not only that, the fact that the Bible does have this human side stops us from setting up the Bible as a 'false absolute'. An absolute is something that can never be challenged / that must always be right: but if the Bible has a human side, we simply cannot treat the Bible in that way: we have to think about, and argue about what it means for us. This leaves room for the *personal* encounter with God that humans can find in the Bible.

# The Church

For the Specification, you need to know about:

## The Church

● The different perspectives of the Protestant and Catholic traditions on the relative authority of the Bible and the Church.

To put this in perspective, here is a quick review / reminder of the different sources of authority in Christianity: these form a 'cascade' of authority beginning with belief in God:

1 For most Christians, **God** is all-powerful and all-knowing, so all other forms of authority are subject to him.

2 **The Bible** is seen as '**special revelation**' from God, which provides knowledge of God and of those of God's teachings that cannot be worked out just by using reason. For example, no amount of reason will lead you to the doctrine of the Trinity or the doctrine of Jesus' **incarnation**. These had to be given through Scripture.

As we have seen, the authority of the Bible can be understood in different ways, ranging from the belief that it is God's inspired and inerrant word to the belief that it is a fully human document which has whatever authority Christians decide to give it.

The Bible also gives authority to other forms of special revelation, such as religious experiences, which we studied earlier. It also shows the ongoing authority of the Holy Spirit in the world.

3 **Reason and conscience** are seen as '**general revelation**' from God. They allow us to understand the place of humans in the world and the purpose for which God created humans. In the section on the Philosophy of Religion, for example, we looked at the Roman Catholic theory and practice of ethics, known as 'Natural moral law'. Natural moral law is worked out by God-given reason, and has complete moral authority for Catholics.

For many theologians, conscience carries God's authority: for example, the Christian theologian St Augustine (354–430CE) sees conscience as literally the voice of God that is informing us concerning right and wrong.

4 **The authority of the Church**

The Church has authority from Scripture, for example: Matthew 28:19–20, where Jesus commissions his disciples to make disciples of all nations, to baptise them, and to teach what Jesus has commanded them. In Matthew 16:18–19, Jesus tells Peter that he is the 'rock' on which the Church will be built, and that he has full authority.

5 **The authority of Church tradition**

Each Church has a body of holy tradition that is part of its authority, and some Churches today claim that their authority goes right back to the tradition that comes directly from Jesus and his **Apostles** (the inner core of Jesus' 12 disciples): for example, the Eastern Orthodox Church, and the Catholic and **Anglican Churches**.

---

## Key terms

**special revelation** Revelation that occurs to specific people at specific times: for example, Scripture; also religious experiences and the ongoing work of the Holy Spirit.

**incarnation** The doctrine that Jesus as the Son of God became *flesh*. In the Bible, this is expressed in the well-known passage in John 1:14:

'the Word became flesh and dwelt among us.'

## Key term

**general revelation** Revelation that is available to all people at all times: knowledge of God that comes through natural means, such as reason and observation of the world.

## Key term

**Anglican Church** A Christian tradition which consists of the Church of England and other Churches that have historical and organisational ties to it.

Each Church tradition has:

- its pattern of worship and ritual
- its approach to the **ecumenical councils** (councils of Church leaders and scholars who met / meet to discuss and decide matters of doctrine and practice)
- its leadership structure and organisation. Each Church has evolved an organisational structure based on its understanding of scripture and tradition, so each tradition considers its structure to be authoritative.

If you look at the 'Road Map' below of the sources of authority in Christianity, it will give you a visual picture of how these various sources of authority relate to each other.

There are three main traditions in the Christian Churches: Orthodox, (Roman) Catholic and Protestant (in this definition the author has included the Anglican Church in the Protestant tradition, although some see it as an independent Church). The two traditions you have to study in this section are those of Catholicism and Protestantism.

Protestants and Catholics have different traditions on the relative authority of the Bible and the Church, and you can see this in outline at the bottom of the Road Map.

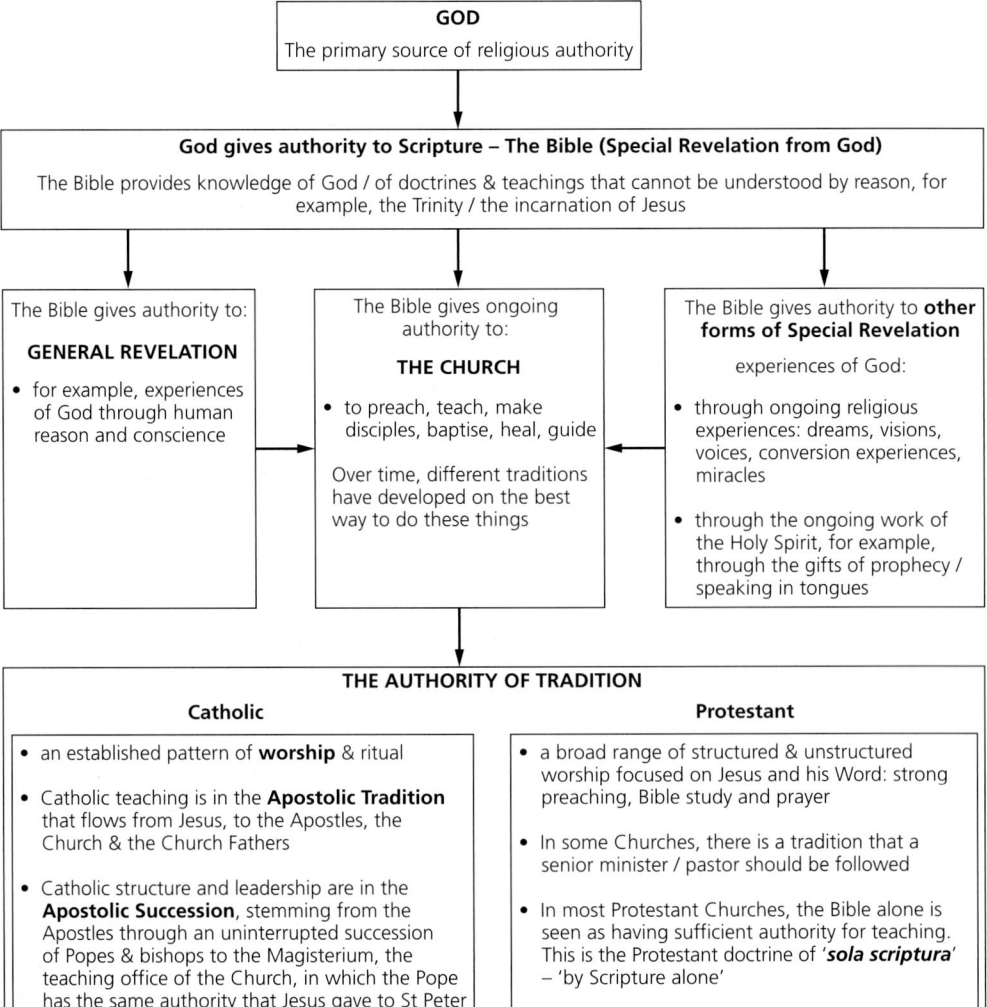

▲ Road Map of sources of authority in Christianity.

Protestants and Catholics have different traditions on the relative authority of the Bible and the Church for reasons that grew out of history and doctrine.

It helps, therefore, to know something about each tradition, and in particular the schism (split) from which the Protestant Churches emerged in the sixteenth century.

**The Catholic Church** is the largest Christian Church, with over a billion adherents. It is also called the 'Roman' Catholic Church, although this was a post-Reformation description that is not popular among all Catholics. Despite its reputation in some quarters for being hostile to intellectual inquiry, the Catholic Church has consistently produced a formidable array of brilliant scholars, not least the thirteenth century-'Angelic Doctor', Thomas Aquinas.

**The Protestant Churches** are those which emerged from the sixteenth century-Protestant Reformation, which was a schism from the Catholic Church. Martin Luther was expelled from the Catholic Church for protesting at what he saw as corrupt Catholic practices, and he and later leaders including John Calvin and Huldrych Zwingli developed distinctively different theology and teachings which form the basis of modern-day Protestantism.

To be called 'Protestant', a Church had to subscribe to beliefs such as: *sola scriptura* ('the sole authority of Scripture'), and *sola fide* ('justification by faith alone'). The number of Protestant Churches today is vast. Main **denominations** (that is, recognised independent branches) include: Baptist, Calvinist, Lutheran, Methodist and Pentecostalist. Some Protestant movements are trans-denominational (reaching out to Christians across different denominations), such as Evangelical Protestantism, which we looked at earlier as an example of a conservative view of the inspiration and authority of the Bible.

We are now in a position to explain the different perspectives of the Protestant and Catholic traditions on the relative authority of the Bible and the Church.

> **Key term**
>
> **denomination** A recognised, independent branch of the Christian Church.

## The Catholic view rests on the Apostolic Tradition and the Apostolic Succession

The Catholic view appears briefly alongside the Protestant view, at the bottom of the Road Map (see page 238).

We have looked at these ideas earlier, explaining Catholic ideas about the inspiration and authority of Scripture, so this will mainly be a reminder of what you have already looked at:

The Bible and the Church have equal authority, since they are inextricably linked through the work of the Holy Spirit.

**The Apostolic Tradition** is the tradition that stems from Jesus' Apostles. Jesus commanded his Apostles to preach the Gospel to all men. This was done orally, from the teachings the Apostles had received from Jesus and from the Holy Spirit; also in writing by the Apostles and by others associated with them, again under the inspiration of the Holy Spirit. Within Scripture, Paul refers to this tradition, for example, when talking to the members of the Church in Corinth:

'I commend you because you remember me in everything and maintain the traditions even as I have delivered them to you.' (1 Corinthians 11:2)

The *ongoing* nature of this tradition is referred to in 2 Timothy 2:

'[W]hat you have heard from me before many witnesses entrust to faithful men who will be able to teach others also.'

The Apostolic Tradition was therefore continued in **the Apostolic Succession**. Jesus' Apostles appointed bishops to be their successors, and the bishops were given teaching authority, and this established a continuous line of succession that would last till the end of time.

Tradition and Scripture are closely connected through the work of the Holy Spirit, who remains active within the Church. The 'rule of faith' for Catholicism is therefore to embrace both Scripture and Tradition, because the Church (and the Church alone) has the authority to interpret Scripture correctly.

The relationship between Tradition and Scripture is explained clearly in the Second Vatican Council's document on divine revelation, *Dei Verbum* ['The Word of God'], and this speaks for itself:

> Sacred Scripture is the word of God in as much as it is consigned to writing under the inspiration of the divine Spirit, while sacred tradition takes the word of God entrusted by Christ the Lord and the Holy Spirit to the Apostles, and hands it on to their successors in its full purity, so that led by the light of the Spirit of truth, they may in proclaiming it preserve this word of God faithfully, explain it, and make it more widely known. Consequently it is not from Sacred Scripture alone that the Church draws her certainty about everything which has been revealed. Therefore both sacred tradition and Sacred Scripture are to be accepted and venerated with the same sense of loyalty and reverence. (Note 9)
>
> Further:
>
> But the task of authentically interpreting the word of God, whether written or handed on, has been entrusted exclusively to the living teaching office of the Church, whose authority is exercised in the name of Jesus Christ. This teaching office is not above the word of God, but serves it, teaching only what has been handed on, listening to it devoutly, guarding it scrupulously and explaining it faithfully in accord with a divine commission and with the help of the Holy Spirit, it draws from this one deposit of faith everything which it presents for belief as divinely revealed.
>
> It is clear, therefore, that sacred tradition, Sacred Scripture and the teaching authority of the Church, in accord with God's most wise design, are so linked and joined together that one cannot stand without the others, and that all together and each in its own way under the action of the one Holy Spirit contribute effectively to the salvation of souls. (Note 10)

## The Protestant view

The Protestant view hinges on the doctrine of *Sola Scriptura* ('by Scripture alone').

This doctrine was developed primarily by Martin Luther during the Protestant Reformation. Whereas the Catholic Church in effect claimed that the teaching of Scripture and the teaching of the Catholic Church are the same, Luther denied this, and claimed that the only true authority is:

> '... the Word of God, through which alone we obtain whatever knowledge we have of God and divine things.' (Note 11)

All that was needed was:

> '... the sure rule of God's Word.' (Note 12)

Luther was concerned that humans should not pass judgement on God's Word, and claim of different parts of Scripture that 'That is true' and 'That is false'. Exegetes have no right to tamper with the text, because to do that is to become a teacher of the Holy Spirit who wrote Scripture and teach him how or what to write:

> '... let us not change the Word of God; we ourselves should be changed through the Word ... It is by the standard of Scripture that the believer is enabled to measure all other teaching. It is in this way that he will put everything to the proof and retain only that which is good.' (Note 13)

Whereas the Catholic Church relies on the teaching authority of the Church and the Pope, according to Luther:

> 'We must learn to adhere solely to the Word of God. It is not who speaks that matters in the Church, but what is spoken. The person is of no consequence; nor is the person's name important, whether it be Peter or Paul. The person is acceptable so long as he teaches faithfully. Therefore let the Word of God be your guide, and assure yourself that this is presented correctly. If the preacher does that, he is above suspicion. But if he does not follow that guideline, then may he be accursed, even if it were ... an angel from heaven.' (Note 14)

Church teaching must be in line with the Bible, and if it is not, then it is false. The Church is the creation of the Word, and not the other way round. Without Scripture, there would be no Church, so the Church cannot be the judge of Scripture. The same reasoning applies to all the authorities of Church and Tradition, such as its councils and its great scholars and Fathers. They are all subject to the authority of Scripture. Christianity stands or falls by the authority of Scripture.

Luther opposed the Catholic belief that salvation is mediated through the priesthood and the sacraments, hence (although he did not use the phrase) he taught the 'priesthood of all believers' – all believers are priests, and all stand equally before God, 1 Peter 2:9:

> 'But you are a chosen race, a royal priesthood ...'

This means that all believers have equal access to God through their prayers, without the need of an ordained priest as an intermediary. All individuals are in effect consecrated as priests through baptism.

It should be clear that the different Christian understandings of the inspiration and authority of Scripture, and of the relative of authority of the Bible and the Church, stem from the fact that religious beliefs can always be interpreted differently. The language and style of the Bible are up to three thousand years removed from our own, and it is not always possible to

## Activity

Read pages 1–4 of: http://www.sgbcsv.org/literature/SolaScriptura.pdf. This gives a perspective on *Sola Scriptura* from the point of view of the Protestant Baptist Church.

understand them fully. If you read Paul's letters to the Christian churches he founded, it is clear that (at a distance of only 20 years or so from Jesus) he felt obliged to correct several misinterpretations that they had concerning 'the Truth': right at the start of his first Letter to the Corinthians, Paul was pleading that there should be no dissensions among them (1:10).

A survey of what different Christian denominations today regard as 'the Truth' might show you that nothing has changed in that respect. As we study the different parts of the Specification on the Christian Religion, it will become apparent that all of its major beliefs are subject to different interpretations. Where it is possible to say that different Christian denominations agree broadly on what they understand as the Truth about Jesus, it is still not possible to say that every member of every denomination (except where composed of only one member) is in complete agreement with every other member.

There are some for whom differences of doctrine are not particularly significant, since it is not the *belief that* something is true about Jesus that is important so much as *belief in* Jesus: belief in Jesus decides how a person should live their life (to revisit this, see the comments about H.H. Price, belief-in and belief-that, in the Philosophy section on Arguments for the Existence of God). This is not to say that differences of belief are unimportant; rather there is no obvious way of resolving them.

# The authority of Jesus

For the Specification, you need to know about:

**The authority of Jesus**

- The authority of Jesus: different understandings of Jesus' authority, including Jesus' authority as God's authority and Jesus' authority as only human.
- Implications of these beliefs for Christian responses to Jesus' teaching and his value as a role model with reference to his teaching on retaliation and love for enemies in the Sermon on the Mount: Matthew 5:38–48.

> We believe in one God,
>
> the Father almighty,
>
> maker of heaven and earth,
>
> of all things visible and invisible;
>
> And in one Lord, Jesus Christ,
>
> the only begotten Son of God ...
>
> (From the Nicene Creed, as modified at Constantinople in 381). [Note 15]

## Jesus' authority as God's authority

The Gospels in particular contain a number of statements which can clearly be taken to mean that Jesus is God in human form. The Christian religion is based on the belief that the historical figure of Jesus, as well as leading a normal human life as a teacher and healer, had, and continues to have, a unique authority from God. This is expressed by the term 'Son of God' in the Nicene Creed. The earliest followers of Jesus were those who encountered him during his lifetime, and even then, some people believed that he spoke and acted with authority from God. A good example of this can be found in the story of the healing of the centurion's servant in the Gospels by both Matthew and Luke.

> As he entered Capernaum, a centurion came forward to him, beseeching him and saying, 'Lord, my servant is lying paralyzed at home, in terrible distress.' And he said to him, 'I will come and heal him.' But the centurion answered him, 'Lord, I am not worthy to have you come under my roof; but only say the word, and my servant will be healed. For I am a man under authority, with soldiers under me; and I say to one, "Go," and he goes, and to another, "Come," and he comes, and to my slave, "Do this," and he does it.' When Jesus heard him, he marvelled, and said to those who followed him, 'Truly, I say to you, not even in Israel have I found such faith …' … And to the centurion Jesus said, 'Go; let it be done for you as you have believed.' And the servant was healed at that very moment. (Matthew 8:5–13)

You can see from this passage that not only does Jesus have the power to control disease, but he also exercises that authority at a distance, without the need to see the centurion's servant. The authority to heal disease was believed to be given by God. In the Old Testament, for example, the prophet Elijah calls upon God's power to resurrect the dead son of a widow, following which the widow says to Elijah:

> 'Now I know that you are a man of God.' (1 Kings 18:24)

After Jesus' resurrection, Matthew shows Jesus claiming total authority from God, when he says:

> 'All authority in heaven and on earth has been given to me.' (Matthew 28:18)

The following verse goes even further and identifies and explains Jesus' authority as that of the Son:

> 'Go therefore and make disciples of all nations … baptizing them in the name of the Father and of the Son and of the Holy Spirit …'

**Key term**

**sustainer** When applied to God, the idea that God sustains creation / maintains it / keeps it in existence / maintains order in a chaotic universe; so that if God ceased to sustain the universe, it would cease to exist.

All the mainstream Churches today believe in the concept of the Trinity. This means that they believe that there is only one God who is indivisible, but that the oneness of God (the Godhead) is understood in three 'persons'. The term 'person' in this sense comes from the Greek word for a theatrical mask, *persona*. Most Christians believe this to mean that God is understood in three roles. As creator and **sustainer** of all that exists, God is 'the Father'. As the source and force of life in creation, and as an ongoing presence in the world, God is the 'Holy Spirit'. As God incarnate (made flesh) the man Jesus is God in human form, or God the Son. Jesus Christ is one aspect of the Godhead, and together with the Father and the Holy Spirit, Jesus is God. This is the view of Orthodox, Roman Catholic, and most Protestant Christians.

Two of the titles used of Jesus in the Gospels are particularly interesting: *Son of God* and *Son of Man*.

243

## Son of God

The expression 'Son of God' is used sometimes in the Old Testament as a special title for a human being; claiming not that the person concerned has a divine nature, but perhaps that as God's representative, that person may be seen as having God's authority. In 2 Samuel 7:14, for example, the title 'Son of God' is given to David, and David is given a promise that his heirs will rule Israel for ever. Since the rule of Davidic kings ended in the 6th century BCE, that promise appeared to fail; however, the Jews came to believe that the Davidic kingdom would one day be restored by a future king/Messiah.

In the New Testament, during Jesus' baptism Mark describes a voice from Heaven saying:

> 'Thou art my beloved Son; with thee I am well pleased.' (Mark 1:11)

Also, at the Transfiguration, God's voice from heaven says:

> 'This is my beloved Son; listen to him.' (Mark 9:7)

For most commentators, Mark is describing Jesus as being by nature the Son of God, and the voice at his baptism declares him to be such. So, for example, Vincent Taylor comments: '... [B]ehind a fully human life, Deity is concealed, but is visible for those who have eyes to see, in His personality, teaching and deeds.' (Note 16) For Mark, Jesus appears to have the same relationship with God that a son has with his father. He has an intimate relationship with God, the same qualities and powers as his father, and he inherits everything that his father possesses. In Matthew's Gospel, Jesus says:

> 'All things have been delivered to me by my Father; and no one knows the Son except the Father, and no one knows the Father except the Son and any one to whom the Son chooses to reveal him.' (Matthew 11:27)

However, the term 'Son of God' also carries a strong theological overtone. Many Jews of Jesus' time were expecting God to send them someone specially chosen and set apart by God to be both a spiritual and a political leader, who would free them from Roman rule and lead the Jews into an age of religious fulfilment. This person would be anointed by God, so he would be the expected King / Messiah ('Messiah' means 'the anointed one') descended from King David. Like David, then, the Messiah would be God's Son. For the early followers of Jesus, it seemed to them that Jesus was the Messiah promised by God. We can see this from Matthew's account of Jesus' trial before the Jewish authorities, when the High Priest says to Jesus:

> 'I adjure you by the living God, tell us if you are the Christ [the Messiah], the Son of God.' (Matthew 26:63)

Both Matthew and Luke stress that Jesus is descended from King David by including a genealogy (a list of Jesus' ancestors).

▲ The Jesse Tree image is often used in stained glass windows to show that Jesus was descended from King David (David's father was called Jesse).

In fact, the two genealogies are quite different, for example, they include different sons of David, Nathan and Solomon. Matthew traces Jesus' ancestors as far as Abraham, but Luke goes back to the creation of Adam, which is another way of indicating that Jesus is the 'Son of God'.

To say that Jesus is the Son of God means, then, that he has God's authority, and this is the sense in which most Christians have understood Jesus' authority.

## Son of Man

Jesus himself is recorded as using the title 'the Son of Man' to describe himself. He uses this as a title for himself in all four Gospels, and in most places it serves to emphasise Jesus' humanity. For example, in Luke 9:58, in reply to a man who asks to follow him, Jesus says:

> 'Foxes have holes, and birds of the air have nests; but the Son of man has nowhere to lay his head.'

Jesus appears to be saying that he is open to the same kind of human hardships as anybody else.

However, the title is also often understood as a way in which Jesus avoided making explicit claims of **divinity** during his ministry. It is clear from the fact that Jesus was crucified by the Romans that making claims to be divine would cause trouble and possibly cut short his ministry. The ambiguous nature of the term 'Son of Man' may therefore have been very useful. To outside observers, he would be doing nothing more than claiming to be a normal human being, but to those who knew his work and teaching, it would hint at his divine mission as a representative of God, as a kind of super-prophet. In Mark's Gospel, scholars suggest that there is a recurrent theme which they refer to as the 'Messianic Secret'. This is the idea that those who most closely encountered Jesus could see that he was the Messiah, but Jesus urged them to conceal this understanding. For example, see Mark 1:43–45 and 8:29–30. In Mark's Gospel, the Messianic Secret is only finally revealed after the death of Jesus, when the centurion who is watching over the crucifixion is recorded as saying:

> 'Truly this man was the Son of God!' (Mark 15:39)

At the moment of Jesus' death, the centurion seems to have seen something godlike in Jesus which marked him out as more than a mere man. Vincent Taylor comments that the centurion's words are '… a confession of the deity of Jesus in the full Christian sense', and adds that Mark probably saw them as a parallel to the phrase he uses at the beginning of his Gospel, that Jesus was 'Son of God'. [Note 17]

Many Christian theologians reached the conclusion that Jesus was both fully divine and fully human, and the use of both 'Son of God' and 'Son of Man' as titles of Jesus gives some support to that understanding of Jesus and his authority.

## Jesus' authority as only human

In general, there are two 'kinds' of Christian who hold that Jesus' authority was only human:

1 Those who, historically, have followed the teachings of a particular sect in which it was believed that Jesus was not divine.

2 Those who take a 'liberal' approach to scripture.

### 1 The approach of different Christian movements

Since mainstream Churches today believe in the idea of the Trinity, the idea that Jesus' authority is only human authority is not a normal Christian understanding. However, historically, there have been movements which viewed Jesus as human rather than divine. Here are four examples:

### Adoptionism

In the early centuries of the Church, Theodotus of Byzantium (particularly active in the late second century CE) and Paul of Samosata (200–275CE) both taught that Jesus was born human, but was later adopted by God at his baptism. Adoptionists accordingly believed that Jesus' authority was something he acquired from God when he was baptised, not something he had as a right because he was God the Son. They base their view on Gospel accounts of Jesus' baptism. This view, called 'Adoptionism', was rejected as heresy by the Church towards the end of the third century CE, at the Synod of Antioch.

### Arianism

In the third and fourth centuries CE, Arius, a priest in Alexandria, and his followers taught that Jesus was not truly divine. They believed that he was created by God to fulfil a specific role, and that the title 'Son of God' was an honour bestowed on him by God. There was a long and bitter dispute between followers of Arius and those who supported a Trinitarian view. In 325CE, the Council of Nicea ruled that Arius was wrong and he was sent into exile. Disagreement in the Church continued for several years, however, until the Council of Constantinople in 381CE re-affirmed the ruling of the Council of Nicea. The statement of faith that is used in many Churches today, known as the Nicene Creed, was put into its final form at the Council of Constantinople.

### The Cathars

Between the eleventh and twelfth centuries, the sect known as Catharism (it is not clear what its followers called it) arose in the south of France. They taught that created matter was too corrupt for the perfect God to become incarnate as Jesus Christ. Because of this, the Cathars concluded that Jesus Christ could not be God in human form. Their views about the authority of Jesus were therefore similar to Arianism, and were condemned by the Pope in 1184 in a papal bull called *Ad abolendam* ('towards abolishing' – abolishing heresy). Catharism did not spread widely in the Church and died out early in the fourteenth century, mainly as a result of a crusade against its supporters proclaimed by the Pope.

### Unitarianism

In the middle of the eighteenth century, the Unitarian movement became popular in Britain. This is a Christian sect which has a **deistic** understanding of God: that once creation was complete, God ceased to act within the created order. For most Unitarians, Jesus has a special place as a great man and a prophet of God, but he is only human and has no divine authority. Some Unitarians believe that Jesus became God's son by adoption, meaning that at his baptism God adopted Jesus as his son, which gives him special status. On this kind of understanding, Jesus' authority is spiritual, but human reason and human experience are the final judge of how people should act. Today there are around 7,000 Unitarians in the UK. (Note 18)

## 2 A liberal approach

Those who take a liberal approach to the Bible would approach the question of Jesus' authority through: (a) their view of the inspiration and authority

> **Key term**
>
> **deist** This refers to someone who accepts the existence of God on the basis of reason and the world of nature. Most deists would reject the idea of special revelation, and would hold that God created the world and then left it to its own free devices.

247

of the Bible, and (b) whether or not any particular claim about Jesus goes against what science sees as reasonable.

### Concerning their view of the inspiration and authority of the Bible

To understand the meaning of the title 'Son of God', liberal Christians might look at how the title 'Son of God' is used in earlier parts of the Bible. As we said earlier, in the Old Testament it is used in connection with beings who in some way represent God's authority, such as angels (Genesis 6:1–4); Israel (Hosea 11:1); and the king (2 Samuel 7:14; Psalm 2:7), so the general sense of 'Son of God' means 'someone close to God'. If we use this kind of thinking with Jesus, then, 'Son of God' might have been used to express the idea that Jesus was close to God as a great teacher, healer and spiritual leader, but was not literally God.

If we take the further point that Mark's Gospel, which is generally considered to be the first of the four Gospels to be written, was composed around 70CE, this would be around 40 years after Jesus' death, and during those 40 years the early Christians, reflecting on who they thought Jesus was, came to the conclusion that he was not just *a* Son of God but was literally *the* Son of God. We get a hint of this developmental process in the very first line of Mark:

**'The beginning of the gospel of Jesus Christ, the Son of God.' (Mark 1:1)**

Older manuscripts omit the title 'the Son of God'.

By the time we get to John's Gospel, which is usually dated to around 90–110CE, this kind of language is much more marked, as in the prologue to the Gospel, in which Jesus is portrayed as the pre-existent 'Word' of God (John 1:1–18).

For a liberal Christian, who believes that the Bible is not so much inspired as inspiring, this developed understanding of who Jesus was is not taken to be literally true. Jesus might be seen as an exceptional human being who, in that sense, could be called 'Son of God', without the need to believe that this was literally the case.

### Concerning their acceptance of the scientific approach

Christians who accept that science gives us an accurate picture of the nature of the world will often apply this acceptance to issues of belief. While many Christians will accept that a creator God is the best explanation for the existence of the universe in the first place, they might still reject anything supernatural, such as miracles, including the miracle of Jesus' resurrection. Jesus' resurrection might mean something like, 'Accepting Jesus brings new life', or 'What Jesus stood for can never die'.

The implications of these different understandings of Jesus' authority are fairly clear. Wherever Jesus makes a pronouncement on how Christians ought to behave, those who take a conservative view of Scripture will be concerned to follow what Jesus says as closely as possible. Those who have a liberal understanding of Scripture will first try to interpret the context and meaning of the text.

The Specification asks you to look at **Christian responses to Jesus' teaching, (specifically in the Sermon on the Mount, in Matthew 5:38–48), in connection with his teaching on retaliation and love for enemies.**

## Christian responses to Jesus' teaching

As we have already learned, the way that Christians respond to these teachings depends on their understanding of Jesus' authority and on the degree to which Scripture gives us a reliable record. If Jesus is the second person of the Trinity, God the Son, then what he teaches is binding on all those who follow God as God is understood in Christianity. If Jesus is merely human, an inspired teacher and prophet, but without divine authority from God, then humans are free to evaluate his teachings and to choose whether to follow them or not. This passage from Matthew's Gospel provides a useful example for this.

> You have heard that it was said, 'An eye for an eye, and a tooth for a tooth.' But I say to you, Do not resist one who is evil. But if any one strikes you on the right cheek, turn to him the other also; and if any one would sue you and take your coat, let him have your cloak as well; and if any one forces you to go one mile, go with him two miles. Give to him who begs from you, and do not refuse him who would borrow from you.
>
> You have heard that it was said, 'You shall love your neighbor and hate your enemy.' But I say to you, Love your enemies and pray for those who persecute you, so that you may be sons of your Father who is in heaven; for he makes his sun rise on the evil and on the good, and sends rain on the just and on the unjust. For if you love those who love you, what reward have you? Do not even the tax collectors do the same? And if you salute only your brethren, what more are you doing than others? Do not even the **Gentiles** do the same? You, therefore, must be perfect, as your heavenly Father is perfect.' (Matthew 5:38–48)

> **Key term**
>
> **Gentiles** A word commonly used in the Bible to mean 'non-Jews'.

## Those who accept Jesus' authority as God's authority

A Christian who believes that Jesus is God incarnate reads the text with the assumption that what Jesus says is what God requires them to do, even though they might qualify this by saying that what the text says needs to be clearly explained and understood. The passage from Matthew's Gospel is very clear. Christians must:

- do nothing to resist an evil person who attacks them
- give freely more than is asked to anyone who makes a demand of them
- lend without expectation of being paid back
- love their enemies
- be perfect.

These expectations are a challenge to normal human behaviour. Most people have the urge to defend themselves if attacked, to limit what they give to charity or to those who ask, give loans only if they are likely to be paid back, and hate their enemies. They generally believe that although trying to be a good person is worth doing, no-one can be perfect. Jesus seems to be telling people to go against human nature.

However, a Christian who assumes that Jesus is teaching with the full authority of God has to take these teachings seriously. For example:

- There are many Christians who are pacifists because they accept the teaching of Jesus as authoritative, so whatever the provocation, they will not resist attack and will try to show love towards those who might be their enemy. During the First World War, many Christians became conscientious objectors and refused to fight with the enemy. Many were punished for their beliefs by imprisonment. Others volunteered to provide medical support on the battlefield. The Religious Society of Friends (more commonly known as Quakers) is a Christian organisation which puts this teaching into practice, by refusing to bear arms or engage in conflict.

● This does not mean that all Christians are pacifists. Many Christians consider this passage in the light of other teachings of Jesus where he appears to allow or encourage conflict, for example Luke 22:36:

> 'He said to them, "But now, let him who has a purse take it, and likewise a bag. And let him who has no sword sell his mantle and buy one." '

## Those who accept Jesus' authority as only human

Christians who believe that Jesus' authority is human authority are free to interpret and evaluate the teaching according to their experience and judgement.

● With regard to the command not to resist attackers, a liberal Christian might point out that Jesus was speaking in the context of the Roman rule of Palestine, where resistance to the Romans could lead to crucifixion as a punishment. The Roman authorities could co-opt any Jewish person to carry a burden for them, so we might imagine Jesus saying, 'If that happens, volunteer to go two miles rather than one, then at least you stay alive.'

● Others might think that Jesus really was saying that pacifism is always the right response to violence, because he contrasts pacifism with the old 'law of retribution' in Leviticus 24:19–20, which laid down the punishment of an eye for an eye, a tooth for a tooth, and so on. In which case, some Christians would say that Jesus was simply wrong: it would be cowardly not to defend your family from attack, for example.

● Yet another approach to what Jesus is saying here is to ask what kind of speech form he is using, because the form of speech governs meaning. The clue might be in the last command in the passage:

> 'You must be *perfect*, as your heavenly Father is perfect.'

Clearly this is an impossible demand, since to carry it out humans would have to have all of God's qualities. Instead, Jesus is probably using hyperbole, which is deliberate exaggeration to achieve an effect. Why would Jesus do this? Jesus appears to have believed, as did St Paul, that the end of the world was not too far away, so those who wanted to get into God's Kingdom should be as near to perfect as possible, so Jesus is saying, 'Don't be satisfied with anything less than the impossible' – it is not the achievement of the impossible that is required, but its attempt.

● To give one more example of the breadth of possible interpretations of this passage, it seems likely that when Jesus commands non-resistance, giving freely more than is asked, lending without expectation of return, loving one's enemies and being perfect, he is telling individuals that this is probably the best way of making moral sense of their lives. For non-resistance and loving one's enemies, we might say that continued violence and hatred have a habit of rebounding on people; moreover being generous in money matters and giving freely in all walks of life is likely to be more productive for individuals than keeping all your assets for yourself.

250

**Activity**

Look at the website: http://www. desiringgod.org/articles/did-jesus-teach-pacifism.

This is entitled, *Did Jesus teach pacifism?* The author (Matt Perman) contrasts some literal and non-literal interpretations of the text we have just been looking at. See whether or not you agree with his conclusions.

- Finally, of those Christian groups which teach that Jesus has only human authority, the position of UK Unitarians with regard to pacifism is very broad:

> On pacifism, as on all issues of personal conscience, each Unitarian is free to come to his or her own conclusions without fear of judgement or censure. So although there are many Unitarian pacifists, there is no explicit requirement or implicit expectation on the matter. Unitarians live with diversity and its potential tensions – on this subject as on many others. A Unitarian congregation may include both pacifists and members of the armed forces. (Note 19)

## Jesus' value as a role model

All Christians, whether they believe Jesus to be divine or human, see Jesus as a role model for Christian living. The more human Jesus is, the more relevant his example is, although perhaps it is then less authoritative. Conversely, perhaps the more divine Jesus is, the more irrelevant his example is (since no human could do likewise), but the more authority it has.

If Jesus is understood to be divine, then clearly human beings should model their behaviour on the qualities of God which Jesus exemplifies. The teaching of Jesus from the Sermon on the Mount is supported by Jesus' own behaviour during his arrest and trial. When he was arrested, he submitted and did not fight to defend himself.

For some Christians (for example, those from Evangelical Christian denominations), the phrase 'What Would Jesus Do?' (usually rendered as 'WWJD?') has been adopted as a slogan reminding them to act in accordance with Jesus' principle of love, applied in all situations. 'WWJD' has merit only if Jesus' example is relevant to, and possible for, ordinary human beings, or human beings empowered by the Spirit.

It is not only Christians who view Jesus as a role model. Mahatma Gandhi, a devout Hindu religious leader who led opposition to British rule in India, did not believe that Jesus was divine, but said this:

> What, then, does Jesus mean to me? To me, he was one of the greatest teachers humanity has ever had … I refuse to believe that there now exists or has ever existed a person that has not made use of his example to lessen his sins, even though he may have done so without realizing it. (Note 20)

However, although the Gospels do not ever show Jesus engaging in fighting, he sometimes found himself in conflict with the authorities. His response to the dealers and money-changers in the Temple precinct was to turn over the tables and drive out the merchants, accusing them of being thieves. For some Christians, this willingness to respond vigorously to injustice provides a model that allows them to do the same.

**Anglican Church** A Christian tradition which consists of the Church of England and other Churches that have historical and organisational ties to it. Its principal head is the Archbishop of Canterbury, who is also the nominal leader of the Anglican Communion, which is a world-wide group of Churches that are in full communion with the Anglican Church.

**Apostles** From a Greek word meaning someone who is 'sent out'; applied particularly to Jesus' original 12 Apostles; also to a wider group of Christian figures such as St Paul.

**The Apostolic Tradition** Is the tradition that stems from Jesus' Apostles. Jesus commanded them to preach the Gospel to all men. This was done orally, from the teachings they had received from Jesus and from the Holy Spirit; also in writing by the Apostles and by others associated with them, again under the inspiration of the Holy Spirit.

**The Apostolic Succession** The Apostolic Tradition was continued in the Apostolic Succession. Jesus' Apostles appointed bishops to be their successors, and the bishops were given teaching authority, and this established a continuous line of succession that would last till the end of time.

**Atonement** Part of the theology of St Paul, who held that after the original sin of Adam, God and the world were 'reconciled' by the sacrificial death of Jesus; for example, Romans 5:1–11.

**canon** A collection of books which a religious group regards as inspired by God, and which therefore forms a body of authoritative scripture, for example, the Christian Canon of the books of the Old and New Testaments.

**denomination** A recognised, independent branch of the Christian Church.

**deist** This refers to someone who accepts the existence of God on the basis of reason and the world of nature. Most deists would reject the idea of special revelation, and would hold that God created the world and then left it to its own free devices.

**disciples** A disciple is a pupil / student / apprentice of a teacher. Jesus' 12 Apostles would have been disciples of Jesus, but not all disciples were Apostles (see Apostles).

**divinity** The state of being divine (God).

**ecumenical councils** Councils of Church leaders and scholars who met to discuss and decide matters of doctrine and practice. 'Ecumenical' comes from a Greek word meaning 'the inhabited world', so the decisions of ecumenical councils were seen as having authority for the whole Church; however, after the various schisms that split the Church into different traditions, the authority of any council was limited to the tradition its members represented.

**evangelism** The Greek 'euangelion' means 'good message' / 'good news'. The word 'Gospel' was its Old English equivalent. To evangelise / evangelism is to spread the good news about Jesus the Messiah. The writers of the four Gospels are also known as the Four Evangelists.

**general revelation** Revelation that is available to all people at all times: knowledge of God that comes through natural means, such as reason and observation of the world.

**Gentiles** A word commonly used in the Bible to mean 'non-Jews'.

**Gospel** see evangelism.

**Holy Spirit** The third person of the Christian Trinity (Father, Son and Holy Spirit), each being an aspect of God.

**incarnation** The doctrine that Jesus as the Son of God became *flesh*. In the Bible, this is expressed in the well-known passage in John 1:14:

'the Word became flesh and dwelt among us.'

**inspiration** In the biblical sense, the doctrine that God in some sense influenced the authors and editors of the Bible, so that what they recorded was 'the word of God'.

**special revelation** Revelation that occurs to specific people at specific times: for example, Scripture; also religious experiences and the ongoing work of the Holy Spirit.

**sustainer** When applied to God, the idea that God sustains creation / maintains it / keeps it in existence / maintains order in a chaotic universe; so that if God ceased to sustain the universe, it would cease to exist.

# Summary of sources of wisdom and authority

## Different Christian beliefs about the nature and authority of the Bible

The issue of the authority of the Bible is complicated because of the many types of literature in the Bible. It is difficult to see how erotic poetry and myth, for example, are inspired and authoritative.

Conservative ideas about the authority and inspiration of the Bible range from those of Evangelical Protestants who tend to regard Scripture as the literal Word of God, inerrant even in passages that are unscientific, to those of Catholics for whom Sacred Scripture is the word of God written through the inspiration of the Holy Spirit, using human authors who were both inspired and allowed to use their human faculties. For Catholicism, the inspiration of Scripture guarantees the truth of all the different forms of literature in the Bible, and guarantees that Scripture is a unity. Scripture must be interpreted and maintained as a unity, through the analogy of faith.

Karl Barth's Neo-orthodox view does not see the Bible as the Word of God but as a human work that becomes inspired when it provides those who read it with a personal encounter with Jesus.

Liberal views take many different forms, ranging from partial inspiration to seeing the Bible as a fully human document. For the Social Gospel Movement, social action is more important than worrying about insoluble matters of doctrine. For Process theologians, God is not the Creator, is not omnipotent and does not intervene in the world.

The idea that the Bible is inspired by God but written by human beings can be seen in the different interpretations of the Catholic Church and Barth's Neo-Orthodoxy.

## The different perspectives of the Protestant and Catholic traditions on the relative authority of the Bible and the Church

The Catholic view is that the Bible and the Church have equal authority, being inextricably linked through the work of the Holy Spirit. The ongoing Tradition of the Church, continued through Apostolic Succession, means that the Church – specifically the Magisterium of the Pope and Bishops – alone has the authority to interpret Scripture correctly. Scripture and the teaching authority of the Church are therefore joined together: neither can stand alone. Under the action of the Holy Spirit, both contribute effectively to the salvation of souls.

For Protestants, authority is focused on Scripture – Luther's doctrine of *Sola Scriptura*. Humans cannot pass judgement on God's Word. The Bible is the sole judge of truth, so the authority of the Church, tradition, councils and Church scholars is subservient in every case to Scripture and cannot contradict it. All believers form a priesthood of believers, consecrated as priests through baptism, by virtue of which all are equal before God and can achieve salvation without the need for intervention by the Church or a priest.

Different Christian understandings of the inspiration and authority of Scripture and of the relative authority of the Bible and the Church, stem from the inevitable fact that religious beliefs can be interpreted differently. For many, the really important thing is the attitude of faith brought about by 'belief in' Jesus, wherever that leads and however it is expressed.

## The authority of Jesus

Most Christians will accept the statements about Jesus given in the Nicene Creed, where Jesus is the Son of God, so has God's authority. The Gospels use a number of titles for Jesus, including Son of God and Son of Man, to indicate his divinity. Nevertheless, some Christians see Jesus' authority as only human. Historically, certain Christian groups viewed Jesus as divine, including those who believed in Adoptionism, Arianism, Catharism and (still today) Unitarianism. Moreover, liberal Christians use textual analysis and science to argue that Jesus was human and not divine, so, for example, where the Gospels tell of Jesus' resurrection from death, they really mean that 'Accepting Jesus brings new life', so all suggestions that Jesus was divine are just the result of the early Christian community reflecting on who Jesus was and coming to an unlikely conclusion.

When we look at Jesus' teachings in the Sermon on the Mount on retaliation and love for enemies, for those who accept Jesus' authority as God's authority, Christians literally should not retaliate and must love their enemies. For those who see Jesus' authority as only human, Jesus' words have to be interpreted in terms of the brutal Roman occupation of Palestine, or in terms of hyperbole, or perhaps in terms of how individuals should confront issues of violence and hatred; not only that, some would simply reject pacifism and love of enemies, arguing perhaps that this is a rare example of Jesus getting it wrong.

Whatever view of Jesus' authority people hold, Jesus can be seen as a role model for Christian behaviour. Where Jesus' authority is held to be merely human, his example becomes more relevant, although his authority decreases. Where Jesus' authority is seen as divine, perhaps the less relevant his example becomes, since it becomes more difficult to copy, although many hold that the important thing for Christians to do is to make the *attempt* to be like Jesus.

# 7

# God

This chapter will cover:
- Christian Monotheism
- God as Personal, God as Father and God as Love
- The concept of God in process theology

## Christian Monotheism

For this, you need to look at:

- Christian **Monotheism**: one God, **omnipotent** Creator and controller of all things, **transcendent** and unknowable
- The doctrine of the Trinity and its importance
- The meaning and significance of the belief that Jesus is the Son of God: the significance of John 10:30; 1 Corinthians 8:6

### Key terms

**monotheism** The belief that there is only one God (which usually entails the belief that God possesses complete power and knowledge).

**omnipotent** All-powerful.

**transcendent** The idea that God is above and beyond space–time; as opposed to immanent, existing within space–time.

For those who make the attempt, trying to describe God can involve paradox and contradiction. In Genesis 3:8, Adam and Eve hear the sound of God 'walking in the garden in the cool of the day', which implies that God has legs and feet and a body to go with them. On the other hand, God is seen also as transcendent – above and beyond the world, as in Hebrews 1:3, where Jesus as God's Son '… reflects the glory of God, and bears the very stamp of his nature, upholding the universe by his word of power'. If we then bear in mind that according to Christian doctrine Jesus was fully human as well as fully divine, the kind of language being used here is difficult to understand.

## Monotheism

This is the belief that only one God exists and is worthy of worship.

- In the Old Testament, Israel did not come to this understanding straight away. Other gods were believed to exist, although they had no power, for example, Exodus 15:11:

  'Who is like thee, O Lord, among the gods?'

  Also, Psalm 86:8:

  'There is none like thee among the gods, O Lord ...'

One of the names for God in the Old Testament is 'Elohim', which in Hebrew is a plural form: 'gods', which underlines the fact that God was seen as the head of a **pantheon** of gods. Each nation was thought to have its own particular deity, and the gods of the nations make up **Yahweh's** Council. The Council is called the 'sons of God'.

- Monotheism seems to have developed in the thinking of the Israelite prophets, particularly in Isaiah 40–55:

  '... I am He. Before me no God was formed, nor shall there be any after me ...' (Isaiah 43:10)

  Also:

  'Thus says the Lord, the King of Israel and his Redeemer, the Lord of hosts: "I am the first and I am the last; besides me there is no god".' (Isaiah 44:6)

## Monotheism in the Bible is *ethical* monotheism

- In the Old Testament, good moral behaviour is at the heart of the **covenant** agreement between Israel and God, whereby God 'adopts' Israel in a special relationship, and in return Israel promises moral and religious obedience (Exodus 19:5–6). The Law given by God to Moses is the 'text' of that agreement, and is centred on the Ten Commandments (Exodus 20:1–17).
- In the New Testament, Jesus tells his followers that whoever weakens in obeying these commandments, or who teaches others to weaken, shall be called least in the Kingdom of Heaven (Matthew 5:19). Many Christians believe therefore that they are bound by the same moral laws. Others, of course, do not (e.g. those who prefer the approach of Situation Ethics).
- In Mark's Gospel (12:29), Jesus quotes from the preface to the first commandment in Deuteronomy 6:4: 'Hear, O Israel: The Lord our God is One'. This phrase forms the heart of the **Shema** prayer in Judaism, and is said to be the ideal expression of ethical monotheistic belief. This is the full text of Mark 12:28–31:

And one of the scribes came up and heard them disputing with one another, and seeing that he answered them well, asked him, 'Which commandment is the first of all?' Jesus answered:

'The first is, "Hear, O Israel: The Lord our God, the Lord is one; and you shall love the Lord your God with all your heart, and with all your soul, and with all your mind, and with all your strength." The second is this, "You shall love your neighbour as yourself." There is no other commandment greater than these.'

Many Christians take this text as morally authoritative, depending on their view of the authority of the text itself and of Jesus.

---

### Key terms

**pantheon** All of the gods / goddesses within any particular religious system.

**Yahweh** The most commonly used name of God in the Old Testament. Ancient Hebrew was written without vowels, so the original pronunciation is not known.

**covenant** In the Bible, this is a formal agreement or relationship, for example, between God and Abraham, Moses and David. Covenants can be conditional or unconditional. That with Moses was conditional, and could bring blessings or curses on the nation, depending upon whether or not they obeyed the Ten Commandments and the rest of the Law.

**Shema** Hebrew (*shama*) – 'to hear', in the context of the *Shema* prayer in Deuteronomy 6:4: 'Hear, O Israel: The Lord our God is One'.

● Moral obedience is at the heart of **salvation**. The appearance in the world of Jesus as God's Son is part of '**Salvation History**'. The ethical teaching of Jesus shows how Christians (by obeying that teaching) can be saved into the Kingdom of God. God (and God alone) has the complete power, authority and love to save humanity from its sins. Again, this is true for some Christians, depending on whether they accept that salvation is by works or by faith, for example.

## God as the omnipotent Creator

For many, to say that God is the only God, means also that he must be omnipotent, the Creator of everything that exists and the controller of all things.

**Since God is the only God, he cannot be challenged by any other power or authority, so Christians have deduced that God must be omnipotent (all powerful).** For example, in Matthew 19:26 Jesus tells his disciples that '… with God all things are possible'.

Christians disagree about what it means for God to be omnipotent, because omnipotence can be defined in different ways:

1 For some, to say that God is omnipotent means that He can do absolutely anything, including the logically impossible; so if God wants to make 1 = 2, or to make murder a morally good act, or to make a stone too heavy for Himself to lift, He can do any of these things.

2 Others think that this is just logical nonsense, and that to say God is omnipotent means that He can do anything that is 'logically possible'.

You will remember that for many Christians, it is important to accept (2) as the right definition because of the problem of evil. If (1) is true, we are faced with the problem of why God does not control evil in the world. Scholars such as Hick and Plantinga maintain that (2) is true, and that it is not logically possible for God to allow humans to be truly free and to get rid of evil at the same time.

You will remember, however, that Process Theologians 'solve' the problem of evil by denying that God is omnipotent in any sense, arguing that the sheer extent of evil in the world shows that God cannot be all-powerful. You will have to make up your own mind on this.

**Most Christians argue that if God is omnipotent, then he must be the Creator of everything that exists.**

Most Christians accept this, although again they disagree about the method of God's creation:

1 Some Christians believe that the universe comes ***ex Deo*** (Latin for 'out of God's own being'), but most reject this idea because it would imply that God and His creation are the same thing, whereas most Christians believe that God is transcendent (beyond space and time) and 'wholly other' (completely different from the material world).

2 Most Christians think that God created the universe literally 'from nothing' (***ex nihilo*** in Latin). This might suggest that the universe is some kind of mental construct by God. Many Christian theologians insist that this idea of 'creation from nothing' can be found in the creation narrative of Genesis 1, where God 'brings forth' the universe by words of creative power: God simply says: 'Let there be …' (for example, verses 3, 6, 9).

> In the beginning God created the heavens and the earth. The earth was without form and void, and darkness was upon the face of the deep; and the Spirit of God was moving over the face of the waters. And God said, 'Let there be light'; and there was light.

It may be true that God created the universe from nothing. The problem is that Genesis does not show this to be the case, because the Revised Standard Version's translation here is almost certainly wrong. A more likely translation of the Hebrew is this:

> In the beginning of God's creating the heavens and the earth, *the earth being without form and void, and darkness being upon the face of the deep;* and the Spirit of God moving over the face of the waters, God said, 'Let there be light'; and there was light.

The words in bold are describing an already-existing, dark, watery chaos. God's creative acts are to bring order to this chaos, hence his first act is to create light to banish the darkness.

3 Those Christians who accept the second translation therefore believe that God created the universe by using already existing chaotic matter, which he put into an ordered state. You will remember that this is the view of Process theologians, who think that God / the material universe have always existed together.

Of the three views explained here, this is the closest to the text of Genesis, not least because the Genesis texts reflect the Babylonian account of creation, the *Enûma Eliš*, which also assumes primeval chaos. Lines 1–5 of the *Enûma Eliš* refer to the mingled waters of heaven and earth, and to 'chaos, Tiamat, the mother of them both'. [Note 1] In Genesis 1:2, Tiamat is reflected in the word *Tehom*, which in the Revised Standard Version translation is 'the deep', referring to the formless primeval waters surrounding the world. The mythological elements are subdued in Genesis; nevertheless the language reflects them.

None of this shows that the doctrine of creation out of nothing is not true – it is just that the Bible makes little effort to make a case for it. It is an idea which, like many others in Christian thinking, has evolved during the ongoing life of the Church. Balanced against that, the idea of creation as God ordering pre-existent chaos is much closer to the ideas of Process Theology, which we refer to elsewhere. The important point is that for most Christians, God is the all-powerful Creator of everything.

There are clear links with the problem of evil here, because if God is perceived as the all-powerful Creator of *everything*, then he must have created evil. Augustine addressed this problem by denying that evil exists as a thing in itself, whereas others claim that what we perceive as evil is created by humanity, so God is not the sole creator of evil. Alternatively, Hick argues that what we perceive as evil provides the stimulus for spiritual development into children of God.

## God as the controller of all things

This idea follows naturally from the belief that God is the omnipotent Creator. If the universe was made by God, and if God is all-powerful, then God must in some sense control everything. Another way of saying this is to refer to God as 'King' or 'Sovereign', since a king has control over his subjects; although as an omnipotent King, God's control over everything is total (Romans 11:36; 1 Corinthians 8:6; 1 Timothy 6:15; Hebrews 1:3).

Perhaps the most important expression of this idea is that 'God sustains the universe', meaning that he holds it in existence and preserves it from destruction: God sustains the fabric of existence itself. This idea is expressed in many ways, for example:

● God preserves the universe from falling back into the watery chaos that He put into structured and ordered form at creation. This a frequent motif in the Psalms, for example, 89:9–10, where God rules the raging of Yam (the sea) and crushes Rahab like a carcass.
● Equally, God '… set the earth on its foundations, so that it should never be shaken' (Psalm 104:5).
● We said above that monotheism for Christians is 'ethical' monotheism, so God sustains human morality by providing a code by which Christians are expected to live: basically, the Ten Commandments and the teachings of Jesus.

**Christians vary in their interpretation of God as the controller of all things.**

● For some, since God is the only God, and since He is all-powerful, He must also be **omniscient** (all-knowing). God must therefore know absolutely all of the past, present and future, which means that the future is fixed and unavoidable. This idea is called 'theological determinism'. Theological determinism comes in various forms, but in its strongest form it means that humans do not have free will, and so God has absolute control over a person's actions.
● One alternative to this view is to follow Aquinas' view that God does not exist in time: rather he exists timelessly. For God, there is no today, tomorrow or yesterday: timeless God sees all times, rather like an unrolled scroll, so sees the entire history of the universe timelessly. Following this idea, some argue that God's omniscience means that God sees the results of our future free choices but does not cause them. On this view, God has the power to intervene and control, but does not – he permits human free choices.

The question of whether or not we have free will is a particularly important one, since many believe that without free will our moral actions are worthless, since we would be nothing more than 'moral robots'. This is an issue that is returned to in the A-Level Specification.

You might find it rather irritating that there seems to be no doctrine or belief that all Christians agree on, but the simple fact is that although some Christians claim to *know* God's nature and God's mind, that is a completely untestable claim. Some regard it as laughable to think that the mind of any creature, human or otherwise, can know the mind of an omnipotent being. For some, this view is strengthened by the Christian belief that God is transcendent and unknowable, which we now turn to.

## God as transcendent and unknowable

To say that God is transcendent means that God is above and beyond the space–time universe.

For Christians who have this understanding of God's nature, God is not a thing or an object: God is not made of anything, and does not exist *in*

> **Key term**
> omniscient All-knowing.

anything (so cannot exist in time or in space, since to do so would limit him). God is eternal, having no beginning and no end. The Catholic doctrine of God's aseity holds that as God is the omnipotent Creator, nothing is responsible for his existence. God was not created by something else; nor did He create Himself; God is his own existence, and God's essence is to exist.

God's transcendence is expressed in many ways in the Bible, for example:

> 'For my thoughts are not your thoughts, neither are your ways my ways, says the Lord. For as the heavens are higher than the earth, so are my ways higher than your ways and my thoughts than your thoughts.' (Isaiah 55:8–9)

> '... No one comprehends the thoughts of God except the Spirit of God.' (1 Corinthians 2:11)

Think back, here, to Chapter 3 Religious Experience, and the section on Rudolf Otto, on numinous experiences of God as 'an apprehension of the wholly other'. Otto focuses on God's holiness, in the sense of his being numinous and transcendent: for example in the narrative of Moses' call (Exodus 2:23–4:17), where God tells Moses to take off his shoes because he is standing on holy ground (3:5).

Texts such as these show that God's transcendence means that God's true nature is unknowable.

This idea is again central to Moses' call narrative. Moses says to God:

> 'If I come to the people of Israel and say to them, "The God of your fathers has sent me to you," and they ask me, "What is his name?" what shall I say to them?' (3:13).

In reply, God says to Moses: 'I am who I am.' (3:14). The Hebrew of this phrase is: *ehyeh ašer ehyeh*, which is an etymology (an explanation of the meaning) of God's name, YHWH, and the etymology can be understood in various senses, including: 'I will be what I will be'. Whatever the precise translation, most Christian commentators see the importance of God's answer in terms of his monotheistic status, and his complete transcendence and unknowability. God is the Creator, and cannot be categorised, known, or understood by any other being.

## The doctrine of the Trinity and its importance

Trinitarian doctrine is not something that Christians put in place of monotheism – rather it interprets it in the light of historical revelation. Not all Christians accept Trinitarian doctrine, but for those who do: historically, God is encountered in the Old Testament revelation as Father, Creator and Judge. In the New Testament revelation, God is encountered as a human being, Jesus, and the revelation of the Holy Spirit is also made explicit – Jesus is conceived by the power of the Holy Spirit (Luke 1:35) and at his baptism the Spirit descends on him in bodily form, as a dove (Luke 3:22). In the ongoing life of the Church, God is experienced in all three persons.

A clear doctrine of the Trinity is not found in the New Testament writings; rather it is 'perceived' within them. To give some examples:

> 'Go therefore and make disciples of all nations, baptizing them in the name of the Father and of the Son and of the Holy Spirit ...' (Matthew 28:19)

'The grace of the Lord Jesus Christ and the love of God and the fellowship of the Holy Spirit be with you all.' (2 Corinthians 13:14)

The understanding of the Early Church that through Jesus they were experiencing God **incarnate** is seen in texts such as:

'I and the Father are one.' (John 10:30)

'And he who sees me sees him who sent me.' (John 12:45)

'He who has seen me has seen the Father ... I am in the Father and the Father is in me ...' (John 14:9–10)

God's presence and action as the Holy Spirit is seen in texts such as:

'Joseph, son of David, do not fear to take Mary your wife, for that which is conceived in her is of the Holy Spirit ...' (Matthew 1:20)

'And I will pray the Father, and he will give you another Counselor, to be with you for ever, even the Spirit of truth, whom the world cannot receive, because it neither sees him nor knows him; you know him, for he dwells with you, and will be in you.' (John 14:16–17)

'When the day of Pentecost had come, they [the 11 disciples] were all together in one place. And suddenly a sound came from heaven like the rush of a mighty wind, and it filled all the house where they were sitting. And there appeared to them tongues as of fire, distributed and resting on each one of them. And they were all filled with the Holy Spirit, and began to speak in other tongues, as the Spirit gave them utterance.' (Acts 2:1–4)

The formal, or classical, doctrine of the Trinity was achieved after centuries of confusion and controversy as the Church wrestled with competing ways of understanding the relationship between the three persons of the Trinity. (Note 2) This affirmed that:

● Father, Son and Spirit are one God in three persons.
● Each person is God, each possessing in equal measure the divine characteristics such as omnipotence (unlimited power) and omniscience (total knowledge).
● Each person differs from the others only in terms of their inner relations; so the Son differs from the Father only in the fact that he *is* the Son and *is not* the Father, and the same is true for the Holy Spirit in relation to the Father and the Son.
● Put technically, God exists as one substance in three persons (hypostases).
● All three persons are eternal and uncreated.

The diagram opposite captures much of this meaning.

If you study the Shield carefully, you will see there are 12 propositions that are the relationships between the persons of the Trinity.

The outer circle shows that the persons of the Trinity remain distinct, because the Father is not the Son or the Holy Spirit / the Son is not the Father or the Holy Spirit / the Holy Spirit is not the Father or the Son.

Each of the persons of the Trinity in the outer circle is linked to the centre circle, so the Father is God, the Son is God, and the Holy Spirit is God / God is Father, Son and Holy Spirit: the Godhead is one. Each person of the Trinity is thus fully and completely God; yet at the same time each of the three persons is unique.

---

> **Key term**
>
> **incarnate** Meaning 'enfleshed'. The doctrine of the Incarnation is that the second person of the Trinity – the Son – took on a human body and nature. He was made flesh by being born in the womb of Mary.

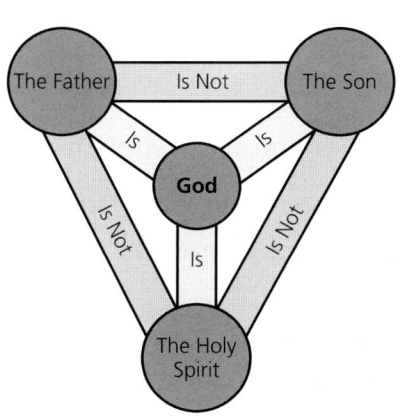

▲ The Shield of the Trinity

## Key terms

***perichoresis*** Greek for 'rotation', used in Trinitarian theology to describe the relation between the three persons of the Godhead, often translated as 'mutual indwelling' – so that the Father is *in* the Son; the Son is *in* the Father, and so on.

**redemption** To buy back, as with the ransom of slaves (Exodus 21:8). 'Redemption' is part of the language of the doctrine of the atonement: the suffering and death of Jesus redeems humanity from sin.

**atonement** The doctrine that Christ's obedience, suffering and death on the cross effected a reconciliation between humanity and God following the original sin of Adam and Eve. Those who accept Christ are thereby redeemed from sin and are reconciled with God.

**immanent** When applied to God, means, 'existing within the space–time universe'.

The technical term for describing the relationship between the persons of the 'Godhead' at the centre of the Shield is ***perichoresis***, which is often translated as 'mutual indwelling' – so that the Father is *in* the Son; the Son is *in* the Father, and so on. John's Gospel is thought to show a perichoretic understanding of God's glory: Jesus says:

> 'Father, the hour has come; glorify thy Son that the Son may glorify thee …'

This follows on from 16:14, where the Spirit brings glory to the Son.

## The importance of the doctrine of the Trinity

Trinitarian doctrine is important in Christianity in any number of ways. Here are three:

1 It brings together the main historical and doctrinal truths of Christianity concerning sin, **atonement** and **redemption**.

Many Christians believe that the relationship between God and humanity was affected by the 'original sin' of Adam and Eve in disobeying God, as the result of which death entered the world, and this made it necessary for there to be an 'atonement' to make up for human sin. The doctrine of the Trinity explains this coherently:
- **God** sent the Son as the atonement, to redeem humans from sin. (Galatians 4:4–5)
- **The Son** is fully human (as well as fully God), and because of this the Son is able to make that atonement through his death on the cross and subsequent resurrection. (1 Peter 3:18–19)
- **The Holy Spirit** gives new birth in Jesus (Titus 3:5) so that humans have the hope of eternal life.

2 The Trinity makes it possible for humans to have a personal relationship with God.

We have been talking about God's transcendent nature as the Creator, the controller of everything, wholly other, unknowable. There is a major problem in thinking about God just by referring to his transcendent characteristics, because most Christians believe that God is **immanent** within creation. An immanent God answers prayer, performs miracles, intervenes in history and relates to persons, and the Bible is full of examples of God doing all these things.

It seems paradoxical to say that God can be both transcendent (above the space–time universe) and immanent (within the space–time universe) at the same time; nevertheless the doctrine of the Trinity allows for this to be the case. The Christian Godhead (the centre of the Trinity Shield) is thought of as transcendent and unknowable; nevertheless as the Father, God is thought of by most Christians as a personal Creator – one who can be known and loved by his creation. Moreover, as the Son, most Christians believe that God became immanent as a human person – Jesus of Nazareth. The Holy Spirit is indwelling in the human spirit and transforms human life, for example, inspiring the human emotion of joy (1 Thessalonians 1:6).

3 The Trinity is seen as a model of personhood.

The relationship between Father, Son and Holy Spirit is one of love, since God is love. Since humans are made in the image of God (Genesis 1:26–27), personal relationships between people are in that sense modelled on Trinitarian love, and are therefore of immense value. Similarly, the German Reformed theologian, Jürgen Moltmann, develops a 'social' account of the Trinity which puts the emphasis on the three persons of the Trinity existing in a community of mutual self-giving and receiving love. (Note 3) This concept of the Trinity is a model for human relationships, emphasising, for example, giving as well as receiving and accepting difference as well as sameness.

## The belief that Jesus is the Son of God

**The meaning and significance of the belief that Jesus is the Son of God: the significance of John 10:30; 1 Corinthians 8:6.**

There is an extended discussion of the meaning and significance of Jesus as 'Son of God' in Chapter 6 Sources of wisdom and authority, pages 244–248, and you should revisit that section at this point. The essential points made there are that whereas mainstream Christian Churches today accept Trinitarian doctrine, and hold that Jesus was literally 'the Son of God', 'liberal' Christians often interpret that title to mean that Jesus was simply 'a son of God', that is, an exceptional / godly man.

The issue is quite simple: if 'Son of God' is taken in the Trinitarian sense, then Jesus' authority is God's authority. If it is taken in the 'liberal' sense, then Jesus' authority is merely human. As noted in the earlier chapter, the solution to this issue has a huge impact on the question of Jesus' moral authority. It is one thing to follow Jesus' ethical teachings if he commands them as the Son of God; whereas it is quite another to follow them if they are merely his teachings as a human being.

The two texts specified for discussion here are key texts that are often referred to when discussing the Trinitarian view.

> I and the Father are one. (John 10:30)

The context of this statement is the Feast of the Dedication of the Jerusalem Temple. Some of the Jews who saw Jesus walking in the Temple portico asked him: 'How long will you keep us in suspense? If you are the Christ, tell us plainly.' Jesus' reply concludes with the statement: 'I and the Father are one.'

So, is this a claim that Jesus is literally God's Son? The answer is that the evidence is ambiguous. The word for 'one' in Greek is *hen*, which some take to mean that Jesus is claiming to be one in essence with God, whereas others suggest that Jesus is simply saying that he and God are one in harmony about Jesus' mission. Jesus uses the same word, *hen*, in John 18:11, where he asks God for 'oneness' between himself and his Apostles just as he himself has oneness with God, and clearly he is not claiming here that he is one in essence with the Apostles, so why should we assume in 10:30 that he is claiming oneness in essence with God?

Against that, his questioners in John 10:30 clearly did think that he was claiming to be God, since they wanted to stone him to death for blasphemy. However, even this proves nothing, because in 10:36–38 Jesus in reply says that he is the Son of God doing his Father's work, and here he seems simply to be saying that by 'Son of God' he means that he is simply doing the work that God wanted him to do.

As a final comment here, those who accept that in 10:30 Jesus was referring to himself in a Trinitarian sense as the Son, point to John 8:58, where he tells his questioners:

> '... before Abraham was, I am.'

Here, Jesus seems to be claiming that he already existed in the remote past before Abraham – in other words, that he was pre-existent and 'one' with God. If that is the case, then that would support the claim that in 10:30 he is also claiming to be one with God. This is stated very clearly in John 1:1-2:

> 'In the beginning was the Word, and the Word was with God, and the Word was God. He was in the beginning with God ...'

We shall have to leave things there, however. There are too many possibilities to be sure of any one interpretation. For a start, Jesus' conversation would have been in Aramaic, but John's Gospel is in Greek, so it is not possible to be sure what Jesus originally meant, since translation can easily change the sense of the original words, and we cannot even be sure that what Jesus actually said was remembered accurately. Moreover, John's Gospel is considered by most New Testament scholars to be the latest of the four Gospels, so it is possible that what we have is John's interpretation of who Jesus was, reached many years after the events described. Here, as so often elsewhere, you will have to decide for yourself where the balance of the evidence points.

> '... yet for us there is one God, the Father, from whom are all things and for whom we exist, and one Lord, Jesus Christ, through whom are all things and through whom we exist.' (1 Corinthians 8:6)

For a start, whereas John's Gospel is generally seen as one of the last books of the New Testament to be written, 1 Corinthians is seen as one of the earliest: perhaps dating from around 57CE, so what Paul says about Jesus comes from a time much closer to Jesus himself.

The context of 1 Corinthians 8:6 is Paul's advice concerning eating meat that had been offered to idols. The 'stronger' members of the Corinthian Church apparently maintained that eating meat offered to idols was acceptable, since: (1) idols do not exist, so (2) eating meat offered to non-existent gods can hardly hurt anybody.

Paul agrees that 'an idol has no real existence', (verse 4), and then affirms monotheism: 'there is no God but one'. Moreover, although there are many so-called gods and lords (verse 5), there is only one (real) God and one (real) Lord. Note the parallelism in Paul's language in verse 6:

| one God, the Father | from whom are all things | and for whom we exist |
|---|---|---|
| one Lord, Jesus Christ | through whom are all things | and through whom we exist |

Paul's audience in Corinth contained both Jews and Gentiles (non-Jews), although the majority of the Corinthian Church members would have been Gentile (Acts 18:6). We need to bear in mind that Corinthian society would mainly have been polytheistic (acknowledging many gods), so Paul seems to be reminding them that:

- there is only *one God*, and the one God is the Creator of all things, humanity included
- there is also only one Lord, Jesus, and Jesus is God's instrument in creation.

As with John 10:30, it is very difficult for us to know exactly what Paul means here in 1 Corinthians 8:6. Some argue that Paul is claiming that Jesus is God, and in support of this interpretation they often point to the *Shema*, the Jewish prayer that is the great statement of monotheism: 'Hear, O Israel: the Lord our God, the Lord is one.' (Deuteronomy 6:4). Since Paul's language in the first half of 1 Corinthians 8:6 seems so close to the *Shema*, then perhaps Paul is deliberately using the language of the *Shema* to equate God as Father with Jesus as Lord.

Against that, however, the Greek word for 'Lord' here is *kurios*, which is a common title used in the New Testament with many shades of meaning, such as: 'sir' (Matthew 27:63), or the owner of a slave (Matthew 10:24), or even 'husband' (1 Peter 3:6), so applied to Jesus it does not have to mean the Lord (God), so where the Revised Standard Version translates *kurios* in 1 Corinthians 8:6 as 'Lord' with a capital L, that might be reading more into the text than is really there. Where Paul describes Jesus as the one 'through whom are all things and through whom we exist', the word 'through' seems to suggest that Jesus is God's *instrument* in creation, but is not identifying Jesus with God.

What can we conclude? Well, obviously at some point the majority of Jesus' followers became convinced that he was God in human form, so perhaps the kind of language we see in John 10:30, 1 Corinthians 8:6 and elsewhere is part of that process. The language of 1 Corinthians is credal, in that it has the flavour of a confession or statement of faith, and it should be remembered that it took the Church until 381CE to produce the definitive form of the Nicene Creed, which laid out what is generally seen as the orthodox version of Christian teaching on the Trinity. Texts like those we have looked at in the Bible could perhaps be seen as stepping stones towards that teaching. For 1 Corinthians 8:6, as for John 10:30, you will have to decide for yourself where the balance of the evidence points.

## Activity

For those who want to go further, you could research:

1 The doctrine of 'Eternal Sonship', and

2 The non-Trinitarian doctrine of Adoptionism.

# God as Personal, God as Father and God as Love

For this, you need to look at:

- The challenge of understanding anthropomorphic and gender-specific language about God
- God as Father and King
- Feminist perspectives

## The Anthropomorphic tradition

So far in this section, we have been looking at two sets of ideas about God: that his nature is on the one hand transcendent, unknowable and wholly other; on the other that God is immanent and can relate to persons. To some extent these different ideas can be reconciled by holding that God is both transcendent and immanent, and we have seen that the language of the Trinity gives us one way of doing this. In particular, to describe Jesus as the Son of God means that as the second member of the Trinity, Jesus was fully God; yet at the same time as God

## Key term

**anthropomorphism** The practice of attributing human characteristics to non-human entities. With regard to God, it is anthropomorphic to describe God in human terms.

## Activity

Look up the following references and note the anthropomorphic features they give to God:

- Exodus 20:5; 1 Samuel 15:35; Jeremiah 30:23–24; Romans 1:18.

- Exodus 7:5; Numbers 6:24; Revelation 19:15.

- John 14:6–7.

- Genesis 1:27; Hosea 11:4 and 13:8; Deuteronomy 32:11–12; Isaiah 42:14; Isaiah 66:13; Psalm 123:2; Matthew 23:37.

incarnate, Jesus of Nazareth was fully human. Most Christians accept this language as a coherent way of talking about God, but one problem with it is that it requires us to talk about God anthropomorphically. **Anthropomorphism** is the practice of attributing human characteristics to non-human entities. With regard to God, it is anthropomorphic to describe God in human terms.

The Bible frequently describes God in human terms. For example, in Genesis 2:2, God 'rested' from the work of creation; in Genesis 3:8–9, Adam and Eve hear the sound of God 'walking' in the garden in the cool of the day, and God 'asks them where they are'; in Genesis 6:6, God is 'sorry' and 'grieved' that he made humanity; in Exodus 32:14, God 'changes his mind' about bringing evil on his people; in Romans 5:5, God's love is poured into human hearts; in Psalm 35:15 God's 'eyes' look toward the righteous, and his 'ears' listen to their cry. In other words, God is portrayed as having human actions, human emotions and a human body. Perhaps the ultimate anthropomorphism in the Bible is that God himself assumes human form as the Son.

There are clear problems in understanding anthropomorphic language about God. For example:

- To describe God as having human actions, human emotions and a human body reduces God to the human level. If God has human physical characteristics, then he presumably shares some of the physical limitations of humans. How can a supposedly all-powerful God be described in limiting terms?
- Equally, to say that God judges, forgives and laments, for example, suggests that God has a conscious brain, since these are brain states that with humans can be seen using magnetic resonance imaging to scan the brain. How are we to understand the concept of a God whose brain states are potentially analysable like our own?
- How can such a God be the Creator of the universe? Presumably the universe cannot have been created from inside itself, so the creator must have been separate from the universe, and must have been transcendent (above and beyond space-time). Anthropomorphic descriptions of God seem to suggest that God is a part of the universe rather than its creator.
- Sigmund Freud (for example) understands the concept of God in terms of wish-fulfilment. We desire a God who forgives / saves / heals / is just / creates peace, and so we invent God in our own image. Perhaps this explains the state of the human race, because such a being simply cannot do what is required.
- How can such a limited God save humans from sin, or be the object of worship?
- In summary, human language has developed over thousands of years, and reflects human concerns, thoughts and values. It is therefore a challenge for us to understand how human language can be used about God and by God.

To illustrate the depth of anthropomorphic language about God, consider, now, what the Christian tradition says about God as Personal / Father / Love / King.

## God as Personal

- To say that God is personal does not mean that God literally 'is' a person; rather this kind of language is analogical and is used to argue that God can be 'related to' as a person. For example, a God who answers prayer or gives people religious experiences, is the kind of God who is experienced in a personal sense. As some people put it, they feel that they have a relationship with God.

- A personal God would therefore be immanent within the world, and in the previous section we saw that whereas the Christian 'Godhead' is thought of as transcendent and unknowable, God as Father, Son and Holy Spirit are thought of as immanent and personal.

- We referred also, in the previous section, to Moltmann's 'social' account of the Trinity which puts the emphasis on the three persons of the Trinity existing in a community of mutual self-giving and receiving love. This offers a model for human personal relationships.

- In Section 6 Ethics and religion, we saw that most Christians (for example, those who follow Catholic Natural Moral Law or Protestant Divine Command Theory) believe that moral standards are not just a matter of opinion: they are objective and given by a personal God.

**Activity**

In pairs, or as a group, read Luke 11:1–13 (sayings on prayer).

Explain briefly the various ways here in which God is portrayed as personal.

## God as Father

The image of the human father stands as a metaphor for a number of qualities, such as strength, power, authority, wisdom and love, but as far as the Bible is concerned, to call God 'Father' is not just a familial metaphor. In the Ancient Near East, society was organised along patriarchal lines, a patriarch being the oldest male in a family, having complete control of the other members of the family. Although some women did achieve positions of power and influence (see the story of Deborah in Judges 4), the adult males held political, economic, domestic and moral power.

Deuteronomy 32:6 describes God as the Father who creates the human race, and in Exodus 4:22 God describes Israel as his first-born son: the son who is rescued from Egypt (Hosea 11:1). In Jeremiah 3:19, God laments the faithlessness of Judah, who he thought would call him Father. In Malachi 1:6, God is the Father who should be honoured. In 2 Samuel 7:14, God announces that he will be the Father of the Davidic dynasty.

To talk of God as Father is, of course, male anthropomorphism. As the God of Israel, Yahweh's role is in effect described as that of the patriarchal Father. After the disobedience of Adam and Eve he exercises punitive justice by ordaining different roles for men and women in which agriculture becomes a matter of toil and sweat for men, and women continue being fruitful and multiplying, but childbirth becomes painful for them (Genesis 3:16–19). In return for protection and security, God lays down absolute religious and moral laws, and does not hesitate to punish breaches of the rules, going so far as to bring about the destruction of the Kingdom of Israel at the hands of the Assyrians (2 Kings 17) and that of Judah by the Babylonians (2 Kings 24:18–25:21).

Perhaps the most anthropomorphic aspect of God's role as the Father is seen in the New Testament, where God becomes incarnate through his Son, Jesus. In the Apostles' Creed, the statement of belief in God 'the Father almighty, Creator of heaven and earth' is followed by that of belief in 'Jesus Christ, his only Son, our Lord'. God is Father in both senses here: the Father Creator all things, and the Father of Jesus.

Jesus himself frequently uses the title Father to refer to God, for example, in teaching the disciples the Lord's Prayer, *Our* Father in Matthew 6:8–9, where that form of address reflects the whole range of reverence, respect and love that all Christians have for God as the heavenly Father. In the wording of the Lord's Prayer, there is a sense in which Christians who use it share the Father / Son relationship of Jesus with God as they pray. The Aramaic word that Jesus would have used of God as Father would have been 'Abba', which can also have the intimate meaning, 'My Father'. Avoid the popular mythology that 'Abba' means 'daddy' in first-century Aramaic (Note 4); however 'Abba' does signify God's approachability as the Father for all people, so in Romans 8:15 (see also Galatians 4:6), Paul suggests that when Christians cry, 'Abba – the Father!' they become 'adopted' sons of God; thus the emphasis on God's fatherly nature is both intimate, powerful and all-inclusive.

### Activity

The only other reference to 'Abba – the Father' in the New Testament is where Jesus makes a passionate appeal to God before his arrest in the Garden of Gethsemane (Mark 14:36):

> **'Abba, Father, all things are possible to thee; remove this cup from me; yet not what I will, but what thou wilt.'**

In your view, what qualities of God as Father is Jesus appealing to here?

## God as Love

Alongside God's main characteristics of complete power and knowledge, the Christian tradition puts an equal emphasis on God's love, holding that God is omnibenevolent – 'all-loving' / 'perfectly good'. This can be a very difficult attribute to comprehend, not least because of the problem of evil. You will remember that in the section on the problem of evil, the logical problem of evil can be stated in terms of the 'inconsistent triad':

1 God is omnipotent (all-powerful).

2 God is omnibenevolent (all-loving / all-good).

3 Evil exists.

An all-powerful God must be able to abolish evil; an all-loving / all-good God must wish to abolish evil. Why then does evil exist? The problem is made worse by adding a fourth proposition:

4 God is omniscient (all-knowing).

At the point of creation, God must have been aware of the sheer extent of evil that would befall the world; so why, then, did he bother to create it?

We looked at three attempts to solve this problem: the Free Will Defence, the Irenaeus-Hick theodicy and the views of Process Theology, and doubtless you will have formed your own opinions as to whether or not any such views offer a satisfactory solution to the problem.

It is probably fair to say that although the philosophical solutions may not work too well, most Christians put their trust in the loving nature of God. Their main evidence for this comes from the Bible:

- **God's love is the basis of the covenant between God and Israel.** In fact, this is a special kind of love, known as *hesed̲*, for example, Deuteronomy 7:9, where it is translated as 'steadfast love':

  'Know therefore that the Lord your God is God, the faithful God who keeps covenant and steadfast love with those who love him and keep his commandments ...'

- **God's love is encapsulated by the suffering and death of Jesus:**

  'For God so loved the world that he gave his only Son, that whoever believes in him should not perish but have eternal life. For God sent the Son into the world ... that the world might be saved through him.' (John 3:16–17)

- **The greatest gift of the Spirit is love**, because it is God's love poured into human hearts. (Read 1 Corinthians 13:1–18, which is Paul's great 'hymn to love'.)

- **God *is* love, and this is the basis for loving others:**

  'Beloved, let us love one another; for love is of God, and he who loves is born of God and knows God. He who does not love does not know God; for God is love ... Beloved, if God so loved us, we also ought to love one another. No man has ever seen God; if we love one another, God abides in us and his love is perfected in us.' (1 John 4:7–8, 11–12)

- **If God is love, then love describes the relationship between the persons of the Trinity**, since they are 'mutually indwelling'. Where, for example, John 3:35 says that 'the Father loves the Son', this is not simply a metaphor: it is part of the nature of the Trinity. In John 17:20–26, Jesus suggests that God's love for him is pre-existent: 'given ... before the foundation of the world'. (verse 24)

- **The fact that God is love requires love to be the basis of human relationships also.** In Matthew 22:34–40, a lawyer asks Jesus which is the greatest commandment, to which Jesus replies: 'You shall love the Lord your God with all your heart, and with all your soul, and with all your mind. This is the great and first commandment. And a second is like it, You shall love your neighbour as yourself. On these two commandments depend all the law and the prophets.' (verses 37–40). By 'the law and the prophets', Jesus means the whole content of law and prophecy in the Bible, so literally the whole sphere of human activity is encapsulated within the commands to love God and other people. Again, this is not just a metaphor: Jesus sets it as the basis for right conduct.

- **The kind of love that Jesus is talking about is *agape*.** *Agape* is Jesus' 'other-person-regarding' love, which comes from the nature of God as love. You will remember that this is why Joseph Fletcher placed *agape* at the centre of Christian Situation Ethics, with direct reference to Jesus' answer to the lawyer.

- **Finally, the belief that humans are made in God's image (Genesis 1:26–27) means that God's love must be reflected in the human capacity for *agape*.** Perhaps the most poignant representation of this is in Michelangelo's fresco painting of *The Creation of Adam*, which in the mirroring of the pose between God and Adam is generally believed to reflect the creation of Adam in God's image. God is portrayed as being accessible and personal, and not as remote and unknowable.

▲ Michelangelo: *The Creation of Adam*, painted on the ceiling of the Sistine Chapel, Vatican, Rome: 1508–1512.

## God as King

The Bible is full of God's kingly titles, such as: Majesty, Lord, Sovereign, God of gods, King of the whole earth. To call God 'King' is an obvious metaphor, since the power of the king in the ancient world was usually absolute. We can see this kind of royal imagery in the prophet Isaiah's vision of Yahweh as an enthroned deity in the Jerusalem Temple:

> In the year that King Uzziah died I saw the Lord sitting upon a throne, high and lifted up; and his train filled the temple. Above him stood the seraphim; each had six wings: with two he covered his face, and with two he covered his feet, and with two he flew. And one called to another and said: 'Holy, holy, holy is the Lord of hosts; the whole earth is full of his glory.'
>
> And the foundations of the thresholds shook at the voice of him who called, and the house was filled with smoke. And I said: 'Woe is me! For I am lost; for I am a man of unclean lips, and I dwell in the midst of a people of unclean lips; for my eyes have seen the King, the Lord of hosts!' (Isaiah 6:1–5)

The throne in this vision is the Ark of the Covenant, which was built during the Israelite wanderings in the wilderness, after the Exodus from Egypt. It was seen as the throne seat above which God was enthroned as 'the King, the Lord of hosts' (verse 5). Yahweh was envisaged as presiding over a heavenly council in much the same way as the earthly king presided over his court, with the difference that Yahweh's council was composed of the gods of the nations who were all subservient to Yahweh. There are reminders of this concept throughout the Old Testament, not least in Genesis 1:26–27, where God says: 'Let us make man in our image', where the 'us' presumably refers to God's attendant court. Not only that, the image is not just male: verse 27 shows quite clearly that humans were created 'male and female', so Yahweh's court included female deities.

Psalms 24, 27, 93, 95–99 are known as 'Enthronement Psalms', because they are hymns celebrating Yahweh's kingship. For example:

'The Lord reigns; let the earth rejoice ...' (97:1)

'For thou, O Lord, art most high over all the earth ... exalted far above all gods.' (97:9)

'He sits enthroned upon the cherubim ... Mighty King, lover of justice ...' (99:1,4)

In Psalm 24, Yahweh is the 'King of glory … strong and mighty … in battle' (verse 8). One of God's main kingly titles appears in verse 10 – he is *Yahweh Sebaoth* – 'The Lord of hosts', which refers to his leadership of the hosts / gods of heaven, picturing Yahweh as a warrior king of ultimate power.

For Christianity, the most important feature of all this royal imagery is how it is used in the New Testament to portray Jesus as the Messiah, a title which means 'king' / 'anointed one'. In Luke 9:20 Jesus asks his disciples who they think he is, to which Peter replies: 'The Christ of God'. 'Christ' is the Greek translation of the Hebrew word for 'Messiah'. The Jews were expecting a warrior king who would get rid of the Romans, but in the New Testament Jesus' role as the Messiah is to bring about the Kingdom of God. The kingly reign of God is announced by John the Baptist: 'Repent, for the kingdom of heaven is at hand' (Matthew 3:2), and Jesus is the one who brings it about.

There are many different interpretations of what the Kingdom of God is, and they are not necessarily mutually exclusive. Some interpret the Kingdom as the new relationship brought about between God and humanity by Jesus as the Messiah, who dies and then is resurrected to atone for the sins of humanity. Some see the Kingdom as an ongoing reality inseparable from Jesus and the life of the Church. Some see it as a future event heralded by the 'Second Coming' of Christ the Messiah, when the forces of evil are finally defeated and the dead are raised to eternal life:

> **'The kingdom of the world has become the kingdom of our Lord and of his Christ, and he shall reign for ever and ever.' (Revelation 11:15).**

We can perhaps summarise these different understandings by saying that Christ's Kingdom is both a present and a future reality for all who believe in him. This forms part of the discussion in the next chapter, on Self, Death and Afterlife.

## Anthropomorphic and gender-specific language about God

**The challenge of understanding anthropomorphic and gender-specific language about God (God as Father and King), including feminist perspectives.**

We have referred already (above) to the challenges of using anthropomorphic language about God: it seems to limit God. God becomes a being with human emotions, human actions and human physical characteristics. How could such a God be the Creator, or save humans from sin, or be worthy of worship? Does all such language merely reflect the human desire for a God who protects, forgives and heals?

Not only that, anthropomorphic language about God is distinctly gender-specific, so God is male, and is described as both King and Father – a figure of authority and power who commands and rules the lives of his subjects, having the power of life and death over all. How are we to understand language which makes so much of male characteristics? Why should we not refer to God as Queen and Mother?

### The use of gender-neutral language:

In response to this, in the past two decades new translations of the Bible have appeared that are gender neutral (using terms that are neither masculine nor feminine). For example:

- 'man' (meaning) the human race becomes 'mortals' / 'humankind'
- 'man' (meaning a male) becomes 'person' / 'anyone'
- 'son' becomes 'child'
- 'father' becomes 'parent'.

Whether this helps with understanding the Bible is a matter for debate. As we have seen, terms such as 'Father' and 'King' are part of the patriarchal culture of the Ancient Near East, and to remove them from the text is to remove them from their proper context. The royal line in Israel was male, with the single exception of Athaliah, who became queen at the death of her son by murdering all the male contenders, ruling for six years until she suffered the same fate at the hands of a surviving male heir (1 Chronicles 22:10 – 23:15). Athaliah is the exception that proves the rule: to refer to God as Father and King is a cultural norm in the context of the Old Testament.

For a good overview of the controversy about the use of gender neutral language in translating the Bible, you should look briefly at Michael Marlowe's account at: http://www.bible-researcher.com/inclusive.html.

### The feminist critique of anthropomorphic and gender-specific language about God:

Feminist critiques of anthropomorphic and gender-specific language about God offer perhaps the most serious attack on the biblical view of God, particularly with the objection that it is irrelevant to half of the human population.

To give an outline of one of the most coherent and consistent feminist critiques, here is an overview from Daphne Hampson. (Note 5)

Whereas feminist theology can be a gender-inclusive theology (using language which does not privilege men over women / avoids bias towards a particular sex) or a non-gendered theology (for example replacing 'Father' with 'Creator'), the language of the Bible is clearly masculine. God is defined as an omni-everything, and so represents what every male would like to be in his wildest dreams: all-powerful, all-knowing; perfect in every way, and clearly and unequivocally male. God is the male patriarch carried to extremes. He is the all-powerful warrior, leader of the heavenly armies, supreme judge, king, ruler and – in fact – unchallengeable male despot. Much of the 'problem' with Christianity, in Hampson's view, is that its 'truths' are fundamentally flawed. Christians insist that there has been, and can be, only one Christ and one resurrection, for example, so the whole Christian story that was 'true' in the first century CE must necessarily be true in the twenty-first century CE, which means that all its patriarchal 'baggage' has to be accepted in the twenty-first century into a society which is becoming increasingly less patriarchal. We no longer (for the most part) live in the kind of tribal, male-dominated society that was characteristic of Jewish life during Old and New Testament times. Hampson puts it as strongly as this:

'... I have concluded that fundamental to the Abrahamic religions is the will to subvert women and establish man as norm. That is to say that, in so far as this is the case, these religions are a form of fascism.' (Note 6)

Monotheism in effect means male monotheism, and why should women be subject to that which is represented as unreservedly male? Why should women pray to a male God? The archetypal prayer Jesus taught his disciples is to 'Our Father'. What happened to 'Our Mother'? To what extent can Trinitarian thought be inclusive of women, when we have a male God the Father, and a male God the Son? There are a few Christian groups who see the Holy Spirit as feminine, on the grounds that the Hebrew for 'spirit' (*ruah*) is feminine, but this is very much a minority viewpoint. Hampson comments that:

'What is to be understood as female is something vague; indeed the Spirit is often designated as neuter. The two "male" persons of the trinity by contrast are anthropomorphically conceived entities, "persons" to whom people direct their prayers. Moreover the Spirit has ever played second fiddle to the male Christ within trinitarian theology.' (Note 7)

Feminist theologians also point to Jesus' apparent lack of commitment to any kind of female equality, not least in that he consistently refers to God as the Father. Jesus was unquestionably kind to women, but the idea that he had any kind of feminist perspective on society is something for which there is no evidence. (Note 8)

Some of these issues are addressed in the A-Level section on 'Christianity, gender and sexuality', but as a final comment here on the anthropomorphic aspects of Christianity, Hampson suggests that just because we can picture God as a person – as a Father and King, for example – it does not follow that God is in fact such an anthropomorphic agent. Feminist analysis of the language of Christian prayer convinces some that belief in a personal God who enters into relationships with people 'requires' anthropomorphism, because God is required to be a being of this kind in order to take part in the dialogue of prayer. In Hampson's view:

'As one's intellectual understanding of what the word God connotes changes, so too may one's practice.'

so that instead of the dialogue of prayer we might think of ourselves as:

'... being open and present to what one conceives to be a greater reality than one's self, knowing oneself as loved and upheld.' (Note 9)

As a critique of anthropomorphic, patriarchal, male-dominated Christian ideas, this is very challenging material, and it is not difficult to see why Hampson thinks that such ideas can no longer serve as a credible approach to religion in the modern era. There are, of course, feminists who disagree. Some point in particular to Jesus' general approach to women, not least his defence of the woman taken in adultery (John 8:1–11), together with the fact that he clearly accepted women as disciples. Had Jesus gone so far as to advocate modern feminist principles in the context of first-century Judaism, he would perhaps have achieved very little.

# The concept of God in Process Theology

For this you need to look at:

● God in Process Theology
● God as neither omnipotent nor Creator

## The Process God as neither omnipotent nor Creator

If you have not come across Process Theology before, you might find it very different from other concepts of God in Christianity. Within this AS book, you will come across Process thought in three different contexts:

● In this chapter, on the nature of God.
● In connection with life after death, Chapter 8 Self, death and afterlife, since the Process view is very different from 'mainstream' Christian thought on this subject.
● In the context of the discussion of the problem of evil, in Chapter 2 Evil and suffering.

Process Theology is not exactly easy to get to grips with, so you will find that Chapter 2 and Chapter 8 cover much the same ground in order to deal with life after death and the problem of evil. The repetition will, hopefully, make it more familiar to you. For the most part, you will be looking at David Griffin's account of Process Theology. The description of this in the section on the problem of evil in Chapter 2 is very full, so what follows here is only the Process view that God is neither omnipotent nor the Creator.

Process thought arose primarily from the work of the English philosopher and mathematician Alfred North Whitehead (1861–1947). Whitehead was fascinated by quantum mechanics, which in simple terms is the science of the very small. Whereas models of the universe from the time of Isaac Newton (1643–1727) tended to see the universe as a gigantic kind of mechanism working by precise mathematical laws, quantum mechanics began to reveal a universe in a constant dynamic of flux and change, and according to Whitehead, God is also growing and changing. This is the background from which Griffin's Process Theology evolved. (Note 10)

## Griffin's rejection of 'creation from nothing', and his rejection of God as the Creator

The main point from which Griffin starts his theodicy concerns the Christian view of *creatio ex nihilo* – 'creation out of nothing', which most Christians assume is the way that God created the world in Genesis 1:1–3. Griffin insists that this is based on a mistranslation of the text. To recap, this is the Revised Standard Version:

> 'In the beginning, God created the heavens and the earth. The earth was without form and void, and darkness was upon the face of the deep; and the Spirit of God was moving over the face of the waters.
>
> And God said, "Let there be light"; and there was light.'

This translation of the Hebrew text shows that God's first creative act is to create the universe ('the heavens and the earth'), and it implies that God called the universe into existence from nothing simply by using words of creative power.

However, a more likely translation of the Hebrew would be:

> 'In the beginning of God's creating the heavens and the earth, the earth being without form and void, and darkness being upon the face of the deep; and the Spirit of God moving over the face of the waters, God said, "Let there be light"; and there was light.'

If you compare the two translations, you will see that the second gives a completely different sense of the passage, because the phrase, 'the earth *being* without form and void' assumes that the universe already exists. What God is creating, therefore, is not the universe: rather he is creating order out of the 'formless and void' chaos.

According to Griffin, then:

● The universe is uncreated, and eternal – it was always there.
● What was there was primitive, unformed matter, that is, chaos.
● God was also always there, and just as human minds and bodies exist together, God and the universe exist together. The technical word is that they exist 'panentheistically', meaning everything is in God. Equally, God is 'in' the universe, so both are eternal and uncreated.
● God's role was therefore creative in the sense that he persuaded matter away from chaos into a state of greater order and complexity. The development of the galaxies we now see is one aspect of this persuasion. The evolution of life on earth is another.

In Chapter 6 Sources of wisdom and authority in Christianity, you will remember that we looked at the stories of creation and flood in Genesis and pointed out that they are in large part copies of earlier Babylonian stories – the *Enûma Eliš* (the creation narrative) and the Epic of Gilgamesh (the Flood story). The Babylonian accounts presuppose that the gods created the world out of chaotic pre-existing matter, so it seems probable that Genesis makes the same assumption.

Put simply, then, most Christian scholars and most Christians assume that God created the universe out of nothing, because they believe that this is what Genesis is teaching. Process theologians such as Griffin beg to differ: they make a very strong case that what Genesis really teaches is that God is a 'persuader': he does not create out of nothing – he persuades what is already there into some kind of order. He persuades order to come out of chaos.

## Griffin's rejection of God's omnipotence

1 Perhaps the main source of the Christian belief that God is omnipotent (all-powerful) is the doctrine of creation out of nothing, because a God who can literally bring the universe into existence from nothing would truly have unlimited power. But, if God did not create the universe from nothing, then he cannot have unlimited power, because there is something he cannot do: he cannot now create the universe, since it has always existed.

2 Not only that, chaotic matter has some power of its own to resist God. Think again of the analogy between human minds and bodies. We only ever see minds that are connected with bodies, so it makes sense to think of God and the universe in the same kind of way: God is 'in' the universe and the universe is 'in' God in the same way that our minds and bodies are both part of one thing – a human being. We are mental and physical unities, and we can understand the idea of God / the universe being a similar unity. Equally, your mind can control some of the workings of its body, but as Jesus says in Matthew 7:27, try adding to your height (or your lifespan) just by being anxious about it. If the mind of God seeks to persuade the vastness of the universe (or the multiverse), it has presumably taken him 13.7 billion years since the Big Bang to organise the universe into the form in which we now see it. God's power on this kind of thinking is immense, but it is not unlimited, so God is not omnipotent.

## Assessing the Process view of God

The discovery through quantum mechanics that, at the sub-atomic scale, reality is a chaotic process of flux and change, gives some support to Griffin's argument that God's creation of the universe was not creation from nothing but instead was the gradual ordering of pre-existing chaotic material.

Whether or not the doctrine of creation from nothing is implied in some biblical texts is a contested point, but Griffin is almost certainly right that the Hebrew of the main creation account in Genesis 1:1–3 is talking about creation from chaotic materials, and this understanding is strongly supported by the fact that the biblical account reflects the Babylonian stories of Creation and Flood.

God's lack of omnipotence in Process Theology can be seen, in some ways, as a strength, for example, it explains why God does not control evil – he cannot. Some consider it to be a major weakness, however, holding that a non-omnipotent God would not be worth worshipping.

Note that Process Theologians do not on the whole claim that it 'is' the case that God is not the Creator and is not omnipotent; rather they claim that what we observe of the universe suggests that this is 'probably' the case. Questions such as this can be considered afresh after looking at the other sections where we consider Process thinking.

**anthropomorphism** The practice of attributing human characteristics to non-human entities. With regard to God, it is anthropomorphic to describe God in human terms.

**atonement** The doctrine that Christ's obedience, suffering and death on the cross effected a reconciliation between humanity and God following the original sin of Adam and Eve. Those who accept Christ are thereby redeemed from sin and are reconciled with God.

**covenant** In the Bible, this is a formal agreement or relationship, for example, between God and Abraham, Moses and David. Covenants can be conditional or unconditional. That with Moses was conditional, and could bring blessings or curses on the nation, depending upon whether or not they obeyed the Ten Commandments and the rest of the Law.

*ex Deo* Latin, meaning 'out of God', as in creation 'out of God's own being'.

*ex nihilo* Latin, meaning 'from nothing', as in the doctrine of creation 'out of nothing'.

**immanent** When applied to God, means, 'existing within the space–time universe'.

**incarnate** Meaning 'enfleshed'. The doctrine of the Incarnation is that the second person of the Trinity – the Son – took on a human body and nature. He was made flesh by being born in the womb of Mary.

**monotheism** The belief that there is only one God (which usually entails the belief that God possesses complete power and knowledge).

**omnipotent** All-powerful.

**omniscient** All-knowing.

**pantheon** All of the gods / goddesses within any particular religious system.

*perichoresis* Greek for 'rotation', used in Trinitarian theology to describe the relation between the three persons of the Godhead, often translated as 'mutual indwelling' – so that the Father is *in* the Son; the Son is *in* the Father, and so on.

**polytheism** The belief in more than one god.

**redemption** To buy back, as with the ransom of slaves (Exodus 21:8). 'Redemption' is part of the language of the doctrine of the atonement: the suffering and death of Jesus redeems humanity from sin.

**salvation** To be saved from sin, for example, through the atonement made by Christ.

**Salvation History** Refers to the unfolding of God's plan throughout history to save the human race from sin and death (after the disobedience of Adam and Eve). God reveals himself by means of his saving acts in human history. Just as God came to the aid of the ancestors of the Jews when they were slaves in Egypt, God also reveals himself personally through Jesus, so the Bible reveals God's *ongoing* salvation of humanity.

**Shema** Hebrew (*shama*) – 'to hear', in the context of the *Shema* prayer in Deuteronomy 6:4: 'Hear, O Israel: The Lord our God is One'.

**transcendent** The idea that God is above and beyond space–time; as opposed to immanent, existing within space–time.

**Yahweh** The most commonly used name of God in the Old Testament. Ancient Hebrew was written without vowels, so the original pronunciation is not known.

# Summary of this section on God

## Monotheism

Religious belief in early Israel moved from polytheismh to monotheism, as encapsulated by the *Shema* prayer in Deuteronomy 6:4: 'Hear, O Israel: The Lord our God is One'. Biblical monotheism is 'ethical' monotheism. In the Old Testament, the covenant agreement between God and Israel is based on God's moral commands: the Law of Moses, centred on the Ten Commandments. In the New Testament, Jesus quotes from the *Shema* to say that love of God and love of one's neighbour as oneself are the greatest commandments. Moral obedience is at the heart of salvation to God's Kingdom.

## God as omnipotent Creator

Although some Christians believe that God created the world *ex Deo* (out of God's own being), most believe that God created the world *ex nihilo* (out of nothing), mainly because creating simply by words of power is the act of an omnipotent / unlimited Creator. Some Christians reject creation *ex nihilo* (for example, Process theologians) on the grounds that this belief is based on a mistranslation of Genesis 1:1–3, which is really suggesting that 'creation' amounted to God putting pre-existing chaotic material into an ordered form.

## God as controller of all things

An all-powerful Creator must by definition control everything and sustain everything. For some, God's omniscience leads to theological determinism, meaning that because God must know the entire future, there is no way the future can be changed, so humans cannot make free choices, and in effect are controlled by God's omniscience. Others follow the kind of view developed by Aquinas, that God is timeless, so he sees the results of our future free choices but does not cause them. To be able to choose freely is particularly important for good moral behaviour.

## God as transcendent and unknowable

Belief in God's transcendence follows from his omnipotence and omniscience: such a God cannot be known by mere human minds, so God must be unknowable and outside space and time. This, for example, is Rudolf Otto's view – that God is holy and numinous.

## The doctrine of the Trinity and its importance

The doctrine of the Trinity is 'perceived' (rather than found) in the New Testament writings. The classical doctrine of the Trinity affirms that Father, Son and Holy Spirit are one God in three persons, each possessing God's characteristics (such as his omnipotence and omniscience) in equal measure, and differing only in terms of their inner relations. God exists as one substance in three persons (*hypostases*). All three persons are eternal and uncreated. The three persons are 'mutually indwelling' (the doctrine of *perichoresis*).

The doctrine of the Trinity brings together the main historical and doctrinal truths of Christianity concerning sin, atonement and redemption. The concept of the Trinity makes it possible for humans to have a personal relationship with God, since the Father and the Son are immanent within creation, although the Godhead remains unknowable and transcendent. The Trinity can also be seen as a model for personal relationships, for example, in Moltmann's idea of the 'social Trinity'.

Study of John 10:30 and 1 Corinthians 8:6 shows us the difficulties in understanding whether the New Testament sees Jesus as literally 'the' Son of God (in the Trinitarian sense) or as 'a' son of God in the sense of someone close to God. **In John 10:30**, the fact that some of the Jews wanted to stone Jesus for blasphemy because they understood him to be identifying himself with the Father, seems to suggest that Jesus did see himself literally as the Son of God. However, another reading of the passage is that Jesus simply told them they were wrong, and that by claiming to be the Son of God he was simply saying that he was doing the work that God had predestined him to do. **In 1 Corinthians 8:6**, some think that Paul is using the language of the *Shema* to equate 'God as Father' with 'Jesus as Lord', but again, the words can be read in a quite different sense, to the effect that although Jesus' mission was so important for the human race that it was right to call him 'Lord', that title does not mean that Jesus was the (Lord) God. Rather, Jesus was God's instrument in creating the world. The Church clearly did come to understand that Jesus was the Son of God in the Trinitarian sense, but the New Testament texts may be stepping stones along the way to this understanding.

## God as Personal, Father, Love, King / anthropomorphic language about God; feminist perspectives

Although the Godhead in the Trinity is seen as transcendent and unknowable, God as Father and as Son are seen as immanent, and are described using anthropomorphic language. This kind of language is seen throughout the Bible, where it does not mean that God is literally a person; rather the language is analogical, showing that God can be related to as a person, for example, through prayer and religious experience.

## God as Father

Calling God 'Father' reflects the practice of patriarchal societies in the Ancient Near East, in which the oldest male ancestor in the patriarchal families had complete power. God reveals himself to Moses as the 'God of the Fathers' (Abraham, Isaac and Jacob). He is the Father Creator, and is also Father in relation to his Son Jesus. His actions are those of the patriarchal father, in that he instructs humans to be fruitful and multiply; he ordains different roles for men and women, and punishes disobedience. He also displays the love of a father for his Son, Jesus. The most anthropomorphic aspect of God as Father is the incarnation of Jesus as God's Son. Within the Trinity there are at least two male 'persons': Father and Son. Jesus frequently addresses God as Father, and taught his disciples to pray to God using that title. The Aramaic for 'Father' is 'Abba', which is the word Jesus would have used – a word that signifies God's approachability as the

Father of all people, and St Paul uses the word to suggest that by crying 'Abba – the Father!', all people become sons of God.

## God as Love

The issue of God's love relates to the question (in the problem of evil) of why an all-loving God allows evil to exist. God's love is the basis of the covenant for Israel. It is encapsulated by the suffering and death of Jesus, since these atone for human sin. The greatest gift of the Spirit is love. God is love, and this is the basis for loving others. If God is love, then love describes the relationship between the persons of the Trinity, and further requires love to be the basis of human relationships also. The kind of love Jesus is talking about is *agape*, which Fletcher uses as the basis for his Situation Ethics. The belief that humans are made in God's image means that God's love must be reflected in the human capacity for *agape*.

## God as King

God's nature as Father links naturally to that of God as King, with its attendant metaphors of God as sovereign ruler. This kind of imagery is seen clearly in Isaiah 6, where the prophet has a vision of God enthroned in the Jerusalem Temple. It is also seen in the 'Enthronement Psalms', where God is portrayed as a warrior king who leads the hosts of heaven. The most important aspect of this royal imagery is its use in the New Testament to portray Jesus as Messiah, although the role of Jesus as Messiah is much wider, since Jesus brings about the Kingdom of God.

## The challenge of understanding anthropomorphic and gender-specific language about God

Understanding anthropomorphic language about God is difficult in the sense that to describe God as having human actions, human emotions and a human body reduces God to the human level. How could such a God be the Creator, or save humans from sin, or be worthy of worship? To describe God as Father and King is clearly gender specific, and relates to the patriarchal model of society in ancient Israel. The royal line in Israel is almost exclusively male, so within that model it would be inappropriate to refer to God as Mother or Queen.

The real challenge here comes from feminist critiques of anthropomorphic and gender-specific language, since it seems very difficult to reconcile the anthropomorphic, patriarchal / male-orientated language of Christianity with feminist concerns. If the revelation through Jesus was binding for all the future, this means that the patriarchal model has to be used in the twenty-first century, whereas that model is arguably redundant. Monotheism, in particular, reinforces the position of the dominant male, and the fact that at least two members of the Trinity are male adds to this problem. Moreover Jesus, although he was kind to women, appears to have had no commitment to feminist principles. Feminist responses vary. Some remain Christian within the Church as it is, arguing that had Jesus taken a feminist stance in the first century CE, Christianity would probably never have got off the ground.

## The Process God as neither omnipotent nor Creator

The view that God is not the Creator stems from the Process reading of the Genesis 'creation' stories. These do not teach 'creation out of nothing'. As the older Babylonian stories show, the Hebrew in Genesis is talking about God creating order out of pre-existing chaotic material. Both God and physical matter are eternal and uncreated, and they exist panentheistically: the universe is in God and God is equally in the universe. God is not the Creator, but is therefore 'creative', persuading the universe into the form that we now see. The ordering of the galaxies and of life on earth is the result of this ongoing persuasion. If God did not create 'from nothing', then equally he cannot be omnipotent, since his power is limited by pre-existing matter. Using the analogy of the unity of human and animal minds and bodies, we can see that God is the mental aspect of reality, and the universe is God's 'body'. Just as the ability of the human mind to control its body is limited, God's power over the universe is limited. Process Theologians argue that the most likely explanation of the universe we observe is that God is not the Creator; nor is he omnipotent. This raises the question of whether or not such a God is worth worshipping.

# 8

# Self, death and afterlife

This chapter will cover:
- The meaning and purpose of life
- Resurrection
- Different interpretations of judgement, heaven, hell and **purgatory**

> **Key term**
>
> **purgatory** A (particularly Catholic) doctrine of an intermediate state after death in which those who are destined to enter heaven are punished / purified in order to make them worthy of heaven.

## The meaning and purpose of life

For this, you need to look at the meaning and purpose of life; the following purposes and their relative importance:

- To glorify God and have a personal relationship with him
- To prepare for judgement
- To bring about God's Kingdom on Earth

At some point, most humans ask themselves: 'What is it all about? Why am I here? What is the purpose of life?' Religious people look for answers to these questions in the teachings and beliefs of their religion, but their search for meaning does not stop there. They also consider their own experiences and things they observe in the world around them. This means that there is no one, simple answer to these questions that applies to all Christians. Not only do different Christian denominations and scholars teach slightly different things, but each individual Christian draws on different personal experience and observations. Because of this, the three purposes that are considered below are only a starting point.

### 1  To glorify God and have a personal relationship with him

Most Christian ideas about the purpose of life have their origin in Christian ideas about God. Because Christians see God as the creator and sustainer of all that exists, they define the meaning and purpose of life with reference to God. One way of doing this is to consider why God created humans. In the Revised Standard Version (RSV) translation, below, it uses 'man' for 'humans' or 'humankind'.

> Then God said, 'Let us make man in our image, according to our likeness; and let them have dominion over the fish of the sea, and over the birds of the air, and over the cattle, and over all the earth, and over every creeping thing that creeps upon the earth.' So God created man in his own image, in the image of God he created him; male and female he created them. And God blessed them, and God said to them, 'Be fruitful and multiply, and fill the earth and subdue it; and have dominion over the fish of the sea and over the birds of the air and over every living thing that moves upon the earth'. (Genesis 1: 26–28)

There are two creation stories in Genesis, and each gives a different account of the beginning of human life.

**In the first creation story** (Genesis 1:1–2:4a), God creates humans in one act of creation by speaking the words:

> **'Let us make man in our image.'**

The writer stresses the fact that humans, being created in God's image, are very like God. God tells them to be fruitful and multiply, to fill the Earth and subdue it, and at the end of the act of creation:

> **'... God saw everything that he had made, and behold, it was very good.'** (Genesis 1:31)

One way of understanding this is to see that humans are God's image in the created order. They represent God's qualities to everything else that God has made, and to one another. By reproducing and filling the Earth, they are supposed to spread the qualities of God that they represent over the whole Earth. For Christianity, the 'Godness' of God is beyond all human understanding, so God's qualities are hard to define in language. The term 'glory' (*kabod* in Hebrew) is used throughout the Old Testament to describe God's essential quality, and the prophet Isaiah links this with the purpose of life:

> **'... everyone who is called by my name, whom I created for my glory, whom I formed and made.'** (Isaiah 43:7)

Early Christians saw this quality in the life, actions and teachings of Jesus. The prologue to John's Gospel says:

> **'... we have beheld his glory, glory as of the only son from the Father.'** (John 1:14)

It follows from this that for many Christians, the purpose of their existence is to represent and spread God's glory, that is, to glorify God. They influence Christians in a number of ways:

- They try to show God's glory in their own life and actions.
- They tell others about God and try to encourage them to become Christians so they too can glorify God.
- They try to make their own lives more God-like in order to represent him better in the world.
- They draw people's attention to God's qualities in the world by talking and writing about them.
- They engage in worship which draws on and reflects back God's glory.

Jesus sums up this agenda in the Sermon on the Mount, when he says:

> **'Let your light so shine before men, that they may see your good works and give glory to your Father who is in heaven.'** (Matthew 5:16)

**In the second creation story** (Genesis 2:4b–3:24), the content is quite different. It depicts a view of God who is intimately involved with the physical act of creation.

> Then the LORD God formed man of dust from the ground, and breathed into his nostrils the breath of life; and man became a living being. And the LORD God planted a garden in Eden, in the east; and there he put the man whom he had formed. (Genesis 2:7–8)

God shows care and affection here for the individual that has been created, and makes animals to be companions, finally creating woman as a partner for him. In this creation story, God walks in the garden and talks to Adam and Eve. This close relationship between God and creation leads to a belief that another part of the purpose of human existence is to share a personal relationship with God. Christians believe that as well as glorifying God in the world, they also need to nurture their own relationship with God.

The relationship between Jesus as a human being and God the Father is, for Christians, the model for the relationship between every human and God. The writer of John's Gospel includes a long prayer by Jesus in which he sets out a wish for both the disciples present at the Last Supper, and for those followers who will come after them.

> I do not pray for these only, but also for those who believe in me through their word, that they may all be one; even as thou, Father, art in me, and I in thee, that they also may be in us, so that the world may believe that thou hast sent me. The glory that thou hast given me I have given them, that they may be one, even as we are one, I in them and thou in me, that they may become perfectly one, so that the world may know that thou hast sent me and hast loved them even as thou hast loved me. (John 17: 20–23)

This prayer shows the intimacy of the relationship between the Father and the Son ('you are in me and I am in you'), and uses that intimacy as a model for the relationship between Christians and God.

By this, Christians are influenced to build a close relationship with God, for example by:

- Communicating through prayer.
- Aiming to know God better through studying the Bible.
- Trying to follow Jesus' teachings, because Christians believe that God can be known through the person of Jesus Christ.
- Trying to model their lives on the life of Jesus.

## 2 To prepare for judgement

Another view of the meaning and purpose of life also has its roots in the second creation story. Humans were created to be with God. After the creation of the world and all its contents, Adam and Eve were persuaded by the serpent to disobey God, and as a result, they were banished from the garden. The close relationship between humans and God was broken, and humans were forced out into a world where they had to work to survive, and where pain and death became part of human experience. But since the original purpose of creation was to allow humans to spend eternity in God's presence, Christianity teaches that God paid for the sin of humanity by suffering.

The idea that Jesus' death can 'make up' for human sin is called the Doctrine of the Atonement. Probably the closest meaning for 'Atonement' is 'reconciliation' – Jesus' death reconciles God and the world:

**'God was in Christ reconciling the world to himself.' (2 Corinthians 5:19)**

In order to complete God's plan for reconciliation, humans must face judgement of their lives at the end of time.

▲ Medieval churches often had an image of the Last Judgement on the chancel arch to remind worshippers that they would have to face judgement. This image was painted in Holy Trinity Church, Coventry in the 1430s.

In the famous Parable of the Sheep and the Goats, Jesus taught his followers that they would be judged according to how they treated those less fortunate than themselves:

When the Son of man comes in his glory, and all the angels with him, then he will sit on his glorious throne. Before him will be gathered all the nations, and he will separate them one from another as a shepherd separates the sheep from the goats, and he will place the sheep at his right hand, but the goats at the left. Then the King will say to those at his right hand, 'Come, O blessed of my Father, inherit the kingdom prepared for you from the foundation of the world; for I was hungry and you gave me food, I was thirsty and you gave me drink, I was a stranger and you welcomed me, I was naked and you clothed me, I was sick and you visited me, I was in prison and you came to me.'

Then the righteous will answer him, 'Lord, when did we see thee hungry and feed thee, or thirsty and give thee drink? And when did we see thee a stranger and welcome thee, or naked and clothe thee? And when did we see thee sick or in prison and visit thee?' And the King will answer them, 'Truly, I say to you, as you did it to one of the least of these my brethren, you did it to me.'

Then he will say to those at his left hand, 'Depart from me, you cursed, into the eternal fire prepared for the devil and his angels; for I was hungry and you gave me no food, I was thirsty and you gave me no drink, I was a stranger and you did not welcome me, naked and you did not clothe me, sick and in prison and you did not visit me.' Then they also will answer, 'Lord, when did we see thee hungry or thirsty or a stranger or naked or sick or in prison, and did not minister to thee?'

Then he will answer them, 'Truly, I say to you, as you did it not to one of the least of these, you did it not to me.' And they will go away into eternal punishment, but the righteous into eternal life. (Matthew 25:31–46) [Note 1]

This leads to a view that the purpose of life is to prepare for judgement. Humanity's ultimate purpose is to be with God, and that will happen after all life on Earth has come to an end. All those who have died will be raised and judged. Those who have treated others with compassion and justice will be welcomed into God's eternal presence, but those who have not will be forever excluded from God.

Many liberal Christians today do not accept the dramatic narrative of a Judgement Day at the end of time as factually accurate. They argue that it is a story designed to show an important truth about the purpose of human existence. However, they do believe that some form of eternal existence in the presence of God is the outcome of striving for moral perfection. For some, judgement happens in response to Christ in *this* life; and being born of spirit and living eternal life is a quality of life in this life.

Yet another approach is taken by the soul-making theodicy of John Hick, which we looked at in detail in the section on the 'Problem of Evil'. (Note 2) In brief, Hick agrees with St Irenaeus (130–202CE) that the existence of evil in the world is not a flaw in God's perfect creation, but an essential part of God's plan for creation. The problem of evil can be stated simply:

God created humans as incomplete beings, with the potential to achieve a 'likeness' with God. The existence of evil allows humans to grow and develop virtues. God could have made humans with ready-made virtues so that they never sinned, but that would not be real moral goodness. Hick argues that God made humans free to choose good or evil, so that true virtues are those gained through freely overcoming temptations and trials; so in Hick's view, the existence of evil is essential to developing moral perfection, and the purpose of life is soul-making in which evil plays an essential part.

Living a life in a world where evil exists means that people can choose to overcome evil. If there is hunger, poverty or exclusion, Christians who respond to those evils with compassion and generosity become better people. In Hick's opinion, this process of overcoming evil continues, perhaps through different levels of existence, until everybody reaches God's Kingdom, so for Hick there is no possibility of God sending anybody to hell.

## 3 To bring about God's Kingdom on Earth

One problem with the two purposes described so far is that they focus on the individual. Glorifying, and building a personal relationship with God, or preparing oneself for judgement; both have a good outcome primarily for the person concerned. A more holistic view is that humans are part of the whole fabric of creation, and that the purpose of everything in creation is to bring to completion God's work by bringing about God's Kingdom on Earth.

The idea has its roots in the understanding of kingship at the time of Jesus. Jewish scriptures take God's kingship for granted because God created everything, but by the time of Jesus, the Jews were expecting a Messiah who would free them from the oppression of Roman rule, as both an earthly king and a spiritual leader. When Jesus refers to the Kingdom of God (Matthew uses the similar term 'Kingdom of Heaven'), he is linking the kingship of God over all of creation to the possibility that there will come a time when all of the created order, on Earth as well as in heaven, will follow God's laws. The Lord's Prayer, a prayer that Jesus taught his disciples, makes this very clear:

**'Your kingdom come, your will be done, on earth as in Heaven.'**

For some Christians, this hope is an eschatological one; that is, it relates to the end of time. They believe that one day, Jesus Christ will return to Earth in glory, and sin and death will be eliminated. However, other Christians see the whole purpose of their existence as a responsibility to work towards creating perfection on Earth. This means that they not only try to build up their own relationship with God, and develop virtues to make them more like God, but that they also work to bring about the conditions of a perfect heaven in their own community and in the world.

Many Christians believe that the coming of Jesus made it possible to imagine the Kingdom of God on Earth. The first thing Jesus is recorded as saying in Mark's Gospel is:

**'The time is fulfilled, and the kingdom of God is at hand; repent, and believe in the gospel.' (Mark 1:15 – the word 'gospel' here means 'good news')**

For this reason, Jesus is referred to as 'the inaugurator of the kingdom'. In order to make this kingdom a full reality on Earth, Christians believe they must first of all repent – turn away from – all that is not god-like, and then work to bring about the qualities of God to fruition on Earth.

The qualities that God's Kingdom on Earth would have are largely drawn from Old Testament texts, especially the prophets and the Book of Psalms. Peace, justice and freedom from want are the key features. Those Christians who see their purpose in this way not only seek these things for themselves, but for all those in the world who are the victims of conflict, injustice and poverty. They do not concern themselves with preparing for God to intervene: they focus on bringing about these qualities themselves as God's stewards.

One such Christian organisation is the Religious Society of Friends (Quakers). This is how they describe their work:

> We believe there is something of God in everyone and this shapes all our relationships and the way we treat others.
>
> It means treating everyone with respect, whatever their circumstances, beliefs, race, age or gender. It also means working to make this world a better place.
>
> Quakers have been, and continue to be, involved in working with and supporting many of those who are the most vulnerable and marginalised including refugees and asylum seekers, prisoners, war casualties and those living with mental health issues.
>
> Quakers work for peace in all aspects of life – locally, nationally and internationally – and we believe that working for peace begins in our own hearts. We do this both individually and collectively. (Website of the British Yearly Meeting) [Note 3]

## Evaluating the relative importance of these purposes for life

Such varied agendas about the meaning and purpose of life suggest that these terms may mean different things for different people. Preparation for judgement can imply simply being good in order to earn a reward, so some might be motivated by fear of punishment. It would be impossible to second-guess how God might view the actions of those whose motivation is fear of judgement as opposed to a desire to do right for right's sake, although presumably many people could be motivated by both self-interest and a desire to follow God's laws.

For those whose desire is to have a personal relationship with God, this could result in a contemplative life – a life-long journey of prayer and contemplation, perhaps within a monastic community, leaving on one side everything that might make the journey less direct. Some might focus on Christian mysticism, working through study, worship and contemplation towards a hoped-for, transformative experience of God.

None of these purposes are mutually exclusive: many Christians work to bring about God's Kingdom on Earth while also developing their own virtues and a closer personal relationship with God. For some Christians, doing God's will, or being a good person, is an end in itself. For others, what they do has a focus and a purpose that is in line with their personal circumstances and abilities.

# Resurrection

For this you need to look at:

- The concept of soul
- Resurrection of the flesh as expressed in the writings of Augustine
- Spiritual resurrection; the significance of 1 Corinthians 15: 42–44 and 50–54.

One of the defining features of Christianity is the concept of resurrection. All four Gospel narratives say that on the third day after his death, Jesus' tomb was found to be empty. Three of the Gospels describe episodes where the risen Jesus appeared to his disciples. It is clear that they knew it was Jesus, but that he was in some ways different to the person with whom they had spent three years. He ate normal food with them, and showed his disciples the injuries he received at the crucifixion, but he was able to appear and disappear at will, and in the story of his appearance on the road to Emmaus (Luke 24:13–35), some of his followers did not recognise him during the course of a long conversation.

Christianity teaches that Jesus rose from the dead. This does not mean that he was merely revived or resuscitated, but that through the power of God, he overcame the power of death, and appeared to his disciples full of life from God. No human has ever experienced this: even those whom Jesus brought to life in his healings would go on to die a normal death at the end of their lives, for example, Lazarus (John 11:1–57). The resurrection of Jesus is symbolic for Christians of the everlasting life that comes from God, the source of all life. Jesus' resurrection shows that death, a consequence of the sin in the world, can be overcome through the power of God. The death of Jesus Christ on the cross has cancelled out the consequences of sin for human beings, and the possibility of eternal life is available to everyone.

## 1 The concept of soul

The Christian concept of soul comes from both Judaism and ancient Greek philosophy. In Judaism, the physical body is infused with the 'breath of life' which comes from God. This concept appears in Genesis 2:7, where God formed the man, Adam, from the dust of the ground, and 'breathed into his nostrils the breath of life', so that he became a *nephesh hayyah* – 'a living being'. Life is not only a quality of humans: for Jews, everything that breathes has the spirit of God within them. *Nephesh* in Genesis 2:7 is usually translated as 'soul', and this is the existence that a creature has as a result of receiving the breath of life from God. Another word with similar meaning is *ruach* (similar to Greek *psyche*), so that in Genesis 1:2, the *ruach elohim* – the 'Spirit' of God was moving over the primeval waters during creation.

In early Old Testament Judaism, people did not believe in life after death, but in the period leading up to the time of Jesus, some had come to believe that since God is eternal, human life which comes from God might not end at death. Something of the person might live on after the death of the physical body. The book of Daniel, written in the second century BCE, contains prophecies about the end of time, including:

> '... many of those who sleep in the dust of the earth shall awake, some to everlasting life, and some to shame and everlasting contempt.' (Daniel 12:2)

The Greek philosopher Plato (who died in 348 BCE) and his later followers believed that there were two modes of existence. The physical world that we see around us is a reflection of a deeper reality which he called the world of **Forms**. The world of Forms is made up of perfect ideas, and the things in the physical world are imperfect copies of the perfect ideas. So, for example, the chair you are sitting on is one of many chairs in the physical world, but in the world of Forms, there is one perfect idea of a chair and all physical chairs are reflections of this idea. Plato believed that the human soul separates from the body at death and goes to the world of Forms, and there contemplates the Form of the Good (this Form being about as close as Plato got to the idea of God), before being **reincarnated** ('re-enfleshed') into the physical world in a human womb. This world view is called 'dualism', so 'soul' is usually a dualistic idea – humans have two aspects: the physical (perishable) body and the spiritual (immortal) soul. Plato believed that the soul eternally pre-existed human life and is immortal in its own right. Our ability to know what things are, he suggested, is the result of the fact that the soul belongs to the world of Forms. Because the soul is familiar with the perfect idea for each thing, it can recognise the imperfect copies in the physical world.

In the early years of Christianity, the Jewish ideas of Jesus and his followers combined with the ideas of Plato and his later followers (Neo-Platonists), which were widely accepted in the world of the first and second centuries CE. The Jewish and Greek ideas of 'soul' were similar enough for early Christians to link them together. They believed that a baby received a soul from God, some time before birth. The soul was the inner existence of a

### Key terms

**Forms** Plato's Theory of Forms is that everything in the physical universe is a particular instance of a perfect idea in the metaphysical world of Forms, so every particular chair is a chair by virtue of being a particular instance of the perfect form of a chair.

**reincarnation** The belief (found in Plato and Hinduism, for example) that at death, the soul at some point is 're-enfleshed' into another body.

human being, inhabiting the body during life, and then leaving the body at death to return to God, from whom it came. The soul was the moral and spiritual dimension of human existence and the source of humankind's response to God:

> My soul magnifies the Lord, and my spirit rejoices in God my Saviour ...
> (From the 'Magnificat' – Mary's 'Song of Joy', Luke 1:46)

Some people today continue to see the human being in dualistic terms as body and soul. In popular thinking, the soul is what makes a person who they are, the source of their beliefs, understanding of self, thought processes, moral judgement and conscience. Others see the human being as a whole creature in whom consciousness and thought are part of their physical reality. For them, there is no existence before conception, and no life beyond death.

Beware of popular myths about souls: in 1901, an American doctor called Duncan McDougall conducted experiments which involved weighing dying tuberculosis patients. He reported that on average, they lost around 21 grams at the moment of death. He concluded therefore that the human soul weighs about 21 grams. This finding has subsequently been shown to be incorrect – there is no loss of weight at death, and few today believe that the soul is something that can be measured scientifically.

Modern psychologists especially since the work of Sigmund Freud at the start of the twentieth century, tend not to use the term 'soul'. Instead they speak of the 'psyche' (the Greek word for *breath* or *spirit*). Freud suggested that the psyche could be divided into three parts, the id (source of basic impulses like desire for pleasure), the super-ego (source of moral judgement) and the ego (source of reason). Ideas about life before conception or after the death of the body are not part of the study of psychology.

## 2 Resurrection of the flesh as expressed in the writings of Augustine

For Christians, the resurrection of Jesus Christ was the event which made it possible for all people to have life after death. By overcoming death on the cross, he restored to humankind the hope of resurrection and eternal life that had been lost through original sin. However, the exact nature of the hoped-for resurrection was not at all clear.

### St Augustine of Hippo (354–430CE)

St Augustine tackled the question of resurrection head on, and his theology continues to inform Catholic teaching today. Born in what is now Algeria, he lost his father as a teenager and had a few wayward years before turning to religion. As priest and then bishop, he wrote with great scholarship, but also with wisdom and insight into human nature. His two most famous books are *Confessions*, an account of his own conversion, and *City of God*.

Augustine believed that sin, caused by the fall of Adam and Eve, had an effect on every human being born, both spiritually and physically. People's souls were stained with sin, and their bodies, senses and desires were also tainted with sinfulness. If the resurrection of Christ offered hope for the resurrection of humans, Augustine was sure that this resurrection must be a bodily, physical resurrection where both the spiritual and physical effects of sin would be removed.

> For if we were only souls, that is, spirits without any body, and if we dwelt in heaven and had no knowledge of earthly animals, and were told that we should be bound to earthly bodies by some wonderful bond of union, and should animate them, should we not much more vigorously refuse to believe this, and maintain that nature would not permit an incorporeal substance to be held by a corporeal bond? And yet the earth is full of living spirits, to which terrestrial bodies are bound, and with which they are in a wonderful way implicated. If, then, the same God who has created such beings wills this also, what is to hinder the earthly body from being raised to a heavenly body, since a spirit, which is more excellent than all bodies, and consequently than even a heavenly body, has been tied to an earthly body?
>
> [...]
>
> But granting that this was once incredible, behold, now, the world has come to the belief that the earthly body of Christ was received up into heaven. Already both the learned and unlearned have believed in the resurrection of the flesh and its ascension to the heavenly places, while only a very few either of the educated or uneducated are still staggered by it. If this is a credible thing which is believed, then let those who do not believe see how stolid they are; and if it is incredible, then this also is an incredible thing, that what is incredible should have received such credit. Here then we have two incredibles – to wit, the resurrection of our body to eternity, and that the world should believe so incredible a thing; and both these incredibles the same God predicted should come to pass before either had as yet occurred.
>
> Augustine: *City of God*, Book 22, ch.4–5 (Note 4)

In other words, it is Augustine's understanding that Jesus Christ rose from the dead in a wholly physical way, and then ascended to heaven in a physical form. If it is possible for this to happen to Jesus Christ, then surely God can perform the same miracle for anything that has been created with a soul? Augustine's view forms the basis of the teaching of the Catholic Church today:

> From the beginning, Christian faith in the resurrection has met with incomprehension and opposition. 'On no point does the Christian faith encounter more opposition than on the resurrection of the body.' It is very commonly accepted that the life of the human person continues in a spiritual fashion after death. But how can we believe that this body, so clearly mortal, could rise to everlasting life?
>
> How do the dead rise?
>
> What is 'rising'? In death, the separation of the soul from the body, the human body decays and the soul goes to meet God, while awaiting its reunion with its glorified body. God, in his almighty power, will definitively grant incorruptible life to our bodies by reuniting them with our souls, through the power of Jesus' Resurrection.
>
> (*Catechism of the Catholic Church* Article 11.1 996–997) (Note 5)

# 3 Spiritual resurrection

As we learned earlier, the idea of an immortal soul is not biblical, but derives from Greek thought. For some Christians, the idea of physical resurrection does not make sense. They argue that the dead body rots away to nothing in the grave or is completely destroyed by fire in cremation. The elements that make up the body are returned to nature and re-used in such a way that resurrection of the flesh is a nonsensical idea. This does not mean, though, that they reject the idea of resurrection. For these believers, it is the soul or spirit of the person that is resurrected. When the body comes to its end in death, the soul lives on with God. They support this view with reference to Paul's first letter to the Church in Corinth. Paul says:

> 'It is sown a physical body, it is raised a spiritual body'
> (1 Corinthians 15:44)

and

> 'We shall not all sleep [die], but we shall all be changed.'
> (1 Corinthians 15:51)

This seems to indicate that the resurrected 'body' will be quite different to the body that has died.

Some think Paul's words imply that there will be some kind of physical aspect to the resurrection, but that the soul may be resurrected into in a new heavenly body that had no physical existence on Earth. Others argue that Paul is trying to explain that a miraculous change will come over physical bodies so that they become perfect, no longer subject to ageing and decay. This too raises questions: What age and condition will the resurrected body be? Will it be the same age as the person was at death, or will all bodies be the same ageless form? Will someone who died in infancy be resurrected as an infant, or as the adult they might have become? Will someone with a missing limb or organ be resurrected whole or as they were at death? Religion does not provide answers to any of these questions.

## The significance of 1 Corinthians 15:42–44 and 50–54

In his first letter to the people in the Church at Corinth, Paul's purpose was to intervene in disputes that risked splitting the community. One of these was about the resurrection. Paul says:

> 'Now if Christ is preached as raised from the dead, how can some
> of you say that there is no resurrection of the dead?' (1 Corinthians
> 15:12)

Clearly, the Corinthians had been struggling to make sense both of the idea of the resurrection of Jesus Christ, and also of the implication that humans too can be resurrected. This chapter of Paul's letter unpacks his teaching on the resurrection of Jesus and its implications for humankind.

Paul's explanation focuses on an insistence that resurrection is possible. Humans can indeed be resurrected and Jesus Christ has been raised from the dead. If the Corinthians do not believe in resurrection, then their faith in Jesus has been pointless. He goes on say:

> 'In fact Christ has been raised from the dead, the first fruits of
> those who have died.' (1 Corinthians 15:20)

In other words, the raising of Christ is the beginning of the resurrection of all humankind.

We can guess some of the things the Corinthians had been saying from what Paul writes: How can this physical body be resurrected as it is? Bodies grow old and sick and decay. Disease and injury leave bodies disfigured and ugly. How could a body like this be resurrected in the Kingdom of God?

> There are celestial bodies and there are terrestrial bodies; but the glory of the celestial is one, and the glory of the terrestrial is another. There is one glory of the sun, and another glory of the moon, and another glory of the stars; for star differs from star in glory.
>
> So is it with the resurrection of the dead. What is sown is perishable, what is raised is imperishable. It is sown in dishonor, it is raised in glory. It is sown in weakness, it is raised in power. It is sown a physical body, it is raised a spiritual body. If there is a physical body, there is also a spiritual body. Thus it is written, 'The first man Adam became a living being'; the last Adam became a life-giving spirit. But it is not the spiritual which is first but the physical, and then the spiritual. The first man was from the earth, a man of dust; the second man is from heaven. As was the man of dust, so are those who are of the dust; and as is the man of heaven, so are those who are of heaven. Just as we have borne the image of the man of dust, we shall also bear the image of the man of heaven. I tell you this, brethren: flesh and blood cannot inherit the kingdom of God, nor does the perishable inherit the imperishable.
>
> Lo! I tell you a mystery. We shall not all sleep, but we shall all be changed, in a moment, in the twinkling of an eye, at the last trumpet. For the trumpet will sound, and the dead will be raised imperishable, and we shall be changed. For this perishable nature must put on the imperishable, and this mortal nature must put on immortality. (1 Corinthians 15:40–42)

This passage is important for a number of reasons. First, it is a very early piece of Christian theology. All of Paul's authentic letters were written before 58CE, and this one is thought to date from sometime between 53 and 57CE. This means that it was written only 20–25 years after the death of Jesus. It shows the development of Christian thought at an early stage, at a time when people who remembered Jesus would still be alive. We can see how Paul uses his certainty that Jesus was raised physically from the dead to argue that belief in the resurrection is both rational and essential for members of the emerging Church.

Second, it forms the basis for Christian teaching on resurrection. According to Paul, the death and resurrection of Jesus was not a one-off spectacular historical event. It was the cause of, and evidence for, the start of a new relationship between humankind and God, one that was no longer damaged by the sin of Adam. Death was not the end, but there was hope for eternal life in the presence of God alongside the risen, ascended Christ.

Third, it provided hope during periods of persecution that the Church would soon experience, and a theological justification for martyrdom. The first period of persecution of Christians was under the Roman emperor Nero in 64CE, after he blamed Christians for causing a fire which destroyed large parts of Rome. It would have been easy for Christians to give up their faith rather than risk imprisonment, torture or death. However, belief in resurrection to eternal life was so attractive that rather than give up their faith, Christians were prepared to die bearing witness to Jesus Christ as Lord. Without these martyrs, Christianity might have died out altogether.

### Within Christian ideas about resurrection, we can see a range of interacting influences at work in Christian thinking:

- Burial rituals from ancient times underline the importance of the body in defining a person. The ancient Egyptians practised mummification for the spirit to return to. As a way of thinking about the importance of persons, then, the Christian concept of bodily resurrection, as expressed for example in the teachings of St Augustine and the Catholic Church, make perfect sense.
- Until 1963, cremation was forbidden in the Catholic Church, since the practice was generally seen as a statement of disbelief in resurrection of the body, and its acceptance after 1963 depended on not being intended as such a statement. Moreover, burial is still recommended over cremation.
- We can see the influence of the idea of bodily resurrection in Christian art, which has countless examples of the bodily resurrection of Jesus and the physical resurrection of the dead in general. Without a physical body, it would be impossible for resurrected beings to experience the physical delights of heaven or the torments of hell.
- The alternative notion that resurrection is a spiritual reality was influenced by the Greek concept of the soul, particularly through the teachings of Plato and his followers. In turn, this influenced the body/soul dualism of Descartes, who believed he had proved philosophically that the mind must survive the destruction of its body. Christians have different ideas about the nature of resurrection depending on which influences are most dominant in their own Church traditions and their own thinking.
- Protestant Churches are more likely to support the idea of cremation, sometimes on the grounds that resurrection is spiritual, so the method of disposing of dead bodies is less important than maintaining a general respect for the dead person.
- Regardless of the method of disposing of dead bodies, belief in resurrection influenced the Christian tradition of martyrdom. A martyr was someone who gave witness or testimony, and came to mean those who testified to the truth of the Christian gospel with a great likelihood of being killed for doing so. The first recorded Christian martyr was Stephen. Just before he was killed, Stephen was upheld by a vision of the resurrected Jesus standing at the right hand of God (Acts 7:56). There was a general belief among Christians that God, being all-powerful, would even reconstitute the bodies of those martyrs who were burned at the stake.

### Key term

**objective immortality** The belief (in Process Theology) that every living thing exists for ever in the mind of God, because they are literally objects 'in' God.

# Different interpretations of judgement, heaven, hell and purgatory

For this you need to look at:

- Judgement, heaven, hell and purgatory as physical, spiritual or psychological realities
- **Objective immortality** in Process thought

Look back at the image of judgement in this chapter (page 283) and re-read the Bible passage after it. This story forms the basis of Christian ideas about judgement, but there are other passages in the Bible, and also many cultural influences, which have shaped Christian thinking. Some of the Old Testament prophetic books and the New Testament book of Revelation describe the events at the end of time.

> Then I saw a great white throne and him who sat upon it; from his presence earth and sky fled away, and no place was found for them. And I saw the dead, great and small, standing before the throne, and books were opened. Also another book was opened, which is the book of life. And the dead were judged by what was written in the books, by what they had done. (Revelation 20:11–12)

The classic idea of judgement, as generally understood in the West until the modern era, was this: at the end of time, the dead, who had been sleeping in their graves, would be awoken by the sound of a trumpet which would herald the end of all things. Christ would come again in glory. He would be seated on a throne surrounded by angels, and each individual would be judged according to their deeds written in the book of life.

- Those who were judged holy would gain immediate entrance to heaven (usually thought of as a holy city), and would be led there by angels.
- Those who were judged sinful would be sent to suffer burning, pain and torture.
- If their sins were unforgiveable (mortal sins), they would spend eternity suffering in hell, tormented by demons.
- If their sins were forgivable (**venial sins**), they would undergo a period of suffering and pain to cleanse (purge) them of the evil in a state called 'purgatory', and after that they would be admitted to heaven. Catholic teaching is clear that purgatory is a state that the soul undergoes in preparation for the final universal judgement:

> 'All who die in God's grace and friendship, but still imperfectly purified, are indeed assured of their eternal salvation; but after death they undergo purification, so as to achieve the holiness necessary to enter the joy of heaven.' (*Catechism of the Catholic Church*, Sect 2, Ch 3, Article 12 1030)

Many of the details that were widely believed about heaven, hell and purgatory became popular from Dante's long poem *The Divine Comedy*. Dante described a journey in which he was conducted through hell, heaven and purgatory by the Roman poet Virgil. It was intended to be an **allegory** describing the journey of the human soul towards God, but the vivid descriptions of the fate of historical characters caught public imagination. Artists like Botticelli (1445–1510) used Dante's description as the basis for images of the afterlife and, at a time when many were illiterate, they influenced the way that people thought about life after death.

The Orthodox Churches of the East have different teaching about judgement. They believe that 40 days after death there will be a 'particular' judgement of each individual Christian, when God will decide where the soul will wait until the second coming of Christ. There will then be a

**Key term**

**venial sin** A 'forgivable' sin that does not result in separation from God and eternal damnation to hell (as opposed to 'mortal sin', which does result in this).

**Key term**

**allegory** For example: a piece of literature which has hidden / symbolic meaning.

293

'general' judgement, when the dead bodies will rise, and Christ through God's grace will grant salvation, although the deeds of individuals will be taken into account as in the Parable of the Sheep and Goats. The judgement of those who are not Christian is not defined in Orthodox theology, but it is thought that they will be judged with mercy.

The Catholic Church today teaches a similar view to that of the Orthodox Churches:

> Each man receives his eternal retribution in his immortal soul at the very moment of his death, in a particular judgment that refers his life to Christ: either entrance into the blessedness of heaven – through a purification or immediately, – or immediate and everlasting damnation [...] The resurrection of all the dead, 'of both the just and the unjust,' will precede the Last Judgment. This will be 'the hour when all who are in the tombs will hear [the Son of man's] voice and come forth, those who have done good, to the resurrection of life, and those who have done evil, to the resurrection of judgment.'
>
> (*Catechism of the Catholic Church*, Sect 2, Ch 3, Article 12 1022 & 1038)

## 1 Judgement, heaven, hell and purgatory as physical

Throughout most of Christian history, people have understood judgement, heaven, hell and purgatory as physical realities. In the same way that they accepted the idea of a physical resurrection, they believed that, once raised, the physical body would enjoy the delights of heaven or the pains of purgatory and hell.

When these doctrines were being developed, people were much more aware of the reality of death than people are today. During the periods of persecution by the Romans, Christians were tortured and killed in painful ways. Even after the persecutions ended, death, pain and suffering were part of normal life. Young women often died as a result of childbirth and young men through injuries or infection. Many children failed to survive childhood, and some diseases and injuries that are now easily treated were fatal before the advent of modern medicine. In the same way, people were more aware of physical suffering. With no anaesthetics and only simple herbal remedies, people who were injured or ill experienced the full force of physical pain more often, and more fiercely, than people today.

They also lived at a time when earthly crime often led to brutal physical punishment by the courts. Serious crimes were punished by death: the criminal might be hanged, burnt at the stake, ripped apart or thrown off cliffs. Lesser punishment included mutilation of eyes, limbs or testicles, or imprisonment under appalling conditions which led to illness and starvation. The rationale behind such punishments was to deter people from crime by making them fear the consequences.

It is no surprise, then, that when they were taught Bible stories about judgement, heaven and hell, with the description of pain and suffering, people had no trouble believing in the literal reality of 'the eternal fire prepared for the devil and his angels' as a punishment for sin. Hell would be a dark, cruel place, not unlike a medieval dungeon, populated by torturing demons and everlasting fire. The Church hoped that by focusing on the suffering of sinners after death, they would deter people from committing individual sins. This purpose became especially important after the Black

Death (a plague which swept through Europe in the fourteenth century). The Church taught that the plague was a punishment from God for human sin, and so it was essential for sinners to repent and avoid sinning in future.

In the same way, the idea of heaven reflects the realities of life at the time. Heaven would be a place where there was no physical suffering or pain, where there was enough to eat, and no labour or sorrow. Because in life these things were the product of wealth, they were more often found in market towns and cities, where the rich lived in comfort and clean conditions with sufficient food and rest. It is no surprise, therefore, that the heaven to which the saved are led by angels is usually shown as a walled city. References from the Bible to a heavenly banquet promise abundant food and celebrations, for example, Luke 14:15–24.

The presence of a doom painting in most churches served to remind people that they were under judgement. The hell section of doom paintings (always at the bottom right of the image to reflect the fact that the 'goats' were sent to the left of Christ the judge) invariably included flames and demons torturing the unhappy damned. Some images went further still: Fra Angelico's *Last Judgement* shows different punishments for each of the seven deadly sins under the direction of demons, and an image of the devil chewing up sinners while wallowing in a vat of body parts.

▲ The hell section from Fra Angelico's *Last Judgement* (painted c.1425–1431)

One outcome of this set of beliefs, was that people feared death so much that they were prepared to go to great lengths to avoid going to hell, and to reduce the amount of time they might spend in purgatory. The Catholic Church developed the teaching on 'indulgences', which gave sinners the opportunity to acquire some of the virtue of the risen saints by going on pilgrimages, visiting and touching relics, or by making donations to the Church. Sinners could be persuaded to do these things at enormous personal cost out of the fear of suffering in purgatory. Over time, the abuse of indulgences to fund an expensive building project in Rome was one of the things that caused Luther to protest, and this led to the Protestant Reformation.

## 2 Judgement, heaven, hell and purgatory as spiritual

In modern thought, the concept of a final resurrection of the dead in bodily form is not so widely held. We have seen that the view that individual bodies might be resurrected whole at the end of time is counter-intuitive, and this leads to the idea that if the resurrection of the dead is a spiritual reality, then so too must be the final judgement; moreover, if purgatory exists, it must be a spiritual purging. If that is the case, the concepts of heaven, hell and purgatory must be adjusted to fit with the idea that the spiritually resurrected souls may be subject to eternal life with God in heaven or eternal suffering apart from God in hell.

This, of course, changes the nature of how people understand both the joy of heaven and the suffering of hell. If heaven is a spiritual reality rather than a physical one, the qualities that the saved enjoy are spiritual rather than material: joy, peace and love, and the pleasure of being reunited with loved ones, in the safe and secure knowledge that God is always present. In the same way, the suffering of the damned is understood as spiritual loss: the eternal absence of God, no source of goodness, joy or peace, eternal separation from loved ones, and endless sorrow and spiritual pain.

For some Christians who believe in the idea of spiritual judgement, ideas about individual judgement and final judgement are conflated. They argue that since for God time has no meaning, there is no difference to God between the time when an individual person dies and the end of time itself. Therefore, there is only one spiritual judgement at the time of death, and the final destination of each soul is decided at that time. Having left the physical world and their bodies behind, the afterlife begins with judgement, and eternity in a spiritual heaven or hell follows. The idea of purgatory loses its force in this world view, since a time of suffering to cleanse the soul would depend on time having some meaning in eternity.

## 3 Judgement, heaven, hell and purgatory as psychological realities

There are many Christians today who find notions of resurrection, judgement and eternal joy or suffering to be out of date. There is no empirical evidence for any kind of existence after death, and so the idea that behaviour in human physical life can make a difference to their experience after death seems pointless. For some Christians, then, eternal life is reinterpreted in terms of the quality of living in this life: if Christ's teachings on right living are followed, then this can bring about heaven on Earth. Some find a basis for this understanding in John 17:3, for example:

> 'And this is eternal life, that they know thee the only true God, and Jesus Christ whom thou has sent.'

A similar, alternative view is that judgement, heaven and hell might be psychological realities, the product of the human mind rather than the external power of God.

This is not an entirely new idea: in Book 1 of *Paradise Lost*, the poet John Milton gives these words to the rebel angel:

> 'The mind is its own place, and in itself can make a heav'n of hell, a hell of heav'n.' (*Paradise Lost*, Bk 1)

Of course, for Milton, this view was wholly wrong, because it is spoken by a fallen angel who has fought against God and been expelled from heaven. However, it does articulate very clearly the notion that the concepts of judgement, heaven and hell may be understood not as part of a supernatural, external process, but as part of the psychology of the human mind.

Modern psychology, as articulated first by Freud, suggested that the human psyche was governed by conscious and unconscious urges, and that conflict between different aspects of the psyche leads to mental suffering. Freud thought that religious belief was merely the result of neurosis, but a student of Freud's, Carl Jung, suggested that religious or spiritual experience is essential as an individual develops towards a full realisation of who they really are.

In either case, it is clear that both joy and suffering may be experienced as psychological realities. A person who is spiritually fulfilled experiences a state of contentment, and one who is spiritually in conflict experiences psychological suffering. Where a person lives a life wholly in harmony with their deepest beliefs and spiritual instincts, they will experience inner peace, contentment and joy akin to the idea of heaven. Where someone's beliefs and spiritual instincts clash with each other and with the way they live their life, the result is inner conflict and suffering, misery and a sense of failure that seems to have no hope, and may lead to self-destructive behaviour – in other words, a psychological hell.

For those who find themselves in a psychological hell, there is the possibility that they may escape through therapy or treatment. Psychoanalysis, which helps a sufferer recognise and confront the causes of their inner conflict, may help in the recovery of psychological wholeness. Self-reflection and small incremental change may help sufferers to leave behind self-destructive behaviour: this is the basis behind the twelve-step programme of Alcoholics Anonymous. Whilst these are not identified in any way with theological ideas of purgatory, it is clear that these are parallel concepts. Therapy and self-reflection may restore those who find themselves in a state of psychological hell, through a process which, over time, allows them to separate from the things that cause them to suffer and offers the possibility of psychological wholeness.

# 4 Objective immortality in Process thought

In the section on Evil and Suffering, (pages 77–82), we looked at the ideas of Process Theology as to why an omnipotent (all-powerful) God allows evil and suffering to exist in the world. In particular, we looked at David Griffin's Process Theology. Process Theology in general rejects the idea that God created the universe 'out of nothing', and proposes instead that both the physical universe and God are uncreated and have always existed. 'Reality', then, is both mental and physical; and just as humans exist as a unity of mind and body, reality as a whole is made up of mind and matter. To describe this relationship, Process theologians say that God and the universe exist **panentheistically**, meaning that the universe is in God, and God is in the universe. Not only that, those Christians (the majority) who believe that God created the universe out of nothing are (according to Process Theology) wrong.

To explain this, try to imagine God and primitive matter existing together without any beginning. Process theologians think that this primitive matter would have been chaotic / without form or structure. By comparison with primitive matter, even an electron has structure. Process theologians argue that God decided to bring chaotic matter into order, and God foresaw that, eventually, matter could become so orderly that it would form intelligent beings, such as ourselves. God's task in creation was therefore to 'persuade' chaotic matter into ever-increasing order. This kind of God, therefore, cannot be all-powerful, because matter that has to be persuaded must always have some ability to resist God's persuasion.

What exists necessarily, then, is what Griffin calls, 'God-and-a-world' (that is, God + the universe). As we learned above: just as humans have embodied minds, it makes sense to think of God as the soul of the universe. Just as the human body's experiences are integrated by the mind, the experiences of the entire universe are integrated by the mind of God. Since God and the universe exist panentheistically, this means further that God must experience every single process within the universe, and it is this belief that dictates how Process theologians think about life after death. Process theologians therefore tend to believe in 'objective immortality': after death, all individual entities in the universe remain forever as 'objects' in the mind of God, so in that sense they never die.

In this view, then, all our actions, thoughts and ideas continue to exist in every minute detail as objects in God's memory, and since God is eternal, in that sense we are eternal also, but objectively and not subjectively. **Subjective immortality**, by contrast, is the view that beings such as ourselves have the potential to exist for ever as 'irreducibly subjective units of experience'; meaning that when we die, we will exist always as thinking, feeling subjects with our own thought processes, memories and continued experiences; and nobody else (not even God) will experience them for us. Most Christians believe in subjective immortality.

To evaluate this briefly: most Christians appear to believe that subjective immortality is for humans, and not for other animals. This is certainly the case for Catholics, who believe that animals do not have souls. The idea of objective immortality does at least do away with the anthropocentric (human-centred) idea that only humans have sufficient value in God's eyes to be granted immortality after death. The idea that humans are

## Key terms

**panentheism** The philosophical view that everything that there is exists 'in God'.

**subjective immortality** The belief that after death the thinking self continues as the same subject of consciousness – the same 'I'.

somehow more valuable than the rest of creation is seen by some to be wishful thinking. With Process Theology, then, all 'entities' have objective immortality; all entities are valued forever and for their own sakes, which sounds like a reasonable and a fair viewpoint.

Having said that, some people think that the idea of objective immortality is a meaningless form of words. After death 'I' am no longer conscious, so 'I' no longer have any subjective experiences about anything; so how can it matter to 'me' that 'I' am objectively present in God's memory?

Similarly, in Christian terms, satisfactory answers to the problem of evil include the belief that those who have suffered injustice in this life will have their suffering redeemed in the next. But if the next life is merely an objective form of immortality, I will not exist subjectively to know that my suffering has been redeemed; so in reality, as far as 'I' am concerned it never will be redeemed.

## Technical terms for self, death and afterlife

**allegory** For example: a piece of literature which has hidden / symbolic meaning.

**Forms** Plato's Theory of Forms is that everything in the physical universe is a particular instance of a perfect idea in the metaphysical world of Forms, so every particular chair is a chair by virtue of being a particular instance of the perfect form of a chair.

**objective immortality** The belief (in Process Theology) that every living thing exists for ever in the mind of God, because they are literally objects 'in' God.

**panentheism** The philosophical view that everything that there is exists 'in God'.

**purgatory** A (particularly Catholic) doctrine of an intermediate state after death in which those who are destined to enter heaven are punished / purified in order to make them worthy of heaven.

**reincarnation** The belief (found in Plato and Hinduism, for example) that at death, the soul at some point is 're-enfleshed' into another body.

**subjective immortality** The belief that after death the thinking self continues as the same subject of consciousness – the same 'I'.

**venial sin** A 'forgivable' sin that does not result in separation from God and eternal damnation to hell (as opposed to 'mortal sin', which does result in this).

# Summary of self, death and afterlife

### The meaning and purpose of life

For Christians, the meaning and purpose of life might include:

1 To glorify God and to have a personal relationship with him. Humans are made in God's image, so their purpose is to reflect God's glory in their lives and actions.

2 To prepare for judgement. The Genesis story reflects the Christian view that the relationship between God and humans was broken. Jesus died on the cross to atone for human sin, and this process is completed by judgement at the end of time. For some, this judgement is literally to heaven or hell; for John Hick, for example, God's love means that in the end everyone will be saved.

3 To bring about God's Kingdom on Earth. Some Christians see the hope of establishing God's Kingdom as eschatological (at the end of time). Others see it as a present reality, thinking that it is possible to establish the qualities of God's Kingdom on Earth.

### Resurrection

Resurrection is the defining feature of Christian belief. It is understood by Christians either as a bodily or a spiritual resurrection.

1 Resurrection of the body is described in the writings of Augustine. The flesh is needed so that both the spiritual and physical effects of sin can be removed, and Augustine presumes from the Gospels that Jesus' resurrection is physical.

2 The idea of spiritual resurrection is influenced by Plato's dualistic philosophy, where a person is essentially a non-material soul housed in a physical body. St Paul seems to support the idea of a spiritual resurrection where he says that what is sown a physical body, is raised a spiritual body, although perhaps Paul's idea of a new, incorruptible, heavenly body retains some kind of physical aspect.

3 1 Corinthians 15: 42–44 and 50–54 is about Paul's responses to those in the Corinthian Church who doubted that humans could follow Jesus' example and resurrect after death. Paul's answer is important as an early piece of Christian theology from a time only 20–25 years after Jesus' death.

### Judgement, heaven, hell and purgatory

The classical ideas of judgement appear in the Parable of the Sheep and Goats, and, for example, in Revelation 20:11–12.

1 Some understand judgement, heaven, hell and purgatory as physical. The reality of pain in the era before anaesthetics made the idea of physical punishment after death a likely one to expect.

Moreover, the bodily suffering of Jesus on the cross was real, so physical pain as punishment for sin was a natural idea.

2 Others understand them as spiritual realities, in which suffering might be seen as a spiritual loss, such as permanent or semi-permanent separation from God.

3 For many liberal Christians, judgement, heaven, hell and purgatory are perhaps psychological realities, generated by the mind, so 'heaven' in this sense might be a life of peace and contentment, whereas those who live in conflict might experience psychological 'hell' from which escape might come through some form of reformation, perhaps through psychoanalysis.

4 Process theologians generally reject any idea of subjective immortality (that is, where the individual retains the same consciousness after death). Since God exists panentheistically with the physical universe, God is the totality of both mental and physical experience. If the universe is 'in' God, then all humans are 'in' God, and in fact when any being dies, it stays as a real and permanent object in the mind of God.

# 9

# Good conduct and key moral principles

This chapter will cover:
- Good conduct
- **Sanctity** of life
- **Dominion** and **stewardship**

## Good conduct

For this, you need to look at the importance of good moral conduct in the Christian way of life, including reference to:

- Teaching about **justification** by works
- Justification by faith
- **Predestination**

> ### Key terms
>
> **sanctity** As in the Sanctity of Life Principle: holy / sacred to God.
>
> **dominion** Meaning power / power over, as in the debate about human dominion over the world.
>
> **stewardship** The view that 'dominion' over the environment should be understood as responsible human care for it, on the understanding that humans are answerable to God for their treatment of the environment.
>
> **justification** When used in 'justification by faith' and 'justification by works' – Christians are counted as righteous before God on the basis of faith or by works, or by both.
>
> **predestination** The view that all events have been willed by God from eternity, specifically the fate of the righteous and of the damned.

If you look back, in particular at Chapter 7 God, you will be aware that Christian thinking about morality is based largely on the view that God is omnipotent and omniscient; and so is the law giver and the controller of all things, and this must therefore mean that God is the controller of morality.

What this means for good Christian moral conduct varies considerably between different Christian groups. For example, we have seen that:

- Those Protestant Christians who follow **Divine Command Theory** believe that an action is morally good only if it is commanded by God.
- Those who follow **Catholic Natural Moral Law** teaching follow the teachings of Aquinas, for whom natural law is that part of God's eternal law that human beings can understand simply through the application of reason.

- Those who follow **Joseph Fletcher's Christian Situation Ethics** focus on one rule only; the law of *agape* (Jesus' other-person-regarding love) and apply this situationally.
- Some deistic Christians believe that since God has left the governance of the world to humans, humans have complete freedom to interpret the Bible as they wish. In particular, **Process theologians** will reject any ethical ideas which tend to separate humanity from its environment. According to Alfred Whitehead, who is commonly regarded as the 'defining' figure in Process Theology, ethics needs to be grounded in the idea of reality as an undivided whole, so ethical decision-making has to include the interests and needs of the environment as a whole. Such a view requires a radical departure from the narrower biblical concerns of Divine Command Theory and of Aquinas' Natural Moral Law. (Note 1)

In summary, then, Christians are agreed about the need for good conduct, but they disagree about what form good conduct should take.

### Why is good conduct important for Christians?

- For many Christians, good conduct is important because it brings the reward of earning a place in heaven, and it also avoids being sent to hell.
- Faith in Jesus is the basis for good conduct, since Christians try to follow Jesus' example in what he taught and the way he behaved: so in Paul's Letter to the Ephesians, Paul urges them to abandon bad conduct and to put on the new moral nature that befits what they learned in Christ (4:17-5:20). For example, they must abandon deceitful lust, speak the truth, put thieves to honest work, indulge in no evil talk, abandon bitterness and anger, abandon slander and malice and be kind/tender-hearted and forgiving towards each other.
- Particularly important is Jesus' teaching in the 'Sermon on the Mount' (Matthew 5–7). At one point, Jesus says, 'Let your light so shine before men, that they may see your good works and give glory to your Father who is in heaven.' (Matthew 5:16). Good conduct therefore glorifies God.
- In Matthew 22:35–40, Jesus says that the greatest commandment is to love God with all one's heart, soul and mind; and that a second commandment is like it, namely to love your neighbour as yourself; because on these two commandments depend the law and the prophets. Good conduct, then, is based on loving God and other people.

### Not all Christians agree about what good conduct is and *why* good conduct is important:

- Some moral commands in the Bible are seen as immoral. For example, in the Letter of Paul to Titus, part of the moral advice given is to slaves, who must be 'submissive to their masters and … give satisfaction in every respect … to show entire and true fidelity …' (2:9–10), which appears to condone slavery by requiring slaves to put up with their situation.

  As another example, those Christians who see Jesus' authority as merely human are perhaps likely to question his command to 'turn the other cheek' (Matthew 5:39). Whether or not Jesus is commanding pacifism here, there is no doubt that many Christians today take the passage in this way, whereas others might find pacifism impractical and immoral, since it does not defend the innocent and allows evil to have its way.

Jesus (in Matthew 19:9) rules that whoever divorces his wife for any reason other than unchastity (marital infidelity), and then marries another, commits adultery, and Christian Churches differ in their interpretation of this principle.

- Some Christians insist that good conduct is not a matter of following rules for the sake of a reward (such as heaven) or to avoid punishment (including that of hell), but is a matter of doing right for right's sake. In the Unitarian movement, for example, it is assumed that members have free will to make moral choices: religious doctrines are an aid to choosing, but it is free reason that makes the choice.
- Some liberal Christians see concepts of heaven and hell as psychological realities, so that those who practise good moral conduct create God's Kingdom here on earth rather than after death.

Many Christians for whom the Kingdom of God is a future reality place particular importance on the New Testament doctrine of the Atonement, which we looked at earlier. It teaches that the suffering, death and resurrection of Jesus atone (make up for) for the original sin of humanity, as expressed in the story of the disobedience of Adam and Eve in the Garden of Eden. The theology is complex, as you have seen in earlier chapters, but essentially, it explains death as a consequence of original sin, and it explains further that Jesus' death restores the relationship between God and humanity, so that those who accept Jesus and God's Holy Spirit can have the gift of eternal life in the Kingdom of God.

Most Christians accept the doctrine of the Atonement, but there is disagreement about what precisely it is that Christians must do to accept this gift: how do Christians 'access' the Kingdom?

This is where the doctrine of 'Justification' (to be declared righteous) comes in. How is it that a sinner can be declared righteous? You need to look at three sets of ideas:

1 That a Christian can be justified by faith.

2 That a Christian can be justified through good works.

3 That a Christian is predestined to enter God's Kingdom.

The theme of justification by faith is developed by St Paul, whereas the idea of justification by works is raised in the Letter of James. For some, their ideas conflict, although for others they do not. We shall start with justification by faith. The debate about justification by faith and justification by works (also about predestination) is very complex, so you will need to understand the main points rather than the detail.

## Justification by faith

'To justify' is *dikaioó* in Greek, and the verb carries several senses, such as 'to make righteous', 'to defend the cause of', 'to plead for the innocence of' (for example, legally). Paul's writing on justification by faith appears principally in his Letter to the Romans, where justification is characteristic of Paul's language. Justification is '**eschatological**' (that is, dealing with death, judgement and the fate of the soul and of humanity). Simply obeying the Jewish Law cannot justify humanity: only God can justify humanity.

Read the full text of Paul's theology, in Romans 3–5. Here are some of the main verses:

> **Key terms**
>
> **eschatological** To do with the last days, that is, the last Judgement / God's Kingdom.

For no human being will be justified in his sight by works of the law, since through the law comes knowledge of sin. But now the righteousness of God has been manifested apart from law, although the law and the prophets bear witness to it, the righteousness of God through faith in Jesus Christ for all who believe. For there is no distinction; since all have sinned and fall short of the glory of God, they are justified by his **grace** as a gift, through the redemption which is in Christ Jesus, whom God put forward as an expiation by his blood, to be received by faith. This was to show God's righteousness, because in his divine forbearance he had passed over former sins; it was to prove at the present time that he himself is righteous and that he justifies him who has faith in Jesus. (3:20–26)

For we hold that a man is justified by faith apart from works of law. (3:28)

For if Abraham was justified by works, he has something to boast about, but not before God. For what does the scripture say? 'Abraham believed God, and it was reckoned to him as righteousness.' Now to one who works, his wages are not reckoned as a gift but as his due. And to one who does not work but trusts him who justifies the ungodly, his faith is reckoned as righteousness. (4:2–5)

Therefore, since we are justified by faith, we have peace with God through our Lord Jesus Christ. Through him we have obtained access to this grace in which we stand, and we rejoice in our hope of sharing the glory of God. (5:1–2)

## Key terms

**grace** God's grace is seen as the free gift of mercy to sinful humanity, for example, through the atonement made by the suffering and death of Jesus. According to Pelagius, God's grace was the gift of free will to humans.

To understand what Paul is saying here:

- Where Paul talks about being justified, the most accepted understanding of the verb 'to justify' in Greek is that it means, 'to count, or treat as, righteous'. [Note 2]
- In 3:20–26, Paul says that no human being will be justified in God's eyes by works of the law (that is, by following the Jewish Law), because for humans to be counted as righteous does not mean that they 'earn' righteousness. Righteousness cannot be 'earned' by following the Law, because all humans have sinned (through original sin) and fallen short of what they should be. (verse 23) Therefore to be judged 'righteous' by God can only be a free gift, by God's grace. (verse 24) This free gift of grace is to redeem humanity through the sacrifice of Jesus, whose death on the cross atones for human sin. (verse 25)

As C.K. Barrett puts it:

> 'Justification ... is the verdict which faith, and only faith, can hear. Outside faith, as outside grace, men can hear (out of the law) only the verdict of guilty, and the sentence of condemnation.' [Note 3]

In other words, if justification came just by people's work in following the law, then everybody would be judged guilty by God. Justification comes only through faith in Jesus. (verse 26)

- So, in 3:28, Paul goes on to state that people are justified by faith 'apart from' the law – **in other words, justification is by faith, and not by works.**
- In 4:2–5 Paul discusses whether the great patriarchal ancestor of the Jews, Abraham, would be justified by God. The point here is important: Abraham lived many centuries before Jesus' atonement for sin, and so on the face of it Abraham could not have been justified by God. Paul says that Abraham can indeed be justified by God, but not because of his good works – only because of the extent of his belief – his faith in God. This would be a powerful reminder to Jewish readers, since Genesis 22 contains a well-known story where God tests Abraham's faith by commanding him to kill his only son, Isaac, and to place his body on an altar as a burnt-offering. When Abraham is on the point of killing Isaac, God stops him because the root of Abraham's obedience is his faith in God. In Romans 4:5, then, Paul says of Abraham that 'his faith is reckoned as righteousness'.

- In 5:1–2, Paul then draws the chain of reasoning to its conclusion: when we have complete faith in God, and rely upon God's grace rather than upon our own works and deeds, we have 'peace with God' – in other words, reconciliation with God, and so we can confidently expect our final destiny to be with God.
- We are justified, therefore, by grace and faith, not by good moral conduct. This seems to say clearly that good moral conduct is less important than having faith.

## Justification by works

Despite Paul's interesting arguments, the author of the Letter of James appears to disagree. Here is what James says:

> What does it profit, my brethren, if a man says he has faith but has not works? Can his faith save him? If a brother or sister is ill-clad and in lack of daily food, and one of you says to them, 'Go in peace, be warmed and filled,' without giving them the things needed for the body, what does it profit? So faith by itself, if it has no works, is dead.
>
> But some one will say, 'You have faith and I have works.' Show me your faith apart from your works, and I by my works will show you my faith. You believe that God is one; you do well. Even the demons believe—and shudder. Do you want to be shown, you shallow man, that faith apart from works is barren? Was not Abraham our father justified by works, when he offered his son Isaac upon the altar? You see that faith was active along with his works, and faith was completed by works, and the scripture was fulfilled which says, 'Abraham believed God, and it was reckoned to him as righteousness'; and he was called the friend of God. You see that a man is justified by works and not by faith alone. And in the same way was not also Rahab the harlot justified by works when she received the messengers and sent them out another way? For as the body apart from the spirit is dead, so faith apart from works is dead. (James 2:14–26)

The argument seems clear:

- What is the point of faith without works? If a brother or sister lacks food or clothing and someone says that they love them without doing anything about it, that is useless; so faith without works is dead.
- Rather, faith can be shown by works.
- Faith on its own is useless, because even the demons believe in God.
- Abraham is a case in point: he had faith, and it was reckoned to him as (i.e. counted as) righteousness, but he showed it by works: he was going to sacrifice Isaac!
- So, a man is justified by works, and not by faith alone.
- In the same way, Rahab, the prostitute was justified in what she did (hiding Joshua's spies to keep them safe) to help the Israelite conquest of Jericho. (Joshua 7)
- So, just as a body without a spirit is dead, faith without works is dead.

So, should Christians:

a prioritise good moral conduct (works), or
b prioritise faith, or
c emphasise the importance of both faith and works?

## Those who prioritise works

- Some Christians accept that the Letter of James is very clear in what it says, particularly the last line of the argument above: '... faith apart from works is dead'.
- Moreover, as James says, even demons must believe in God, but by nature their works are demonic. In other words, demons are judged by their demonic works and not by the incidental fact that they happen to believe in God.
- Many Christians across all **denominations** accept the need for works on the basis of Jesus' Parable of the Sheep and the Goats, on the judgement of the nations, Matthew 25:31–46 (referred to on page 283 but reproduced here for ease of reference).

> **Key term**
>
> **Denomination** A recognised branch of the Christian Church.

When the Son of man comes in his glory, and all the angels with him, then he will sit on his glorious throne. Before him will be gathered all the nations, and he will separate them one from another as a shepherd separates the sheep from the goats, and he will place the sheep at his right hand, but the goats at the left. Then the King will say to those at his right hand, 'Come, O blessed of my Father, inherit the kingdom prepared for you from the foundation of the world; for I was hungry and you gave me food, I was thirsty and you gave me drink, I was a stranger and you welcomed me, I was naked and you clothed me, I was sick and you visited me, I was in prison and you came to me.' Then the righteous will answer him, 'Lord, when did we see thee hungry and feed thee, or thirsty and give thee drink? And when did we see thee a stranger and welcome thee, or naked and clothe thee? And when did we see thee sick or in prison and visit thee?' And the King will answer them, 'Truly, I say to you, as you did it to one of the least of these my brethren, you did it to me.' Then he will say to those at his left hand, 'Depart from me, you cursed, into the eternal fire prepared for the devil and his angels; for I was hungry and you gave me no food, I was thirsty and you gave me no drink, I was a stranger and you did not welcome me, naked and you did not clothe me, sick and in prison and you did not visit me.' Then they also will answer, 'Lord, when did we see thee hungry or thirsty or a stranger or naked or sick or in prison, and did not minister to thee?' Then he will answer them, 'Truly, I say to you, as you did it not to one of the least of these, you did it not to me.' And they will go away into eternal punishment, but the righteous into eternal life.

Jesus' message here is very clear:

- God makes no mention at all of whether those who are sheep-like or goat-like are full of faith or lacking in faith.
- The sheep go to eternal life in God's Kingdom for the simple reason that they have done good works: they have fed the hungry, given drink to the thirsty, visited the sick in prison and more besides. The goats, by contrast, have failed to live up to these examples of good works.
- Moreover, many Christians feel that to follow Jesus is to follow his commands. Many of these are specified in Matthew 5–7, including the need to keep all the commandments (5:17–20). Christians are to keep them and teach them (verse 19), so Jesus himself is emphatic about the need for good works, hence he says, 'Let your light so shine before men, that they may see your good works and give glory to your Father who is in heaven.'

## Those who prioritise faith

- It is easy to see why many Christians follow this line, not least because it seems to be stated explicitly by St Paul. Aside from what he says in Romans, see for example, Ephesians 2:8–10:

> For by grace you have been saved through faith; and this is not your own doing, it is the gift of God— not because of works, lest any man should boast. For we are his workmanship, created in Christ Jesus for good works, which God prepared beforehand, that we should walk in them.

Here again is the emphasis on faith as the channel for salvation. It is not a person's faith that saves, but God who saves the person through the channel of their faith.

## Martin Luther (1483–1546)

Luther was a religious reformer and prolific author. He initiated the sixteenth-century Reformation when, in 1517, he published the 95 Theses in Wittenberg, where he was a professor. He attacked the excesses of medieval religion, seeking a simpler and more direct form of religion, based on scripture and personal faith.

◀ Martin Luther: German monk and professor of theology. Changed Christianity irrevocably when he began the Protestant Reformation.

● The best-known advocate of justification by faith alone is Martin Luther. Luther based his understanding of justification on Romans 1:16–17:

> For I am not ashamed of the gospel: it is the power of God for salvation to every one who has faith … For in it the righteousness of God is revealed through faith for faith; as it is written, 'He who through faith is righteous shall live.'

### Key term

*sola fide* Latin, refers to Luther's doctrine of justification by 'faith alone'.

On the basis of this text, Luther proclaimed the doctrine of *sola fide* – 'justification by faith alone'. He believed that God pardons guilty sinners on the basis of their faith alone, without reference to their works. Through Jesus' atonement, God grants sinners justification. God's verdict on the sinner is not based on anything the sinner has done. Moreover, the faith of the sinner is passive, not active. Justification is not brought about by human achievement or works but by what God brings about through Jesus Christ. The righteousness of Christ is literally attributed by God to the believing sinner.

In much of Protestant theology, then, following Luther's line, righteous works are the result of being justified by God and born again through the Holy Spirit.

Luther considered the doctrine of *sola fide* to be so important that to ignore it was literally to preach a false gospel: the Church stands or falls in accordance with whether or not it accepts this. In fact, Luther considered *sola fide* to be one of five interlinked and equally fundamental doctrines, the others being: *sola scriptura* (by Scripture alone), *sola gratia* (by grace alone), *solus Christus* (Christ alone) and *soli Deo gloria* (to the glory of God alone). Together they emphasise Paul's argument that salvation is through Christ alone, through his work of atonement.

### Those who emphasise the importance of both faith and works

● Luther's insistence on *sola fide* did not impress the Catholic Church at the time, and at the Council of Trent (1545–1563), the Catholic Church clarified and

> '… codified its understanding of the doctrine of justification, which the Council said was predicated upon both faith *and* good works.' (James R. Adair) (Note 4)

Whereas Luther insisted that grace was received in an entirely passive manner, purely on the basis of faith, the Catholic Church took the view that some human effort had to be involved in the process of justification.

307

The division between Catholic and Protestant thinking on this issue was such that it:

> '... caused many Catholics to accuse Protestants of preaching an antinomian (lawless) gospel that minimised the importance of following Jesus' life and teaching in their daily lives. In return, many Protestants accused Catholics of preaching a doctrine of justification by works, as though one could work one's way to heaven without the necessity of God's grace.' [Note 5]

● Catholic teaching is that grace comes to the individual through baptism. Baptism is the sacrament of faith, so that faith is then developed in the context of the Church. For the baptised, faith grows 'after' baptism. In turn, this leads to a new life in Christ, the outcome of which is good works through living in the light of Christ. (John 3:16–21)

● From the Catholic perspective, belief is not just 'intellectual assent' to God's existence and Jesus' sacrifice, because as the Letter of James says, even the demons have that: it must entail obedience and good works. Moreover, in 1 John 2:3–6 we find the following:

> And by this we may be sure that we know him, if we keep his commandments. He who says 'I know him' but disobeys his commandments is a liar, and the truth is not in him; but whoever keeps his word, in him truly love for God is perfected. By this we may be sure that we are in him: he who says he abides in him ought to walk in the same way in which he walked.

Without a positive response (by works) to grace, salvation is not possible.

● On this interpretation, the passage in James 2:14–26 is comparing two kinds of faith: the kind that leads to good works, and the kind that does not. The kind of faith possessed by demons (James 2:19) is of the first kind – they have faith in God since they believe in God; but that kind of faith does not lead to good works, and faith without works is dead (verse 17).

## Summary

So far, we have looked at three views about how Christians are justified and admitted to God's eternal Kingdom.

1 Justification by faith.

2 Justification by works.

3 Justification by faith and works.

However, what happens if we add to these the doctrine of predestination?

## Predestination

1 In theology, predestination is the view that all events have been willed by God.

In particular, here, predestination is the view that the fate of each individual, with regard to his or her place in the Kingdom of Heaven, has also been willed by God. If this is the case, then this seems to imply that their conduct is morally good because God has willed that also, and this implies further that good moral conduct in human beings is less important than God's will. Whatever God decides will happen.

**2** What does the Bible have to say about predestination?

During the Old Testament period, there was a general belief that Yahweh was the God of history, particularly in God's 'election' of Israel as a chosen nation, for example, Deuteronomy 7:6–8.

In the New Testament, the doctrine of predestination appears in more explicit form, for example, in Romans 8:28–30:

> We know that in everything God works for good with those who love him, who are called according to his purpose. For those whom he foreknew he also predestined to be conformed to the image of his Son, in order that he might be the first-born among many brethren. And those whom he predestined he also called; and those whom he called he also justified; and those whom he justified he also glorified.

In this passage, Paul is suggesting that God predestined some people to 'be conformed to the image of his Son', that is, to lead Christ-like lives; moreover, those who were called were thereby justified (*edikaiosen*). If that is the correct understanding of Paul, then as we said above, this implies that God predestines some people to good moral conduct: they lead Christ-like lives not through their own choice but by God's.

So, who is justified through predestination, and who is not? Some argue that Paul is teaching that all *Christians* are justified, excluding members of other religions and unbelievers. Others argue that he believed in the salvation of *all human beings*, although that seems unlikely. In Romans 6:23 he says that, '… the wages of sin is death, but the free gift of God is eternal life in Christ Jesus our Lord'. So perhaps Paul thought that those who were not predestined to eternal life simply died without entering God's Kingdom.

**3** Whatever Paul really thought about predestination, the doctrine was developed in the first place from the view that God is all-powerful and all-knowing.

Although beliefs about the omnipotence and omniscience of God are not developed philosophically in the Bible, we have seen that the biblical authors believed that all power and knowledge were in God's hands as the Creator. The inevitable conclusion to be drawn from such beliefs was that God's control of the world is complete, and therefore God must control all of history, and this in turn includes the lives of every being that he has created.

**4** One problem with thinking in this way is that it clashes with the idea of human free will.

From Genesis 1:26–27, Christians derive the belief that humans are created in God's image, and for most Christians this includes the ability to be moral beings and the ability to reject God's commandments. If you think about it, we can only be morally good by 'choosing' the good, because if people do good works for fear of punishment, then they are not really making a free choice. It is easy to make someone obey by threat of punishment, but their obedience then is through fear rather than choice.

Regardless of what Paul thought about the fate of those who rejected Jesus, the Gospels, which were written several decades after Paul's **Epistles**, make it fairly clear that the fate of those who reject Jesus is rather dire. The word 'hell' in the New Testament is used as a translation for a variety of different terms, referring mainly to fiery torment (for example, Matthew 5:22) or to a gloomy pit of darkness (*tartarus* – 2

309

**Key term**

**epistle** The Greek word for 'letter'. There are 21 epistles in the New Testament, 13 of which are attributed to the apostle Paul, although the authorship of several of these is disputed.

Peter 2:4). In the Parable of the Rich Man and Lazarus, Jesus refers to 'Hades' as a place of torment (Luke 16:23). The problem should be clear: if humans freely choose to reject God, then torment awaits them – hardly a 'free' choice at all. If humans are God's 'children', what human parent would offer their children such a choice and think it morally good?

If we then add to that the idea that God 'predestines' humans to heaven or hell, then serious questions can be asked about the goodness of God. Why should Christians have good moral conduct when God has already decided that they will go to heaven or hell?

You can see that theologians in the early years of the Church had a problem: if God gives humans free will because they are created in God's image, how does that square with any idea about predestination? What real reason do Christians have for good moral conduct?

5  According to Pelagius, freedom and predestination do not 'square' at all, although Augustine disagreed.

Pelagius argued that everything God created was good, so God could not possibly have created humanity in a state of original sin. As far as Pelagius was concerned, 'grace' was nothing more nor less than God's gift of free will to humans, so the idea of predestination had to be nothing more than moral nonsense. The human will therefore needs no help from God in choosing between good and evil

Pelagius seems to have a strong argument. What would be the point of God creating humans with such a weak degree of free will that they were unable to make free good choices? What sense is there in the idea that humanity as a whole inherits the 'original sin' of Adam and Eve when no individual has any choice in the matter of being born or not?

Despite this, Augustine (whose ideas on the problem of evil you have encountered briefly in connection with John Hick's theodicy) disagreed.

● In opposition to Pelagius, Augustine insisted that it is not by human merit that the elect are predestined to God's Kingdom: 'Holiness is the *result* of election, not its source' (Note 6) and is decided by 'the inscrutable will of God.' (Note 7)
● Because God is all-knowing, his **foreknowledge** means that he infallibly knows who will be saved.
● Augustine worked his way to a doctrine of **double predestination**, meaning that God (1) predestines some to God's Kingdom through his grace, but (2) leaves others immersed in their sin to be condemned to hell through both their choice and their works.

6  The doctrine of predestination reached its most familiar form through the work of John Calvin during the Protestant Reformation.

'**Luther revived the full Augustinian doctrine, together with a new stress on the total depravity of fallen man. Since, in Adam, all are guilty before God, all deserve eternal damnation, and therefore it is no injustice in God if some are lost; rather, it is a sign of infinite love if some are saved.**' (Note 8)

Calvin reaffirmed Augustine's doctrine of double predestination in a more uncompromising form:

'**... some are eternally ordained to glory, through the sheer will of God, and the rest are ordained to eternal torment.**' (Note 9)

**PELAGIUS**
*Accurst Pelagius with what false pretence
Durst thou excuse Mans foule Concupiscence:
Or cry down Sin Originall, or that
The Loue of God did Man predestinate.*

▲ Pelagius: c.357–418: Irish theologian / moralist, declared a heretic by the Council of Carthage because he rejected the doctrine of predestination as so much nonsense, and asserted against it the doctrine of free will. The caption below the picture calls him 'accursed' because he rejected the idea of original sin along with that of predestination.

### Key terms

**foreknowledge** When applied to God, the doctrine that an all-knowing God knows the entire future, so knows from eternity who will accept the gift of grace and who will reject it.

**double predestination** God predestines some to the Kingdom through His grace but leaves others immersed in their sin to be condemned to hell.

> By predestination we mean the eternal decree of God, by which he determined with himself whatever he wished to happen with regard to every man. All are not created on equal terms, but some are preordained to eternal life, others to eternal damnation; and, accordingly, as each has been created for one or other of these ends, we say that he has been predestinated to life or to death.
>
> Calvin: *The Institutes of the Christian Religion*, Book III, Ch. XXI, Sec. 5. (Note 10)

7 The Protestant Churches and the Catholic Church today have a variety of approaches to the idea of predestination.

An online search on predestination will reveal the official position of the different Churches, but the debate about predestination is incredibly complex, and it is not necessary that you should get immersed in the detail. In the opinion of some, after almost 2,000 years of debate, Christian scholars have got no closer to expounding a version of the doctrine that has even the remotest chance of being accepted by all Christians.

8 The philosophical problems with the idea of predestination.

As noted earlier, it is not difficult to see why various Christian scholars and Churches have paid so much attention to the idea of predestination: it is the inevitable result of the view that God is omniscient (all-knowing). You will recall that when looking at Evil and Suffering in Chapter 2, you learnt that 'God is omniscient' is the fourth statement that can be added to the 'inconsistent triad':
i  God is omnipotent (all-powerful).
ii  God is omnibenevolent / perfectly loving.
iii Evil exists.
iv  God is omniscient.

This suggests that there is a major philosophical / ethical problem with the idea of predestination: If God is omniscient, then he must have known in advance of creating the universe who will be worthy of heaven and who will be worthy of hell. Why, then, would God bother to create beings who would inevitably go to hell?

Here are five thoughts on this question for you to consider:

1 In Chapter 7 God, we looked at the Christian understanding that God is love, and that love defines the nature of the relationship between the three persons of the Trinity. If we are to take this understanding as being literally true, it is a strange kind of love that condemns anybody to eternal hell, whether that condemnation is predestined or is simply the consequence of rejecting God / doing evil deeds. Can infinite love be reconciled with the idea of infinite punishment?

2 To look at the other side of the argument, you will recall that Hick's conclusion is that if God is a God of love, then eternal damnation to hell cannot exist. Instead, after an indeterminate number of lifetimes, Hick suggests that every human will freely come to acknowledge God, since God's loving persuasion has infinite patience and the certainty of eventual success. It might therefore seem as if Hick is teaching a doctrine of predestination to universal salvation; but if God is sure of success, then it appears that humans have no real freedom to reject God, since in the end there will be no single instance of a human rejecting God.

Moreover, if universal predestination to heaven is true, then what value does the doctrine of the Atonement really have? Humans will eventually reach God's Kingdom regardless of (1) whatever atrocities they might commit on the way, and (2) regardless of Jesus' suffering and death as an atonement for sin.

3 For some people, the most acceptable form of the doctrine of predestination is similar to what Paul teaches in Romans, that God knows, through his foreknowledge, who will freely accept him, so these are predestined to salvation whereas those who reject him will simply die and cease to exist.

This idea sounds reasonable, but it has a well-known problem: if God knows that you will make a choice (X) at a given time (Y), then it would seem that you cannot avoid choosing X at time Y, since God knows absolutely what you will do and when you will do it. On this understanding, then, God causes all your choices, so your choices cannot be 'choices at all', and this seems to make a mockery of any doctrine that God knows who will freely accept him.

4 The usual answer to this is to say that God exists timelessly. To understand this, think of God existing beyond space–time: he would presumably see the whole history of the universe simultaneously, like an unrolled scroll, from its beginning (if it ever had a beginning) to its end. God would timelessly see the results of our free choices, but would not cause these choices.

5 We saw above that Pelagius argued that God's gift of grace to humanity is simply the gift of free will, and that the human will therefore needs no help from God in choosing between good and evil. On this view, the idea of predestination is redundant, and humans are fully responsible for their own moral conduct. In effect, then, Pelagius offered strong support for the Free Will Defence that we considered as a response to the problem of evil. He also supported the view that justification is through good moral conduct. Did Pelagius get it right?

## Activity

Discuss the following questions concerning predestination and the need for good moral conduct.

1 Do you think that the idea of timeless God rescues the doctrine of predestination?

2 Does the doctrine of predestination need rescuing in the first place?

3 Would a loving God predestine people to hell?

4 Hick's theodicy seems to offer a doctrine of universal predestination to heaven. In terms of the need for good moral conduct, does this idea raise more problems than it solves?

5 Process theologians, whose ideas we have looked at in several connections, argue that God-and-the-universe are evolving *in* time. The future is unknown, and cannot be predestined, for the simple reason that the future has not yet happened. Does this view offer a more realistic assessment of the future than the doctrine of predestination? If the future is unknown, does this make the need for good moral conduct more important?

6 In your view, if predestination is wrong, what would Christians need to do in order to reach God's Kingdom? Discuss this from the Christian viewpoint.

# Sanctity of life

For this you need to look at:

- The concept of the sanctity of life
- Different views about its application to issues concerning the embryo and the unborn child
- The Just War theory and its application to the use of weapons of mass destruction

## The concept of the sanctity of life

1 To say that life has sanctity means that it is holy, or sacred to God.

In Christian teaching, this has developed as a central ethical teaching known as the Sanctity of Life Principle.

2 The Sanctity of Life Principle derives from two main texts: Genesis 1:26–27 and Genesis 2:7.

The first of these is the text which says that humans are born 'in the image of God'. From this, most theologians have argued that what is created in the image of the Creator must be sacred to him. Genesis 2:7 is from the creation story in Genesis 2:4b–3:24:

> '... then the Lord God formed man of dust from the ground, and breathed into his nostrils the breath of life; and man became a living being.'

In the phrases 'the breath of life' and 'living being', both 'breath' and 'being' are from the Hebrew *nephesh*, which is usually translated as 'soul'. Since this method of giving life is described only in connection with the creation of humans, and not with any other form of life, most theologians have assumed that humans are the only beings with souls. In Chapter 8 Self, death and afterlife, we saw that belief in the soul features in Christian beliefs about either a bodily or a spiritual resurrection. In either case, belief in the existence of souls is an important part in the Christian belief that human life is sacred to God.

3 The Sanctity of Principle holds that human life has **intrinsic value**.

Something that has intrinsic value has value 'in itself'. Human life has value in itself because it is a gift from God. There are any number of conditions caused by accident or disease that can lead to humans being in the most dire and weak physical and mental conditions; nevertheless all such lives are valued and must be respected.

Job 1:21 is often referred to here. Having lost everything: home, possessions and children, Job still says:

> '...the Lord gave, and the Lord has taken away; blessed be the name of the Lord.'

4 Some theologians distinguish between a 'strong' and a 'weak' form of the Sanctity of Life Principle.

The 'strong' form is sometimes used to argue that all human life is sacred to God, and it is therefore morally impermissible to allow contraception, abortion or euthanasia, for any reason, or to turn off a life-support machine, even if the person concerned has no detectable brain activity.

> **Key term**
>
> **intrinsic value** Something that has value for its own sake, for example, human life in the Sanctity of Life Principle.

The 'weak' form generally takes the view that although human life is sacred to God, and the Sanctity of Life Principle must always be considered in issues of life and death, the situation must also be taken into account when deciding what to do.

5 Some theologians appeal to a 'Quality of Life Principle' alongside the Sanctity of Life Principle.

This is usually the approach taken by those who support the weaker form of the Sanctity of Life Principle. For example, someone who is on a life-support machine, who has no real hope of recovery (for example, where brain scans show that the brain has atrophied to a point where it could never support life functions unaided); who perhaps has shown a clear wish not to be kept on life support in such a condition; and where the family and the doctors are in agreement with the patient's wishes, may be judged to have a quality of life where the principle of sanctity no longer applies. In such cases, it may be judged that humans have a God-given right to autonomy (self-determination) that also follows from the fact of being made in God's image, so they have the right to decide.

## Applying the Sanctity of Life Principle

**Different views about applying the Sanctity of Life Principle to issues concerning the embryo and the unborn child.**

The general issues to be discussed here concern the issue of embryo research and the issue of abortion.

The relevant issues / principles include:

- The Sanctity of Life Principle, strong and weak
- Questions about personhood
- The right to life
- The Quality of Life Principle
- UK law

Bear in mind the following when you do your own research and investigations:

- This section is *not* a complete review of the issues concerning embryo research. You have already looked at these in the section on practical ethics, from the point of view of Natural Moral Law, Situation Ethics and Virtue Ethics. It is good idea to refresh your memory of these at this point.
- Further, this section is *not* a review of the issues concerning abortion. The same comment applies as for embryo research.
- This section *is* about the application of the Sanctity of Life Principle.

1 Applying a strong Sanctity of Life Principle to issues concerning the embryo and unborn child depends largely on the logic of 'personhood'.

- At the point of conception, when the sperm fertilises the egg, in biological terms a new life is created.
- There is of course a debate in Christianity about if and when this biological life form becomes a person with an inviolable right to life.
- The strong Sanctity of Life Principle holds that personhood begins at conception, since all the necessary genetic material that will form the person that is born is already present.

- The Catholic Church supports this understanding, and argues that there is a 'continuous development' of each life from conception to birth.
- In the Church's *Declaration on Procured Abortion*, 1974, article 12 points out:

**'Any discrimination based on the various stages of life is no more justified than any other discrimination. In reality, respect for human life is called for from the time that the process of generation begins. From the time that the ovum is fertilized, a life is begun which is neither that of the father nor of the mother, it is rather the life of a new human being with his own growth. It would never be made human if it were not human already.'** (Note 11)

2 The conclusion of the strong Sanctity of Life Principle can be supported by Scripture, for example:

- Psalm 139:13:

**'For thou didst form my inward parts, thou didst knit me together in my mother's womb.'**

- Job 31:15:

**'Did not he who made me in the womb make him? And did not one fashion us in the womb?'**

- Jeremiah 1:5:

**'Before I formed you in the womb I knew you, and before you were born I consecrated you; I appointed you a prophet to the nations.'**

Although these verses do not address specific biology, they support the principle that life is sacred to God, and in the case of Jeremiah, this principle holds even before conception.

3 The Incarnation of Jesus was a normal process of conception, so human conception must have the same implications.

The account of the incarnation of Jesus in Luke's Gospel suggests that Jesus was conceived and gestated in the womb as a normal human child:

**'... you will conceive in your womb and bear a son ...'** (Luke 1:31)

One would hardly suggest that Jesus at conception was a legitimate target for embryo experimentation or abortion; so the same principle holds for all human embryos at the point of conception. The sanctity of Jesus' human life began at his conception; so the sanctity of all human life must begin at the same point.

4 The strong Sanctity of Life Principle therefore suggests the following:

- Because UK law (following the Warnock Report) gives special status to the human embryo after 14 days, following the appearance of a rudimentary nervous system (the so-called 'primitive streak'), the law in effect denies the embryo the right to life that it possesses at the point of conception.
- According to the strong Sanctity of Life Principle, experimentation on human embryos at any time before or after day 14 therefore breaks the commandment against murder.

- Despite the potential of embryonic stem cell research and therapeutic cloning to cure a range of debilitating diseases, all such procedures are profoundly immoral. Harvesting embryonic stem cells destroys the donor embryo, and is equivalent to murder. Cloning is also seen as 'playing God' by manipulating life that is sacred to God.

- The process of genetic selection of embryos (Pre-implantation Genetic Diagnosis – PGD), although it means that doctors can check for conditions such as Down's syndrome and cystic fibrosis, could contribute to a dystopia where parents who can afford it create a kind of super-race, whereas those who cannot are seen as second-class citizens. The strong Sanctity of Life Principle requires that children are valued for what they are, since they are made in the image of God. All children should be valued for what they are, which means that PGD should be rejected because it rejects some lives as not worth living.

5 The conclusions of the strong Sanctity of Life Principle apply also to abortion at any stage.

Life is sacred because it is created in God's image. Abortion destroys that image. Our care of life should be by good stewardship rather than ownership of the embryo.

These principles can be followed, for example, even in the case of pregnancy through rape, where the child's 'sanctity of life' / 'right to life' can override the 'quality of life' of the mother. At the time of writing, in October 2016, Poland is considering tightening its anti-abortion laws, to the extent of criminalising all abortions, with the mother facing up to 5 years in prison. (Note 12)

6 Christians who support the weak Sanctity of Life Principle reach different conclusions.

- This is because although they may accept the value of the embryo at all stages of development, they also take into account both actual and potential situations, not least with embryo experimentation and abortion.

- The Church of England, for example, takes this approach to abortion. (Note 13) It applies a Quality of Life Principle to the life of the mother. If the mother is pregnant as the result of rape, or if her life is in danger as a result of the pregnancy, or is she is in a situation where she or the child could suffer abuse, then the importance of the quality of her life in such situations can override the sanctity of the embryo's life.

- For many Protestant Christians, a Quality of Life Principle applies also to the foetus: if the foetus faces a life with severe mental or physical disability, then again, this may override the right to life of the foetus. With Fletcher's situation ethics, for example, the primary concern is the application of agape love as opposed to any considerations of rights or sanctity.

- The Church of England uses the same principle to allow Pre-implantation Genetic Diagnosis for serious disorders, and to allow embryo experimentation under strict control. The Church of England believes that God-given knowledge should be used, wherever possible, to improve the human condition, while at the same time holding to the sanctity of life. Different Protestant groups may therefore accept the 14-day rule concerning embryo experimentation, in so far as the benefits of such research help us to recognise the sanctity of the lives of the millions who suffer from diseases that are currently incurable.

7 How should we evaluate the Sanctity of Life Principle itself?

Some of the arguments in its favour:

It protects life as sacred, and promotes a positive approach to the value of life, including the value of a human life suffering under different forms of disability. The weaker form of the principle is in line with Jesus' teachings on agape and on loving one's neighbour. Also, the weaker form is often seen as more in line with the realities of life, recognising, for example, that abortion is not necessarily an arbitrary choice but is often linked to the inadequacies of the way in which countries do or do nor protect their citizens:

**'The Church must also stand in opposition to the restricted life chances, poverty and in particular inadequate housing and social services which continue to limit and stunt too many people's lives.'**
(Note 14)

Some of the arguments against it:

The principle – particularly in its strong form – rests on a pre-scientific assessment of human value (and of the way the embryo develops, for example) made some 3,000 years ago. It ignores scientific findings concerning evolution and natural selection. These show beyond reasonable doubt that human beings are not a special life form – they are merely part of what has evolved, and in that respect are no different from other animals. To say that humans are made in God's image is not only anthropomorphism; it reinforces a patriarchal model of society in which women are not equal with men in their choices (concerning abortion, for example).

## Activity

Consider the following questions, some of which overlap:

1 What gives *your* life quality and value?

2 On the face of it, therapeutic cloning violates the Sanctity of Life Principle because it blocks the embryo's potential to become an actual person. However, others argue that the embryo is nothing more than a non-integrated clump of cells that has no interests or rights, and so cannot be harmed by not becoming a person. Which view do you think gets closest to the truth? (Note 15)

3 Does the embryo's right to life outweigh any potential benefits to existing people who might benefit from experimentation on that embryo?

4 Do you think that *existing* people (i.e. those already born) 'embody' the Sanctity of Life Principle, or do embryos?

5 As far as we know, embryos cannot suffer, whereas existing people can. Do you think that the suffering of existing people is morally worse than creating and destroying embryos? (If you do, then therapeutic cloning should be permitted.)

6 Consider this statement from Judson G. Randolph (Surgeon in Chief, Children's Hospital National Medical Centre, Washington DC):

**'If a severely handicapped child were suddenly given one moment of omniscience and total awareness of his or her outlook for the future, would that child necessarily opt for life? No-one has yet been able to demonstrate that the answer would always be "yes". In my judgement, the perspectives of the Christian tradition on life and its meaning, would suggest that in some instances the answer would be "no".'** (Note 16)

Apply this suggestion to the case of a severely disabled foetus. Does your answer suggest that judgements about the *quality* of life *should* be used to guide our concerns for the *sanctity* of life?

# The Just War theory

**The Just War theory and its application to the use of weapons of mass destruction.**

The Just War Theory is clearly an issue to which the Sanctity of Life Principle applies, since war is generally an issue of life and death, and in effect war overrules the sanctity of life, or makes the right to life conditional.

1 Development and rationale

- Just War Theory was mainly developed in Christian circles, primarily because Christian authorities found a tension between Jesus' commands to resist violence (Matthew 5:38–41) and situations in which they found violence to be necessary.
- Both Augustine and Aquinas were influential in the development of the theory. The theory has mainly been set within a natural law framework, where there is a principle of defending one's own life and the lives of the innocent.
- There are two main elements in Just War Theory:
  *Ius ad bellum* – These are the conditions under which it would be legitimate to go to war.
  *Ius in bello* – These are the rules under which a war must be fought once it has begun.

2 The Just War clauses in outline form

*Ius ad bellum* principles

1 There has to be a **just cause**.

2 War can only be declared by a **legitimate authority**.

3 The war must be fought with the **right intention**.

4 There has to be a reasonable **probability of success**.

5 War must be the **last resort**.

6 There must be **proportionality** – the benefits expected from waging war must be proportionate to the expected harm caused.

*Ius in bello* principles

1 There has to be a principle of **discrimination** – non-combatants must not be directly attacked.

2 **Proportionality of means to ends** – the means used to fight the war must be proportionate to the ends required.

3 Further explanation of these criteria, and some of the difficulties they present:

*Ius ad bellum*

1 A just cause would be, for example, to restore peace, to defend the innocent, or to resist attack. *Who decides whether or not a cause is just? In most wars both sides believe their position to be the just one.*

2 A just war can only be started by a competent political authority, meaning a political system that promotes genuine justice. Hitler's dictatorship would not qualify as a legitimate authority. *Who decides*

---

**Key term**

*ius ad bellum* Latin for the laws / conditions under which it is legitimate to go to war.

*ius in bello* Latin for the rules under which a war must be fought once begun.

*that an authority is competent? If we regard the United Nations as a competent authority, how successful has the UN been in controlling the start of war since 1945?*

3 A right intention would be war in a just cause, for example, to restore peace. *A right intention should arguably include forceful intervention to stop barbaric actions such as genocide. Had Hitler not declared war in 1939, it would arguably have been a right intention to declare war on Hitler because of his attempt to exterminate the Jews and others whom he thought 'undesirable'.*

4 A probability of success means that unless the war is winnable it is pointless, because to fight an unwinnable war would be futile. *Whether or not a war can be won cannot necessarily be known at its start. Much might depend on others seeing the legitimacy of a cause and deciding to assist once the war has started.*

5 The last resort criterion means that all other means to settle a conflict have been tried. *As a criterion, this is dubious, because by definition pacifists will use any means to avoid war, including making concessions and having protracted negotiations, whereas the strategy with the best chance of success may be to launch an immediate attack.*

6 The proportionality clause means that waging a war must be proportionate to the evil or harm that is being threatened. *In the 2003 Iraq War, Tony Blair committed the UK to joining a US-led coalition to invade Iraq a second time, for the purposes of removing an alleged arsenal of nuclear, chemical and biological weapons that the US and British officials called an immediate and intolerable threat to world peace. The evil of the war was considered to be proportionate to the potential harm that would be caused by the use of these weapons. Such weapons failed to materialise, and the effects of the war were arguably out of all proportion to the achievements. Casualties were estimated at somewhere between 150,000 and 600,000 deaths, depending on the source consulted; the region has been politically and militarily destabilised, and the conflict has bred a deep-seated resentment of US interference in the Muslim world. In other words, complying with a proportionality clause can amount to crystal-ball gazing: the principle of proportionality is unworkable, because it is impossible to know the outcome in advance.*

*Ius in bello*

1 The principle of discrimination means, for example, that non-combatants should not be targeted in a war. It would also not be legitimate to target civilian areas for bombing without there being legitimate military targets in those areas. *One obvious problem with this, is that it is sometimes impossible to define whether or not civilians are involved with a war effort. During the Second World War, one Allied tactic was the saturation bombing of Dresden, carried out on 14 February 1945, in which the city was reduced to an inferno where between 25,000 and 40,000 civilians died. The rationale for attacking Dresden included the fact that its rail network linked eastern and southern Germany with Berlin, Prague and Vienna. The Dresden raid was also considered as a legitimate reprisal for the German 'terror' Blitz on Coventry and for the German tactic of firing thousands of V-1 and V-2 rockets at southern England during 1944–45, causing thousands of civilian deaths. The Nazi propaganda chief, Joseph Goebbels, coined the word 'Koventrieren', ('to Coventrate') meaning 'to reduce to rubble', so both sides in the conflict evidently accepted that civilians were legitimate targets. Is the theory of a Just War, which was developed*

*centuries earlier, even applicable to the kind of warfare experienced in modern times?*

2 The proportionality of the means to ends clause means that when actually fighting the war, the amount of force used must always be morally proportionate to the threat. It includes, for example, the rejection of intrinsically evil methods of war, such as rape and genocide. In the 1994 genocide against the Tutsi people in Rwanda, rape was used as a weapon of war to humiliate and terrorise women and young girls. During 100 days, an estimated 500,000 to 1,000,000 Rwandans died. Some of those who carried out the executions called themselves the 'Army of Jesus', believing that they were acting legitimately against the enemies of God. Proportionality would also include the rejection of the use of biological weapons and nuclear weapons, which are likely to be indiscriminate in whom they kill. *Again, there is an issue of practicality here: how practical are such criteria in modern theatres of war? We shall turn to this question now, in considering the application of the theory to weapons of mass destruction.*

## Application of the theory to weapons of mass destruction

You do not need to be an expert on the technicalities of weapons of mass destruction. This section gives a brief overview of their nature and capabilities.

### What are weapons of mass destruction?

**By 'weapons of mass destruction', we are referring here to three broad types of weaponry.**

1 Nuclear weapons

The effects of a thermonuclear explosion include primarily heat, blast and radiation. The heat from an exploded bomb reaches several million degrees. A 20-megaton blast would produce third-degree burns at a distance of up to 38 km, and would probably level civilian buildings up to 20 km away, with lethal radiation effects at a distance of up to 5 km. The environmental damage caused by nuclear weapons would be severe, with contamination of topsoil, existing crops and water supplies. In April 1986, an explosion at the Chernobyl Nuclear Power Plant in the Ukraine released a cloud of radioactive dust over 200,000 km² of land. The effects of a global nuclear war are incalculable, particularly in terms of environmental damage.

2 Chemical weapons

These can cause injury, incapacitation or death. When used as far back as the First World War, mustard gas and phosgene gas caused blindness, lung damage and death. Phosgene was responsible for about 85 per cent of the 100,000 deaths from chemical weapons. Sarin gas can be around 16 times more deadly than cyanide, and VX gas is about 100 times more deadly than Sarin. Several countries have stockpiles of chemical weapons. Most chemical agents can be delivered to their target by a shell or a warhead, which explodes to spread the agent. Chemical weapons such as VX gas can be used to make a combat no-go area, so human and animal life forms would be inevitable casualties.

▲ Effects of the detonation of the atomic bomb on Hiroshima, 1945.

▲ USA 'Honest John' missile warhead cutaway, showing M134 sarin bomblets (c.1960).

**3** Biological weapons

These include bacteria and viruses, and in some ways biological weapons are the most feared form of warfare. Entomological warfare uses insects to deliver biological agents such as plague. Insects can be used to carry infectious pathogens that are transmitted when the insect bites a victim. Botulinum toxin can be distributed by aerosol or by contamination of water and food supplies; it is so deadly that one gram of the toxin can kill a million people if inhaled. (Note 17)

## All such weapons appear to lie outside the boundaries drawn by Just War theory

**1** Discrimination

Most theologians argue that, at the very least, the use of weapons of mass destruction can never discriminate, since they are equally likely to kill non-combatants as they are to destroy military targets; so they breach the principle of discrimination (Principle 1, *ius in bello*).

**2** Proportionality

Most theologians argue, also, that weapons of mass destruction meet neither of the proportionality clauses. For Principle 6, *ius ad bellum*, the harm done by such weapons can never be proportionate to the good that is aimed at. For Principle 2, *ius in bello*, using weapons of mass destruction during a war can never be proportionate to the ends desired. This is particularly true of nuclear weapons, where their use is likely to render any affected area contaminated and unusable for decades.

**3** Probability of success

Fighting an unwinnable war would be futile. With airburst nuclear weapons, for example, the range of contamination could be as deadly to the aggressors as to the intended victims. A full-scale nuclear confrontation would result in massive casualties and environmental destruction for all sides in the war. With the current progress in weapons development, it will probably be possible within a few decades to destroy the Earth entirely. All of this goes against Principle 4, *ius ad bellum*, since such wars have no probability of success.

## Can Just War theory be applied to weapons of mass destruction?

**1** Many Christians argue that Just War theory cannot be applied to weapons of mass destruction, because the evil threatened or caused by them would be out of all proportion to any hoped-for good effects, and could *never* be just. The position of the Christian Churches varies, although many appeal to Just War theory in describing nuclear weapons as 'intrinsically evil'.

Since 2013, Pope Francis has urged the abolition of nuclear weapons, and many of the Protestant Churches take a similar line, for example, in recommending that Trident (the UK's submarine-based nuclear deterrent) should not be renewed.

**2** Other Christians see such arguments as unrealistic and unworkable. Chemical, biological and nuclear weapons cannot be uninvented, and it would be naïve, for example, to imagine that countries will voluntarily give up their nuclear weapons. Smaller nations with a nuclear capacity that is big enough to deter larger and more powerful countries would think it suicidal to give up a nuclear deterrent, since they would then have nothing capable of deterring those countries from mounting a full-scale attack. If Czechoslovakia had possessed a nuclear deterrent in 1939, Hitler would have been unable to invade that country without a retaliation that would have obliterated much of Germany.

In this kind of thinking, the threat and the use of nuclear weapons (and potentially of biological and chemical weapons also) could be justified by Christians, for example on the grounds that: the threat of their use is the best deterrent to a potential attacker. For some, invasion and conquest by another country could be a worse evil than using nuclear weapons against the attacker: the atrocities committed by invading armies are arguably as unspeakable as the use of nuclear weapons. Also, the abolition of nuclear weapons would merely return us to conventional forms of warfare, and conventional weapons are rapidly becoming as deadly as nuclear weapons.

## Activity

Research and discuss the following questions:

1   If there is something 'intrinsically evil' about weapons of mass destruction, in what lies the evil – in the weapons themselves or in humans, who make them?

2   If life is sacred to God, does this mean that *all* war is against God's wishes?

3   Some Christians are pacifists because they believe that Jesus commanded a non-violent response to threats (Matthew 5:28–31). Just War theory rejects pacifism because the theory takes the Aristotelian approach that although life is indeed a value that must be preserved, it is not right to sacrifice all other values to preserve it, and this includes the values of independence and liberty. Do you think that pacifism is a better response than the Just War approach to threats from weapons of mass destruction?

4   Some modern nuclear weapons have been developed to be far less powerful than in previous decades and have very accurate guidance systems to enable 'surgical strikes'. Do you think that Just War theory can allow their use in war to pinpoint attacking forces?

5   Can Just War theory be applied to international terrorism?

6   How far do you think that 'Justifiable' War theory might be a more appropriate description than 'Just' War theory? How might the use of weapons of mass destruction be included in such a theory?

7   The death toll from the atomic bombs dropped on Hiroshima and Nagasaki is estimated at 200,000, yet if the Allies had invaded Japan using only conventional weapons, then depending on the degree to which Japanese civilians resisted the invasion, estimates at the time ran into the millions for Allied casualties and tens of millions for Japanese casualties. (Note 18) In the light of this, was the use of atomic weapons to end the war on Japan 'justified', or not?

# Dominion and stewardship

For this you need to look at:

● The belief that Christians have dominion over animals
● Beliefs about the role of Christians as stewards of animals and the natural environment
● How changing understandings of the effects of human activities on the environment have affected that role

# The belief that Christians have dominion over animals

## Dominion as virtually unrestricted power over animals / the environment

Dominion means 'power over', and there are a number of reasons why many Christians believe that Christians do, and should have, power over animals.

1 Humans are described as having been made 'little less than God' and as having dominion over what God has made.

 The Bible leaves us in no doubt about the status of humanity in the created world. Psalm 8, for example, is a hymn celebrating God's glory in which the status of humans is clear:

> When I look at thy heavens, the work of thy fingers,
> – the moon and the stars which thou hast established;
>  what is man that thou art mindful of him,
> – and the son of man that thou dost care for him?
>  Yet thou hast made him little less than God,
> – and dost crown him with glory and honor.
>  Thou hast given him dominion over the works of thy hands;
> – thou hast put all things under his feet,
>  all sheep and oxen,
> – and also the beasts of the field,
>  the birds of the air, and the fish of the sea,
> – whatever passes along the paths of the sea.          (Psalm 8:3–8)

 If humans are believed to have been made 'little less than God', it is little wonder that humanity has a high opinion of its own importance. Moreover, humans are said to have dominion over 'the works of God's hands', which means the rest of creation.

2 Human power over creation is reinforced by the belief that humans were created *Imago Dei* – in the image of God – which means literally that they 'look like God'.

 This is the implicit meaning of a text we have looked at several times: Genesis 1:26–28:

> Then God said, 'Let us make man in our image, after our likeness; and let them have dominion over the fish of the sea, and over the birds of the air, and over the cattle, and over all the earth, and over every creeping thing that creeps upon the earth.' So God created man in his own image, in the image of God he created him; male and female he created them. And God blessed them, and God said to them, 'Be fruitful and multiply, and fill the earth and subdue it; and have dominion over the fish of the sea and over the birds of the air and over every living thing that moves upon the earth.'

Again, the status of humanity is clear: humans are made in God's image. The Hebrew word for 'image' here is *tselem*, and both Jewish and Christian writers have generally taken this to mean that humans have a God-given capacity to use reason and to be moral beings. This, however, is reading more into the text than really exists, since *tselem* is not used in the Old Testament with this meaning. *Tselem* really means 'image' in the sense of a physical copy, and is often used to refer to the images

323

of various gods that should not be worshipped, for example, Numbers 33:52; 2 Kings 11:18; Psalm 73:20. This is the kind of image that can be modelled, as for example in Amos 5:26, and probably represents a stage of belief when human beings were thought literally to look like God, so in both understandings of the word 'image', Genesis 1:26–28 reinforces the verdict of Psalm 8, that humans are 'little less than God'.

3 Human dominion means that the Earth is to be subdued and that humans are to be feared by all other creatures.

In the same text, (Genesis 1:28), the command that humans are to 'subdue' the Earth is from the verb *cbsh*, which literally means to 'subjugate' – 'to bring into subjection', for example, Jeremiah 34:11,16; Numbers 32:29. This word is followed immediately by the verb *rdh*, meaning 'to have dominion over' – literally, 'to rule over'.

Further, after the flood with which God destroys the world, God blesses Noah and his sons, and tells them:

> Be fruitful and multiply, and fill the earth. The fear of you and the dread of you shall be upon every beast of the earth, and upon every bird of the air, upon everything that creeps on the ground and all the fish of the sea; into your hand they are delivered. Every moving thing that lives shall be food for you … (Genesis 9:1–3a)

The passage ends with a repetition of the command to multiply the human race on Earth (9:7).

4 What we have in the Bible, then, is a strong anthropocentric and anthropomorphic tradition which in several respects is detrimental to care of the environment.

We might conclude, from what we have seen so far, that whereas the status of humanity is only a little less than that of God, the Bible places no particular 'intrinsic' value on animal life or on the life of any other living thing. These have value only in so far as they serve human desires. Thus one can say that the Bible has a strong anthropocentric view of the environment as a whole; humans see themselves as the pinnacle of creation against which everything else is measured and found to be of lesser value. 'Anthropocentric', then, means centring the universe on humans; regarding humans as the central fact of the universe. Given the absolute minuteness of this galaxy (let alone this planet) in relation to the rest of the universe, this is a mind-set which can readily be understood from the perspective of ancient Israelite culture, but which has no relevance in relation to modern cosmology. Arguably, it encourages humans to be arrogant and uncaring about anything non-human.

A similar word is anthropomorphic, which means representing God as having human form, personality or attributes. We looked at anthropomorphism and gender-specific language about God in Chapter 7 God, so you have some knowledge of this already. Anthropomorphism also means ascribing human characteristics to what is not human, including animals. The fact that animals, and even God, are given human characteristics also shows the extent of human intellectual arrogance. Animals are not valued for what they are, but for how human they might be. An example of this might be seen by some to be the posters of smiling chickens, apparently delighted to be served up for human consumption, outside various chicken fast-food outlets. Even God has a human likeness, which is simply another device which makes humans greater than they are. When the environment is judged by anthropocentric and anthropomorphic values, you can see, therefore, that there are likely to be few checks on human behaviour that treats the world as a means to the end of human pleasure. Instead of being respected and maintained as an environment that is essential to our own well-being, the world is plundered for raw materials to help people get rich at the expense of everybody and everything else. If the Bible encourages anthropocentricity and anthropomorphism, then the Bible encourages environmental destruction.

5 We can see the effects of this kind of thinking on Christian thought and action.

Christians who take the view that 'dominion' means 'power over' believe that humans are entitled to use the environment to satisfy their needs. This interpretation is often supported by referring to the 'Fall' of humanity, where the world was corrupted by Satan, and by the sin of Adam and Eve. Some Christians assume that after the Fall, the role of humans was to control an environment that had already been damaged by sin, and had to be kept in submission.

Something of this kind of view can be seen in the philosophy of Thomas Aquinas, and we have looked at this in Chapter 4.1 Natural Moral Law. According to Aquinas, humans have only indirect duties to animals. Aquinas followed Aristotle's view that animals are just part of the human food chain. Aquinas did object to cruelty to animals, but only because he believed that cruelty to animals bred cruelty in humans themselves. Mistreating animals was basically a kind of property damage.

Most Christians believe that animals do not have souls. Scholars such as Aquinas and Descartes believed that without souls, animals were not self-aware, and so could not feel pain. Descartes thought of animals as automata, and thereby as not meriting compassion from humans. If Christians believe that animals have no souls, then they have a strong reason for not caring too much about animal experimentation and factory farming. Refer back to Chapter 4 for what was said about these in the discussion on practical ethics.

When the Industrial Revolution began in England and Germany, the accumulation of lots of money was seen by Protestants in those countries as a sign of God's approval. Unfortunately much of this wealth was achieved at the cost of huge environmental damage.

Although mistreatment of the environment is not solely due to Christian or other religious perspectives, religious views clearly do not always encourage humans to attach much significance to the non-human world. Among the most damaging texts, in terms of the treatment of the environment, is Genesis 9:2–3, where God tells Noah and his sons:

**'The fear of you and the dread of you shall be upon every beast of the earth, and upon every bird of the air, upon everything that creeps on the ground and all the fish of the sea; into your hand they are delivered.'**

Take a look back at Chapter 5 Application of Ethical Theories, to the issues of non-human life and death, and the range of issues discussed there: the use of animals as food, intensive farming, use in scientific procedures, and blood sports, and other things perpetrated by humans on the animal world. You might consider that the licence granted for cruelty in Genesis 9 has been fully exploited by humans.

There is, however, another tradition about human dominion over the environment, which also stems from the Bible, in which the 'dominion' of humans over the environment is interpreted in terms of the human duty to be 'stewards' of the world.

## Beliefs about the role of Christians as stewards of animals and the natural environment

### Dominion as caring stewardship of animals / the environment

1 'Dominion' as 'stewardship'

An alternative way of thinking about the environment can be found in the views of those Christians who argue that to have 'dominion' over the environment really means that humans should act as 'stewards' of the entire environment – as caretakers of God's creation, fully responsible to God in that duty. The world belongs to God because God created it, along with humans. As the most intelligent species, humans have a responsibility to look after it, because they alone have been made in God's image.

2 This way of thinking is also rooted in the Bible. The focus here is not on the 'Fall' of the world from perfection but on those statements in Genesis that God viewed his creation as 'good' (Genesis 1:4.10, 12, 18, 21, 25, 31). According to this view, the environment has intrinsic value because God made it, and, by definition, it must therefore reflect God's goodness.

There are several passages in the Bible that show the value of the non-human creation to God. Creation itself is said to rejoice at God's rule, for example:

> Let the heavens be glad, and let the earth rejoice; let the sea roar, and all that fills it;
>
> let the field exult, and everything in it! Then shall all the trees of the wood sing for joy before the Lord ... (Psalm 96:11–13)

Being made in God's image, Christians have a responsibility to look after the world, and they have a duty to reflect God's love for its goodness.

3 It is also reflected in Augustine's 'Principle of Plenitude'.

This principle began with Plato, and it suggests that all the forms of existence that are possible in the universe will exist somewhere. St Augustine used a version of this principle to suggest that a universe with many species is much better than a universe with only one, because having a huge variety of species shows the depth of God's power and the beauty of his creation. Creation is perfect because of this range and diversity, which reflect God's omnipotent creativity. [Note 19]

On this kind of approach, humans are therefore just one of an infinite range of entities, both organic and inorganic. The natural environment includes all of heaven and Earth, including lakes, rivers and seas, mountains and the atmosphere. Levelling of the rainforests and pollution of lakes, rivers and seas has reached crisis proportions, and much of the natural beauty of the landscape has been spoiled. If the entire environment belongs to God, then stewardship must be of the entire environment, and not just of humans and other animals.

## Activity

Below are samples of biblical passages that illustrate the view that Christians should be responsible stewards of the whole environment. Study a selection of the texts and note their relevance for the understanding of dominion as 'responsible stewardship'. [Note 10]

- God as the Creator of everything: Nehemiah 9:6; John 1:3; Colossians 1:15–16.
- God as the owner of creation: 1 Chronicles 29:11; 1 Corinthians 10:26.
- God's love and compassion for creation: Psalm 33:5; Psalm 145:9.
- God sustains creation: Job 12:10; Psalm 65:9-13; Hebrews 1:3.
- God redeems creation: Romans 8:18–25; Colossians 1:20.
- Creation's praise of God: Psalm 148:1-10; Isaiah 55:12.
- God's care for animals: Genesis 9:9–10; Hosea 2:18; Luke 12:6; Isaiah 11:6–9.
- God's commands for stewardship: Leviticus 25:2–7; Numbers 35:31-34; Deuteronomy 20:19.
- God's anger at those who defile the land: Hosea 4:1–3; Jeremiah 12:4; Isaiah 5:8–10.

It is probably the case that a changing understanding of the effects of human activities on the environment has brought about the increased popularity among Christians of the idea that they should be stewards of the natural environment.

## Christians as stewards of animals and the natural environment

Changing understandings of the effects of human activities on the environment have affected the role of Christians as stewards of animals and the natural environment.

From the late twentieth century to the present, we have come to understand that the degradation of the environment has reached crisis proportions. There are many symptoms of this degradation, for example:

- Global warming, where the burning of fossil fuels: coal, oil and natural gas, has produced toxic gases that contribute to an overall increase in the planet's average temperature. The Earth's temperature is kept warm by the 'greenhouse effect', where certain gases in the atmosphere prevent the Sun's energy from bouncing back off the Earth's surface, and this effect has been increased by burning fossil fuels. The increase in temperature has resulted in a huge meltdown of the ice at the Earth's poles. In some places, the ice sheets have thinned by over 40 per cent since the 1970s. Sea levels have been predicted to rise by around 90 cm by the year 2100 and by considerably more thereafter. Some scenarios are far worse, including the prediction that three-quarters of the UK will be submerged. The effects on low-lying areas will be catastrophic. Huge storms are becoming common: in 2005, Hurricane Katrina caused a storm surge that breached the New Orleans flood barriers, inundating three-quarters of the city and killing over 1,300 people.

- Water pollution has increased drastically, for example, by the increased release of waste products like sewage and factory chemicals into river drainage systems, much of which then ends up in the sea. Oil pollutes the seas and oceans, killing millions of seabirds and fish every year. Freshwater systems are polluted by industrial settlement and the introduction of dams, which often submerge large areas of natural beauty, with a resultant loss of biodiversity.
- Soil pollution occurs when chemicals are released by accident or by design. Some of the worst soil contaminants include herbicides and pesticides, produced on a large scale by the farming industry and on a local scale by people using them in their own gardens. There is much concern about the long-term effects of genetically-modified crops, not least in their possible effects on biodiversity.
- Radioactive pollution occurs as the result of the work of nuclear power stations, and through research into nuclear weapons. Contamination is by radioactive dust or through dumping radioactive waste. In 1986 there were a number of unexplained bone cancers in young children in southern Ireland, which some researchers suggested were caused by radioactive fallout (from the explosion at the Chernobyl nuclear power plant) on grazing land, which then entered the food chain.
- Human population pollution occurs where excess population intensifies most of the other types of pollution. The effects of all these pollutions are disproportionate because 20 per cent of the world's population controls 80 per cent of the world's resources.

The ethical issues include, primarily:

- The treatment of other humans in ways that go against their interests.
- The treatment of other species in ways that go against their interests.
- The treatment of the general environment of rocks, plants and trees, in ways that go against the interests of both humans and animals, and of the planet as a whole.

## The reaction of Christian scholars

The reaction of Christian scholars interested in the role of religion has generally been that there must be an increased emphasis on stewardship of the environment as a whole.

Some examples:

- **Victoria Harrison** (focusing on Judaism and Islam as well as Christianity):

  'By the end of the twentieth century, many had come to believe that this situation posed an immediate threat to the continuation of life on the planet. Given the possible magnitude of this threat, it is not surprising that religious thinkers from each of the Abrahamic faiths felt the need to address some of the issues. The result was eco-theology, which consists in an attempt to develop a theology that can respond to the environmental crisis.' (Note 21)

- **Lynn White Jr** (Note 22) argues that many of the problems at the root of the environmental crisis have been shaped, in the Western world, by the Judaeo-Christian tradition, particularly by its belief that humans have dominion over the environment as a whole. Not all Christian thinkers accept this, since some argue that the crisis has developed because of our increasingly secular and scientific / mechanised culture, where our ethics have not kept up with our technological ability.
- **Sallie McFague** is a Christian feminist writer who argues that the current environmental crisis is largely the product of patriarchal Christianity, where God is seen as transcendent and apart from the world, which encourages humanity's subjection of nature. We need to develop new models of God, particularly where God is immanent and involved within the entire world, so that Christians see the world literally as God's body. (Note 23)

The response of Christian organisations in promoting the idea of stewardship of the environment has been widespread.

### Activity

Look, for example, at https://ctbi.org.uk/environment-links and take some notes on the variety of Christian organisations and development agencies currently involved in a wide range of initiatives for environmental stewardship.

Using the examples that you find, write 300 words on your concept of the role of a Christian steward in caring for the environment.

### Key term

**eco-theology** The approach to environmental issues focusing on establishing the right relationship between religion and nature. It stems from the perception that our current environmental problems are due in large part to religious misunderstanding.

### Where does Christianity stand at the end of this debate?

1 There is no doubt that there is a significant increase in Christian attempts to develop a consistent **eco-theology**.

2 Many Christians still take the view that dominion over animals means virtually unrestricted power over them. Among those Christians who prefer to think that animals have intrinsic value as part of God's creation, comparatively few are vegetarian, so their main emphasis might be on good treatment of animals before killing them humanely for food production.

3 In 2015, Pope Francis issued *Laudato Si* ('Praise be to you'), a detailed encyclical addressing a wide range of environmental concerns. (Note 24) In particular, he called for better care for the environment as a whole. In article 67, he admits that the Church has at times interpreted the Scriptures incorrectly, so:

> '... we must forcefully reject the notion that our being created in God's image and given dominion over the earth justifies absolute domination over other creatures.'

He also rejects 'misguided anthropocentrism', and suggests that:

> 'There can be no renewal of our relationship with nature without a renewal of humanity itself.' (118, 119)

Much of the call to action in the encyclical advocates 'dialogue'. Do you think that Christian Churches should, rather, *instruct* their followers?

▲ Fishermen prepare to fish, amid floating rubbish off Manila Bay in the Philippines.

Would it be a reasonable action for the Church leaders to instruct Christians (where feasible) to reject food that originates from factory farms or intensive farming methods?

4 Have a look at the Church of England's environmental campaign: 'Shrinking the Footprint', for example, at: http://www.churchcare.co.uk/shrinking-the-footprint. How far do you think this goes in terms of Christian stewardship of the environment?

5 As a final comment to focus your mind on the extent of the environmental problem, you might do an online search on plastic pollution. For example, look at: https://www.theguardian.com/environment/2016/jan/24/plastic-new-epoch-human-damage.

Plastic pollution is now so extensive that it has sunk to the deep ocean floor. With reference to the plastic 'invasion', some scientists are suggesting that we have brought about a new geological epoch – the 'Anthropocene'.

It seems undeniable that environmental issues really are at the centre of all questions about the survival of life on Earth, and that religions need to be more proactive in what they do as well as what they say.

## Technical terms for this section on Key Moral Principles

**Denomination** A recognised branch of the Christian Church.

**dominion** Meaning power / power over, as in the debate about human dominion over the world.

**double predestination** God predestines some to the Kingdom through His grace but leaves others immersed in their sin to be condemned to hell.

**eco-theology** The approach to environmental issues focusing on establishing the right relationship between religion and nature. It stems from the perception that our current environmental problems are due in large part to religious misunderstanding.

**eschatological** To do with the last days, that is, the last Judgement / God's Kingdom.

**foreknowledge** When applied to God, the doctrine that an all-knowing God knows the entire future, so knows from eternity who will accept the gift of grace and who will reject it. In the modern debate, the question is whether or not God's foreknowledge (omniscience) is causal – does it cause human actions? If so, then there is a problem with the concept of predestination to heaven or hell.

**grace** God's grace is seen as the free gift of mercy to sinful humanity, for example, through the atonement made by the suffering and death of Jesus. According to Pelagius, God's grace was the gift of free will to humans.

**intrinsic value** Something that has value for its own sake, for example, human life in the Sanctity of Life Principle.

***ius ad bellum*** Latin for the laws / conditions under which it is legitimate to go to war.

***ius in bello*** Latin for the rules under which a war must be fought once begun.

**justification** When used in 'justification by faith' and 'justification by works' – Christians are counted as righteous before God on the basis of faith or by works, or by both.

**predestination** The view that all events have been willed by God from eternity, specifically the fate of the righteous and of the damned.

**sanctity** As in the Sanctity of Life Principle: holy / sacred to God.

**Sanctity of Life Principle** The idea, based on the concepts of (1) being made in God's image and (2) having (uniquely) a soul, that human life is sacred to God.

***sola fide*** Latin, refers to Luther's doctrine of justification by 'faith alone'.

**stewardship** The view that 'dominion' over the environment should be understood as responsible human care for it, on the understanding that humans are answerable to God for their treatment of the environment.

# Summary of Key Moral Principles

**Justification by faith or works?**

This is Paul's doctrine, found principally in Romans, that humans are 'counted as righteous'/'declared innocent' by faith in Jesus Christ. Justification is eschatological and cannot come simply by obeying the Jewish Law: only God can justify humanity. Justification is the free gift of God's grace, because all have sinned through Adam, so God freely redeemed humanity through the atoning suffering and death of Jesus. Justification includes those who died before Jesus was incarnated: they too (as with Abraham) are justified by faith. We are justified, therefore, by grace and faith, not by good moral conduct. This seems to say clearly that good moral conduct is less important than having faith. The Letter of James, however, argues that Christians are justified by works. If we ignore someone who has no food or clothing, then our faith is useless – 'faith without works is dead'. Rather, faith is shown '*by*' works. Even the demons believe in God! Abraham was justified by works – he was going to sacrifice Isaac; equally, Rahab the prostitute was justified in what she 'did' to help Joshua's conquest of Jericho.

Who is right? The priority of works is suggested by Jesus' emphasis on works in the Sermon on the Mount and in his Parable of the Sheep and the Goats, in which he makes no mention of faith, and the righteous are sent to heaven / the unrighteous to hell precisely because they have ignored works. However, those who prioritise faith point to Ephesians 2:8–10, where Paul explicitly states that Christians are saved by faith and not by their own works: God saves the person through the channel of their faith.

Martin Luther, especially, defended justification by faith alone (*sola fide*). Justification comes through Jesus' atonement. The faith of the sinner is passive, not active, and justification is not brought about by human achievement or works but by what God brings about through Jesus Christ. The righteousness of Christ is literally attributed by God to the believing sinner. Righteous works are the 'result' of being justified by God and being born again through the Holy Spirit.

Others insist on the importance of both faith *and* works, and this was the position taken by the Catholic Church in response to Luther, at the Council of Trent: some human effort must be involved in the process of justification, since Jesus himself constantly emphasised the need for good works. Grace comes to the individual through baptism, which is the sacrament of faith, so faith is developed in the context of the Church. This leads to new life in Christ and to good works. Faith is not just intellectual assent to God's existence: it must entail obedience and good works:

'He who says "I know him" but disobeys his commandments is a liar.' (1 John 2:4).

On this interpretation, then, James is comparing two kinds of faith: the kind that leads to works and the kind that does not, and the second kind of faith is 'dead'.

**Predestination**

Predestination is the view that all events have been willed by God, and that the fate of each individual with regard to the Kingdom has also been willed by God. Paul gives an explicit statement of predestination in Romans 8, in which he says that God 'conformed to the image of his Son' those who in his *foreknowledge* he knew would be righteous. If this is the case, then this seems to imply that their conduct is morally good because God has willed that also, and this implies further that good moral conduct in human beings is less important than God's will. Whatever God decides will happen. As for those who are not predestined to heaven, in Romans 6, Paul says that, '... the wages of sin is death, but the free gift of God is eternal life in Christ Jesus our Lord', so perhaps Paul thought that they simply died without entering God's Kingdom.

There is a logical problem with predestination in that it clashes with the belief that God gave humans free will. Pelagius rejected predestination on this basis, rejecting also the idea of original sin, and arguing that God's 'grace' was God's gift of free will to humans.

In opposition to Pelagius, Augustine proposed the doctrine of 'double predestination': God predestines some to the Kingdom through his grace, but leaves others immersed in their sin to be condemned to hell. During the Reformation, John Calvin added to this by arguing that God ordains some to glory and some to eternal torment.

The modern debate about predestination links to the debate about the problem of evil, because of the doctrine of God's omniscience: if God knew, before creation, that some would inevitably merit hell, why did God bother to create such beings in the first place? How do we reconcile hell with the idea of a God of love? Does Hick's theory of universal salvation help or does this in effect destroy the doctrine of the Atonement? How do we reconcile the idea of predestination with the concept of human free will and the issue of God's relation to time? Is there any realistic way of reconciling predestination with the belief held by most Christians that good moral conduct is essential to Christian living and Christian faith?

### The concept of the sanctity of life

To say that life has sanctity means that it is holy or sacred to God, and this is the basis of the Sanctity of Life Principle. The principle derives from the Genesis texts that humans are made in the image of God (1:26–27) and have a soul (2:7), which together are taken to mean that humans are sacred to God because they reflect his image and alone were given a soul. The principle therefore holds that human life has intrinsic value. The principle is sometimes described as 'strong' (forbidding any kind of killing, for example, through contraception, abortion, euthanasia or removal of life support) or 'weak', which argues that the situation should be taken into account. The weak form of the principle is also associated with a 'Quality of Life Principle', which suggests that there are some human conditions where the quality of life is such that a strong Sanctity of Life Principle is inappropriate, and that humans have been given reason and free will to judge these conditions.

### Different views about applying the Sanctity of Life Principle to issues concerning the embryo and the unborn child

Applying the Sanctity of Life Principle to these issues is largely about the question of 'personhood'. The strong Sanctity of Life Principle holds that personhood begins at conception, because all the necessary genetic material that will form the person is present. The Catholic Church supports this understanding, arguing that there is a continuous development of each life from conception to birth. The strong Sanctity of Life Principle is founded in Scripture, and human conception can be seen as analogous to the incarnation of Jesus 'conceived in Mary's womb'. The strong Sanctity of Life Principle rejects the Warnock Report's 14-day limit for experimentation on human embryos, regarding it as a licence to murder.

Equally it rejects embryonic stem cell research and therapeutic cloning, along with Pre-implantation Genetic Diagnosis, and rejects abortion at any stage and for any reason: the child's right to life overrides the quality of life of the mother.

Although the weak Sanctity of Life Principle shares the same scriptural basis as the strong principle, those who support the weak Sanctity of Life Principle reach different conclusions, since the weak Sanctity of Life Principle takes into account both the situation and a Quality of Life Principle. The Church of England allows abortion for quality of life considerations for both the mother and the foetus, and different Protestant groups use the same kind of logic to argue that the various forms of embryo experimentation can be legitimate because they support the sanctity of the lives of all who suffer from disease or disability.

The strong Sanctity of Life Principle protects the value of life, and protects those who suffer disabilities, and the weak Sanctity of Life Principle is in line with Jesus' teachings on love and compassion. However, the strong principle can be seen as unscientific, ignoring the evolution of all species, and ignoring the fact that scientifically, human life is no more special than any other form of life. The view that humans are made in God's image can be seen as an anthropomorphic / gender-specific red herring leading to speciesism.

### The Just War theory

Just War theory was mainly developed in Christian circles, for example, Augustine and Aquinas, mainly within a natural law tradition, in order to clarify (for example, in relation to Matthew 5:38–41) the idea of justifiable violence. It outlines the principles of *ius ad bellum* (conditions under which it would be legitimate to go to war) and of *ius in bello* (rules under which a war must be fought once it has begun). *Ius ad bellum* principles include: just cause, legitimate authority, right intention, probability of success, last result, proportionality. *Ius in bello* principles include: discrimination (re non-combatants) and proportionality of means to ends. There are difficulties with each of these principles, not least their application to modern weapons of mass destruction.

### The application of the Just War theory to the use of weapons of mass destruction

As a term, weapons of mass destruction refers primarily to nuclear, chemical and biological weapons. All of these appear to lie outside the boundaries drawn by Just War theory. Most theologians argue that weapons of mass destruction cannot discriminate between military and civilian targets (principle 1 of *ius in bello*); also that they meet neither of the proportionality clauses (principle 6, *ius ad bellum*; principle 2, *ius in bello*). It is also doubtful that they could meet the possibility of success clause (principle 4, *ius ad bellum*). If, then, Just War theory cannot be applied to weapons of mass destruction, does this mean that the theory is pointless? The weapons cannot be uninvented, and if smaller countries give up a nuclear deterrent, they would be incapable of resisting attack from a more powerful country. Many of the Christian Churches describe nuclear weapons as 'intrinsically evil' and advocate global nuclear disarmament, although most see this approach as unrealistic and potentially as more dangerous than retaining a nuclear deterrent. Some Christians argue that a nuclear deterrent is justifiable, since that gives the greatest chance of avoiding the use of weapons of mass destruction.

**Dominion and stewardship: the belief that Christians have dominion over animals**

Dominion as virtually unrestricted power over animals.

Psalm 8 describes humans as having been made 'little less than God' and having dominion over what God has made. This understanding is reinforced by the belief that humans were created in the image of God. This concept of dominion means that the Earth is to be subdued and ruled over by humans, to the extent that the fear and dread of humanity should be over all animals. This understanding has a strong anthropocentric and anthropomorphic understanding

that is detrimental to the care of the environment, so that animals are not valued for what they are but for how useful they are to humans. Some Christians therefore use the environment to satisfy their needs, regardless of the effects of this policy. The problem has arguably been made worse by Aquinas' teaching that mistreating animals is a kind of property damage; by the Protestant view that accumulating wealth is a sign of God's approval; and by the Christian belief that animals do not have souls.

**Beliefs about the role of Christians as stewards of animals and the natural environment**

Dominion as 'caring stewardship of animals and the entire environment'.

Other Christians interpret 'dominion' as caring stewardship of the entire environment, seeing humans as caretakers of God's creation who are fully responsible to God in what they do. This view is also rooted in the Bible (for example, in God's description of creation as 'good'). It is also reflected in Augustine's Principle of Plenitude.

**How changing understandings of the effects of human activities on the environment have affected that role**

The rejection of 'dominion' as 'unrestricted power over' has been accelerated by a new Christian understanding of the effects of environmental degradation brought about by human activities, and a number of Christian scholars argue that there must be an increased emphasis on stewardship of the environment as a whole, for example, through eco-theology.

# 10 Expressions of religious identity

This chapter will cover:
- Baptism
- Holy Communion
- The mission of the Church

**A note about the text**

Whereas elsewhere the text refers simply to the 'Catholic Church', in this section 'Roman Catholic Church' has been used, this is because in various places the word '**catholic**' (with a small 'c') appears, which means 'all-embracing', that is, 'the whole body of Christians world-wide'.

Further, when 'church' refers to an actual building, the place where Christians worship or the congregation of that church, a small 'c' is used. Where the word refers to a particular denomination, an upper case 'C' is used, as in: Orthodox Church, Protestant Church, Catholic Church, Baptist Church, the Early Church, and so on. It is worth noting that some cases are ambiguous, so do not get too anxious about it!

**Key term**

**catholic** (With a small 'c') 'all-embracing', that is, 'the whole body of Christians world-wide'.

One way that people express their religious identity is through the practices of their religion. All religions have their own specific practices: some are related to rites of passage (births, attaining religious adulthood, death), and others are practices which have a community dimension. In this chapter, we shall look at two key practices of Christianity. **Baptism** is a rite of passage related to birth and religious adulthood, and **Holy Communion** is a community practice. We shall also look at mission, which is how the Church as a body expresses its religious identity in society and the world.

## Baptism

For this, you need to look at:

- The significance of infant baptism in Christianity with particular reference to the Catholic and Baptist traditions.
- Arguments in favour of and against infant baptism.

The word 'baptism' comes from the Koine Greek word *baptizo* which means 'to dip' or 'to dunk'. Rituals using water as a symbol of cleansing or membership are used by other religions. In Judaism, ritual washing in water is required in several different circumstances, for example, after contact with a dead body and during consecration as a Cohen (priest). Jewish women attend a Mikveh, a ritual bath, each month when their period ends. In Sikhism, initiates take part in the Amrit Sanchar ritual, during which they drink sweetened water and have it sprinkled on them: this is how they join the *Khalsa*, the community of Sikhs.

The roots of baptism in Christianity go back to Jesus' lifetime. Jesus, of course, was a practising Jew. After growing up in relative obscurity, Jesus left his home and went into the desert to see his cousin, John. John was a wandering holy man who taught people that they needed to be cleansed from their sins by baptism to prepare for the coming of the Messiah (the expected king who would get rid of the Romans, feed the hungry and perform miracles). Although the Gospel accounts of the event differ slightly, they all agree that Jesus was baptised by John, that this event exposed Jesus' special relationship with God, and that this marked the start of his public ministry.

> John the baptizer appeared in the wilderness, preaching a baptism of repentance for the forgiveness of sins. And there went out to him all the country of Judea, and all the people of Jerusalem; and they were baptised by him in the river Jordan, confessing their sins. Now John was clothed with camel's hair, and had a leather girdle around his waist, and ate locusts and wild honey. And he preached, saying, 'After me comes he who is mightier than I, the thong of whose sandals I am not worthy to stoop down and untie. I have baptised you with water; but he will baptize you with the Holy Spirit.'
>
> In those days Jesus came from Nazareth of Galilee and was baptised by John in the Jordan. And when he came up out of the water, immediately he saw the heavens opened and the Spirit descending upon him like a dove; and a voice came from heaven, 'Thou art my beloved Son; with thee I am well pleased'. (Mark 1:4–11)

It is not clear from the New Testament whether or not Jesus himself baptised people – John's Gospel suggests he did, but the other Gospels do not. Certainly, Jesus' disciples did baptise people when they became followers of Jesus, so for them it had become not only a ritual of cleansing, but also a way of bringing someone into membership of the group. In John's Gospel, Jesus tells a potential convert:

> **'I say to you, unless one is born of water and the Spirit, he cannot enter the kingdom of God. That which is born of the flesh is flesh, and that which is born of the Spirit is spirit.' (John 3:5–6)**

This seems to suggest that Jesus saw baptism as both a physical and a spiritual event.

After the death of Jesus, two of the Gospel writers describe how Jesus gave instructions to his disciples to continue to bring people into the religious movement he had started through baptism (although Mark's account is part of the 'Longer Ending' of his Gospel, which is generally thought to have been added later by the Church).

> Now the eleven disciples went to Galilee, to the mountain to which Jesus had directed them. And when they saw him they worshipped him; but some doubted. And Jesus came and said to them, 'All authority in heaven and on earth has been given to me. Go therefore and make disciples of all nations, baptizing them in the name of the Father and of the Son and of the Holy Spirit, teaching them to observe all that I have commanded you; and lo, I am with you always, to the close of the age'. (Matthew 28:16–20)

Christian practices concerned with baptism are mainly based on these Bible passages. There are three contrasting viewpoints about the importance of baptism in Christian Churches.

- For Orthodox Christians, Roman Catholics and some parts of the Church of England, baptism marks an irreversible spiritual change to a person's soul.
- For most Protestant Christians, it is a symbol of their public commitment to the Christian faith.
- Some denominations, for example, Quakers, do not practise baptism at all, because they believe that you show your membership of the Church by living a Christian life rather than through a ritual.

## Baptism in the Catholic tradition

The Orthodox Churches, the Roman Catholic Church and parts of the Church of England share a broadly catholic understanding of the nature of baptism. For them, it is a mystery (Orthodox) or a **sacrament** (Roman Catholic and Church of England). This means that the simple act of using water in a cleansing ritual, through God's grace, makes a profound and irreversible change to the person's spiritual existence. There is a strong element of mystery and symbolism in baptism which reflects its history as a mystical initiation into an alternative spiritual existence. We shall look at this in detail through the teachings and practice of the Roman Catholic Church.

Roman Catholic Christians believe that all human beings are born with the stain of original sin, because the sin of Adam and Eve was passed on seminally (through reproduction) to Adam's descendants – the whole human race. Even new-born babies, who have done nothing themselves that could be considered sinful, inherit the taint of sin through their human family. The only way to free someone from this sin is to link them with Jesus Christ, whose death on the cross overcame the consequences of original sin. They do this, both by re-enacting death and rising again, and by joining the spiritual community of the Church. Both of these happen during a baptism service.

It is for this reason that Roman Catholics normally practise infant baptism (**paedobaptism**). Through a formal ritual which links the child with Christ, the soul of the infant is washed clean of original sin. The key parts of the ritual are these:

- The priest, or the person performing the baptism, makes the sign of the cross on the child's forehead to symbolise that the child belongs to Christ.
- The adults who bring the child for baptism (parents and godparents) reject evil and sin on behalf of the child. They make a declaration of faith

### Key terms

**sacrament** A ceremony seen as imparting spiritual grace. In the Roman Catholic Church there are seven sacraments: baptism, confirmation, the Eucharist, penance, anointing of the sick, ordination, and matrimony. In the Protestant Churches the main sacraments are the Eucharist (Holy Communion) and baptism.

**paedobaptism** Infant baptism.

in God the Father, God the Son and God the Holy Spirit on behalf of the child. This is formally accepting the terms of membership of the Church.

- The person performing the baptism asks God to make holy the water used for baptism through the Holy Spirit, so that the infant will be 'born of water and the Spirit'.
- The baby may be immersed three times in the water, or have water poured over its head three times, as the person performing the baptism says:

> **'I baptise you in the name of the Father, and of the Son, and of the Holy Spirit.'**

This symbolises both the washing away of sin, and also death (going under water) and resurrection (coming out of water).

- The baby is then anointed with perfumed oil consecrated by the bishop, which is a symbol of the gift of the Holy Spirit. This means he or she is now a member of the Church. The child is given a candle, lit from the Easter candle, to symbolise that the child has died to sin and risen to new life with Christ.
- The child may be dressed in new white clothes as a sign of a new life free from sin.

A similar procedure is used for the baptism of a new adult Roman Catholic. The Roman Catholic Church teaches that baptism should be followed by education (**catechism**) as the child develops. When the child is old enough to understand the real meaning of baptism and of living as a Christian, he or she takes on responsibility for the baptism promises through a ritual called 'confirmation', when he or she confirms the promises made at baptism.

In an emergency, for example, if a new-born baby is very ill, a baptism can be performed by anyone who understands what baptism is. Any water can be used, and the person performing the baptism says 'I baptise you in the name of the Father, and of the Son, and of the Holy Spirit,' while wetting the baby's head with a little water.

Because Catholics believe baptism makes a permanent change to the child's soul, it is impossible to undo or annul a baptism.

## Baptism in the Baptist tradition

The Baptist Church is a Protestant Church. You will remember that in the sixteenth century, a Roman Catholic priest, Martin Luther, protested against things that he believed were wrong with the teaching and practice of the Roman Catholic Church. As a result, he was excommunicated (expelled) and he started a new Church which was separate from, and had different teachings to, the Roman Catholics. One of the new Churches that grew out from the Protestant Reformation was the Baptist Church. As the name suggests, baptism is very important for Baptist Christians.

Baptists do not believe in sacraments. They believe that symbols are not necessary, and that Christians instead should read the Bible to learn about the life of Christ and then copy what Jesus did to live a life as God wants. The Baptist Church teaches that Jesus showed people how to live a life in accordance with God's plan, and so humans must imitate Jesus and follow his instructions. Baptists believe that Jesus gave a specific instruction when he told the disciples to:

> **Key terms**
>
> **catechism** Teaching: a summary of the principles of the Christian religion, given in question and answer style.

## Key terms

**ordinances** Any form of law or instruction, for example, from Jesus, such as the instruction to his disciples to make disciples of all nations and baptise them. An ordinance also means a religious ceremony, sacrament, statute or regulation.

**credobaptism** Believer's baptism.

**'Make disciples of all nations, baptizing them in the name of the Father and of the Son and of the Holy Spirit' (Matthew 28:19)**

They call direct instructions from Jesus '**ordinances**', so for Baptists, Baptism is an ordinance which must be taken very seriously.

Because Baptists try to do things the same way that Jesus did, they do not baptise infants. Jesus was already an adult when he was baptised by John, so Baptists practise adult baptism. They do not believe in original sin, which is a Catholic teaching, so they do not consider it necessary to wash it away early in a person's life. Instead, they see baptism as a ceremony of membership and commitment, as someone prepares to start their adult ministry in the world. It is a public confirmation that a person believes and trusts in God: Father, Son and Holy Spirit, and has been admitted to membership of the Church. For this reason, adult baptism in Protestant Churches is called 'believer's baptism' or **credobaptism**. Normally, teenagers or adults who wish to be baptised join Bible study groups and prepare for baptism by learning all they can about the Christian faith as it is understood by the Baptist Church. Baptists believe that baptism can only be meaningful when those who are being baptised know and understand fully what they are committing to. During this period of preparation, they may spend extra time in study and prayer with an experienced member of the church who will act as a sponsor.

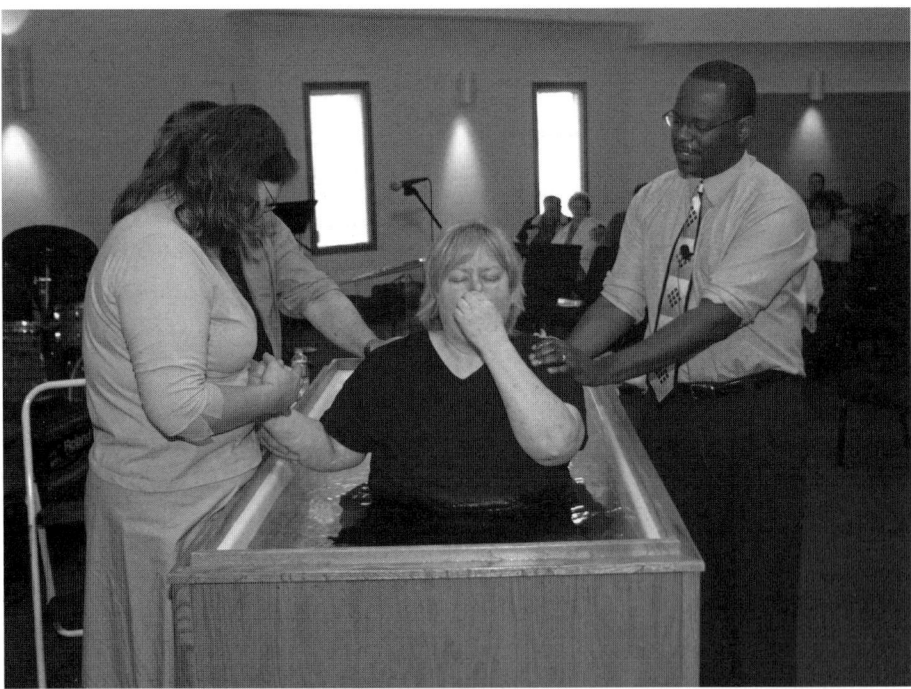

▲ In believer's baptism, the adult makes a declaration of faith, and is then immersed fully in water, usually in a purpose-built baptismal pool in the church.

The normal practice for believer's baptism in most Baptist churches is this:

- A sponsor, who is a member of the church already and knows the candidate, presents the person to the church community.
- The person who is being baptised makes a short speech called a testimony, which outlines how they believe God has been working in their life. This may be a short biography, or they may describe a single event which led them to accept Jesus as Lord.

# Holy Communion in the Roman Catholic Church

According to the *Catechism of the Catholic Church*:

> 'Sacraments are perceptible signs (words and actions) accessible to our human nature. By the action of Christ and the power of the Holy Spirit they make present efficaciously the grace that they signify.' (*Catechism of the Catholic Church*, 1084)

In other words, they are physical words and actions that act as signs of God's grace acting on human souls.

A sacrament has three aspects:

- the ritual actions and words (form)
- some physical substance (matter)
- the understanding and intention of the person performing it (intent).

Because of this, Roman Catholic Holy Communion is always celebrated by an ordained priest, who has the training and authority to make sure the sacrament is conducted correctly. Only those who are baptised and have been admitted to communion are allowed to receive bread and wine. Children are usually given their first communion around the age of seven or eight after a period of education and preparation, some time before they are confirmed.

In baptism, you have learnt that the priest uses specific words and actions (form) and water (matter) with the intention to baptise. In Holy Communion (Mass), the priest also uses specific words and actions, and matter (bread and wine) with the understanding and intention to celebrate Mass. The bread is usually unleavened wheat wafers (symbolising the unleavened bread of Passover) and fermented grape wine.

After a section of the service devoted to reading and explaining Bible texts, bread and wine are brought to the altar, as an offering. The core purpose of an altar, historically, was as a place of sacrifice. In Catholic theology, celebrating the mass is also re-enacting the sacrifice of Christ on the cross for human sin.

During the prayer of consecration (making sacred), the priest makes symbolic actions which include cupping his hand over the bread and wine as a symbol of calling down the Holy Spirit (**epiclesis**), raising the bread and wine above his head (elevation) and kneeling to show reverence to the sacrament (**genuflexion**). As a result of these actions, and the words of Jesus which are repeated during the prayer, Catholics believe that the bread and wine are transformed into the body and blood of Christ (the Real Presence). This is called '**transubstantiation**'. After this, the bread is broken (**fraction**) to re-enact the way that Jesus' body was broken in death on the cross – this is the representation of sacrifice. Members of the congregation go to the front of the church and the priest gives each one a wafer, sometimes into their hand and sometimes into their open mouth. In most Catholic churches, they are also given a sip of wine from the chalice.

For Roman Catholics, therefore, receiving consecrated bread and wine is a deeply spiritual action, because they are receiving Christ into their body. Many Catholics fast for at least two hours or overnight before receiving communion as a way of preparing their body for such an important meal, and they confess their sins to a priest to be forgiven before Mass. As a sacrament, it makes a spiritual change to them as they receive the bread and wine. Any left-over bread and wine remain holy, and are consumed

▲ A Roman Catholic priest celebrating Holy Communion.

## Key terms

**epiclesis** The part of the Eucharistic prayer in which the presence of the Holy Spirit is invoked to bless the elements of bread and wine or those taking part.

**genuflexion** The bending of the knees or kneeling, as an act of reverence (for example, to God).

**transubstantiation** In the Roman Catholic Church, the change of substance by which the bread and wine used in the sacrament of the Eucharist during the Mass become, literally, the body and blood of Jesus.

**fraction** The breaking of the bread at the Eucharist, as a symbol of the breaking of Christ's body on the cross.

prayerfully by the priest, and the vessels used are carefully wiped to make sure there are no leftovers thrown away. After the service is ended, the members of the congregation are sent out into the world spiritually stronger, ready to share their faith and live better Christian lives.

## Holy Communion in the Baptist Church

For Baptists, the focus of Christian life and worship is on the Bible, which they regard as God's communication with humankind. Baptists believe individual Christians can learn all they need to about God, Jesus Christ and Christian living by studying the Bible carefully with prayer. The status of Holy Communion in worship is therefore of less importance than reading and explaining the Bible.

Baptists celebrate Holy Communion because Jesus said, 'Do this to remember me', and they therefore see it as an ordinance (a direct instruction from Jesus). For them, it is a community memorial meal. When they take part in it, they focus on remembering the actions and words of Jesus during his last meal with his disciples before his death. Because of this, there is little symbolism or ritual attached to the Baptist celebration of Holy Communion. The service is normally conducted by a minister, but can be conducted by someone who is not a minister, provided the person is authorised by the congregation to do so.

In a service that includes the Lord's Supper, there are readings from the Bible and a sermon to explain the readings. Then a table is prepared with cubes of bread or a broken up loaf and individual cups of grape juice (wine is sometimes used). Baptist churches do not normally have an altar, though many do have a communion table. The minister or person who presides reads the words of Jesus from Paul's account of the Last Supper, and may break the loaf of bread as they read the narrative. Then the members of the congregation pass around the bread and wine, serving one another. Generally, there is no restriction on who can receive Holy Communion – the usual invitation is to 'all who love the Lord Jesus' or a similar form of words, and it is normal for even very small children to share in the Lord's Supper. Individual Baptists do not do anything special to prepare for Holy Communion – they do not practise fasting or confession.

Baptists believe that the bread and wine do not undergo any spiritual or physical change: they remain just plain bread and wine, and leftovers can therefore be thrown away or washed down the sink.

Baptists do not believe that there is any particular spiritual change associated with Holy Communion. The main value of the Lord's Supper is to bring the community together in a special memorial meal to remember the life and death of Jesus, and especially the way that his death offers salvation from sin. This means Baptists have a 'memorialist' understanding of Holy Communion.

## Different Christian understandings of the significance of Jesus' actions at the Last Supper

And he took a cup, and when he had given thanks he said, 'Take this, and divide it among yourselves; for I tell you that from now on I shall not drink of the fruit of the vine until the kingdom of God comes.' And he took bread, and when he had given thanks he broke it and gave it to them, saying, 'This is my body which is given for you. Do this in remembrance of me.' And likewise the cup after supper, saying, 'This cup which is poured out for you is the new covenant in my blood'. (Luke 22: 17–20)

## The Jewish context of this ritual is important

Jesus' Last Supper was a Passover meal, when Jews remember the way that God freed the Israelites from slavery in Egypt. Passover meals include bread and wine which have symbolic importance: the unleavened bread remembers that the women did not have time to let their dough rise to make bread for the journey out of Egypt and wine remembers the way God restored the people of Israel from exile.

When Jesus used these elements at the Last Supper, he was deliberately taking things that already had a symbolic importance and role, and giving them a deeper, extended meaning for his followers. He told his disciples that through his death, the bread would symbolise not just freedom from slavery, but also freedom from sin. Wine would symbolise not just restoration from exile, but the restoration of the relationship between God and humankind.

Luke's account is important because it was written for early Christians who did not have a Jewish heritage. He refers to 'the new covenant' (Luke 22:20), that is, a new contract between God and humankind that is symbolised by the breaking and sharing of bread.

As we have seen above, different Christians assign different kinds of importance to the words and actions of Jesus at the Last Supper. For some Christians today, the Passover symbolism, overlaid with the extra symbolism which Jesus gave the bread and wine, is important. For them, Holy Communion is full of layers of symbolism about freedom from slavery, freedom from sin, restoration from exile and restoration of the relationship with God. For others, Holy Communion is an uncomplicated meal shared with other disciples, to remember that Jesus died for humankind.

For Roman Catholics, Orthodox and some Church of England Christians, Jesus was instituting a formal ritual, where bread and wine would forever after have deep spiritual significance to individual Christians and to the Church. Their highly ritualised, symbolic use of the words of Jesus and the carefully crafted actions help to imbue Holy Communion with a very special status. Once consecrated, the bread becomes the embodiment of the actual presence of Christ in the gathered community. In many Catholic churches, a wafer is kept after the service and placed in a sacred safe (tabernacle) or a special display frame (monstrance) so that people can pray in the physical presence of Christ.

Mass is celebrated regularly, at least once every week, and many Catholics receive Holy Communion several times a week. It is compulsory for confirmed Catholics to attend Mass at certain festivals, including Christmas, Corpus Christi and All Saints' Day. Excommunication (barring Catholics from receiving Holy Communion) is a very serious punishment which is reserved for major breaches of Church discipline.

Because Roman Catholics believe the sacrament has a special effect on the soul, most Catholics want to receive it at key moments in their life, especially marriage and just before death. After someone has died, his or her family and friends may ask the priest to say a mass especially for the deceased person. People who are about to undertake a spiritual or life-changing task, or who face a personal challenge, may also ask for a mass to be said for their special intention.

In contrast, Protestant Churches, like the Baptist Church, do not attach so much special importance to Holy Communion. The members of the local congregation value the celebration of the Lord's Supper as an aspect of the worship of the community, but it has no extra symbolic role in the life of the church or of individual Christians. Holy Communion is only one of the many things that Jesus told his disciples to do. Baptism is the other Protestant ordinance, and it has a higher status for Baptists than Holy Communion. Jesus' teachings to feed the hungry, care for the sick and bring an end to oppression are all equally important for Christians, because leading a good Christian life and sharing the good news of Jesus Christ with others are the ways that people can help to bring about God's plan for the world.

Holy Communion is not celebrated very often in Baptist churches: usually around once a month. The normal weekly service includes prayers, readings and hymns; and Holy Communion is added into this, rather than being celebrated as a different and separate kind of service. There is no requirement for Baptists to receive Holy Communion and many Baptists consider it an optional extra rather than a normal part of their worship.

# The mission of the Church

For this you need to look at:

● The mission of the Church: developments in Christian ideas of 'mission' from the early twentieth century to today.

Christians, who have different understandings about many things to do with Christian practice and teaching, all agree that belief in Jesus Christ as Lord and Saviour is central to the faith. Most Christians also share the core belief in one God, Father, Son and Holy Spirit, as set out in the Nicene Creed. They all share the same core texts in the Bible, especially the New Testament Gospels. For this reason, it is reasonable to talk about all Christians, however different their beliefs and practices, as 'the Church'.

We saw earlier that in Matthew's Gospel, Jesus' last instruction to his disciples was to, 'make disciples of all nations'. In the chapter on self, death and the afterlife (pages 283–284), you studied Jesus' Parable of the Sheep and the Goats, where he made it clear that people were expected to do good things for people who were less fortunate than themselves. Both of these contribute to the Church's view of what it should do as the body of people who follow Jesus Christ.

The word 'mission' comes from the Latin word *mittere*, which means 'to send'. Christians believe that when Jesus said, 'Go, therefore, and make disciples', he was not only talking to his disciples who were there with him, but to everyone who would follow him in the future. In John's Gospel, Jesus similarly says:

'As the Father has sent me, even so I send you.' (John 20.21)

Mission is therefore at the heart of Christian religious identity. Christians believe that they have been sent out to do God's work in the world.

The Church of England puts it this way:

'For Anglican Christians God's mission is about transformation – transforming individual lives, transforming communities and transforming the world.' (Note 1)

Christians of most denominations have put this into action in different ways since the start of the twentieth century, and these can be usefully considered by looking at three ways that the Church has engaged in mission.

## 1 Mission as evangelism

From the earliest days of Christianity, people have tried to persuade other people to become Christians: this kind of mission is called 'evangelism'. In the first century CE, St Paul travelled around the Mediterranean, visiting synagogues and communities of people who did not know about Christianity, to tell them about Jesus Christ and often persuading them to join the community of Christians. For many people today, especially those Protestants who regard themselves as evangelicals, this remains the main task that the Church should undertake.

One example of a Christian organisation that engages in evangelism is the **Church Missionary Society** (CMS), which was founded in 1812 after the merging of several other missionary societies. During the nineteenth century, the CMS sent missionaries to parts of the world where the majority of people were not Christian. They engaged in mission in Africa, Australasia, the Indian subcontinent, the Middle East, Japan and the Pacific Islands. Men were trained in Europe to teach from the Bible, and sent to live with their families in their mission field. They got to know the local people and learnt their languages, and offered health and social care as well as sharing their faith. They set up churches and trained local people to be ministers, so that when they returned to Europe, the new local churches would continue. They also set up schools so that local children could be raised and educated as Christians.

The CMS continued their work throughout the twentieth century. One way they funded this was to partner missionary families with UK churches. The missionaries would send personal letters to the church community in the UK about their work in the mission, and in return, the church would support them with prayer and financial support. This meant that all members of a church could feel that they too were participating in missionary activity. Over time, the CMS partners were less concerned with converting foreigners, and instead focused on supporting the work of local churches by helping to run outreach projects. For example, in Cairo in the 1980s, CMS missionaries worked alongside the clergy of Cairo Anglican cathedral to run child-care projects among the Christian 'Zabaleen', the people who earn a living by recycling rubbish in the municipal rubbish tips on the outskirts of the city. Christians are a minority in Egypt, so the missionaries helped them both to improve their living conditions and to remain firm in their religious faith.

Another organisation that engages in Christian Mission is **The Evangelical Alliance Mission** (TEAM), which was set up in 1890, and continues to engage in mission today. TEAM missionaries who are qualified doctors, nurses, pharmacists and teachers work in teams to set up and staff churches, hospitals and schools in countries where Christianity is not the local religion. Alongside offering medical care and education to poor families, they openly share their evangelical beliefs and encourage local people to attend their church services to learn about Christianity, in the hope that they will convert. One example of a TEAM project is the Karanda Mission Hospital in Zimbabwe.

> Our goal is to provide an authentic Christian witness by: demonstrating the compassion of Christ through medical work; establishing and strengthening the local church through participation in spiritual ministry to patients and in outreach to local communities; educating and training Christian professionals for the medical ministry (hospital and nursing school) and to facilitate the training of leaders for the local church. (Karanda Hospital Mission Statement) [Note 2]

In the 1970s, secularism was on the rise and people were starting to be concerned about the fall in the number of worshipping Christians in the UK. In 1977, the vicar of Holy Trinity Church Brompton, in London, started a new course in evangelism, called the **Alpha Course**. It was aimed first at members of the church, but as it developed, he also encouraged them to bring friends and neighbours to the church. Each course involved ten weekly sessions, in which churchgoers and their invited non-churchgoing guests shared a meal, listened to a talk about aspects of the Christian faith and then discussed it. The Alpha Course is not unlike a sales pitch for a business: it aims to persuade people that they want to 'buy into' the Christian faith. It has since spread throughout the UK and around the world. The Alpha Course operates in a similar way to a franchise – churches buy books and recorded material to run their own courses.

We can see from this how evangelism has changed during the twentieth century. It was originally aimed at converting people of other faiths, in other countries, first by direct preaching and teaching, and then through the provision of healthcare and education. It has now become something that happens as much in post-Christian Britain as it does around the world.

## 2  Mission to the poor and disadvantaged

Another aspect of the work of the Church is to help the poor and needy. When Paul travelled round his new churches, he collected money from them to help support the members of the Church in Jerusalem. Wealthy Christians provided schools for pauper children and housing for the elderly poor during the middle ages, and during the nineteenth century, rich people often left money to provide bread to poor parishioners in their wills.

In 1881, the **Children's Society** was formed in London. As a result of the Industrial Revolution, there was widespread poverty and illness in cities, and poor children were often left as orphans when their parents died young. With the backing of the Archbishop of Canterbury, Edward Rudolph, a Sunday School teacher, set up the charity to give homeless children an upbringing in a loving family environment. He set up cottage homes with around ten children living in each house, with a matron and master who acted as parents. In this way, the charity was feeding and clothing them, and providing homes for the homeless. From the 1970s onwards, there were fewer homeless children, and the Children's Society changed its focus towards helping young people deal with illness, stress or poverty in family day-care centres. Since 1990, they have worked for social justice for the poorest and most disadvantaged young people, challenging government and society to address the needs of vulnerable children.

Another Christian organisation that has a mission to the poor is **Christian Aid**. Formed in the aftermath of the Second World War, Christian Aid is an agency of 41 British and Irish churches. They provide short-term, medium-term and long-term aid to less economically developed countries to improve the standard of living of some of the world's poorest communities. They also provide emergency aid following major disasters. Christian Aid does not seek to convert people to Christianity. The basis of their work is the call of Jesus to feed the poor, clothe the naked, tend the sick and house the homeless. Christian Aid is funded partly from the UK overseas aid budget and partly by donations. During Christian Aid Week each May, local volunteers in each community in the UK drop off envelopes and invite people to make a donation in the envelopes to Christian Aid. This means that people in local communities can feel that they are sharing in the work of Christian Aid by collecting and donating money.

In 1985, the Archbishop of Canterbury's Commission on Urban Priority Areas produced a report called *Faith in the City*. It identified large-scale poverty in urban areas and, as a result, the Church of England set up the **Church Urban Fund** (CUF). Today the CUF provides financial and practical support to churches and communities in poor urban areas to improve the quality of life of local people and to support work for social justice for the poor.

> CUF was established by the Church of England as a practical response to unmet need and has been active in local communities for over 30 years. Our vision is to see people and communities all over England flourish and enjoy life in all its fullness.
>
> We work through the Church of England's local parish networks, and alongside other faith-based and secular organisations, to bring about positive change in neighbourhoods.
>
> We work by building trust, empowering local people to have a go at addressing the areas of greatest need in their communities, and speaking out against injustice. (Church Urban Fund website – 'About Us') [Note 3]

So, we have seen how attitudes to mission to the poor and disadvantaged changed during the twentieth century. At the start of the century, wealthier Christians gave money to charities or worked themselves to provide clothes, food and housing for poor people. After the Second World War, Christians became more conscious of the poor and disadvantaged in other countries. As the century drew to a close, Christians and Christian organisations became more concerned with fighting the causes of poverty through work with poor communities and social justice campaigns.

## 3 Mission to the Christian community

The Church also has a duty to care for faithful Christians in their own communities. For this reason, all the churches see serving the local congregation as part of their mission.

At the start of the twentieth century, most people in Britain were Christians and went to church regularly. The mission of the Church, therefore, was to provide facilities and staff for worship and religious instruction. The building, care and maintenance of churches, the provision of clergy, and money to support Sunday Schools and other services were priorities. Many new churches were built in the second half of the nineteenth century

## Key terms

**ecumenism** The drive to promote unity between the different Christian Churches.

**ecumenical** Promoting unity among the different Christian Churches, for example, by services in which different denominations take part.

▲ The Church of Christ the Cornerstone, Milton Keynes.

to accommodate growing urban populations following the Industrial Revolution, but it was not always easy to find suitable ministers. Poor city dwellers often needed financial help and social care from their church as well as worship, so part of the mission of the Church was to raise money and recruit and train clergy to work in such parishes. New dioceses were created in the Church of England, centred on the new industrial cities, for example, Birmingham in 1905 and Sheffield in 1914.

As provincial towns grew after the two world wars, new churches were built to serve these new communities. In some cases, different Christian denominations agreed to share facilities between them and work together to serve the local community. In the 1960s, **Local Ecumenical Partnerships** started to spring up as local congregations for two or more Christian denominations agreed to work together or share buildings. A new spirit of **ecumenism** (relationships between different denominations) led to **the British Council of Churches** rebranding itself in 1987 as **Churches Together in England**. One example of the Church community that works on an ecumenical basis is the Church of Christ the Cornerstone in Milton Keynes. This church building is used by the Church of England, Baptists, Methodists, the Roman Catholic Church and the United Reformed Church. The members of all these denominations work together to provide care and support in the local community.

In the twenty-first century, Churches are again re-thinking how to engage in mission in local communities. As fewer people go to church, the Methodist Church and the Church of England set up a new movement called **Fresh Expressions**. This is a way to take Christianity to people where they are, rather than expecting them to come to church. New worshipping communities are being set up in places where people gather, such as cafés, a surfer centre in Cornwall and a skateboard park in Essex. Worship in these new 'churches' is focused on the interests and concerns of the people in the congregation, and fits in around the times that people are there, rather than having services at traditional times on a Sunday. Fresh Expressions churches deliberately set out to attract people to Christianity, but they are also very much engaged with the cultures they serve.

So we can see that the mission of the Church to local communities has evolved since the start of the twentieth century. In 1900, the Church's main task was to serve a majority Christian country through local churches of each denomination. As the patterns of religion and worship changed, the Church has responded by developing links and partnerships between denominations and more recently has begun to export the idea of 'church' to other kinds of communities.

## Different views about mission

Some Christian groups do not engage in mission in all of the ways described above. They may, for example, serve the local community and the poor and needy, but not engage in evangelism. **The Religious Society of Friends** (Quakers) believes that God speaks directly to the hearts of people, and so evangelism is wrong because it interferes with God's work in the lives of individuals. Some groups put a much larger focus on one or two of these kinds of mission. For example, **The Salvation Army** sees its mission as serving the poor and needy, and although they do serve their own worshipping congregation and evangelise, they put the majority of their effort into caring for the homeless and looking after the most deprived and vulnerable members of society. There are also some groups who do not see mission as important at all. **The Exclusive Brethren**, a small denomination which split off from the Plymouth Brethren, believe that the whole world is contaminated by sin. They believe that in order to be saved, they must cut themselves off from mainstream society as far as possible, and keep their work and worship free of sin. The idea of mission depends on Christians believing that God wants them to work with other people, and in the view of the Exclusive Brethren, God wants them to separate themselves from others, so mission is impossible.

## Technical terms for expressions of religious identity

**catechism** Teaching: a summary of the principles of the Christian religion, given in question and answer style.

**catholic** (With a small 'c') 'all-embracing', that is, 'the whole body of Christians world-wide'.

**covenant** In the biblical sense, this refers to an agreement between God and humanity, as in the covenants with Adam, Noah, Abraham and Moses. The New Testament refers to the new covenant effected through Jesus.

**credobaptism** Believer's baptism.

**ecumenical** Promoting unity among the different Christian Churches, for example, by services in which different denominations take part.

**ecumenism** The drive to promote unity between the different Christian Churches.

**epiclesis** The part of the Eucharistic prayer in which the presence of the Holy Spirit is invoked to bless the elements of bread and wine or those taking part.

**fraction** The breaking of the bread at the Eucharist, as a symbol of the breaking of Christ's body on the cross.

**genuflexion** The bending of the knees or kneeling, as an act of reverence (for example, to God).

**liturgy** The pattern for worship used by a particular denomination, in line with its particular beliefs and traditions.

**ordinances** Any form of law or instruction, for example, from Jesus, such as the instruction to his disciples to make disciples of all nations and baptise them. An ordinance also means a religious ceremony, sacrament, statute or regulation.

**paedobaptism** Infant baptism.

**sacrament** A ceremony seen as imparting spiritual grace. In the Roman Catholic Church there are seven sacraments: baptism, confirmation, the Eucharist, penance, anointing of the sick, ordination, and matrimony. In the Protestant Churches the main sacraments are the Eucharist (Holy Communion) and baptism.

**transubstantiation** In the Roman Catholic Church, the change of substance by which the bread and wine used in the sacrament of the Eucharist during the Mass become, literally, the body and blood of Jesus.

# Summary of this section on expressions of religious identity

**Baptism**

Baptism (as the washing away of sins) in Christianity goes back to John the Baptist, who baptised Jesus in the River Jordan (Mark 1:9–11). Jesus himself (according to John 3:5) seems to have seen baptism as both a physical and a spiritual event. Jesus commanded his disciples to baptise people in the name of the Father, the Son and the Holy Spirit.

In the **Catholic tradition**, baptism is a sacrament that makes a profound and irreversible change to a person's existence. Baptism enables the baptised person to overcome the stain of original sin by re-enacting dying and rising again, and by joining the Church. This is the main reason that Roman Catholics practise infant baptism.

In the **Baptist tradition**, Baptists do not believe in sacraments. Baptism is important simply as an ordinance from Jesus. Jesus was baptised as an adult, so Baptists do not practise infant baptism. Instead they practise credobaptism, which is a service of membership and commitment to the Church, and the individual has to know the meaning and importance of the ceremony.

## Arguments in favour of infant baptism include:

(1) it has sacramental value, for example, infant baptism for Catholics; (2) it has value as a mystery: for Catholics, baptism is part of God's grace and its mystery can never be fully understood, so it applies to infants also; (3) it acts as a remedy for original sin; (4) it signifies the start of life in the Christian Church; (5) the story of mothers bringing their children to Jesus suggests that Jesus might perhaps have approved of infant baptism; (6) the Early Church seems to have practised infant baptism. If it was acceptable to the Early Church it is acceptable today.

## Arguments against infant baptism include:

(1) baptism is an ordinance that babies cannot understand; (2) Jesus was about 30 when baptised, so we should follow his example and practise adult baptism; (3) baptism is the washing away of sins and this concept cannot really be understood by infants; (4) children are born into God's grace, but cannot understand how to live in faith until they become adults; (5) despite the story of the mothers and their children, Jesus probably did not baptise infants, so neither should we; (6) the argument that the Early Church practised infant baptism is weak: household baptism was probably of the adults.

## Holy Communion

As with baptism, different Christian Churches have different understandings of the meaning and purpose of Holy Communion. For Roman Catholics, Holy Communion is a sacrament; for Protestants it is an ordinance. Quakers and the Salvation Army do not celebrate Holy Communion at all, preferring to express their faith in Christian life rather than in symbolic rituals. Holy Communion is called the Eucharist in the Church of England, Mass in the Roman Catholic Church, Divine Liturgy in the Orthodox Churches and The Lord's Supper in the Baptist Church; each name emphasising different understandings of the nature of the ritual.

In the **Roman Catholic tradition**, the focus of the Mass is on transubstantiation. Mass is celebrated as a sacrament by an ordained priest, and is given only to those who are baptised. Celebration of the Mass is a service full of symbolism and mystery, including the re-enaction of Christ's sacrifice on the cross. Preparation for the Mass may involve fasting and confession.

In the **Baptist Church**, as in most Protestant Churches, the focus is on the Bible. Baptists celebrate the Lord's Supper because it is an ordinance from Jesus:

'Do this to remember me.'

The Lord's Supper is usually conducted by a minister, but can be led by someone authorised by the congregation. The Lord's Supper will involve Bible readings and a sermon to explain them. There is no belief in transubstantiation of the bread and wine, which remain, for Baptists, ordinary bread and wine.

### Different understandings of the significance of Jesus' actions at the Last Supper

For Catholics, and some Church of England churches, Jesus was instituting a formal ritual based on the Jewish Passover meal. The Catholic focus on transubstantiation means that the sacrament has a special effect on the soul that makes it fitting for Catholics to receive it at key points in life, such as at marriage and just before death. In the Baptist Church, Holy Communion has a lower status than baptism. It is one ordinance among others from Jesus.

### The mission of the Church

Jesus' last instruction to his disciples was that they should go and make disciples of all nations, and this is the substance of the Church's mission. Mission today is understood in several different senses:

- **Evangelism**, for example, in the work undertaken variously by the Church Missionary Society, the Evangelical Alliance Mission, and the Alpha Course.
- **Mission to the poor and disadvantaged**, for example, The Children's Society, Christian Aid, and the Church Urban Fund.
- **Mission to the Christian community**. This led to a spirit of ecumenism, which in turn led to the British Council of Churches, rebranded as Churches Together in England (1987). The Methodist Church and the Church of England set up Fresh Expressions to take Christianity to people where they are (as opposed to bringing people to a church).
- Other views about mission. Quakers think that evangelism is wrong because it interferes with the lives of individuals. The Salvation Army put its efforts into serving the poor and needy.

# The Exam: Specimen assessment materials

> There is no doubt that the prospect of sitting an examination raises a host of different emotions in the minds of the sitters. I read recently an account of a university student who ran out of socks on the day of his exam, so was forced to wear a Christmas comedy pair. Unfortunately they turned out to be fitted with a miniature musical box which, when pressed (intentionally or inadvertently), churned out a Christmas tune; hence the invigilators were scandalised when the strains of 'Rudolph the Red-nosed Reindeer' shattered the silence of the exam hall. (Note 1)

The only moral of this story is that doing well in exams comes from good preparation, be it in terms of in-depth knowledge, plenty of practice, wide reading, breathing exercises or an appropriate choice of socks.

Here is some advice from which you can hopefully profit.

## Preliminary advice

- This textbook is exactly half of the full A-Level, so you can use it in order to sit an AS exam after 1 year, or as the first half of the full 2-year A-Level.
- Your teachers might decide to study the Specification in a completely different order, in which case you will be using the textbook in order to support whichever part of the Specification your teachers are dealing with at the time.
- The textbook is written to an A-Level standard, so if you sit an AS exam you will be well prepared!
- Be sure that you know the details of your course. Here is a grid for you to check the content of the different components. The column on the left is the AS content. On the right are the additional bits for A-Level. So: if you are just doing AS, you study only what's on the left, whereas for A-Level you study all of it. (See also the additional notes below the table.)

| Component 1 – PHILOSOPHY OF RELIGION and ETHICS | |
|---|---|
| **Section A – Philosophy of Religion** | |
| • Arguments for the existence of God<br>• Evil and suffering<br>• Religious experience | |
| | • Religious language<br>• Miracles<br>• Self and life after death |
| **Section B – Ethics and Religion** | |
| • Ethical theories (Natural Moral Law, Situation Ethics, Virtue Ethics)<br>• Issues of human life and death<br>• Issues of animal life and death | |
| | • Introduction to meta-ethics<br>• Free will and moral responsibility<br>• Conscience<br>• Bentham and Kant |
| **COMPONENT 2 – Study of Religion and 'Dialogue'** | |
| **Section A – Study of Religion** | |
| • Sources of wisdom and authority<br>• God<br>• Self, death and afterlife<br>• Good conduct and key moral principles<br>• Expressions of religious identity | |
| | • Religion, gender and sexuality<br>• Religion and science<br>• Religion and secularisation<br>• Religion and religious pluralism |
| **Section B – The Dialogue between Philosophy of Religion and Religion** | |
| | (How religion is influenced by, and has an influence on philosophy of religion in relation to the issues studied) |
| **Section C – The Dialogue between Ethical Studies and Religion** | |
| | (How religion is influenced by, and has an influence on ethical studies in relation to the issues studied) |

- The AS content is exactly half of the full A-Level, so the textbook just splits the course in half. Your Centre / teachers might do the A-Level in a *completely* different order.

- If you are doing AS after 1 year, *and you are going to stop after AS*, you study everything in the left column and you follow the AS exam format (every question = 15 marks).

- If you are doing full A-Level at the end of 2 years, you study everything in both columns, and you are examined on it using the A-Level exam format, at the end of the 2 years.

- *This (Volume 1) textbook is written to the A-Level standard*, so if you go on to do the full A-Level, what you have studied in volume 1 of the textbook does not have to be 'topped up' in any way.

- If you are studying the AS content in Year 1 (following this textbook), your Centre might (or might not) enter you for the AS exam. In either case, you sit the A-Level exam at the end of 2 years and you are examined on **both** columns.

- If your Centre does enter you for the AS exam after 1 year (some Centres will do this as a 'diagnostic' of how you are getting on, and to give you exam practice) and then enters you for the A-Level at the end of year 2, you will end up with both an AS and an A-Level grade. That could be useful if you got a high grade at AS and a not-so-high grade at A-Level!

# 1 The Specimen Assessment Materials

**These appear only on the AQA website, and you should print a copy.** They will show you the structure of each exam paper, the exam rubric (that is, the instructions which you should follow to the letter), and the format of the questions themselves.

You will also be able to look at the Mark Scheme for each question, the Levels of Response for the two Assessment Objectives and some specimen answers.

## The Mark Scheme

● The Mark Scheme is a set of suggestions from those who write the papers to the examiners who mark them, giving some indication of the kind of thing that might be written by candidates answering each question.

● You are **not** expected to write about everything that appears in the Mark Scheme. So long as what you write directly answers the question set, the examiners will credit any **relevant** material.

● If a question has two parts, the Mark Scheme might instruct examiners that candidates who answer only one part of the question can achieve no higher than a certain Level. In other words, make sure you answer all parts of a question.

## The Levels of Response for the two Assessment Objectives

● These are the criteria by which examiners mark your answers. Each answer is judged to be within one of five Levels, Level 5 being the highest.

● There are two sets of Assessment Objectives: AO1 and AO2. Very broadly, AO1 tests knowledge and understanding and AO2 tests your ability to evaluate.

● There are no other criteria by which your essays are judged, so it is important to study them closely. We shall come back to the Levels / Assessment Objectives in a moment.

## Specimen Answers

● These are answers written by examiners for you to revise and discuss in pairs. Some specimen answers are included at the end of this section.

It is very important that you should read the Specimen Assessment Materials and become thoroughly acquainted with the layout of exam papers. To do so means that you can avoid making some silly mistakes, such as:
  – Answering too many questions or too few.
  – Running out of time / spending too much time on some questions and too little on others.
  – Answering the question that you think you see rather than the question that is really there.
  – Forgetting which Assessment Objective you are supposed to be addressing.
  – Panicking because you are unfamiliar with the paper layout.
  – Answering only one part of a two-part question.

## 2 The course components, exam paper structure and timing

As indicated in the grid, you need to be clear about whether or not you are sitting an AS-Level exam after 1 year of study or an A-Level exam at the end of 2 years.

### If you are sitting an AS exam after 1 year of study

**To remind you, there are two components for AS:**

**Component 1**: Philosophy of religion and ethics

**Component 2**: Study of (one) religion from:

- 2A Buddhism
- 2B Christianity
- 2C Hinduism
- 2D Islam
- 2E Judaism

This textbook (both Volume 1 and Volume 2) is written from the perspective of Christianity, although the exam structure is the same regardless of which religion is studied.

- The AS exam for Component 1: Philosophy of religion and ethics – is 2 hours.
- The AS exam for Component 2: Study of (Christian) religion) – is 1 hour.
- Component 1 is weighted at 67% overall (50% Philosophy of religion and 50% Ethics).
- Component 2 is weighted at 33% overall.
- All questions have two parts. The first part tests AO1 and the second tests AO2.
- Component 1 has four questions in two Sections:
  - Section A is Philosophy of religion: two questions, each worth 15 marks AO1 and 15 marks AO2.
  - Section B is Ethics: two questions, each worth 15 marks AO1 and 15 marks AO2.
- Component 2 has two questions, each worth 15 marks AO1 and 15 marks AO2.
- So, both AO1 and AO2 are weighted at 50%.
- **All questions are compulsory.**

### If you are sitting an A-Level exam at the end of 2 years

Further information for the A-Level will of course appear in Volume 2 of the A-Level textbook. The grid above will give you sufficient information for now, and here are the A-Level basics again, together with a summary of the exam format:

**Component 1**: Philosophy of religion and ethics

**Component 2:** Study of Religion and 'Dialogues'. In the 'Dialogues' Sections, you are not going through new material: you are linking the ideas you have studied and learned in Components 1 and 2. The 'Dialogues' Sections test the claims, coherence and relevance of religion according to Philosophy and Ethics. Another name for the 'Dialogues' Sections is to call them 'Synoptic' ('seeing together').

- The A-Level exam for Component 1: Philosophy of religion and ethics – is 3 hours.
- The A-Level exam for Component 2: Study of (Christian) Religion and 'Dialogues' – is 3 hours.
- Component 1 is weighted at 50% overall (25% Philosophy and 25% Ethics).
- Component 2 is weighted at 50% overall (25% Religion and 25% Dialogues).
- All questions are worth 25 marks.
- Component 1 has two Sections:
  - Section A (Philosophy of Religion) has 2 questions.
  - Section B (Ethics) has 2 questions.
- All questions in Component 1 are 10 marks AO1 and 15 marks AO2 each.
- Component 2 has three Sections:
  - Section A (Religion) has two questions worth 10 marks AO1 and 15 marks AO2.
  - Sections B & C (Dialogues) are marked holistically out of 25 using the same balance of AO1 and AO2.
- The exam for each Component therefore requires you to answer four 25-mark questions:
  - Two Philosophy and two Ethics for Component 1.
  - Two Religion and two Dialogues for Component 2.
- So, for each question in Components 1 and 2 you have 45 minutes, writing time.
- In the Dialogues questions the AO1 and the AO2 do not have to be kept separate. Critical analysis is best addressed throughout the answer.
- Note that the weighting between AO1 and AO2 at A-Level is tilted even more towards AO2: the AO1 is 40% and AO2 is 60%.
- **All questions are compulsory except for Dialogues**, where you have a choice of 1 question out of 2 for the Dialogue between Philosophy and Religion, and 1 question out of 2 for the Dialogue between Ethics and Religion.

# 3 The new AS-Levels of Response, and writing AO1 answers

## Level descriptors

| Level | Response | Marks |
|---|---|---|
| 5 | <ul><li>Knowledge and understanding is accurate and relevant and is consistently applied to the question.</li><li>Very good use of detailed and relevant evidence which may include textual / scriptural references where appropriate.</li><li>The answer is clear and coherent and there is effective use of specialist language and terminology.</li></ul> | 13–15 |
| 4 | <ul><li>Knowledge and understanding is mostly accurate and relevant and is mostly applied to the question.</li><li>Good use of relevant evidence which may include textual / scriptural references where appropriate.</li><li>The answer is mostly clear and coherent and specialist language and terminology is used appropriately.</li></ul> | 10–12 |
| 3 | <ul><li>Knowledge and understanding is generally accurate and relevant and is generally applied to the question.</li><li>Some use of appropriate evidence and / or examples which may include textual / scriptural references where appropriate.</li><li>The answer is generally clear and coherent with use of specialist language and terminology.</li></ul> | 7–9 |
| 2 | <ul><li>Knowledge and understanding is limited and there is limited application to the question.</li><li>Limited use of appropriate evidence and examples which may include textual / scriptural references where appropriate.</li><li>Some clarity and coherence and limited use of specialist language and terminology.</li></ul> | 4–6 |
| 1 | <ul><li>Knowledge and understanding is basic.</li><li>Isolated elements of accurate and relevant information, and basic use of appropriate subject vocabulary.</li></ul> | 1–3 |
| 0 | <ul><li>No accurate or relevant material to credit.</li></ul> | 0 |

Table heading: **Levels of Response: 15 marks AS-Level – A01**

You can see from this that there are three main criteria by which examiners will assess your AO1 essays:

1 Relevant knowledge and understanding applied to the question.

2 Use of appropriate evidence and examples.

3 Clarity and coherence, using specialist language.

You will also see that each criterion is judged on an ascending scale, so the AO for **relevant knowledge and understanding**, for example, goes from *basic* (L1) to *limited* (L2) to *generally accurate and relevant* (L3) to *mostly accurate and relevant* (L4) to *accurate and relevant* (L5). As the wording suggests, it is not just a case of knowing relevant material: you also have to understand it. Some candidates can give endless details of what they know, but it may also be clear that they do not understand what they have written, and have recited it parrot-fashion.

You can see for yourself that progressing through the Levels of Response for **use of appropriate evidence and examples** follows much the same kind of pattern. Much of this is common sense. Look at *Question 02-1 on the Specimen Paper for 7061/1 Paper 1: Philosophy of Religion and Ethics*:

*'Explain religious views about the nature of the following type of religious experience: visions.'*

If you are writing about visionary religious experiences, the **evidence** suggests that some are corporeal, some are imaginative, and some are intellectual, and you should be able to explain these terms and give **examples** of each kind.

For *clarity and coherence, using specialist language*, try this tip: when you write practice essays, assume that you are explaining the topic to someone of roughly your own ability level. Get someone else to read it, and if they can understand it, then you are on the right lines. If they can't, then you will know precisely where to look to find what you yourself are unsure about. In the Specimen question on visionary religious experiences, the words *corporeal, imaginative,* and *intellectual* are chief among specialist terminology that you need to know about and to be able to explain. Check the *Mark Scheme Question 02-1* for the question above.

There are 3 marks for each Level, so examiners can differentiate (for example) between candidates who are just into a Level, those who are squarely in it, and those who are at the top end of it / on the verge of the next Level. The Level you achieve for your answer takes account of all three criteria.

## 4 The new AS-Levels of Response and writing AO2 answers

### Level descriptors

| Levels of Response: 15 marks AS-Level – AO2 | | |
|---|---|---|
| **Level** | **Response** | **Marks** |
| 5 | <ul><li>Reasoned and evidenced chains of reasoning supporting different points of view with critical analysis.</li><li>Evaluation is based on the reasoning presented.</li><li>The answer is clear and coherent and there is effective use of specialist language and terminology.</li></ul> | 13–15 |
| 4 | <ul><li>Reasoned and evidenced chains of reasoning, with some critical analysis, supporting different points of view.</li><li>Evaluation based on some of the reasoning.</li><li>Specialist language and terminology is used appropriately.</li><li>The answer is largely clear and coherent.</li></ul> | 10–12 |
| 3 | <ul><li>Different points of view supported by evidence and chains of reasoning.</li><li>The answer is generally clear and coherent with use of specialist language and terminology.</li></ul> | 7–9 |
| 2 | <ul><li>A point of view relevant to the question with supporting evidence and chains of reasoning.</li><li>Some clarity and coherence and limited use of specialist language and terminology.</li></ul> | 4–6 |
| 1 | <ul><li>A basic response to the question with reasons given in support.</li><li>Isolated elements of accurate and relevant information, and basic use of appropriate subject vocabulary.</li></ul> | 1–3 |
| 0 | <ul><li>No accurate or relevant material to credit.</li></ul> | 0 |

There are three main elements referred to in the Levels of Response:

1 Critical analysis / reasoning / evidence.

2 Evaluation / reasoning.

3 Coherence and clarity of argument as well as specialist language and terminology.

**Point 1 *critical analysis*,** asks you to discuss an argument or viewpoint and to analyse whether or not it works, and what its flaws might be. Analysis looks at the parts of an argument – their elements and structure. It might break them down into smaller parts to get a better understanding / to interpret them. Analysis is *objective* – it does not depend on your opinion. By the time you have done this, it should lead you naturally to evaluation.

**Point 2** *evaluation* means what the word says – it decides on the value of an argument – whether the argument is good or bad, valid or invalid. Evaluation is *subjective* – it is your view backed up by the reasons you have for holding it. You should reach a final *conclusion* based on what you decide are the most important factors, and you should justify your conclusion.

**Point 3** *coherence and clarity of argument* means exactly what it says: you need to be clear in what you say, and you must ensure that what you say makes sense. Again, if you give one of your practice essays to your friends, they should be able to make sense of it.

Here is a schema to help you use these three elements in any AO2 question:

You do not have to stick like glue to this schema, but it is a good place to start. Think of putting your answer into three boxes (boxes in your head, that is), so that the three criteria in the Levels of Response are all clearly addressed:

---

### Box 1

Try starting with the third element in the Levels of Response: Coherence and clarity of argument as well as specialist language and terminology.

**Coherence and clarity** have to be present all the way through, of course, but you can set the scene at the start by briefly presenting the evidence for the view that you have been asked to evaluate, using the right **specialist language and terminology**.

---

### Box 2

Next, analyse critically the view you have just referred to. Two important points here:

1 **Critical analysis** can be done by considering a number of possible flaws in the argument, for example:

— **Assumption**: does the argument just assume something without giving evidence for it?
— **Consistency**: does the argument become inconsistent at any point?
— **Evidence**: does the argument give reasonable evidence for what it claims, or does it make unsupported claims? Does it ignore other evidence or alternative interpretations of the evidence it has used?
— **Exaggeration**: does the argument exaggerate its claims?
— **Generalisation**: does the argument make generalisations from a single example, for example, that because *some* people make false claims about religious experiences, *all* claims about religious experiences are false?

— **Objectivity**: does the argument lose objectivity at any point? For example, is the writer / are the writers failing to be impartial and fair-minded in what they say?
— **Omission**: does the argument omit one or more steps?
— **Unreasonableness**: does the logic of the argument fail at some point?

*This is not an exhaustive list: it is simply an indication of some of the ways you can give a critical analysis of a piece of writing.*

2 You can show quite clearly where you are giving critical analysis by using specific **trigger words**. Four of the most common are:

— however
— moreover
— furthermore
— nevertheless

*Before going any further, think of at least three other such words or phrases.*

## Box 3

The value of doing the critical analysis like this is that it leads you straight into **evaluation**.

- Your critical analysis might lead you to think that the argument fails
- Or, it might lead you to think that it is right
- Or, you might conclude that the evidence is ambiguous.

Your critical analysis should lead you to two or more different viewpoints about the statement you have been asked to evaluate. On the whole, you only need to consider *two* different viewpoints, and if you have studied the material conscientiously, you should have no problem with this.

'Evaluation' is literally the process of assessing the *value* of an argument.

Do note in the Levels of Response that you cannot get a mark higher than Level 2 without referring to 'different points of view'. This does not necessarily mean *opposing* points of view – just 'different' points of view.

To illustrate all this, here is a sample evaluation of *Question 02–2 from the Specimen Paper for 7061/1 Paper 1: Philosophy of Religion and Ethics:*

**'Science makes it unreasonable to believe that visions are a form of religious experience.' Assess this view. [15 marks]**

Here is a sample answer using the format shown above, so the three boxes show:

**1** the argument

**2** critical analysis of the argument

**3** evaluation which follows on from, and is part of, the critical analysis.

Bear in mind that once you have got used to the format, you should be able to make it much less rigid, as in the two examples given below, in Notes 10 and 11.

Before reading this sample answer, make sure that you print off the Mark Scheme for Question 02–2.

## Box 1 – the argument

Scientists who claim that it is unreasonable to believe that visions are a form of religious experience do so because they believe that religious visions have no reality outside the brain or that they are unreliable because they cannot be tested by the scientific method. Science can also claim that religious visions are nothing more than alterations in the way the brain works: they might happen through the effects of drugs, or through brain conditions such as temporal lobe epilepsy, so it does seem unreasonable to claim that God is involved at all.

## Box 2 – critical analysis of the argument

These arguments are also strong because science can duplicate some of the effects of religious visions through devices such as Persinger's Helmet; nevertheless it is not obvious that religious beliefs should be tested scientifically, because they are not scientific phenomena. Imaginative visions, for example, are not seen by 'normal' sight – they are seen by the 'eye' of the mind, so they cannot be tested, but that does not mean that they are false. Things like love and artistic appreciation are of great value to humans, but they are not testable by science, so it is reasonable to believe that although religious visions cannot be tested by science either, they are still of great value, and may be experiences of God.

## Box 3 – evaluation which follows on from, and is part of, the critical analysis

Despite the reasonableness of this view, however, I am inclined to think that religious visions are indeed inventions of the brain. If we look at the corporeal visions of Bernadette Soubirous at Lourdes, for example, it seems unlikely that she saw the Virgin Mary whereas her sister and friend did not. Furthermore, imaginative visions are often experienced in dreams, and very few scientists can accept the idea that dreams can give factual information of the kind that Joseph received from the angel (Matthew 2). The **key word** in this question is: 'unreasonable', and in my view corporeal, imaginative and intellectual visions are not 'reasonable' at all – they ask us to believe in supernatural experience and accept it as more trustworthy than scientific reason. Reason is the basis of science, and science gives us all sorts of benefits, such as vacuum cleaners, air travel and electricity, whereas religious visions are about faith, not reason.

## Exercise

1 Memorise main points in the essay and seeing how long it takes you to write the essay yourself. This will give you some idea of whether you are likely to be able to write as much, or less, or about the same, and to practise your own essay style accordingly.

2 'Trigger words' are discussed on page 360. What are the trigger words in box 2.

3 Make a list of the key pieces of specialist language from box 3.

4 The expression 'key word' is in bold type in the third box. Why?

# 5 The new A-Level Levels of Response and writing AO1 essays

The A-Level Levels of Response are more detailed those for AS, although there are only 10 marks available for AO1 at A-Level as opposed to the 15 marks at AS, because of the increased value of AO2 at A-Level.

## Level descriptors

| Levels of Response: 10 marks A-Level – AO1 | | |
|---|---|---|
| Level | Response | Marks |
| 5 | • Knowledge and critical understanding is accurate, relevant and fully developed in breadth and depth with very good use of detailed and relevant evidence which may include textual / scriptural references where appropriate.<br>• Where appropriate, good knowledge and understanding of the diversity of views and / or scholarly opinion is demonstrated.<br>• Clear and coherent presentation of ideas with precise use of the appropriate subject vocabulary. | 9–10 |
| 4 | • Knowledge and critical understanding is accurate and mostly relevant with good development in breadth and depth shown through good use of relevant evidence which may include textual / scriptural references where appropriate.<br>• Where appropriate, alternative views and / or scholarly opinion are explained.<br>• Mostly clear and coherent presentation of ideas with good use of the appropriate subject vocabulary. | 7–8 |
| 3 | • Knowledge and critical understanding is generally accurate and relevant with development in breadth and / or depth shown through some use of evidence and / or examples which may include textual / scriptural references where appropriate.<br>• Where appropriate, there is some familiarity with the diversity of views and / or scholarly opinion.<br>• Some organisation of ideas and coherence with reasonable use of the appropriate subject vocabulary. | 5–6 |
| 2 | • Knowledge and critical understanding is generally accurate and relevant with limited development in breadth and / or depth shown through limited use of evidence and / or examples which may include textual / scriptural references where appropriate.<br>• Where appropriate, limited reference may be made to alternative views and / or scholarly opinion.<br>• Limited organisation of ideas and coherence and use of subject vocabulary. | 3–4 |
| 1 | • Knowledge and critical understanding is basic with little or no development.<br>• There may be a basic awareness of alternative views and / or scholarly opinion.<br>• Isolated elements of accurate and relevant information and basic use of appropriate subject vocabulary, | 1–2 |
| 0 | • No accurate or relevant material to credit. | 0 |

# 6 The new A-Level Levels of Response and writing AO2 essays

For AO2, the A-Level Levels of Response are still out of 15 marks, but the criteria are more specific.

## Level descriptors

| Level | Response | Marks |
|---|---|---|
| 5 | • A very well-focused response to the issue(s) raised.<br>• Perceptive discussion of different views, including, where appropriate, those of scholars or schools of thought with critical analysis.<br>• There is an appropriate evaluation fully supported by the reasoning.<br>• Precise use of the appropriate subject vocabulary. | 13–15 |
| 4 | • A well-focused response to the issue(s) raised.<br>• Different views are discussed, including, where appropriate, those of scholars or schools of thought, with some critical analysis.<br>• There is an appropriate evaluation supported by the reasoning.<br>• Good use of the appropriate use of subject vocabulary. | 10–12 |
| 3 | • A general response to the issue(s) raised.<br>• Different views are discussed, including, where appropriate, those of scholars or schools of thought.<br>• An evaluation is made that is consistent with some of the reasoning.<br>• Reasonable use of the appropriate subject vocabulary. | 7–9 |
| 2 | • A limited response to the issue(s) raised.<br>• Presentation of a point of view relevant to the issue with some supporting evidence and argument.<br>• Some attempt at the appropriate use of subject vocabulary. | 4–6 |
| 1 | • A basic response to the issue(s) raised with some evidence in support. | 1–3 |
| 0 | • No accurate or relevant material to credit. | 0 |

This is Question 01–2 from the *Specimen Paper for the A-Level 'Christianity and Dialogues'*, Section A: *Study of Christianity*:

**'Christianity is not relevant in a secular society.' Evaluate this claim. [15 marks]**

Below is a sample response to this question. This is a real essay, written in response to a very similar question, by a student who in his early months of study had a very limited idea of the nature of evaluation. Take heart, because in the end he worked his socks off and got a high grade. As you read it, try to formulate a clear idea of how it might be improved.

NB: This essay refers to named scholars that students are not required to study, but *may* refer to if relevant. No questions will be set that refer to named scholars who are not mentioned in the Specification. The paragraphs are numbered for ease of reference.

1  Pope John Paul II says that we are living in a time of crisis for civilisation because of secular challenges to religion and religious authority. Secularism is the movement to remove religion from the world on the grounds that it is no longer relevant. Pope John Paul says that this keeps God at a distance and makes society poorer.

2   Richard Dawkins is a secular humanist who says that evolution proves that God is not needed in the world. Dawkins says that children do not have to inherit their parents' preferences in food or sport, so why should they have to inherit their views on religion so that they are Catholics or Protestants from birth? This means that they do not think for themselves, which proves that Christianity is not relevant in a secular society.

3   John Polkinghorne says that this is wrong because society needs science and religion and a lot of scientists do not know as much about science as they should do. The laws of nature are so finely tuned that they must have been designed by God, so there must be a purpose to the universe. Dawkins needs to realise that the universe is not like a mechanical clock. In fact it is so unlike a mechanism that it is incredible that we can understand it all. The fact that we do understand it means that God must have brought about the evolution of brains to understand the universe. This shows that Christianity is relevant in a secular society.

4   The psychologist Sigmund Freud had a psychological critique of religion and said that we should abandon religion and live in a secular society. God is just the product of human psychology. We are scared of the unknown and of death, so we invent the idea of God as a divine Father in order to be able to cope with fear. God protects us as a Father. In The Future of an Illusion he claimed that all religious beliefs are illusions, so religion is neurotic and should be abandoned so that society is secular, because it is based on the idea of God as a perfect person, and there can be no such thing, so Christianity is not relevant in a secular society.

5   However John Hick says that in creating the idea of God as Father, Freud has actually uncovered how God makes himself known to us, because we can all understand the idea of a protective human father, so we can easily make sense of the idea of a divine Father, so religion is still relevant in a secular society.

6   Jean Paul Sartre said that religion is irrelevant morally, because existence precedes essence, so a human being exists before having his nature formed and not the other way round. Religious morality is therefore irrelevant, because a man is nothing more than what he makes himself. All the commands in the Bible and the Church are irrelevant, because we cannot be free if we have to obey moral commands, and neither can we be truly moral, because true morality means making moral choices. Sartre gave the example of a young man who had the choice of staying with his mother or joining the Resistance. There was no right choice, because the only thing required was the act of choosing. Christian morality should therefore be abandoned in a secular society, so this proves that Christianity is not relevant in a secular society.

7   Peter Kreeft rejects most of what Sartre says about religion. Kreeft says that religion is not meaningless, and that Sartre is wrong to reject ideas about love, responsibility, honesty and Christian values in general. Society would be a better place by following Christian values. Therefore Christianity is relevant in a secular society.

8 In conclusion, scholars such as Richard Dawkins, Sigmund Freud and Jean Paul Sartre say that Christianity is irrelevant in a secular society because of challenges from biology, psychology and morality. Pope John Paul II, John Polkinghorne, John Hick and Peter Kreeft say that these challenges do not work, and we are better off with a society which has religious values. Therefore this proves that Christianity is relevant in a secular society.

---

## Exercise

First in small groups, and then as a class, mark this essay using the A-Level AO2 15-mark Levels of Response. Which set of statements form the best fit to describe the value of this essay? An essay can reach different Levels for different criteria: you need to pick the closest Level overall.

---

# 7 Some general rules for answering questions (AS and A-Level)

1 **Don't start essays with statements of intent.** If the question asks you to 'Explain the nature of the Bible and its authority for Christians' (*Question 02 – 1 on the Specimen Paper for Christianity, AS*), do not begin (as many do) by parroting the question: 'In this essay I am going to explain the nature of the Bible and its authority for Christians' – what else would you be doing?

2 **Do use paragraphs for your ideas.** As a general rule, use a new paragraph for each main idea.

3 **Make sure your hand-writing is legible.** If you have problems with your hand-writing, and they are problems that you can cure by diligent practice, then practise diligently. If they are problems that you cannot cure, then your teachers will be able to help in other ways. Remember that what examiners cannot read they cannot mark.

4 **Select, plan and be relevant.** Some candidates cannot resist the temptation to go for quantity over quality. This usually results in much irrelevance, a lack of focus in the essay, and legibility issues. Spend a minute or so in some form of embryonic plan, however short, selecting *only* what is relevant to the question asked. Cross out the plan at the end. Do not write out a plan in full sentences, because you will end up writing the essay twice, which unfortunately is by no means uncommon.

5 **Answer the question set.** Rather than answer the question set, some candidates will answer the question they wanted to be set, or which they had carefully prepared on a related topic. One common practice is to prepare near-perfect essays on the previous year's questions, and then to be unable to resist the temptation to reproduce one of them in answer to a completely different question.

6 **Make sure that you spell technical words correctly.** Another way of improving your performance is to read widely, because reading around your subject will have the inevitable effect of improving your knowledge, style and achievement. Some misspellings are more common than others – check you know how to spell every word you've spelt wrong in the past.

7 **Try not to confuse scholars / schools of thought.** For scholars, Aquinas and Anselm, Paley and Swinburne, and Fletcher and Mill often exchange identities. Schools of thought can similarly be confused under the stress of exam conditions, so make sure that you know enough about those to whom you refer.

8 **Pay attention to chronology.** It is not uncommon for candidates to invent imaginary conversations between scholars who lived centuries (or even millennia) apart. Hume and Dawkins, Descartes and Plato, Irenaeus and Hick feature prominently on the list. Such pairings will make examiners smile, but they will not be impressed.

9 **Practise timed essays as much as you can.**

# 8 Effective preparation and revision

1 Make sure you are aware of the importance of the Assessment Objectives for the exam questions.

2 As a general piece of preparation advice, make sure that you can deal with the different question styles, for each area of the Specification.

3 **Remember that you do not need to know everything in the textbook.** You need to know enough about each area of the Specification. Try to remember the weighting of each question according to the different AOs.

4 **Memory can be trained like muscles.** If you have ever tried weightlifting, or some other form of sport that increases muscle size and density, you will know that putting on muscle is a sure and steady process. You will also know that as soon as you stop exercising, your muscles will return to their previous size. The same is true with your memory. If you set aside an hour or more a day memorising subject material, your memory can improve significantly in 2 or 3 months, and in many cases by more than this. If you stop the process, your memory capacity will go back to normal. The benefits, if you stick at it, can be enormous.

5 **Ignore those who tell you that last-minute revision does not work.** It does. This does not mean (of course) that you should ignore long-term memory training. Short-term memory can last for 24 hours, and can complement long-term memory. Not only that, but long-term memory can improve your short-term memory, so make the most of both. Even the last look at a page before you go into an exam can pay dividends. Try it with a revision partner: it will work.

6 **Develop your own revision devices.** One useful technique, faced with a practice-essay, for example, is to revise a set of key words, so that the

key words remind you of arguments. Before writing the essay, write down the key words in any order, then depending on the question organise the key words into a coherent pattern so that your answer has an orderly flow to it (as opposed to being a collection of thoughts in any old order). Use any device that works for you. One useful technique is to rehearse arguments out loud, which trains your auditory memory. If you have a patient dog or cat, or even a budgie, they can make an effective (if uncritical) audience. Practise *remembering* – don't just read things through.

7 **If you are exceptionally nervous with exams, try some relaxation techniques.** There are any number of books and websites that can help you, and they will be useful even if you are not particularly nervous. Breathing techniques and meditation techniques can stop your heart from feeling like a sledge-hammer, can improve your concentration and memory, and can boost your confidence, because you will feel that you can do something positive to take control of the exam.

8 **Finally, avoid the common error of using the word 'all' in connection with what people believe.** You do not need to shoe-horn Christians (or members of any other religion) into a single category for any kind of belief or practice. The suggestion that all Christians believe X, whatever X might be, is simply wrong. If you type in the words 'Christian denominations' into a search engine, the number of different denominations alone is staggering, and their existence testifies to the fact that their beliefs do differ; and the beliefs of the individuals within each denomination differ as well. 'Belief' and 'faith' are not measurable: they are states of mind, and as such are unquantifiable.

With ethics in particular, about 50% of candidates who write essays on situation ethics will suggest, for example, that everyone who follows that theory will be in favour of embryo research, whereas the truth is that this depends the exact situation in which it is proposed to use embryo research and on how the demands of love are interpreted. Fletcher specified the working principles for the theory, but its application depends on individual interpretation. Try suggesting how individuals *might* think rather than how they *do* think.

## 9 Student sample answer 1

*Explain the differing approaches to proving that God exists taken by the cosmological and ontological arguments.*

The ontological argument holds that God's existence is a matter of logical necessity. By contrast, the cosmological argument sees God's existence as a matter of factual necessity: God is the first cause of the universe, meaning that God explains why the universe exists, and is also the first cause of everything that happens here and now (Aquinas).

The ontological argument takes the view that God's existence can be deduced from premises. Anselm's premise is that God is defined as 'that than which none greater can be conceived', so cannot not-exist. By contrast, the cosmological argument is inductive, arguing back from what we see in the world to the supposed cause: so Aquinas argued back from our observation of the universe to the existence of God as the uncaused cause, unmoved mover and necessary being. Deductive arguments are logically certain, so for the ontological argument, God's existence is logically necessary, whereas for the inductive cosmological argument, its inductive basis can only make God's existence is no more than probable.

The ontological argument is 'a priori', known by reason alone; whereas the cosmological argument is 'a posteriori', meaning that it comes after sense experience: when we look at the world, it leads us to look for an explanation for what we see. For the ontological argument, we can know that God exists just by thinking about God's definition.

For the ontological argument, the claim 'God exists' is analytic: we can know it to be true just by analysing the words used. For the cosmological argument, 'God exists' is synthetic, so its truth or falsity can only be determined by sense experience. For the ontological argument, the structure of the sentence 'God exists' shows the truth of the claim, since the subject (God) contains the predicate (exists). In fact, it contains the predicate 'exists necessarily', because when we think of God, we have to think of a being who exists necessarily, because if he existed contingently he would not be God. For the cosmological argument, the subject (God) is separate from the predicate (exists), because by 'exists' we mean that 'God is the reason for the existence and nature of the universe'.

The ontological and cosmological arguments are not mutually exclusive approaches, since some hold that God's existence can be known both logically and factually.

## Exercise

In making a plan for the essay here, you might find it helpful to list the specific key terms and facts relating to the ontological argument and then the contrasting terms or facts about the cosmological argument.

The key points about the ontological argument are listed in the table below. In pairs, add the contrasting points about the cosmological argument.

| Ontological | Cosmological |
|---|---|
| God's logical necessity | |
| deductive | |
| a priori | |
| analytic | |
| predicate of necessary existence contained within the subject (God) | |

# 10 Student sample answer 2

*'A deontological system of ethical decision-making is unsatisfactory.'*
*Evaluate this claim.*

This seems to be a very sweeping claim, because in effect it is saying that all deontological ethical systems are unsatisfactory, whereas they can hardly be unsatisfactory to those who follow them.

The term 'deontological' comes from the Greek word meaning 'duty', or 'obligation', so deontologists hold that ethical decisions should be reached by following the moral rules that duty points us towards. There is an immediate problem here, however, because different deontological systems have different rules, and we can hardly obey them all. Divine Command theorists hold that we must obey the rules of the Bible, yet the Bible contains immoral rules, for example, Exodus 21:20–21 suggests that a slave is mere property, and can be beaten to any extent short of death (excluding damage to eyes or teeth). Such ideas are rooted in the past, when slavery was common, whereas most people today reject slavery as obviously immoral.

It is possible to find fault with any deontological system. Catholic Natural Law does preserve high moral standards, but its approach to issues such as abortion, contraception and AIDS, does not seem very practical. For example, in 2010, Pope Benedict allowed condom use for male sex-workers, but that still left millions exposed to the virus. The Catholic Church is one of the biggest charitable organisations dealing with AIDS, but it cannot deal practically with the spread of AIDS because its primary precepts, rooted in an ancient moral theory, forbid contraception (which makes the Pope's exception for male sex-workers seem inconsistent).

What of Kantian deontology? Basically, it ignores both the emotions and the consequences of our moral decisions, but it can hardly be satisfactory for any moral system to ignore either of these. Does this mean that deontological systems are unsatisfactory and teleological / consequentialist theories are better? If space permitted, we could raise equally telling objections to these systems. For example, Situation Ethics, ignores the fact that agape love is subjective, so can potentially justify any kind of atrocity.

The usual answer to the weaknesses of both deontological and teleological systems is to suggest a compromise, for example, in rule utilitarianism. Rule utilitarianism, according to some, has the best of both worlds, since it caters for minorities and keeps moral rules where appropriate. Is deontology satisfactory in this hybrid form? I am not sure that it is, for the simple reason that it has to deal with situations where following the rule leads to undesirable consequences. This might happen, for example, with the complex rules currently in place in the UK concerning embryo research.

Nevertheless, I would want to insist that following moral rules can make for a satisfactory life. If (for example) we define murder as unjustified killing, then I can see nothing wrong with making the rule against unjustified killing absolute. The whole point of morally *good* behaviour is to enrich life for as many people as possible, so holding to a deontological system must be satisfactory for those who obey the laws.

To draw some of these ideas together, three conclusions can be offered. First, even if we admit that all forms of deontological ethics are unsatisfactory (either completely or in part), it must nevertheless be true that if millions of people follow them, then they must each be satisfactory for those who accept them. Second, although all deontological systems, religious or otherwise, seem to have unsatisfactory elements; much the same can be said of any ethical theory, deontological, teleological or hybrid. Third, deontological principles, are crucial if we want to live in an ordered society, and history tells us that few would not. Deontological principles, then, are deeply satisfactory and they are necessary.

As Martin Luther King once said: 'It may be true that the law cannot make a man love me, but it can stop him from lynching me, and I think that's pretty important.'

## Exercise

1 In pairs, use different colours to show which parts of this essay deal with the specific criteria for AO2:
- focus on the issue raised / relevance
- perceptive discussion of different views / scholars
- appropriate evaluation fully supported by the reasoning
- precise use of appropriate subject vocabulary.

You might underline different parts in more than one colour.

2 Are there any criticisms you would make of the essay / suggestions for improvement?

3 If the essay is longer than you think you could write in the exam what would you shorten or omit?

# A time chart of theologians, philosophers and others

Use this for reference, reminder and comparison; and for the avoidance of inventing conversations between people in the past with people in the future!

The parts in bold type indicate a philosopher / theologian or topic named directly or indirectly in the Specification.

| Born | Died | Name | Did |
|------|------|------|-----|
| not | not | GOD | **Invented all those below** (and lots of other things as well, including having a sense of humour). |
| 470/469 BCE | 399BCE | SOCRATES | Greek (Athenian) philosopher; one of the founders of Western philosophy; Plato was a student of Socrates. |
| 428/427BCE or 424/423BCE | 348/347BCE | PLATO | Founded the Athenian Academy, first centre of higher learning in the Western world; considered to be the number 1 philosopher, particularly in the Western tradition; huge influence on Christian thought; rationalist: saw reality as being centred on the metaphysical world of Forms. |
| 384BCE | 322BCE | ARISTOTLE | **Most things; Virtue Ethics; main influence for Aquinas' Cosmological argument; main influence for Aquinas, Natural Law Ethics; earliest form of Virtue Ethics;** Greek philosopher and scientist / empiricist; studied under Plato; huge influence on Judaism, Christianity and Islam. |
| 341BCE | 270BCE | EPICURUS | **'Epicurean paradox' of God's omnipotence – problem of evil;** Greek philosopher. |
| 7-2BCE | 30-33CE | JESUS of Nazareth | Described as 'Son' of first entry above; Jewish teacher, prophet and ethicist; central figure of Christianity. |
| *c.*5CE | *c.*67CE | PAUL, Saint | Main architect of the Christian Church in the first century CE; founded churches in Asia Minor and Europe; wrote about half of the books in the New Testament; probably martyred in Rome by beheading. |
| ? | *c.*64CE | PETER, Saint | One of Jesus' 12 Apostles; leader of the Early Christian Church; considered by the Catholic Church to be the first Pope; probably crucified in Rome under the emperor Nero Augustus Caesar. |
| first half of second century | ? | IRENAEUS, Saint | **Irenaeus-Hick theodicy;** Bishop of Lugdunum in Gaul, in the Roman Empire. |
| 354CE | 430CE | AUGUSTINE of Hippo, Saint | **Theodicy; conscience;** theologian and philosopher; very influential in the Catholic and Anglican Churches; should have read Irenaeus before writing his theodicy. |
| *c.*1033 | 1109 | ANSELM, Saint | **Ontological Argument;** Benedictine monk; Archbishop of Canterbury 1093–1109. |
| eleventh century | | GAUNILO of Marmoutiers | **Ontological Argument;** Benedictine monk; did not like Anselm's Ontological Argument. |
| 1225 | 1274 | AQUINAS, Thomas | **Cosmological Argument; Natural Law ethics; conscience;** Dominican friar; philosopher and theologian; the most famous proponent of natural theology. |
| 1483 | 1546 | LUTHER, Martin | **Very influential in the Protestant Reformation;** German theologian, priest / monk. |
| 1509 | 1564 | CALVIN, John | **Very influential in the Protestant Reformation;** French theologian; differed from the Lutherans, for example, over the issue of the real presence of Christ in the Eucharist. |

| 1596 | 1650 | DESCARTES, René | **Dualism of body and soul**; refused to trust his senses; famous for his *cogito* ('I think, therefore I am'); French philosopher, scientist and mathematician; known as the 'father of Western philosophy'; allegedly dissected his wife's pet dog alive, under the conviction that animals cannot feel pain because they do not have souls. |
|------|------|------|------|
| 1711 | 1776 | HUME, David | Did not like **design arguments; critique of miracles; critique of Aquinas' cosmological argument**; Scottish empiricist; had a well-developed sense of humour. |
| 1724 | 1804 | KANT, Immanuel | **Critique of Ontological Argument**; ethical theory based on the 'categorical imperative'; German philosopher; woken up from his 'philosophical slumbers' by David Hume. |
| 1743 | 1805 | PALEY, William | **Watchmaker design argument**; English Anglican clergyman and philosopher; natural theology; utilitarian; Arch-deacon of Carlisle. |
| 1842 | 1910 | JAMES, William | **Analysed mystical religious experiences**; American psychologist and philosopher. |
| 1844 | 1900 | NIETZSCHE, Friedrich | Famous for suggesting that 'God is dead'; German philosopher, philologist. |
| 1869 | 1937 | OTTO, Rudolf | **Numinous experiences and the 'wholly other'**; German Lutheran theologian. |
| 1872 | 1970 | RUSSELL, Bertrand | **Critique of Aquinas' cosmological argument**; philosopher and logician; wrote 'A History of Western Philosophy', (which the author recommends should be read). |
| 1884 | 1976 | BULTMANN, Rudolf | **Form critic; aimed to 'de-mythologise' the New Testament**; German Lutheran theologian. |
| 1886 | 1967 | STACE, Walter | **Mystical religious experiences as non-sensuous and non-intellectual union with the divine**; British philosopher, theologian and epistemologist. |
| 1886 | 1968 | BARTH, Karl | **Interpreted Anselm's ontological argument as a faith statement**; very influential Swiss Protestant theologian; like Tillich, Barth was fiercely critical of Hitler and left Germany after refusing to swear allegiance to Hitler and the Nazi party. |
| 1905 | 1991 | FLETCHER, Joseph | **Christian Situation Ethics**; American academic and Episcopal priest who later decided he was an atheist; talked a lot about love and apparently suggested that someone with Down's Syndrome is not a person. |
| 1917 | 1981 | MACKIE, John | **Clarified and rejected the Free Will Defence [for the problem of evil]**; wrote 'The Miracle of Theism', meaning that it would be a miracle if any person of sense believed it. |
| 1922 | 2012 | HICK, John | **Irenaeus-Hick 'soul-making' theodicy**; British philosopher of religion and theologian. |
| 1923 | 2005 | WILES, Maurice | **Views on miracles**; learned Japanese after Pearl Harbour, and employed on code work during. |
| 1934 | | SWINBURNE, Richard | **Principles of credulity and testimony (religious experience)**; British philosopher; converted from the Church of England to the Eastern Orthodox Church. |
| 1939 | | GRIFFIN, David | **Process theology / Process theodicy**; American philosopher of religion and theologian. |
| 1944 | | HAMPSON, Daphne | **Emphasised necessity to overcome patriarchal religion;** wrote 'Theology and Feminism', 1990. |
| 1946 | | SINGER, Peter | **Influential in the field of animal ethics**; utilitarian; Australian bioethicist / moral philosopher. |

# Some background information about the Bible

## The terms 'Bible' and 'Old and New Testaments'

The word 'Bible' comes from the Greek *ta biblia*, which literally means 'the books', that is, the holy books of the Christian religion. There are two main sections of the Christian Bible, commonly referred to as the Old Testament and the New Testament.

The word 'Testament' in both cases refers to the covenant (meaning an agreement or dispensation) between God and the Jewish people. In the Old Testament there are various covenants, including the Mosaic Covenant, the substance of which is given in Exodus 19:5–6:

> **'Now therefore, if you will obey my voice and keep my covenant, you shall be my own possession among all peoples; for all the earth is mine, and you shall be to me a kingdom of priests and a holy nation.'**

Moses acts as the covenant mediator on Mount Sinai, and by means of a *theophany* (a manifestation / appearance of God), God tells the people, 'I am Yahweh, your God, who delivered you from the land of Egypt', and then delivers the Ten Commandments (Exodus 20), which are the main text of the covenant agreement. They are part of the moral structure of both Judaism and Christianity.

## The contents of the Old and New Testaments of the Bible

### The Old Testament

The Old Testament is based primarily on the Hebrew Scriptures, which date from the first millennium BCE, and which are also known as *Tanakh*. Each of the main divisions of the Christian Church favours a somewhat different version of the Hebrew Scriptures.

To summarise briefly the Old Testament contents:

1 The Law of Moses

   The first five books (Genesis to Deuteronomy) are known as the Law of Moses, also as the *Pentateuch* (Greek for 'five scrolls'), and they tell the history of Israel from the creation of the world to the death of Moses. They also contain the instructions and laws given to Moses on Mount Sinai, including the Ten Commandments.

**2** Historical writings

Joshua, Judges, Samuel, Kings, Chronicles, and Ezra-Nehemiah, form a history of Israel from the conquest of Canaan down to the second half of the fifth century BCE.

**3** The prophetic books

A significant part of the Old Testament is taken up with the prophetic books, including 'major' prophets such as Isaiah, Jeremiah and Ezekiel, and the 'Book of the Twelve' – the 'minor' prophets such as Hosea, Amos, Micah and Zechariah. Prophets were individuals who announced God's will to the nation by means of prophetic oracles.

**4** The wisdom literature

Another significant section includes the 'wisdom literature', for example: the Book of Job, Psalms, Proverbs, Ecclesiastes and the Song of Songs. The Book of Job, for example, contains much of the thinking of the wise about the problem of evil, and why wicked people seem to prosper whereas good people often suffer throughout their lives.

The Old Testament contains a great variety of literature: cosmogonic myths, historical writing, prophetic and priestly oracles, structured laments, proverbs, riddles, moral stories, apodictic law, general rules and regulations, humorous anecdotes, scandal, love songs and erotic poetry just to mention a few. The language of the Old Testament is Hebrew (aside from a few sections in Aramaic).

You should perhaps take from all this that the Old Testament gives a complete cross-section of Jewish culture from its origins to the period shortly before the birth of Jesus. The Old Testament is different from the New, not least because its scope is much wider. Some Christians have a tendency to 'judge' the Old Testament as being in some way inferior, or secondary, to the New Testament, but this is inappropriate. Bear in mind, for example, that where the New Testament mentions 'the Scriptures', it is the Hebrew Scriptures that it refers to. In Matthew 5:17–19, for example, Jesus insists that he has come to fulfil the Law and the Prophets, and not to abolish them: not the smallest detail of God's Law will disappear until that fulfilment is accomplished. Remember, also, that Jesus was Jewish, and was raised in that culture. When (in John 10:30) Jesus says, 'I and the Father are one', the 'Father' he refers to is the God of the Old Testament.

## The New Testament

The New Testament is a collection of books written mainly in the first century CE. As with the Hebrew Scriptures, the New 'Testament' refers to a covenant – an agreement between God and humanity. In 1 Corinthians 11:23–25, St Paul writes:

> 'For I received from the Lord what I also delivered to you, that the Lord Jesus on the night when he was betrayed took bread, and when he had given thanks, he broke it, and said, "This is my body which is for you. Do this in remembrance of me." In the same way also the cup, after supper, saying, "This cup is the new covenant in my blood. Do this, as often as you drink it, in remembrance of me".'

The continuity with the Old Testament here is clear. The new covenant is confirmed in the blood of Jesus, just as the 'old' covenant was confirmed in the blood of animals sacrificed on the altar (for example, Exodus 24:8). There is continuity, then, between the ancient ceremonies of covenant renewal and the Christian ritual of the Eucharist / Holy Communion, which is at the heart of the New Testament.

To summarise briefly the New Testament contents, there are 27 books with 4 main types of writing:

1 The Gospels

The word 'Gospel' comes from the Greek *euangelion*, meaning 'good news', so the four Gospels of Mark, Matthew, Luke and John are accounts of the good news about Jesus. They are a record of Jesus' teachings, and they are also biographical, recording where Jesus came from, his ministry, passion (his arrest, trial, suffering and crucifixion) and resurrection.

Further, the Gospel-writers are known as 'evangelists', and 'evangelism' is the preaching of the gospel. 'Gospel', by the way, usually takes a capital G when referring to one of the four Gospels, as in 'The Gospel of Mark'; and a small g when it refers to the good news in general, as in 'spreading the gospel'. The Gospels of Mark, Matthew and Luke are known as the 'synoptic' Gospels (from a Greek word meaning 'seeing together'), because most scholars believe that Matthew and Luke used Mark's Gospel as a source for writing their own. These Gospels have many parallel passages, and if the parallels are placed in adjacent columns, the synoptic content can be seen clearly. John's Gospel is considered by most scholars to be later than the synoptics, dating perhaps from the early second century CE. Although there are many points of similarity between John and the synoptics, John has a very distinctive style and theology, not least in his identification of Jesus as the *Logos* / Word: 'And the Word became flesh and dwelt among us, full of grace and truth; we have beheld his glory, glory as of the only Son from the Father.' (John 1:14)

2 The Acts of the Apostles

Most modern scholarship agrees that the author of Luke's Gospel was also the author of Acts, so Luke-Acts is a two-part book. Luke concludes with the death and resurrection of Jesus and Acts begins with the ascension of Jesus to heaven (1:6–11) and the subsequent activities of Jesus' disciples. The first half of Acts deals mainly with the Jerusalem Church, whereas the second is dominated by the figure of St Paul, and charts the progress of the spreading of the word about Jesus until it reaches Rome itself.

3 The Epistles

The word 'epistle' comes from the Greek word for 'letter'. There are 21 epistles in the New Testament, 13 of which are attributed to the apostle Paul, although the authorship of several of these is disputed. The longest and the most influential is the letter to the Romans, so this would be a good one to read to get a flavour of Paul's thinking and teaching. In 1 Corinthians 15 Paul summarises the gospel message:

'Now I would remind you, brethren, in what terms I preached to you the gospel, which you received, in which you stand, by which you are saved, if you hold it fast – unless you believed in vain.

For I delivered to you as of first importance what I also received, that Christ died for our sins in accordance with the scriptures, that he was buried, that he was raised on the third day in accordance with the scriptures ...' (1 Corinthians 15:1–4)

The Epistles as a whole are written to the various churches founded by missionary activity, and contain words of encouragement, explanations of particular doctrines, instructions about behaviour and advice on resolving disputes.

4  The Book of Revelation

The Book of Revelation is also called 'Apocalypse', or the 'Apocalypse of John', or just 'Revelation'. The word apocalypse is a Greek word meaning 'uncovering', or 'disclosure', so it means 'lifting the veil of revelation'. The author's energies are directed towards 'lifting the veil' over the Last Judgement, and this makes rather terrifying reading. Much of the writing and the imagery is symbolic, with figures such as the Four Horsemen of the Apocalypse, the Whore of Babylon and the Beast from the Earth, and there are any number of interpreters who will claim to give you infallible information about the meaning of the imagery.

# The Canon of the Bible (the books that Christians see as authoritative)

A 'canon' is a collection of books which a religious group regards as inspired by God, and which therefore forms a body of authoritative scripture.

The canon of both the Old and New Testaments was formed over a long period of time; moreover, different Christian groups accept or reject different books. Owing to two major schisms (splits) in the Church, Christianity now has four main traditions: the Orthodox, Catholic, Anglican and Protestant. Whereas the New Testament canon for these traditions is very similar, there are significant variations concerning the Old Testament, so whereas most Anglican and Protestant groups accept a canon of 39 Old Testament books, Catholics accept 46 and the Eastern Orthodox Church accepts 51.

Perhaps the main criterion by which the Early Church judged a book to be canonical was the belief that it is part of God's inspired and authoritative revelation to humans.

# Notes

## Introduction

**Note 1** Taken from http://www.filmsite.org/wiza.html.

## Chapter 1.1 The Design Argument

**Note 1** Paley, William: *Natural Theology; or, Evidences of the Existence and Attributes of the Deity. Collected from the Appearances of Nature.* p.1 http://darwin-online.org.uk/content/frameset?itemID=A142&pageseq=1&viewtype=text.

**Note 2** Hume, David: *Dialogues Concerning Natural Religion.* For example: http://www.anselm.edu/homepage/dbanach/dnr.htm.

**Note 3** Hume, David: *Dialogues Concerning Natural Religion*: http://www.anselm.edu/homepage/dbanach/dnr.htm.

**Note 4** Swinburne, Richard: *The Existence of God*, Revised Edition, Clarendon Press, Oxford, 1990, pp.141–142.

**Note 5** Paley, William: *Natural Theology; or, Evidences of the Existence and Attributes of the Deity. Collected from the Appearances of Nature*, p.492.

**Note 6** Paley, William: *Natural Theology; or, Evidences of the Existence and Attributes of the Deity. Collected from the Appearances of Nature*, p.525: 'the contrivances of nature decidedly evince intention'.

**Note 7** There is a good discussion of 'Great Pumpkin' objections in: Michael Peterson, William Hasker, Bruce Reichenbach & David Basinger: *Reason and Religious Belief: An Introduction to the Philosophy of Religion,* Oxford University Press, 1991, pp.122–127.

**Note 8** Price, H.H. 'Belief "in" and belief "that"'. In: *The Philosophy of Religion*, ed. Basil Mitchell: Oxford Readings in Philosophy, OUP, 1971. Ch. VIII, pp. 143–167, reprinted from *Religious Studies*, 1 (1963), 1–27 (CUP). The PDF is available at: http://philosophicalfragments.com/pdf/The_Philosophy_of_Religion.pdf

**Note 9** Price, H.H. 'Belief "in" and belief "that"'. In: *The Philosophy of Religion,* ed. Basil Mitchell: Oxford Readings in Philosophy, OUP, 1971. Ch. VIII, p.143, reprinted from *Religious Studies*, 1 (1963), 1–27 (CUP).

**Note 10** Price, H.H. 'Belief "in" and belief "that"'. In: *The Philosophy of Religion*, ed. Basil Mitchell: Oxford Readings in Philosophy, OUP, 1971. Ch. VIII, p.166, reprinted from *Religious Studies*, 1 (1963), 1–27 (CUP).

**Note 11** Price, H.H. 'Belief "in" and belief "that"'. In: *The Philosophy of Religion*, ed. Basil Mitchell: Oxford Readings in Philosophy, OUP, 1971. Ch. VIII, p.167, reprinted from *Religious Studies*, 1 (1963), 1–27 (CUP).

**Note 12** Price, H.H. 'Belief "in" and belief "that"'. In: *The Philosophy of Religion*, ed. Basil Mitchell: Oxford Readings in Philosophy, OUP, 1971. Ch. VIII, p.167, reprinted from *Religious Studies*, 1 (1963), 1–27 (CUP).

## Chapter 1.2 The Ontological Argument

**Note 1** Palmer, Michael: *The Question of God: An Introduction and Sourcebook*, Routledge, London & New York, 2001, p.4.

**Note 2** Palmer, Michael: *The Question of God: An Introduction and Sourcebook*, Routledge, London & New York, 2001, p.31.

**Note 3** Palmer, Michael: *The Question of God: An Introduction and Sourcebook*, Routledge, London & New York, 2001, p.7.

**Note 4** Palmer, Michael: *The Question of God: An Introduction and Sourcebook*, Routledge, London & New York, 2001, p.32.

**Note 5** Kuehn, Manfred: *Kant: A Biography*, Cambridge University Press, 2001, p.26.

**Note 6** Descartes, René: *Meditations on First Philosophy*, Cambridge Texts in the History of Philosophy, ed. John Cottingham, Cambridge University Press, 1986. Meditation V, 66.

**Note 7** Palmer, Michael: *The Question of God: An Introduction and Sourcebook*, Routledge, London & New York, 2001, p.26.

**Note 8** Stanford Encyclopedia of Philosophy, http://plato.stanford.edu/entries/anselm/.

# Chapter 1.3 The Cosmological Argument

**Note 1** Hawking, Stephen: *A Brief History of Time*, Bantam Books, 1988.

**Note 2** Loewenstein, Werner R.: *Physics in Mind. A Quantum View of the Brain*, Basic Books, New York, 2013, p.21.

**Note 3** The Existence of God (Three Articles) – (3) Whether God exists: Reply to Objection 2, http://www.sacred-texts.com/chr/aquinas/summa/sum005.htm.

**Note 4** Davis, Stephen T.: *Reason and Theistic Proofs*, Edinburgh University Press, 1997, p.66.

**Note 5** Russell, Bertrand: *History of Western Philosophy*, London, George Allen & Unwin Ltd, 1961 edition, p.453.

**Note 6** The transcript of the debate can be read online, for example, at: http://www.scandalon.co.uk/philosophy/cosmological_radio.htm.

**Note 7** Stanford Encyclopedia of Philosophy, http://plato.stanford.edu/entries/cosmological-argument/.

**Note 8** Reichenbach, B. R.: *The Cosmological Argument: A Reassessment*, Charles C Thomas Pub Ltd, 1972. Ch.5 quoted in http://plato.stanford.edu/entries/cosmological-argument/.

**Note 9** Hume, David: *Dialogues Concerning Natural Religion*, Oxford University Press, 1998, p.92.

**Note 10** To read this online, see: http://www.anselm.edu/homepage/dbanach/dnr.htm [188].

**Note 11** To read this online, see: http://www.anselm.edu/homepage/dbanach/dnr.htm [190].

**Note 12** Hughes, Gerry J.: *The Cosmological Argument*, Richmond Journal of Philosophy 9 (Spring 2005), p.2. Online at: http://www.richmond-philosophy.net/rjp/back_issues/rjp9_hughes.pdf.

**Note 13** Hughes, Gerry J.: *The Cosmological Argument*, Richmond Journal of Philosophy 9 (Spring 2005), p.4.

**Note 14** Hare, R.M. Edited by Mitchell, Basil: *The Philosophy of Religion*, Oxford Readings in Philosophy, Oxford University Press, 1971: I: 'Theology and Falsification', pp.15–18.

**Note 15** Hare, R.M. Edited by Mitchell, Basil: *The Philosophy of Religion*, Oxford Readings in Philosophy, Oxford University Press, 1971: I: 'Theology and Falsification', p.17.

# Chapter 2 Evil and suffering

**Note 1** Mother Julian of Norwich, quoted by John Hick in: *Evil and the God of Love* (1966), Macmillan Press, 1985 edition, p.289. Quoted in turn by Hick from *The Revelations of Divine Love of Julian of Norwich*, translated by James Walsh, S.J. (London: Burns & Oates. 1961), chap. 27.

**Note 2** Mother Julian's visions were subsequently written and published in 1395 as *Revelations of Divine Love* – the first book to be published in English by a woman.

**Note 3** There is a beautiful reading of the *Epic of Gilgamesh* by Richard Padstow at:

https://www.youtube.com/watch?v=Kde-P_jffqk The best place to start is 1:20:15, with the decision by the despairing Gilgamesh to seek Utnapishtim the Faraway.

**Note 4** This is Paul's doctrine of 'Justification by Faith', and this is studied in detail in the section on Key Moral Principles, in the Religion section.

**Note 5** Quoted from: http://www.scrapbookpages.com/AuschwitzScrapbook/History/Articles/Selection2.html.

**Note 6** Hospers, John: *An Introduction to Philosophical Analysis*, Second Edition, 1967, Routledge & Kegan Paul, London, p.461. In his *Dialogues*, Hume took up the question from Epicurus; see, for example: http://plato.stanford.edu/entries/humereligion/# ProEvi (section 5).

**Note 7** The text of Augustine's argument concerning evil can be followed at: http://oregonstate.edu/instruct/phl201/modules/Philosophers/Augustine/augustine_evil.html.

**Note 8** http://science.nasa.gov/science-news/science-at-nasa/2002/28jan_extinction/.

**Note 9** www.eyewitnesstohistory.com/pompeii.htm. Pliny noted that, 'Many besought the aid of the gods, but still more imagined there were no gods left ...'

**Note 10** Dostoyevsky, Fyodor: *The Brothers Karamazov*, 1880. The extract is from chapter 4 of the novel. The text can be read at: http://www.bibliomania.com/0/0/235/1030/17183/1/frameset.html.

**Note 11** Rowe, W: 'The Problem of Evil and Some Varieties of Atheism', *American Philosophical Quarterly, 16,* 1979, pp.335–341.

**Note 12** Mackie, J.L.: 'Evil and Omnipotence', *Mind,* 64 (254), April 1955, pp.200–212. For an online version, see: http://www.ditext.com/mackie/evil.html. Plantinga's response to Mackie is in: A. Plantinga: 'God, Freedom, and Evil: Essays in Philosophy', George Allen & Unwin, 1975, pp.7–64 & pp.85–112. Mackie took up the argument again in: *The Miracle of Theism; Arguments for and against the existence of God,* Clarendon Press, Oxford, 1982, pp.150–176.

**Note 13** Mackie, J.L.: 'Evil and Omnipotence', *Mind, 64* (254), April 1955, p.209.

**Note 14** This account of Plantinga's argument is necessarily abbreviated. To follow a longer version online, see, for example: http://www.iep.utm.edu/evil-log/#H4.

**Note 15** From a letter written by the poet John Keats to his brother and sister-in-law, George and Georgiana Keats, 1819. For example, see: http://www.lewisiana.nl/painquotes/keats-on-soul-making.pdf.

**Note 16** Hick, John: *Evil and the God of Love,* Macmillan Press, Second edition, 1977. Part IV: 'A Theodicy for Today.'.

**Note 17** Hick, John: *Evil and the God of Love,* Macmillan Press, Second edition, 1977, p.246.

**Note 18** Hick, John: *Evil and the God of Love,* Macmillan Press, Second edition, 1977, p.254, quoting Hebrews 2:10 & Romans 8:17.

**Note 19** St Augustine: *City of God,* Book 21, Chapter 9. For example: https://en.wikisource.org/wiki/The_City_of_God/Book_XXI/Chapter_9.

**Note 20** Griffin's theodicy here is given from Chapter 4 of: Stephen T. Davis (editor): *Encountering Evil: Live Options in Theodicy,* T. & T. Clark Ltd. Edinburgh, 1981. 'Creation out of Chaos and the Problem of Evil'.

**Note 21** Griffin, D.R.: *Reenchantment without Supernaturalism. A Process Philosophy of Religion,* Cornell Studies in the Philosophy of Religion, Series, editor W.P. Alston, Cornell University Press, Ithaca & London, 2001, pp.140–144.

**Note 22** Griffin, D.R (edited by Stephen T. Davis): *Encountering Evil: Live Options in Theodicy,* T. & T. Clark Ltd. Edinburgh, 1981, p.107.

**Note 23** For various reasons, Griffin rejects Darwinian evolution in favour of a model in which God persuades organisms to evolve in incremental steps. Griffin, D.R.: *Reenchantment without Supernaturalism. A Process Philosophy of Religion,* Cornell Studies in the Philosophy of Religion, Series, editor W.P. Alston, Cornell University Press, Ithaca & London, 2001, Chapter 6.

**Note 24** Griffin, D.R (edited by Stephen T. Davis): *Encountering Evil: Live Options in Theodicy,* T. & T. Clark Ltd. Edinburgh, 1981, p.110.

**Note 25** John K. Roth, commenting on Griffin, D.R (edited by Stephen T. Davis): *Encountering Evil: Live Options in Theodicy,* T. & T. Clark Ltd. Edinburgh, 1981, p.121.

**Note 26** Griffin, D.R (edited by Stephen T. Davis): *Encountering Evil: Live Options in Theodicy,* T. & T. Clark Ltd. Edinburgh, 1981, p.113.

**Note 27** Griffin, D.R.: *Reenchantment without Supernaturalism. A Process Philosophy of Religion,* Cornell Studies in the Philosophy of Religion, Series, editor W.P. Alston, Cornell University Press, Ithaca & London, 2001, p.392.

**Note 28** Data from: http://encyclopedia.1914-1918-online.net/article/influenza_pandemic.

## Chapter 3 Religious experience

**Note 1** Butler, Alban: *Lives of the Saints,* first published 1756–1759 as: *The Lives of the Fathers, Martyrs and Other Principal Saints).* The extract is taken from the online version edited by Herbert J. Thurston, S.J. & Donald Attwater: https://archive.org/stream/ButlersLivesOfTheSaintsCompleteEdition/ButlersLivesOfTheSaintsCompleteEdition_djvu.txt.

**Note 2** St Augustine: *De Genesi ad litteram* (The Literal Meaning of Genesis), composed 401-415CE.

**Note 3** von Rad, Gerhard: *Genesis. A Commentary,* (Old Testament Library Series), translated John H. Marks, SCM Press Ltd., London, second edition 1963, p.370.

**Note 4** Skinner, John: *A Critical and Exegetical Commentary on Genesis* (The International Critical Commentary Series), second edition, T. & T. Clark, Edinburgh, 1930, p.469.

**Note 5** From: *The Life of St. Teresa of Jesus of The Order of Our Lady of Carmel,* written sometime before 1567. Online version, translated from the Spanish by David Lewis, 1904: http://www.catholicspiritualdirection.org/lifeofteresa.pdf Chapter.27, p.149.

**Note 6** From: *The Life of St. Teresa of Jesus of The Order of Our Lady of Carmel,* written sometime before 1567. Online version, translated from the Spanish by David

Lewis, 1904: http://www.catholicspiritualdirection.org/lifeofteresa.pdf pp.149–150.

**Note 7** From the New Advent, Catholic Encyclopedia: http://www.newadvent.org/cathen/10663b.htm.

**Note 8** Published in 1917 as: *Das Heilige – Über das Irrationale in der Idee des Göttlichen und sein Verhältnis zum Rationalen* ('The Holy – On the Irrational in the Idea of the Divine and its Relation to the Rational').

**Note 9** Otto, Rudolf: 'The Idea of the Holy', Chapter 22 in: *'Historical Selections in the Philosophy of Religion'*, edited by Ninian Smart, SCM Press Ltd., London, 1962, p.424.

**Note 10** Lewis, C.S.: *The Problem of Pain*. Fount Paperbacks 1977 (first published 1940, Geoffrey Bles), p.14.

**Note 11** Lewis, C.S.: *The Problem of Pain*. Fount Paperbacks 1977 (first published 1940, Geoffrey Bles), p.15.

**Note 12** Macquarrie, John: 'The Experience of the Holy.' Chapter 64 in: *Twentieth-Century Religious Thought*, SCM Press, fourth edition, 1988 (first published 1963), pp.214–215.

**Note 13** James, William: The book is the collected Gifford Lectures, given at Edinburgh in 1901–1902: *The Varieties of Religious Experience: A Study in Human Nature*. The page references here for **Notes 13–26** and **39–40** are to the Fount Paperbacks edition, January 1977. Or, an online version can be found here: https://ebooks.adelaide.edu.au/j/james/william/varieties/index.html.

**Note 14** James, William: *The Varieties of Religious Experience: A Study in Human Nature*, Fount Paperbacks edition, January 1977, p.19.

**Note 15** Nock, Arthur Darby: the introduction to James, William: *The Varieties of Religious Experience: A Study in Human Nature*, Fount Paperbacks edition, January 1977.

**Note 16** James, William: *The Varieties of Religious Experience: A Study in Human Nature*, Fount Paperbacks edition, January 1977, p.491.

**Note 17** James, William: *The Varieties of Religious Experience: A Study in Human Nature*, Fount Paperbacks edition, January 1977, p.499.

**Note 18** James, William: *The Varieties of Religious Experience: A Study in Human Nature*, Fount Paperbacks edition, January 1977, p.464.

**Note 19** James, William: *The Varieties of Religious Experience: A Study in Human Nature*, Fount Paperbacks edition, January 1977, pp.367–368.

**Note 20** James, William: *The Varieties of Religious Experience: A Study in Human Nature*, Fount Paperbacks edition, January 1977, p.371, quoting from Charles Kingsley's *Life*, i.55, quoted by Inge: *Christian Mysticism*, London, 1899, p.341.

**Note 21** James, William: *The Varieties of Religious Experience: A Study in Human Nature*, Fount Paperbacks edition, January 1977, p.373.

**Note 22** James, William: *The Varieties of Religious Experience: A Study in Human Nature*, Fount Paperbacks edition, January 1977, pp.378–379.

**Note 23** James, William: *The Varieties of Religious Experience: A Study in Human Nature*, Fount Paperbacks edition, January 1977, p.385, quoting from the experiences of Dr. Bucke.

**Note 24** James, William: *The Varieties of Religious Experience: A Study in Human Nature*, Fount Paperbacks edition, January 1977, p.386, quoting from: Vivekananda, *Raja Yoga*, London 1896.

**Note 25** James, William: *The Varieties of Religious Experience: A Study in Human Nature*, Fount Paperbacks edition, January 1977, pp.394–395.

**Note 26** James, William: *The Varieties of Religious Experience: A Study in Human Nature*, Fount Paperbacks edition, January 1977, p.469.

**Note 27** James, William: *The Varieties of Religious Experience: A Study in Human Nature*, Fount Paperbacks edition, January 1977, p. 469.

**Note 28** James, William: *The Varieties of Religious Experience: A Study in Human Nature*, Fount Paperbacks edition, January 1977, p.475.

**Note 29** James, William: *The Varieties of Religious Experience: A Study in Human Nature*, Fount Paperbacks edition, January 1977, p.492.

**Note 30** From James Ward Smith's 'Walter Terence Stace 1886–1967', *Proceedings and Addresses of the American Philosophical Association*, (41) 1967–1968, pp.136-138. See: https://philosophy.princeton.edu/about/great-and-good/w-t-stace.

**Note 31** Stace, W.T.: *Mysticism and Philosophy*, 1960, The Macmillan Press Ltd, pp.71–72.

**Note 32** Stace, W.T.: *Mysticism and Philosophy*, 1960, The Macmillan Press Ltd, p.63, quoted by Rudolf Otto: *Mysticism East and West*, New York, The Macmillan Company, 1932, p.61.

**Note 33** Stace, W.T.: *Mysticism and Philosophy*, 1960, The Macmillan Press Ltd, pp.120–121.

**Note 34** Stace, W.T.: *Mysticism and Philosophy*, 1960, The Macmillan Press Ltd, pp.131–132.

**Note 35** Stace, W.T.: *Mysticism and Philosophy*, 1960, The Macmillan Press Ltd, p.131.

**Note 36** Tinoco, C. A. & Ortiz, J. P. L.: *Journal of Consciousness Exploration & Research*, April 2014, Volume 5, Issue 3, pp.234–257: 'Magnetic Stimulation of the Temporal Cortex: A Partial "God Helmet" Replication Study.' The account given in this textbook can be found at: http://www.feelguide.com/2015/06/14/neurotheology-team-proves-god-helmet-is-real-eliciting-mystic-states-visions-god-like-presence/, which has a link to the full results of the study.

**Note 37** A later follow-up and critique of this experiment can be read at: https://www.erowid.org/plants/mushrooms/mushrooms_journal2.pdf.

**Note 38** James, William: *The Varieties of Religious Experience: A Study in Human Nature*, Fount Paperbacks edition, January 1977, p.385, quoting Dr. Bucke.

**Note 39** James, William: *The Varieties of Religious Experience: A Study in Human Nature*, Fount Paperbacks edition, January 1977, p.386.

**Note 40** Swinburne, Richard: *The Existence of God*, Revised edition, Clarendon Press, Oxford, 1991 (first published 1979), pp.257–276.

**Note 41** Swinburne, Richard: *The Existence of God*, Revised edition, Clarendon Press, Oxford, 1991 (first published 1979), p.254.

**Note 42** Swinburne, Richard: *The Existence of God*, Revised edition, Clarendon Press, Oxford, 1991 (first published 1979), p.254.

**Note 43** Swinburne, Richard: *The Existence of God*, Revised edition, Clarendon Press, Oxford, 1991 (first published 1979), p.254.

**Note 44** Swinburne, Richard: *The Existence of God*, Revised edition, Clarendon Press, Oxford, 1991 (first published 1979), p.272.

**Note 45** Swinburne, Richard: *The Existence of God*, Revised edition, Clarendon Press, Oxford, 1991 (first published 1979), pp.272–273.

**Note 46** Swinburne, Richard: *The Existence of God*, Revised edition, Clarendon Press, Oxford, 1991 (first published 1979), p.273.

## Chapter 4.1 Natural moral law

**Note 1** Cicero: *De Republica*. This translation is taken from: http://www.nlnrac.org/classical/cicero/documents/de-republica.

Translated by David Fott. Ithaca, N.Y.: Cornell University Press. 2014. Books 1 and 3.

**Note 2** All references to Aquinas' *Summa Theologica* are taken from http://www.sacred-texts.com/chr/aquinas/summa

**Note 3** The author is indebted to his good friend Dr Mike Wilkinson for his advice on this and other points concerning Natural moral law.

**Note 4** Servais Pinckaers, O.P.: *Morality. the Catholic View*. Preface by Alasdair MacIntyre, translated by Michael Sherwin, O.P., 2001, St Augustine's Press, South Bend, Indiana, p.27. Original French edition, *La morale catholique*, 1991, Les editions du Cerf.

**Note 5** Taken from: http://www.vatican.va/archive/ccc_css/archive/catechism/p3s1c1a7.htm.

**Note 6** http://www.sacred-texts.com/chr/aquinas/summa/sum320.htm.

**Note 7** Pojman, Louis P.: *Ethics: Discovering Right and Wrong*, third edition, Wadsworth Publishing Company, 1998.

**Note 8** Pojman, Louis P.: *Ethics: Discovering Right and Wrong*, third edition, Wadsworth Publishing Company, 1998, p.47.

**Note 9** Pojman, Louis P.: *Ethics: Discovering Right and Wrong*, third edition, Wadsworth Publishing Company, 1998, p.47. The description of double effect that follows is Pojman's.

**Note 10** There is some dispute about the tendency of morphine to hasten death in such cases: for example, *The National Catholic Bioethics Quarterly 3, Spring 2011*: 'End-of-Life Decisions and Double Effect How Can This Be Wrong When It Feels So Right?' Rita L. Marker, p.110. See online at: http://www.patientsrightscouncil.org/site/wp-content/uploads/2012/03/NCBQ_11_1_8_MarkerArticle_99-119.pdf. Use of morphine may in some of these cases prolong rather than shorten life. This does not invalidate the example given in cases where morphine has the effect referred to.

**Note 11** This example is from the online Stanford Encyclopedia of Philosophy: http://plato.stanford.edu/entries/double-effect/#applications.

**Note 12** Pojman, Louis P.: *Ethics: Discovering Right and Wrong*, third edition, Wadsworth Publishing Company, 1998, p.49.

**Note 13** Servais Pinckaers, O.P.: *Morality. the Catholic View.* Preface by Alasdair MacIntyre, translated by Michael Sherwin, O.P., 2001, St Augustine's Press, South Bend, Indiana, p.37. Original French edition, *La morale catholique*, 1991, Les editions du Cerf.

**Note 14** Servais Pinckaers, O.P.: *Morality. the Catholic View.* Preface by Alasdair MacIntyre, translated by Michael Sherwin, O.P., 2001, St Augustine's Press, South Bend, Indiana, p.40. Original French edition, *La morale catholique*, 1991, Les editions du Cerf.

**Note 15** Taken from McCormick's obituary in the American 'National Catholic Review', April 8, 2000: http://americamagazine.org/issue/288/article/he-lived-wisdom-richard-mccormick-1922-2000.

**Note 16** Hoose, Bernard: *Proportionalism. The American Debate and its European Roots.* Georgetown University Press, 1987.

**Note 17** Vardy, Peter & Grosch, Paul: *The Puzzle of Ethics*, Fount, 1999 (first published 1994), p.48.

**Note 18** Hoose, Bernard: *Proportionalism. The American Debate and its European Roots.* Georgetown University Press, 1987, pp.137–138.

**Note 19** Waters, John: http://www.quodvultdeus.com/Resources/KS5%20A%20level/NaturalLaw/OtherResources/si_naturallaw-notes.pdf.

**Note 20** For example, see: http://americainclass.org/sources/makingrevolution/rebellion/text8/decindep.pdf.

**Note 21** Pojman, Louis P.: *Ethics: Discovering Right and Wrong,* third edition, Wadsworth Publishing Company, 1998, p.50.

## Chapter 4.2 Situation ethics

**Note 1** Fletcher, Joseph F.: *Situation Ethics. The New Morality,* Westminster John Knox Press, Louisville, Kentucky (Introduction by James F. Childress), 1997 reprint Library of Theological Ethics series). First published 1966, W.L. Jenkins. The page references here for **Notes 2–21** and **23–32** all refer to this book.

**Note 2** Fletcher, Joseph F.: *Situation Ethics. The New Morality,* Westminster John Knox Press, Louisville, Kentucky (Introduction by James F. Childress), 1997, p.34.

**Note 3** Fletcher, Joseph F.: *Situation Ethics. The New Morality,* Westminster John Knox Press, Louisville, Kentucky (Introduction by James F. Childress), 1997, p.13 & p.15.

**Note 4** Fletcher, Joseph F.: *Situation Ethics. The New Morality,* Westminster John Knox Press, Louisville, Kentucky (Introduction by James F. Childress), 1997, p.45.

**Note 5** Fletcher, Joseph F.: *Situation Ethics. The New Morality,* Westminster John Knox Press, Louisville, Kentucky (Introduction by James F. Childress), 1997, p.19.

**Note 6** Fletcher, Joseph F.: *Situation Ethics. The New Morality,* Westminster John Knox Press, Louisville, Kentucky (Introduction by James F. Childress), 1997, p.19.

**Note 7** Fletcher, Joseph F.: *Situation Ethics. The New Morality,* Westminster John Knox Press, Louisville, Kentucky (Introduction by James F. Childress), 1997, p.30.

**Note 8** Fletcher, Joseph F.: *Situation Ethics. The New Morality,* Westminster John Knox Press, Louisville, Kentucky (Introduction by James F. Childress), 1997, p.43. Fletcher quoting from William James: 1907. *Pragmatism*, 1907, Chapter 2.

**Note 9** Fletcher, Joseph F.: *Situation Ethics. The New Morality,* Westminster John Knox Press, Louisville, Kentucky (Introduction by James F. Childress), 1997, pp.43–44.

**Note 10** Fletcher, Joseph F.: *Situation Ethics. The New Morality,* Westminster John Knox Press, Louisville, Kentucky (Introduction by James F. Childress), 1997, p.45.

**Note 11** Fletcher, Joseph F.: *Situation Ethics. The New Morality,* Westminster John Knox Press, Louisville, Kentucky (Introduction by James F. Childress), 1997, p.49.

**Note 12** Fletcher, Joseph F.: *Situation Ethics. The New Morality,* Westminster John Knox Press, Louisville, Kentucky (Introduction by James F. Childress), 1997, p.57.

**Note 13** Fletcher, Joseph F.: *Situation Ethics. The New Morality,* Westminster John Knox Press, Louisville, Kentucky (Introduction by James F. Childress), 1997, p.59.

**Note 14** Fletcher, Joseph F.: *Situation Ethics. The New Morality,* Westminster John Knox Press, Louisville, Kentucky (Introduction by James F. Childress), 1997, p.64.

**Note 15** Fletcher, Joseph F.: *Situation Ethics. The New Morality,* Westminster John Knox Press, Louisville, Kentucky (Introduction by James F. Childress), 1997, p.65.

**Note 16** Fletcher, Joseph F.: *Situation Ethics. The New Morality,* Westminster John Knox Press, Louisville, Kentucky (Introduction by James F. Childress), 1997, p.69.

**Note 17** Fletcher, Joseph F.: *Situation Ethics. The New Morality,* Westminster John Knox Press, Louisville, Kentucky (Introduction by James F. Childress), 1997, p.74.

**Note 18** Fletcher, Joseph F.: *Situation Ethics. The New Morality,* Westminster John Knox Press, Louisville, Kentucky (Introduction by James F. Childress), 1997, p.80.

**Note 19** Fletcher, Joseph F.: *Situation Ethics. The New Morality,* Westminster John Knox Press, Louisville, Kentucky (Introduction by James F. Childress), 1997, p.87.

**Note 20** Fletcher, Joseph F.: *Situation Ethics. The New Morality,* Westminster John Knox Press, Louisville, Kentucky (Introduction by James F. Childress), 1997, p.103.

**Note 21** Fletcher, Joseph F.: *Situation Ethics. The New Morality,* Westminster John Knox Press, Louisville, Kentucky (Introduction by James F. Childress), 1997, p.105.

**Note 22** Fletcher, Joseph F.: *Situation Ethics. The New Morality,* Westminster John Knox Press, Louisville, Kentucky (Introduction by James F. Childress), 1997, p.111. Fletcher quoting S. Kierkegaard, *The Works of Love,* tr. D.F. & L.M. Swenson (Princeton University Press, 1946), p.17.

**Note 23** Fletcher, Joseph F.: *Situation Ethics. The New Morality,* Westminster John Knox Press, Louisville, Kentucky (Introduction by James F. Childress), 1997, p.116.

**Note 24** Fletcher, Joseph F.: *Situation Ethics. The New Morality,* Westminster John Knox Press, Louisville, Kentucky (Introduction by James F. Childress), 1997, p.120.

**Note 25** Fletcher, Joseph F.: *Situation Ethics. The New Morality,* Westminster John Knox Press, Louisville, Kentucky (Introduction by James F. Childress), 1997, p.123.

**Note 26** Fletcher, Joseph F.: *Situation Ethics. The New Morality,* Westminster John Knox Press, Louisville, Kentucky (Introduction by James F. Childress), 1997, p.123.

**Note 27** Fletcher, Joseph F.: *Situation Ethics. The New Morality,* Westminster John Knox Press, Louisville, Kentucky (Introduction by James F. Childress), 1997, pp.124–125.

**Note 28** Fletcher, Joseph F.: *Situation Ethics. The New Morality,* Westminster John Knox Press, Louisville, Kentucky (Introduction by James F. Childress), 1997, p.133.

**Note 29** Fletcher, Joseph F.: *Situation Ethics. The New Morality,* Westminster John Knox Press, Louisville, Kentucky (Introduction by James F. Childress), 1997, p.134.

**Note 30** Fletcher, Joseph F.: *Situation Ethics. The New Morality,* Westminster John Knox Press, Louisville, Kentucky (Introduction by James F. Childress), 1997, pp.135–136.

**Note 31** Fletcher, Joseph F.: *Situation Ethics. The New Morality,* Westminster John Knox Press, Louisville, Kentucky (Introduction by James F. Childress), 1997, p.139-140.

**Note 32** Fletcher, Joseph F.: *Situation Ethics. The New Morality,* Westminster John Knox Press, Louisville, Kentucky (Introduction by James F. Childress), 1997, p.162.

**Note 33** Respectively: Leviticus 20:15–16 (the animal was condemned to death as well); 20:11–12; 20:10; 20:13; 21:9; Deuteronomy 22:13–21; 22:23–24).

**Note 34** Barclay, William: *Ethics in a Permissive Society,* 1971, Chapter 4 on 'Situation Ethics'. This can be read online at: http://www.clydeserver.com/bairdtrust/node/51.

## Chapter 4.3 Aristotle's virtue ethics

**Note 1** Aristotle: Nicomachean Ethics, 1098a20. The references to Aristotle's Nicomachean Ethics used throughout this section are from: 'Aristotle's Nicomachean Ethics, translated, with an interpretative essay, notes, and glossary', by Robert C. Bartlett & Susan D. Collins, The University of Chicago Press, Chicago & London, 2011.

**Note 2** Anscombe, G.E.M.: 'Modern Moral Philosophy': *Philosophy,* vol. 33, no. 124, 1958.

**Note 3** Bartlett & Collins: 'Aristotle's Nicomachean Ethics', p.xvi.

**Note 4** Bartlett & Collins: 'Aristotle's Nicomachean Ethics', p.243.

**Note 5** Prior, William J.: *Virtue and Knowledge. An Introduction to Ancient Greek Ethics*, Routledge, London & New York, 1991, p.154. Prior's exposition is very clear, and the author in indebted to him for much of the selection here.

**Note 6** See, for example, Martha Nussbaum: http://virtueethicsinfocentre.blogspot.co.uk/2008/02/morality-and-emotions.html.

**Note 7** The AREA categories are for the most part from A. W. Price, *Virtue and Reason in Plato and Aristotle*.

# Chapter 5 Application of ethical theories

**Note 1** Cardinal, D., Jones, G. & Hayward, J.: AQA A2 Philosophy, Hodder Education 2015, p.7.

**Note 2** See Note 1 above. There account of the virtues and dispositions involved is given on pages 160–161 of their textbook.

**Note 3** Catechism of the Catholic Church online text: http://www.vatican.va/archive/ENG0015/__P8K.HTM.

**Note 4** This conclusion is thoroughly grounded in what Aristotle says about the need to take into account the 'common opinions of persons with broad life experience' as well as the views of those who have been 'brought up in good habits' (1095a 4 & 1095b 5 respectively). Online, look at http://www.iep.utm.edu/ross-wd/#H4, Section 4 on W.D. Ross and virtue theory.

**Note 5** Fletcher, Joseph F.: 'Ethical Aspects of Genetic Control', Extract 2 in: Michael Palmer: *Moral Problems in Medicine. A Practical Coursebook*. The Lutterworth Press, 1999, p.172.

**Note 6** Fletcher, Joseph F.: 'Ethical Aspects of Genetic Control', Extract 2 in: Michael Palmer: *Moral Problems in Medicine. A Practical Coursebook*. The Lutterworth Press, 1999, p.173.

**Note 7** Simonds, Thomas Andrew: *Aquinas and Early term Abortion*, The Linacre Quarterly, Vol. 61, No.3, Article 4, August 1994. Online at: http://epublications.marquette.edu/cgi/viewcontent.cgi?article=2118&context=lnq.

**Note 8** Pojman, Louis P.: *Ethics: Discovering Right and Wrong,* third edition, Wadsworth Publishing Company, 1998, p.48.

**Note 9** Pojman, Louis P.: *Ethics: Discovering Right and Wrong,* third edition, Wadsworth Publishing Company, 1998, p.48.

**Note 10** Fletcher, Joseph F.: *Situation Ethics. The New Morality,* Westminster John Knox Press, Louisville, Kentucky (Introduction by James F. Childress), 1997, pp.37–39.

**Note 11** Hursthouse, Rosalind: 'Virtue Theory and Abortion', Chapter 11 in: *Virtue Ethics*, edited Roger Crisp and Michael Slote, Oxford Readings in Philosophy, Oxford University Press, 1997.

**Note 12** Hursthouse, Rosalind: 'Virtue Theory and Abortion', Chapter 11 in: *Virtue Ethics*, edited Roger Crisp and Michael Slote, Oxford Readings in Philosophy, Oxford University Press, 1997, p.235.

**Note 13** Hursthouse, Rosalind: 'Virtue Theory and Abortion', Chapter 11 in: *Virtue Ethics*, edited Roger Crisp and Michael Slote, Oxford Readings in Philosophy, Oxford University Press, 1997, pp.235–236.

**Note 14** From: http://www.telegraph.co.uk/news/worldnews/1582333/Euthanasia-debate-woman-found-dead-at-home.html.

**Note 15** The relevant part of Fletcher's discussion is printed in Extract 19, 'Euthanasia', in: Robin Gill: *A Textbook of Christian Ethics*, pub. T. & T. Clark Ltd, Edinburgh, 1985, pp.480–488.

**Note 16** Robin Gill: *A Textbook of Christian Ethics*, pub. T. & T. Clark Ltd, Edinburgh, 1985, p.481.

**Note 17** Cardinal, D., Jones, G. & Hayward, J.: AQA A2 Philosophy, Hodder Education 2015, p.150.

**Note 18** Cardinal, D., Jones, G. & Hayward, J.: AQA A2 Philosophy, Hodder Education 2015, p.150.

**Note 19** Pojman, Louis P.: *Life and Death. A Reader in Moral Problems*. Second edition, Wadworth Publishing Company, 1999, p.361.

**Note 20** Wilcockson, Michael: *Issues of Life and Death*. Second Edition, Hodder Education, 2009 (first published 1999), p.108.

**Note 21** See, for example, The Cambridge Declaration on Consciousness, 2012: http://fcmconference.org/img/CambridgeDeclarationOnConsciousness.pdf.

**Note 22** Chimpanzees cannot speak because their vocal chords are positioned higher up in the throat than in humans.

**Note 23** Barad, Judith: 'Aquinas' inconsistency on the nature and the treatment of animals.' p.108, http://digitalcommons.calpoly.edu/cgi/viewcontent.cgi?article=1692&context=bts.

**Note 24** http://www.vatican.va/roman_curia/ pontifical_academies/acdlife/documents/rc_pa_acdlife_ doc_30091997_clon_en.html.

**Note 25** https://www.theguardian.com/science/2015/ dec/23/uk-couple-await-birth-of-two-clones-of-dead-dog.

**Note 26** http://www.roman-catholic.com/Roman/ Articles/Cloning1.htm.

**Note 27** From: http://www.catholicmedicalassociation. org.uk/ethics/Articles/department-of-health-xenotransplantation.htm.

**Note 28** Data from The World Food Programme: https://www.wfp.org/hunger/stats.

**Note 29** From: http://www.peta.org.uk/issues/animals-not-experiment-on/.

**Note 30** Hursthouse, Rosalind: essay on 'Applying Virtue Ethics to Our Treatment of Other Animals', p.153 – appearing in, 'The Practice of Virtue', Classic and Contemporary Readings in Virtue Ethics, editor Jennifer Welchman, 2006, Hackett Publishing Company; reproduced online at http://www. hackettpublishing.com/pdfs/Hursthouse_Essay.pdf.

## Chapter 6 Sources of wisdom and authority

**Note 1** Catechism of the Catholic Church, Part 1, Sect.1, Ch.2, Articles 2-3: taken from: http://www.vatican.va/ archive/ccc_css/archive/catechism/p1s1c2a2.htm & http://www.vatican.va/archive/ccc_css/archive/catechism/ p1s1c2a3.htm.

**Note 2** *The Gift of Scripture*. Catholic Bishops' Conferences of England and Wales, and of Scotland, published by the Catholic Truth Society, 2005. Taken from: file:///C:/Users/John/Downloads/gift-of-scripture-2005%20(2).pdf.

**Note 3** *The Gift of Scripture*. Catholic Bishops' Conferences of England and Wales, and of Scotland, published by the Catholic Truth Society, 2005. Taken from: file:///C:/Users/John/Downloads/gift-of-scripture-2005%20(2).pdf, p.21.

**Note 4** Taken from paragraph 2 of the introduction to the International Theological Commission's: '*Sensus Fidei*' in the Life of the Church. (2014).

**Note 5** Catechism of the Catholic Church, Part 1, Sect.1, Ch.2, Article 3, II. 105 (online source as in Note 1).

**Note 6** Adair, James R.: *Introducing Christianity*, Routledge, 2008, p.313.

**Note 7** *The Gift of Scripture*. Catholic Bishops' Conferences of England and Wales, and of Scotland, published by the Catholic Truth Society, 2005, p.19. Taken from: file:///C:/Users/John/Downloads/gift-of-scripture-2005%20(2).pdf .

**Note 8** https://joshuahoffmann1.wordpress. com/2013/02/28/karl-barths-doctrine-of-scripture/.

**Note 9** Dogmatic Constitution on Divine Revelation *Dei Verbum* Solemnly Promulgated by His Holiness Pope Paul VI on November 18, 1965. II, 9. Taken online from: http://www.vatican.va/archive/hist_councils/ii_ vatican_council/documents/vat-ii_const_19651118_dei-verbum_en.html.

**Note 10** Dogmatic Constitution on Divine Revelation *Dei Verbum* Solemnly Promulgated by His Holiness Pope Paul VI on November 18, 1965. II, 10.

**Note 11** From: http://biblicalstudies.org.uk/pdf/asw/ captive/captive-to-the-word_11.pdf, p.120.

**Note 12** From: http://biblicalstudies.org.uk/pdf/asw/ captive/captive-to-the-word_11.pdf, p.120.

**Note 13** From: http://biblicalstudies.org.uk/pdf/asw/ captive/captive-to-the-word_11.pdf, p.121.

**Note 14** From: http://biblicalstudies.org.uk/pdf/asw/ captive/captive-to-the-word_11.pdf, p.122.

**Note 15** Taken from http://www.earlychurchtexts.com/ public/nicene_creed.htm .

**Note 16** Vincent Taylor: *The Gospel According to St. Mark. The Greek Text, with Introduction, Notes, and Indexes.* 2nd edition Macmillan. St Martin's Press, N. York, 1966, p.121.

**Note 17** Vincent Taylor: *The Gospel According to St. Mark. The Greek Text, with Introduction, Notes, and Indexes.* 2nd edition Macmillan. St Martin's Press, N. York, 1966, p.597.

**Note 18** Data from: http://www.bbc.co.uk/religion/ religions/unitarianism/ataglance/glance.shtml.

**Note 19** From: https://www.unitarian.org.uk/pages/ frequently-asked-questions-faq.

**Note 20** *The Modern Review*, October 1941, p.406.

# Chapter 7 God

**Note 1** The *Enûma Eliš* can be read online, for example at: http://www.sacred-texts.com/ane/stc/stc04.htm.

**Note 2** McEnhill, Peter & Newlands, George: *Fifty Key Christian Thinkers*, Routledge, London & New York, 2004, p.285. The summary here is from the same source.

**Note 3** McEnhill, Peter & Newlands, George: *Fifty Key Christian Thinkers*, Routledge, London & New York, 2004, p.192.

**Note 4** Barr, James: *Journal of Theological Studies*, New Series 39, Oxford, Clarendon: 1988, pp.28–47: "Abba Isn't 'Daddy' ", p.46.

**Note 5** This is a brief synthesis from: Daphne Hampson: *Theology and Feminism*. Signposts in Theology series, Blackwell, 1990, and a lecture given by Hampson at an Academy Conferences symposium, Oxford, April 2016.

**Note 6** Daphne Hampson, Academy Conferences lecture, Oxford, April 2016.

**Note 7** Hampson, Daphne: *Theology and Feminism*, Signposts in Theology series, Blackwell, 1990, p.95.

**Note 8** Hampson, Daphne: *Theology and Feminism*, Signposts in Theology series, Blackwell, 1990, pp.89–90.

**Note 9** Hampson, Daphne: *Theology and Feminism*, Signposts in Theology series, Blackwell, 1990, p.169.

**Note 10** Griffin's views here are summarised in Chapter 4 of Stephen T. Davis (editor): *Encountering Evil: Live Options in Theodicy*, T. & T. Clark Ltd. Edinburgh, 1981, 'Creation out of Chaos and the Problem of Evil'.

# Chapter 8 Self, death and afterlife

**Note 1** The author has inserted the paragraph breaks for clarity.

**Note 2** Hick, John: *Evil and the God of Love*, second edition, New York: Palgrave Macmillan, 2007 (1966).

**Note 3** From: http://www.quaker.org.uk/about-quakers/our-faith/what-quakers-do.

**Note 4** Augustine: *The City of God against the Pagans*: online PDF: http://www.unilibrary.com/ebooks/Saint%20Augustine%20-%20City%20of%20God.pdf.

**Note 5** *Catechism of the Catholic Church*: http://www.vatican.va/archive/ENG0015/__P2H.HTM.

# Chapter 9 Good conduct and key moral principles

**Note 1** Griffin, D.R.: *Reenchantment without Supernaturalism. A Process Philosophy of Religion*, Cornell Studies in the Philosophy of Religion, Cornell University Press, Ithaca & London, 2001, Chapter 8: 'Religion, Morality and Civilization'.

**Note 2** Barrett, C.K.: *A Commentary on the Epistle to the Romans*, Adam & Charles Black, London, 1962 (first printed 1957), p.75.

**Note 3** Barrett, C.K.: *A Commentary on the Epistle to the Romans*, Adam & Charles Black, London, 1962 (first printed 1957), p.76.

**Note 4** Adair, James R.: *Introducing Christianity*. World Religions Series, ed. Damien Keown & Charles S. Prebish, Routledge, New York & London, 2008, p.364.

**Note 5** Adair, James R.: *Introducing Christianity*. World Religions Series, ed. Damien Keown & Charles S. Prebish, Routledge, New York & London, 2008, p.364.

**Note 6** *A New Dictionary of Christian Theology*, ed. Alan Richardson & John Bowden, SCM Press, 1983, p.460.

**Note 7** *A New Dictionary of Christian Theology*, ed. Alan Richardson & John Bowden, SCM Press, 1983, p.460.

**Note 8** *A New Dictionary of Christian Theology*, ed. Alan Richardson & John Bowden, SCM Press, 1983, p.461.

**Note 9** *A New Dictionary of Christian Theology*, ed. Alan Richardson & John Bowden, SCM Press, 1983, p.461.

**Note 10** Calvin, John: *The Institutes of the Christian Religion*, first published 1536. The reference here is from an 1845 English translation by Henry Beveridge: http://www.ccel.org/ccel/calvin/institutes.v.xxii.html.

**Note 11** This document can be read online at: http://www.vatican.va/roman_curia/congregations/cfaith/documents/rc_con_cfaith_doc_19741118_declaration-abortion_en.html. The emphasis in the last sentence is the author's own.

**Note 12** For example, see https://www.theguardian.com/world/2016/oct/03/polish-women-strike-over-planned-abortion-ban.

**Note 13** The Church of England's Briefing Paper on Abortion can be found at: https://www.churchofengland.org/media/45673/abortion.pdf.

**Note 14** Conclusion of the Church of England Briefing Paper on Abortion: https://www.churchofengland.org/media/45673/abortion.pdf.

**Note 15** Questions 2–5 here were suggested with reference to: Glannon, Walter: *Biomedical Ethics: Fundamentals of Philosophy Series*, Oxford University Press, New York & Oxford, 2005, pp.90–91.

**Note 16** Taken from: McCormick, Richard: 'The Quality of Life, the Sanctity of Life', *Theological Issues in Bioethics. An Introduction with Readings*: ed. Neil Messer; Darton, Longman & Todd, 2002, p.43.

**Note 17** See, for example: http://www.army-technology.com/features/featurethe-worlds-most-dangerous-bioweapons-4546207/.

**Note 18** Data from: http://thediplomat.com/2014/08/how-hiroshima-and-nagasaki-saved-millions-of-lives/.

**Note 19** See Hick: *Evil and the God of Love*, Macmillan Press, 1985 (first published 1966), 70ff.

**Note 20** These categories are suggested by the website: http://www.earthcareonline.org/.

**Note 21** Harrison, Victoria: *Religion and Modern Thought*, SCM Press, 2007, p.263.

**Note 22** White Jr,. Lynn: 'The Historical Roots of our Ecological Crisis,' *Science*, 155, 1967, pp.1203–7.

**Note 23** McFague, Sallie: *Models of God: Theology for an Ecological, Nuclear Age*, Fortress Press, 1987.

**Note 24** See this at: http://w2.vatican.va/content/francesco/en/encyclicals/documents/papa-francesco_20150524_enciclica-laudato-si.html.

## Chapter 10 Expressions of religious identity

**Note 1** From: https://www.churchofengland.org/our-faith/mission/missionevangelism.aspx.

**Note 2** Karanda Hospital Mission Statement from: http://www.karanda.org/about/.

**Note 3** Church Urban Fund: http://www.cuf.org.uk/about-us.

## The Exam

**Note 1** https://www.theguardian.com/education/mortarboard/2012/jun/01/exam-hall-horror-stories.

### Text and photo credits

The publisher would like to thank the following individuals, institutions and companies for permission to reproduce copyright illustrations for this book/

**Text credits**

p349 text written by the Church Urban Fund; p285 text written by Quakers in Britain.

Works quoted throughout: *Situation Ethics: A New Morality* by Joseph Fletcher, 2nd ed. (Westminster John Knox Press, 1997); *Nicomachean Ethics* by Aristotle, translated by Robert C. Bartlett and Susan D. Collins (University of Chicago Press, 2012); *Catechism of the Catholic Church*, © Libreria Editrice Vaticana.

**Photo credits**

p2, 20, 36, 51, 87, 118, 121, 141, 161, 179 © Stefanos Kyriazis - Fotolia; p2 © The Granger Collection/TopFoto; p4 *l,r* © Horologicam/Topfoto; p6 © HIP/TopFoto; p7 © Jeff J Daly/Alamy Stock Photo; p11 © joingate/123rf; p22, 26, 38 © The Granger Collection/TopFoto; p27 © NumisMaster; p31 © ullsteinbild/Topfoto; p37 © jager/Topfoto; p40 © Library Thing; p51© epnd7n; p54 *t* © ACTIVE MUSEUM/Alamy Stock Photo, *b* © Daniel BOITEAU/Alamy Stock Photo; p56 © Les Gibbon/Alamy Stock Photo; p72 © Topfoto; p77 © Davidraygiffin; p79 © Stefano Bianchetti/Getty Images; p89 *l* © The Granger Collection/TopFoto, *r* © Carsten Koall/Getty Images; p91 © Chronicle/Alamy Stock Photo; p92 © Ullstein bild/ullstein bild/Getty Images; p95 © Pictorial Press Ltd/Alamy Stock Photo; p99 © Walter Sanders/The LIFE Picture Collection/Getty Images; p104 © Michael Persinger; p107 © Photograph by SueAnne Bergmann; p113 M.C. Escher's "Three Worlds" © The M.C. Escher Company-The Netherlands. All rights reserved. www.mcescher.com; p122 © World History Archive/TopFoto; p125 *l* © David Arky/Getty Images, *m* © Christian Martinez Kempin/123RF, *r* © Carol M. Highsmith's America, Library of Congress, Prints and Photographs Division; p133 © Glen Martin/The Denver Post/ Getty Images; p141, 149 © TopFoto; p150 © Heritage Images/TopFoto; p152 © Bettmann/Getty Images; p155 © United States Holocaust Memorial Museum; p162 © VPC Travel Photo/Alamy Stock Photo; p166 Daniel Cardinal, Gerald Jones & Jeremy Hayward: *AQA A2 Philosophy*, publ. Hodder Education, 2015, p.129; p193 © Scott Camazine/Alamy Stock Photo; p207 © Ian Hinchliffe/Alamy Stock Photo; p208 © imageBROKER/Alamy Stock Photo; p217 © epa european pressphoto agency b.v /Alamy Stock Photo; p228, 255, 280, 301, 334 © Stephen Meese - Fotolia; p245 © Philippe Lissac/Getty Images; p270 © Peter Barritt/Alamy Stock Photo; p283 © MyLoupe/UIG/Getty Images; p288 © Lanmas / Alamy Stock Photo; p295 © DeAgostini/SuperStock; p307 © Portrait of Martin Luther (1483–1546) as an Augustinian Monk, c.1523–24 (oil on vellum on panel), Cranach, Lucas, the Elder (1472–1553)/Germanisches Nationalmuseum, Nuremberg, Germany/Bridgeman Images; p310 © Hulton Archive/Getty Images; p320 *t* © Pictorial Press Ltd/Alamy Stock Photo, *b* © Library of congress, Prints and photographic Division [ HAER COLO,1-COMCI,1–191 ]; p338 © Tom Carter/Getty Images; p343 © Imagestate Media Partners Limited - Impact Photos / Alamy Stock Photo; p350 © Jim O Donnell / Alamy Stock Photo.

# Index